A History of St Lucia

There was nothing they wanted, nothing I could give them
but this thing I have called "The Light of the World"

Derek Walcott, The Arkansas Testament

A History of St Lucia

Jolien Harmsen
Guy Ellis
Robert Devaux

LIGHTHOUSE
ROAD

Lighthouse Road Publications
Cape Moule à Chique, Vieux Fort, St Lucia

www.lighthouse-road.com

ISBN 978-976-95340-0-1

Designed by Cécile Wiltshire
First published 2012
Reprinted 2014

Cover design by Cécile Wiltshire
Cover illustration:
An uncommon depiction of two women's teams playing a cricket match (*Ca.* 1900). The original caption reads '*Caneway-versus-Cariere*', perhaps a reference to Conway and Carrière. Postcard courtesy of Robert Devaux.

Contents

List of Illustrations

20. Eighteenth century cattle mill used for crushing sugar cane.
21. Nineteenth century water wheel at Balembouche Estate. The wheel bears the inscription *G. Fletcher London.*
22. Cutting and carrying sugar cane was hot and arduous work. This picture was published in 1876 in *The Graphic*, a British illustrated newspaper.
23. View over Vieux Fort, 1888. Note the central sugar factory, St Paul's Anglican Church and the hill at Beanefield (which has since been partly quarried).
24. Soufrière Valley covered in sugar cane in 1888. Visible are the Soufrière River, the village of Soufrière just south of that, and a number of estates scattered around inland.
25. Using an antiquated still to make illegal rum in the bush, circa 1898.
26. HMS *Comus* coming in at the Northern Wharf to load coal. The coaling industry started in Port Castries in 1863.
27. A two-penny coaling token, only used during wartime.
28. A one-shilling coaling token, paid to the riggers.
29. A day token (marked 'D'), generally worth one penny.
30. A night token (marked 'N') worth one-and-a-half times the value of the day token.
31. Female coal carriers (some smoking clay pipes) getting ready for work. Only in St Lucia and Nagasaki (Japan) did coal workers carry baskets weighing over 100 pounds.
32. A ship coaling at Port Castries, 1917. The industry waned and died in 1942 due to the advent of oil-fuelled ships and the Panama Canal.
33. Walking from Morne Fortuné into Castries town, 1833. Clearly distinguishable are the Anglican Church and the Prince Alfred's Basin, which has since been filled in.
34. The Conway land reclamation project in 1890. Nowadays, this is the Castries Waterfront with Government Buildings. The Conway River still flows at this same spot.
35. Prince Alfred's Basin in 1890, showing two of Castries' leading merchants, *messieurs* de Minvielle and Chastanet in conversation with Vicar-General Fr Tapon.
36. Hustle and bustle around Minvielle & Chastanet's first department store, here seen in 1905. The building was originally constructed in 1864.
37. Looking south down a cobble-stoned Bridge Street in 1890. Note the lack of telephone lines and electrical wires.
38. Old Castries in 1898, before it was partly destroyed by the fire of May 1927.

39. Coasting steamer RMS *Tees* loading passengers and cargo in Prince Alfred's Basin, 1900.
40. A police officer in colonial uniform (white with yellow trim) guarding the bridge on Bridge Street, 1900. Note behind him the Police Headquarters, Royal Gaol and Dispensary.
41. Barnard & Sons on the south-west corner of Jeremie and Bridge Streets (1900) with students from St Joseph's Convent and St Mary's College congregating outside.
42. The same south-west corner of Jeremie and Bridge Streets 100 years later, now home to the modern head office of the Bank of Saint Lucia.
43. Bridge Street looking south (circa 1908), showing telephone poles and gas lamps. The first telephone call in St Lucia was made on Christmas Day, 1895.
44. Brazil Street looking west (circa 1910), looking down the Castries River and across to what is the oldest remaining Roman Catholic cemetery on the island.
45. Looking north along the Chaussée Road in 1916. Nobel Prize laureate Derek Walcott grew up in this area a few decades later.
46. St Joseph's Convent and St Mary's College on Micoud Street, circa 1916. The college is the building to the fore.
47. Grace Anglican Church at River Dorée is the second-oldest Anglican church and housed the island's first school for emancipated black children.
48. The Carnegie Library, originally built in June 1924.
49. Victoria Hospital, completed in 1887, was named to honour the occasion of Queen Victoria's Golden Jubilee.
50. A lovely example of Caribbean architecture is this office of the curator at the botanical garden in Castries.
51. Church-goers milling about near Columbus Square after Sunday Mass. The picture shows the church still with its domed belfry. In 1895, the building was enlarged and the main entrance moved to Micoud Street.
52. The new Government House was completed in January 1896 for Administrator V.S. Gouldsbury. Horseback was the main mode of transport at the time.
53. St Louis Street looking east, around 1900, blissfully uncongested.
54. Government buildings and Peter & Company, both built after the 1927 fire. The Peter & Company building survived the 1948 fire and is now one of Castries' historical highlights.
55. Anse la Raye Village was named after the impressive-looking manta ray fish which used to frequent the bay in large numbers.

56. The west-coast fishing village of Canaries got its name from the Amerindian clay cooking pots of that name.
57. Soufrière Town in 1909. The original layout remains unchanged up to this day.
58. A group of cadets from the Royal Navy (circa 1880) being shown around the Sulphur Springs by local tour guides.
59. Soufrière *en fête* in 1910. People clearly enjoyed the chance to dress up.
60. Drying cocoa beans on the Soufrière waterfront (circa 1910). The beans were spread out on tarpaulins which could be used to cover them in case of rain.
61. Ecuelling limes to extract the precious oil from their skins (circa 1930). This was done at various estates around Soufriere, including Diamond Estate.
62. Choiseul (circa 1900), with its large Catholic church, long jetty and fishing canoes lined up on the beach.
63. Laborie Village as seen from the jetty (circa 1910) has changed remarkably little.
64. The fishing village of Vieux Fort only came to life on weekends, when people came in to visit the market and attend Mass.
65. The Vieux Fort mangroves, once rich fishing grounds, were partially drained in the 1940s due to concerns over malaria.
66. Vieux Fort celebrating First Communion. Showing the lower end of Clarke Street looking down towards the Caribbean Sea.
67. *Ma Gilbert* (born circa 1880) in the doorway of her home in Church Road, Vieux Fort. Photographed in the 1970s by her nephew, Antoine Theodore, former MP for Vieux Fort, pharmacist and avid amateur photographer.
68. Micoud (circa 1910) was originally located further south at *Vieux Bourg*, where it was destroyed by the great hurricane of 1780.
69. Praslin Village was once an important sugar-producing area. Heading into the twenty-first century, Praslin seemed set to enter the age of tourism.
70. Dennery Village was described in 1893 as 'a most beautiful place on the seashore. [I]f it were in Europe instead of the West Indies, it would be the most fashionable of watering places.'
71. The waterfront of Gros Islet Village, named after the 'big island' in its bay, Pigeon Island. Note the fishing nets spread out to dry in the sun.
72. Traditionally, whoever helps to pull in the seine fishing nets gets a share of the catch for their efforts.
73. A countryside *kay pay* ('straw house') with walls of woven sticks and a roof of thatched coconut branches or grass. Kerosene drums were

used to store water and cook ground provisions. Circa 1920.

74. Fishermen mending nets and shooting the breeze near a make-shift shelter by the seaside, around 1920. Note the double-masted canoe and the bamboo fish pots.

75. A St Lucian belle dressed in an eighteenth century style *wob dwiyèt*. The head dress is called the *calendeuse*, the scarf a *foulard* and the full skirts the *madras*.

76. A pedlar carrying coal pots to the market, circa 1910. They are still a popular means of cooking, allowing dishes to simmer for hours and adding a unique flavour.

77. The first motorcar in St Lucia was owned by George Barnard (second from the right). It got stuck in the mud of the Choiseul River during one of its first outings, in 1913.

78. During the First World War, the presence of Canadian soldiers created welcome income through various forms of entertainment for the troops (Vigie, 1916).

79. Canadian soldiers adopted the village of Canaries in an effort to help improve living conditions there. Here shown at their favourite rum shop, 1916.

80. People wandering through the desolate, smoking ruins of Castries after a large part of the town was burnt down in May 1927. The Carnegie Library stood unscathed.

81. This 1922 certificate of the *United Negro Improvement Movement* demonstrates that Black Power existed in the West Indies, including St Lucia, well before the 1970s.

82. Watching the horse racing at Choc Pavilion, in 1916.

83. For centuries, women washing clothes in the river was a familiar sight all around St Lucia.

84. A barber at work in the cooling sea breeze of a late afternoon.

85. The first airmail delivered to St Lucia was carried on board a plane flown by Charles Lindbergh himself (22 September 1929). In 1930, there was a parking ramp for amphibian planes at La Toc.

86. On 22 November 1938, erosion and heavy rain caused a mountainside at Ravine Poisson to collapse, killing 100 people and leaving 700 homeless.

87. The three soldiers' barracks at Vigie, built in the 1890s. One was demolished to accommodate the Vigie Airport; the others now house foreign embassies.

88. A private of the West India Regiment is awarded a military medal during a ceremony on Columbus Square (early twentieth century).

89. St Lucia observed full black-outs after a German submarine torpedoed

two ships in the harbour of Castries on 9 March 1942, leaving twenty dead and nineteen injured.

90. In October 1941, American troops raised the 'Stars and Stripes' in Vieux Fort. The wooden barracks were used as offices for administrative and engineering staff.
91. Pay-day for the local staff at the American Base in Vieux Fort, 1942. Workers came from far and wide to find employment in Vieux Fort.
92. The Great Fire of 20 June 1948 laid four-fifths of Castries into ashes, forever changing its face and character.
93. The destruction of Castries levelled not only buildings but social hierarchies as well.
94. George F.L. Charles, founding member of the St Lucia Labour Party and Chief Minister from 1960 to 1964.
95. Sir Frederick J. Clarke became St Lucia's first native-born Governor-General when the island attained Associated Statehood in 1967.
96. The banana industry often involved all members of a household, particularly on harvesting day. Here, women are seen washing bananas by hand.
97. Packing bananas in plastic bags (Roseau or Cul de Sac, 1967). The wagons were pulled along railroad tracks (a remnant of the sugar days) by a horse or small locomotive.
98. Bananas were initially (1967) loaded onto the refrigerated Geest boats by women carrying large bunches of the fruit on their heads.
99. Prime Minister John Compton joined in the work during a 1960s self-help programme to bring pipe-borne water to a community in his Micoud-south constituency.
100. The charismatic, controversial George Odlum enthralled and outraged St Lucians with his work as political leader, journalist and commentator - but rarely bored them.
101. Aerial view of Reduit Beach, Rodney Bay and the marina in 1975. Before 1970, this area consisted mostly of mangrove swamps. Now, it sports much sought-after real estate.
102. Independence Day, 22 February 1979, which Princess Alexandra attended on behalf of Queen Elizabeth II. John Compton was later called *'the father of Independence'*.
103. Sir William Arthur Lewis, St Lucia's first-ever Nobel Prize laureate (Economics, 1979).The Community College on the Morne bears his distinguished name.
104. Derek Walcott brought home the Nobel Prize for Literature in 1992, making St Lucia the country with the highest density of Nobel Prize winners per capita in the world.

105. Dame Pearlette Louisy was appointed Governor-General in 1997, the first woman to hold this office in St Lucia.
106. Kenny Anthony came to power in a landslide election in 1997 and was re-elected with a handsome majority in 2002.
107. United Workers Party supporters congratulating Sir John Compton on his party's victory on election night, 11 December 2006.

Biographies

Jolien Harmsen

Jolien Harmsen *(the Netherlands, 1966)* is a historian, journalist and author. In 1993, she received a degree in Social History based on her study of an Aboriginal Catholic mission in Central Australia, for which she was awarded the Jan Romein Prize for best MA-thesis in twentieth century history in the Netherlands. She has been studying St Lucian history since 1994, resulting in a Ph.D in 1999 (Erasmus University Rotterdam). She is also the author of *Sugar, slavery and settlement. A social history of Vieux Fort* (Saint Lucia National Trust, 1999) and *Rum Justice*, a crime novel published in 2008 by MacMillan Caribbean. She has lived in Vieux Fort since 1994.

Guy Ellis

Guy Ellis (*St Lucia, 1944*) started his career in journalism after leaving St Mary's College and, in May 1962, became a reporter with *The Voice of St Lucia*, the island's leading newspaper. He worked at *The Voice* for more than thirty years during three spells, including 19 years as managing editor. He resigned from that position in 1994 to co-found the weekly *St Lucia Mirror* and become its managing editor. Guy Ellis has covered St Lucia extensively for several international news agencies including Reuters, United Press International and Associated Press. He was the AP correspondent for St Lucia for nearly three decades. He is also a founding correspondent of the Caribbean News Agency, with which he has worked for more than 20 years.

Guy Ellis has two tourist guide books to his name: *St Lucia* (1981, Editions Delroisse) and *Saint Lucia: Helen of the West* (1986, MacMillan). He is also the scriptwriter for a comic book on the life of Nobel laureate Sir Arthur Lewis, which was published by the Trinidad & Tobago publishing house Imprint, as part of its National Heritage Series on Caribbean Heroes. In 1980, Ellis was the first winner of the M&C Fine Arts Award for Creative Journalism. In 2003, he was made a Member of the Most Excellent Order of the British Empire for his services to journalism.

Robert Devaux

Robert Devaux *(St Lucia, 1934-2013)* spent a lifetime studying the history, ecology, landscape and culture of St Lucia. As a field engineer, he kept a close eye on possible archaeological finds. In his subsequent role as director of the Saint Lucia National Trust, he contributed in many practical ways to the preservation of the island's historical, natural and cultural heritage. In the course of his long career, Robert Devaux published several books and articles, including the monumental *St Lucia Historic Sites* (1975). Also by his hand are *A century of coaling in St Lucia* (1975), *History and analysis of coastal processes at Pigeon Island* (1993) and *They called us Brigands: the saga of St Lucia's freedom fighters* (1997).

In 1961, Devaux founded the St Lucia Research Centre (incorporated in 1994), producing dozens of research papers on a wide range of topics, usually following a request by government, corporate or private entities for information on (occasionally obscure) details of St Lucia's past. The decades of meticulous research spent on those papers have been put to good use in this general history of St Lucia. Robert Devaux was made an Officer of the Most Excellent Order of the British Empire in 1991. In 1993, he received a Paul Harris Fellowship Award, followed a year later by the Pigeon Island Museum Dedication. He was inducted into the Tourism Hall of Fame in 1996 and won the M&C Fine Arts Award for Literature in 1998.

Robert Devaux passed away at his home on 16th April 2013.

Acknowledgements

Jolien Harmsen

This book has been a labour of love fifteen years in the making. My gratitude goes out to my two co-authors, our chief whip Suzy Barnard, Nick Gillard and Louisa Browne at MacMillan Caribbean and my former academic tutor, Michiel Baud. The early stage of this project was spearheaded by Ed Phelps of Canada, who until his death in 2007 remained a regular provider of obscure and sometimes hilarious publications. During the mid 1990s, I collected the life histories of some sixty people in the Vieux Fort area. I thank them all. Ms Jean Lascaris was a huge moral support, as were the late Unita *'Nan'* Romain, Myrtle Isaac, Gregor and Deirdre Williams, Rex Tasker and Ria Hodgson. I would also like to acknowledge David Clifford, Olivia Hackshaw, Seton and Joyce Campbell, Barbara and the late Jane Tipson, Maria Grech, Rosie Brown, Damian *Sappie* Edward, Claire Louisy, Mavis Emmanuel, Dian Chase, Lorraine Royall, Michaeline Crichlow, Anderson Reynolds, the late Alan *Kaf* Smith, Alice Bagshaw, Pam Devaux, Matthias Burt, Yves Renard, Sylvester Clauzel, Olivette Wallace, Patrice Esper, Cheddi St Juste, Louise Riley-Francis, Michael Walker, Cécile *Toni* Wiltshire and my family in the Netherlands and at The Reef in Vieux Fort.

On behalf of Suzy Barnard, who kept this project going, I would also like to thank the late Dr S.J. Drouilhet of Moorshead University Minnesota, who was constantly on call for information from his personal archives. The illustrations were made possible by the generosity of Nancy Dowd, who proffered her entire collection of postcards for our selection and Robert Devaux, who provided photographs and other material from his personal collection. Some of the pictures stem from Suzy's own collection, while the St Lucia National Archives, the Folk Research Centre, Guy Ellis, the *National Geographic* and the late Mrs Idalia Theodore also generously consented to the use of their materials.

Guy Ellis

I am grateful for the use of the records and documents of the Castries Central Library and the St Lucia National Archives in researching this book. Thanks also to my journalistic colleagues David Vitalis, Rick Wayne and Willie James whose writings became useful in getting this project done.

Robert Devaux

I am eternally grateful to Thomas Ferguson, antiquarian, whose wonderful stories and recollections awakened in me at the age of ten a curiosity and lifetime interest in the history of my island home. He continued tutoring me over the next four years before he lost most of his manuscripts in the tragic Castries fire of 1948. To Anthony Fanis, better known as *Lazar*, fisherman of Micoud, I owe a debt of gratitude for introducing me to my first Brigand site and for sharing so much of his knowledge of folk culture. My wife Pam tolerated my many hours of scrutinizing old newspapers and fragmented records, while putting up with the clutter of dusty papers being sorted on the dining room table. To my co-authors, I say thanks for helping to make our journey both enjoyable and rewarding. My main sources of information were several overseas repositories as well as the St Lucia National Archives.

Introduction

St Lucia may be a tiny speck of an island on the world map but its history is a tale of grand things: of tragedy and death, cruelty and persistence, fear and bravery, corruption and success. It is a dazzling, kaleidoscopic journey that comes with unexpected twists and turns, sweeping vistas, occasional dead-ends and, from time to time, little-known resting places that offer us a glimpse of life in the past so intimate, and so moving, that we can almost touch and speak with the people involved. It is a great privilege to have St Lucia crack open her past for us and let us drink from the rich stories she has harboured for all these centuries.

There are many avenues into the past. In putting together this history of St Lucia, we have used as many as we could: archaeological findings, historical correspondence, maps, recorded events, oral history, secondary sources and literature. Writing a history is like building a house, where one uses raw bricks and planks but also prefabricated materials such as doors, windows and roofing. As historians, we reach higher ground only by standing on the shoulders of those who have gone before us. We go to the archives and research primary sources, we dig in the landscape and try to imagine what may once have been, and we leaf through big dusty tomes of newspapers. But we also try to lay our hands on, and read, every last bit of history already written by others. St Lucia has never had a comprehensive, detailed general history written before but many specific periods, events and aspects have already been researched. While much of the text ahead rests on our own interpretation and analysis of primary sources, we have not hesitated to embrace the work of others before us and we are proud to showcase their work, sometimes in great detail, and always with full kudos, as part of the greater story that is St Lucia's past.

St Lucian historian Barry Gaspar has written sound, detailed studies on the French Revolution in St Lucia and the position of free people of colour. Austrian historian Ernestine Kolar spent months sifting through the colonial archives in London, resulting in a highly detailed Ph.D-thesis on slavery in St Lucia, with many primary sources reproduced in their entirety. In 1989, Eugène and Raymond Bruneau-Latouche collated an impressive number of French documents relating to St Lucia's early colonial history, including Jean François Lefort de Latour's report and detailed maps of 1784, showing land ownership for each district. *Sainte-Lucie fille de la Martinique* is a typographed manuscript which was never widely distributed and is now virtually unobtainable. In 1844, English administrator Henry Breen produced a history of St Lucia that is an entertaining concoction of description, fact and gossip, which has added considerable colour to this book. Father Charles Jesse, the English priest who worked in St Lucia in the mid-twentieth century, provided us (amongst other things) with a highly useful, albeit somewhat staccato, overview of the past in his *Outlines of St Lucia's History*, which has deservedly been reprinted many times. More recently, Nobel Prize laureate Derek Walcott captured the history of St Lucia's soul in his epic poem *Omeros* – an almost impossible task.

Several others have added other patches, angles and insights to the quilt that is the folklore and history of St Lucia: from John Nicholl, Cooper Willyams and John Jeremie to Charles Wells, Robert McHugh, Charles Gachet, Harry Simmons, Arthur Lewis, Thomas Ferguson, John Pilgrim, Sullivan d'Auvergne, Bertrand Easter, Leo *Spar* St Helene, Dunstan St Omer, Roderick Walcott, Francis Carasco, George F.L. Charles, Stanley French, Morgan Dalphinis, Vernon Cooper, Reginald Clarke, Douglas Midgett, Charles Cadet, Stanley Reid, Peter Adrien, Woodville Marshall, Roy Augier, Michael Louis, Gregor Williams, George Odlum, Winville King, Patricia Charles, Patrick *Paba* Anthony, Kennedy *Boots* Samuel, George *Fish* Alphonse, Joyce Auguste, Rupert and Eric Branford, Willie James, Earl Long, Garth St Omer, Jacques Compton, Alice Bagshaw, Pearlette Louisy, Michael Aubertin, Embert Charles, Kenny Anthony, Wayne Louis, Sylvester Clauzel, Michaeline Crichlow, Curtis Jacobs, Lennox Honychurch, Manfred Kremser, Rosamunde Renard, Rochelle and Coleman Romalis, Jane Beck, John Robert Lee, Jane King, Kendel Hippolyte, McDonald Dixon, Richard Cheddie, Jim Drouilhet, Céline Foster-Walker, Jason Sifflet, Kyneata Joseph, Anderson Reynolds and Rick Wayne - to name just a few...!

Colonial officers sometimes kept diaries, such as Major-General John Moore who fought the Brigands in 1796 and Surgeon-Major D.W.D. Comins who, in 1891, kept a diary of his encounters with recently immigrated Indian labourers in St Lucia. In the case of such sources, where the original documents are almost impossible to come by, we have occasionally quoted at length. The same goes for many of the original historical records we have used. The underlying rationale for this practice is that other researchers of St Lucia's history, perhaps with different objectives, may find additional meaning in the original words.

1

Geological formation, flora and fauna

The island of St Lucia first rose from the ocean about 50 million years ago, which makes it relatively young in geological terms. Its birth must have been a sight to behold: the awesome power of two tectonic plates - crusts of solid material floating atop the fiery hot, fluid inner centre of our planet earth - grinding into each other until the Atlantic plate was forced downwards, where it rippled and melted, and the Caribbean plate pushed up until land rose above the waters of the ocean, laying dry the extreme north and south parts of the island. Red-hot fluid rock *(magma)* accumulated under the crust of the earth. Earthquakes, caused by the continuous grinding of the tectonic plates eventually broke open this crust, allowing torrents of flammable gas, ashes, rocks and boulders to rush upwards and out into the open sea and air. In a long series of such volcanic explosions, the central, northern and eastern parts of St Lucia were created. The initial result was high, sharp-edged mountains separated by deep chasms - but over millions of years, these tall peaks were blunted by the erosive effects of rain, wind and gravity. Boulders slid down hillsides and filled up the deep ravines, creating the expansive, fertile alluvial valleys now known as Roseau, Cul de Sac, Mabouya, Fond d'Or, Marquis and Troumassée. Erosion also wore down the mountain range that runs along the spine of St Lucia - the *Barre de l'Isle* - until today, it reaches just 900 feet above sea level. The hard, basalt-like 'nozzles' of the original volcanoes remain today as some of the island's highest peaks: La Sorcière, Piton Flore, Morne La Combe and Piton St Esprit.

Yet St Lucia had still not reached the shape it has today. A third geological stage started approximately 26 million years ago, when a fresh round of volcanic eruptions created tall mountains in the west and centre of the island, including Morne Gimie, Piton Canaries, Morne Paix Bouche, Morne Tabac, Morne Parasol, Morne Houelmon, Morne Grand Magazin, Petit Piton and Gros Piton. Having had less time to erode, these mountains remain steeper today, with jagged edges and steep ridges.

Near Soufrière, the collapse of a huge crater caused an area of land six kilometers in diameter to drop, forming a bowl-like impression in the landscape now known as the Qualibou Caldera. On the floor of this crater, a series of very violent volcanic explosions subsequently took place, throwing up glowing avalanches of gas and ashes and ejecting boulders with such force that some landed as far as thirteen kilometers away, lending them the nickname 'volcanic bombs'. Periods of volcanic eruption were interspersed by long periods of torrential rainfall and flooding, causing massive mudflows *(glacis)*, some of them over 40 meters deep. Gros Piton and Petit Piton came into being as the result of magma inside the 'nozzles' of two volcanic mountains cooling down more slowly than the surrounding rock, making this core concomitantly harder. As erosion wore down the domes and skirts of the mountains, their triangular-shaped cones remained, making them unique landmarks to St Lucia.

Today, the only evidence of active volcanism are the sulphurous steam vents just south of Soufrière, where the constant bubbling release of heat and gas through cracks in the earth have gained the town fame for having the Caribbean's only drive-in volcano. It is thought that this constant release makes for relative safety, but other volcanoes in the Lesser Antilles remain active today, including ones in Montserrat (which started erupting again in the mid 1990s), St Vincent (1979), Martinique (where, in 1902, gas eruptions killed thousands of people), Dominica, Guadeloupe and St Kitts. Near Grenada, underwater volcano Kick 'em Jenny also continues to stir.

The last alteration to St Lucia's landscape came when a final volcanic blast in Soufrière caused a giant glacis and mud covered the whole south-west, from Soufrière to Vieux Fort. Like melted sugar being poured into a tray of peanuts, this huge, fan-shaped flow of wet sediment filled up ravines, inundated hills and skirted mountains. Its effects are particularly clear around Vieux Fort, where only an occasional mountaintop 'drowned' in mud interrupts ten square kilometers of perfectly level land. As a result, the oldest phase of geological formation now lies shoulder-to-shoulder with the newest, as Cape Moule à Chique rises protectively over the glacial plains of Vieux Fort.

Where tall mountains continue to stand guard over mud-filled valleys - in Laborie, Piaye, River Dorée and Choiseul - rivers have cut narrow gorges *(ravines)* through the coastal plains. Consequently, construction of roads has been difficult here. A bridge in Mont Lézard is colloquially known as 'the Devil's Bridge' because, as folklore holds, the planter who built it had to promise Satan the soul of the first living being that crossed it. He cunningly chased his dog across and, so the tale goes, the poor animal vanished forever.

Climate and ecology

St Lucia lies in the southern Lesser Antillean arc, at 13.85 degrees north and 61 degrees west. The nearest island is Martinique, 30 kilometers north across the usually choppy St Lucia Channel. St Vincent lies 40 kilometers to the south and Barbados 160 kilometers south-east. The nearest mainland is South America. St Lucia is just 42 kilometers long by 22 kilometers wide with a shoreline of 155.7 kilometers. The average temperature is 27 degrees Celsius (78 Fahrenheit), with

75 per cent humidity. During the wet season (from June till November), tropical storms and hurricanes sometimes hit the island with devastating wind, huge waves and torrential rain.

The east coast is washed by the Atlantic Ocean and the west by the Caribbean Sea. St Lucia receives steady northeasterly trade winds almost year round. The windward Atlantic shore offers few natural harbours and no easily accessible anchorages but the leeward, Caribbean side easily makes up for this. The natural harbours of Castries and Marigot - both drowned volcanic craters - though small, are well-protected anchorages and Marigot Bay is renowned Caribbean-wide as a hurricane hole.

Because of its topography, this 616.4 square kilometer (238 square miles) dot of land is surprisingly varied in micro-climates, flora and fauna. About one-third of the island is considered tropical dry forest, which includes most of the coastline and river valleys. Another one-third consists of subtropical wet forest, which originally was covered in primary forest. Both of these zones have in recent centuries been converted into agricultural lands. Most of the remaining one-third is (sub)-tropical wet or moist forest, which consists of lush vegetation on steep gradients. The shallow soils in this zone are easily depleted and eroded once the original vegetation is removed for agriculture. Only at Cap Estate in the north and Moule a Chique in the south do we find tropical dry forest, with stony and shallow soils covered in thorny scrubs and cacti, unsuitable for agriculture. The other ecological extreme is found on the cloud-covered tops of Mount Gimie, Morne La Sorcière and Gros Piton, where the average temperature is just 19 degrees, rain falls almost constantly and trees are covered with parasitic and epiphytic plants. These are the rare elfin woodlands of St Lucia.

Although useful, this geological and ecological summary of St Lucia does little to convey the island's vulnerability and stunning beauty, the...

> *... dramatic landscapes with unexpected streaks of sunlight, green shadows, giant ferns, ledges, perched boulders, dark canyons, hanging valleys, waterfalls and ever-changing skylines. Beneath the surface, always lacey green, there lurks in a slightly menacing but not depressing way the ever-present risk of flash floods, land slips, rock falls and the lesser nuisances of isolation, dampness, mold, mud, and the long walk back up the steep and slippery track.*[1]

Flora

The first seeds took root while St Lucia was still being formed, washing ashore from South America or being dropped by birds. As erosion created soil out of rock, primary forests evolved. It is crucial to understand that the island's fertility resides not in the soil but in the canopy between the ground and the tops of the trees. Once the rainforest is cut down, this storehouse of humidity and nutrients disappears also. What grows back is a collection of scrub bush that can survive on nutrient-poor soils. Moreover, exposing the ground to direct rain and wind causes erosion and a thin layer of fertile soil that has taken thousands of years to develop, can wash away in mere days, leaving behind just a sterile mixture of clay, iron compounds and quartz.

A 1949 study established that St Lucia contained 151 species of trees. Those with small seeds (that can be carried by birds) dominate the interior: gommier, châtaignier, mahaut, palmiste, bois côte, paletuvier, bois de masse, l'encèns, goyavier, laurier canelle, bois pain marron, balata chien, corosol marron, bois blanc, casse and grigri, while high up on the mountainsides mérise, feuille dorée and balata are found also. Trees with large husky seeds that float are commonly found along the coast, such as morning glory, Madagascar periwinkle, seagrape, Indian almond, manchineel, white cedar and casuarina. Exotic to St Lucia but nowadays grown on plantations are mahogany, blue mahoe, Caribbean pine, teak, eucalyptus and leucaena.

Popular trees and bushes in the countryside are those which provide fruits, wood, shade, bush medicine and colourful flowers, or which can be used as fences, windbreaks, animal fodder and garden furniture. Commonly found are hibiscus, red ginger, anthurium, ixora, heliconia, philodendron, poinsettia, bougainvillea, flamboyant, royal palm, bamboo, tamarind, gliricidia (or *glory cedar*), calabash, castor bean, saman (or *massav tree*), sea island cotton, logwood, aloe vera, sugar cane, banana, plantain, avocado, cocoa, breadfruit, mango, dasheen, guava, pigeon pea, eddo, tannia, nutmeg, papaya (or *pawpaw*), soursop, passion fruit and a range of citrus trees including orange, grapefruit, lemon, lime, sour orange and tangerine.

Not all are native to St Lucia, or even the Caribbean. The banana (*Musa sapientum*) was brought from the Canary Islands in the late fifteenth century on board Spanish ships. By the time Englishmen first stumbled across St Lucia in 1605, the Amerindians were happily growing plantains (*Musa paradisiaca*), which they had probably carried in their canoes from the Spanish-dominated islands.

The coconut palm (*Cocos nucifera*), despite being so inextricably bound up with the popular image of the Caribbean, is not native either. Portuguese explorers carried these from Asia around Africa into the Atlantic realm and the same applies to the mango (*Mangifera indica*), which was first introduced by the Portuguese to Brazil, brought to Barbados from there (in 1742) and quickly spread to the other islands. Also imported were dasheen (*Colocasia esculenta*) and pigeon peas (*Cajanus cajan*), possibly by African slaves. Native food crops that are still in use since the time of the Amerindians are: cassava, arrowroot, sweet potato, papaya, cocoa, tomato, pepper, peanut, christophene, edible canna lily, maize, avocado, pineapple, tannia, sugar apple, mammey apple and soursop.

Fauna

Once plant life developed, the world of animals followed close behind. St Lucia still harbours three unique species of fauna: the St Lucia parrot, the blue ground lizard and the St Lucia grass snake. The parrot (*Amazona versicolor* or *Jacquot*) almost became extinct in the 1970s but thanks to strict protection has recovered to more viable numbers. Such help came too late for the now extinct Semper's warbler, while the St Lucia wren is endangered. Other endemic (sub)species are the St Lucia black finch, St Lucia oriole and the whitebreasted thrasher. In all, some 150 species of birds are thought to exist, or have existed, in St Lucia, including pelicans, cormorants, frigate birds, herons, ducks, hawks, falcons, rails, coots, plovers, stilts, sandpipers, gulls, pigeons, cuckoos, night jars, swifts, hummingbirds, kingfishers, flycatchers, swallows, wrens, mockingbirds, thrushes, vireos, warblers, honey creepers, orioles and finches.

The uninhabited Maria Islands near Vieux Fort are the only place where imported predators such as mongooses and rats never reached and this is now the last sanctuary for the multi-coloured ground lizard (*Cnemidophorus vanzoi* or *zandoli tè*) and a small grass snake (*Liophis ornatus* or *kouwès*). Also endemic to St Lucia are the tree lizard (*Anolis luciae*), pygmy gecko (*Sphaerodactylus microlepis*), fer-de-lance snake (*Bothrops caribbaeus*), a sub-species of boa constrictor (*Boa constrictor orophius*), the little worm snake (*Leptotyphlops sp.*), a subspecies of hercules beetle (*Dynastes hercules baudrii*) and the St Lucia muskrat (*Megalomys luciae*) - a mammal now presumed extinct. Other distinctive animals are three species of regionally endemic bats, four species of endangered marine turtles (hawksbill, leatherback, loggerhead and green turtle), the agouti, the iguana and the red-necked pigeon. The Amerindians introduced agoutis around 1000 years ago, while opossums were introduced by a European collector in 1902.

The only animal which poses a serious threat to human life in St Lucia is the fer-de-lance, but vigorous government campaigns in past centuries (between 1870 and 1874 alone, 60,784 snakes were killed!) ,[2] have resulted in a situation where one can live on the island for a lifetime without ever crossing one's path.

2

The doom of the Caribs: early European claims on St Lucia

Popular modern writing on St Lucian history almost invariably repeats the notion of 'war-like Caribs' conquering the 'peaceful' Awaraks, murdering the men and taking their women as wives. The main evidence for this recital lies in the fact that at some stage in the past, between 600 and 800 AD, the Amerindians' pottery style changed from being uniform, thin and finely decorated to coarser, thicker and more varied. While it is possible that one Amerindian society was overpowered by another, it can also simply indicate a process of peaceful cultural change - in which case the producers of typical 'Arawakan' pottery were the ancestors of those who made typical 'Carib' pottery at a later stage.

Amerindians: historical and archaeological sources

At the root of this sort of uncertainty is the fact that two fundamentally different types of source inform us about Amerindian life: archaeological evidence and historical documents. They are sometimes difficult to reconcile. The historical records we have consist of journals, logbooks and reports written from 1492 onwards by European seafarers, missionaries and settlers. These are biased sources, written by men who came with particular cultural, religious and political preoccupations and specific goals: to enslave, conquer, settle or convert. What is more, they increasingly describe a changing world. In the sixteenth century, the Spanish raided the Caribbean islands for Amerindian slaves to work their mines in South America. In the seventeenth century, the British and French began to colonize the Lesser Antilles. Besides being murdered outright, thousands of Amerindians also died from influenza, measles, smallpox and other 'European' diseases against which they had no natural resistance. Thus, far from describing 'traditional' Amerindian peoples, these historical records actually describe societies crumbling under colonial assault.

Archaeological evidence, on the other hand, consists of tools and sculptured objects made of stone or shell, shards of pottery, bone, rock basins, engravings in stone (*petroglyphs*), post holes where houses once stood, burial sites, refuse heaps and other man-made material evidence, all of which provides us with clues about what the Amerindians ate, where they lived, what they used for digging, hammering, fishing, sewing, weaving, spinning and cooking, how long they lived, what physical deformities they suffered from or inflicted upon themselves, how they buried their dead, and so on. By their very nature, archaeological remains cannot talk. This renders them harder to understand, but also less biased. Unable to speak, they also do not lie as readily. What archaeological material can*not* reveal is what names people used for themselves and each other, or what languages they spoke.

Columbus had learned from Amerindians in the Greater Antilles that they were very afraid of 'those of *caniba* or *canima*'.[3] From this, the Spanish minted the terms *canibal* and *carib*. Terms commonly used in historical studies to denote various Amerindian groups are 'Taino', 'Ciboney', 'Arawak' and 'Carib'. Archaeologists, instead, usually prefer to base their categories on the finding places of characteristic pieces of pottery. As a result, two classifications co-exist to describe one historical reality, sometimes overlapping, sometimes contradicting one another. Trying to compile a coherent narrative out of historical sources and archaeological evidence sometimes feels like trying to compose a jigsaw puzzle with 90 per cent of the pieces missing and the remaining 10 per cent belonging to two different images!

The earliest settlements in the Caribbean were small and isolated. They are known as Saladoid, named after Saladero in eastern Venezuela, where a type of pottery was found that was later also discovered in the Antilles. Saladoid ceramic dates to the period from 400 BC to AD 600-850 and is uniform, delicately shaped and elaborately decorated. Saladoid cultures were eventually replaced by more complex stratified political systems which were ruled by local chieftains known as *nitainos* or *mitaines*, under one supreme chief or *cacique*. From the word *nitainos*, the people of this culture became known as the *Tainos*. The Tainos traded goods between the Greater Antilles, the Lesser Antilles and South America, primarily objects of green stone and metal (gold, copper and silver alloys) which formed the political and economic basis of the power of the caciques. In archaeological terms, this period is simply known as *post-Saladoid*. Post-Saladoid pottery is coarser, more varied and less elaborately worked than Saladoid material. Archaeologists believe this change indicates a diminishing symbolic value of ceramics (to the gain of green stone and metal objects) and perhaps also the disappearance of a class of specialized craftsmen and women. In post-Saladoid culture, settlements became larger than before, with villages of up to 1000 people in the Greater Antilles, and between 30 and 70 people in the Lesser Antilles. Post-Saladoid ceramics found at Troumassée in St Lucia have lent this period its alternative name: *Troumassoid*. The post-Saladoid/ Troumassoid period started between AD 600 and 850.

While realizing that one ought not to stick historical labels on archaeological evidence, sterile archaeological categories do little to bring the human tale to life.

For the purposes of this book, therefore, we have decided to follow Hulme and Whitehead and speak of 'Amerindians' and 'Caribs' to indicate the inhabitants of St Lucia at the time of European invasion - even though, in truth and fact, the first label is too general and the second too specific.[4]

Early Carib life in Ioüanalao

The first-ever recorded encounter between Europeans and Amerindians in the Lesser Antilles took place in St Lucia and, as luck would have it, this is one of the most elaborate narratives of such a meeting to survive. In 1605, the ship *Oliphe Blossome* set out from England for British-Guiana in South America. It drifted off course, a mutiny broke out and 67 of those on board were left behind on an island of which they knew nothing except the name given to it by European discoverers a century earlier: *Santa Lucia*. The Englishmen spent six weeks in St Lucia, living close to the Amerindians, who knew their island as *Ioüanalao* (*Hewanorra* or 'there where iguanas are found'). One of the surviving Englishmen afterwards wrote: *'These Carrebyes ... did seeme most strange and ugly, by reason they are all naked, with long blacke haire hanging downe their shoulders, their bodies all painted with red, and from their eares to their eyes, they do make three strokes with red, which makes them looke like divels or Anticke faces'*.[5] Alas, what the Caribs thought of the Englishmen has not been preserved for posterity.

Who were these stocky, red-skinned people with their thick, straight black hair and prowess of the sea, whose ancestors had arrived in *Ioüanalao* long before the beginning of the Christian era? We must begin by forgetting what the region looks like today. Where nowadays, the sea is a barrier between political nation states, in Amerindian days, the sea was a channel of communication, trade, exchange and movement. The Amerindians were great sailors, who built their settlements near mangroves and beaches where fresh water could be found, or else on promontories with easy access to the sea. Carib remains have been found all over the south-east and south-west of the island: in the Micoud district at Anse Capitaine, Anse Ger, Beauford, Kajouka, Patience, L'Islet Point, Mascare (Massacre), Point Canelle, Pointe de Caille, Troumassée and Vieux Bourg. Closer to Vieux Fort, Pointe Sable, La Tourney and the St Urbain mangrove are known sites while areas around Laborie, Black Bay, Banse, Béranger, Des Catières, Gertrine and Piaye all harbour remains. In the Choiseul district - where Carib blood still runs in people's veins - Morne Lézard, Ravine Chute d'Eau and Pointe Caribe are well-known, while other remains have been found at Praslin, Dennery, Anse Louvet, Grande Anse, Dauphin, Anse Lavoute, Gros Islet, Pigeon Island, Choc, Wingsville and Gros Piton.[6] Rock engravings (*petroglyphs*) on the banks of rivers and in gorges are thought to be at least 1000 years old and so belong to some of the earliest Amerindian cultures of St Lucia - even though their cartoon-like designs of humans, animals, the sun, moon and stars jump across time with surprising directness.[7] For many generations, Amerindian people in *Ioüanalao* taught their children about the natural resources of land, rivers and shores. Boys and girls were taught to hunt and gather food and the uses and dangers of the animal and plant life around them. They learned how to read the skies and navigate, how to make the tools and artefacts needed for survival, how to address and behave towards the people around them, how to relate to the deities, and how to deal with disaster, illness, fear, death and all the other inevitable challenges of life. The boys underwent protracted initiation rites at puberty, after which they went to live in the men's house (*carbet*). Women and children lived separately in smaller family huts. Storage platforms were used to keep foodstuffs and valuables out of harm's way. The Caribs ate cassava, yam, sweet potato, corn, beans, various fruits and hot peppers as well as agoutis, iguanas, birds and almost any form of life offered by the sea, mangroves and rivers. They hunted and fished using bows and arrows, with arrow tips made from sharpened shell, dipped in manchineel tree poison, or tied with a blunt object to stun birds they wanted to catch alive. They tamed parrots as pets and kept a small bark-less breed of dog - although it is unclear whether dogs were off-menu pets or hunting companions, since dog bones have occasionally been found in food refuse heaps as well.

These refuse heaps are usually full of remains from fish, shellfish, lobster, conch, crab, manatee and turtle. Sea food was caught by hand or with baskets, shot with bow and arrow or harpoons, trapped in rock pools or man-made structures or stunned with the juices of pounded poisonous leaves. Parties of Caribs also regularly paddled to nearby islands to collect food. A mixture of cassava-juice with crushed peppers and lime juice (*coüi*) helped to preserve their food almost indefinitely - much like the *cazirib* still used today in Guyana to cook *pepperpot*.

The Caribs were natural sailors who navigated by the stars and currents. Their vessels - *canouas*, origin of our word canoe - were propelled with shovel-like paddles and could hold up to 30 or 40 people. Canoes were made from gommier trees, hollowed out with axes, fire, hot stones and water, and with wooden ribs inserted to obtain the shape. This method of canoe-making survived in St Lucia until the late twentieth century. Another Amerindian invention which quickly gained fame in the Old World were hammocks. Typically, these measured twelve by six feet and were woven from spun cotton. A small fire was lit underneath if someone felt ill or cold. Hammocks were quickly adopted by Europeans on board ships and in the armed forces. Amerindian women were also experts at basketry and dyeing, and they made all sorts of knapsacks and other carriers with intricate designs.

The Caribs wore little more than a cotton loincloth hung like an apron around their waists, but they bathed daily and painted their bodies with bright red annatto (*roucou*), using clay stamps to print geometrical designs on their skins in white, black and ochre. Such body paintings served to protect them from the sun and biting insects but were also ornamental, and sometimes ceremonial.

Amerindian women tied cotton straps around their legs to increase the bulge of their calves, which was a mark of beauty. Men (and perhaps women too) pierced their ears and lips and wore shell and bone ornaments. As a mark of distinction, some men wore crescent-shaped jewellery on their chest, made of hammered gold or copper. A widespread habit was that of flattening the foreheads of newborn infants by tying a board across it, a practice believed to strengthen the skull and enhance beauty.

Post holes show that Amerindian houses were round, constructed around a central pole. They had thatched roofs and sometimes contained graves as well. Archaeological digs performed by the University of Vienna (1983-7) at Pointe de Caille revealed, amongst other things, 26 burial sites dating back to AD 830 (plus or minus 70 years). The deceased had been buried in a seated position, with knees bent towards the chest. From this and other burial sites we know that Amerindian burials were extensive and prolonged ceremonies. In some cases, more than one person had been buried in a grave, at different times. Often, graves were not filled in immediately and were re-opened some time after the burial to remove or replace parts of the skeleton. It is perhaps from this custom that the Amerindians gained the reputation of being man-eaters. The very word Carib (which in their language simply meant 'human being') lies at the root of the word cannibalism. The Spaniards and other colonizers ardently believed that Caribs habitually ate human flesh out of vengeance. Modern research shows that if Caribs ate human flesh at all, the amounts were probably minimal and the settings ceremonial. Warriors, for instance, might chew a small piece of the body of a slain enemy (and possibly spit it out again) to demonstrate and encourage each other to be valiant in battle.

The elaborate burial rites indicate that Amerindians had a strongly developed ancestor cult. Selected men were trained as *boyez*, whose task it was to placate evil spirits (*mabouyas*), induce benevolent spirits to protect and nourish them, act as medicine men and cast spells (*piai*). Recurring items in archaeological digs are three-pointed or conical stones and clay objects carved or shaped with human or animal figures. These are known as *zemis* and were used as amulets or oracles in religious ceremonies. Household pottery was often decorated with small animal or human figures (*adornos*) as well, but whether this served a spiritual purpose is unclear. The three-pointed *zemis* were believed to be the embodiments of spirits, in particular *Yokahu*, the Giver-of-Food (from the Amerindian *Yok-ahu* or Manioc-Giver). It is interesting to note, in this context, the striking similarity between such zemis and a large stack of rock protruding from the sea off Mammelles Point at Fond d'Or Bay, near an area still commonly known today as Mabouya Valley. It is not inconceivable that Caribs named the area in reference to this feature.[8] In similar vein, Robert Devaux has posited that Gros and Petit Pitons fulfilled a divine astronomical function in Amerindian spiritual beliefs and that their shape is what first inspired Amerindians to create these three-pointed, triangular spiritual vessels or *zemis*, not just in St Lucia but in other islands of the Lesser Antilles as well.

Amerindian resistance to European invasion: the sixteenth century

On 3 November 1493, Christopher Columbus completed his second successful crossing of the Atlantic Ocean in a fleet of seventeen ships, carrying some 1500 men. At the break of dawn, the crews spotted an island and, as it was a Sunday, christened it Dominica. Unable to find a safe harbour, the fleet sailed on northwards. Over the next few days, Columbus saw and named Marie-Galante, Guadeloupe, Montserrat, Nevis, St Christopher, St Eustatius, Saba, St Croix and the Virgin Islands and moved on into the Greater Antilles: Puerto Rico, Hispaniola, Jamaica and Cuba.

Columbus was hardly the first man to reach the Americas. Prehistoric hunters had crossed from Siberia into North America 20 000 years earlier; the Norse reached Greenland and Newfoundland in the tenth century and a school in academic thought maintains that West Africans set foot in Middle America two centuries before Columbus did.[9] Nor can it be said that Columbus 'discovered' the Caribbean - a feat performed by the Amerindians long before. What Columbus did discover was a new route from Europe to America - even if he himself continued to believe he had reached India (hence the term 'West Indies').

Columbus did not notice St Lucia on this second voyage in 1493, nor is it likely that he spotted it during his third voyage in 1498, when he made landfall at Trinidad, named Tobago, Grenada and Isla Margarita and continued on to Hispaniola. In 1499, a private voyage was made by Alonso de Hojeda, with Amerigo Vespucci and Juan de la Cosa on board. The latter was a skilled navigator who had accompanied Columbus on his second voyage. In 1500, Juan de la Cosa drew a map which features St Lucia under the name *El Falcon* and an island immediately south as *Las Agujas:* Spanish for 'The Needles'. Since the Pitons resemble needles, it is possible that de la Cosa transposed the two. Other historians believe that Columbus spotted St Lucia on 15 June 1502, during his fourth and last voyage, when Spanish ships made landfall in *Martinico*

(Martinique) and travelled northward to Hispaniola. On a clear day, St Lucia can be seen from Martinique with the naked eye - but the absence in the ship's log of an island south of *Martinico* considerably weakens this theory.

Either way, it is beyond doubt that Europeans knew of St Lucia by the start of the sixteenth century. A Spanish Cedula of 1511 considered *Sancta Lucia* a Spanish domain; a Vatican globe of 1520[10] depicted *Sancta Lucia* and a Spanish map of 1529 bore *S. Luzia* on it. In 1550, a French book referred to a small island, two-and-a-half leagues away from *Matelyne* (Martinique) not as St Lucia but as *Fatigate* (meaning 'restless' or 'tiresome'), possibly because St Lucia was then an infamous pirate hide-out. Why is there a connection with the Virgin Martyr of Syracuse, if neither Columbus nor Juan de la Cosa were anywhere close on the patron saint's feast day? An old but persistent legend in St Lucia holds that before the island appeared on any official map, French sailors were shipwrecked on its shores and, it being the 13th of December, named the island in honour of Sainte Lucie.

The Great Dying

The sixteenth century in the New World is known as The Great Dying. Within four generations, slavery and disease spelled death for hundreds of thousands, perhaps millions of people. The Greater Antilles were raided first, followed by Middle and South America. Hispaniola, when Columbus first entered it in 1492, contained almost one million inhabitants. Forty years later, in 1530, these had been all but wiped out. By the Treaty of Tordesillas (1494), a papal bull allowed Spain and Portugal to divide the New World between them. In no time at all, Portuguese sugar plantations covered half of South America (Brazil) and Spaniards were mining gold and silver in Central and South America and Mexico, destroying age-old indigenous empires, and wreaking havoc in the Greater Antilles as well. Spain was Europe's super power and its Crown spent heavily on military pursuits, running up millions of ducats in debt. The New World had a seemingly endless supply of bullion and between 1503 and 1660, more than seven million pounds of silver crossed the Atlantic Ocean in Spanish ships, tripling the amount of silver circulating in Europe.

Spain started bringing African slaves to Hispaniola as early as 1503 (and to Jamaica, Cuba and Puerto Rico from 1517), but the majority of slaves mining the gold and silver during this first century of exploitation were Amerindians. The result was genocide. In 1512, Spain specifically authorized its *conquistadores* by royal edict to capture and enslave the Amerindians on '*the islands of Los Barbados, Dominica, Matinino, Santa Lucia, San Vincente, La Asuncion (Grenada) and Taraco (Tobago)*' also. They attempted a few slave raids but soon learned to be wary of these small islands. Dominica was attacked in 1514 by a Spanish fleet of nineteen ships and 1500 men but the Caribs' poisoned arrows chased them off within four days. In 1525, a similar battle sent the Spaniards scuttling from Guadeloupe. Consequently, for most of the sixteenth century, the Spanish bypassed the small islands in the south, deciding that the small number of natives did not warrant the perils of capturing them. When European ships landed in the small islands at all during the sixteenth century, it was to obtain water, wood and provisions. Early on, Spanish ships introduced cattle, sheep, goats and pigs to these islands to provide their crews with easy hunting in case of an emergency. British and French privateers, of course, were happy to help themselves to such feral stocks and throughout the seventeenth and early eighteenth centuries, St Lucia was a favourite hunting ground for settlers from nearby islands and crews from passing vessels. Until about 1700, though, Europeans could never be sure of the kind of reception the Caribs would give them. They might barter with them one day, but attack mercilessly the next.

It must be remembered that by then, the Caribs in islands like St Lucia were fully aware of events in the Greater Antilles, as refugees carried news of Spanish atrocities south. Sometimes, Carib refugees arrived from the Greater Antilles carrying tales of horror. Other times, people themselves travelled and witnessed the atrocities first-hand. There is the case of an Amerindian chief in St Lucia who, in 1605, told the Englishmen of the *Oliphe Blossome* that he could speak a little Spanish since he had been '*a slave to the Spaniard in the Ile of Margareta.*'[11] Occasionally, Spanish vessels loaded with treasure got shipwrecked while passing through the island chain. Legend has it that on 13 March 1597, a storm sank the Spanish galleon *San Fernando,* two miles north-east of the southern-most tip of St Lucia. If this was one of the ships referred to by the crew of the *Oliphe Blossome* in 1605, then it was quickly stripped clean by the Caribs.

> *A little before our arrivall, three Spanish ships were cast away, and much of the goodes these Indians had saved with their Boats, and hid it in the Woods, they had so much Roan cloath, that all their Periagoes had sayles thereof. They also had great store of stuffe, Sirge, and Spanish woollen cloath, cloakes and apparell: insomuch that if we had had a Barke of fortie tons burthen, wee could have loaden her home with such commodities as would have made a saving voyage.*[12]

In 1621, the *Santisima Trinidad* sank in the same waters. Worth noting is the mention of *roan cloath* used for sails on canoes which traditionally were paddled. The Caribs had been astounded to see the use of sails on European ships but in St Lucia, the innovation appears to have been adopted very quickly.[13]

Shipwrecks also sometimes brought survivors ashore, as did the occasional retaliatory attack by Caribs on a European settlement or ship. An unknown number of European deserters, African runaway slaves and prisoners-of-war were thus absorbed into pre-colonial Carib society. In Dominica in 1569, more than 30 Spaniards and 40 Africans lived amongst the native Amerindians.[14]

In short, while the Caribs of St Lucia remained in control of their homeland during the sixteenth century, they were fully aware of disruptions taking place nearby. As a result, they were wary of European advances, ready to defend themselves, and keen to participate in occasional revenge attacks. It is not even inconceivable that the Caribs carefully nourished and encouraged their image of warlike, man-eating savages!

Against this background, let's take a look at the story of the *Oliphe Blossome* and the *'most lamentable miseries, and distressed Calamities'* that befell its crew in St Lucia in 1605 - not only because this tale is considered *'the most detailed and valuable account of Carib-European contact before the full-scale attempts at settlement in the Lesser Antilles in the 1620s'*[15], but also because it describes the first attempt at English settlement anywhere in the West Indies. It heralded a crucial transition, namely the encroachment by France and England on Spain's possessions in the Caribbean. Since Spain had never managed to conquer the Lesser Antilles, this was precisely where France and England started nibbling at the Spanish empire first. As it turned out, St Lucia became one of the - if not *the* - most hotly-contested island in the Anglo-French wrangle for power in the Caribbean.

The mutiny of the Oliphe Blossome

Two years after his hair-raising ordeal, one of the survivors of the *Oliphe Blossome,* John Nicholl, returned to London and published an account of his adventures. *An Houre Glasse of Indian Newes* brims with detailed descriptions of the south of St Lucia at a time when the island firmly belonged to the Caribs. We can retrace Nicholl's every step and picture what he saw with his own eyes in 1605: the distant Pitons, waves crashing on the reef near Maria Island, the Carib garden at La Retraite where he stole tobacco and yams... we can even feel the occasional fierce mosquito sting. Ultimately, Nicholl described the day his companions were murdered by the *Carebyes* and he himself narrowly escaped death. One can stand at Anse de Sable Beach today and almost hear the cries of fear and victory; the rushing around of attackers and victims; the sound of Englishmen desperately loading their muskets to counter-attack; the *whoosh* of arrows flying out of the bush; the Englishmen's panic as they wade out into the sea to try and escape the arrows, and the look in the Amerindian chief's eyes when, bow drawn, he finally faces the fugitive Nicholl. We can even understand why the Caribs may have felt compelled to attack.

How did it all start?

The *Oliphe Blossome* left England on 12 April 1605 to bring supplies and settlers to the budding colony of British-Guiana. Dissent smouldered from the start and relations deteriorated further when the ship drifted off course. Food and water rations were cut and *'many fearful & dangerous mutinies'* occurred. After seventeen miserable weeks at sea, the crew sighted St Lucia. No sooner did the *Oliphe Blossome* anchor *'but the Carebyes came in their Periagoes or Boats aboard us with great store of Tobacco, Plantons, Potatoes, Pines, Sugar Canes, and diverse other fruits, with Hens, Chickens, Turtles, & Guanas ...'*

Seeing the welcome, 67 Englishmen decided to stay in St Lucia *'and there to live untill it should please God to send some meanes to bring us a way'*. They were set ashore with some food and tools, a musket each, one *great Piece* (cannon) with ten round bullets and four barrels of gun powder. Soon after, bad feelings resurfaced. Shots were exchanged and the captain told some Amerindians that the 67 deserters *'were bad people, and would take all they had from them, and would cut their throats.'* For four weeks, the *Carebyes* and the English lived in peace. The Caribs sold the English *'five or seaven houses planted by a fresh water River'* (at the mouth of the old Vieux Fort River) where the Caribs had a small fishing settlement. Their main village was located a mile or two to the north-east, on the reef-protected Atlantic coast. Here lived their chief Anthonie, the *Captaine* who had once been a slave in Margarita.

Anthonie and his men daily visited the Englishmen, trading *'for all manner of victuall, as Plantons, Potatoes, Penas, Papaians, Pumpins, Callobashoes, Pappes, Mammies, Guiavas, with diverse other fruits, and Tobacco aboundance, all verie pleasant to eate. Also they brought Turtles, Guanas, Hens and Chickens, Woodcocks and Snipes, with some Pellicans.'* The English bartered *'hatchets, knives, beads, fish-hooks, and thimbles, with other trifles.'*

After their harsh sea journey, life could not be better. The English built a fence and stayed close to their huts but otherwise lived in peace. Every night, they caught turtles and made *'White-pots and Puddings'* with cassava, turtle eggs and turtle fat. Also *'we had a Net, with the which wee would get at one draught as many fish of diverse sorts, as would serve all our companie a day.'* The English and Caribs even dined together *'but by no meanes wee could not make them eate salt: for they use to eate all their meate seasoned with Ginnie Pepper.'*

But things turned sour when Anthonie's brother arrived from St Vincent. According to Anthonie, this Augraumart was furious that the English occupied the huts near the river and planned to *'bring twelve Periagoes loaden with Carrebyes to kill us.'* Anthonie advised the Englishmen to kill his brother. They, however, had *'found this Augraumart verie kinde onto us'* as he had shown them how to make a cassava grater out of sharp stones and a piece of wood. Before long,

Augraumart in turn told the Englishmen *'that Anthonio would cut our throates, and therefore bid us kill him. This made us doubtfull which to trust to.'*

The situation worsened when one of the Englishmen sold a sword to Anthonie, thereby defying a rule never to sell a weapon to the Caribs. A dozen Englishmen under Captain Alexander Sen-Johns set out to visit Anthonie in his village and reclaim the sword. They *'found him in his ... Hamaco, with a little fire under him because he was not well, and the Sword standing by him, which yong Sen-Johns tooke and brought forth to us. This drove him into a great rage against us, for never after that would he be familiar with us.'*

Not long after, the Englishmen noticed some Carib men wearing *'for an ornament upon the small of their naked armes a four-square plate, which maister Browne a Gold-finer told Captaine Sen-Johns had three partes of it Golde.'* Sen-Johns asked the Caribs where they had found this gold and they pointed to *'a great Mountaine on the North-west part of the Island whose toppe we might see from the place where wee dwelt'* - probably Gros Piton. Not everyone trusted it, but sixteen men insisted on a gold-finding mission, using the group's only boat in what should have been a one-week trip. But John Nicholl's suspicion that it was an ambush ploy by the Caribs seems to have been correct, for the sixteen were never seen nor heard of again.

Meanwhile, the Caribs ceased their daily trading visits and the Englishmen ran short of provisions. Nicholl and some men visited Anthonie's village where, to their surprise, they found only a handful of men, while the women were *'making great preparation of victuals: some baking of Cassada, others roasting and boyling of great fishes and Turtles.'* The women refused to barter any food and the Englishmen, perhaps nettled, decided to find some for themselves. They walked west-north-west for three miles (probably towards La Retraite) until they

> *... passed through many goodly Gardens, wherein was abbundance of Cassada, Potatoes, Tobacco, Cotton-wool-trees, and Guiava trees ... fearing that wee shoulde bee benighted, wee returned the same way againe, with as much greene Tobacco, Potatoes, and Cassada, as wee could carrie, which did much content our men at home for the Indians had not brought any victuals in three dayes before.*

The following day, a large group of Caribs led by Augraumart and his father came to see the Englishmen, who instantly anticipated trouble. But Augraumart was nicer than ever, bringing roasted land crabs and inviting them back to the village for more. The Englishmen hesitated but were swayed when Augraumart promised them hammocks, for which they had begged him many times as *'a meanes to save us from the Stings of a certaine Flye called a Musketo, the which would so torment us with their poysoned stings, and cause us to swell as though we had the Leprosie, for they would sting through three payre of Stockings.'*

With anticipatory gratitude, they invited the Caribs into their settlement, where an impromptu party ensued. Even the normally sour Master Tench '*did show himselfe so extraordinarie pleasant, that hee fell a singing of Catches with the Carrebyes, and caused them to drink carouses of Agua vitae and water.*'

In the midst of the drunken party, one Englishman thought he overheard an Amerindian saying that '*the Captaine of the English had his hande cutte off at the Mount.*' Anxiety about the fate of the sixteen gold-seekers was rekindled and the English realized that this was their chance to kill the Caribs as '*wee had a hundreth and above of them within our houses without either bowe or Arrowes.*' The attack was debated but Master Tench objected, '*saying: God would not be pleased with such a bloudie Act, agaynst such harmlesse people*' and the conspiracy was abandoned.

The Caribs left shortly after, but Augraumart and his father stayed on for a meal. That done with, eighteen Englishmen along with Augraumart and his father set out for Anthonie's house to fetch the desired hammocks. Augraumart and his father carried no bows and arrows, only a '*Brasell sworde*'. The English carried their firearms but '*did not regarde either to charge them, or to light our match*', not fearing treason. '*In this carelesse and secure manner*', wrote Nicholl, they walked from the Vieux Fort River across the lower slope of Moule à Chique onto Anse de Sable Beach, *which was so extraeme hote with the reflexion of the Sunne that wee were not able to travail apace, being loaden with our Peeces.*'

Carrying heavy weaponry, wearing unsuitable clothes and probably boots, the Englishmen must have plodded through the soft deep sand, panting and sweating and quite possibly cursing the heat. Only one Englishman was enjoying himself. '*Maister Alexander had put off his Doublet, and gave his Boy his Peece, & went jesting and playing arme in arme with the two Carrebyes a good space before us, until wee came to a point of Land a quarter of a mile from Anthonios house ...*'

Master Alexander and the two Carib men had arrived at Pointe Sable: a place where the beach protrudes into the sea and is surrounded by water on two sides, and thick undergrowth on another. Unaware of any danger, Master Alexander allowed Augraumart to embrace him. Then, suddenly, Augraumart clasped Master Alexander's rapier with one hand and his dagger with the other '*and his Father with a great Brassell Sword strooke him downe before we could come at him, but he recovered againe.*'

Horrified, the Englishmen realized they were trapped. '*Then came the Arrowes so thicke out of the wood, that we could not get our match in the Cocke for pulling the Arrowes out of our bodyes: so amongst us all was but five or sixe peeces discharged, which when the Indians saw give fire, they did fall flat on the ground, shouting and crying with a moste hellish noyse, naming us by our names when they hit us.'* The English tried to retreat but were met with another volley of arrows. When they threw away their muskets and unsheathed their swords, this only encouraged the Amerindians,

> *... for when they see wee could not hurt them with our peeces, they would come so neere us, as though they purposed to make choyce in what place to hit us, of some they shot in the faces, others through the Shoulders, and of others, they would naile their feete and the ground together. Maister Budge and Robert Shaw ranne into the sea, and there were both drowned and kild with Arrowes, Maister Tench had a little Buckler, with the which hee did save himselfe a long time, but at the last an Arrowe passed through both his legges, that hee could not goe, and stooping to pull it out, they kild him, and if anye of us offered to runne at one or two of them, they would runne away, and of a suddaine twentie or thirtie would enclose us, and still shoote Arrowes in them til they were downe, and then they with a great Brassell sword beate them to death, and after would rifle them.*

And so it went on: with the Englishmen's attack as inconsequential as their defence. Three times, Nicholl tried to save a mate and three times, he was forced to leave him, dead or dying. Desperate, Nicholl and another man tried to break through the Amerindian lines. They entered a narrow path through the bush, pursued by Amerindians. Nicholl's companion was shot in the head and died.

> *Then came there two Arrowes and hitte mee in the back, the one directly against my hart, the other through my shoulder blade: so (with my sword in my hande) I ran upon them desperatly, thinking (before I had died) to have ben the death of some of them. And in my running, I saw Captaine Anthony, with an Arrow in his Bow drawne against me, who stood untill I came very neere him (for he purposed to have sped mee with that shot) which when I see come, I thought to put it by with my sword, but it light on my hand, & passed therein the handle of my sword, and nayled both together: but I continued running at him still; and before he could nocke another, I made him, and all the rest turne their backs, and run into the sands againe: which oportunity when I espyed, I leapt into the wood, downe to the valley, where I found a great Lake: And hearing them, with great showts and cry, which they use in signe of triumph and victory, pursue mee still, I leapt into the Lake, with my sword nayled to my hand, and two arrowes in my backe, and by the helpe of God swamme over, but with much ado: for the further side was shallow water, but I waded in mud up to the waste, which had almost spent me.*

Nicholl managed to get back to his compatriots before the Caribs did, and discharge of their cannon caused the Caribs to retreat hurriedly. For three days, the Englishmen fortified their settlement. When the Caribs attacked again, by land and sea at once, they managed to set fire to the huts with burning arrows but all the Englishmen - except two - saved themselves behind their cannon which '*drove them all backe, with most lamentable shrikes and cryes: no doubt but that shot was the death of many of them: for she was charged with stones.*' The Caribs eventually blew their horns and retired.

Without shelter or food, the Englishmen's situation seemed untenable. Surprisingly, not long after the attack, other Caribs arrived with cassava, potatoes and plantains and, ostentatiously placing their bows and arrows on the ground, traded with the English as though nothing had happened. But the respite did not last. For a whole week, three or four hours every day, the Englishmen were attacked. Hurt, hungry and desperate, they offered a truce. Anthonie agreed to give them a canoe and some cloth in exchange for hatchets, knives, beads, spades and shovels. He also warned them that Augraumart was due to arrive from St Vincent the following day with twelve canoes full of armed men. On the 26 September 1605, shortly after midnight, the nineteen surviving Englishmen pushed off in their Carib canoe - without a compass and using their garters as ropes for the sail. With their hurried departure came an end to the first English settlement in the Caribbean.

Amerindians under attack, 1605-1732

By 1600, France, England and Holland started challenging Spain's dominance in the Caribbean, quietly welcoming the privateers who attacked the silver fleet convoys carrying silver from the Americas to Spain. One of these pirates, a one-legged Frenchman by the name of Francois le Clerc - nicknamed *Jambe de Bois* because of his wooden stump - used St Lucia as his base, roaming as far as Cuba. It is believed that in 1554, he captured and looted four Spanish galleons and hid part of the bounty in a cave on the north side of Pigeon Island.[16] Since Spain had never penetrated the Lesser Antilles, this was a logical place for France and England to start chipping away at the Spanish empire and with typical expansionist arrogance, the two European crowns staked out their claims. Even while Amerindian resistance was still in full bloom, Barbados was soon thought of as 'rightfully' English, and Martinique and Guadeloupe as 'rightfully' French. But colonial ownership of other islands remained disputed - and nowhere more so than in St Lucia. For two centuries, the French and English bickered over St Lucia, with the Caribs caught in the uncomfortable middle, ceding now with this side, then with the other. Although they fought a brave and strategically cunning battle, by the time St Lucia was finally ceded to England (in 1814), the last remaining Caribs had long since died out or become assimilated into the new African and European populations.

Early European claims and counter-claims

The first successful European settlement in the Lesser Antilles was established in January of 1624, when Thomas Warner, his family and thirteen colonists set up camp in St Kitts. They survived the first year and in 1625, Warner secured a commission from King Charles I giving him full power *'to order and despose of any landes'* in St Kitts, Nevis, Barbuda, Montserrat *'and any other neighbour Islandes to them ... not beinge in the possession or government of any other Christian Prince, State or Potentate.'* Meanwhile, a Frenchman named Pierre d'Esnambuck had started a colony on the other side of St Kitts. By striking up an ad-hoc alliance against the Amerindians, these normally fierce European adversaries gained their first successful footholds in the Lesser Antilles. From St Kitts/Saint Christopher, the English went on to colonize Barbados and Antigua, and the French occupied Guadeloupe and Martinique.

In 1627, the King of England granted *Letters Patent* to Jacques, Earl of Carlisle, giving him ownership of *'all the Caribbee Islands'* including St Lucia, Grenada, St Vincent, Barbados, Mittalanea (Martinique), Dominico, Marie Galante, Deseada, Todosantes (the Saintes), Guadaloupe, Antigue, Montserrat, Redendo, Barbuda, Nevis, Statis (St Eustatius), St Bartholomew, St Martin, Anguilla, Sembrera, Enegada *'and other islands, before found to his great cost.'* Settlements were tried in several of these but not without Amerindian opposition. In 1635, Caribs from Dominica burnt down a settlement in Marie-Galante. The French retaliated by massacring an entire Carib village in Dominica. In 1640, Caribs almost wiped out a settlement of 40 English families in Antigua, killing Thomas Warner's son Edward, who had been in charge, and abducting his wife and children. It was suspected that they had received support from the French. True enough, France took over control of Antigua soon after (but had to cede the island back to England in 1667 at the Treaty of Breda).

It is unclear which of the two nations first colonized St Lucia. One English document holds that the Earl of Carlisle settled the island *'in 1635, and 1637, by English Colonies from Bermuda, in 1638 by a Colony from St Christopher and in 1640, 1644 and 1645, by Colonies from Barbados.'*[17] Other English records claim that the first settlement occurred in 1639 by a Captain Judlee, commissioned by Thomas Warner from St Kitts. Judlee's camp was allegedly located at Praslin Bay and consisted of 300 or 400 Englishmen (including 120 from Somers Island in the Bermudas).

French documents, on the other hand, claim that Monsieur d'Esnambuck first settled St Lucia, having received letters of patent on 8 March 1635. D'Esnambuck died before he could subdue the Caribs but his nephew, Monsieur du Parquet (who was made captain of Martinique and St Lucia in December 1637) had almost managed to chase the Amerindians out of St

Lucia when, in 1639, some English adventurers took advantage of the upset and established themselves. This, in French historiography, was Judlee's settlement: a rogue enterprise, non-commissioned and without a governor.

Either way, Judlee's little colony failed within eighteen months. Caribs attacked it in revenge for an incident in Dominica involving an English ship. Caribs had boarded the ship without suspicion, mistaking it for a French ally. The English captain entertained them in style but, mid-party, quietly weighed anchor and abducted his guests. Most Caribs managed to jump overboard but four were captured and enslaved. In retaliation, Amerindians from Dominica, Martinique and St Vincent massacred Judlee's colony in St Lucia. The attack lasted three weeks, from 20 September until 12 October 1640. The Caribs smoked out the Englishmen with red pepper, burnt down their huts and pilfered their stores. The Governor and most men died. Only a handful of survivors made it safely to Montserrat.

French settlement under de Rousselan and successors

The attack on Judlee greatly tempered the English Crown's desire for colonizing St Lucia, as they judged it too far from Barbados and St Kitts for adequate protection. France, on the other hand, was sorely tempted by the extra land and resources St Lucia offered its settlers in Martinique, just a few hours' sailing away. Besides, St Lucia was strategically well-placed relative to France's other possessions in the Antilles. In 1642, King Louis XIII ceded St Lucia to the French West India Company (FWIC). Eight years later, Captain du Parquet of Martinique, who had never given up his vision of a French colony in St Lucia (and who happened to be a shareholder of the FWIC) pooled his resources with a Monsieur Houel (later the Governor of Guadeloupe) and jointly, the two Frenchmen bought Martinique, St Lucia and most of Grenada from the FWIC for 41 500 livres (1660 pounds Sterling).

Without delay, 40 Frenchmen crossed the Martinique Channel and constructed a fort '*aupres du Petit Cul-de-Sac et de la rivière du Carénage*' - probably on the La Toc or Tapion headland. They were led by a French officer called de Rousselan who, interestingly, was married to a Carib woman. Although the Frenchmen were wary of the Caribs and lived and planted most of their crops (ground provisions, tobacco, ginger and cotton) inside a fort protected by cannons, double palisades and a moat, the settlement flourished for three years. But de Rousselan's death in 1654 put an end to the relative peace. His successor, de la Rivière, moved to live outside the fort and was clubbed to death by visiting Caribs before the year was out. His wife, two children and a slave were carried off. This, incidentally, is the earliest mention of the presence of a slave in St Lucia - whether of African or Carib origin remains unclear.

The next Governor, Hacquet, survived for two years until a fateful day in October 1656 when some Caribs invited him to inspect a catch of turtles for sale. '*They lunged for him and threw him into the sea, but he came up with drawn, albeit wet, pistol, and they hit the ground in terror. He backtracked to the fort but one arrow hit him, and he died three days later of gangrene*'[18] in Martinique. His successor, le Breton, did not last long either but for once, the demise was self-inflicted. Le Breton's behaviour reportedly caused such an outcry that his own officers attempted to murder him. He escaped into the woods and eventually found his way back to Martinique, while his would-be assassins escaped prosecution by boarding an English ship.

After le Breton, Governor du Coutis held the fort for a year, being relieved in 1657 by Diel d'Aygremont, who was a relative of du Parquet (the *Captain* of Martinique and co-owner of St Lucia). Following the natural death of du Parquet in 1658, ownership of St Lucia was transferred to du Parquet's wife and their two minor sons, while the boys' uncle, Diel de Vaudroques, acted as mentor and interim-Governor for Martinique, St Lucia and Grenada. Under Diel d'Aygremont's rule, the French settlement in St Lucia finally flourished for the first time.

This greatly worried the English, and they quickly reiterated their old claim to the island. They organized a fleet in Barbados and in (or just before) 1659 landed in St Lucia with cannons and men to besiege the French fort. A bitter battle ensued. The French eventually managed to drive off the English invaders, who had to leave several wounded and dead men behind, and France maintained its tenuous foothold in St Lucia.

Meanwhile, in 1654, some Dutchmen had built a redoubt in the south of the island, to use as a refueling station for water and wood en route to their new colony in Tobago. Nothing much had changed since the days of the *Oliphe Blossome* and the Dutch constantly needed '*to protect themselves from the attacks of the Caribs, who were vexed at seeing foreigners act as if they were the masters in the midst of their very huts.*'[19] The Dutch fort was soon succeeded by a small French redoubt, located near a bay with '*a very beautiful and very good harbour*' (Vieux Fort Bay)[20]. It was staffed by twenty men whose main task was keeping track of English naval movements.

The Caribs' sale of St Lucia

In 1660, France and England struck up a temporary alliance to once and for all bring the Caribs of the Lesser Antilles under control. They opted for diplomacy over warfare and, on 30 March 1660, at a meeting in Guadeloupe, the French and English signed a peace treaty with the *Sauvages Caraybes*. The Amerindians were represented by fifteen principal chiefs; the English by Monsieur Houel, the French Governor of Guadeloupe who had brokered the deal, while the Governor of Martinique, Diel de Vaudroques, sent his deputees Laubières and Renaudot, to sign on behalf of Madame du Parquet, her two sons, and all the French inhabitants of Martinique, St Lucia and Grenada. The treaty stipulated that the Caribs of the Lesser Antilles would renounce all rights of ownership to the islands occupied by France and England but would be allowed to keep Dominica and St Vincent '*for their sole and unique retreat.*'

The French attached a great deal of value to the treaty, considering it the final stamp of legitimacy to their occupation of St Lucia. But English historical records hardly mention the treaty at all and, in truth, little changed after 1660. D'Aygremont remained in charge of the French fort in St Lucia, which expanded under his leadership with the construction of a line of fortifications along *Chocque* Bay but in 1663, like so many of his predecessors, he was murdered by Caribs. He was replaced by Monsieur la Lande.

The treaty also did not diminish England's desire for ownership of St Lucia. A meeting was arranged and on 6 April 1663, 600 Caribs from all over the Lesser Antilles sailed or paddled their canoes to Barbados and formally signed over to Francis Lord Willoughby '*Captain General over all the Carribbee Islands*' the '*full and absolute purchase*' of St Lucia.[21] A central role in this event was played by Thomas *Indian* Warner - a man who merits some attention. Indian Warner was the illegitimate son of Sir Thomas Warner, the pioneer Governor of St Kitts, and an unnamed enslaved Carib woman. Born in 1630, Indian had been acknowledged by Thomas Warner as his natural son and was raised alongside his legitimate half-siblings. But soon after Sir Thomas' death, Indian's English stepmother put him to work in the fields alongside the slaves. Indian eventually escaped and went to live in his mother's Carib village in Dominica, where he emerged as a local chief. No documentary evidence remains to explain what Indian Warner and the Caribs aimed to achieve with the sale of St Lucia in 1663. Perhaps they were playing divide-and-rule, hoping to fan the flames of conflict between England and France. Indeed, the French furiously denounced the sale as a hoax involving nothing but a few casks of *eau de vie*.

After the treaty was signed, 1100 Englishmen in five ships-of-war accompanied by 600 Amerindians in seventeen pirogues left Barbados and proceeded to invade St Lucia. According to French records, only fourteen men guarded the garrison at Choc Bay at the time of the invasion, and they quickly surrendered on condition they be allowed to travel to Martinique.[22] With the French out of the way, a formal hand-over ceremony took place and '*four Indian Princes or Captains ... gave and delivered in a Solemn Manner by Turf and Twig, on behalf of themselves and the rest of the Indian Proprietors, all their Rights, Title and Interest to* [St Lucia].*'*[23] Colonel Carew was appointed Deputy Governor and for a while, St Lucia became English. The new occupants seem to have favoured the south of the island. A 1742 map by Houel shows in detail where in 1663, English troops maintained a fort, battery and retranchements (ruins of which remained in 1742) on top of what is now Convent Hill in Vieux Fort town. One battery guarded the river mouth, another stood on top of Raphael Hill and retranchements followed the beach from the river mouth to *Ance Grougrous* (now the Fisheries complex). These guns and defences could be carried across to Anse de Sable Beach to guard the Atlantic coast as well. An even earlier English map (1722) indicates that in a sandy bay in the far south of the island (presumably Vieux Fort bay), '*the English made the first Settlement, about forty years since, and was then about 1500 people upon it, and Governour.*'[24] It is plausible that this refers to the same 1663 settlement.

Renewed Anglo-French contestation

Once again, the English settlement did not last. Disease swept through it and when a Martiniquan fishing boat landed in St Lucia a few months later, the crew found the old French fort at Choc Bay empty and not an Englishmen in sight (the source does not mention the Vieux Fort settlement). They reported to the *Conseil Souveraine de la Martinique* and before 1663 was over, colonists, tools and provisions were being shipped from Martinique to St Lucia. La Lande had died but du Parquet's widow's brother, a Monsieur Bonnard, was appointed Governor.

By June 1664, however, the English were back. They forced Governor Bonnard to capitulate the fort at Choc and regained possession for sixteen months until, on 20 October 1665, diplomatic negotiations reinstated St Lucia to France. Not pleased with the way in which the heirs of du Parquet had managed the island, the King of France forced his widow to sell the colony back to the FWIC and in this manner, the island that had been bought fifteen years earlier *along* with Grenada and Martinique for 41 500 livres, was sold back to the FWIC in 1665, *singly*, for 240 000 livres - showing that St Lucia's value had increased five or tenfold. The English, however, were not fazed and before 1665 was out, they had returned and chased the French off once more. Yet again, English settlement failed. Dysentery, famine and Carib attacks created a situation so desperate that by January 1666, a group of Englishmen sailed to Martinique and begged the French authorities to help them get safely back to Barbados.

Once more, France assumed control of St Lucia. The occupation was ratified in 1667 by the Treaty of Breda, which brought a halt to Anglo-French warfare in Europe and the Americas for almost two decades. Throughout that period, St Lucia remained French - with the footnote that in 1674, formal ownership was transferred back from the FWIC to the King of France, who governed St Lucia as a dependency of Martinique, with Count de Blénac in charge. Finally feeling secure in its possession, the French Crown started giving land titles to settlers.

Yet still the English did not give up. In 1683, the Governor of Barbados wrote to the French Commander of the West Indies claiming that St Lucia, Dominica and St Vincent rightfully belonged to the English and ordering him to evacuate the islands. The French ignored the demand. Three years later, in 1686, after nineteen years of relatively peaceful French occupation, the English sent a 54-gun warship to St Lucia under the command of Captain du Temple, in a mission ordered by King James personally. The monarch had heard that in St Lucia, Frenchmen '*under Cover of Hunting, Fishing and cutting Wood - for the use of Martinico ... built houses, and made some small Settlements there.*' Displeased, King James ordered '*to cause all Foreigners, unless they submitted themselves and acknowledged the King of England's Sovereignty over that Island, to remove from thence, and to take possession of their Habitations.*'[25]

When the French refused to comply, Du Temple's troops pillaged and burnt their settlements. En passant, the English also '*took away the free mulattoes*' - which is the earliest mention (1686) of the presence of free people of colour in St Lucia. Most likely, these *mulattoes* were settlers in their own right, having come to St Lucia from Martinique or Guadeloupe in search of land to cultivate. What fate befell them is unknown: perhaps they were subjected to slavery in a British colony. It does show, however, that from the very start, St Lucia was being colonized by both whites and free people of colour. A treaty was eventually negotiated and on 11 December 1687, the English abandoned their claim to St Lucia on condition they be allowed to come ashore to cut wood. They also promised not to disturb the French settlers, who soon returned. A subsequent peace treaty (Ryswick 1697) reconfirmed France's occupation of St Lucia. But by 1700, the English were back at it, ordering the French to evacuate and threatening violent action. The French coolly replied that they would defend their colony at all cost, and no war ensued.

Meanwhile, under the relative peace of French occupation, the island was becoming a sort of tourist destination *avant-la-lettre* for well-to-do inhabitants from neighbouring islands (both French and English) who sailed across to hunt, fish and relax on St Lucia's shores. Population numbers grew steadily, as missions of settlement continued. In 1713, a group of French deserters - soldiers, sailors and '*stray squatters*'[26] - arrived in St Lucia, and the French Crown allowed Marshal Count d'Estrées to start giving out parcels of land. More and more families from Martinique migrated to St Lucia, accompanied by a major military force. On 24 July 1719, this *prise de possession* was celebrated with a religious-military ceremony held at Pointe St Victor, a spot on the Vigie side of the Castries Harbour. It is the first recorded occasion of Catholic Mass being said in St Lucia (although a church or chapel may have existed as early as 1664). The officiating priest's name was Suffret de Villeneuve.

St Lucia anno 1719: Lillington's report

The English, of course, objected. They claimed anteriority of settlement and rightful purchase of St Lucia from the Caribs in 1663, conveniently ignoring the fact that France had spent much more time and resources colonizing the island. Back in Europe, these claims and counterclaims were negotiated in a civilized but facetious manner. When, in 1719 or 1720, the Earl of Stairs invited the Maréchal d'Estrées for dinner, he requested that he '*carry the Treaty, by which England had ceded the Island of St Lucia to the French.*'[27] The Earl had probably read a report received by the Lords Commissioners of Trade in England, written by a Mr Lillington, concerning his recent visit to Barbados and St Lucia.[28] In it, Lillington lauded St Lucia's potential but warned of progressive French settlement. The island, he wrote, was covered '*with the best of Timbers much wanted in our Islands, for building Houses, Mills and all such like necessary Works for our Plantations and for frames of small sloops which are much used in those parts, and employ many vessels a year in fetching those commodities thence, and ... considerable quantities of Turtle for the subsistence of our Inhabitants, and of fustick sent for Great Britain for Dying.*'

The soil, too, was of fine quality, he said, and could produce cocoa for England which would earn an income without competing with the other colonies' crops. Lillington claimed that St Lucia had been '*until the late Peace possessed by the native Indians and Negroes - which run off in Boats and other Vessels from the adjacent Islands.*' He proclaimed surprise at the '*many and often repeated Reports*' in recent years '*that the French were settled on Sta. Lucia with three hundred Families, were building Houses, were clearing and planting ground with sugar Canes, and at last that they had erected a Fort or Battery with several pieces of Cannon and the French Arms flying thereon*'.

According to Lillington, the French had suffered several setbacks, and their hunger for slaves had landed them in hot water shortly before August 1719, when they '*with a considerable armed Force had attempted to take and carry off the Negroes from St Vincent, but were repulsed with Loss by the Desperateness of the Negroes, who had killed many of the Wifes and Children to prevent them falling into the French Hands, and declared themselves under the English Subjection and fought under their Colours.*'

Piracy was another concern. A '*New York Privateer*' landed in St Lucia '*and having reed some Affront or Disgust from the French settled thereon, landed his Men, hawled down the French Colours which were flying, nail'd up their Cannon and took away their Stores of Ammunition.*'

Lillington's report compounded England's fear that after half a century of *de facto* French occupation, St Lucia was fast becoming a full-blown agricultural colony, modelled after Martinique and Guadeloupe. The French Antilles seemed to be on the brink of developing into a mighty socio-economic bloc and being so near to Martinique, St Lucia's bountiful stocks of fish, wood and fertile soil could well be the deciding factor in lending France decisive strategic control over the area. Hence, while France's primary interest in St Lucia was agricultural and economic, England was first and foremost inspired by political and military motives (a fact further borne out by its consistent refusal to trade St Lucia for French-held Tobago).

In August 1720, France and England agreed that settlers from both nations ought to withdraw and that St Lucia, along with Dominica and St Vincent, would become neutral territories. The King of France acted accordingly, annulling his grant and ordering his settlers to evacuate - which they did - but he soon discovered that the cunning English had never intended to live up to their part. By 1722, the King of England was once again granting letters of patent for St Lucia: this time to John, Duke of Montague. The Duke lost no time and 40 000 pounds Sterling later, an expedition under the command of Nathaniel Uring set sail for St Lucia, casting anchor on 17 December 1722 at Pigeon Island Bay. They built a fort (Montague fort) on a hill along a creek just north of Castries harbour, using '*negro labour*'. The French Commander of the Lesser Antilles soon got wind of the settlement and before long, an army of 1400 men, including soldiers and prospective colonists[29] from Martinique, Guadeloupe and other French islands, under the command of the Marquis de Champigny, landed in a north-eastern harbour (probably the bay of l'Espérance or Marquis). They '*cut a path across the Island, and joynd their camp at the Shocque*'.[30] Just one month after making landfall, Nathaniel Uring was forced to sign the Treaty of Choc, promising on behalf of England to restore St Lucia to a state of neutrality.

European settlement taking root

Officially, St Lucia remained neutral throughout the 1720s and 30s. Unofficially, Martiniquan settlers busied themselves building roads and towns and planting cocoa, coffee, cotton and tobacco. A worried report from a Mr Forbes, written on 4 July 1728 and addressed to the Board of Trades in England, mentioned that '*there are now already upward of 1200 French Families there settled, and daily increasing. 'Tis true that they are - at present - very courteous and civil to the few English that are amongst them, but it may be justly fear'd that the very first opportunity that offers, they will readily embrace to dispossess them.'*[31] Nothing was done to check the expansion and eighteen months later, someone else reported '*that the French are now about three thousand settled at St Lucia, + that their numbers are daily encreasing from Martinique.*'[32]

The French had ambitious plans. A 1732 map shows they had planned to build a road right across St Lucia, from *Cul de Sac de l'Espérance* to *l'Ance du Gros Islet*, with a second road running from Gros Islet south along the spine of the island to Soufrière. They called it the *Chemin de la longue Chasse ou de la Souphrière* - but it never got beyond the drawing board. Meanwhile, settlers were establishing farms on the windward coast and a small group of Irishmen had joined French planters in the south. A 1742 map of the south shows that Frenchmen were growing cotton and cassava (*magnoc*) in the '*Plat Paijs*' (now the international airport) and on Cape Moule à Chique. They would have been whites or free people of colour, relying on family labour, white indentured workers and a (still relatively small) number of African slaves to get the work done. They came from neighbouring French islands or were fortune-seekers from Europe. How the Irishmen ended up in St Lucia is not clear - perhaps they were deserters from British ships or the army.

Since St Lucia was neutral, the colonists had no taxes to pay, no administration to maintain and no troops to feed. Most importantly, between the 1720s and 1740s, the island acted as a free haven where English vessels traded with French ships, circumventing the strict trade barriers that were in force elsewhere. English ships collected wood from St Lucia and it was said that numerous Martiniquans only survived by the grace of being able to spend six months of every year in St Lucia, where they hunted, fished and collected wood. Many buildings in Martinique were constructed of St Lucian timber - to the extent that that by 1784, the *Quartier de Gros Islet* was already said to suffer from deforestation and worsening droughts.

During the state of neutrality, small incidents occurred (French settlers for instance complained regularly about English ships stealing their piles of cut and prepared timber) but, on the whole, the relative peace of the 1720s, 30s and 40s may be considered the cradle into which St Lucia's plantation economy was born.

The doom of Amerindian society

Meanwhile, the Carib threat slowly faded away. Houel's 1732 map mentions *Carbet Caraïbes* ('Carib houses') at Ance Mabouya (Fond d'Or Bay) - but only as a curiosity, a remnant of antiquity. The census of 1730 recorded seventeen

Sauvages résidents dans l'Isle plus twenty *Sauvagesses*, making for a total of 37 Caribs. At the same time, there were 100 white males bearing arms; six white women; two white girls of marriageable age; 33 married *Mulatresses, méstises et négresses libres* (free black and coloured women); nineteen free black and coloured girls (presumably also of marriageable age); seventeen white children under the age of twelve; 74 children under the age of twelve born of free coloured and black women; 137 working slaves, and 38 *Négrillons* (slave children), making for a total of 463 souls (including the Caribs).[33] This means that by 1730, the Caribs of St Lucia had been decimated: reduced to less than eight percent of the total population. Two years later, they no longer even merited a separate entry but had literally been reduced to a footnote. '*A l'Ance Louvet, il y a trois Carbets de Caraïbes contenant 12 hommes et femmes*', it reads in the margin of the 1732 census: 'At Anse Louvet, there are three Carib houses containing 12 men and women'.[34]

As a people, by 1730, the Caribs had entered the genetic pool of African and European heritage. Records from Soufrière, for instance, show a marriage on 24 February 1778 between Victoire, the illegitimate daughter of a '*red Carib*' woman by a white man, with a mulatto man from St Vincent (who, incidentally, was her own slave): '*24.2.1778. Victoire, of Choiseul 28 ans, métisse libre, illégitime et naturelle de feue Lisette ROCQUEMONT caraïbesse rouge, avec Dominique ou Caliacoua (St Vincent) 25 ans, mulâtre, son esclave, naturel et illégitime de Dorothée négresse esclave de Guillaume QUEMIN.*'[35]

As a society, by 1730, the Caribs were dead. The last mention of them as rightful owners of St Lucia dates to December 1719, when a Captain Chapelle from Martinique conceived of the bright idea to buy St Lucia from the *sauvages* (by then headquartered in St Vincent). Once France owned St Lucia, Chapelle reasoned, England would have to give up its assumption of ownership. And so, 56 years after the English bought the island from Indian Warner, a zealous French captain purchased it all over again. Upon his triumphant return to Martinique, Chapelle's superiors judiciously asked him to keep the treaty a secret. It was the final, pathetic act in the tragic dispossession of the Amerindians of St Lucia.

3

Conflict and colonization 1731 - 1793

Seigneur de Vieillecourt could not believe his ears! Muttering dangerously under his breath, a vein throbbing in his left temple, he strode to the scene of calamity, where he could hear the roll of a drum and the loud, bragging voice of an Englishman. 'How dare he,' de Vieillecourt muttered, 'How dare he!' He turned a corner and stopped dead in his tracks. His face first turned pale and then flushed a deep red. There, in the heart of the island Ste Alouzie of which he was the proud commanding officer, stood an English captain with a drum strapped across his chest reading a proclamation. '... the state of neutrality to be enforced and therefore ordering all inhabitants to leave this, the island of St Lucia!' An English flag turned lazily in the afternoon breeze behind him. De Vieillecourt dashed behind a house, grabbed a gòlèt and a man's shirt that lay bleaching on a shrub and, holding his make-shift white flag high, stepped forward to face the Englishman. The prettily-dressed captain faltered just long enough for de Vieillecourt to cut into his proclamation. In heavily accented but perfectly clear English, he asked the captain for his name. Self-importance turned into arrogance and the answer came as a sneer. But de Veillecourt was so angry, the King of England himself would not have intimidated him. 'To be sure, Captain Hawck,' he replied icily, holding his flag high to make it catch the breeze, 'Ste Alouzie is neither French nor British. She is neutral. But let it be known that if one country has the right to plant the colours of her nation in the soil of this island, that she be France!'

1731-1778: a plantation economy emerges by leaps and bounds

Some more expletives may have passed between the two men - certainly, de Vieillecourt lodged a formal complaint to the British Governor of the Windward Islands about Captain Hawcke, whose behaviour he considered rude, premature and inappropriate. It was 1740 and, true enough, the French Governor of St Lucia, de Champigny, had been informed by his British counterpart in Barbados that England wanted to see the state of neutrality reinforced in St Lucia, Dominica and St Vincent. But that did not excuse the impertinent manner in which Captain Hawck had strolled into St Lucia and told the French settlers to start packing their bags.

For years, St Lucia's state of pseudo-neutrality had been a thorn in the side of both French and English regional administrators. Under the Navigation Act, free trade between French planters and English merchant ships was strictly forbidden but being neither one nor the other, St Lucia was a no man's land and its planters made the most of it: acquiring cheap slaves, cheap provisions to feed the slaves, and fetching high prices for their crops. When, in early 1731, a slave trader from Nantes in France by the name of Roy sold 200 *blacks* from Guinée in West Africa to planters in St Lucia, French administrators complained bitterly that even more illegal trade seemed to be going on in St Lucia, and between St Lucia and Martinique, than they already suspected.[36]

At this point, for the first time in history, it is possible to speak of 'St Lucians' as a group of people with shared objectives, objectives which sometimes clashed with those of their European administrators. St Lucian planters - mostly Frenchmen from Martinique, a few Englishmen, Irishmen and a sizeable group of free coloureds of mixed white and African descent with some Carib blood mixed in - increasingly shed their cultural differences in favour of a common interest as plantation owners in St Lucia. This embarrassed the French administrators who, whilst hating the free trade, were happy to see Martiniquan planters succeed in St Lucia by virtue of it.

Both France and England would have preferred to occupy St Lucia outright - but neither dared provoke the other. A sort of cold war ensued. '*[W]e have no warships strong enough to oppose those which the English keep there all the time. They are master of Carénage. The English ships and the French who wish to trade with them, do so within the range of English cannons*', a French official complained in 1730.

In 1731, the British and French Governments decided that the only way to end the free trade was by evacuating St Lucia altogether. The order reached St Lucia in August of 1733. Understandably, it was not welcomed by the nascent St Lucian plantocracy and they, in response, resorted to subterfuge, replying that all available ships were in such disrepair that everyone would surely perish. Fresh orders followed in 1735, from both France and England to their respective patriots. Again, nothing happened. In 1740, the British considered seizing and fortifying St Lucia but '*the times were not favourable*' and no attack ensued. The French faced a similar situation the following year, when they planned an invasion of St Lucia but had to abort when 60 English warships showed up in the area. While this miniature cold war occupied the military strategists, Martiniquan, English, Irish and free coloured planters developed their estates, English loggers cut wood and English merchant ships traded freely at the harbour of Carénage.

In 1742, the French administration in Martinique sent its Chief Engineer, Monsieur Houel, to St Lucia to spy on the works undertaken by the insidious settlers. In his report to Governor-General de Champigny, Houel stated that '*considerable plantations*' had been set up in St Lucia by leading (Martiniquan) planters, including a Monsieur Culant, and that they had even gone so far as to mark the boundaries between properties. De Champigny quickly publicly denied having given settlers permission to do so, knowing that the English authorities would be angered if they found out. He also realized that, given the chance, many more planters and even military officers would abandon Martinique for St Lucia '*and that Martinique would be deserted.*'

The temptation was enormous for the authorities in Martinique to seize St Lucia: they hungered for the island's copious resources of land and lumber and were keen for its profits to flow into the coffers of their merchants in St Pierre. Equally importantly, they wanted to check its growing independence. England's interest in St Lucia was strategic and simple: they did not want France to possess it.

The first militias

While free trade was a boon to the mixed bag of planters, St Lucia's perpetual state of insecurity and recurring threats of evacuation did hinder agricultural development. So much so, that when in 1744 France finally *did* seize St Lucia and made it a full dependency of Martinique, troops reported that St Lucia's inhabitants were surviving by nothing but the grace of the land and the abundance of game and fish. They grew only cotton and provisions and lived in '*a type of barracks*', it was said. No towns existed yet and the '*main location of the island*', Carénage, was still '*covered in woods*'.

Proper land surveys were carried out in 1745 and from this time, it is possible to speak of villages, towns and bourgs - keeping in mind that these were little more than hamlets of fishermen's huts, located near navigable bays and defended by some type of military works (usually batteries with a few cannons). The militiamen responsible for the defence of the districts were for the most part not professional soldiers quartered in barracks, but ordinary men who had gained a little military experience, by virtue of which they held a rank of some sort. In daily life, they lived and worked on plantations around the island, to be called upon for military service when needed. The officers were without exception white, while the lower ranks and common troops probably contained some free men of colour also.

By 1745, there were militias island-wide, in locations which eventually grew into towns and villages. These *compagnies* were typically named after their commanding officer, who was usually the largest settler in the district. Gros Islet was defended by the *Revue de la Compagnie de Littée*: a militia consisting of five officers and 36 militiamen. On the leeward side was a battery with two eight-pounder cannons. On the windward side, at the *Port de l'Espérence,* no battery existed yet in 1745 but the recommendation was to bring in two or three cannons.

Marquis was defended by the *Revue de la Compagnie de Dubocage,* with two officers and 31 men, while further south, the *Revue de la Compagnie de Depincher* was stationed at Trois Islets, now known as Praslin Bay. Two officers and 49 fusiliers protected the anchorages at Trois Islets and Anse Canot.

The compagnie in Vieux Fort did not have a commanding captain or any cannons in 1745 but there were a lieutenant, two *enseignés* and three fusiliers looking after a considerable length of anchorable coastline in the south. It was recommended that Vieux Fort be assigned a commandant and a compagnie of troops and receive some cannons: not just for protection against foreign invasion but also to ensure that the residents remained loyal to the King of France, whose authority *'for the most part, they have never recognised.'*

River Dorée on the south-west coast had the *Revue de la Compagnie de Duqueisac,* comprising four officers and 33 militiamen who were responsible for the coastline from River Dorée to l'Islet à Caret (now Laborie). It was considered a coast easily defended against enemy landings, even with just ordinary musket fire since the only way to land troops was via a narrow entrance in the reefs between l'Islet à Caret and the mainland.

Soufrière, which by 1745 was rapidly becoming an important agricultural district, was defended by the *Revue de la Compagnie de Devaux* with six officers, one aide-major and 40 fusiliers. The bay of Soufrière was deep and easily accessible for ships, which could come very close to shore. More than once, the residents of Soufrière had come to the aid of French ships pursued by English *corsaires.* In 1745, Soufrière contained a battery with two six-pound cannons, only one of which was in working order. It was recommended that three more be added.

The main district of the island, Carénage, was protected by the *Revue de la Compagnie Pichery Desrivières,* with four officers and 74 fusiliers. They were responsible for the protection of a long stretch of coastline, including the main harbour and Choc Bay. Enemy ships could easily land troops and pillage the town, so Carénage was protected by 100 garrisoned troops, spread out over several batteries: five at the entrance to the port with 24 cannons in all (two 24-pounders, four 18-pounders, sixteen 12-pounders and two 8-pounders) and two more

12-pounders at Choc Bay. Marigot Bay was uninhabited in 1745. Although enemy troops could easily land there, for the time being, the bay remained undefended.

A nascent plantation society

Once St Lucia was brought back under French control in 1744, agricultural expansion soared. Coffee and cotton plantations were established or expanded and where in 1730, just 463 people lived on the island (175 of them slaves of African or Creole descent), by 1745 the total population had boomed to 3455, including 2573 slaves. The militias were increasingly used not just for coastal defense but also as protection against 'the threat within': the slaves. Militiamen were deployed to suppress slave uprisings and to track down and return runaway slaves. Just as the mixed bag of planters had emerged in the 1730s as a stakeholder *vis-à-vis* the French and British authorities, so did the African and island-born slaves emerge as a distinct stake holding group in the 1740s. As population numbers grew and the economy expanded, a new social order emerged - and a contentious one at that.

Under Governors-General Marquis de Caylus, Martin (1744-45) and de Longueville (1745-48), St Lucia remained French for four years but by the Treaty of Aix-la-Chapelle (1748), it was declared neutral once again. *De facto*, however, France retained possession and de Longueville remained in the saddle until February 1762. The year 1756 saw the start of the Seven-Year-War between France and England and, as always, hostilities soon spilled over into the Caribbean. England conquered Martinique in 1762 and subsequently waltzed into St Lucia virtually without a fight. It was a significant omen that the planters never considered defending St Lucia by force, evidently fearing loss of property more than British rule. Instead, they surrendered and negotiated a favourable capitulation prize. As it turned out they chose well, as British rule was short-lived and the Treaty of Paris in 1763 ceded St Lucia back to France.

The administrators in Martinique had waited for this moment. Almost immediately, a host of French and Creole planters crossed the channel to settle in St Lucia, among them Joseph Gaspard de Tascher (Chevalier Seigneur de la Pagerie) and his wife Rose Claire Desvergers (*née* de Senois). Married two years earlier in Trois Islets church in Martinique, the young couple came to St Lucia to occupy a 68-carré estate (about 180 acres) at Morne Paix Bouche. It was here that, on 23 June 1763, their daughter Marie Josephine Rose Tascher de la Pagerie was born: the girl who went on to become the first wife of Napoleon Bonaparte and Empress of France.[37]

The flow of immigrants was augmented by French planters fleeing Grenada and St Vincent, which had fallen prey to the British. Most brought their slaves with them and the influx of people, capital and other resources after 1763 caused a great acceleration in the development of St Lucia's plantation economy. It also pushed the island into an altogether new phase by introducing the crop that was to shape and dominate St Lucia's landscape and destiny for two centuries to come: sugar cane.

Sugar's debut in St Lucia

The first sugar estate was established in Vieux Fort in April 1763 by two planters, Levacher and le Blond. Between them, they owned a stretch of flat land from La Ressource to Beausejour, St Urbain and Aupicon. Easily accessible from the *Chemin Royal,* it was ideal for a sugar plantation (*sucrérie*).[38] The example was swiftly followed by other colonists and in 1767 there were five *sucréries* operational in St Lucia. In 1769, there were sixteen; in 1771, there were 33 and in 1777, the total was 53. The acreage of land under sugar cane increased equally rapidly: from eighteen carrés in 1764 to 1040 carrés in 1771; 2003 carrés in 1777, and 3271 carrés in 1784. Sugar plantations sprang up in every district, usually close to a river. Until the mid-nineteenth century, such *sucréries* were small-scale operations using basic equipment and crude techniques to grind juice out of the sugar cane, boil that into syrup then allow the syrup to crystallize into sugar. Until the 1870s, almost every estate manufactured its own sugar: a crude variety known as *muscovado* (from the Spanish word *mascabado* which means 'lowest quality').

To understand the impact sugar had on St Lucia in terms of human costs, physical landscape, technology, economy, labour relations and social hierarchy, we first need to have an idea of what is practically involved in its production.

From cane to sugar: the process

Sugar cane grows as a tall, bushy grass with sharp-edged blades and juicy, fibrous stalks. The canes take between twelve and eighteen months to mature. Planting was traditionally done during the wet season (June to November) and harvesting eighteen months later, during the dry season (January to May). Canes naturally grow fresh shoots but to optimize the sugar content, stalks were replanted every two to five years. Pieces of stalk one foot long were buried in holes three feet square and one foot deep and covered with soil and manure. A gang of 30 field slaves could plant about two acres in a day but digging and covering the stalks in muddy conditions was a filthy and arduous job. The most detested job, however, was manuring, which required slaves to carry baskets filled with animal dung and cane trash weighing up to 80 pounds and distribute the contents over the fields. Child gangs were employed in weeding the canes and killing rats and vermin.

Manually harvesting sugar cane is tortuous work, as the sharp blades of cane lacerate the skin and cause it to itch painfully. A hook was used to gather together stalks which were then cut with a sickle. The leaves were slashed off and the bare stalks bundled together, loaded onto ox-carts and taken to the mill. Cane trash was collected separately and used for fuel, manure and bedding in the stables.

At modern-day ruins of sugar estates, the most eye-catching feature is usually the mill. Complex contraptions were built for the sole purpose of turning three or five heavy rollers with sufficient power to crush the thick cane stalks and extract the juice. Animal-drawn mills were the simplest ones to construct: three hardwood rollers connected with cogs to a vertical axle were set in motion by horses or oxen which, harnessed onto two long sweeps, plodded round and round. Animal mills were often fixed but mobile ones were also in use from the earliest days of sugar cane cultivation. These were dragged from field to field by oxen, mules, horses or donkeys and rented on shares to adjoining plantation owners. At Morne Courbaril Estate, for instance (south of Soufrière, owned by Philippe Devaux), mobile cattle mills were used from 1771 until 1778, when a water mill was built powered from a reservoir and canal on nearby Terre Blanche Estate.[39] At other estates, mobile animal mills remained in use for much longer, sometimes even after permanent mills were built.

Along the windy Atlantic coast and in the elevated area between Choiseul and Soufrière, windmills were common and ruins of stonework bases are still evident today. The design was Dutch in origin, brought to Brazil by Sephardic Jews, on from there to Barbados and eventually to St Lucia. The third common model was the waterwheel mill. This provided the most constant power but often required elaborate aqueducts to channel water from a point higher up the river to the factory.[40]

Whichever way the mill was powered, slaves were required to pass cane stalks back and forth through the heavy rollers. It was a dangerous job, in which a moment's lapse in concentration could result in the loss of a hand, arm or worse. A popular horror story is that of one slave feeding canes into the rollers while another stood guard with a machete, ready to cut off his arm and save his life should his fingers get caught.

Sites for sugar factories were chosen carefully, usually on slightly sloping land. Canes were carried in carts or on donkeys' backs to the highest point near the factory and unloaded onto a stone platform beside the mill house. They were then pushed through the mill and squeezed dry. The left-over pressed stalks (known as *bagasse*) were used as fuel for the ovens. From the rollers, the cane juice drained into a gutter and ran by gravity towards the first and largest of five large copper vessels in the boiling house. Boiling thickened and reduced the juice. The scum was skimmed off and the liquid ladled into vessels of decreasing size, until thick syrup remained. The skimming from the third and fourth boiling pots was mixed with molasses and distilled twice to make a powerful type of rum. The skimming from the first and second pots was discarded. The boiling vessels were heated by ovens built in underneath them. These ovens were linked together by a network of vent pipes that led to a tall stone chimney. To clarify the boiling juice, lime or ashes and water were added. A specialist job was that of the boiler watching the fifth and last copper, for he had to know when the brew was ready to crystallize. At his sign, the bubbling liquid was carried in great two-handled ladles to the cooling cistern, and poured into tapering wooden barrels known as *hogsheads*: sixteen inches square at the top and 26 or 28 inches deep. These were then left to cool in the filling-room. After two days, they were tested by rapping the outside: good sugar made a ringing sound, bad sugar a dead one. The hogsheads, which had small drain holes in the bottom, spent four weeks in the curing-house to allow the molasses to drain from the sugar crystals. (Nowadays, the same result is achieved in just a few minutes by spinning to apply centrifugal force). The curing-house was kept as airtight and warm as possible and coal fires were lit if necessary. The molasses was drained and used to make rum, which was a profitable by-product and often made the difference between profit and loss.

The continuous ladling of hot syrup in the sweltering heat of the boiling house was an exhausting job and teams of slaves had to be relieved every four hours. Raw sugar juice spoils quickly so that on large estates, during crop season, the fires were doused for just one full day per week: from Saturday midnight until 1 a.m. on Monday morning. Other than that, sugar boiling continued day and night during the harvest. After four weeks, the hogsheads were turned upside down and knocked hard on the ground to force the pyramid of muscovado sugar out. Muscovado could be refined further but, this being an elaborate process involving water and clay being drained through it for four months, St Lucian planters rarely bothered.

As it was, weighing about 30 pounds and standing two feet tall, light yellow at the base and deep brown at the top, these hogsheads of muscovada sugar were what planters lived, and slaves died for. Almost literally worth its weight in gold, West Indian sugar was king and tyrant all at once.

Sugar and slavery expansion

From the 1770s onwards, no amount of human suffering was allowed to stand in the way of the money to be made from sugar. The sweetness of the crop could not have contrasted more bitterly with the human experience it dragged in its wake. Planting, growing, weeding, cutting, grinding and boiling sugar was dirty, hard and debilitating work. It also required a labour force that was up to three times larger than that needed for traditional crops such as coffee, cotton or cocoa. As the amount of land under sugar cane doubled and tripled, so did the slave population. Between 1772 and 1789 alone, more than 5000 new slaves were imported into St Lucia:[41] an average of almost 300 people per year.

Where in 1764, there were 5069 slaves out of a total population of 6336 (with 18 hectares in sugar cane, 717 in coffee and 621 in cotton); only five years later, in 1769, the number of slaves had almost doubled to 10 278 (out of a total population of 12 794) and sixteen *sucréries* were up and running. Another ten years on, by 1779, there were 16 003 slaves (total population 19 230) and 44 sugar plantations. Over the two decades between 1764 and 1784, St Lucia's slave population tripled from 6000 to 18 000 souls. Around the same time, the number of slave *owners* increased by less than one-third: from 2468 in 1765 to 3227 in 1779: an increase of just 759 people.

So while, as a percentage of the total population, slaves increased from 73 to 84 per cent, slave owners *de*creased from 27 to 16 per cent. Put differently, where in 1765 there were 3.7 slaves to each slave owner, by 1779 there were 6.25.

Slaves and owners: the role of free people of colour

Not every slave was born in Africa or was of full African descent, and not every slave owner was born in Europe or of full European descent. While it is true that in St Lucia, no whites were ever slaves, it is also true that people of mixed African/European descent found themselves on both sides of the divide, as slaves and slave owners. For this reason, the terms 'slave' and 'slave owner' are used rather than 'blacks' and 'whites'.

As a late-comer to the plantation economy, St Lucia tended to attract free people of colour and poor whites (*petits blancs*) who lacked the capital to buy plantations in more established plantation colonies such as Martinique, Guadeloupe, Antigua or Barbados. Poor white men usually entered into sexual relationships with coloured or black women, which in turn served to expand the coloured segment in the population. The same applies to white planters sexually abusing or otherwise fathering children with black or coloured women, both enslaved and free.

Children were given their mother's legal status, so if she was a slave, so too were her coloured children. If the mother was free, so were her children, even if their father was a slave. Occasionally, slave owners manumitted their mixed-descent children, setting them up for an independent existence by virtue of a trade or some land. A few families arrived directly from Africa as settlers in their own right: the Floissacs, for instance, reportedly came from Senegal to St Lucia as free people.[42]

By 1787, 1500 free people of colour (*gens de couleur libres*) owned 170 of the 881 plantations operational in St Lucia, and about one-seventh of the land. This means that between one-fifth and one-third of St Lucia's plantocracy was made up of free people of colour. Like their white counterparts, they owned and managed agricultural estates on which they grew a range of crops, including sugar cane, and employed slave labour. Not much quantitative research has been done on this topic but it is safe to make at least a few observations.

First of all, the number of free people of colour as a proportion of the total planter's class increased over time and, by 1799, free people of colour outnumbered whites in St Lucia (1364 free coloureds versus 1195 whites).[43]

Secondly, while initially, free coloureds owned proportionally less land than their white counterparts (in 1787, free people of colour formed one-fifth of the population but owned just one-seventh of the land), by the late eighteenth or early nineteenth century, this balance of ownership had tipped in their favour.

Thirdly, while free people of colour owned plantations and slaves, they generally employed fewer slaves than whites did, and their slaves were more often personal slaves rather than field slaves.

Fourthly, despite initially being a minority, free people of colour played a significant role in the agricultural development of St Lucia right from the start. As early as 1745, the second-largest slave owner in St Lucia was a free coloured man: a certain Nouet, '*mulatre libre*' of the *Compagnie de Pichery* (an estate in the Castries area). Nouet owned '*46 negres, 24 negresses, and 23 negrillons*', making for a total of 93 slaves. Only one white man had a larger plantation: Dubuq Letang, who owned Dezincher in Trois Islets (Praslin) and had 109 slaves (50 men, 23 women and 36 children).[44]

Free people of colour: land ownership

In 1771, Governor-General Baron de Micoud ordered surveys to be drawn up specifying land ownership in St Lucia per district (*quartier*). These maps provide a wealth of information showing, amongst other things, the following data on land ownership by free people of colour.

In the *Quartier du Carénage* (Castries), *La négresse Charlotte* owned 1 carré of land (in the heart of what is now Rodney Bay). The *famille libre Dugue* owned 30 acres at Choc/Marisule, adjacent to land owned by Dugue de la Touche (to whom the *famille libre Dugue* possibly owed not only their name but also some of their genes).

The *Quartier de l'Ance la Raye* had no free coloured land owners in 1771, but Soufrière had five: Francoise, *mulâtresse libre,* 7 carrés; Stanislas, *mulâtre libre,* 20 carrés; the widow of Martin, *mulâtresse libre,* 27 carrés; Budin, *mulâtre libre,* 20 carrés and the widow of Duc, *mulâtresse libre,* 15 carrés. Soufrière was by then an up-and-coming town, with three sugar producing plantations: Belfond estate immediately east of the town, owned by Devaux (65 carrés) and two along the coast just south of the Canaries river, owned by Prevost (96 carrés) and Ferret Marnoux (35 carrés).

Choiseul, in 1771, had two free coloured land owners and, interestingly, also three landowners indicated as *Caraïbe,* which shows that a few individual Caribs continued to survive. Lizoni, *mulâtre,* owned 5 1/3 carrés on the L'Ivrogne river; Marie Rose, *mulâtresse,* owned 4 1/3 carrés, and Rabaca, Zabeth and Marianne, all *Caraïbes,* owned 2, 3 and 11 2/3 carrés respectively in an area known up to today as Pointe Caraïbe.

The district of Laborie, at the time known as *Quartier de l'Islet Caret,* had no coloured landowners, and neither did Vieux Fort. The *Quartier de Micoud,* on the other hand, had 24 *gens libre,* all with land of between 2 1/2 and 10 carrés in size and one with 25 carrés. Their lots were clustered together in three sections located around the mouth of the Anse Ger River, just south of Ti Rocher at Des Blanchard and also around Rameau/Latille. They grew cotton, foodstuffs and some cocoa. Their names were *veuve* (widow) Bonnet, Helenne, Jean Denis, Dugay, Nicolas, Victor, Marianne Barbay, Francois Bernier, Inagne, Lambert, Dial, Babet, Gilles, Thomas, Delila, Pierre Marianna, Catin Lacariere, Jean Francois, Mathiana, Jeanne Dada, Marie Thomas, Radigua, Budin and Noel.

The *Quartier Praslin* had no free coloured landowners in 1771 but Dennery had three, two of whom had either died or abandoned their estates. They were la Garde, *mulâtre,* 35 carrés; Francois *mulâtre,* 15 carrés, and the widow of Louison, *mulâtresse,* 10 carrés.

Gros Islet had four free coloured landowners: Marie Rose and Francoise Martininq, *libre,* 10 carrés; Elisabeth Brisefer, *libre,* 33 1/3 carrés; Mimy Ridier, *libre,* 33 1/3 carrés, and Rigout, *libre,* 29 carrés. Finally, the *Quartier du Dauphin* had a sizeable free coloured land owning class: sixteen altogether, all of whom were simply indicated in the records as *libre.* They were Duhamel, 10 carrés; La Norrat, 15 3/5 carrés; Louise Soyer, 10 carrés; Dubernay, 10 carrés; Francois Grand Champ, 21 2/3 carrés; Colas Dada, 6 carrés; Frambourg, 32 3/4 carrés; Ferol Lacour, 10 carrés; Bernard, 3 2/3 carrés; La Diorant, 22 3/4 carrés; Marie Magdeleine, 12 carrés; Remond Dampierre, 20 3/4 carrés; Blancherot, 20

1/3 carrés; Charles Dada, 10 carrés; Boniface Gaud, 30 carrés and Toussaint Blancherot, 12 carrés.

Dreams of progress: snapshots from 1765-67

Back under French rule, in 1763 St Lucia's new Governor, Baron de Micoud set out to try and make St Lucia catch up with Martinique and Guadeloupe. Two years later, in 1765, two Frenchmen were sent out to report on the island's progress and potential: Monsieurs d'Ennery and de Peynier. D'Ennery was impressed with what he found and wrote: '*This island is capable of producing very large amounts and of being entirely cultivated.*' Large numbers of French colonists fleeing British control of Dominica and St Vincent had found refuge in St Lucia and this had '*pushed the colony forward by ten years: it has increased by at least one-third in whites and negroes over the past 6 months, and several new villages have been established.*'[45]

Governor de Micoud was praised outright as the man who '*leads this nascent colony with much wisdom, forthright activity and firmness.*' [46] D'Ennery made a complete tour of the island during his three-week-stay and found that '*the roads are passable, partly on foot, partly on horseback ... and that is a lot, considering that only six months ago one could only communicate by sea.*'

De Micoud had re-established the militias, creating fourteen companies with 700 men under arms. '*I am very satisfied with the militias*', d'Ennery wrote. '*They are almost all dressed in uniform.*' Surviving militia records providing names, family connections, dates of birth and origins,[47] when set against lists of estate ownership, underscore the depth to which military and economic interests were intertwined.

Since '*the citizenry has a need for regulation*', de Micoud encouraged priests to keep registers of baptism, marriage and burial - something to which they had '*brought little punctuality and attention*' until then. The '*disorderliness of the registries*' was remedied by Mr de Peynier and, following a second visit in 1767, d'Ennery hoped they would now '*be kept in the order he has demanded, and the priests will now be able to keep this in hand*'. It is thanks to this intervention that some 600 marriage acts from the period 1752 to 1789 still exist.[48] They relate primarily to Soufrière and Castries, where the population was more dense and longer-established, and provide invaluable information about St Lucia's white, coloured and black population in the late eighteenth century. They also clearly show the intricate family connections that existed with Martinique, Guadeloupe, Grenada, St Vincent, the Grenadines, France and other places in the world.

Amidst the praise, d'Ennery raised one serious concern: the layout and location of the capital, Carénage, which he said was '*totally barbaric; and it is this detestable placement which is almost uniquely to blame for the death of the majority of people who have been sent there. ... A lot of new inhabitants who had come ... to this island have died, and it has put fear in some, who have returned to the English islands and several others have gone to Martinique and Guadeloupe.'*

D'Ennery ordered an immediate relocation. '*We have decided that the new place for the town of Carénage will be at the back of the harbour, and at the foot of the Morne Ferlande, on both sides of the Carénage River. Henceforth, we will no longer build at the place where the old town is located.* And so the capital was moved from the main fortifications at Choc Bay and Vigie Heights (near the swampy area of Conway), to the south side of the harbour: at Morne Fortuné, La Toc and Tapion. The government spent 40 000 Pounds to acquire the plantation of Madame Dubucq on Morne Fortuné, and moved the troops and hospital there. When d'Ennery visited again eighteen months later, in 1767, the relocation was almost complete. '*The inhabitants have moved very promptly and voluntarily. All roads have been built and are quite beautiful for such a new colony, one can now easily ride all around the island on horseback.*'

Despite the obvious challenges ahead, D'Ennery was optimistic about the future and he believed that *'despite the deaths, the fever and the snakes, we will manage to finish settling the inhabitants on this murderous soil, in total liberty and at no expense, and when the island is opened up, she will from then on be as healthy as all our other Windward Islands.'*

How much of this dream came true?

Dreams tempered: the reality of 1773-8

In the decade after d'Ennery's account, two more reports came out concerning the state of affairs in St Lucia under French occupation: one in 1773 (by de Nozière and de Tascher) and a second in March 1778 (by Marquis de Bouillé). De Nozière and de Tascher attested that St Lucia had been pulled *'from the state of inertia in which she had languished all along'* but found the island not as prosperous as d'Ennery had hoped for, eight years earlier. '*It is at the moment very rare to see inhabitants of Martinique migrate to St Lucia. The settlements that remain to be created in this island must now solely depend on foreigners.*'

They quoted from the 1773 census, which found that St Lucia contained:

> *... 2199 whites, 960 free people of colour and 13 782 slaves, with a total population of 16 941. There are animals to the number of 2102 cattle, 1035 horses and mules, 3661 sheep and goats, thus a total of 6798 heads. The plantations in sugar cane occupy 1120 quarrés of lands divided between 39 sugar estates. One counts 6 602 400 coffee plants and 1 365 350 cocoa plants. 404 quarrés are used for the cultivation of cotton. ... When the island reaches its peak of cultivation, it would have 50 to 60 000 blacks.*

Carénage was still just a little town, tucked behind a sandy beach at the head of the Grand Carénage Bay and flanked by two mangrove swamps.

> *In our vanity, we had hoped that the docks which have been established at Carénage would have contributed, by their very activity, to the expansion of this port destined to become the capital of the island. These hopes were misplaced, in light of the uselessness of the docks themselves, the unhealthiness of the air, the slowness and difficulties of the trade, the wasting away of animals, the rising prices of the syrup and the taffia* [strong rum] *because of the cost of transportation to the docks and of the commission, all of these inconveniences have repelled, and will always continue to repel, the foreigners one had hoped would have contributed to this growth.*

The high death rate in Carénage continued to be a major obstacle to the town's development.

Ten years after d'Ennery and five after de Nozière and de Tascher, a third Frenchman reported on the state of affairs in St Lucia. '*The population of this island is small*' wrote Marquis de Bouillé in March 1778. '*Because of the bad air, not many children can be raised here. It has been said that in Carénage, not one child has yet been raised.*'[49] He roundly called Carénage *'a grave'* and added that '*Nine-tenths of the people who go there will die within a year.*' For fifteen years, no merchants had wanted to set up in business in Carénage and hence only a *'few minion officers of justice and government'* lived there. With the military seat removed to Morne Fortuné, which was healthier and easier to defend, the town was rendered completely vulnerable. '*In its present position, the English can burn down Carénage and none of the military forces at Morne Fortuné would be able to prevent it.*'

De Bouillé saw only one solution: move the capital from Carénage to Soufrière,

> *which is, at the moment, the most fully developed town of the island and the locality of which offers the possibility of eventually creating a considerable city here, being at the heart of the colony and close to the richest quartiers, and whose bay offers all the appropriate securities, both against the dangers of the sea and the undertakings of the English. ... One could eventually put here the seat of justice, and even of government, while the military establishments remain at Morne Fortuné, which from then on could be considered a citadelle where the military force of the island must reside. The advantages which Soufrière has altogether will attract merchants and eventually business houses ...*

The recommendation was not executed due to subsequent warfare and other disasters but for a while, Soufrière did surpass Castries in terms of social and economic growth. However, Soufrière never replaced Castries as the island's capital, as is sometimes suggested.

In 1769, Soufrière had 151 agricultural estates, Castries 126 and Vieux Fort 100. Traditional crops such as cotton, cocoa and coffee remained important but by 1789, St Lucia also boasted 43 estates dedicated exclusively to sugar: six in Castries, four in Anse la Raye, nine in Soufrière, five in Laborie, eight in Vieux Fort, one in Micoud, three in Praslin, one in d'Ennery, two in Dauphin and four in Gros Islet. Only Choiseul had none. At the same time, the island counted 180 coffee plantations, 57 cotton plantations and 88 cocoa plantations.[50] Traditional crops slowly declined, while sugar plantations continued to spread, reaching a record number of 102 in 1819.

For extended periods between 1769 and 1835, Soufrière had the largest number of inhabitants (both free and enslaved), the most land under cultivation (both in sugar and other produce) and exported the largest amounts of produce (both legally and illegally). From a tentative plan on paper in 1746, Soufrière had grown into a lively district centre - a position it maintained until 1835, when it had to concede to Castries once again. Incidentally, in 1785, Carénage was renamed Castries but both names were commonly interchanged until 1803.[51]

Despite Soufrière's success and the French administrators' valiant attempts to engineer the economic and infrastructural development of St Lucia, growth was hampered by several factors. Marquis de Bouillé described some of these in 1778. '*Trade is nil in the colony. A few English merchants have established themselves and hold the inhabitants to ransom. No business house from St Pierre has wanted to set up here.*'[52]

The justice system did not help. '*Justice has done a lot of harm in this colony: they have hastened to set up a jurisdiction which levied 200 000 pounds of taxes from the population and which, on the whole, consists of brigands (robbers).*' Nor did the church. '*The matters of the clergy and religion are in disorder due to the choice of priests who, on the whole, are bad characters. Too many parishes have been established, the inhabitants are in no position to maintain them, and the majority of churches and presbyteries have fallen into ruin.*' Finally, as de Bouillé observed: '*The cultivation of coffee, for which the soils of St Lucia are generally poor, has ruined a lot of estate owners; almost all of them are now geared towards sugar and cotton. The high mortality of the negroes has also contributed to stopping the progress of agriculture.*'

But the biggest obstacles to the progress of St Lucia's plantation economy were not internal, but came from outside: food shortages and famine due to the American War of Independence, renewed Anglo-French warfare in 1778 and a massive hurricane in 1780.

1778-84: the Battle of Cul de Sac and English occupation

The American War of Independence (started in 1776) cut off the regular shipping routes from North America and resulted in famine and disease in the West Indies. Slaves were particularly affected, as they depended largely on imported flour and salt fish. To cope with the situation, they were given time off to work their provision grounds and new trees were introduced: the ackee and mango from West Africa and India, and breadfruit from Tahiti (imported in 1793 by Captain William Bligh)[53]. Nevertheless, by 1777, malnutrition was taking its toll and '*a strange illness among the slaves*'[54] broke out. One source claims that in St Lucia, 5000 people died (out of a population of 14 000) but more likely, 5000 is the total number of (mostly) slaves who perished or disappeared between 1776 and 1784: be it through malnutrition, the 1780 hurricane, marronage or relocation to other islands.

Outright war came to St Lucia in 1778, when France entered the war on the side of the rebels opposing British rule in America. Before long, England and France were back at the old game of grappling for power in the Caribbean. England once again cast an avaricious eye towards St Lucia, which was ideally located to intercept ships coming from windward - something for which Barbados was too far upwind and Antigua too far north. Sensing the threat, and aware that St Lucia's forts had fallen into disrepair, Deputy-Governor Baron Claude Anne Guy de Micoud (nephew of the previous Governor Baron de Micoud)[55] repeatedly appealed to the Governor-General in Martinique for reinforcements. But to no avail. On 27 October 1778, Sir Henry Clinton, from the English headquarters in New York, ordered Major-General James Grant to attack '*& if practicable reduce and take possession of*' St Lucia.

Grant sailed from Sandy Hook to Barbados, where he joined up with Admiral Samuel Barrington's fleet. Coincidentally, on the same day, a French fleet under Count d'Estaing left Boston with orders to attack English-held St Vincent and Grenada. On 13 December 1778, the English arrived in St Lucia with 6000 men in 59 transports under Major-General Grant, and ten battleships under Admiral Barrington. They landed their troops at La Pointe beach on the south side of Grand Cul de Sac Bay, safe from the feeble guns of the Ciceron Battery. They quickly erected batteries on Morne Delzin (now Morne Cabrit, Hess Oil) to prevent a French counter-attack from the south and, with surprise on their side, within 24 hours the British captured Ciceron Battery, Morne Fortuné (including '*the Governor's House, the Hospital, the Barracks with all the Stores and Magazines belonging to the Island*') and the fort at Vigie. French troops put up a brief resistance but there were only 180 men of the Martinique and Guadeloupe Regiments, about 60 militia volunteers and a few regular army troops, 28 of whom were sick in hospital.[56] Before long, the motley French army under de Micoud was forced to withdraw to Morne Paix

Bouche, seven miles inland. De Micoud did however manage to send some pleas for help to Martinique, one of which reached Admiral Count d'Estaing there, who was in the midst of preparing his fleet for an attack on St Vincent and Grenada. D'Estaing lost no time and by the evening of December 15th, a considerable French sea force consisting of twelve battleships, 68 transports and 9000 troops dropped anchor off Choc and Reduit Bay. It was the start of what has become known as the Grand Battle of Cul de Sac.

At first light, D'Estaing's fleet sailed into Carénage Harbour where it planned to set up a stronghold to force the English out of Cul de Sac. They received a nasty shock when their own guns at Vigie, now manned by English troops, opened fire on them. D'Estaing retreated and instead sailed with ten men-of-wars to Cul de Sac, hoping to deliver the British a direct hit. But Barrington had anchored nine warships across the mouth of the bay, keeping his transport ships safely anchored in the inner bay. Twice, the French attacked. Twice, they were met with devastating broadside gunfire as well as artillery fire from the batteries on shore. Forced to retreat once more, D'Estaing changed tactics and decided to concentrate on ousting the 1300 English troops from Vigie. He left 4000 men guarding the south-side of Carénage Harbour to repel British reinforcements and, on December 18th, 5000 French troops attacked the Vigie stronghold.[57] They were met with heavy cannon fire and a bayonet counter-attack. The English Major-General Grant afterwards reported that '*their two first Attacks were made with the impetuosity of Frenchmen and they were repulsed by the determined bravery of Britons - they made a third attempt but were soon broke and retreated in confusion leaving their killed and many of their wounded in Our power. They were permitted to bury the Dead and to carry off the Wounded.*'

The slaughter had been awful, with more than ten Frenchmen wounded to every single British soldier. '*The Enemy had 400 Men killed upon the spot,*' Grant reported, '*500 dangerously wounded so as to render them unfit for Service and 600 slightly wounded. This is their own account. We had only ten men killed and 130 Wounded some of them have already joined their Corps and our loss upon the whole will be under Fifty.*' Some British soldiers plucked the white cockades from the caps of dead Frenchmen and dipped them in blood in defiant triumph. One English major later wrote feelingly: '*None of us had ever seen so many dead upon so small a spot.*'[58] A moratorium was eventually declared to allow the French to carry their dead and wounded (assisted by a few Englishmen) to a makeshift field hospital at Morne Pleasant. For ten days, Admiral d'Estaing's battered fleet lingered indecisively outside Carénage Harbour. On December 29th, it set sail for Martinique. Deputy-Governor de Micoud and his French colonists, watching the fleet disappear over the horizon, had no choice but to surrender to the English the following day.[59]

The change of hands badly disrupted daily life: planters lost their lines of credit and other services from Martinique and under the terms of the capitulation, they were obliged to pay fines and lend out their slaves as labourers to British military construction sites. Then, as though matters were not grave enough already, Mother Nature dealt a second severe blow to St Lucia's nascent plantation economy.

The hurricane of 1780: mayhem and marronage

In 1780, the Windward Islands were struck by the most devastating hurricane in recorded history. St Lucia took a hammering which lasted for 36 hours: from the evening of October 10 until the morning of the 12th. Approximately 800 people died, along with countless animals. Trees, crops, houses and roads were destroyed and washed away. Only two houses remained standing in Castries and half of the British fleet in St Lucia was lost, including HMS *Vengeance* which was driven up onto the rocks on the south side of Carénage Harbour and smashed to pieces.

A telling piece of evidence was uncovered in 1964 during construction of a bridge over the Roseau River. Heavy equipment digging 18 feet deep uncovered an anchor 6 feet tall with a chain attached to it and surrounded by tree trunks, all lying in a north-south direction. It is believed that they are the remains of a ship trying in vain to shelter from the 1780 hurricane.[60] Less than two weeks later, on 23 October 1780, a second violent storm struck. As always, the aftermath of these hurricanes (in the form of epidemics of *témisme*, dysentery, measles and small-pox) claimed several more victims still.[61]

Hundreds of slaves took advantage of the mayhem and ran away to the mountains. This in addition to the unrest that had resulted from the British take-over two years earlier left the (mostly French) planters at their wits' end. They accused the British of agitating the *gens de couleur libre* against them, promoting marronage and furnishing slaves with weapons, while at the same time undermining the planters' usual defenses.[62] One-third of the '*tormented French planters*' (as a contemporary source called them) packed up their belongings and with their remaining slaves moved to *La Trinité Espagnole* (Trinidad), which was offering asylum.

Between the 1778 take-over and the 1780 hurricane, St Lucia lost hundreds of slaves: because their owners moved them overseas and as a result of '*famine, hunger, the misery after the hurricane, war duties and abductions by English ships which have caused the colony to lose more than 2000 negroes which is almost one-fifth or one-sixth of all working slaves.*'[63]

The war duties mentioned consisted of military defenses built by Admiral Rodney at Pigeon Island, ruins of which remain today. These were built between 1779 and 1782 by coloured artisans, other free people of colour and confiscated slaves. In 1781, Rodney even proposed to use slaves as seamen in order to help sail ships back to England for refitting, intending to grant them freedom upon their return.[64]

In 1781, France tried to reconquer St Lucia. But their invasion of Gros Islet was ill-advised, and British guns opened fire from Pigeon Island before the Frenchmen could even disembark, forcing them to abandon anchor and beat a fast retreat. Pigeon Island proved to be a strategic goldmine and it was from Fort Rodney that in early April 1782, Admiral Rodney spotted a French fleet leaving Fort Royal in Martinique. Rodney gave chase with his British squadron and on 12 April, intercepted the French fleet at Les Saintes, between Dominica and Guadeloupe. The British defeat of the French navy, including its flagship *Ville de Paris* (the largest war ship in the world at the time) commanded by Admiral de Grasse, has become known as the Battle of the Saintes. The victory saved Jamaica and won England the upper hand in the 1783 peace treaty.[65]

But glorious as Rodney's military victories might have been, they did nothing for St Lucia's economy. By 1784, 300 plantations lay abandoned and only a few working estates near the coast remained. Meanwhile, a thousand or more runaway slaves were living as maroons in the mountainous interior, accompanied by the occasional white army or navy deserter. Eighteen months before the great hurricanes, in April 1779, James Grant had already reported that '*there were 704 Maroon Negroes in the whole island*'[66] and at any one time, an estimated 5 per cent of the slave population lived out in the woods as free runaways. But the 1780 hurricanes and the opportunities for escape during war duties had easily doubled or tripled this number.

1784-1793: Baron de Laborie and a period of relative peace

By the Treaty of Versailles (September 1783), St Lucia was re-instated to France. Actual power was handed back in early 1784. Between 1765 and 1778, Baron de Micoud and his successors had kick-started St Lucia's plantation economy for the first time. British rule and the hurricanes of 1780 had reversed much of that work but back under French rule from 1784, St Lucia entered its second phase of development, this time under Governor Baron de Laborie.[67] One of de Laborie's first concerns was to reduce the number of runaway slaves in St Lucia. He chose persuasion over force with an amnesty which reportedly brought '*many*' slaves back to the estates. He also clamped down on army deserters and reduced the number of public holidays, because '*On the day following the holidays there was little work done, many Negro slaves did not behave properly or over drank on holidays, traveling from one quarter to the other, sometimes escaping from their masters.'*[68] Even so, marronage remained a fact of life in St Lucia until Emancipation.

Another priority for de Laborie was infrastructural improvement. Mangrove trees on the flanks of Castries Harbour were cleared to extend the town boundaries; the roads of Castries were paved; a timber jetty was built; the public service was improved; discipline was brought to the military; new forms of agriculture were introduced; baths were built near the Sulphur Springs in Soufrière, and all the roads originally cut by de Micoud (but destroyed in the hurricane and further neglected by the British) were repaired. De Laborie also suggested three ambitious new roads: one to run east-west across the island from Soufrière to Micoud along the Soufrière and *Thoumacé* (Troumassée) Rivers; another from Castries to Dauphin to meet the coastal road at Marquis, and a third to run through the interior from Castries (in the north-west) to Vieux Fort (in the south-east), more or less following the spine of the Barre de l'Isle, with branches stretching into each district.[69] Without this third road, de Laborie believed, the interior of St Lucia could never be fully opened up for the kind of economic development he envisaged: 70 to 80 000 slaves and a national income of seventeen to eighteen million Pounds in sugar crops annually. The interior road was started but never completed (although stretches of stone-paved road colloquially known as 'the French Road' can still be found today) but the *Chemin Royal* was: a circular road from Castries to d'Ennery, Vieux Fort, Soufrière and back to Castries.

Another of his hobby horses was free trade. De Laborie fervently believed that free trade had been the crucial factor in St Lucia's first spurt of economic development. The level to which free trade and smuggling occurred was perhaps best exemplified by the number of different currencies that were simultaneously in use, with traders accepting and paying in '*sols, deniers, livres, Louis d'ors, "three-man pieces", British pennies and "Leeward Island Dogs",*'[70] as well as the *Portuguese gold Johannes*, commonly known as *Joes*.[71] For sixteen years, St Lucia had been a free haven for merchants trading under all kinds of flags[72] and when he first arrived, de Laborie was pleased to note that English business houses wanted to stay on despite the change in administration, simply because of the '*freedom they enjoy* [to] *make their sojourn in St Lucia agreeable and useful; we have regular arrivals of several negro-traders and numerous ships come from England loaded with salted beef and utensils for the manufacturers, there is abundant codfish, and the colonial crops sell well and are well paid for.*'[73]

But shortly after de Laborie was appointed, in 1784, French authorities clamped down on free trade and ordered that all goods henceforth must be imported and exported via merchants in Martinique. This drastically cut into St Lucia's profits and so Governor de Laborie started his campaign for financial independence from Martinique in general, and re-instatement of free trade in particular.

It was with this purpose in mind that he instructed *Arpenteur Générale* Jean François Lefort de Latour to put together a *General and Descriptive Report* of St Lucia, accompanied by a geometrical map. The report was meant to attract new settlers as well as to convince the French authorities that free trade was absolutely necessary for St Lucia's economic development. The report used strong words, arguing that, like Guadeloupe, St Lucia must shake off the yoke of Martinique if she were ever to flourish and achieve her full potential. Lefort de Latour's 1784 report was reprinted in Paris in 1989 as part of a collection of historical records on St Lucia brought together by Eugène and Raymond Bruneau-Latouche under the title *Sainte-Lucie. Fille de la Martinique.* In it are Lefort de Latour's maps of each *Quartier* (showing all existing property boundaries, tables with landowners' names, the size of their estates and crops grown) as well as detailed descriptions of each district. It reads like a guided tour of St Lucia in the year 1784 – surely an opportunity too good to pass over!

Snapshots of St Lucia in 1784

Le Quartier de Castries

Lefort de Latour started off by lauding the useful deep-water harbour of Castries. The town itself contained 100 houses by then. Having been relocated in 1769 from La Vieille Ville (on the south-side of Vigie) to the windward side of the swamps at the foot of Morne Fortuné, living conditions had improved a little but Castries continued to struggle with '*unhealthy air*' and disease. Most of the *Quartier de Castries* had only mediocre soils and ill-chosen plantation sites, except for *Pais-Bouche,* which boasted the best coffee and cocoa estates of all St Lucia, and the valleys of the *Rivière de La Brelotte* and *Grand Cul de Sac,* both of which could support many more sugar factories than they did. Lefort de Latour believed that while 2000 slaves worked on plantations in Castries district in 1784, the area was capable of occupying 15 000 or 20 000. '*The shortage of hands is so dire that one often sees good crops perishing in the fields for lack of negroes to harvest the crops.*'

Le Quartier du Joubert (Marigot and Roseau)

The second district Lefort de Latour visited was the *Quartier du Joubert,* which had been dismembered from the *Quartier de Lance Laray* by a previous Governor, de Joubert. Encompassing the Marigot and Roseau bays, Lefort de Latour described this as one of the least developed areas on the island despite its excellent soils, with neither church nor *bourg* (although a village was planned for *Lance des Roseaux*). He extolled on the safety of Marigot Bay, which could hold 50 or 60 ships. The rivers were numerous and large enough to support several sugar mills but much of the land in the interior had not yet been given out. At the time of the report, there were only seven sugar estates in the *Quartier du Joubert*, employing about 1500 slaves, where he believed 20 or 30 estates could function with 10 000 slaves.

Le Quartier de L'ance-La-Raye

The *Quartier de L'ance-La-Raye* had been named after the abundance of rayfish found in this bay along the west coast. The district also contained '*l'ance Gallet, l'ance Cochon, l'ance Laverdure et les Canaries.*' It was difficult terrain, admitted Lefort de Latour, due to the many steep mountains, but he complimented the inhabitants for their industriousness. Although the soil was not ideal for coffee or cocoa, the valleys were perfectly suitable for sugar cane and the air and water were of very good quality also. In 1784, there were four *sucreries* in the area with less than 1000 slaves, where the district could support twelve or fifteen sugar estates, and 6000 or 7000 slaves. Nine-tenths of the district was still covered in bush, making for very picturesque views from the hills, said Lefort de Latour, albeit it of the '*genre sombre*'.

Le Quartier de la Souffrière

Le Quartier de la Souffrière was, in 1784, St Lucia's main economic district. It was named after the volcano, which had several craters including one that was 900 feet in diameter. The 1780 hurricane had changed the volcano's shape, wrote Lefort de Latour, with some craters being buried and new ones opening up. Some craters were hot and soft and could not be walked upon - although Governor Baron de Laborie had reportedly done just that shortly after the hurricane, when broken trees covered the surface. De Laborie and his brother had also thrown boulders of seven or eight pounds apiece into the craters and watched the vents throw them five or six feet back up into the air. The most recent volcanic activity, according to Lefort de Latour, had been some twenty years earlier, when the earth wall to the north-west of a small volcanic lake (étang) suddenly gave way, spilling its contents violently into the sea. Lefort de Latour made special mention of the medicinal qualities of the sulphur springs water and, more unexpectedly, also reported the presence of a deposit of coral and seashells '*on top of one of the highest mountains in the quarter.*' Along with Anse la Raye, Soufrière was the most mountainous part of St Lucia, with the characteristic *Sugar Loaves* (the Pitons) standing with '*their feet in the sea and their heads in the clouds.*' Hills and mountains were cultivated almost up to their summits, producing the richest crops of cocoa and bananas on the island. Soufrière had been very badly damaged in the 1780 hurricane but was on the road to repair and still the second-largest town. Merchants had re-built their shops and Lefort de Latour believed that with freedom of trade, business would soon bloom again. The town had a good bay where just 50 yards from shore the water was already 60 or 70 yards deep. The air in the town, although pungent with sulphur, was considered very healthy and the river water was clean and potable. In 1784, Soufrière had twelve sugar estates and about 2000 slaves, where 30 estates could easily employ 10 or 12 000 pairs of hands. Labour shortage was a huge concern - in Soufrière as elsewhere.

Le Quartier de Choiseul

Just south of Soufrière was the *Quartier de Choiseul*, previously known as *L'ance Citron* but re-named after the Peace of 1762 in honour of the Duc de Choiseul *'for his care and attention in ensuring that the island would be and remain in French hands.'* The village was well-placed, with a pretty river running between the houses and a good anchorage on the main beach. Some smaller anchorages were rather exposed to the currents of the St Vincent Channel. The *quartier de Choiseul* was bounded to the north by the *Rivière de L'Ivrogne* and to the south-east by the *Rivière Dorée.* The soil in the district was light and of mediocre quality, but cocoa and coffee were cultivated with some success and sugar and cotton could get by. There was little flooding, as rain easily drained into the ground and the area was shaped like an amphitheatre, running off towards the sea. The plantations presented a pleasant picture to the eye, the air and water were pure and the Choiseul area had never been visited by epidemic disease. There were a few merchants in Choiseul, who did relatively good business. In 1784, there were seven sugar estates employing 1500 slaves, where 20 could be sustained, using 6000 or 7000 workers.

Le Quartier de l'Islet à Caret (Laborie)

Next, Lefort de Latour visited the *Quartier de l'Islet à Caret*, which was later re-named after Baron de Laborie but which originally gained its name from a small island in the bay, on whose white sand banks hundreds of turtles (*carets*) laid their eggs. This *l'Islet à Caret* was an important resting ground for marine birds as well. It was already partially destroyed (possibly during the 1780 hurricane) when Lefort de Latour first saw it and disappeared altogether not long after. Ironically, the village was renamed just in time because already at the time of this report, turtles here were hunted so extensively for their meat and shells (to be carved into precious objects for the European market) that their abundant presence was soon to be a thing of the past. Geologically, the district was flatter than Choiseul and the soil was generally good. There were six sugar estates, with 1600 or 1700 slaves, where 15 or 18 *sucreries* could exist, worked by 7000 or 8000 slaves. There were enough small rivers in the area to turn waterwheels, roads were good and horse-drawn carriages could easily travel around. The anchorage at *l'Islet à Caret* was safe enough but the entrance into the bay was dangerous due to submerged rocks and reefs. The river water was not very clean and rain water was used to supplement drinking purposes. In 1784, this village was the third-largest population centre on the island.

Le Quartier du Vieux Fort

In the deep south of the island, demarcated by the *Rivière des ances noirs* (Black Bay River) on the west and a line running from Morne Grand Magazin to the *Baye des Savannes* on the east, lay the *Quartier du Vieux Fort.* According to Lefort de Latour: '*There is no district on this island as beautiful as this one. It is almost one unified plain, well cultivated, covered in sugar cane and estates. ... A few hills are elevated above the plains, but since they are cultivated almost up to their summits, they add to the embellishment of the countryside.*'

The Caribbean bay of Vieux Fort offered a safe anchorage and being within easy sailing distance of Tobago and Barbados, Lefort de Latour felt that the town ought to be attractive to merchants. On the Atlantic side of the Moule à Chique peninsula, Anse de Sable Bay offered safe anchorage but reefs one kilometer off-shore near *Islet Maria*[74], combined with strong cross-shore trade winds made entry hazardous. Soils around Vieux Fort were good and produced excellent sugar canes while inland, several beautiful coffee plantations flourished also. Transport of produce went smoothly as roads were easy to maintain. Despite the presence of several swamps, the air was very healthy and water from the Vieux Fort River, other streams and springs was good to drink. In the village of Vieux Fort, where seawater made the river brackish, cisterns of rain water complemented the supply.

Despite its natural advantages and clear potential, Vieux Fort in 1784 consisted of little more than a few fishermen's huts and the district as a whole contained just six sugar estates, with 1400 slaves. Lefort de Latour estimated that Vieux Fort could easily sustain 15 or 16 plantations and 7000 or 8000 slaves employed in various forms of agriculture.

Le Quartier de Micoud

Before it was re-named in honour of Governor de Micoud, this east coast district had been known as *Le Thoumacé,* after the Troumassée River. Micoud was more hilly than Vieux Fort but not as mountainous as the west coast districts, and had a sloping coastline. Soils were good for a range of crops but anchorages were problematic. Port du Volet, just north of Micoud village, accommodated some smaller vessels but it was Port de Savannes, right in between the Vieux Fort and Micoud districts, which acted as the district's main port. Micoud had many rivers, of which Troumassée was the largest, with good drinking water. Every river was also capable of supporting several water mills - more so, in fact, than any other district in St Lucia. Yet in 1784, there were just five sugar plantations in *le Quartier de Micoud* with 1200 slaves, where Lefort de Latour saw scope for at least 20 estates and 12 000 or 15 000 slaves.

Le Quartier du Praslin

By 1784, Praslin (named after the French Minister of Marine Affairs) was important enough to have been dismembered as a separate district. The land had been subdivided into large lots, resulting in relatively few inhabitants and a small number of estates. The district's best-known inhabitant was Baron de Micoud, the infamous Deputy-Governor who had been forced to surrender St Lucia to the English in 1778. He was married to Marie Anne Devaux, whose white French family owned extensive property in Soufrière also. At Praslin, she was known as Madame de Micoud or, in common parlance, *Mamiku* - which today is still the name of this old estate and the river flowing through it. Lefort de Latour thought the soil in Praslin mediocre but even so, sugar cane, cotton and cocoa were all produced here in 1784. The rivers were small and could power only a few mills but the district's main bay (*Le Ports des Trois Islets,* named after its three islands) was deep and safe enough for smaller vessels. The French surveyor advised that the existing six *sucreries* with 600 or 700 slaves be expanded to 12 estates, with 6000 slaves.

Quartier d'Ennery

Originally known as *Lance Canot* and *Le Grand Mabouya,* this district had been re-named after Count d'Ennery: the man who had written such comprehensive reports on St Lucia in 1765 and 1767 and had gone on to become Governor-General of the Windward Islands. There were no decent ports or anchorages except for a mediocre landing site in the village itself, and the lack of safe shipping hampered the export of crops. It explains why, despite the ample fertile soils of Mabouya Valley and the presence of some beautiful cocoa and coffee estates, in 1784, the majority of the *Quartier d'Ennery* was still covered in forest. Along with the district of Joubert (Marigot/Roseau), d'Ennery had some of the most fertile, yet least cultivated land in St Lucia. Lefort de Latour estimated that the district could easily employ 8000 slaves on 15 sugar estates, where at the time only 1100 slaves worked on five estates.

Quartier du Dauphin

North of d'Ennery, *le Quartier du Dauphin* contained steep mountains and only mediocre soil, but offered a safe port at *Lespérance,* which had lent the district its name until Governor de Micoud re-named it after Monsieur le Dauphin. The district's main village, le Mouflet, had the only intact church of the island after the 1780 hurricane. The Lespérance and Marquis Rivers could each turn several waterwheels, yet in 1784, Dauphin had no more than five *sucreries* and 1200 slaves, where 12 plantations and 7000 or 8000 slaves would bring the district up to full working capacity, according to Lefort de Latour. He did however mention the existence of several beautiful cotton and coffee estates, covering whole mountain sides including Morne La Sorcière, where coffee grew almost up to the summit.

Quartier de Gros-Islet

His last stop brought Lefort de Latour to the very north, *le Quartier de Gros-Islet*, named after St Lucia's largest off-shore landmass: Pigeon Island. In recent years, the British had used Pigeon Island for recuperation purposes, to get away from the *maladies* that pestered Castries, and to keep track of movements of the French navy in nearby Martinique. Considering the quality of the look-outs and batteries, it was a miracle, wrote Lefort de Latour, that the military base at Pigeon Island had not inflicted still more harm on the French. The Gros Islet bay could easily hold the biggest of ships while cannons on the mainland, at Morne Piment, could effectively protect the entire bay. The only reason Pigeon Island never became St Lucia's main naval station lay in the fact that there were no rivers or wells, and the British had to rely on a rain cistern for drinking water.

On the mainland, the soils were light and sandy but of good quality. The Gros Islet district was susceptible to droughts, though, especially in the north-east. As early as 1784, Lefort de Latour noted that '*The destruction of all the forest in this district did not help the droughts*'. He advised '*that it would be wise to adopt the axiom that without woods, no rain, and without rain, no crops!*'[75] As a result, there were just five sugar estates in Gros Islet, employing 1600 or 1700 slaves. Some cotton was grown also, of a quality even better than that grown in Dauphin, and so Lefort de Latour recommended that up to 6000 slaves be employed in Gros Islet, producing various crops including, but not limited to, sugar.

Governor de Laborie's legacy

Baron de Laborie's zealous dedication between 1784 and 1789 went a long way towards boosting St Lucia's plantation economy. By the time he died, in April 1789, 43 sugar estates were once again in production, plus another 143 coffee and 88 cocoa plantations. The largest number of sugar estates was located in the district of Soufrière (nine), with Vieux Fort (eight) a close second. Castries came next (six), followed by Laborie (five), Anse la Raye and Gros Islet (four each), Praslin (three), Dauphin (two) and Micoud and d'Ennery (one each). The district of Choiseul still had no sugar estates.[76] Cotton fetched high prices, with some 200 planters setting up or re-establishing cotton plantations and by 1789, cotton merchants had set up business houses in Castries, Soufrière,

Laborie, Micoud and Gros Islet. In fact, until 1803, cotton remained St Lucia's primary export crop and by rights, the true dominance of sugar as St Lucia's main crop is only a nineteenth century phenomenon.

With the increased need for agricultural labour came the expansion of the slave population: growing by 5197 people between 1772 and 1789 to a total of 18 218.[77] It was to be the highest recorded number of slaves ever in St Lucia's history, as a thorough study of various records[78] suggests:

Year	Slaves	Free Coloureds	Whites
1745	2,470	790*	-
1772	12,795	663	2,018
1789	18,218	1,588	2,181
1799	13,391	1,364	1,195
1810	14,397	1,878	1,210
1825	13,530	3,871	1,194
1834	13,300	-	2,200
1835	-	3,919	-
1838	14,000	-	1,109

Table 1

Development of the population of slaves, free people of colour and whites between 1745 and Emancipation (1838).
** free coloureds and whites together*

In summary, the three decades between 1765 and 1794 saw two periods of dedicated development of a plantation economy in St Lucia based on sugar cane and other crops (cotton, cocoa and coffee). Both periods were characterized by French rule: from 1765 until the end of 1778 under Governor Baron de Micoud and his nephew Deputy-Governor de Micoud, and again from 1784 until 1793 under Governors de Laborie (1784-1789) and his successors Governors de Gimat, de Ricard and Goyrand. The interruption in this economic spurt, as usual in St Lucia, took the form of Anglo-French warfare. Although it was not their intention to undermine the plantation economy, when the English captured the island in late 1778, their military priorities seriously interfered with crop production. The few remaining working plantations were subsequently wiped out by the hurricanes of 1780.

It took the French authorities, under governorship of Baron de Laborie, five years to get St Lucia's plantation economy and infrastructure back on its feet. De Laborie's successors continued to keep the island on this track until 1793, when the French Revolution dramatically impacted on life in St Lucia and the wider Caribbean.

4

The Brigand Wars: French Revolution in St Lucia 1794-1804

'Liberty, Equality and Brotherhood', the fiery wish of the working masses of France, culminated on 14 July 1789 in the siege of the Bastille Prison. By August, a new National Assembly proclaimed the Declaration of Rights of Man and of the Citizen and France was having its revolution. Once the poor masses rose up against centuries of absolute reign by King and nobility, there was no holding back the tidal wave of change and for a decade-and-a-half, the reverberations of the French Revolution rippled around the globe in waves of frantic and frightening events, with the guillotine becoming its most chilling symbol. As many as 35 000 or 40 000 enemies of the revolution lost their heads,[79] not just in France but in the Caribbean as well. It is said that when Victor Hugues, agent of the Revolutionary Government, sailed into the West Indies, he carried a guillotine '*shrouded in the bows of his ship and, as he approached the shore, he tore off the tarpaulin sheet and the sunlight glittered on its steel blade.*'[80]

Jean Joseph de Gimat had been Governor of French-held St Lucia for exactly four weeks when the Bastille was stormed in Paris. News of the revolution took a while to travel to the Caribbean but on 15 September 1789, a public celebration was held in Martinique. St Lucia followed closely behind, with conventions in Gros Islet and Castries where, on 20 October, an enthusiastic crowd gathered at the square. Although there was no official support for the revolution, out of fear that the slaves might rebel, the 14th of July was declared a public holiday in St Lucia and the mood was generally expectant. Naturally, the ideas of the revolution were most appealing to those most discontented with their lot: the *petits blancs* (poor whites) and the *gens de couleur libre* (free people of colour), not to mention the 18 000 slaves, who monitored events with huge hope in their hearts, having nothing to lose and everything to gain.[81]

The editor of the *Gazette de Ste Lucie*, a local newspaper, took up the cause and added *Nationale et Politique* to its name. His views were moderate but supportive of the revolution and he made a concerted effort to guide the reading public through the new political philosophies of the day. In those early days, before aristocratic blood had stained the streets of Paris, planters in St Lucia were not overly alarmed by the wind of change in their mother country. B.H. Easter was probably correct in his estimation that

> *... the colonists, so far away from those happenings in Paris, accepted these changes in the spirit of loyal submission to the effective home government, however it might have been established. They were probably disheartened by the hurricane of 1780, debilitated by yellow fever and, like all colonists, disgruntled with the home government .... Moreover, the only alternative to the Republican French Government was British rule from which they had only lately been delivered. Better a bad Frenchman than a good Englishman!*[82]

It took less than two years for white planters to realize, to their intense horror, that their survival in fact depended entirely on British support.

The French Revolution took an ominous turn on 2 November, when a new decree authorized the confiscation of Church property. The atmosphere grew more volatile. In March 1790, the St Lucia Royal Volunteers were called on to help keep order in Martinique, where the Government (still representative of the now-besieged King of France) felt increasing pressure from an agitated revolutionary population. Further north, in Ste Domingue, matters took a more radical turn with the Black Jacobin revolution which resulted in the creation of Haiti as an independent black nation.

In St Lucia, people of all colours and classes studied events intently, thrashing out their own views. In March 1790, the editor of the *Gazette de Ste Lucie, Nationale et Politique* moved to Martinique but the paper kept its name and continued to report on St Lucia. Slaves across the French Antilles began to openly question their bondage, and free people of colour their inferior position. Under the *Code Noir* of 1685, free people of colour had held the same rights as whites. But in 1766, this had been overturned in all French islands and was replaced by restrictive measures which prohibited free coloureds from serving in the militias, carrying weapons or holding legal posts. Even their clothes were prescribed for them. The British island governments had implemented somewhat less restrictive but equally frustrating laws to keep free people of colour down[83] - which perhaps shows just how threatened the white minority felt by the expanding numbers of free people of colour and their rise to economic power. The restrictions had caused '*a smouldering resentment which eventually caught fire.*'[84] In April 1790, a group of free people of colour in Castries presented an address to the *Assemblée Coloniale* in which they clamoured for equal rights. By June, the free people of colour from Anse la Raye were holding meetings. On 8 July, the Government established municipalities and free people of colour became hopeful that they would soon be allowed to hold government jobs.

A grimmer face of the French Revolution showed itself on 24 August 1790, when a proclamation in France authorized state control of the clergy. At the same time, the National Assembly in France remained undecided on the issue of emancipation of slaves, and a sense of impending anarchy filled the air in St Lucia. In October 1790, an insurrection took place among French soldiers stationed at Morne Fortuné, who apparently felt intimidated by white and coloured revolutionaries. In December, the Martinique Government passed a law promoting tranquillity in all the French Antilles but instead of calming matters down, it failed to comfort the planters while raising the hopes of the slaves.

Violence erupted in St Lucia three weeks later. On New Year's Day 1791, slaves belonging to a Monsieur Viet[85] in the district of Soufrière, somehow convinced that in Martinique all slaves had been set free, revolted and demanded their liberty. '*The Soufrière authorities moved quickly. Before the rebellion could spread, several ringleaders were seized and executed. Their heads were cut off and displayed prominently in different parts of the area.*'[86] It shows that at the start of 1791, despite mounting support for the French Revolution, the traditional, royalist powers-that-be still held the upper hand in St Lucia - just.

In late January, the National Assembly appointed four *Commissaries* for the West Indies: Jean Lacoste, Louis Magnitot, d'Eau de Montdenoix and Jacques Linger, mandating them to spread the philosophies of the revolution and implement them in law. The *Commissaries* were denied entry into Martinique and Dominica but the authorities in St Lucia allowed them access. Before long, de Montdenoix and Linger raised the tricolour flag and began reorganizing the Colonial Assemblies.

The *Commissaries* encountered mixed reactions in St Lucia. The most conservative royalist faction was that of the émigrés: aristocrats who had fled France for fear of losing their heads under the guillotine, who sought to preserve their old positions of power and supported the return of monarchical rule in France. The majority of white planters however (in an address to the Governor of Martinique on 20 February) still expressed support for the revolution although condemning the bloody anarchy it carried with it (undoubtedly with the Soufrière uprising still fresh on their minds). On the other side of the spectrum were the free people of colour and slaves, who had everything to gain by radical change. Small factions of atheists, counter-revolutionaries and abolitionists added their voices to the political confusion.

In April 1791, Pope Pius VI condemned the civil constitution of France. Almost immediately, priests became victimized, which added considerably to the complexity of the situation. For another year or so, revolutionary change occurred within the bounds of regular law. In March 1792, for instance, the Assembly in St Lucia allowed free men of colour to vote in parochial assemblies and made them eligible for all posts, provided they were qualified. But not long after, the rising revolutionary tide began to wash over the confines of legal niceties. On 14 August 1792, a second French Revolution took place in Paris and King Louis XVI was arrested and imprisoned. Reprisal, victimization and acts of terror followed. A month later, the National Convention took over and proclaimed the Republic of France, causing great anxiety around Europe. Britain (still licking its wounds from the American War of Independence and not at all keen to engage in another war with France) persisted in its aloof, wait-and-see attitude. But in St Lucia, law and order were breaking down. A second revolt rocked Soufrière on 23 August, and while this one, too, was short-lived, in subsequent weeks, slaves began to abandon estates everywhere. Governor de Gimat, as the appointee of King Louis XVI, realized his power was becoming untenable and deserted the island, leaving St Lucia teetering on the brink of anarchy. Control devolved upon Lieutenant-Colonel Laroque-Montel, the highest-ranking available officer. The citizens of Castries grabbed their chance and, on 26 September 1792, formed a temporary assembly which became a full-blown Colonial Assembly four weeks later. To demonstrate the new Government's revolutionary tenor, one of its first feats was to dissolve a counter-revolutionary newspaper that had been started in Castries: *Le Journal de Ste Lucie ou le Patriote des Antilles Française.* The paper's main message, opposition to the liberation of slaves, no longer stood a chance in the now openly revolutionary island.

Royalists, in turn, began to vocally condemn the French Revolution. From 'preferring a bad Frenchman to a good Englishman', white planters in St Lucia now begged the British King for help. By then, however, the republicans had gained the upper hand.

In December 1792, Lieutenant Jean-Raymond la Crosse landed in St Lucia as commander of the fregate *La Félicité.* He circulated revolutionary pamphlets (which were for the most part enthusiastically received) and began to organize and arm St Lucia's *patriots*, which is what the republican poor whites and free people of colour had started calling themselves. For two months, la Crosse acted as unofficial Governor-General of St Lucia, Martinique and Guadeloupe. In recognition of its support for the revolution, St Lucia was re-named *St Lucie La Fidèle* ('St Lucia the Faithful'). Castries became *Félicitéville* and Soufrière *La Convention.* By early 1793, slaves island-wide had abandoned the plantations. Only a few women with children and the elderly and infirm stayed behind, growing food for themselves while leaving the cash crops to wither in the fields. Trade ground to a halt.[87]

On 21 January 1793, the French Revolution turned from grim to bloody with the execution by guillotine of King Louis XVI. It was the final straw for Britain, which severed all diplomatic ties. On 1 February, France declared war on England and Holland and the old adversaries were back at it once again. Republicans in British-held islands began to encourage slaves to rebel and in Soufrière, the St Lucia Patriotic Party did the same. In February, General Nicolas Xavier de Ricard replaced la Crosse as Governor of St Lucia (although la Crosse continued to lead the St Lucia patriots for some time longer) and republican terminology was formally adopted in all interactions. Thus, people of all colours started calling each other *citoyen* or *citoyenne* ('citizen'). Inspired by the example of Ste Domingue, the St Lucia Jacobin Club flourished, with a republican-minded Frenchman by the name of Raymond Drouilhet as its secretary. Meanwhile, the white planters - who were by and large royalists - were fast descending into ruin. The rift became deeper still when the Colonial Assembly announced in February that, as a colony of the Republic of France, St Lucia must be defended against royalist enemies. That these were not just hollow words became evident the following year.

The First Brigand War

By January 1794, it was clear that England was planning an invasion of St Lucia. Governor de Ricard wanted to arm St Lucia's black people so they could help defend the island, but the remaining white planters were terrified of the prospect and persuaded him to delay the plan. It left de Ricard with limited options and a lot of worries. In the end, the National Convention in Paris decided the matter for him. Aware of the mounting threat of an English attack on Martinique, Guadeloupe and St Lucia, on 4 February 1794, the National Convention in Paris finally bit the bullet and abolished the enslavement of all '*negro people*' in its colonies. Henceforth, all inhabitants, without distinction of colour, were to be French citizens with full constitutional rights.[88] It had taken years of stalling and an urgent opportunistic cause but finally, France was making *Liberté, Egalité and Fraternité* count for its slaves as well.[89]

Ironically, by the time the decree reached St Lucia (around September 1794) it was too late: the English had recaptured the island.

Martinique fell first, on 23 March 1794, and St Lucia ranked next on General Vaughan's hit list. Governor de Ricard desperately tried to mobilize a defence force but the planters were useless: being by and large royalists, they welcomed English invasion as a means of salvation from the republican threat to their power, property and safety. At the same time, the slaves, free people of colour and republican-minded whites, although abundantly motivated to fight the English invaders, were not yet sufficiently organized or trained.

And so it was that the British recaptured St Lucia with hardly an ounce of resistance. On 1 April 1794, Vice-Admiral Sir John Jervis with a Brigade of Grenadiers commanded by his Royal Highness Prince Edward landed his troops at Ance du Cap, Choc beach and Roseau Bay '*with little resistance, and no loss.*'[90] The battery at La Toc was taken and shortly after Prince Edward personally took down the tricolour at Morne Fortuné, hoisted the British flag and renamed it *Fort Charlotte*, after his mother. Castries (*Felicitéville*) now became Charlotteville.

The English proudly reported the '*entire Conquest*' of St Lucia.[91] But this would turn out to be a grossly premature boast. Although they had captured the main defensive posts and forced Governor de Ricard to surrender (along with a garrison of 300 men, troops of the line,[92] some artillery and a few people of colour), England's true enemy had rushed off into hiding. In the densely forested mountains, a republican resistance army was emerging that would become one of England's worst nightmares.

At the head of the resistance army were two French soldiers, Kermené and Sabathier Saint-André.[93] Within weeks, they turned their motley troops into something the English army had never yet had the misfortune to face: a self-styled *L'Armée Française dans les Bois* ('French Army in the Woods') which was extremely well-adapted to the topography and climate of St Lucia, well-armed, infused with black, coloured and white people's skills and techniques, capable of maintaining long lines of communication with republicans on other islands and, most important of all, deeply committed. Unlike the regular British soldiers, these members of *L'Armée Française dans les Bois* did not fight for prize money or booty: they fought for their own destinies. Considered runaway slaves, insurgents and *brigands* (bandits) by British and French royalists, and faced with the threat of a return to bondage as long as British occupation lasted, they literally fought for their lives. Moreover, their commitment was undoubtedly peppered with vivid memories of the humiliations suffered under slavery and the bloody suppression of recent slave uprisings. As for the free people of colour, poor whites and the handful of French soldiers who joined *L'Armée Française dans les Bois*, they all had reasons of their own, but equality and respect would have been paramount to them also. Finally, a small number of white planters, covertly and overtly, supported the rebel army, partly out of disgust with the way in which the English army was abusing the prize-money system.

Exhilaration at freedom, a longing for equality, revenge, hatred, idealism and a certain amount of desperation: they all went into the mixture that fuelled *L'Armée Française dans les Bois* - or, as the British came to call them: *the Brigands.*

1794: British attempts at restoring order

Following the British invasion, Sir Charles Gordon was left in charge of St Lucia. One of his first actions was to round up and deport '*undesirables and suspect persons*': people with republican sympathies suspected of spreading the '*seeds of insurrection*'. Several people were arrested and some of them sent to England as prisoners-of-war. The policy eventually became Gordon's downfall, after he succumbed to the temptation of accepting protection money from suspects.[94] It led to his arrest and disgrace - but not before the first few clashes with the insurgents. In August of 1794, British troops marching from Fort Charlotte to Dauphin came across a Brigands' camp. They attacked it at daybreak, killing and wounding eleven and hanging two. The others escaped. The English lost one man and had four wounded. Their commander later wrote: '*... the Rascals are in such Numbers and the Woods impenetrable that I am much afraid they will not be easily quelled particularly as I cannot well spare more men from this Garrison*'.[95]

Sickness, mortality and desertion undermined the British troops and General Grey tried to raise troops locally. He organized the island's '*British gentlemen*' into the St Lucia Royal British Volunteers and armed the planters, but soon realized that the latter could not be counted on for much. They were '*so extremely timid as to prove hurtful rather than serviceable to us, under continual apprehension of the Guillotine, and ever apprehensive of an Insurrection amongst the Negroes, in consequence of the Note of Emancipation of the French Government.*'

St Lucia's economy limped through the year 1794, with the few remaining planters trying to keep their estates afloat with the handful of slaves who had not yet absconded, but whose allegiance they deeply distrusted.

By the end of 1794, Grey's successor in the West Indies, Lieutenant-General Sir John Vaughan, decided to fight fire with fire. Planters continued to oppose the thought of placing loyal slaves under arms alongside regular soldiers to fight the Brigands, so Vaughan compromised and sent the Black Carolina Corps (based in Martinique) to St Lucia instead. This corps had been formed in 1779 in South Carolina from slaves and free coloureds loyal to the Southerners during the American War of Independence. Their first mission was to destroy a Brigand outpost in the mountains, a task which Vaughan judged '*to be a Service of more Fatigue than Danger*' and hence '*a proper Enterprize on which to employ the Blacks, and to save our own Soldiers.*' Seventy soldiers of the Black Carolina Corps attacked the Brigands (who had one white man among them), killing several but also losing fourteen of their own, including two officers. They did however destroy the camp, burning the palisades and levelling everything inside it.

Vaughan also tried to lure the Brigands with promises of an amnesty. Eight people surrendered but, within a month, the Brigands were back on the offensive, attacking a detachment of the Black Carolina Corps while it crossed the centre of the island and killing several of them. It was the final straw. General Vaughan finally overrode local planters' objections and brought 120 black soldiers from Martinique to St Lucia. Known as *Malcolm's Rangers* or the *Black Rangers,* they had been raised from royalist slaves in Martinique. They were the predecessors of the West India Regiment, which was established the following year to become the first black regiment in the British army. By now, Vaughan was convinced that the only way to fight *L'Armée Française dans les Bois* was with the help of '*a strong Body of Blacks*'. In the meantime, Governor Gordon was recalled from St Lucia over the debacle with protection money and replaced by Brigadier General Stewart.

Victor Hugues: horror of all royalists

During the second half of 1794, the British in Martinique, St Lucia and Guadeloupe came under increasing pressure, both from Brigand armies and from the Republic of France. In late 1794, France recaptured Guadeloupe and the island was placed under the command of a man who haunted the sleep of every Briton and royalist in the West Indies: Victor Hugues. Hugues was a fearless and ferocious man, still only in his mid-twenties and a protégé of Robespierre, the leader of the French Revolution, himself. Hugues had been born in France of poor parents and sent to Guadeloupe as apprentice to a hairdresser. His subsequent careers included being a petty innkeeper, captain of a small trading vessel and lieutenant in the French navy. Hugues distinguished himself during the French Revolution and caught the eye of Robespierre, who delegated him to the National Assembly. In 1794, Hugues was appointed *Commissaire* of Guadeloupe with full control over the army and navy - a role in which he was '*nearly as savage, remorseless and bloody as Robespierre himself.*'[96]

One of Hugues' first acts (and his favourite boast) after he captured Guadeloupe was to guillotine 1200 royalists. His was reportedly the only guillotine that ever operated outside of revolutionary France.[97] Even some fellow republicans, including St Lucia's *Commissaire* Goyrand, spoke with distaste about Hugues' predilection for cruelty and bloodshed, and Goyrand's sidekick, artillery officer Pierre Jacquin, called him a '*terrible little man*'. Victor Hugues' appearance and demeanour apparently matched his reputation for ugliness. He was described as being of less than medium height, with a corpulent torso and thick stocky legs: a man dressed in too-tight clothes, with a face pitted by smallpox, abrupt in his manner, jerky in his movements and rarely looking anyone in the eye - '*but, when he did, his small grey eyes inspired either terror or repulsion.*'[98]

From his stronghold in Guadeloupe, Hugues directed and supplied the insurgents in St Lucia, St Vincent and Grenada. On 21 February 1795, he decreed that for every republican put to death, one British officer would be guillotined. A fortnight later, Hugues sent two representatives to St Lucia: black republicans by the names of Massade and Jean-Joseph Lambert. They landed in Dennery with a proclamation which declared all slaves free men and women, and instructing all inhabitants, from newly freed slaves to royalist planters, to join in the fight against the enemies of the Republic on pain of death. Hugues appointed Jean-Joseph Lambert commandant of St Lucia.

It was the start of a systematic guerrilla war against the British and royalist French in the Lesser Antilles. Hugues roused insurgent republican troops, supplied them with food, weapons and ammunition and maintained constant lines of communication across the various islands, putting the British under tremendous pressure. In St Lucia, thanks to regular supplies from Hugues, the Brigand army was gaining a foothold in the south, where it opted for a 'war of posts': wearing out the British while remaining frustratingly elusive. Before long, Governor Stewart reported miserably that *'despite all efforts, the Brigands are gaining ground.'*[99] By the end of March 1795, the Catholic Church abandoned St Lucia and the two remaining priests (Abbé Petroné from Anse la Raye and Abbé Bourcière from Praslin) joined *L'Armée Française dans les Bois.*

By April, the British army still commanded Fort Charlotte (Morne Fortuné) and Charlotteville (Castries) but was losing its grip on the rest of St Lucia. Soufrière, like Vieux Fort, was a hot-bed of republicans and had it not been for the exertions of the Black Rangers, Stewart believed, the island would already have been lost. The Rangers had been supplemented by *'a small body of Negroes, lately recruited (in February) in St Lucia,'* who had *'shown remarkable bravery in action'* but in March, 150 of these men were sent to assist the British in Grenada instead.

While Governor Stewart was waiting for reinforcements, in early April 1795, the *Commissaire* from Guadeloupe, Goyrand, landed with two ships in republican-controlled Soufrière. He encountered no resistance and even managed to intercept a passing British schooner laden with flour and eggs: a welcome catch.[100] Goyrand's first act was to establish a tribunal in St Lucia. A guillotine was set up in Soufrière and two planters were beheaded: Auguste Jean de Sauzay and Gillis du Chaumont. Between February, when Hugues first arrived in the West Indies, and June 1795, when the British abandoned the island, St Lucia experienced its own Reign of Terror.[101] By then, most plantations had been abandoned as planters and their families had fled to the villages or left the island altogether. The few remaining men formed volunteer corps to try and defend their properties against frequent Brigand incursions.

Headquartered in Guadeloupe, Hugues conducted a terrifying and strategically brilliant guerrilla war, driving out not only the British but most of the island's plantocracy as well. A century later (in 1906) local historian Tom Ferguson described some of the silent ruins of this period[102] while another source described how a *mulatto* Brigand, Marin Pèdre, defeated a superior force of British soldiers at Camp Décedé on Piton Flore, near Morne La Sorcière. With the help of 60 Brigand warriors (including women, children and a few old men) Marin Pèdre lured some soldiers into a trap, consisting of a deep pit with sharp sticks stuck upright. While the survivors extricated themselves, he blew a trumpet pretending to muster reinforcements. The ruse convinced the other soldiers that they were outnumbered and they beat a hasty retreat.[103] There were several other minor battles like it. But one major Brigand battle, in April 1795, formed a turning point in the history of St Lucia.

The Battle of Rabot

In April 1795, Governor Stewart and General Vaughan decided to launch one last, desperate attack on the towns of Vieux Fort and Soufrière, which had become virtual Brigand strongholds. They mustered what soldiers they could and on 15 April, Stewart set sail from Charlotteville (Castries) with 1000 men under arms: 400 blacks and 600 whites.[104] They headed for Vieux Fort and disembarked the following morning '*in a neighbouring bay*' (probably Black Bay) to avoid the heavy guns in town and on Mathurin Point at Moule à Chique, which were all in Brigand hands. Stewart's men encountered surprisingly little resistance during their attack on Vieux Fort, and the fleeing Brigands left behind a considerable quantity of stores and ammunition, recently arrived from Guadeloupe and not yet moved to camps in the interior. Given this, it is likely that the Brigands had expected the British to attack Soufrière from the north, not via Vieux Fort in the south. The Brigands maintained several camps near Canaries and probably had ambushes prepared in the narrow ravines along that way.

Leaving a garrison in charge of Vieux Fort, on 18 April, Stewart began to march the rest of his troops towards Soufrière, with seamen from HMS *Blanche* pitching in to drag the heavy pieces of artillery over land while '*the remainder of his stores followed him by sea.*'[105] Stewart found both Laborie and Choiseul evacuated, which again suggests that the Brigands were not prepared for an attack from the south. Stewart continued the march on 20 April, following the *Chemin Royal* from Choiseul, over the ridges of Mongouge, Etang and Rabot, heading for Soufrière. The Brigands quickly reorganized themselves and tried to delay the British advance. A first ambush was probably organized from a camp near Choiseul, known today as Mokoji. A second one came from a Brigand camp on Gros Piton, where today we find the community of Fond Gens Libres ('Valley of the Free People'). This camp, on the north side of the L'Ivrogne River and within striking distance of the road from Choiseul to Rabot, was under the command of a coloured woman by the name of Flore Bois Galliard, '*a prominent leader of the revolutionary party at that period*' whose name lives on in Piton Flore.[106]

Two ambushes and an uncomfortable night later, during which '*the exhausted troops bivouacked for the night under continual showers of tropical rain,*'[107] Stewart's troops reached the spot of a third ambush. It was eleven o'clock in the morning of 22 April 1795. The British found the road (a narrow pass) to the south of Lake Rabot blocked and Brigands positioned behind it. More rebels were positioned to the west, at Morne la Croix, and a third group to the east, while to the south-east (at a spot known today as La Bastille) Brigands cut off the British retreat. The main body of Brigands, meanwhile, was entrenched above the lake on Morne Rabot, to the north. The spot was well chosen and rendered the British vulnerable on all sides. Stewart sent troops to the west, north-west and east to try and distract the main body of Brigands but when he sent a company directly forward, they were met with a terrific volley of gunshot. This precipitated a reaction and for a considerable time, Englishmen fired bullets at an invisible enemy, while the Brigands lay hidden, enjoying the spectacle and firing off the occasional shot to keep the British occupied. Only with great difficulty did Stewart eventually check the random fire but in that first hour of battle, his men had spent much of their precious ammunition.

At noon, the Brigands took the initiative. Fortescue wrote:

> *The brigands then advanced in dense columns along the road upon Stewart's guns, with a coolness and intrepidity which was quite new to them; nor were they finally driven back ... until they had made two attacks and suffered very heavily. ... The action was prolonged from noon till seven in the evening without any decisive result, when, the British having spent all their ammunition and thrown away, under the stress of the tropical sun, the provisions supplied to them for the march, Stewart was compelled to fall back to his nearest depot of supplies and stores at Choiseul. He retreated accordingly at eight o'clock in the evening, and reached Choiseul in safety, though the men were so exhausted that they could hardly drag their guns.*

Governor Stewart's campaign had lasted a week and cost the British nine officers and over 160 men, more than 100 of whom were killed during the eight-hour Battle of Rabot. Fortescue later called the Brigands' skills '*disconcerting*'. Stewart did not dare leave troops at Choiseul or Laborie but he did leave '*a garrison of about two hundred men, chiefly negroes*' in Vieux Fort before sailing back to Morne Fortuné with the rest of his men. They got away just in time: republican troops had been sent from Soufrière to chase the retreating British army, headed by a French artillery officer called Pierre Jacquin (who later wrote an eyewitness account). They arrived just in time to see a couple of pirogues filled with English *red-coats* fleeing Vieux Fort. Jacquin and his men did not attack the Black Rangers who had been left behind to protect Vieux Fort that day but Governor Stewart knew that without reinforcements, his men did not stand a chance. He was right. Not long after, the republicans did attack Vieux Fort and the Black Rangers were forced to surrender. While there is no report of their exact fate, in other instances, Brigands took harsh revenge on black soldiers in British uniform who, understandably, they would have considered the ultimate traitors. One can only imagine the enormous stress those 200 Black Rangers must have felt at their isolated post, anticipating the inevitable Brigand attack.

The Battle of Rabot proved crucial. Had the Brigands been defeated at Rabot, it is unlikely that they could have mustered another ambush before the British reached Soufrière, and the republicans may well have had to surrender the whole town. As it turned out, the Brigands held Soufrière, recovered Vieux Fort and gained full control of the south, south-east and south-west of St Lucia.

'Vive la République'

During the month of May 1795, yellow fever ravaged the British troops in St Lucia. The Brigands, who seemed immune to the scourge, let the disease run its lethal course, meanwhile stockpiling supplies from Guadeloupe. In the absence of British reinforcements, Governor Stewart raised additional black troops. Malcolm's Rangers (also known as 'Whyte's Foot') along with troops from the Black Carolina Corps and the Dominica Rangers were amalgamated into the 1st West India Regiment. In similar vein, between April and September 1795, the 2nd, 6th and 8th West India Regiments were raised from all over the Windward and Leeward Islands. From this time onwards, black soldiers fought side by side with whites in the British army, having shown bravery, steadfastness and loyalty in battle and indispensability in the tropical climate and rugged terrain. Nevertheless, their numbers were always insufficient, as planters were reluctant to lose their few remaining slaves to the army. After all, chances of survival were uncertain and the idea of returning a trained soldier to slavery was unthinkable. And so the shortage of soldiers could not be alleviated in time to save St Lucia for Britain.

By the middle of 1795, the situation had become critical and Governor Stewart knew that a republican attack on the remaining British posts was imminent. He tried to strengthen the garrisons at Fort Charlotte, Vigie, La

Toc and Pigeon Island but when the Brigands attacked Pigeon Island on 6 June 1795, the fort fell without difficulty. His men, *'completely worn down by death, sickness and fatigue, had lost all heart; and there were even a few who, in desperation, deserted to the enemy.'* Eleven days later, the republicans attacked Vigie, which fell equally easily, and started closing in on Castries. The British still held La Toc but most soldiers had retreated into Fort Charlotte on Morne Fortuné, where they were joined by the remaining terrified royalist planters and their families. Knowing that a Brigand attack was inevitable and realizing that port Castries would be closed off as soon as the Brigands secured La Toc, Stewart decided to abandon St Lucia.

During the night of 18 to 19 June 1795, British troops quietly boarded two ships at Tapion Bay, under the protection of nearby Fort Edward. They carried 1400 troops, of whom 400 were sick or wounded, plus some white planter families. Some 100 women and wounded men were left behind at Fort Charlotte. When Brigand troops under the command of Goyrand (along with our eyewitness officer, Pierre Jacquin) stormed the slopes of Morne Fortuné early the following morning, waving their sabres, they found an empty fort. From the heights, *'they saw, emerging out of the morning mists, a fleet of ships, conveying the English forces away from St Lucia in the direction of Martinique'*. Goyrand pulled down the British flag that had been placed there by Prince Edward himself on 9 April of the previous year, hoisted the tricolour once more and triumphantly hailed '*Vive la République!*'

Unlike his counterpart Victor Hugues, Goyrand proved himself a man of occasional mercy. In his memoirs *La Terreur sous les Palmes*, Jacquin described how General Stewart, in his haste, had left behind 60 sick and wounded men, as well as

> *... some 30 frightened women. They were English, wives of officers for the most part. The unfortunates thought that their last hour had come. Goyrand went to see them and soothe them. 'The Republicans do not make war on women. You have nothing to fear from us. As soon as we can, we will arrange your return to one of the British possessions.' I recall the expression of relief and joy which passed over their faces. There were in the group several pretty blondes, rosy and fresh as the daughters of Albion always are.*[108]

Under Goyrand's republican command

As Governor of St Lucia under the Republic of France, Goyrand had his hands full restoring law and order in a country where agriculture, trade and commerce had been devastated and a radically new social order was emerging. His first victory consisted of convincing the ex-slaves-turned-soldiers that slavery would not be re-instated. Next, Goyrand appointed literate black and coloured men as heads of some of the municipalities to work side-by-side with white republicans. By 1796, Goyrand proudly reported that *'thus I proved that all enjoyed civil liberty and political equality according to the French Constitution.'*[109]

With most of the crops and sugar factories destroyed or abandoned, Goyrand started requisitioning provisions to feed the inhabitants. He commandeered land and used compulsory paid labour and military labour to harvest crops. During his ten months of governorship, St Lucia was peaceful enough, but little agricultural work got done. Although slavery had been abolished, most former slaves preferred to remain in the mountains: hunting, gathering and growing provisions in make-shift gardens rather than returning to the estates or villages as paid labourers. It did little to restore planters' confidence and so, despite the relative calm, few colonists risked returning to their estates between late 1795 and early 1796.

With St Lucia fully under republican control, Victor Hugues turned his attention to fighting the British elsewhere. By now, he commanded 11,000 men in eight islands. In Grenada, the slaves were rebelling under the leadership of Julien Fédon and in St Vincent, slaves and Carib Indians had come together under young Chatoyer. St Lucia became a supply depot for the islands to its south, sending over stores, arms and ammunition as well as trained guerrilla fighters. In August 1795, a detachment of 500 soldiers under the command of a black St Lucian by the name of Marinier sailed to St Vincent where they *'surprised the post of Owia ... killed about eighty of the garrison, and compelled the remainder to take refuge in some small vessels, leaving behind them their cannon and large quantities of provisions and stores.'*[110]

A month later, another 500 men led by a black St Lucian Captain of the Grenadiers, Marin Pèdre *'so completely turned the scale ... that the British were forced to abandon their principal position and retreat in dismay to Kingstown.'* Pèdre went on to become the Brigand leader in St Vincent (possibly after Marinier was killed) and later played an important role in peace negotiations between the Brigands and the British in St Lucia. In October, a third detachment of St Lucian Brigands left for Grenada, where they landed *'200 men and some supplies, the whole of which arrived without opposition in the rebel camp.'* This revived the local insurgents, who soon captured Charlotte Town and forced the British commander to retire to St George's.

Meanwhile, in France, the Thermidorean Reaction was humanizing the revolution and effectively ended the Reign of Terror in France. But as long as Victor Hugues was in charge in the West Indies, he continued to reign with unchecked aggression - his only disadvantage being that his influence in Paris was now weaker than that of his British counterparts in London.[111]

By early 1796, St Lucia was the main distributor of provisions to insurgent troops in St Vincent and Grenada, and the British were keen to regain control over St Lucia and cut off these lines of supply. Goyrand knew that a counter-invasion loomed. With just 4000 black troops and a handful of white engineers and artilleryman under his command, he concentrated his energies on fortifying the coast from Gros Islet to Cul de Sac, and improving the defences at Morne Fortuné.

The British invasion came on 26 April 1796 at Point du Cap, in the far north. General Abercrombie and a large force of men (the exact number is disputed but they were likely around 12 000 strong)[112] attempted three different landings under cover of his fleet: the first one at Longueville Bay (named after the owner of Cap Estate), the second at Choc Bay and a third at Anse la Raye. Brigadier-General John Moore was in command of the first landing and proceeded to neutralize the forts protecting Choc Bay, including those on Morne Chabot and Morne Duchasseau. Among Moore's troops was the 2nd West India Regiment, made up of seasoned black veterans from the Brigand battles of the previous year. Initially, the republicans performed well against the onslaught of the British. Morne Fortuné was defended by approximately 2000 black and coloured veteran soldiers and it took Moore and his men a whole month to conquer the prized fort. In the end, the 27th Foot and Light Artillery (Inniskilling Regiment) ascended the steep Morne ridge and attacked the fort from the rear: an approach that until then had been considered impossible. Brigadier-General Moore later wrote in his diary:

> *The negotiations ended in a capitulation, and the General did me the honour to order me to take possession of the fort ... We formed a lane from the gate, and the garrison, to the amount of 2000, marched out, laid down their arms, and were conveyed to the Vigie, and from thence on board transports. The garrison consisted chiefly of blacks and men of colour.*[113]

The British soldiers' intrepidity was helped by the fact that a week earlier, on 17 May, Castries had been accidentally set alight by misdirected bombs from British warships aiming for Vigie, causing the inhabitants to panic and rush up to Morne Fortuné for safety. Possibly as many as 2000 civilians were crowded into the confines of the fort, putting stress on the scarce drinking water and food. In the end, it may well have hastened the republicans' surrender.

John Moore and the Second Brigand War

On 25 May 1796, Brigadier-General John Moore was appointed Military Governor of St Lucia. His first task was to restore order: not an easy one, given that hundreds of republican soldiers had once again taken to the mountains, neatly slipping back into their roles as Brigand soldiers of *L'Armée Française dans les Bois*. Moore was distressed by the prospect of an irksome clean-up operation and lamented in his trusted diary: *'I am involved in a most disagreeable scene; a considerable number of the Negroes are in the woods in arms. ... Everything military or civil is in the greatest confusion, and the rainy season has commenced; whilst it lasts it is almost impracticable to do anything.'* Moore had between 4000 and 5000 men fit for duty, including O'Meara's Black Corps.[114] Meanwhile, the insurgents were getting ready for round two of the Brigand War. As before, they had the overwhelming majority of black and coloured people on their side, both covertly and overtly. Once again, pro-British and royalist French and Creole planters fled to town, leaving their estates unprotected and the few remaining slaves to do as they pleased. Moore judged the escape of the Brigands a strategic blunder on the part of his own army command.

> *The General and Admiral think they have cleared themselves from all trouble by running away from it. They have, however, hurt their character as military men. The moment the fort had surrendered large detachments under proper officers ought to have been detached to different parts of the island to encourage or support the proprietors and disarm the blacks. A week or ten days would probably have done this ... As it is, the island is left in the most precarious state.*

Moore was most unimpressed with his new job as Military Governor. He found his troops sickly and miserable, his personal assistant *'completely absurd'* and the countryside in a state of upheaval.

> *The reports of the devastation done by the negroes in the woods on the side of Souffriere and Vieux Fort increased daily; the inhabitants were demanding troops; I had no confidence in the officer who commanded in those parts ... I was displeased with the proprietors for leaving their habitations and assembling in the towns on the coast, because I was convinced that those in arms in the woods were few, and that the proprietors by remaining upon their estates and treating their negroes kindly would more effectually prevent their joining those in arms, than I should by dispersing the troops through the country. I also suspected that the proprietors wished for troops in order to overawe and tyrannise over the negroes, a system I was determined by no means to countenance. The reports of the numbers of brigands and their acts of violence came from all quarters. The village of Micoud was burnt.*

Moore's initial approach was two-fold. He offered a pardon *'to the people of all colours and descriptions who would come in with their arms'*. At the same time, he took an unusually uncompromising stance against slave owners, making it clear he would not tolerate any acts of revenge. He delivered this message in person, travelling from Dennery to Vieux Fort, Laborie, Choiseul and Soufrière.

> *I had an opportunity at those country places of conversing with all the country people whom fear had driven from their habitations. I encouraged them, and assured them of protection. I said that I should post the troops so as to protect their plantations, that they must then return to them with a determination not to quit them. I said that something must be risked to preserve their property, and that, above all, it has become necessary from policy, if not from humanity, to treat their slaves not only with lenity, but even with kindness; that men after having been told they were free, and after carrying arms, did not easily return to slavery and labour. It would require management. Kind treatment and good feeling could alone do it. When those in the woods saw the others comfortable and happy, they would naturally join them. The troops would be employed to catch such as did not, but it would not permit the masters to treat their negroes with harshness. That, for my part, I saw no reason why a man should be treated harshly because he was black or of colour. All men were entitled to justice, and they should meet with it from me without distinction or partiality, whether white or black, republican or royalist.*

Many planters, especially the radically royalist émigrés, found Moore's stance hard to swallow. In turn Moore himself, as an Englishman not naturally inclined to entertain French aristocratic arrogance, was not at all impressed with the émigrés. He made it his duty to '*curb their insolence*' and felt that '*instead of profiting by their misfortunes,* [they] *seem only to have increased their prejudices, and in their banishment pant for the moment to gratify their revenge and tyrannise over their fellow-creatures. The terms of* canaille, coquin, &c., *are ever in their mouths, and applied to every person in the lower ranks of life.*'

It demonstrates just how intensely personal the upheaval in St Lucia had become: for the Brigands as well as the royalist planters. Moore's approach was that of the objective professional military man who assessed a conflict in terms of strategy and policy. But for the Brigands, it was the prospect of a return to slavery. For the royalists, it was a sense of terror at having lost control over 'their' slaves, mixed in with a deep-seated, plaguing resentment against the free people of colour.

The depth of these emotional charges on both sides must be kept in mind when trying to understand the levels of ferocity and bloody-mindedness that characterized the following fourteen months of guerrilla warfare. History books often singularly emphasize the atrocities committed by Brigands but royalist planters had set a gruesome tone from day one, when, following the slave uprising at Monsieur Viet's plantation in Soufrière back on New Year's day 1791, the ringleaders had been decapitated and their heads displayed on spikes around the area.

Under Governor Moore, the British objective was to harass the Brigands, destroy their provision grounds and prevent them from receiving supplies from Guadeloupe or St Vincent. The British hoped that sheer destitution would force the Brigands back to the estates. But they faced a daunting task in the rugged interior, where Brigand hide-outs were difficult to find and the risk of being ambushed along an isolated ravine was ever-present. After some deliberation, Moore established a line of military posts along the south-west coast, from Vieux Fort to Soufrière.

> *The habitations extend to the foot of the mountains, which are covered with wood, from whence the negroes in arms sally to pillage and murder. By keeping detachments at certain points in the line of the habitations nearest the mountains, by patrolling from post to post, and even sending small parties into the woods, the plantations and the whole country from thence to the sea is protected.*

He mostly used abandoned estates. '*The houses all around are burned,*' he noted, but '*they have spared the sugar houses and mills alone, and these form both good barracks and posts for the troops.*' Coves, bays and beaches were guarded by officers patrolling from post to post, with occasional parties sent out to scour the woods. Very few Brigands were captured during these early months but Moore took no risks. Four men arriving in a boat from St Vincent were captured in Soufrière (four others escaped) and shot on Moore's orders. '*I ordered several people, who could give no reason for remaining in the island, to be shipped off*', and a number of known republicans were arrested. Rupez Roche, a white Frenchman and '*principal agent of the Republic*' was arrested in Vieux Fort and charged with acts of violence, inciting slaves to rebel and supporting the Brigands.[115] Some of these *agitators* were imprisoned; others deported to England, including Victor Hugues' representative, Lambert. Yet Moore still continued to receive reports of Brigand attacks '*on the side of Grosislet, Dauphin, &c. &c., and a letter from Major Lindsay stating that upon his arrival with his detachment at Praslin he had been attacked three times by the brigands, who were 300 in number, 150 only being armed; that he had repulsed them, and killed and wounded twenty or thirty of them, with the loss of two men wounded.*'[116]

Moore sent 190 men to Gros Islet and provisions to Dauphin and Dennery. On 25 June, he headed a contingent of men marching from Gros Islet to Acquart's Estate in Dauphin, while 200 men of the Black Corps under Major Campagne approached the estate from the side of Morne Fortuné. Moore reached Acquart's at seven in the morning, only to find that the house had been burnt down the day before. He captured one Brigand and had him hanged. The plantation slaves, he wrote, *'would give no information till the prisoner was hanged and they were threatened with the same.'* Not until evening did the manager finally offer to lead the British to the Brigand camp (probably Camp Bamba) but when Moore and Major Campagne approached it from two sides, they found it abandoned. Moore spent three days gathering information and concluded that *'the negroes on both Acquarts and Ostia's estates are in league with those in the woods. I pardoned several, but ordered one man to be hanged, against whom there was strong proof of guilt.'*

Leaving Major Campagne and several troops at Ostia's, Acquarts and Dauphin Bay, Moore marched his own men to Osteris Estate, near Dennery. *'Upon our appearing on the heights the whole country was set on fire; upon our approach to this house we could see a few fellows running off. The men were too much fatigued to follow them.'*

Moore's provisioning vessel had not yet arrived in Dennery and when he sent a dozen men out to collect some cattle, they were immediately attacked by forty or fifty Brigands and forced to retreat. Moore and his soldiers went back to the same place a few hours later and found a large stockpile of provisions and cattle, and Brigands running off in all directions. Most escaped, probably to Morne Sorcière. Moore believed there were not actually very many of them. Over the next few days, *'Negroes, chiefly women, come in daily. They were told we should put them to death. This fear will, I hope, gradually wear off, and as they find they are sure of protection they will come in.'* He believed that many plantation slaves were caught in the middle of the conflict. *'The negroes, male and female, of the estates who refuse to join or follow them are obliged to escape into the woods to avoid being put to death.'* He hoped that the Brigands' own actions, *'the burning of the negroes' houses and the cruelties they have committed will ... make the negroes less attached to them.'*

Leaving troops behind at Dauphin and Dennery, Moore and 70 men marched southwards to Praslin to meet up with Major Lindsay, in whom Moore had become very disappointed. '[H]*e is frightened and does not know what he is about. He treats the poor brigands, ill led and unarmed, with as much respect as if they were a regular disciplined body. His communication from Vieux Fort to Praslin is stopt, and the country devastated.'* Praslin was an important landing site for the Brigands and they roamed freely from nearby camps at Wayon Nèg and Duroché - so much so that Moore sourly noted: *'The Brigands, I understand, display colours, and are posted near Praslin.'*

On reaching the British post at Praslin (based at Baron de Micoud's estate house), Moore found that Major Lindsay had left for Vieux Fort a few days earlier. He spent a day inspecting the post, expressing his pleasure with the Black Corps, whom he found *'the very best troops for that country; for the heat of the sun did not distress them; and they could march with much greater celerity than the British soldiers.'* He then set out for Mr Rigby's plantation at Canelles with an escort of twenty men. Near the old site of Micoud village (south of Troumassée River),

... we were fired on by a party of brigands from a height in our rear. I formed the men on the opposite side, but having a village on my flank in which more brigands might be placed, I continued my march. I also, as it was late, dreaded being detained till dark. The brigands took the continuation of our march for a flight, and began to follow with loud shouts. I saw ground at a little distance which was open and favourable. I therefore continued with my march, wishing to encourage them to approach. When, thus encouraged, they came pretty close, I ordered the men to halt and front; we gave them a fire, and charged them with bayonets. They ran off, leaving the box with their ammunition. We emptied that and continued our march unmolested. Their firelocks did not exceed twenty-four or twenty-five, but there were above a hundred, some with pikes, some quite unarmed. Some of our servants when the firing commenced had run off to give the alarm to the detachment at Rigby's, and we met an officer and forty or fifty men coming to our support.[117]

At Rigby's Estate and also in Vieux Fort, a few days later, Moore found everyone '*in the greatest consternation. Wherever Major Lindsay has been this is the case. He is nervous himself and makes every one else so.*'[118] It presented a stark contrast to Soufrière, Moore's next stop (travelling by sloop this time) where he found Major Wilson had matters firmly in hand.

Back at Morne Fortuné, Moore reported to his superiors that '*The negroes in the island are to a man attached to the French cause; neither hanging, threats, or money would obtain for me any intelligence from them. Those upon the estates are in league with and connected with those in the woods.*' He warned that '*Any disembarkation from Guadeloupe of ever so few men and 800 or 1000 stand of arms, will force me to abandon the country, retire my post, and concentrate everything in the Morne Fortuné.*'

Although not personally intimidated by them, Moore had a healthy respect for the Brigands' courage. '*Their attachment and fidelity to the cause is great; they go to death with indifference. One man the other day denied, and persevered in doing so, that he had ever been with them or knew anything about them. The instant before he was shot he called out 'Vive la république'*.

Not one for extensive bed rest, the next day (9 July, 1796) saw Governor Moore back on a sloop headed for Soufrière. '*I saw as I passed the Canarie and Ance la Raye, burning.*' There were Brigand strongholds at Camp Dieu Soutien and on Morne Parasol, where the southern ravine is still known today as Wavin Konba ('Combat Ravine') and the one to the north as Wavin Gens Libres ('Ravine of the Free People'). Two days later, Moore was back at Rigby's Estate at Canelles, a few miles north-east of Vieux Fort. '*I had arranged an attack on one of the brigand camps before I went to the Morne. Owing to bad execution it only partly succeeded. They were, however, dispersed to the number of 700 or 800, one-half women, ten or twelve only killed.*'

A similar thing happened when Major Campagne attacked a camp at Morne Sorcière, which Moore believed harboured as many as a thousand Brigands. A musket was fired prematurely - whether accidentally or not will never be known - and all Brigands escaped except for about two dozen, who were killed in action.

While all this was going on, Brigands attacked a British post at Angiers plantation, near Choiseul, killing and wounding eight soldiers. The British officers botched the counter-attack and in the end, all Moore could do was have '*the negroes' houses in the wood and on the heights to be burned, and the ground provisions to be destroyed.*' On yet another tour, while marching near Vieux Fort, Moore was informed of the existence of a large Brigand camp (probably Camp Morne Michel) on Morne Forcieuse, known today as Morne Caillandre. He mobilized a large force and proceeded to attack. Once again, a musket went off prematurely, giving the alarm at which the Brigands dispersed. The British troops killed one or two Brigands and destroyed the camp.

Moore realized that his troops did not stand a chance as long as the Brigands continued to receive supplies from Guadeloupe. '*I am obliged to go from post to post myself, and have the constant dread of arms being landed from Guadeloupe. A vessel under American colours attempted to land a cargo at Esperance. I had fortunately a detachment there, and she was prevented.*' Complete disruption of Brigand supply lines was required, so when British soldiers discovered a cave along the coast south of Rivière Canot near Dennery (at Attense), they blew in the roof with explosives. Brigands used to approach the rocky shore in small boats and unload the cargo inside the cave, then remove it through a hole in the roof for transfer to their inland depots. A similar landing post was discovered on the northern promontory of Anse Lavoutte (north of Anse des Canaries) where a series of ten holes and interconnecting tunnels were used for hiding Brigand stores. Moore's troops blocked the holes with large boulders, rendering the tunnels inaccessible, but the area is still known today as Kai Solda ('Soldier's House').

The British offensive had its successes, especially after Moore received a reinforcement of 300 black troops, but the going was tough. His white officers were demoralized to the point where they seemed to '*wish their men to die that they may get home*' and in a letter to his father, dated 20 August 1796, Moore wrote despairingly of the challenges of his campaign.

> *These last six weeks have been employed in eternal movement round the island; visiting the different posts and attacking the Brigands whenever I could get intelligence of their being assembled. The difficulty of this country is prodigious - mountains, deep and rugged ravines and woods. These are extremely favourable to such an enemy. The country,*

I. Amerindians making a canoe using fire, water and stone implements.
(Picture by Penny Watson, courtesy of Robert Devaux).

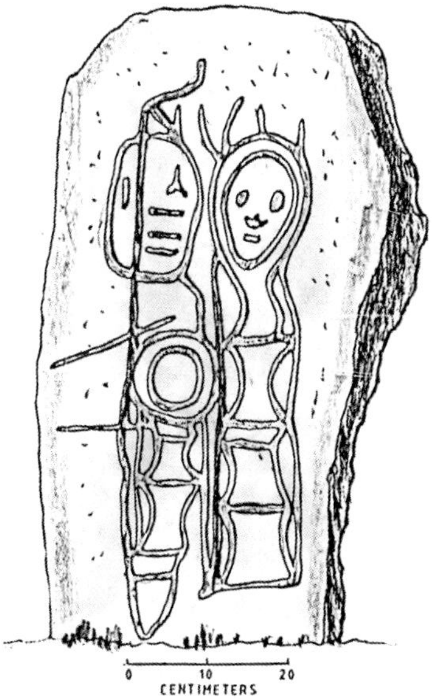

2. Amerindian rock carving at Dauphin.
(Picture courtesy of Robert Devaux)

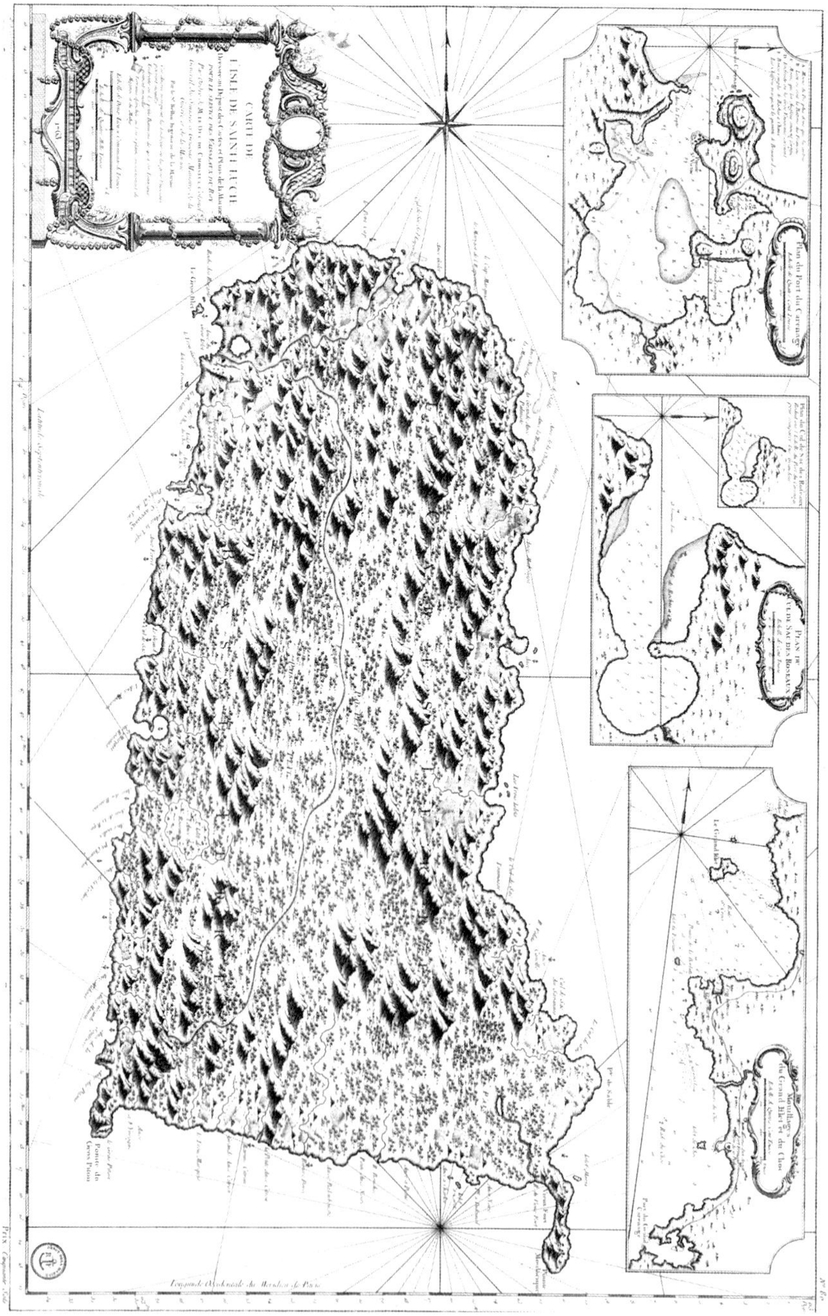

3. Map of St Lucia in 1763, drawn by Marine Engineer Bellin for Baron de Choiseul.
(Map courtesy Suzy Barnard collection).

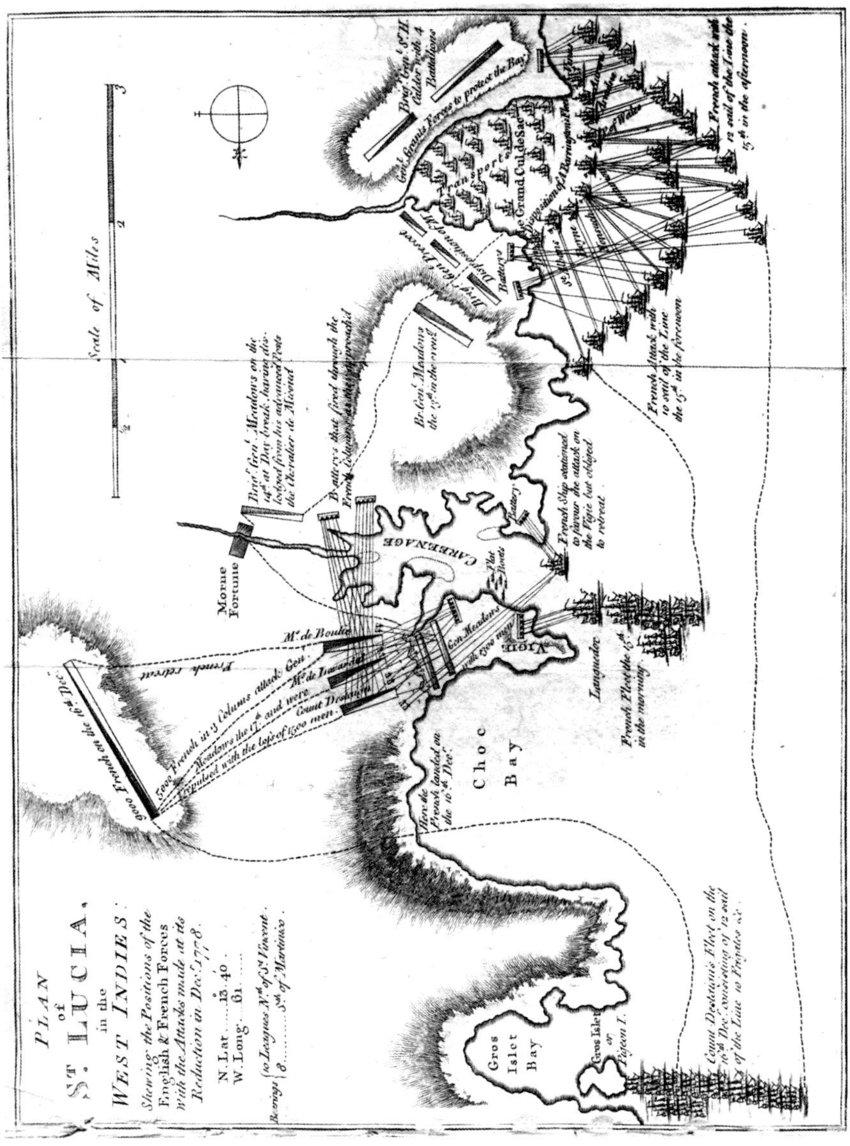

4. Plan of attack for the Great Battle of Cul de Sac, December 1778.
(Map courtesy Robert Devaux collection).

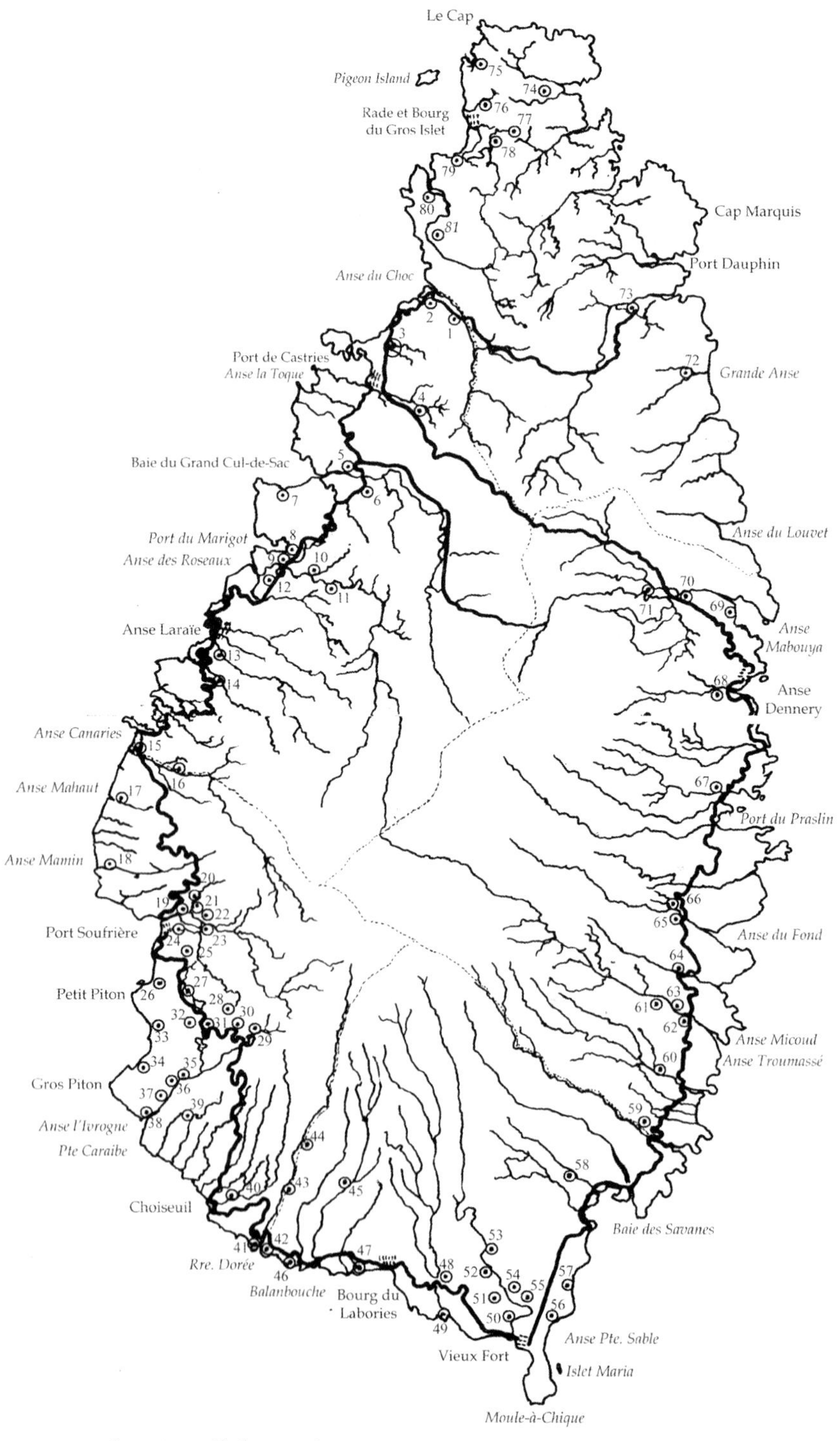

5. Map showing all the working sugar estates in St Lucia, by Detaille and Jamet, 1847. (From: Report on the Blue Book for 1848. London: HMSO) Courtesy Ed Phelps

6. Working sugar estates in St Lucia - 1847 (Map)

1. Union
2. Choc
3. Vide Bouteille
4. Entrepot
5. Incommode
6. Soucis
7. La Pointe
8. Marigot
9. Perle
10. Perou
11. Mont d'Or
12. Roseau
13. Mont Plaisant
14. Anse Gallet
15. Deux Amis
16. L'Esperance
17. Anse Mahaut
18. Anse Mamin
19. Palmiste
20. Reunion
21. Rubis
22. Perle
23. Diamant
24. Soufrière
25. Morne Coubaril
26. Malgrétout
27. Rabot
28. Belle vue
29. Belle plaine
30. Imbert
31. Dauphine
32. Fond-doux
33. Pitons
34. Beau Séjour
35. Espérance
36. Chateau Belle-air
37. Union Vale
38. Anse Ivrogne
39. Delser
40. Réunion
41. Riviére Dorée
42. Des Gatiéres
43. Mon Lizard
44. Parc
45. Beausejour
46. Balanbouche
47. Saphir
48. Black Bay
49. Anse Noir
50. Tourny
51. Ressource
52. Retraite
53. Beau sejour
54. Beau sejour
55. Mon repos
56. Pointe Sable
57. Bellevue
58. Savanne
59. Cannelles
60. Fond Cajou
61. Beauchamp
62. Trou Masse
63. Mondesir
64. Volet
65. Fond Lauréol
66. Orangerie
67. Praslin
68. Anse Canot
69. Fond d'Or
70. La Caie
71. Richefond
72. Grande Anse
73. Marquis
74. Espérance
75. Cap
76. Bellevue
77. Beausejour
78. Boneterre
79. Reduit
80. Bois d'Orange
81. Corinthe

7. The old coat-of-arms and motto of St Lucia (1837) depicting Port Castries flanked by the Pitons and the citadel at Morne Fortuné. The motto 'Statio Haud Malefida Carinis' means 'A safe harbour for ships'.
(Courtesy St Lucia National Archives)

8. The coat-of-arms St Lucia adopted upon attaining Associated Statehood in 1967. It bears the motto 'The Land, the People, the Light'

9. The modern coat-of-arms of St Lucia, designed in 1979 by Sydney Bagshaw.

10. St Lucia's landmark Pitons were formed at the end of the Pliocene period, between 5 and 1.8 million years ago.
(Photo courtesy Suzy Barnard collection)

11. The Sulphur Springs, now famous as the Caribbean's only drive-in volcano.
(Photo courtesy Robert Devaux collection)

12. Caribs attack the English camp at Vieux Fort, 1605.
(Theodor de Bry, *America*. Frankfurt-on-Main, 1634. The Bodleian Library: Mason B.B. 62. Picture courtesy Robert Devaux collection)

13. A Spanish dollar, worth eight reales, marked *Carolus III Dei Gratia 1774* ('Charles III by the grace of God'). Spanish dollars, first minted in 1497, were commonly cut into eighths, quarters, halves and one-third pieces and counterstamped with the initial of the island where they were legal tender. S/L or S.Lucie represented St Lucia.

14. One-half piece of eight, counter-stamped SL, dated 1806.

15. One-quarter cut piece of eight, counter-stamped SL, taken from a 1974 postage stamp.

16. The Battle of the Saintes, April 1782, where Admiral Rodney won a strategically crucial victory over the French.
(Picture courtesy Robert Devaux collection)

17. Pigeon Island seen from the north in 1833. The aquatint was made by Canadian military artist Lieutenant John Herbert Caddy (1801-1883).
(Print courtesy Robert Devaux collection)

18. Stamp depicting the peace agreement of November 1797 between the Brigands (led by *Commandant* La Croix of *L'Armée Française dans les Bois*) and the British army (led by Colonel James Drummond).
(Stamp courtesy Robert Devaux collection)

19. The West India Regiment on parade at Vigie. These were the first-ever black troops in the British army. (Postcard courtesy Robert Devaux collection)

20. Eighteenth century cattle mill used for crushing sugar cane.
(Postcard courtesy Nancy Dowd collection)

21. Nineteenth century water wheel at Balenbouche Estate. The wheel bears the inscription *G. Fletcher London.* (Photo: Cécile Wiltshire)

22. Cutting and carrying sugar cane was hot and arduous work. This picture was published in 1876 in *The Graphic,* a British illustrated newspaper.
(Picture courtesy Suzy Barnard collection)

23. View over Vieux Fort, 1888. Note the central sugar factory, St Paul's Anglican Church and the hill at Beanefield (which has since been partly quarried). (Postcard courtesy Robert Devaux collection)

24. Soufrière Valley covered in sugar cane in 1888. Visible are the Soufrière River, the village of Soufrière just south of that, and a number of estates scattered around inland. (Photograph courtesy Robert Devaux collection)

25. Using an antiquated still to make illegal rum in the bush, circa 1898.
(Photograph courtesy Robert Devaux collection)

26. HMS *Comus* coming in at the Northern Wharf to load coal. The coaling industry started in Port Castries in 1863
(Picture from *The Graphic*, courtesy Suzy Barnard collection)

27. A two-penny coaling token, only used during wartime.

28. A one-shilling coaling token, paid to the riggers.

29. A day token (marked 'D'), generally worth one penny.

30. A night token (marked 'N') worth one-and-a-half times the value of the day token. (Photos: Robert Devaux)

31. Female coal carriers (some smoking clay pipes) getting ready for work. Only in St Lucia and Nagasaki (Japan) did coal workers carry baskets weighing over 100 pounds. (Postcard courtesy Nancy Dowd collection)

32. A ship coaling at Port Castries, 1917. The industry waned and died in 1942 due to the advent of oil-fuelled ships and the Panama Canal.
(Postcard courtesy Nancy Dowd collection)

33. Walking from Morne Fortuné into Castries town, 1833. Clearly distinguishable are the Anglican Church and the Prince Alfred's Basin, which has since been filled in.
(Aquatint by John Caddy, print courtesy Suzy Barnard collection)

34. The Conway land reclamation project in 1890. Nowadays, this is the Castries Waterfront with Government Buildings. The Conway River still flows at this same spot. (Photograph courtesy Robert Devaux collection)

35. Prince Alfred's Basin in 1890, showing two of Castries' leading merchants, *messieurs* de Minvielle and Chastanet in conversation with Vicar-General Fr Tapon. (Photograph courtesy Robert Devaux collection)

particularly the interior, abounds in ground provisions, upon which the Negroes, who are extremely temperate, live and are satisfied.

Nevertheless, by August 1796, Moore believed the Brigands were beginning to lose heart, especially after a British attack killed more than 100 of them, bringing the total number of insurgents '*killed, wounded and hanged*' to 300 or 400. Moore also continued to arrest whites and free people of colour whom he suspected of assisting the Brigands with provisions, ammunition and intelligence. He used increasingly violent means, which '*at first I had flattered myself would not have been necessary.*' Moore set great store by the help of his Black Corps troops. In a letter to Abercrombie dated 2 September 1796, he wrote: '*I have had occasion to observe them of late. They possess, I think, many excellent qualities as soldiers, and may with proper attention, become equal to anything.*'

While some Brigands returned to the plantations, the majority remained in the mountains, waiting for reinforcements from Guadeloupe. These arrived in September, with a shipment of arms and stores which were quickly dispersed to various camps along the windward side. When Moore received intelligence of this, he immediately sent out detachments and, intent on overseeing the action in person, set out from Morne Fortuné by canoe. Off the coast of Soufrière, however, his vessel was intercepted by Brigands. Moore's party veered off course and frantically started to head for St Vincent instead. A prolonged chase followed, which the Brigands only gave up hours later. Much later that night, Moore landed at Vieux Fort, unharmed but chastened by the experience.

Moore continued to move from post to post in relentless pursuit of Brigands, until finally fever overtook him. He spent almost two months recuperating and it was not until the middle of November 1796 that he could resume his offensive against *L'Armée Française dans les bois.* In the meantime, the playing field had shifted somewhat and Moore used his period of forced rest to plot out a new strategy. On 2 October 1796, Marin Pèdre, commander of the Caribs and Brigands in St Vincent, had surrendered after receiving assurances from the British as to the safety of himself and his fellow freedom fighters. Pèdre brought in several hundred Brigands and sent word to the remainder to surrender also '*so that tranquility was nearly restored in the island*'. Moore set great store by this event.

As Marin Pedre is an inhabitant of St Lucia, and has great weight with the blacks here, I wrote to General Hunter [in St Vincent] *that I should restore to Marin Pedre his property if he would undertake and succeeded in bringing in the brigands of St Lucia. The General had informed me that since his surrender he had employed him repeatedly to*

> *return to the woods to negotiate with those who refused to surrender, that he had executed everything he had undertaken, and in every transaction with him had behaved with great honour.*

Moore gave some surprisingly subtle insights into the motivations and concerns of Marin Pedre, who reportedly came from a family of '*free blacks and mulattoes ... his brother is a boatman at Grosislet.*' As events of the first and second Brigand Wars unfolded, Pedre had been forced to cast his allegiance. '*His character in this island is extremely good*', Moore wrote. '*Before the war he was an industrious, honest man, and since the troubles he had behaved with moderation, and was the means of preserving numbers from the guillotine. He first took up arms because of the oppression of Sir Charles Gordon, who embarked about 300 people without cause, and then sent emissaries to agree with them for their release upon their paying certain sums according to their means.*'

Evidently, Governor Gordon's protection money scam had disgusted men like Pedre to the point of wanting to take up active armed resistance against the British. According to Moore, Pedre and Marinier had '*commanded the negroes in the woods till the arrival of Goyrand from Guadeloupe.*' Goyrand promoted Pedre to '*Captain of Grenadiers*' and he had '*served as such until General Stuart evacuated the island.*' With the British evicted, Goyrand promoted Marin Pedre to Colonel and sent him to St Vincent, along with '*considerable reinforcements.*' (Interestingly, Moore believed that Goyrand secretely '*dreaded*' Pedre's influence over the blacks in St Lucia). When the British captured St Vincent, Pedre had refused to surrender, saying that since his predecessor Marinier, after being caught by the British had not capitulated, neither would he. Nor would he betray the Carib insurgents. Instead, he had retired with them into the woods, hoping to obtain terms for them. Having done so successfully in St Vincent, Pedre told Moore '*he would be happy if he could persuade the blacks who were in the woods here to surrender upon the same terms as those of St Vincent, and he thought he could if I would promise them their pardon. He wished of all things to see tranquility restored to this island, where all his relations were.*'

Moore was obviously impressed. '*Marin Pedre is a plain man, with great apparent goodness of heart; he can neither read or write, but possesses good sense and shrewdness. All the negroes are perfectly acquainted with him. He assumes no airs, and though dressed in his national uniform with two epaulets, he shakes hands and speaks kindly and familiarly with them all. He shows great attachment to and anxiety for his relations.*'

And so it was that Marin Pedre accepted the difficult task of trying to convince the Brigands of St Lucia to surrender to the British, without appearing to be a traitor himself.

But before sending in Pedre to open the negotiations, Moore wanted to shift the balance of power a little more to his advantage. The Brigands were still on a high after having received ammunition and supplies from Guadeloupe and Moore judged it wise to '*give them a drubbing*' first. For four weeks, from 17 November until mid December 1796, detachments of British soldiers relentlessly attacked Brigand camps between Morne Fortuné and Soufrière, destroying their depots and breaking up their lines of communication.

> *I then allowed Marin Pedre to commence a negotiation with them, keeping at the same time detachments constantly in the woods. On the 19th December I received a letter from La Croix, 'commandant', as he signed himself, 'of L'Armée française dans les bois', offering to treat, and wishing to know the terms I would give him. I answered that upon surrendering with arms and ammunition he and the armed force should be treated as prisoners of war. The negroes, male and female, who had quitted the estates must return to them, and should be treated with humanity. He asked a month to assemble his people, during which hostilities should cease. I gave him forty-eight hours. He wrote that he should immediately set about assembling his different detachments, consult the chiefs, and send me an answer in eight days. During this time Marin Pedre had seen La Croix frequently, and assured me that his wish was to surrender. At the expiration of the eight days, however, no message was sent.*

Unfortunately, during the eight days' ceasefire, a young French officer who lived with Moore's family had gone hunting in the woods and was murdered by Brigands. '*This, Marin Pedre told me, had frightened La Croix, and was the cause of his not approaching our posts to communicate.*' In deference to Pedre's assurances, Moore gave la Croix an additional eight days to surrender. But still no message came. Pedre even went into the woods to search for la Croix himself, but by then, Moore was losing heart. '*I rather think still that La Croix and the principal chiefs were sincere in their wish to surrender, but they have since been frightened and persuaded by disaffected people not to come in. These people, who have always communicated with them and assisted them, are averse to their coming in, lest they should be discovered and punished.*'

Moore was very disappointed with the failure of a truce, and his disenchantment deepened in subsequent months to the point where he finally decided that his trust in Marin Pedre had been misplaced.

On 10 January 1797, Brigands attacked and captured the post at Praslin, killing fifteen and wounding twenty of the seventy British soldiers. The surprise attack was '*a bolder measure than the brigands had ever attempted, and more suggestive of the advice of Marin Pedre than of any one who had hitherto directed them*', Moore noted sorely in his diary. The English captain had been asleep in the house with

> *... most of the men at the river below the post washing themselves. The men on guard upon the height above were either asleep or drunk. They were bayonetted without resistance. The captain had just time, because of some halt the brigands made, to get part of his men under arms. Some of the men ran off, as might be expected, when surprised. This enraged the captain so much that he lost his head, and was incapable of giving orders. He exposed himself much, was wounded twice, and when he saw his men giving way, and that a retreat with the rest had become necessary, he drew out his pistol and shot himself.*

In retaliation, six days later, Moore's troops surprised and destroyed a Brigand camp, killing twelve or fourteen and capturing 27 stands of arms and some ammunition which had been taken from Praslin the previous week. Another 70 firearms were taken from Brigands shortly after and in the months that followed, Moore pushed on with grim and renewed determination. The Brigands fought back smartly, though, and around 17 March 1797, attacked the British post at Dennery, killing three soldiers and wounding twelve - but also losing '*at least sixty*' people themselves. The Brigands had been much in the majority but the post was heavily fortified and over the course of a three-hour fight, the British repelled the attack. At the end, the Brigands '*were seen taking away as usual their killed and wounded during the engagement.*'

A few days later, in another brazen attack, Moore's personal secretary, Duthrie, was injured. He had been in a boat returning from Soufrière when he noticed some *Chasseurs* (black soldiers) calling out to him from a bay along the way. Duthrie

> *... did not perceive that they were brigands till he was close to the shore. The moment he ordered the boat to be put about fifty or sixty brigands got up from the bushes and fired. A negro woman was killed, and Mr Duthrie wounded in the neck. The wound is bad, but not dangerous. Detachments of the Chasseurs were instantly sent after them, found their camp, killed a very few, and took thirteen muskets.*

Nine months into the second Brigand War, Moore believed his command was as perilous as ever. '*A small force if landed will force me to withdraw my outposts and expose the inhabitants to be murdered, the country to be plundered and devastated. If the officers commanding detachments are not alert, they will risk being cut off from the Morne.*' Unfortunately, there are no historical records to describe the state of affairs within *L'Armée Française dans les Bois* at this stage, nor of la Croix or Marin Pedre's precise activities.

At the end of May 1797, Governor John Moore's role in St Lucia came to an end. He was overcome by fever once more, aggravated by an abscess in his hip, and in late May, Abercrombie recalled him to Martinique and sent Colonel James Drummond to replace him. Unfortunately, with Moore's departure also comes an end to our detailed eyewitness reports of the Brigand Wars.

What we know is that Drummond basically followed Moore's strategy of fighting fire with fire: executing guerrilla-style attacks on Brigand camps in much the same way the Brigands attacked English military posts. In October, soldiers of Druault's Black Corps shot and killed a Brigand chief (a man by the name of Stanislaus).[119] Following this death, Brigand attacks appear to have waned somewhat.[120] One month later, in November 1797, la Croix and most of the remaining Brigands surrendered to a conditional cessation of hostilities. '*The only stipulation they made was that, as they had borne arms for so long a period, and had enjoyed the immunities of freemen, under the sanction of the Republican laws, they should not be again reduced to slavery. The British authorities, glad to get rid of such troublesome 'Citoyens' upon any condition, formed them into a regiment, which was sent to the coast of Africa.*'[121]

More research is needed to trace the fate of these ex-Brigands who, ironically, were inducted into the army of their former enemy, as soldiers of the West India Regiment serving (initially, at least) in West Africa (Sierra Leone). Possibly, some of them may have returned to the Caribbean when their regiments were deployed in battles in Guadeloupe, Grenada and elsewhere, but much more research is needed to bring their intriguing tale to light.

Other Brigands capitulated on condition that they were allowed to leave St Lucia voluntarily. John Jeremie recorded in 1831 that '*large bodies of the insurgents*', both black and coloured, had travelled to Guadeloupe after their surrender.

> *Some of these persons who were slaves, or the children of slaves, are generals at this moment in the French service. General Pelage, a common agricultural slave from St Lucia, and who first got his notice from his conduct in the field among the insurgents, subsequently became governor of Guadeloupe, and held that government down to 1803. His administration is said to have been firm, judicious, and enlightened. On delivering up the government, he continued in the French service, and was ultimately killed, in Spain, at the head of his regiment. His son, who is now residing at St Lucia, is quite dark as was his father: he is a respectable inn-keeper, and a man of great intelligence. Generals in our service, and captains in the navy, have also been men of colour.*[122]

Brigadier-General George Prevost (who took over from Colonel James Drummond in July 1798), calculated that during the course of the preceding decade, St Lucia's slave population had been diminished by more than 4000 souls: from 18 406 in 1790 to just 13 391 in 1799.[123] Barry Gaspar (in his monumental article 'La Guerre des Bois. Revolution, war, and slavery in

Saint Lucia, 1793-1838') wrote: '*Many were killed, sent away as prisoners of war, captured as insurgents and deported or executed, or joined up with the insurgents at St Vincent. ... Many more also died as a result of the famine caused by the fighting in 1796-1798, when cultivation of provisions on the plantations was abandoned.*'[124]

Many of the ex-Brigands who had not been inducted into the West India Regiment or joined the French military continued to hide out in the mountainous rainforest of St Lucia: no longer actively fighting the British but refusing to return to the plantations and re-submit to slavery all the same. From the time of the Brigand Wars until Emancipation in 1838, and despite occasional incursions of '*Native Troops*'[125] looking for runaways, several hundreds of black and coloured people (with perhaps a handful of whites among them) continued to live as Maroons (*Nèg Mawons*) in the interior of St Lucia, with the intermittent arrival of runaway slaves supplementing their ranks.

Survival in the forest: the lifestyle of Brigands and Maroons[126]

Maroons and Brigands had to be resourceful, cunning and independent to survive in the wild and their frequent incursions on estates and military posts required discipline, good communication and well-supplied base camps. They were masters at exploiting St Lucia's mountainous terrain with its deep narrow valleys, isolated interior, abundance of natural resources and easy but secluded access to the coast. Maroon and Brigand camps were usually located in a depression or plateau near a mountain top, where boulders were piled to form walls, framed with green sticks and covered with grass. One of the best-positioned and disguised sites was the ridge near the top of Morne Souf, which had a commanding view of Soufrière and the surrounding countryside. In another camp above L'Ivrogne River on the southern slope of Gros Piton, Brigands used huge boulders to form a parapet wall overlooking the river 60 meters below. Caves were used as well (such as the one at Fond Gens Libre which could hold twelve people) and some camps, such as a site near Anse La Verdure, consisted of elaborate structures with interconnecting tunnels through rocks and into the ground. A tunnel located on a tributary of Galet River led into an underground chamber which had an emergency exit as well. Caves near La Sorcière, Dernière Rivière and all along the coast were used as outposts and (temporary) depots for ammunition and other supplies. Brigand lookouts have been identified on Morne La Feuillet, Morne Duroché and Morne La Combe. These sites served as communication stations and emergency depots.

The Maroons developed communication posts around the island, using strategic mountain tops such as Morne Forcieuse in the south, La Sorcière in the northeast and Gros Piton in the west, with intermediate signal camps to link them together. Skilled drummers could practically talk using the drum. Less sophisticated smoke, trumpet and conch shell signals were used mostly for emergencies. The *abeng* consisted of a carved cow's horn or a length of wood used as a flute. The Maroons of Jamaica developed an alphabet of sounds and could single out a person by *abeng* communication over a distance of five kilometers. Brigands on sentry duty also used birdlike sounds or whistles to warn others of approaching danger.

Maroon women and children were hidden in camps deep in the forest, where crops could be freely grown. *Joupas* were erected over a trampled earth floor, with green sticks for the frame and balizier leaves for the roof, bound together with vines. Another type of shelter was made with boulders that were rolled together and the spaces between them covered with sticks and grass or leaves. Abandoned long-term camp sites have been found on the plateau of Bef Mo between Morne Gimie and Morne Houelmon and on the plateau of Gros Piton. These sites were isolated, well protected and almost impenetrable.

Cooking was usually done on fires located within a clump of trees so as to contain and disperse the smoke. Cooking utensils were iron or clay pots and the fact that pieces of fine chinaware and other ceramics have been found scattered around some Brigand sites suggests that they also took objects useful for survival away from the estate houses they looted. At Fond Bérangé and Canaries Valley, abandoned ovens have been found carved into the rock.

Maroon women grew various crops, including cassava, corn, cucumber, dasheen, papaya, pepper, plantain, pumpkin, sweet potato and tanya, while root esculents such as *banja* grew in great profusion naturally and wild passion fruit (*pomme de lien*) and nuts such as *aralie* could be easily harvested from the forest. Maroons also hunted rainforest birds - pigeons and parrots foremost - and used a special gum from a tree called *la gli* to trap small animals such as agouties, muskrats, iguanas and tree lizards. Crayfish, crabs and oysters were reasonably plentiful in the ravines and mangrove swamps and a few hours spent along the shore of an isolated bay would produce a sack full of shellfish such as *bwigo* (whelks) and *lambi* (conch).

What Maroons could not grow or find in the wild, they raided from nearby plantations. The chicken coop was always a prime target for a hungry runaway and goats, pigs, rabbits, sheep, cows and the occasional dog or cat were caught and slaughtered on the spot or herded off to the nearest camp. Many plantation slaves covertly assisted the Maroons by creating some sort of confusion to divert attention, or by secretly sharing food from their own garden plots and rations.

The lifestyle of Maroons and Brigands was, of necessity, a temperate one. A diet of vegetables and fruits, supplemented occasionally with fresh meat, fish and seafood kept them physically fit. Fresh water for cooking, drinking and washing was readily available from the many forest ravines. If Brigands ever drank rum captured from a plantation's distillery, they did so in moderation, mindful of the need to remain alert. General Moore explicitly commented on their temperance. By contrast, British troops fighting the Brigands elsewhere were reported to suffer from '*an almost constant state of drunkenness.*'[127]

For entertainment, Maroons used simple musical instruments and drums to accompany their singing and dancing. Another favourite diversion was the wawi game, which is of African origin: a thick board with cups carved into it, from which seeds are moved around in various combinations. At night, *flanbos* (torches) made from a green branch of flanbo nwe (*Erithalis fruticosa*) or pencil cedar (*Juniperus barbadensis*) were used, both of which burn with a bright flame. Lamps or *chals* were made from a bottle filled with oil and a cloth wick. Maroons' weapons consisted of a cutlass (machete), occasionally a sword, a musket with a pouch containing gunpowder and as much shot as possible, a few extra flints and a rod. They usually travelled with bare feet and bare back but sometimes covered their heads with a cloth. They might also carry a cloak if staying out overnight in the open. Only on fighting expeditions did they wear the long, tight-fitting soldier's cotton underwear (*long Johns*) which were the standard clothing of male plantation slaves. On the whole, though, clothes were considered an encumbrance and Maroons wore little else other than a loin cloth (*kal fouk*).

They faced some deadly natural enemies, particularly scorpions and snakes, whose bites could be fatal. Some 25 people died every year from the bite of the fer-de-lance (*se-pen*) and deaths from scorpion stings (*eskoupion*) were estimated at two per year. While Maroons developed some cures for snake bites and also wore charms (*cham bwa*) to prevent being bitten in the first place, snakes must have been a real threat, particularly in the central forest between Dennery/Praslin and Anse la Raye/Canaries.

5

The '120 Year's War': slavery in St Lucia, 1719-1838

Writing the history of a subjugated people by using official documents easily leads to a distorted picture, since formal records usually disregard the experiences of those who are deemed powerless, believing them unimportant in defining the course of events. Wherever slaves are mentioned in the colonial records, they almost always remain faceless and nameless, pawns in a larger game: necessary for their labour but tiresome in their physical needs and irritating in their unwillingness to meekly submit to slavery.

During the first century of slavery in St Lucia (from the 1720s until 1815), not even the names of slaves were recorded. Only in 1815 was a slave register started and updated every three years until abolition, in 1838. The register provides not only the name of the estate, estate owner or tenant, size of plantation, crops and number of slaves employed but also a list of slaves' names (usually only a first name or nickname) and some additional information on age, identifying marks and ethnic origin (if known).[128] From that time onwards, slaves' voices can also occasionally - if dimly - be heard in documents kept by the Protector of Slaves, who sometimes recorded slaves' complaints and evidence long-hand.

But just because slaves did not speak up as actors in their own history does not mean they were merely passive recipients of the brutal challenges imposed on them. Far from it. Slaves used various survival strategies to mitigate the brutalities of slavery. Barbadian historian Hilary Beckles, in this context, has coined the term '*200 Year's War*' to describe what he conceived of as '*one protracted struggle launched by Africans and their Afro-West Indian progeny against slave owners*', a struggle which took place in the British West Indies between 1638 and 1838.[129]

Slave resistance took various forms: from day-to-day acts (aimed not so much at overthrowing the system of slavery but at frustrating its efficiency) to revolts, rebellions and marronage. Slaves used their wits and sabotaged, covered up, misappropriated, ran away, revolted, ridiculed and insulted their self-appointed superiors. They assessed their situation and circumstances and grabbed opportunities as they occurred, making the best of a bad situation. They were brave, sly, smart, persistent, original, sullen, strong-headed and quick. They loved, mourned, hated, feared, regretted, betrayed, celebrated, enjoyed, suffered, hoped, worried, forgot and remembered.

The Brigand Wars show beyond the shadow of a doubt the tremendous level of force, resourcefulness, audacity and strategic overview which African people and their offspring who had been submitted to slavery carried from the cane fields of St Lucia onto the battle fields of the Caribbean. At other, less opportune times, they shaped their destinies in more covert and personal ways. But they were always persistently grinding away at the very foundations of oppression. There can be no doubt that slave owners, overseers and their families were often rattled by slaves' insolence, disobedience, (covert) threats and acts of sabotage, and felt intimidated by the occasional sound of drums at night-time gatherings.[130] White people's level of physical security - and certainly their *sense* of security - was often flimsy at best. Racial arrogance and harsh physical punishments kept slave owners' sense of dominance real - but only just. The fact that they were nettled into a virtually permanent state of anxiety, distrust, irritation and dislike, directly attests to the effectiveness and relative success of slaves' strategies of resistance. Through explicit subversion (running away or revolting) and covert resistance (sabotage, insolence, ridicule and stalling) the men and women who were designated slaves by their so-called owners, although to some extent submitting to it, never internalized or acknowledged the legitimacy of the system of slavery in their lives. This may not be borne out by the official records of the day but it is nevertheless the calibrating benchmark against which the history and experience of slavery in St Lucia must be read and understood. To paraphrase Beckles, slavery in St Lucia is best understood as 'The 120 Year's War' (1719-1838): a war of '*ongoing psychological warfare and intermittent bloody battles.*'[131]

The Middle Passage

The first English trader who carried enslaved Africans from the Sierra Leone region across the Atlantic to the Caribbean (in 1562-3) was John Hawkins, who sold his human cargo to the Spaniards in Hispaniola. Half a century later, in 1626, African slaves were first introduced in the Windward Islands when Thomas Warner brought 60 *negro slaves* to work in the nascent sugar industry of Barbados. From 1650 onwards, Africans were landed in Barbados and the Leeward Islands in growing numbers. St Lucia followed some 70 years later.

St Lucia's slave population was never more than just a fraction of the total number of Africans forcibly abducted from their homelands. Not all researchers agree, but estimates hold that a total of approximately twenty million African men, women and children were enslaved, half of whom died in the holding camps in Africa or during the Atlantic crossing known as the Middle Passage. It is estimated that during the 419 years between 1451 and 1870, a total of 9 566 100 enslaved Africans reached the Caribbean and American coasts alive: an average of 22 830 per year.[132]

But that figure belies the explosive growth of the slave trade. Between 1451 and 1600, approximately 275 000 Africans arrived in the New World alive.[133] Once sugar was introduced, around 1650, slave arrivals escalated. Some 1 341 000 Africans were shipped to Jamaica, Ste Domingue and other Caribbean islands between 1650 and 1700 alone, and over the course of the eighteenth century (from 1701 to 1810), another six million slaves or more survived the gruelling Middle Passage. Even after England abolished the slave trade in 1807, two million more Africans were shipped (between 1810 and 1870) to French, Spanish and Dutch colonies in the New World and, especially, to Cuba and Brazil.

From Senegambia in the west to Angola in the south-west and the Swahili-speaking coast in the east: West Africa, Central-Western Africa and even parts of East Africa were the hunting grounds for slave traders capturing and exporting people from an area which itself, around 1800, contained not more than 30 million people. The insatiable demand for slaves in the New World coincided with indigenous processes of state formation in Africa, cruelly tying African elites and European traders into a macabre bond of military and commercial activities which made possible the abduction and forced replacement of such mind-boggling numbers of people.

Earliest slaves in St Lucia

The earliest mention of slavery in St Lucia dates back to 1654 when Amerindians murdered Governor de la Rivière and carried off his family '*and a slave*'. It is not certain if this referred to an African slave but it is possible. In 1686, there was mention of '*free mulattoes*' in St Lucia who were part of an attempted French settlement. In 1699, an English document claimed that '*some French had employ'd Negro's to clear the Grounds, & intended to make Settlements there.*'[134] Next, in 1719, a '*large group*' of inhabitants from Martinique sailed across to take possession of St Lucia, asking for concessions of land and bringing with them '*more than 100 negroes.*'[135] In December 1722, Martiniquans reported that Nathaniel Uring was building a fort near Carénage '*avec des troupes et des nègres*' ('with troops and negroes').[136]

Slavery did not take a real hold in St Lucia until the mid or late 1720s. By 1730, there were 463 people living in St Lucia, including 175 African slaves. It would seem that some of these slaves had escaped from Martinique and were living in St Lucia as runaways, for in 1726 and 1727, a French militia captain twice asked the Martiniquan authorities for permission to go to St

Lucia and '*chase the maroon negroes of St Lucia.*'[137] In March 1731, a slave trader from Nantes by the name of Roy sold 200 slaves from Guinée to planters in St Lucia.[138] In 1736 and again in 1742, reports in Martinique lamented the clandestine trade in negro slaves that was taking place at Entrepôt in St Lucia, due to an increasing demand for, but lacking supply of, 'legitimate' slave ship arrivals.[139]

By 1745, there were 2573 slaves in St Lucia, 216 free people of colour (73 adults and 143 children) and 666 whites.[140] There were repeated complaints about the lack of slave arrivals and a report in 1746 stated that the advancement of the colony of St Lucia was slow due to the lack of negro slaves. It also mentioned: '*sold in one afternoon 400 negroes captured by a corsaire; increased price for slaves (1200 to 1300 pounds).*'[141]

In the course of the 1730s, slaves and free people of colour began to outnumber whites in St Lucia once and for all. The largest number of slaves ever in St Lucia was approximately 18 000 (in 1789) but it must be borne in mind that '*during the continuance of the slave trade ... if a newly purchased slave lasted five years, the speculation was a good one. In thirteen years the whole labouring population was said to be renewed.*'[142]

Origins of slaves in St Lucia

Reconstructing the African origins of St Lucia's slaves is not easy. In the holding camps in Africa, slaves were separated from their ethnic affiliates to minimize the risk of uprisings. Furthermore, St Lucia's sugar industry was late to develop (from 1763 onwards) so that most slaves were imported not directly from Africa but from neighbouring sugar colonies: Barbados, Martinique, Antigua, St Vincent, Grenada and elsewhere, where they had arrived earlier from Africa, or had been born into slavery. Hence, only snippets of information guide our research.

French planters allegedly preferred slaves from Angola and the Cape Verdes and so Martinique and Guadeloupe received a lot of slaves from the coasts of Guinea, Angola and Senegal and from the Cape Verdes. At some stage after 1750, Martinique imported slaves from Barbados of whom '*the surplus*' was sent to St Lucia. After the Brigand Wars, in 1799, negotiations were set in motion in St Lucia for the importation of 300 or 400 slaves from Ste Domingue but it is not certain if this ever materialized. In a document dated 6 July 1799, the slaves in question were described as '*French Negroes who followed the Fortunes of their Masters on our evacuation of the Posts, which are held in St Domingo*' and were said to be '*very well-behaved.*' Brigadier-General Prevost responded by saying that St Lucia could well use that number of slaves but that '*from the distresses of the planters in general*' they would not be able to pay for them until after the next harvest.[143]

Between 1799 and 1801, 238 slaves arrived in St Lucia from Grenada, Martinique and St Vincent and on 8 February 1800, the slave ship *Prince John* arrived in St Lucia with 175 slaves on board. Unfortunately, its port of embarkation is not recorded. In 1805, two more slave ships arrived: on 3 May the *Marriott* with 219 *Negroes* from Africa ('*Part of the Coast not described*') and on 16 July the *Backhouse*, also from Africa, with 153 *Negroes* on board.

After England abolished the slave trade in 1807, slaves were still brought to St Lucia from other Caribbean islands - sometimes legally, other times not. On 16 May 1817, 41 slaves arrived from Kingstown in St Vincent on board the *Sloop Grenada Planter*: thirteen *negro men* and thirteen *negro women* (field slaves), seven boys, one male (*domestic*), one female (*domestic*), three girls and three young boys. On 18 March 1818, 11 slaves arrived from St John's in Antigua on board the *Sloop Samuel Lamb*: Jack a sailor, Henry a labourer, John Thomas a mason, George, Charles and Sam (children), Sally, Chloe and Amelie (washers), Madelaine (*Color'd a Drudge*) and Diana (a child). In June 1818 arrived Sophie, *a negro slave*, from Saint John in Antigua. In 1819, a further 50 slaves (23 men and 27 women, no names mentioned) arrived from Antigua (twelve), Barbados (five), Dominica (seven), Grenada (two), St Kitts (one), Saint Vincent (fourteen), Trinidad (two) and Martinique (seven).

There also survives an 1819 list with 37 names of slaves living in St Lucia at the time, noting their first and last names, age and places of origin.[144] Some of the family names still ring familiar today: Anicette Jean (22) Creole; Maril Louise (22) Creole; Marie Hyacinthe Marie Rose (10) Creole; Figurdie Francoise (26) St Lucia; Anastazie Fazie (32) St Lucia; Joseph Fazie (5) St Lucia; Evelina Fazie (16) St Lucia; Jean Calotin (21) Guadeloupe; Antoine Johnston (17) St Lucia; Angelique Fatin (27) *Africain*; Laurette Laurent (15) St Lucia; Calisete Pereau (17) St Lucia; Cecile Belle (36) St Lucia; Laurencino Josephe (45) St Lucia; Sophie Josephe (8) St Lucia; Felix Augustin (2) Creole; Cecille Bailiff (43) *Moco*; Honore Bailiff (20) St Lucia; Mathurine Bailiff (12) St Lucia; Philip McClaire (20) Creole; Jean Louis (17) *Africain*; Auguste Aimée (5) St Lucia; Saint John Theotiste (33) *Africain*; Rainette Francois (27) St Lucia; Marie Equerre (55) *Ibo*; Pierre Louis Equerre (18) St Lucia; Annette Equerre (15) St Lucia; Marguerite Equerre (12) St Lucia; Bernardine Suivante (27) St Lucia; Arsine Suivante (6) St Lucia; Louison Louis (45) *Congo*; Marie Louise Lorette (25) St Lucia; Rosilette Negress (15) St Lucia; Alphonsine Lapointeuse (12) St Lucia; Jean Michel Judith (2) St Lucia; Mathurine Judith (4) St Lucia; Marie Madelaine Duchosé (58) St Lucia.

Ibo referred to the area now known as Nigeria (south-east of the river Niger) and the term *Moco* possibly referred to people of the *Móko* language, in Western and Eastern Cameroon, Gabon and Rio Muni. Between 1821 and January 1825, another 82 slaves arrived in St Lucia from other islands in the Lesser Antilles - all of them mentioned by name.[145]

Not all slaves entered the island legally after 1807. Some St Lucian planters travelled to Martinique (which still allowed slave imports from Africa) to buy 'fresh' slaves. In 1815, two such planters, Monsieurs Tharel and Valeton, illegally brought sixteen recent African arrivals from Martinique to work at *Lacaille estate* near Dennery.[146] The sloop that carried the sixteen was called *the Rose* and was navigated by slaves from Lacaille under cover of night. This breach of law was not uncovered until seventeen years later, in 1832, by which time some of the sixteen Africans had died. Five men, three women and their children still lived at Lacaille Estate but the others had been sold. One male slave by the name of Sassal had ended up in the possession of a Madame Jacob in Castries (the Jacobs were an influential coloured family in Castries at the time)[147] and a female slave, Celine, belonged to a Monsieur Ruand (or Ruaud), also in Castries.[148] Three other men, Louis and Michel Coredaine and John, were also still alive.

Another series of illegal slave imports occurred in early 1814 by a planter called LaPorte who reportedly made '*frequent voyages to Martinique*' and '*often returned with Negroes who after a short interval were sent to his Estate at Lesley or at Vieux Fort.*' According to witnesses, LaPorte was '*in the constant habit*' of smuggling slaves from Martinique. In 1819, though, he perished in the act when a storm sank his ship *en route* to Dominica where he was headed to buy illegally '*a certain quantity of negroes.*'[149]

Slave exports

Slaves were not only imported but also exported from St Lucia. In 1819, 38 slaves were legally exported and between 1821 and 1825, another 26 followed the same fate, presumably accompanying their owners to new destinations.[150] At least one instance of illegal slave exports is recorded also: an act which impelled the then-Governor to offer a reward of £4000 for the arrest of the planter and other men involved. On 5 September 1832, fourteen slaves belonging to a Victor Graendcour (or Grandcour), '*late of Anse-L'Ivronge, in the Quarter of Soufriere*' were put on board a schooner in that bay and carried away, probably to Martinique. According to the members of a special Commission of Investigation, this Victor Graendcour had been assisted by '*Clermont Belmar, Monjoli Belmar, and Laferronnay the Younger, otherwise called Beaubrun, the three latter all resident or lately resident at or near Anse l'Ivroigne aforesaid, and of no profession known to the said Commissioners, and who stand charged with having been, in conjunction with others yet unknown, principally concerned as pirates, felons and robbers upon the High Seas, in the embarkation of the said Slaves.'*[151]

It is unclear whether Graendcour, the Belmars or Beaubrun were ever caught. With hindsight, the abduction was particularly dramatic for the fourteen slaves involved, who would have been freed six years later had they remained in St Lucia. In Martinique, slavery lasted another 30 years.

The surviving lists with names, ages and origins of slaves in St Lucia do not provide much depth in terms of life experience but they do at least put a little flesh and features on the men and women who figure so prominently in St Lucia's past and communal memory.

'Saltwater slaves' and Creole slaves

Slaves brought in fresh from Africa were nicknamed 'saltwater slaves'. There are no accounts of slave auctions in St Lucia but we do have a British chaplain's account of a public sale in Barbados in 1794 and, considering that many slaves came to St Lucia via Barbados or one of the other islands, their experiences were probably similar.

> *... there were about forty men, women, and children, sitting on benches round a large room, with no other covering than a cloth round their waists. Some of them were decorated with beads, given to them by their captors, and bracelets round their wrists and ancles, and were much tattooed on their faces and breasts, which ... was a mark of distinction in their own country. I was also informed that they had buried one hundred and forty-nine on the passage, having had a very bad and protracted voyage: the crew had suffered equally, and had buried one third of their original complement. As soon as the planter has fixed on a slave he retires with him and the salesman to another room, there concludes the bargain, and departs with his purchase to his plantation, where the new comer, being clothed in a coarse jacket, and provided with a hat, knife, and other trifles, is placed with one of the old negroes, by whom he is instructed in his business.*[152]

The mortality rate among newcomers was very high. In Antigua, one in three slaves died within the first three years of arrival and there is no reason to believe that they fared any better in St Lucia. Creole slaves - those born in the Caribbean - had somewhat better survival rates but very high mortality nevertheless severely curbed the growth of the slave population. It did not help that planters commonly felt that '*It is cheaper to buy than to breed.*'[153]

New arrivals were put to work in the fields, in gangs directed by Creole slave drivers. For skilled positions in the sugar factories, Creoles were usually imported from islands with a longer tradition of sugar processing - mainly boiler men and coopers (for making the hogsheads). Another important social distinction was that between slaves of full African descent and those of mixed African and white ancestry. Elaborate schemes of distinction existed throughout the West Indies, depending on the exact measure of 'black' or 'white' blood, ranging from the 'fifteen-sixteenth white' *Mustifino*, to *Mustees* ('seven-eighth white'), *Quadroons* ('three-quarters white'), *Mulattoes* ('half white') and *Sambos* ('one-fourth white').[154] In the records for St Lucia, the common terms are *mulatto* and *mulatress* ('half black, half white') and *métis* or *métisse* (one black and one *mulatto* parent). In general, slaves of mixed descent more easily found employment in the planter's house (as cooks, maids, nannies, seamstresses, washerwomen, butlers, footmen, grooms and coachmen), in supervisory positions on the estates, and as tradesmen (blacksmiths, masons, carpenters, wheelwrights, coopers and sugar boilers). Up to the present, the distinction between *field slaves* and *house slaves* is a potent verbal tool in St Lucia, the latter term implying collaboration with a perceived oppressor for personal gain.

Slave laws: prohibitions and obligations

Until the mid 1820s, the *Code de la Martinique* formed the legal basis for defining the rights and obligations of slaves in St Lucia, containing as it did Louis XIV's *Code Noir* of 1685, with rules and appendices added over the years by both the French and English authorities. In St Lucia, the laws of slavery (before the ameliorations of 1823, which came into effect in 1826) can be classified into prohibition laws and 'protection laws'.[155]

Prohibition laws

Slaves were considered moveable property and as such could be mortgaged, pawned and sold. They themselves could not own property. Slaves from different plantations could only congregate with special permission from the *Procureur du Roi* (District Attorney). Slaves were forbidden to hold public positions or to act as agents, merchants, arbitrators or witnesses. They were forbidden to make and use drugs or medications or to treat diseases (with the exception of snake bites) unless they had special permission from their owner. Slaves were forbidden to sell sugar cane, coffee or cotton (even *with* permission from their owner, who then also risked punishment) and needed written permission from their owner to sell fruit and vegetables or grass for feeding cattle. Slaves were also forbidden to buy or sell cattle (with or without their owner's permission) or to butcher and sell meat (with the exception of pork). Slaves were forbidden to carry weapons, except when their owner sent them out to hunt, in which case they needed permission in writing stating the nature of the weapon and the amount of gunpowder issued. Slaves could not act as witnesses in a court of law either in civil or criminal matters other than to assist the judge with a deposition which could be neither presumption nor admission of proof. Slaves could neither be plaintiffs nor defendants in civil matters, although their owners could act for, and defend them in civil matters and demand reparation on their behalf. From 1738 onwards, slave testimonies were admitted in courts of law if there were no white witnesses available, but slaves were not allowed to testify against their owners. A slave who hit his owner, owner's wife or owner's children in the face or drew their blood could be punished with death. Theft of a horse, donkey or cattle also carried the death penalty.

Certain clauses in the slave code were reinforced in later years: often an indication of the frequency of infractions rather than the strictness with which they were imposed. The prohibition on slaves from different estates to congregate, for instance, was reiterated in 1783 and again in 1826. In 1783, carnival was specifically mentioned as a time when congregations should not be allowed *'from the disorders which ensue.'* Slave owners allowing congregations without permission from the *Procureur du Roi*, and those lending their buildings for the purpose, were fined £100 and £300 respectively.

The laws on carrying weapons also became more detailed in the 1780s, which seems to indicate that slave owners felt increasingly threatened and worried about acts of violence and organized slave uprisings. Article 38 stated: *'Slaves arrested as runaways, and found with side or fire-arms of any description, to be punished with death. Those found with cutlasses or knives other than those called jambette (like a garden knife) to suffer corporal punishment, even death if necessary.'*

'Protection laws'

Another part of the *Code Noir* stipulated the so-called protection laws. Slaves had the right to complain to the *Procureur du Roi* if they felt unfairly treated. Owners were obliged to feed and clothe their slaves and provide medical care. All slaves over the age of ten were to receive weekly *'two and a half pots (Paris measure) of farine manioc, or three cassavas, each weighing two pounds and a half at least, or its equivalent, with two pounds salt beef, or three pounds fish, or other things in proportion; and to infants, from the time being weaned, until they shall have attained ten years, half of the above allowance.'*[156]

From 1786 onwards, the law further stated that each slave was to be given a small portion of estate land *'to be cultivated for their profit and advantage.'* Each slave was to receive *'weekly the quantity of provision necessary for subsistence, in salt-fish, salt-beef, farine, sirup and vegetables, exclusive of any provision which the Slaves may have raised in their own gardens, which are never to enter as compensation for a lesser allowance.'*

As for clothing, owners were obliged to give each slave yearly two changes of clothes or four ells of linen, *'for the men, shirts and trowsers, for the women, shifts and petticoats, and for children, shirts.'*

By law, owners' obligations towards their slaves stretched from birth to death. '*Slaves, infirm either from age, sickness, or otherwise, whether the disorder may be incurable or not, shall be fed and maintained by their Masters; and, in the event of their being abandoned, the said Slaves shall be sent to the hospital, and the Masters obliged to pay ten sols per diem for the maintenance of each Slave.*' To this was added in 1786 the regulation that every slave owner had to furnish a hospital building on the estate, '*to be situated in an airy and healthy spot, and to be cleanly kept. To be furnished with camp-beds, mats, and coarse coverlets. Forbidding Masters to suffer their Slaves to lie on the floor.*'

Slave owners over twenty years of age had the right to manumit their slaves. Married or common-law couples and their pre-adolescent children could not be sold separately. Slaves ought to be Christianized and to be allowed, with permission from their owner, to marry. Children born of slaves became the property of the owner of their mother. If the mother was a slave and the father a free man, the children remained slaves. If the mother was a free woman of colour and the father a slave, then the children were born free. However, article IX stated that a free person who had a child with a slave, as well as the owners of such slaves permitting it, were subject to a penalty of 2000 pounds of sugar. '*If the master of the slave be father of the children, he is deprived of slave and children, who become confiscated for the good of the hospital, and lose the right of ever being freed. If, however, the father be unmarried, by marriage with his slave (if his property) she becomes free, and the children legitimate.*'[157]

In practice, this law was not followed and it was in fact fairly common for the illegitimate children of a white slave owner and a female slave to be manumitted as teenagers and thus allowed to join the ranks of free people of colour.[158] Having said that, it must also be kept in mind that instances of white fathers dissociating themselves from their coloured children and leaving them in slavery would not have found their way into wills or other formal records, so their incidence is inevitably under-reported.[159]

Crossing boundaries of colour and slavery: mixed marriages

Marriages across the boundaries of slavery and colour occurred with some frequency - more so than one might perhaps have expected. A close reading of the marriage acts from various districts in St Lucia between 1763 and 1788 yields not only the expected combinations (white men marrying white women; free men marrying free women of colour) but also several examples of white men marrying free women of colour; white, free coloured or free black men marrying enslaved black or coloured women; white women marrying free men of colour; and free women of colour marrying enslaved black or coloured men. In fact, the only combination *not* found in these records is that of a white woman marrying a slave (black or coloured). Some real-life examples of marriages across the divides of colour and slavery may help to underscore the intricacies of social relations in eighteenth century St Lucia.

The instance of a marriage between a white woman and a free man of colour was demonstrated by Lambert Larche, a free *mulatto* man (born in Grenada) who, on 18 June 1765, married Marie Jeanne Nicolas Henry, the widow of René Brisefert.[160] Absence in the records of any further indication of colour or legal status always implies that the person was white: in this case, Marie Jeanne can safely be presumed white. A similar marriage occurred on 10 January 1785 between Jean Pierre Buiret, a free *mulatto* born in Martinique and Rose Despujols, presumably white.[161]

In the cases where a free man (white or coloured) or woman (free coloured) married a slave, the latter usually had been his or her property (although not always). Where one spouse was enslaved, according to the slave laws, the act of marriage itself set him or her free from slavery.

On 13 August 1765, in Ance la Raye, Pierre Beau, a white man, married his black slave Brigite Bernege (born in Grenada).[162] Six years later, on 7 January 1771, Jean Boniface, himself a *free Negro* (and the son of Jean, a *negro slave* and Jeanne Marie, a free black woman) married Eugénie, a black woman who was his own slave.[163]

On 4 May 1776, Alexandre (also known as Nouet, born at Choc at Carénage as the natural son of Marianne Rousseau, a *free mulatto* woman) married Nicole, a *Creole Negresse* who was his slave.[164] It is possible that this Alexandre was a descendant of Nouet, the *mulatre libre* owner of de Pichery Estate near Castries who, in 1745, had been the second-largest slave owner in St Lucia.[165] Nine years later, on 19 July 1785, a black slave owner by the name of Télémaque married his slave Geneviève.[166]

Most unexpected perhaps, are the instances of female slave owners (free black or coloured women) who married slaves. On 15 April 1776, for instance, Jeanette, a free black woman, married Jean Baptiste, also known as La Fleur, who was a field slave and belonged to her.[167]

On 21 January 1766, Anne Jarde, a 31-year-old free coloured woman who had been born in Vauclin (Martinique) and was the widow of a free man of colour, married again, this time to an enslaved man of colour by the name of Gilles, 36 years old and born at Diamant (Martinique). Gilles belonged to Anne Jarde herself and was the illegitimate son of a white man, Honoré Roblot, and a free black woman by the name of Angélique Gatteau.[168] Why Gilles, as the child of a free black woman, should himself have been a slave, remains unclear from this record.

Two years later, on 31 October 1768, Rose Saint Onge, born in Grenada, free woman of colour (*métisse*) and widow of a free man of colour (*métis*), married her *mulatto* slave Philippe, who had been born in Vieux Fort as the illegitimate son of Cyprien Sallibus (a white man) and Catherine, a black slave woman belonging to Sieur Pugens.[169]

Yet another case of a woman marrying her own slave is that of Marie Jeanne, 36 years old and a *capresse libre* (born in Grenada as the illegitimate daughter of Joseph, a free *mulatto* and Jeanne, a *negro slave* belonging to Sieur Chanteloup). On 24 July 1769, Marie Jeanne married her *mulatto* slave Gabriel, who had been born at Fort Royal in Martinique as the illegitimate son of a *mulatto* slave by the name of Charles, belonging to Monsieur Dugard Duhaumont, and Louise, a black slave woman belonging to Madame Turgis.[170]

Some years later, on 23 January 1776, Marie Anne, 20 years old and born in Soufrière as the illegitimate daughter of a free *mulatto* woman (Julie Flore), married her 38-year-old slave Jean Baptiste, born in Maigrin (Grenada) of *mulatto* and black slave parents.[171] In similar vein, on 1 December 1787, Sophie, *négresse libre*, born in Soufrière, married Isidore, born in St Lucia, '*nègre, son esclave*'.[172]

Finally, there are one or two cases where a free woman of colour married a slave who did not actually belong to her. On 6 May 1788, for instance, Anne Marie, a free *mulatto* woman born at Diamant in Martinique of a free black mother (Barbe) and an unnamed white father, married Jacques Bruneaux, *Mulâtre esclave* who belonged to the heirs of Bruno Petit.[173]

Laws of punishment

On the subject of punishment of slaves, the sheer number of regulations and communications alone indicate that corporal punishment was a crucial ingredient in maintaining the system of slavery. Use of the whip and shackles was permitted, but owners did not by law have the right of life and death over their slaves. Articles XLII and XLIII of the *Code Noir* of 1685 stated that:

> *Masters, when they consider their Slaves deserve punishment,* [are] *permitted only to chain them, and flog them with rods or cords. They are prohibited putting them to torture, or mutilating their limbs, under pain of confiscation of the Slaves, and the Master being proceeded against extraordinarily. Masters or Commandeurs, (Drivers), who kill a Slave under their order or protection,* [are] *to be prosecuted criminally and punished according to the nature of the offence.*[174]

Under this law, in 1745, St Lucia's largest slave owner, Dubuc l'Etang, was arrested, imprisoned in Martinique and fined £6000 for spreading pamphlets around St Lucia offering a prize for the head of a runaway mulatto woman.[175]

In 1786, the following clause was added: '*Forbidding Masters, on any pretext whatever, to give their Slaves more than fifty lashes, or to beat them with sticks, or to mutilate them, or to make them perish by any kind of death.*'[176]

Owners, attorneys and managers who were convicted of having given a slave more than 50 lashes were to be fined £2000 for the first offence '*and for the second, to be declared incapable of owning Slaves, and to be sent to France.*'[177] Mutilation of a slave was to result in capital punishment for the offender and in the slave being manumitted. The owner or manager who killed a slave was to be prosecuted for murder. The latter clause was strengthened in 1804, to state that '*if any person shall wantonly, or willingly or bloody mindedly, kill, or cause to be killed, any Negro or other Slave, such person so offending, shall on conviction be adjudged guilty of felony, without benefit of Clergy, and shall suffer Death accordingly for such offence.*'

The practice of punishment: John Jeremie and amelioration

It will come as no surprise to hear that the law and actual practice on the matters of slave protection and punishment were worlds apart. For one, although it was legally forbidden for masters to kill, mutilate or torture their slaves, local courts did not hesitate to punish convicted slaves severely. On 14 March 1748, the *Conseil Supérieur* in Martinique ruled that a *mulatto* slave belonging to a Monsieur Ollivier, settler in St Lucia, was to be quartered alive and his *negro accomplices* to be hanged and burnt in punishment for having set fire to a house in which they had believed their master was locked up, and for having tried *other assassinations.* Four years later, a *négresse* of St Lucia was condemned to be burnt alive for having attacked her master (with the help of other *nègres marrons*) with four pickets, slit his throat, cut off his ears and burnt down his house. The *nègres marrons* involved were also condemned to death by fire.

In or just before 1817, two slaves convicted of '*the most inhuman murder of an indulgent mistress*' were hanged and gibbeted on the spot where the murder had been committed. Their case was mentioned merely to show that '*inhumanity forms no part of my Character*', as Governor Seymour wrote to the Earl of Bathurst in London, having stopped the slaves from being broken alive on the wheel. As Seymour insisted: '*I would not hear or allow any such Sentence.*'[178]

To add insult to injury, when a slave was sentenced to death by a court of law or was killed as a runaway by Maroon hunters, not only was his or her death considered a legal action for which no one was incriminated, but the slave's owner was financially compensated for the loss of his property. As early as 1766, a special tax was levied on the colonists, with their own consent, to meet this increasing cost. The fund was called the *caisse des Nègres Justicés*.[179]

Secondly, although there were clear laws forbidding slave owners to mutilate or kill their slaves and clear laws as to which forms and measures of punishment were, and were not, permissible, there was a general culture of disregard for slaves' lives and more than once, acts of cruelty and murder were casually covered up. According to Sir John Jeremie, who in the 1830s became one of the strongest critics of St Lucian slave society, the prevailing culture was rooted in deep racist prejudice against black and coloured people, underscored by a general carelessness regarding the value of human life per sé.[180]

After five years as Chief Justice in St Lucia, Jeremie wrote *Four Essays on Colonial Slavery*, which was published in 1831. Jeremie had become thoroughly disgusted with the way slaves were treated in St Lucia and with the abuse of past decades. His stance was outspoken and he made many bitter enemies amongst the 150 or so merchants and planters *cum* slave owners, many of whom were highly respected and powerful men in society. Confrontations between Jeremie and the upper-class of Castries were usually petty, occasionally ridiculous and once or twice downright dangerous.[181]

Jeremie found himself in St Lucia at a particularly turbulent juncture in time and it is fair to say that while he was fearless and uncompromising, a good deal of the uproar he caused was also simply a sign of planters' general resistance to the introduction of ameliorative slave laws, and of St Lucia's somewhat exceptional position (along with Trinidad, Berbice and Demerara) as a Crown Colony. By the Treaty of Paris in 1814, St Lucia had been placed directly under the administration of the British Government. Unlike other British West Indian islands, which were governed by Representative Assemblies that could vote on laws made in England if these concerned them, the Governor of St Lucia had no choice but to implement whatever ordinances England imposed on the island. This placed considerable limitations on the powers of the local plantocracy. Being the man responsible for implementing and ensuring compliance to the new amelioration laws, Chief Justice Jeremie took the full brunt of planter resistance.[182]

In July of 1823, the English Secretary of State, Earl Bathurst, instructed all British colonies to introduce the new slave laws. Under amelioration, slaves were to receive religious instruction and Christian marriages between slaves were to be encouraged. Slaves would also be allowed to act as witnesses in a court of law, own property and manage savings accounts. Slaves were to be empowered and allowed to buy their freedom, even without their owner's consent, and new social facilities for the care of children, the sick and elderly were to be introduced. Furthermore, new laws regulating the sale of slaves prevented the members of a given slave family from being sold separately and slaves could only be sold as part and parcel of the estate where they lived.

With respect to corporal punishment, the whip was no longer allowed to be used on women and became banned from the fields altogether. Corporal punishment was only allowed 24 hours after the perceived misdemeanour (to allow for a cooling-off period) and all punishments consisting of more than three lashes with the whip had to be recorded and reported twice yearly. Other ameliorations were included as well, such as specific regulations concerning hours of work and rest.

As said, the amelioration laws did not go down well with St Lucia's ruling class. The *Procureur du Roi*, the *Sénéchal* and even Governor Blackwell himself all strongly denounced the laws, giving voice to planters' objections. They felt that matters introduced in these laws were either already provided for, or were impossible to execute. The planters also argued that amelioration would have the opposite effect of what was intended. Slaves, they said, would misinterpret the new laws to mean that they could perform less work without fear of punishment. As a result, the planters said, slaves would end up being punished more frequently and more harshly, rather than less, and relations between masters and slaves would deteriorate.

In 1823, it was falsely rumoured in St Lucia that slaves believed amelioration would soon be followed by full abolition of slavery and that they had begun to rise up in anticipation. Word had it that on outlying estates, slaves were attacking their masters and had begun to burn property and cane fields. Planters themselves were the first to spread such rumours and deliberately painted a picture of gloom and doom to the authorities in London. With the terrifying events of the Brigands' War (only two decades earlier) undoubtedly fresh in every planter's mind, such images of bloody insurgencies would not have been difficult to conjure up!

By February 1826, after three years of dragging its heels, the Privy Council in St Lucia had no other choice than to finally adopt the amelioration laws. They came into effect in July 1826. Governor Mainwaring implored everybody to behave themselves. '*As the Slave Law will be this day for the first time in operation, I, in the most public manner, caution both Masters and Slaves against the erroneous impressions which many apparently entertain respecting the proper intent and meaning of these regulations.*'[183]

The rumoured insurrections turned out to be hogwash. But while Governor Mainwaring's successor, Governor Stewart admitted that the conduct of the slaves was '*in substance correct*' and planters had been '*too gloomy*'[184], many planters nevertheless continued to bewail the new laws. And so John Jeremie found himself in the unenviable position of having to implement and adjudge amelioration against a tide of hostility from his fellow-whites - the same people with whom he, as Chief Justice, would normally be expected to identify and socialize.

On arrival in St Lucia, in February 1825, the new Chief Justice announced his dedication to implementing *'the full spirit'* of Earl Bathurst's amelioration laws *'to the local circumstances of this colony, and to give the Slave the advantage of every benefit intended for him.'*[185] Jeremie not only implemented the laws but also doggedly oversaw their full execution in practice. He investigated abuse and infringements on slaves' working hours and even went so far as to dig up 'cold cases' of slave abuse from decades earlier. And John Jeremie was not a man afraid to speak up. He repeated time and again that in his view, the only sound, long-term solution to the slave question was full abolition. Unsurprisingly, slaves in St Lucia carried Jeremie's name on their tongues.

Planters, for their part, considered Jeremie an irritating and authoritarian figure, best fought with ridicule. But after Jeremie exposed St Lucia as a cesspit of covert cruelty to slaves, they became livid. The abolition movement in England quoted at length from Jeremie's *Four Essays* and he was a popular speaker at anti-slavery meetings.[186] It left a large faction of St Lucia's plantocracy feeling sorely betrayed. Not only had Jeremie given them so much trouble as Chief Justice, drawing a high salary paid for out of their taxes, but now he was exposing their dirty laundry all across Europe. Jeremie's most vociferous enemies were two anonymous '*Inhabitants of St Lucia.*' In a publication of their own, the duo provided blow-by-blow attacks on the examples Jeremie gave in his four essays, attempting to expose him as a naïve tyrant. What particularly stung them was that, in their view, the planters were being demonized simply because the English Government had had a change of heart with respect to the moral acceptability of slavery.[187] They deeply resented being made into scapegoats.

> *Not the planters - not the present slave-holders; they never trafficked to Africa - they never bartered for slaves, nor sold them from their native country; they were never the inhuman traders in human flesh, nor could aught but a monstrous misconception of justice ever expect that they, and they alone, should be called upon to atone for the sins of centuries past, and of every government who sanctioned, enforced, and fostered this traffic, from the age of Elizabeth, who created it, down to the present time.*

In other words, these two self-appointed spokesmen for St Lucia's plantocracy did not dwell on the inhumanity of their action, but defended its legality. They also alleged that Jeremie did not understand *the Negro mind* the way that they, who had owned slaves all their lives, did. Jeremie was criticized for not understanding what was '*required*' to make slaves work and what was sometimes required to protect slaves from themselves. '*Every one, who is conversant with the negro character, must conclude, that to devise any means of keeping at home slaves who are addicted to desertion and depredation, would be an act of kindness and humanity towards them, in comparison to exposing them to this succession of floggings, chains, hard labour, and death.'*

Their racist ideology was as deep-seated as it was crude. With few exceptions, Africans were said to be '*extremely indolent*', '*careless about future welfare*', naturally deceptive and untrustworthy since '*they don't think murder, adultery and theft is in any way sinful. ... The wants of the natives are but few, and so easily satisfied, that such people, I am positive, will never, either by persuasion or example, be urged to pursue agriculture, to a greater degree than they have done.*'

If not for the whip, slaves would never work a stroke in their lives and even *with* the whip, argued the two planters, '*it is perfectly manifest, that the proportion of labour performed by slaves, even under the dread of punishment, is quite trifling compared to what is performed by labourers in Britain. What then would their labour be if left entirely to themselves?*'

It is from the bowels of this society, with its powerful white minority rule steeped in racist ideology and a culture that allowed violent excesses to pass without sanction, that Chief Justice Jeremie stumbled across, and dragged up for all to read, some horrific examples of the treatment of slaves in St Lucia between approximately 1800 and 1830. There was no reason to believe, wrote Jeremie, that matters had been any better before 1800, just less covert - although, if Jeremie's critics are to be believed, planters used to feel more paternalistic and protective of their slaves before amelioration. Jeremie described how, in 1826

> ... *a negro came before* [me] *with a collar riveted round his neck, from which projected three prongs of about ten inches each in length, and at the end of either of these prongs were inserted three smaller ones about an inch long, and these were attached to a chain, reaching to fetters joining round his ancles. His back and limbs were wealed from neck to foot, and he declared that this collar was kept on him by day and by night; that he worked with it in the field; and on his return was immured in a solitary cell; and that this course had been practised for some months in order to prevent his running away, the crime with which he was principally charged.*

Jeremie sent investigators to the estate where this slave lived, and they reported '*that there were three other men, at the time, on the estate, with collars of the same description, and that those collars were in use in the country.*' They also found '*that there was a woman covered with sores, who was found in chains, and who had been so chained for near two years.*' To Jeremie's amazement, they further '*reported that the estate was well managed, and that the arrangements were good! - This was not at a remote period, but in the year 1826.*'[188]

The practice of chaining was unlawful and so was the form of punishment which had come to replace it: '*The women were hung by the arms to a peg, raised so high above their heads that the toes alone touched the ground, the whole weight of the body resting on the wrists of the arms or the tips of the toes.*' The amelioration laws had recommended alternative forms of punishment, including the use of field stocks. Jeremie himself had initially defended the stocks. It was not until he saw the method in practice, that he realized its tortuous character. It is

> *... nothing less than the most cruel picketing. They are in the shape of a pillory, the hands of the slave are inserted in grooves, which may be raised to any height above the head, and the feet are inserted in other grooves at the bottom of the instrument, the toes alone being made to touch the ground: the body is thus suspended in mid-air, its whole weight resting on the wrists and toes. In Trinidad they fix leaden weights to the wrists, which of course adds considerably to the torture. It is a legalised substitute for the whip, and even pregnant women are not exempted from it.*

St Lucian planters admitted that the grooves sometimes had tin sheeting nailed around them in order to prevent a small (woman's) hand from slipping out. Other reports mentioned that such sheet metal was often sharp and caused laceration of the skin.

Jeremie also investigated cases of slave murder. He related a legal battle between a planter and his manager over unpaid wages in which the owner argued in court that the cost of two of his slaves should be deducted from the wages he owed the manager, '*For the value of John the cooper, flogged to death by you, and then buried in the cane piece, 400 dollars! And for the price of the negress Mary Clare, who died by bruises received from you, 300 dollars.*' What made this careless view of slaves' lives even more poignant is the fact that the planter in question was himself a former Chief Justice of St Lucia and had held a seat in the Royal Court for thirteen years.

In another case related by Jeremie, a planter in a private quarrel accused another planter of having killed six or eight of his own slaves '*in as many years*'. These were excessive cases, admitted Jeremie, but none the less firmly documented in court records.

Theoretically, slaves had the right to complain to the *Procureur du Roi* if they were treated in contravention of the slave laws. To do so, however, they required their owner's permission to travel to Castries to lodge the complaint. The *Procureur du Roi* was himself a slave owner and if their complaint was rejected, slaves could be severely punished for their efforts. Jeremie concluded that slaves were faced with a 'conspiracy of silence': a pervasive culture of casual cruelty and disregard for their lives and welfare. Around 1808, the situation was such that a judge admitted: '*Every planter might have assassinated his slaves, yet, unless the public prosecutor proceeded against them, I should not, as a judge, have carried on criminal proceedings against them: fortunately there are not so many* [slave murders] *as the prisoner pretends.'*

Even during Jeremie's tenure, in the late 1820s, cases could only be brought to court if there was an informer. Since slaves could not bear testimony against whites, the informer had to come from the planter's own inner circle. This person then needed to go to the district attorney or prosecutor first, before a judge could proceed against the accused. The witness was examined in secret, the court was composed of planters, and the judgement was secret. Jeremie, with good reason, wondered how anyone was ever going to be convicted in such a system. In St Lucia's small, tightly-knit and racially divided society of the eighteenth and early nineteenth century, it was considered 'impolitic' to make a fuss about the fact that sometimes, slaves died at the hands of their masters. Nobody dared, or cared, to cast the first stone - not least because so many were themselves guilty of breaking slave laws. Even if a planter or other free person might at times feel upset about the level of violence used against slaves, to express this sentiment publicly or to act on it would have made his or her own position in society untenable - as indeed John Jeremie's position soon became. Jeremie wrote: *'even those who were shocked at the crimes committed deemed it prudent to conceal them; ... no public officer dared to take up these cases, except at the expense of his future quiet and reputation; - and ... slave murder was too common, and might ... be committed with impunity.'*[189]

The virtual impossibility for whites to break rank cut deep. White solidarity *vis-à-vis* slaves was official policy and, according to a 1771 instruction from the Crown, fundamental to maintaining the system of slavery. *'It is only by leaving to the masters a power that is nearly absolute, that it will be possible to keep so large a number of men in that state of submission which is made necessary to their numerical superiority over the whites. If some masters abuse their power, they must always be reproved in secret, so that the slaves may always be kept in the belief that the master can do no wrong in his dealing with him.'*[190]

It appears that coloured slave owners generally adopted the same approach. Although they occasionally clamoured for change, until the advent of the revolutionary years in the 1790s, the situation in St Lucia was much the same as that which David Geggus described for Haiti, where *'the free coloreds acted like the slave owners they were and were careful not to have their cause confused with that of the black masses.'*[191]

Even after the amelioration laws were in place, including the institution of an independent office of Protector of Slaves, it remained difficult and risky for slaves to lodge complaints against their owners. Jeremie recorded that in 1826, seven complaints by slaves were reported to the Protector of Slaves. Five of these were found not to be substantiated. In 1827, there were eleven complaints by slaves; seven found not substantiated. In 1828, there were two complaints, both substantiated. Over the same period, slave masters brought 95 complaints against slaves (including domestics) and only one was found to be unsubstantiated. The Protector of Slaves independently brought eleven charges against slave owners: four were acquitted, four convicted and in three cases both master and slaves were judged to have been in the wrong.

Abolitionist movement

Changes to the system of slavery invariably emanated from London, where the Colonial Office administered the Crown Colony of St Lucia. In Britain, resistance to slavery had begun in the late eighteenth century. In 1787, Quakers established 'The Society for Effecting the Abolition of the Slave Trade'. In 1788, a limit was imposed on the number of people that could be stashed in the hold of a slave ship. In 1807, Britain abolished the slave trade and in 1808, all Englishmen were prohibited from engaging in such trade. In July 1823, Britain proclaimed the amelioration laws, which were enforced in St Lucia from 1826 onwards. Britain finally proclaimed full abolition of slavery in 1838. Clearly, Jeremie's strongest supporters were in London.[192]

To illustrate this point: in 1831, a British official intervened and reversed the sentence of a judge in the Royal Court in Castries who had ordered a slave by the name of Neptune '*to receive 200 lashes in the public Market place of Castries, and to wear a chain during seven years upon his Master's property for having assaulted a free person, and struck his Master with his fist while he was endeavouring to separate him from the person whom he was assaulting.*'

However, as the British official discovered: '*The slave appears to have been intoxicated and to have struck his Master by accident. You will therefore on the receipt of this dispatch grant to the slave a free pardon, for that part of his sentence which refers to his working in chains.*'[193] By then, of course, the unfortunate Neptune had already suffered 200 lashes of the whip.

The humanitarian wind of change in British governance was evidenced by the introduction of the office of Protector of Slaves. Under amelioration, slave owners were obliged to report to the protector which slaves were punished, for what perceived misdemeanour or crime, and who witnessed the punishment. Disrespect to the overseer or driver, running away, being late for work, theft, fighting, drunkenness, absence or neglect of duty and carelessness with animals were the most common offences, with men more often being punished for fighting and women for insolence and disrespect.

A random selection of offences and punishments from the half-yearly returns to the Protector of Slaves in 1827-28 shows the following trespasses and punishments: 'disrespect to the driver' (seven hours in the stocks and twenty lashes), stealing sugar (six hours stocks, ten lashes), beating another

Negro (25 lashes), eating dirt (25 lashes), letting the cattle ravage in canes (ten lashes), getting drunk in the kitchen (25 lashes), stealing & killing a sheep (ten lashes), stealing canes (four days in the fetters).

During the 1820s, between ten and 25 lashes with the 'cat' (a whip with up to nine strips) was a common punishment on plantations, as were confinement in the *cachot* and use of the stocks. By then, running away incurred lesser punishment than it had done in the seventeenth and eighteenth centuries. The old *Code Noir* used to specify that slaves who were absent for more than one month were to have both ears cut off and a *fleur-de-lis* branded in one shoulder. A second offence was to result in having '*his hams cut*' (severing the muscles of the upper legs from the bone) and having a *fleur-de-lis* branded in the other shoulder. A third offence carried the death penalty. This was changed in 1763 to lifetime on a chain gang.

Where punishments were as severe as this, slave owners and governors could not but be aware of the strong resentment this created amongst the general slave population. In 1817, five runaway slaves by the names of Philippe, Gabriel, Jean-François, Jean-Baptiste alias Congo and a woman known as *négresse* Marie-Françoise, belonging to a planter by the name of Taillasson, were all sentenced to having their ears cut off and a mark branded on one shoulder. Governor Seymour, however, changed the punishment so that only the two '*most dangerous Characters*' would have '*part of their Ears cut off (a very small portion of the top which is not even perceptible when the hat is on)*' and be branded, while the other three were given 29 lashes each in the public market in Castries.[194] Despite this relative leniency, an insurrection broke out and '*large bodies of 30 & 40 having collected together in the woods, I was obliged in many instances to send Detachments of the Military after them*', Seymour complained.

To a large extent, punishments appear to have been motivated by the private fears, whims and dislikes of owners, managers and overseers. Generally speaking, plantations that belonged to absentee-owners (who left the day-to-day management of their estates to an overseer or manager) reported higher instances of punishment than those run by resident owners. Smaller estates with fewer slaves generally had fewer punishments, as did the fairly significant number of estates run by widows and other female slave owners.

Jeremie remarked on this phenomenon as well. He compared the six estates with the highest returns of punishment to the six estates with the lowest returns of punishments. On the first six estates, he found 820 instances of punishment, delivered on a slave population of 831 souls, over a two-and-a-half year period.[195] On the latter, during the same period, there were 253 punishments on 1332 slaves. Of the first six estates, five were run by managers and one by a proprietor. Of the latter six, five were run by proprietors and just one by a manager. On the first six estates, the death-to-birth ratio was 90:43.

On the latter six estates, the death-to-birth ratio was 92:106.[196] From this, Jeremie concluded that there was a clear correlation between management style and the birth and death rate of slaves, to the point where '*In short, the character of the manager could, almost to a certainty, be ascertained by the births and deaths in his gang.*'[197] Jeremie's opponents fiercely denied this, but they did concede that managers might have more cause to punish slaves than resident-owners. '*Slaves have a most uncontrollable desire of trying the temper of any new manager, and it is not until they have been punished and compelled, that they can be brought into obedience or subjection: this is a trait in the negro character on which Mr Jeremie has remained silent.*'[198]

As the final days of slavery drew nearer, some managers and proprietors appear to have taken out their grievances and frustrations on their slaves even more than usual.[199] There is the case, for instance, of Noel Boirond (aged about 48) and Jean Marie (about 28). Both men were slaves at Savannes Estate in the Quarter of Vieux Fort. On 28 April 1834, Noel and Jean Marie appeared before James Drysdale, the Protector of Slaves, '*complaining of having been punished severely and unjustly*' by their manager, Denys Lesfauries.[200] Noel Boirond testified:

> *On Thursday morning of the week in question I carried canes until breakfast time with my mule. I began early in the morning - after breakfast I went to the boiling house, where I worked until near midnight. The next morning I overslept myself. The overseer called me, and as the sun was rising I was harnessing my mule. The overseer returned, and gave me himself ten lashes with the cat. I then worked with my mule the whole day with the exception of my noon time. On Saturday the overseer called me again, and I went to work carrying canes until breakfast time. I had my breakfast time. After this I was ordered to attend in the boiling house. When I arrived there my master ordered the overseer to tie me to a ladder, and I was again flogged with the cat. I suffered so much that I could not count the lashes. Toussaint begged pardon for me, but it was not granted.*

His friend Jean Marie testified of no less cruel treatment. '*On Saturday morning about fifteen days ago, I had been at work cutting canes in the field. I went to breakfast and after breakfast I was ordered to go to work in the boiling house. The overseer Mr Dantzick arrested me. I was tied to a ladder & received a considerable number of lashes. My master told me it was for his pleasure.*'

Witnesses confirmed the events, with one slave testifying that he '*counted 50 lashes*' being inflicted on Jean Marie '*and could not count any longer.*' Another witness said of Jean Marie's flogging: '*I do not know how many lashes he received, but he was flogged until he cry out no longer.*' Both witnesses agreed that Jean Marie and Noel Boirond had been punished '*without cause.*'

The manager, Denys Lesfauries, and the overseer Dantzick, defended their actions by saying: '*That the infliction of punishment had been indispensable, from the insubordinate conduct of the gang of the Savannes Estate, and that the punishments had been confined within the bounds prescribed by law.*' The judge, however, found Denys Lesfauries guilty of breaking the slave laws and fined him £20 plus costs.

While the case was before the courts, Noel Boirond, Jean Marie and four other slaves belonging to Savannes Estate (presumably witnesses) were kept at the Castries Gaol. The process lasted between four and eight weeks. After his conviction, Denys Lesfauries wanted to return his slaves to Savannes Estate but found that '*the gaoler would not deliver them without my paying the expences they incurred during their detention.*' Lesfauries was irate. In an acrimonious letter to the Acting-Governor, he demanded that the Protector of Slaves pay for the upkeep of the six slaves and, he added, '*Methinks even that he ought to pay me the loss of time of my slaves - and to the same slaves their own loss of time, as allowed by law.*' Again, Lesfauries lost his case and in July 1834 (just one month before the introduction of the apprenticeship system, which was a forerunner to the full abolition of slavery), Lesfauries was forced to pay up for the return of his slaves.

By the 1830s, the system of slavery had become untenable for its human degradation as well as its economic irrationality. But before we move on to the Emancipation and post-abolition years, let us first pick up the thread of St Lucia's history from the end of the Brigand Wars, in 1804.

6

The disenchanted status quo: 1800-1838

The start of the nineteenth century saw a St Lucia still dazed from the ferocious upheavals of the Brigand Wars of the 1790s. With thousands dead and an equal number living in the mountains or banished overseas it was a hesitant, almost reluctant, beginning to the new century. In the absence of a viable alternative, St Lucia slowly returned to the old way of doing things. Governor George Prevost (1798-1802), in February of 1799 reported: '*On my arrival to take command in July last, several respectable Inhabitants who had been driven away, returned. I found the disposition of the people much changed & the Brigands who remained in the woods, so much reduced, as by a little exertion with the stationed Troops, to render them no longer to be dreaded.*'[201]

Before the Brigand Wars, St Lucian planters were already in debt to the tune of £500 000, mostly for the purchase of slaves.[202] With half the country uncultivated, planters scrambling to re-establish their factories and creditors demanding payment, the British Governor resorted to public auctions: offering slaves and abandoned estates for rent or sale.[203] It helped to attract '*several respectable persons*' to St Lucia as prospective settlers.[204] Prevost also re-established the judicial and administrative systems.

A list dated 13 November 1800 names the members of the Council of St Lucia, who were among the first planters to return to resume their businesses: (A.M.) Fayolle, Doyan (*President*), le Chevalier de Marsange, Lamothe Hosten, Pierre de Glapion, (Thomas) Naçaburn, (Gerôme) de Noroy, (Michel) le Vacher, Cornibert Duboulay, William Alexander, Robert Ewing, John McCall, Butel de Montgai (Honorary Member and *Sénéchal*) and (J.M.) Aubert (*Procureur-Général*).[205] Other planters mentioned by name in various documents in 1802 were Thomas Rigby, John Rovelet, John Galvey, Basil Freeland, Devaux St Philip, the brothers de Monchy, Ackey Lawrence and E. Raphel.[206] What this shows is that, at the start of the nineteenth century, St Lucia's plantocracy was once again a combination of French and British, with some other European and African strains mixed in. Some had been born in Europe; others were Creoles, native to the West Indies. Even those planters who had supported the French Revolution - most of them free people of colour, some of them whites

- were turning their minds away from ideological issues and back to matters of agriculture and trade.

And the blacks? Those who had not died during the Brigand Wars or left the island had the unenviable choice between marronage and re-submission to slavery. With the exhilarating prospect of self-governance removed, the dreariness of a life on the run must have loomed large. Especially for women with children, the elderly and the sick, the appeal of regular rations of food, clothing and a permanent roof over their heads on the plantations must have held some lure, even if the daily regime was harsh and humiliating.

It was a disenchanted return to an uncomfortable status quo. By the turn of the century, 3100 men and 5060 women had returned to the estates.[207] Still, it was a far cry from the almost 18 000 slaves St Lucia had counted just a decade earlier. On 25 March 1802, peace negotiations culminated in the Treaty of Amiens and St Lucia was declared a French possession once again. But it no longer mattered to the slaves: that very same year, after eight years of freedom and equality for all, Napoleon Bonaparte reinstated slavery in all French colonies, and once again it was business-as-usual in the French West Indies.

For St Lucia, it was to be a last, brief spell of French administration. Within fifteen months, the British invaded the island once more. French Governor Brigadier-General Nogues '*stood little chance against Commodore Samuel Hood with his 74-guns* Centaur *and* Courageux, *backed by a squadron which sailed into Choc Bay in June of 1803. The Vigie Heights and Castries were soon taken, as usual, and a 4 a.m. assault on Morne Fortune was successful.*' The British lost 21 men, had 110 wounded and took 640 French prisoners-of-war. On 26 June 1803, Brigadier-General Robert Brereton was appointed Governor of St Lucia and from that day (through being officially ceded to England in 1814) until Independence in 1979, St Lucia remained a British colony. It was the end of 160 years of Anglo-French struggle for dominion over the 'Helen of the West'.

Breaking barriers: social hierarchy, 1800-1838

With the failure of the Brigand Wars, St Lucian society reverted to its pre-war three-tier social hierarchy: a small white minority at the top of the apex wielding most of the economic and all of the legal and political power; a smallish but fast-growing free black and coloured group in the middle with some economic power but no legal or political influence; and a large majority of re-enslaved black and coloured people at the bottom, with no economic power and whose brief military and political might had been crushed into nothingness once again. As said, it was a disenchanted return to an uncomfortable status quo. And one which could not last.

What slave revolt had failed to accomplish was eventually achieved via the routes of political and legal action. The four decades from 1800 to 1838 saw a protracted political movement which, slowly but surely, forged fundamental change in the legal foundation of the island's power structure. Some legal distinctions of colour were eliminated on 8 February 1826. The remainder went on 15 January 1829, followed by full abolition of slavery in 1838. The engine that drove this change, whilst rooted in the abolitionist movement and the Government halls of Britain, was fuelled by the enthusiasm, support and lobbying of the coloured and black people of St Lucia itself. If the changes were accompanied by loud creaks and groans of protest - as indeed they were! – then these emanated exclusively from the small, dominant white plantocracy which feared the loss of the very basis of its economic, political and social supremacy.

We already discussed the battle waged by the President of the Royal Court, Chief Justice John Jeremie, who was in charge of implementing the slave amelioration laws in the late 1820s, and the bitter opposition he encountered from the ruling plantocracy. Jeremie's main supporters, besides the Colonial Office in London, were the slaves and free people of colour. The position of the latter, however, was a paradoxical one. As one author put it so well: '*In a society in which slavery was associated with race, a free colored person was "a third party in a system built for two"*.'[208]

Free people of colour: 1800-1834

Free from the hardships of slavery, well-adjusted to the climate and not given to the frequent alcoholic excesses of many of the whites (Breen estimated that half the deaths of whites were attributable to rum!),[209] over the late eighteenth and early nineteenth centuries, free people of colour showed by far the healthiest population growth of any group in society. The number of whites halved between 1772 and 1843, while those of free people of colour increased almost eight-fold.[210] Add to that the manumissions (between 1818 and 1824 alone, more than 500 men and women were manumitted)[211] and by the 1820s, it was clear that keeping free people of colour relegated to the wings of the social stage was going to be difficult. Throughout the eighteenth century, white domination over free people of colour had relied on '*liabilities, heavy penalties, and galling distinctions.*'[212] John Jeremie, in 1831, gave an overview of just how pettily insulting the colour laws were.

> *In St Lucia, persons of colour were not, by law, at liberty to wear the same dress as a white man. There was a positive enactment, strictly adhered to, by which, however wealthy, they were not to be called in any*

> *legal document 'Mr' or 'Madam,' but were designated as 'le nommé, la nommée,' 'that man and that woman.' Thus every paper they were parties to bore proof of the contempt with which they were viewed, and it is scarcely conceivable how much ill blood this single unmeaning distinction - this wanton and paltry insult - engendered. The white man who harboured a slave, paid a trifling fine; a man of colour was sold into slavery with all his family. The coloured were not at liberty, by law, to take the same names as white persons, but were expected to retain their African name, or that by which they or their ancestors had been known as slaves. The very humblest office, even a sheriff's officer's clerk, they were excluded from, nor could they be either apothecaries or druggists' shopmen, or receive testamentary benefactions from whites though their own parents. A coloured gentleman could not invite his friends to dine with him, without the permission of the public procureur ... If a coloured man, under any provocation, resented the affront of a white man, the former, however respectable, the latter, however disreputable; the coloured man was subject to the most dreadful penalties; in some cases, it is said to have extended to the loss of limb.*

These laws applied not only to those with one black and one white parent but '*to the remotest generation, however it might in the mean time have intermingled with whites. However fair their complexions, however legitimate their descent, however exemplary their conduct, a single drop of African blood was a pollution of the whole stock.*' In some ways, Jeremie argued, free coloureds were worse off than slaves, '*because any white man can raise his hand against him, and there is no one to protect him - the law is administered by his tyrant.*'

Free people of colour formed between one-third and three-quarters of the entire free population at any given time.

Some authors argue that as a sub-culture, they were basically African-Creole in outlook.[213] Free coloureds, they argue, were a 'new people', with a shared history, common origin and allied concerns. They primarily interacted with each other and black slaves and as such formed a coherent social group with essentially African-Creole norms and values. Whilst aspiring to equal rights *with* whites, this school of thought holds, it is wrong to infer that therefore, free people of colour wanted to *be* like whites.

Other authors argue that there was actually a distinction *within* the group of free coloureds between those of mixed blood, and the free blacks. They feel that free coloureds '*increasingly came to regard persons without white blood as inferior to those who had*'[214] and were '*deriving self consequence from the approximation of their Colour to the whites*'.[215] Barry Gaspar, for instance, found that in St Lucia, free coloureds aspired to the power and prestige that rested in white hands, seemingly effortlessly overlooking the plight of black slaves. While determined to have their own disabilities in law removed, they were in no way abolitionists.

> *In pleading their case they betrayed their dislike at being in any way classified with slaves, asking the governor and the higher authorities whether it could be considered either generous or just that they, many of whom were wealthy and educated, should be categorized with slaves that were in a state 'little better than that of primitive ignorance.' What they sought was upward mobility leaving behind their slave connections. They had no common cause with the slaves.*

The two views (free blacks and coloureds sharing an essentially Afro-Creole lifestyle versus free coloureds aspiring to leave all things African behind) are perhaps not as paradoxical as they might appear.

First of all, it is probably true that free coloureds interacted more with each other and slaves than with whites. The majority of free people of colour lived in town, where they worked as independent masons, carpenters, sailors, fishermen, tailors and small merchants, or owned and rented out personal slaves. In 1824, the total population of Castries town consisted of 253 whites, 1260 free coloureds and 1150 slaves. The free coloureds that lived in the countryside usually operated small estates of their own, with some slave labour. One thing free coloureds could be counted on *not* to do was rent themselves out as labourers on white-owned and operated plantations. On the contrary, it was the slaves who almost always worked under white supervision, and hence interacted with whites. Secondly, also true is the fact that from fairly early on, and certainly following the Brigand Wars, free people of colour in St Lucia developed a strong sense of shared history, group consciousness and solidarity - something which was reinforced by their steady increase in numbers and the continuation of oppressive laws against them. Faced with the same legal obstructions, they joined hands in their opposition.

However, having said that, there were undoubtedly also significant social distinctions *within* the group of free coloureds, based on skin colour and longevity of freedom. Recently manumitted free people, especially if they were not of mixed blood and had emerged from the countryside, had very different lifestyles from those fair-skinned, well-educated free people of colour who had been free for several generations and lived in Castries town. It was from this last group that the spokesmen for reform stepped forward.

Considering that the total number of free people of colour was close to 4000, it should give pause for thought that only a very small number actively agitated for equal rights. The petition of 15 January 1824 was signed by just 35 free men of colour - as far as we can tell all well-respected, relatively wealthy and educated members of society. Why was there no mass-protest, such as we find just two decades later, during the peasant revolt of 1849? Did the black, African-oriented free people of colour not care about bettering their legal position? That seems highly unlikely. Did the respectable leaders of the free coloured movement not *want* to include them? Quite possibly. Was this exclusion a deliberate strategy on the part of those leaders? Almost certainly. With the benefit of historical hindsight, did that strategy work in the best interest of *all* free people of colour? Absolutely.

When free people of colour began to push for equality and civil rights, they did so gently, almost apologetically. To understand this, and to appreciate the strategic dilemma within which they operated, we must call to mind the immediate historical context. Emerging from the Brigand Wars and faced with a return to business-as-usual, those free people of colour who had been active supporters of the French Revolution had lost their tenuous hold on equality. Like the Brigands, they had seen their high-spirited dreams of universal freedom, equality and brotherhood shot down in flames. Like the slaves, they too must have suffered a terrible ideological hang-over and for them, as for the slaves, the return to the strict colour-coded three-tiered hierarchy was an uneasy one.

Certainly, many free people of colour had themselves been slave owners before the Brigand Wars and returned to being slave owners after the war. Admittedly, their estates were generally smaller, with fewer slaves, and it is also true that free people of colour more often lived in towns and villages where they kept just a few personal slaves.[216] Ironically, from a business point of view, the interests of free people of colour who ran plantations and other businesses ran entirely parallel to those of whites: a need for law and order, stable government, good infrastructure, regular shipping facilities, cheap lines of credit, low taxes, and so on.

But with the return to the status quo, free people of colour had been relegated once again to the position of second-class citizens. They were kept at a stiff arm's length from the privileges and rights of whites and, if anything, were regarded with even more suspicion than before due to their republican sympathies during the Brigand Wars. Even in its mildest form, an appeal for equal civil rights for free people of colour was akin to taking an axe to the very root of social hierarchy, implicitly attacking the legitimacy of slavery as well. So the quandary in which the free people of colour found themselves was that whilst clamouring for equal rights of citizenship for themselves, they had to meticulously dissociate themselves from the slaves, lest their struggle be interpreted as a return to the radical ideologies of the French Revolution - something which was sure to turn the white minority against them and undermine their lobby. Hence, free people of colour moved very carefully. If, in hindsight, their approach seems almost pathetically conservative,[217] particularly in light of their republican sympathies and sometimes militant roles during the Brigand Wars, then this is the context in which that reticence must be understood.

As said, it was a small group of economically successful and respectable free men of colour who took the lead in the fight for equal rights in St Lucia. John Patterson was their primary spokesman. Other signatories to the first petition, on 15 January 1824, were John Baptiste Floissac, Pierre Jean Marie, Laurent Larcher, Louis Jacob, Antoine Luc, Joseph Virginy, Josias Morgan, Edmond Jacob, Louis Glaudon, Cyril Imbert, Louis George, Darzol Decaille, Louis Pilage, William Hepburn, Pierre Sanders, Henry Fahie, François Percin, Baptist Looby, George Aubert, Joseph Girard, Louis Aubert, James Johnston, Jacques D. Decaille, William Well, Amable Arsenne, Dubois (fils), Pierre Cornan, Ste Luce Simon, Bastien Lacoste, Louis Borie, F. Robert Ferdinand, Louis Dalma Borie, Michel Common and Pierre Fournier. Some of these men's life histories are known; others still need to be lifted from the dusty recesses of memories and archives.

John Patterson was a Protestant who, in 1819, lived in Castries and owned seventeen personal slaves whom he rented out to work for others. James Johnston's life and career were explored in a 1983 article by Barry Gaspar. Johnston was a free man of colour, born in Antigua, who later moved to St Lucia where he overcame many hurdles and disappointments during his career in the civil service. He eventually rose from the position of clerk (1819) and principal and confidential clerk (1820) to that of special magistrate (1838, a position he held until the 1860s) but only after having been turned down on several occasions for other, intermediate posts for reasons that could only be attributed to the colour of his skin.[218]

Chief Justice John Jeremie recounted the life story of another man who, although remaining nameless, was almost certainly a signatory to the petition as well.

> *A young gentleman, the son of a judge of* [St Lucia], *by a dark coloured woman, had received from his father a good plain education in Liverpool; he spoke English and French, and wrote both languages with ease and fluency; but being from his descent, inadmissible to any office of respectability, his father had had the good sense to bring him up to a respectable trade, that of a watchmaker. Soon after I arrived in St Lucia, this young man was recommended to me as a clerk. Having kept him in that capacity for six years, an opportunity offered of bringing him to the bar. He accordingly obtained a commission; and I have the satisfaction of knowing that this young gentleman is now one of the leading advocates of the court and enjoying, in a high degree, the public confidence.*[219]

François Percin, finally, is another signatory about whom certain facts are known. Originally a seaman from Trinidad, he married into a well-to-do St Lucian family. Although he was considered a successful member of society, Percin never ceased to be deeply bothered by the racial obstacles which he, as a coloured man, found in his way - which is what must have spurred him to sign the petition. He was a man with keen ambitions, not only for himself but also for his son, Henry (born in 1817), whom he managed to send to school overseas. Henry eventually obtained a law degree in Paris and returned to St Lucia in 1839 to practice his profession.[220] He showed himself to have been very much imbued with the zeal of his father, when he volunteered to represent the leaders of the 1849 peasant revolt in court. Henry Percin eventually took his father's fight for equality to the kind of radical level that remained so conspicuously absent from the free coloured movement of the 1820s.

In their 1824 petition, these 35 men of colour outlined their grievances. They emphasized that free coloureds comprised the majority of the free population and that many of them were landed proprietors, tax-payers and instrumental in maintaining the internal tranquillity of the colony.

> *The Man of Colour however competent his abilities, however unblemished his character, or considerable his fortune is debarred, from Complexion alone, the participation of many of those civil rights enjoyed by the White Class. He sees the White Alien actuated by pecuniary views become a resident in his native land & enter at once in the enjoyment of its highest privileges, while he is condemned to stand aloof a patient Spectator, condemned or despised.*[221]

Equal rights were granted in 1829 but another petition was signed in 1831 to object to lingering prejudices which prevented free people of colour from obtaining certain public posts. The signatories included Louis Aubert ('*A Gentleman of unimpeachable character a Merchant and Proprietor in the Town of Castries*' and a non-commissioned officer in the artillery company) and, once again, John Patterson. The advocates for equal rights always carefully projected an image of themselves as patient men, loyal subjects and faithful employees: as men of '*unblemished character*'. John Jeremie made a 'social inventory' of the free coloureds shortly after they were granted equal civil rights in 1828. He found that there were about 5000 free coloured and black people in St Lucia, one-eighth of whom (about 625) were manumitted slaves, many of whom in turn now possessed land and slaves. Another 80 were '*discharged negro soldiers*'. [222] The free coloureds were '*tranquil, humble, and most unassuming*' and since having received equal rights, their conduct had been '*truly astonishing. They enjoy the esteem and consideration of the white class, nor was any disturbance ever known among them.*' They formed the bulk of the militia, lacking neither '*intelligence nor zeal*' and there was a militia composed of free coloureds alone which was responsible for the protection of property in Castries.

Two or three free men of colour were sugar planters. Numerous others owned coffee, cocoa and provision plantations, '*possessing each from ten to forty slaves.*' In all, free people of colour possessed 2350 slaves, or about one-sixth of the total. Of these, 1202 were plantation slaves and 1148 personal slaves (almost half the total of all personal slaves). As much as one third of the island's trade was in the hands of free people of colour. '*There are two first-rate merchants, and a large number of second-rate merchants and retail dealers, among them. ... The dry-good trade they possess almost exclusively; and they are remarkable for probity in their dealings, and for punctuality in their payments. The generality are retail merchants and small proprietors, nor are they by any means so embarrassed as the whites.*'

In Castries, free people of colour owned '*more than one half the rental of the town, and full half the registered shipping in number and value*', leaving no doubt as to their economic prominence.

Fifteen years later, in 1844, Henry Breen dubbed the coloured class '*the staple population of the Colonies*'. By then, Breen's relatively progressive view was widely shared by the white minority.

> *Few as yet have become owners of the soil to any considerable extent; but much of the property in houses and land, both in Castries and Soufriere, is possessed by them. Some are opulent merchants; others respectable shopkeepers; and many industrious tradesmen. The advantages of education, too, begin to be more generally appreciated: not only are the clerkships in the public offices held by persons of colour; but the Medical Profession, the Press, the Bar, the Legislative Council, the offices of Crown Lawyer, Stipendiary Magistrate, Justice of the Peace, Deputy Registrar, Deputy Marshal, and Notary Public, are aspired to by candidates from amongst their ranks, and filled with credit and distinction.*[223]

On 8 February 1826, some of the more blatant restrictions were repealed, including those differentiating people of colour in judicial and notary acts. On 15 January 1829, the remaining discriminatory laws were revoked as well and free coloureds finally found themselves the legal equals of whites. Legal equality did not by any means eliminate colour distinctions or racial prejudice, but it was a major breakthrough nonetheless. What is more, even though the free coloured lobby had not linked its cause to the plight of the slaves - may even have deliberately avoided the obvious connection - once the glass ceiling between whites and free people of colour was broken, the ideological legitimization for slavery also lay shattered. There could be no doubt left in anyone's mind that the full abolition of slavery was inevitable.

'Après nous la fin du monde': the white minority, 1800-1838.

With St Lucia's formal handover to Britain in 1814, how did the island's numerous French and French-Creole inhabitants fare? Legally and linguistically, nothing much changed at first. By the 1814 cession it was agreed that French would remain St Lucia's first language, including in court, and this remained so until the 1830s. Even after that, French remained the official second language until 1 January 1842.[224] In 1836-7, two English visitors, Thomas Harvey and Joseph Sturge, were amazed to find that '*The French language is almost exclusively spoken by all classes. The lady of the Chief Justice, informed us that there were only two ladies in the colony who spoke English till the arrival, a few days since, of the wife and daughters of one of the Stipendiary magistrates.*'[225]

Until the 1820s, Anglo-French relations were tense, with a lot of '*ill-will and nagging*' between the two, according to Breen. Centuries of warfare had left scars of humiliation, grievance, arrogance, distrust and antipathy. In 1819, it almost came to a duel between five Englishmen and five Frenchmen at a secluded spot near Vieille Ville. The adversaries stood with weapons drawn when the timely intervention of the Attorney-General prevented actual bloodshed.[226] Over time, however, intermarriage between the island's principal families served to intertwine the interests of the old French planters with those of the leading English merchants and public servants. Faced with a continued influx of 'fresh' immigrants, laws were drawn up in 1826 which declared all pre-1814 French occupants British subjects, and as such entitled them to participate in all public offices of trust and emolument. All post-1814 non-British immigrants were considered 'aliens' and on that basis were excluded from public services.

Social distinctions, at the time, existed not only between British and French but also between Creole and European-born. While the island-born Creole whites felt that they more belonged to St Lucia and St Lucia more belonged to them (acting, one could say, as an 'island aristocracy'), the European-born whites tended to look down on the Creoles whom they often perceived as ill-educated and uncivilized (despite the fact that many Creole children were sent to school in France or England). The Creole whites, in response, could be heard to complain about the perceived arrogance and conceited superiority of European-born whites.

Some of the European-born whites came out to St Lucia with the intention of becoming planters. They usually ended up marrying into one of the local white families. Others were career-makers who came for contracted periods of time only, to take up posts in merchant houses or the public service. These were, one could say, ex-pats *avant-la-lèttre*. A few of these also married locally and remained on the island. Finally, there was a small group of poor whites (*petits blancs*) in St Lucia, either native born or newly immigrated, who made ends meet by working as tradesmen, petty clerks, entertainers or small merchants. St Lucia, however, has never known the distinctive, often miserably poor, deeply racist and widely despised poor white communities of, for instance, Barbados (where they were known as *Red Shanks*), the Bahamas, Suriname, Jamaica or Grenada.[227] In any case, by the turn of the nineteenth century, most poor whites had either been assimilated into the class of free people of colour or had emigrated.

Rosemund Renard, in a study of the sugar industry in Vieux Fort, stated that the French sugar plantocracy, '*confronted by growing financial difficulties and a hostile British administration, capitulated around 1830 and their lands were bought over by British-born planters.*'[228] While it is true that most estates changed hands at least once during these first three decades of the nineteenth century, the French by no means disappeared from the social scene. French planters, like their British counterparts, were almost invariably heavily indebted to the British bankers *cum* merchants who shipped and sold the crops on their behalf. These merchants acted '*not only as the agent who sold the planter's sugar, but also in a way as his accountant and his banker and his buying agent.*'[229] Large sums of money were advanced on the value of the estate and its main capital interest: the slaves.[230] Breen explained: '*Thus reduced to the degrading condition of a trustee or manager of his own property, the planter, unmindful of the past and regardless of the future, appeared solicitous but to satisfy the present wants of himself and his family. His device was: 'Après nous la fin du monde'; and his object to prevent the estate from passing into other hands during his lifetime.*'[231]

Numerous plantations did change hands, however, often more than once. Mamiku Estate in Praslin, for instance, was sold ten times between 1818 and 1906.[232] In the process, some properties were consolidated by British planters who acted like corporate businessmen rather than landed gentry (as the French had traditionally done). Other plantations were cut up into smaller pieces, allowing small aspiring landowners such as the free coloureds (and, after abolition, freed slaves) an opportunity to enter the business of agriculture. During the 1800s, 1810s and 1820s, all sorts of systems of double-dealing, fraud and corruption were prevalent.

> *Unable to satisfy at the same time the mortgagee in England, and the more clamorous creditors on the spot, the planter had recourse to every species of deception. To the one he promised a cask of sugar; to the other two casks; but he frequently disappointed both, and gave the whole to a third party, offering to supply the wants of the moment: and in this way he kept shifting from store to store until every merchant and even shopkeeper in the island had obtained a lien upon his estate.*[233]

It was a ruinous system and one that was only remedied by Chief Justice John Jeremie in the late 1820s. An immediate measure was to attach all slaves employed on estates to the soil so as to prevent them from being seized by creditors and sold separately. Under Jeremie's tenure, also, British commercial law replaced the French, and in July 1829, he established an office for the registration of deeds and mortgages so that everyone could see who was indebted to whom. Once all mortgages were registered, the records showed 1918 mortgages, totalling a debt and liability of £59 498 249 or almost sixty million pounds! With the colony thus on the brink of bankruptcy, in 1833, Jeremie authorized the seizure and sale of immoveable property.

'*Soon after the promulgation of this law several estates were levied upon and brought to the hammer, and the same process has continued until almost every estate in the island has now been disposed of by judicial sale.*' The decade between 1833 and 1844 saw 76 estates sold by judicial sale, some more than once. As Breen reasoned, most planters had long since lost financial ownership anyway, and the judicial sales allowed a new class of capable planters to emerge: men who brought money back into circulation and could '*put their cultivation on a new footing of respectability and independence.*'

St Lucia's plantation economy never reached the level of prosperity of long-established colonies such as Barbados and Martinique. Not during the eighteenth century, despite valiant efforts under French Governors de Micoud and de Laborie, and not during the early nineteenth century, despite the absence of Anglo-French warfare. Rosemund Renard correctly described St Lucia's economy as lurching from crisis to crisis, without much benefit from the brief moments of reprieve.[234] The progressive monoculturization of the economy towards sugar production (to the detriment of coffee and cocoa) meant an ever greater need for reliable and pliable labour. The abolition of the slave trade in 1807, followed by the introduction of amelioration laws in the late 1820s and the looming prospect of full abolition, put the planters in an almost impossible position. John Jeremie keenly understood this. '*Perfect slavery,*' he wrote, '*requires a large consumption of human fuel; the supply is stopped, and prices are become ruinous; and doubly ruinous must this state of things be when the slave holder has to compete with free labour on the one side, and with the slave trade on the other; - with India and Brazil.*'[235]

Pure logic prescribed only two possible solutions: extinguish slavery altogether or re-introduce the slave trade. '*The planter cannot discharge his workmen; his capital being invested in the purchase of the slaves, he must forfeit that or work them on. ... Now indeed the planter is truly wretched, for his fetters only remain, and he clings to them from habit and necessity. Weighed down ... by the very nature of his property, he works, and feels he must work on, to his all-but-inevitable ruin.*

To make matters worse, most planters were heavily indebted and owned their estates in name only - until judicial sale caught up with that. With little or no prospect of improvement and a British Government that did not particularly care whether St Lucia produced a whole lot of sugar or no sugar at all as long as the island remained hers militarily,[236] the planters really must have felt, as Breen phrased it: '*Après nous la fin du monde*' ('After us the deluge').

It was as if no white planter really believed in his own efforts anymore – but could not think what else to do. So sugar he produced, as best he could, for as long as he could. The few who prospered were those who successfully merged the roles of planter and merchant, thereby avoiding the debt situation. Actual sugar exports rose between 1807 and 1832 (with a few brief periods of decline) and by 1832 exports reached 4398 tons: more than double the amount of pre-revolutionary years. But the following year saw a serious drop again (2511 tons) and 1834 was no better, with just 2398 tons of sugar exported from St Lucia.[237]

A cynic might say that in St Lucia, the sugar industry never really took off - and then took a mighty long time to die.

Calamities: fire, hurricanes and tropical storms, 1805-1831

The reconstruction of the plantation economy was not helped by some spells of bad luck, which caused death, destruction, scarcity and hunger. On 15 October 1805, from eleven o'clock in the morning until half past two in the afternoon, a fire raged through Castries, laying '*the better half of the Town to the number of about 200 Houses*' into ashes, including '*the most considerable of the Merchant Stores.*' All military troops were sent down from the Morne to help but the weather had been very dry and '*a smart breeze prevailing at the time*' rendered them virtually helpless. To make matters worse, all houses in town were constructed of wood and there was no fire engine. Brigadier-General Robert Brereton, by letter of 27 October 1805, informed London of the calamity. '*By this fatal Event property to an immense amount has been lost to many individuals ... on rough calculation it is estimated at about one Hundred and fifty Thousand Pounds Sterling. Several of these unfortunate sufferers who were before in affluence are by this melancholy Event not only deprived of their Habitations, but also of the Means of Subsistence.*'[238]

Neighbouring colonies jumped to St Lucia's assistance: St Vincent sent 150 barrels of flour and 50 barrels of salt beef and pork and other islands promised similar aid. Governor Brereton (1803-7) grasped the opportunity to implore London to alleviate a more structural problem: the lack of regular arrivals of British ships with provisions. In the same letter which reported the fire, Brereton petitioned the Colonial Office to allow '*American and other*

Neutral Vessels' into Port Castries so that planters could exchange their rum, molasses and some sugar for salted fish, pork and beef, *'as it rarely happens that any of these Commodities are sent to St Lucia from any of the British Colonies in North America and but a very small supply of Provisions from Ireland.'*

It is unlikely that people were actually starving, considering the tropical abundance of fruit and vegetables, but there was definitely a lack of imported staples such as rice, flour, salted cod, beef and pork. Brereton's plea was eventually answered and from March 1807, for a number of months, American and other neutral ships were allowed to trade at Port Castries. It was none too soon as by then, the population had been reduced to *'extreme Distress ... And that to Windward of the Island there is absolutely no Provision of any Kind and the Negroes have begun to Kill Oxen & even Mules for their Subsistence.'*[239]

Another fire raged through Castries on 6 April 1813, again partly destroying the town. The dilemma in construction was always between lumber, which burnt more easily, and masonry, which was more lethal in case of earthquakes - as Martinique discovered to its horror on 11 January 1839, when a 40-second quake buried 500 people in rubble in Fort Royal, killing 261. The same earthquake badly damaged Soufrière and Castries but thankfully nobody died in St Lucia. The worst recorded earthquake in the Eastern Caribbean occurred a few years later still, on 8 February 1843, killing 5000 people in Pointe à Pître in Guadeloupe alone, creating scenes from hell.[240]

Storm records for the Lesser Antilles date back as far as 1756. In the 75 years between 1756 and 1831, St Lucia experienced six hurricanes. The biggest occurred on 10 October 1780 and killed an estimated 22 000 people in Barbados, St Lucia, St Vincent and Martinique combined. On 21 October 1817, another killer storm arrived on the shores of St Lucia, killing 46 slaves along with Major-General Richard Seymour, who died in the ruins of Government House.[241] Eyewitnesses described how *'not a Building remains entire. The Country is Devastated and the Abundant Crop of Canes, which in a very short time would have been cut, are either torn out of the ground or laid flat by the violence of the wind. The whole of the Provision Grounds are completely destroy'd and the Negroes, whose owners have not the means of alleviating their Hunger, are wandering about for Shelter.'* Also dead were 160 mules and horses and more than 300 head of *'Horned Cattle, together with an immense number of Sheep, Hogs, &c.'* The Privy Council, in a petition to King George *'most humbly throw ourselves at Your Royal Highness's feet for Succour'* and estimated the total loss at £550 807.[242]

Barely on the road to recovery, a tropical storm hit the island just two years later, in 1819, causing disastrous flooding and landslides and once more destroying property, animal life and crops. Subsequent years saw several more earthquakes and yet another bad hurricane (in August 1831) which claimed 1500 lives in Barbados and caused much suffering in St Vincent. St Lucia escaped relatively lightly with the loss of ten or twelve lives and some damage to housing, crops and shipping.[243]

Marronage and refugees: 1829-1838

Overall, the first four decades of the nineteenth century can best be described as a period of uneasy apprehension. The sugar economy was debt-ridden and barely surviving; the rising class of free coloured people cautiously but consistently chipped away at the legal inequalities in society; a succession of fires, hurricanes and earthquakes destroyed life and property - and throughout it all, the slaves hungered for the abolition of slavery which the French Revolution had failed to deliver.

Chief Justice John Jeremie had put the slave amelioration laws of 1826 into effect but just as he was keen to report positive results, so were some of the planters hell-bent on demonstrating the upheaval they caused. In June 1829, planters reported that in various locations around the island, gangs of runaway slaves were preparing to attack the estates. Governor David Stewart (1829) believed the planters and on 6 April 1829, and again on 29 September, reported to London that actual insurrections were taking place. The September revolt, he wrote, was the direct result of

> *... the injudicious interference of a gentleman, who, in presence of more than one hundred negroes, severely reprimanded the manager of an Estate for permitting a cat in the hands of the driver: ... the public interference was construed by the Slaves into an absolute freedom from labour, seeing that the First President* [John Jeremie] *had said, that there was to be no more whip, no more punishment. ... That week, there were only two hogsheads of sugar made by these people, instead of nine, the usual number. Work was nearly at a stand. The news rapidly spread. Slaves not only refused to work, but when compelled, they destroyed their master's property ... and in all parts of the country, numbers left their masters and fled to the woods and mountains.*[244]

Stewart sent investigators to the out-districts but they found little or no evidence of violence, beyond a few slaves who had run away '*deceived by false reports, & led to believe, that the king had made them free, and that they were to work no more for their masters ... it would be cruel to punish poor ignorant people; I therefore gave directions to explain to the Slaves in the clearest manner the nature of the new law, and to caution them as to their future conduct.*[245]

Stewart also sent militiamen into the woods '*with directions to make a great noise - to fire blank cartridges in every place, where there was an appearance of the runaways being, and to make large fires in short, to frighten & show these misguided people, that the woods were no shelter for them as they had hitherto been ... and that their masters' house was their surest place of safety.*' At the same time, he ordered estate owners not to punish returning runaways. Within a fortnight, Stewart reported to London, '*The deserters came in, and surrendered themselves in all parts of the Colony. Fifteen people returned to one estate in a body. ... One slave came in, who had been 16 years in the mountains. ... One man who had been out 8 years; - in endeavouring to make his escape down a precipice, when surprised by a party of the militia, fell over a rock, and was so much injured, that he died in a few days. Since then, the slaves have been quiet.*'

John Jeremie later described the September revolt as a panic caused by deliberate '*agitation*' of '*the ultra-colonial party in the Colony*': a relatively small group of planters who felt that the amelioration laws were making them the laughing stock of their relatives in Martinique and Guadeloupe. Twice in 1829, wrote Jeremie, they raised the alarm, only for Governor Stewart's militias to find that the dreaded insurrection consisted of '*exactly eight negroes in the bush, including females.*'[246]

Martiniquan refugees in St Lucia

Although essentially a non-event, the September revolt of 1829 may have had an unforeseen effect on slaves in the neighbouring island. Within weeks, runaway slaves from Martinique started arriving on the shores of St Lucia. Initially, their number was small and the St Lucian authorities were unsure how to respond. Under the British prohibition on slave trade, Governor Stewart was neither allowed to accept them as slaves nor to sell them on. In the end, he sent some back to Martinique and others on to Sierra Leone in Africa. In the debate that followed, it was discovered that a directive *did* in fact exist: a ruling known as Dr Lushington's Bill, which declared that a foreign slave upon reaching a British colony was automatically freed.[247] Governor Stewart had been unaware of this at the time but after his death in late 1829, the *Procureur du Roi* informed the remaining Martiniquan runaways that as long as they behaved themselves, they would come under the protection of the British Government and could stay on in St Lucia as free men and women.[248]

Word of this must have found its way back to Martinique and the following year (1830) saw more than 100 Martiniquan slaves risking the dangerous crossing to St Lucia – or, as one unhappy planter described it: '*swarms of them deserted to St Lucia every week.*'[249] The period 1831-8 saw a steady flow of runaway slaves from Martinique arriving in St Lucia and although no records were kept, by the end of the period their total number was estimated at 600 to 800. How many were lost at sea is unknown but hundreds may have drowned, since '*it is no unusual occurrence to see twelve or fifteen men and women land on the coast of St Lucia, from a canoe in which five persons could not sit at their ease.*'[250]

The crossing was at best twenty miles long, and more often 30 or 40 miles, depending on where the refugees set out from. The waves in the St Lucia Channel are high and treacherous and in bad weather, a small boat or canoe can easily capsize or go adrift. Some boats may have had sails but most refugees appear to have used oars to paddle across. Besides these natural challenges, Martinique soon developed a system of espionage to prevent runaways from leaving. The coastguard was highly vigilant as well, to the point where in 1836, a French ship pursuing a refugee boat with three women and one man on board came so close to the coast of St Lucia that Lieutenant-Governor Dudley Hill (1834-7) ordered an artillery officer to shoot at the French ship.[251] It is believed that in more cases than one, runaway slaves chose to jump overboard and swim or drown rather than be caught by the French coastguards. One source mentioned that '*No less than ten corpses have been lately thrown ashore together, in one small bay of Gros Islet*'[252] - all presumed to be Martiniquan refugees.

Besides the 'pull' of promised freedom in St Lucia, political events in Martinique in 1831 also helped to induce slaves to leave friends and family behind and risk the crossing. In July 1830, France experienced a bourgeois revolution which brought to power the entrepreneurial and well-to-do middle class under the monarchy of King Louis Philippe I. This event became known as the July Revolution. Notions of equality, freedom and opportunity for all were voiced once again in France and by late 1830, these notions were being picked up in Martinique and Guadeloupe as well, carried there by publications and political-minded travellers.[253]

This naturally set off echoes of the French Revolution and before long, slaves in Martinique were conspiring to revolt. Originally planned for 24 December 1830, they had had to delay their uprising until 9 February 1831. On that morning, eleven sugar estates and three houses were set on fire. But by then, the planters had gotten wind of the plans and the troops were prepared.[254] Martial law was declared and numerous people were arrested. Henry Breen, who happened to be in Martinique, attended the two-week trial in which 22 ringleaders (including a free man of colour, Chéry) were handed the death penalty. Breen also attended the public execution. Not a man ordinarily given to much sentimentality, he was clearly intimidated by what he saw on the black and brown faces around him: '*the strained resignation of the multitude, and the studied composure of their looks, the rage and rancour of the boiling spirit within.*'[255] Breen later recalled that '*the most striking circumstance connected with* [the execution] *(apart from the shocking spectacle of so many persons put to death on the same gallows) was the* sang-froid *with which most of the prisoners met their fate. There was no sign of faint-heartedness, no irresolution; and each man in his turn walked up the ladder, before the hangman, without assistance.*'[256]

Martinique had a much larger slave population than St Lucia (70 000 against St Lucia's 16 000 in 1803) and the deep hatred and resentment following the failed 1831 insurrection prompted hundreds of them to flee to St Lucia or Dominica (also British-held). It is estimated that in total, some 4000 people fled Martinique: some succeeding, others perishing in the act.[257] In July 1831, 204 Martiniquan refugees were reported to be living in St Lucia; 301 by September 1832; 400 by March 1836; 600 by December 1836, and '*more than 600*' and possibly as many as 800 by 1838.[258]

The planters in Martinique were hugely indignant at the British Government's refusal to send back their runaway slaves and in St Lucia, many planters were embarrassed by their Government's support and alleged 'encouragement' of the '*deserters*' and '*vagabonds*'. This atmosphere perhaps explains the diversity of public opinion held about the refugees. Stipendiary magistrates in some districts echoed the conservative planters' view, saying the Martiniquan refugees '*form, with few exceptions an indolent Class, whose ambition is only ... to be usurpers of small tracts of Land in the interior, where they grow provisions and burn charcoal for the market. The greater number constantly lounging about the Streets in Castries satisfying their natural wants with the small stipends occasionally bestowed upon them by the persons employing them.*[259]

The stipendiary magistrate for Vieux Fort and Laborie reported that the refugees worked, but that '*steady industry*' was not their forte. '*They are Logwood-Cutters, Charcoal-Burners, Squatters, Jobbers, Fishermen and Boatmen by terms as suits their convenience. They are any thing and every thing but field labourers, and prefer any mode of livelihood to that gained by steady industry.*'[260]

What this actually reveals is that the Martiniquans clearly relished their independence. They were not shy of working hard (charcoal-making and cutting logwood were some of the most physically demanding jobs) but they refused to perform a slave's labour on agricultural estates. Autonomy was the key word in their labour strategies - the one thing they had never had as slaves. And it was exactly this aspect of their lifestyle which so irritated government officials. The stipendiary magistrate for Micoud, Praslin and Dennery conceded that he had '*never entertained a favourable opinion of the Martinique Refugees.*' They spread over St Lucia '*without being under the slightest degree of surveillance - one day a party of them may be found at one point, the next gone. ... they straggle where they please leading a wandering life - The greater part of their time passed in listless idleness - by night they traverse the Country after the Women ... at dances they perform a prominent part, keeping up intelligence with the runaway Apprentices, and informing them of all the movements of the Police &c.*'[261]

Other stipendiary magistrates held more positive views. The official for Gros Islet and Dauphin, for instance, reported in 1838, that '*there are from 50 to 60 Refugees, (with the exception of 5) - located upon lands either hired by them or ...* [which] *have been abandoned ... where they are chiefly occupied in planting Provisions and burning Charcoal. The five individuals, before alluded to, are employed on the Grand Anse Estate as field labourers and receive a monthly allowance of 16/8 Stlg., with sufficient ground for gardens.*'[262]

In Soufrière/Choiseul, the stipendiary magistrate reported that:

> *... there are not more than twelve to fourteen of them resident and all of them are industrious and I can add sober in their habits - Three are employed in the Pirogues, two or three have made permanent engagements as agriculturalists on some of the neighbouring Estates. The only female Refugee in this Quarter is an industrious washer-woman - and one Man is the head-workman in the newly established Pottery of Mr Tesné. This last individual deserves much grace as he has introduced the manufacture of tiles, bricks, &c., which promises much benefit to this Colony.*'[263]

Pottery seems to have been pioneered in St Lucia by Martiniquan refugees. John Jeremie recalled that, in 1831

> *... about twenty-six had clubbed together and placed themselves under the direction of a free coloured man, an African - one of the persons deported from Martinique in 1824. These last had erected a pottery at a short distance from Castries: they took a piece of land, three or four cleared it, others fished up coral and burnt lime, five or six quarried and got the stones and performed the mason-work, the remainder felled the timber and worked it in; and the little money that was requisite was supplied, in advance, by the contractor for the church, on the tiles to be furnished for the building. This pottery was completed, a plain structure, but of great solidity, and surprising neatness. Thus had they actually introduced a new manufacture into the country, for which it was previously indebted to our foreign neighbours, or to the home market. All this had been effected simply by not interfering with them, by leaving them entirely to themselves: they were mustered once a month, to shew that government had an eye on them, and then allowed full liberty. One man only was sick in the hospital, and he was supported by the contributions of his companions.*[264]

Jeremie's opponents derided the pottery scheme, saying it had '*turned out to be a complete failure*'[265] and calling the men involved vagabonds and robbers. But Sturge and Harvey, who visited in December 1836, corroborated Jeremie's findings.

> *There are six hundred refugees in this island, and it is allowed that they contribute to the prosperity of the colony. They introduced at Castries, the manufacture of tiles, and the porous water jars, so extensively used in the West Indies. One gentleman, whom we visited, has one of them in his service as a groom, and spoke highly of his industry and good behaviour. The young man himself told us he did not love his own country, 'it was no good.' The majority of the refugees, it is said, bear an indifferent character, but it is only surprising that they are not totally demoralised and discouraged by the conduct of the government and proprietary body towards them.*[266]

The sort of discouragement they encountered was exemplified by the plight of one Martiniquan refugee who lived on a hillside in the Roseau Valley. '*One of them has a little plantation of canes, which he manufactures into sugar, in a small, crudely constructed mill, and sells in Castries. This display of industry and enterprise, excited the jealousy of a neighbouring planter, who prosecuted the man for stealing two trees from his estate, to make a boat.*'

The refugee managed to prove that '*he felled the trees on the bit of ground which had been given him to clear and cultivate for himself*' - but it shows the kind of petty-minded oppression they experienced. As we will see, the rise of an independent class of wage labourers, peasants, fishermen and charcoal burners after Emancipation in 1838 evoked similar responses and comments from those in authority.

Slavery was abolished in the British islands in 1838 and in the French islands ten years later, in 1848. Martiniquan refugees continued to arrive in St Lucia after 1838 but now having to compete for jobs and land with 15 000 newly freed people, many chose to move on to other British colonies, such as Demerara (British Guiana) and Trinidad.[267] Even after 1848, newly freed men and women continued to travel from Martinique to St Lucia, attracted by '*the fertile soil, the cheapness of the price of land, and very often by their family connexions.*'[268] After 1848, some return migration occurred also, with refugees rejoining their newly liberated families in Martinique. Basically, since 1848, as one official put it: '*People come and go as they please*' between Martinique and St Lucia.

St Lucian refugees in Martinique

Surprisingly, after 1831, some St Lucian slaves sought refuge in Martinique as well. The reason for this sudden movement is not entirely clear. One possible explanation is that St Lucian slaves had heard of the 1830 July Revolution in France and believed that slavery would soon be abolished in the French colonies again, as it had been in 1794. Another explanation was suggested by

Governor James Farquharson (1832-1834), who told of a rumour circulating in St Lucia to the effect that '*the Governor of Martinique has offered asylum and a peculiar reward of a dabloon each to all Slaves who can escape from hence and reach the Island he governs.*' Farquharson sent an investigator to Martinique to ascertain the truth of this rumour but the findings of that inquiry are unknown.

Whatever or whoever prompted it: on the night of 13 June 1831, two-and-a-half miles off the coast of Martinique, a French schooner (the *Jopaze*) picked up a canoe with ten slaves belonging to two estates in St Lucia. They were brought to the slave prison at Fort Royal in Martinique and later returned to their respective owners in St Lucia '*upon security that no punishment shall be inflicted.*' A year later, in October 1832, a boat with seven or eight slaves from the Roseau Estate was intercepted before reaching Martinique and a second canoe with thirteen slaves (twelve belonging to Perle Estate in the valley of Roseau and one from Bois d'Orange Estate) was captured in the Caribbean Sea just off Marigot des Roseaux.

Other St Lucian slaves were more successful in their bids for freedom. They invariably seem to have originated from plantations in the Grand Cul de Sac and Roseau areas along the north-west coast, '*arising no doubt from the facility they have of secreting Boats in the Rivers of these Quarters.*' The authorities in St Lucia reinforced existing laws which forbade slaves to own or use boats without written permission from their owners or managers, but the escape attempts continued. By November 1832, '*about 21 have effected their escape and landed in* [Martinique], *where I understand, they are employed by the Government of that Colony in cutting timber for some public purpose but I cannot ascertain whether as bond or free men.*' In November 1832, two planters sailed to Martinique to personally investigate the matter. One of them, a Mr Noel, discovered

> *... that they are caused to work from 6 o'clock in the morning until 6 at night, that they receive 5 dogs per day wages (about 3/2 Sterling) and fed and clothed by the French government. And that the nominal list of them is called every night when they are shut up until the hour of labour the following morning ... that the Slaves from Mr Muter's Estate of Roseau declared that they were well used upon that Estate but that nevertheless they preferred their present line of life as to being upon a plantation. They are employed in filling up a swamp.*

The other investigator, a planter by the name of James Scott, spoke with eight slaves who had also escaped from the Roseau Estate. They told him '*they would not return as they were well clothed, fed and lodged, that they had white bread and beef, the same as the soldiers, and some received 12 and the rest 8 sous per day.*'

A few weeks later, seven of the 21 St Lucian refugees in Martinique voluntarily decided to return to their estates in St Lucia and had done so by January 1833. After that, new extensive restrictions on the use of boats in Grand Cul de Sac and Roseau cut down on the number of escapees, although it did not stop the phenomenon altogether. As late as December 1836, six men and one woman from Roseau Estate were convicted as criminals for having attempted to run away to Martinique, '*at the instigation of a refugee, who had persuaded them, that the French, by way of reprisal, had determined to set all British apprentices free, who came over to them.*' All seven were sentenced to six months imprisonment and hard labour. '*At the request of the proprietor, they were allowed to remain on the estate, working under the superintendence of the rural police, and being locked up at night.*'[269]

7

The rise of a free peasantry: 'from whip to wages'

The special midnight Mass of 31 July 1834 was well attended throughout the British West Indies. In St Lucia, 13 285 men, women and children thanked the Lord for setting them free from slavery at long last. All across the British colonies (except in Antigua), slavery was replaced by the apprenticeship system: a transition period allegedly needed to teach ex-slaves how to handle the privileges and obligations of full freedom. For personal slaves, apprenticeship was meant to last four years and for field slaves six. But full freedom was granted to all on 1 August 1838. Under apprenticeship, ex-slaves continued to be tied to their former masters for 40 hours of unpaid labour per week. After that, they could do as they pleased: grow their own provisions, work extra hours as estate labourers, perform a trade or not work at all. Apprenticeship was neither slavery nor full freedom but apprentices soon learned to test their new autonomy by demanding increasingly higher wages during crop time. Disagreements abounded, which were dealt with by special magistrates to whom both planters and apprentices could appeal.

Apprenticeship was a concession granted by the British Government to the West Indian planters, who feared that immediate and full Emancipation would cause an exodus of workers from the estates. Planters' primary concern, always, was to control labour and to do so at the lowest possible cost. Planters feared that ex-slaves would become indolent in a climate which easily satisfied their basic needs; they feared the emergence of an independent peasant class (reasoning that if peasants started growing food crops, labour was diverted away from sugar production) and they even feared the idea of ex-slaves becoming sugar cane farmers, resenting the bargaining power this would inevitably give them. And so, planters' primary aim was, and remained, to control the labour output of the freed slaves.

But the planters did not hold a strong hand of cards. For one, St Lucia did not have a high population density like Barbados or Antigua, where land was scarce and the onus was on freed workers to find willing employers in order to survive. St Lucian planters also lacked the cash to increase wages to attract labourers. With profits already marginal, higher wages would push the cost of production beyond revenue levels. Finally, while some of the larger colonies (such as British Guiana, Trinidad and Jamaica) managed to initiate extensive labour immigration projects, St Lucia's scale of operations was too small for this. As we will see in the next chapter, there actually was some immigration of European, African and East Indian contract workers into St Lucia but this had no real impact on the labour market issue- certainly not immediately after Emancipation.

And so the only instrument open to the ruling class in St Lucia to control the labour force was legislative action. For half a century, the plantocracy opposed and sabotaged the rise of an independent peasant class in any legal way it could think of. The sheer fact that a peasantry *did* nevertheless emerge attests to the immense drive shown by the freed population in wanting to become independent, land-owning economic and social operators. What is more, the injustices they suffered in trying to gain access to the soil on which they had been born, created a new sense of class awareness. By the end of the nineteenth century, working men and women in St Lucia understood the value of their labour and were learning how to strategically use this as a political tool. It was the bud that eventually flowered into an indigenous trade union movement.

Compensation payments

Apprenticeship gave planters a first taste of what full Emancipation would bring. In many a planter's mind, imminent ruin loomed large. Some planters waited only long enough to cash in on the compensation payments and then bailed out. The majority, however, stayed on, hoping to use the money to eliminate debts and place their estates on a new footing. Initially, Britain had offered a £15 million loan to appease the slave owners and quell opposition to Emancipation. But the still-powerful planters' lobby persuaded the Colonial Office that an outright grant of £20 million would be much more effective. Compensation payment was calculated according to the relative value of slaves per island, and the age and status of each individual. In St Lucia, planters received a total of £342 155 for 13 285 slaves. A break-down shows that they were paid £31 on average per slave for 8725 field slaves; £30 per slave for 1600 non-field slaves, £8 per slave for every child under the age of six (of whom there were 1960) and £8 for every aged and infirm slave, of whom there were exactly 1000.[270]

The rationale behind compensation was that England had originally allowed the system of slavery to exist, thereby encouraging planters to invest their private money into buying and maintaining slaves. Now that the British Government had changed its mind - and laws - on the issue, it was effectively confiscating capital investments (slaves) from hitherto lawful owners (planters), and so it ought to compensate the planters for their financial loss. Once that was done, planters could fairly be expected to pay a living wage in return for labour received. '*From whip to wages*' was the catch-phrase of the day.[271]

No consideration of monetary compensation for the ex-slaves entered into the equation - although Chief Justice John Jeremie admitted that England, '*In justice ... owes a vast reparation*' and the West India Royal Commission of 1897 expressed the sentiment that Britain had a '*special and unusually strong obligation*' towards the freed slaves, since '*We have placed the labouring population where it is, and created for it the conditions, moral and material, under which it exists, and we cannot divest ourselves of the responsibility for its future.*'[272]

The irony of exodus

Full emancipation came on 1 August 1838. This memorable day, too, passed without the upheaval and disruptions feared by the authorities. Even the planters' main trepidation - an exodus of freed people from the estates - did not immediately occur. When workers eventually *did* leave the estates, it was not so much to flee the memories of the horrors of slavery but, ironically, came as a result of planters' attempts to make them stay. During slavery, planters had held certain obligations towards their slaves: they had had to provide shelter, provision grounds, rations of food and clothing and medical care. With Emancipation, these responsibilities expired and the sick and elderly, in particular, found themselves in a difficult position, suddenly dependent on relatives and friends. Local administrators eventually put in place taxes and institutions to deal with the tasks of providing hospitals, pauper asylums and schools but this all took some time to come on stream.

An even bigger shock to the newly freed people was that they lost the free use of their homes and gardens. Few ex-slaves in St Lucia were actively evicted after 1 August 1838 but the possibility existed and planters were quick to introduce this into their negotiations with workers. It was a costly mistake. Knowing only one mode of interaction with the former slaves - confrontation and complete domination - planters did not pause to consider what aims and aspirations the newly freed people themselves held. Instead, they second-guessed freed people's motivations, feared what they anticipated (an exodus from the estates, labour shortages and financial ruin) and tried to forcibly prevent this. Ironically, in doing so, their fears became a self-fulfilling prophecy.

As Douglas Hall argues (1993), much as they had obviously hated working under the whip, ex-slaves were actually quite attached to their houses and provision gardens on the plantations, which they perceived of as private space: 'home' in a hostile environment. Many freed people were reluctant to pack up and leave the place where they had been born. Given freedom from slavery and a genuine choice, most were happy to remain near the large plantations: growing provisions in their gardens for themselves and the local market, and working for cash whenever they chose to. Not taking this sentimental attachment to 'home' into account, planters began to use their newly gained right of eviction as a means of controlling labour.

Initially, they proposed that freed slaves could only continue to live in their houses and grow their gardens free of rent if they donated their labour to the estates as and when needed. Workers deeply resented this, feeling that while freedom was given to them with one hand, the other hand robbed them of the roofs over their heads and the gardens that sustained them.

In an alternative proposal, planters allowed ex-slaves to stay on as tenants paying rent. Although obscuring the connection between work and home/garden somewhat, this continued to tie workers into a bond with one particular planter – and many opted to leave instead. The third option was one whereby the labourer paid rent for his house and garden but was at liberty to work at any estate of his choice. This conclusively severed the hated tie with *massa* and was for many freed workers the most congenial solution.

Just as with the Martiniquan refugees a decade earlier, it was their sense of autonomy that primarily motivated freed workers' labour strategies, not a blind revulsion of estate labour. And so the harder planters tried to restrict and control the movement of labour, the more the former slaves felt the need to exert their new-found autonomy. When freed people left the estates, they did so not to escape the memories of slavery but to protest the inequities and disappointments of freedom.

Caught between colonial officers and planters

Unable to rely on land scarcity or high wages to tie labourers to their estates, planters in St Lucia applied their power in local Government to pass laws which made it difficult for labourers to gain access to land as tenants or owners. Land prices were artificially inflated and vagrancy laws put into effect. The imposition of a land tax and licensing fees on horses and other means of transport further hampered provision agriculture and the marketing of produce.

Until the 1890s, British government officials acquiesced to the planters' notion that the growth of an independent peasant class was likely to undermine social and economic stability. Colonial administrators and planters alike continued to perceive of St Lucia primarily as an agricultural export economy in the service of Britain. Logically then, maintaining the plantation system was their number one priority. There was little or no conception of the needs of the vast majority of people who *made up* St Lucia's society. Society had to mould itself around the demands of the economy, and agricultural export was the only economic scenario planters, merchants and administrators could envisage. It was a dangerous case of tunnel vision.

Meanwhile, freed people were developing their own agendas. Maintenance of the plantation export economy was obviously not *their* first priority (although they were not averse to exploiting it when it suited them). Their first priority was ownership or tenancy of land. Despite constant opposition and sabotage from the plantocracy, during the second half of the nineteenth century, many ex-slaves managed to carve out a niche for themselves in the local economy as free peasants. Slowly (and increasingly so as the years rolled on), their successes prompted policy makers in the Colonial Office in London to remove their blinkers, as it dawned on them that there was intrinsic social and economic value in the development of an indigenous peasantry.

It is important to keep in mind that at the time, St Lucia was governed as a Crown Colony. This meant that although the island had a Legislative Council (made up of *official members* such as the Governor, Treasurer and Attorney-General, and an equal number of *unofficial members* appointed by the Governor and chosen from the ranks of prominent planters and merchants) with some law-making powers, this council came under direct orders of the Secretary of State for the Colonies, who was based at the Colonial Office in London. The (Lieutenant-)Governor, who reported directly to the Colonial Office, held two votes on the Legislative Council, and hence could usually sway a stalemate. On broad policy lines, Orders in Council from the Colonial Office in London dictated what could, and could not, happen in St Lucia. The Governor and the Legislative Council in St Lucia sent reports and (tax) proposals to the Secretary of State, decided how the local budget was spent and passed on petitions and memoranda from members of society. But in essence, St Lucia was governed from London.

It was the Colonial Office in London which had forced through amelioration and the abolition of slavery against the wishes of local planters - creating the conditions in which a colonial officer such as President of the Royal Court, John Jeremie, had to walk a hazardous tightrope. But Jeremie was an exception. More commonly, the various Englishmen sent out to St Lucia were career civil servants whose main priorities were their next assignments, personal comfort and, in some cases, financial gain. The less upheaval they encountered, the easier their temporary postings were. Hence, as a rule, British colonial officers did not seek to rock the boat - especially not on behalf of the labouring majority, whom they usually could not understand, had little interaction with, and no particular reason to care about. Their main diversion and entertainment usually lay in monitoring and commenting on each other's affairs and those of the upper-class Creole St Lucians (planters, merchants and professionals) with whom they interacted. Gossip and meddling were favourite pastimes of the upper-class, occasionally resulting in pretty outrageous public feuds.[273]

Meanwhile, the island's large planters (most of whom lived on estates in the out districts), while using what influence they had in Government to keep workers dependent on wages, repeatedly found themselves at loggerheads with the colonial administrators, particularly over the issue of taxation.[274] The salaries of public servants in St Lucia were paid for by the export tax and import duties taken from the pockets of the planters, and they resented every penny of it. They pleaded with the Colonial Office to have at least the Governor's salary paid for out of imperial funds instead of their own allegedly meagre pockets, but to no avail. Although planters were represented in the Legislative Council as unofficial members and had easy social access to the powers-that-be (yielding them a measure of political influence the masses could only dream of), they did not have a direct vote or direct representation. And so the mid and late nineteenth century was characterized by mounting frustrations among large planters who, while controlling almost all of the island's economic resources, had virtually no direct political power. As we will see shortly, a huge fraud scandal in the treasury office further marred relations between planters and administrators. Ironically, the more planters clamoured for direct political power, the more the Colonial Office felt it needed to protect the completely powerless class of peasants and labourers, and the less it was inclined to yield to the planters' requests.

In this complicated political and administrative context, a peasant class emerged in St Lucia after 1838, against enormous odds. Peasants were so successful that by 1890, they not only provided the local market with food crops but also contributed about one-fifth of all sugar cane grown in St Lucia. By the end of the century, St Lucia's export economy had become quite dependent on the contributions of small peasants. A crucially important mechanism which enabled this rise of an independent, land-owning peasantry from the ranks of the landless ex-slaves lay in a system of land tenure known as *métayage*.

Métayage and the rise of a peasantry

Métayage (or *métairie*) is a form of sharecropping originally developed in the middle of the twelfth century in France, when money first penetrated rural life there.[275] Métayage is said to have been used in St Lucia on the earliest cotton and coffee estates,[276] presumably back in the seventeenth and early eighteenth centuries when estates were worked primarily with white labour.

It was rekindled shortly after Emancipation, in 1839 or 1840. Basically, a métayer is someone who works on another man's land, using that man's tools and equipment, in exchange for half the produce thus cultivated. With labour in short supply, ex-slaves searching for autonomy and a lot of planters so seriously indebted that they did not have the cash to pay wages, the system was ideally suited for St Lucia. Métayage agreements were usually verbal and deliberately vague, which worked to the advantage of the planter. The planter supplied the labourer with one carré of land (about 3 1/3 acre) to be cultivated by him in canes. The métayer was responsible for planting, weeding and manuring the canes and sometimes also for cutting and hauling them to the factory at crop time. In other cases, the costs of cutting and hauling were shared equally by planter and labourer. The planter was responsible for providing the land, tools, carts, animals and a mill or factory to process the canes. In return for his labour, the métayer received half the sugar produced from the canes on his carré of land. The planter received the other half, as well as all the rum and molasses. If a métayer was given a field of canes already in ratoons (eliminating the need to plant) his share of the proceeds was lower (one-third or one-fourth). Usually, the métayer had to wait until the planter had shipped the sugar to England before he was paid. In some cases, he was given his share of sugar, which he could then sell back to the planter (in return for cash, at the going market rate), sell to someone else, or ship to England himself.

Métayage was often a source of dispute. The agreements gave the métayer little guarantee of rights of possession, security of tenure or claim on crops. Métayers were dependent on planters' honesty in calculating their shares and many disputes resulted from suspicions of swindling. Métayers frequently accused planters of not dividing the sugar equally, of overcharging them for the cost of cutting, haulage and processing, and of fiddling the accounts. They also complained that planters preferred to make more molasses than sugar or that planters processed their own canes first, leaving the métayers' canes in the field until the sugar content had dropped or the canes had become infested with rats. In rare cases, métayers' canes were never harvested at all.

Although métayage contracts were agreed upon for a number of years, métayers had no real security for the future. They sometimes cleared land, dug canals for drainage, built homes and enclosures and planted canes from scratch - only to be evicted at the end of the first season. Stipendiary magistrates, who had been appointed at the time of Emancipation to mediate in conflicts between labourers and employers, tried to resolve métayage conflicts - but the métayer's legal position was unclear and hence even the magistrates could exercise little judicial power. The problem was that métayers considered themselves tenants who leased land and paid their rent in kind, while planters considered métayers labourers who were paid their wages in kind. The difference proved key and it took two important court cases and a new Ordinance to settle the matter.

The first court case resulted from a conflict on Sapphire Estate (near Laborie) in 1843. It is described in detail by Woodville Marshall.[277] The estate had been leased out, but the lessee had fallen badly behind on his payments and so the owner obtained a court order allowing him to seize all the sugar produced that year, by way of compensation.

> *The metayers, with oral contracts, had been unaware of the lessee's indebtedness and they only discovered their error of omission when their sugar was seized along with the rest of the estate's sugar. The stipendiary magistrates and the Attorney General interceded on their behalf, but without success. The Chief Justice ruled that since he could find no evidence of a metayage contract (and in any case the lessee had no authority under his lease to use the metayage system) the metayers were entitled to one month's wages. Clearly, the Chief Justice was inclined to treat the metayers as labourers.*

But a year later, the Attorney General overturned a local court decision which had refused to let two métayers at Rabot estate claim their crops when the heavily encumbered estate was sold by judicial sale. The Attorney General argued that the métayers' contract was in effect a lease of land, not a labour contract and that therefore métayers had the rights of tenants, including ownership of their crops. The Attorney-General's enlightened view was backed up by local and metropolitan opinion and by 1844, both the Colonial Secretary, Lord Stanley, and St Lucia's Governor, Grey, advised that the métayer was '*a tenant paying rent in kind*' and that it was important to encourage his long-term security. '*The longer the term, indeed the greater the interest in the land, and the approximation to ownership which it is so important to encourage.*' It was the first time colonial authorities went out of their way to argue that the rise of a peasantry would enhance social stability in the colony - and it is important to note this, because it is often believed that until the 1890s, British officials tacitly supported the plantocracy's opposition to the rise of an independent peasantry.[278] The Colonial Office even undertook attempts to 'export' métayage to other British West Indian islands (in particular Tobago and Grenada).

But the plantocracy in St Lucia remained largely unconvinced of the long-term social and economic benefits of métayage and continued to fret about losing control over labour and land. The planters were afraid of becoming dependent on an autonomous class of farmers who, they believed, were essentially apathetic and indolent in nature. To planters, métayage was '*a desperate expedient*': a necessary evil to be used only in dire times and to be abandoned as soon as possible. They used métayage to retain ownership of their estates and to produce a crop at times when profits were marginal - but only to 'tread water' while waiting for better prices on the world market.

> *Renee Augier proprietor of Mount Lizard estate in St Lucia and one of the first planters to convert an estate* [to] *metayage cultivation, spoke for many planters when he declared in 1842: 'From the impossibility to which I find myself reduced and with the full knowledge I have of the country ... I consider that there remains but this experiment in the art of cultivation to sustain our manufactories until more prosperous times may, with the blessing of Providence, arrive.'*

Labourers, for their part, leapt at métayage with alacrity and enthusiasm and between 1840 and the mid 1850s, the system boomed in St Lucia. Marshall wrote:

> *As early as December 1840, the proprietor of Beau Sejour estate had received so many applications for metayage contracts that he said that within two years he could cultivate his estate completely on the system. In 1844, M. Beauce proprietor of Anse Canot estate, was encouraged to buy the neighbouring estate so that he could 'meet the demands of his labourers for more land to clear away and plant in canes' on the metayage system. Stipendiary magistrate de Brossard reported that the neighbouring planters were so impressed by this display that they were following Beauce's example. By the end of the same year, all estates appeared to be using the system to some extent, and by 1848, metayage was responsible for a quarter of the sugar cane cultivation. Stipendiary magistrate Drysdale reported in 1848 that metayage labour had produced 8768 cwts of one district's total sugar crop of 19 881 cwts.*

Peter Adrien, in his study of métayage in St Lucia, concluded that métayage allowed many labourers to accumulate enough money to buy land and become independent peasants, thus creating socio-economic diversification within the class of freed slaves. In 1840, one métayer had been so successful at growing canes that he had earned '*by his industry £60 per annum ... In addition, these canes were cultivated on Saturdays, holidays and during his spare time only, whilst all the rest of his time was spent working and receiving daily wages as a general labourer on the property, with free tenancy of house and provision grounds. His young children also ... acquired habits of industry and knowledge whilst assisting their parents by carrying plants and manure to his cane piece.*' Adrien calculated that this man probably earned £12 10s per year as a general labourer. '*Therefore ... he obtained at least five times the yearly income of a first class labourer for that year. In another district metayers cultivating 184 acres of canes produced over 285 hogsheads of sugar for an approximate share of £24 1s 6d.*'[279]

While planters initially adopted métayage as a stopgap measure, the continuing crisis in the sugar industry between 1846 and 1855 forced them to accept it as a more permanent feature. In 1846, England passed the Sugar Duties Act which removed preferential treatment of sugar from British West Indian colonies in the British market, forcing it to compete with sugar from elsewhere. The changes were gradually effected between 1846 and 1854 but the act was received with '*gloomy forecasts of utter ruin*.'[280] Brazil, Cuba and Louisiana all produced sugar at significantly lower prices than the British West Indies and the competition was crushing. In 1848, a Commission of Enquiry recognized the serious distress caused by the Sugar Duties Act but did not have it repealed. Instead, some financial assistance was provided to the larger West Indian islands for labour immigration schemes and the like. The overall effect of the Sugar Duties Act was a concentration of the sugar industry in a few favoured territories (Barbados, St Kitts, Antigua, Trinidad and British Guiana) and a rapid decline in the other islands. Matters only became worse when, in 1849, England repealed the Navigation Acts, abolishing protection in favour of free trade.

And so the crisis in the sugar industry deepened. Following the bankruptcy of several West Indian sugar merchant houses in Britain, the Legislative Council in St Lucia lamented the disastrous state of commerce in the island and its repercussions on the labouring population. Already, wages had been cut by 25 to 50 per cent and with the prospect of no more capital forthcoming from English merchant houses or the Colonial Bank, planters were hard-pressed to find ways of paying even these reduced amounts. By 1851-2, it was estimated that there was less than £10 000 in species circulating in St Lucia and only half that amount in notes. Planters and merchants often lacked the cash to pay workers and in the end resorted to a system of IOUs whereby labourers received a note to say how much money the planter owed them. Quickly, the system became so pervasive that the IOU notes virtually replaced cash money, with shop keepers accepting IOU notes in exchange for goods of equal value. The system was abused occasionally (e.g., when shopkeepers forced labourers to sell their IOUs at a discounted rate) but on the whole, it acted as a successful shadow system of monetary exchange which saved the local economy from total collapse at a time of grave monetary constraint.[281]

Unsurprisingly, 1847 and subsequent years were boom years for métayage, with métayers reportedly earning up to twelve and fourteen times more per annum than able-bodied first-class labourers. The main advantage métayers had over planters when it came to cultivating sugar cane at a low cost lay in the fact that they had access to free or very cheap labour, using family labour and *coup-de-main* (a reciprocal non-monetary labour arrangement). Only the largest métayers occasionally hired wage labourers.[282]

An analysis of production costs on six estates in St Lucia during 1847 by Lieutenant-Governor Charles Henry Darling (1848-51) revealed that the only two estates that showed a profit were those operating on métayage - one completely and the other partially. All others incurred losses.[283] It was quite obvious that planters and métayers had common interests and that during periods of crisis, métayage was the only respite from complete ruin for many estates, large and small. And yet planters continued to bemoan métayage and oppose its extension and formalization. They lamented their loss of control over the labour force, claiming that métayers often practiced slovenly and un-'planter-like' cultivation practices which reduced the sugar content of the canes. Planters also resented their dependence on the co-operation of métayers in the sugar manufacturing process at the factory, which they felt was unreliable and put the entire operation at risk.

Some of St Lucia's stipendiary magistrates (including James Johnston: the man who had advocated legal equality for free people of colour back in the 1820s) heralded the cause of the métayers and tried to convince planters of the advantages of '*establishing an intermediate class of tenant employees*' rather than continue their '*interference with the distribution of labour*' which only served to raise the cost of production. But to little avail. Johnston sadly concluded that too many planters were either '*blind to their own interest*' or '*considered it a species of unworthy apostasy to yield to anything bearing the character of an innovation.*'

Yet it was thanks to métayage that the amount of land under sugar cane increased even though the supply of waged labour steadily declined. Métayage was '*Emancipation in action*': drawing into agriculture a range of people who had either left the sector or had always looked down on work in the cane fields. They included

> *... the residents in the newly established villages and the creole lower middle class. The appearance of the latter was especially significant. This class included the poor whites and the coloureds, the 'respectable' individuals, 'people of higher class than mere labourer,' and 'numerous small proprietors and tradesmen free from birth and who can look forward for a year or two.' Earlier, these individuals had considered labour in sugar cane as 'degrading,' but now they sought metayage contracts and ... 'generally do well.'*

This was especially important because it brought about a degree of social cohesion between the old-time free people of colour and the newly-freed slaves that had been unknown up until that moment. James Johnston himself remarked that métayage helped to promote '*that good understanding which has always been so desirable but which has not been hitherto manifested by the old free and later emancipated class towards each other.*'

Supporters of métayage lauded the socially stabilizing effects of a middle class of métayers and peasants. As land owners, they naturally identified their own interests with the peace and prosperity of the country as a whole. In 1843, for example, a group of labourers established a *Métayer Association* in Dennery for the purpose of co-operatively cultivating six acres of land, as well as paying the costs of worship and the expense of an agricultural school for the children in the Quarter of Dennery. Opponents of métayage, on the other hand, felt that métayage disturbed the social equilibrium '*by giving the illiterate classes a degree of weight and importance which should be the concomitants as well as the rewards of intelligence and education*' - as Henry Breen put it in 1861.

By the late 1850s, world prices for sugar rose once again and planters sought out alternative ways of solving their labour problems: looking primarily at immigration of indentured labourers and mechanization. Just as they had predicted, as soon as the price of sugar increased, planters withdrew land from métayage agreements, sending the practice into decline. Métayage did not disappear completely in St Lucia until the twentieth century (Peter Adrien mentions 1957) but it never regained its previous importance. In the end, as Marshall concluded, métayage remained '*a stopgap while pointing to a new frontier.*' While it is true that the system's full potential was never explored, even in its stunted form, métayage formed an important stepping stone for thousands of landless labourers in St Lucia and, as such, was crucially important in the rise of a peasantry.

The 1849 tax revolt

As soon as slavery was abolished, planters pushed for laws which made it difficult for ex-slaves to rent or own land, and taxes which would force them to earn cash money. As early as 1834, a Road Ordinance was introduced. By 1840, this law called for eight days' service on the roads per year or else a money payment to Government. The law was highly unpopular but non-compliance meant a prison penalty or a fine. In 1845, a law was proposed to tax the raw produce of agriculture - with the exception of sugar, rum and other by-products of the sugar industry. In effect, this taxed the provision crops of small peasants whilst sparing the plantocracy's cash crops. Around the same time, licensing fees on horses, guns and dogs were removed but export duties were introduced on charcoal, cocoa and wood, along with licensing fees for hucksters and boats - again, all exactly the kinds of economic activities undertaken by a diversifying labouring class.

In 1848, Lieutenant-Governor Henry Darling proposed a new direct land tax of four shillings per annum, to be paid by the occupant of every house regardless of whether he or she owned it. If the house came with more than three acres of land, the occupant was taxed one shilling extra for every acre of land, cultivated or uncultivated.[284] However, houses with more than nine acres of land were exempted. Thus, the new tax protected large planters while targeting the newly emancipated class of peasants and tenants. Darling intended to use the proceeds of the land tax for agricultural advancement and education of the children from the lower classes. In a letter to his superior officer, he admitted that part of the rationale behind the new tax was to give the planters some financial relief for fear that the unofficial members of the Legislative Council (i.e., the planters) would otherwise vote against the overall tax proposals for 1849. And Darling needed tax income badly, since he had found the treasury chest empty when he first took up his post in St Lucia (in January of 1848) leaving him unable to pay for much-needed repairs to Government House.[285] Although Darling did foresee some teething problems with the new land tax,[286] he obviously (but mistakenly, as it turned out) feared the wrath of the small peasants less than that of the large planters.

The new land tax was highly unpopular and many people defaulted from the start, particularly in the districts of Gros Islet and Dauphin. When pressed for payment, resentment erupted in riots in Castries, leaving eight or more people dead, dozens wounded, many more arrested and a handful of estate buildings burnt to the ground. This revolt became known as the 1849 tax revolt.[287] It was the first riot of its kind, and the first time that free working class people in St Lucia came together in what may be deemed a true form of political action.

Opposition to the tax started peacefully enough on the morning of 26 February 1849, when two '*respectable looking men of the Laboring Class*' walked up to Government House with a petition for Lieutenant-Governor Darling, asking him to have the land tax rescinded. The letter was signed: '*The Labouring Class of St Lucia*' and stated '*that in consequence of the low price of Provisions, and the very high price they have to pay the owners for the land rent ... renders it entirely out of their Power to pay any additional tax, and which they consider a very great imposition, and are not inclined to pay it at all hazards, as they would thereby deprive themselves and their families of the means of support.*' The letter humbly and respectfully begged the Lieutenant-Governor to '*have the law rescinded, and have it as formerly so that poor people may have it in their power to earn a small living for themselves.*'[288]

Although it was common practice for members of the middle and upper-classes to present letters, petitions and memoranda to the Lieutenant-Governor to be passed on to the Governor of the Windward Islands (based in Barbados) or the Secretary of State for the Colonies in London, this was the first time members of the labouring class used this medium to voice their complaints. Henry Darling was dumbstruck. The petition was brought to him in the midst of a meeting with his commanding officer Governor Colebrooke but Darling was so puzzled by '*the peculiar Language of this Document, and the Words, with which it was subscribed'* that he excused himself and asked to see the petitioners. In an impromptu meeting, Darling told the two men that he could not accept their petition because it lacked a signature. He also explained that even if he wanted to, he did not have the power to rescind the tax. Darling then turned the tables and started questioning the men. '*I endeavoured to ascertain from them the number of people, on whose behalf they appeared, and the right they had to come forward on behalf of the Laboring Class of Saint Lucia generally; and I also enquired who had drawn up their Petition.*' The duo wisely refused to divulge who had penned the petition and also would not say on whose behalf they were acting, beyond stating '*c'est nous tout*' ('it is all of us').[289] Darling later reported: '*they left me after some Conversation although in apparent good humour yet clearly dissatisfied that they had not at once obtained the object of their Petition.*'[290]

The following day was a Thursday. Darling was attending to business at the government office in town when a group of eight or ten men and women asked to see him, once again carrying the petition. Again, Darling conceded to speak with them. '*The Interview lasted for ten minutes or a quarter of an hour, and on this occasion, I had not only the assistance of a person who understands their peculiar Language, but one of their principal Spokesmen having been employed as a Sailor at Bermuda, both spoke and understood English.*' Darling's private secretary, Lieutenant Henry Whatley Tyler, was present at both the first and this second meeting. He later testified that while Lieutenant-Governor Darling's manner had been '*mild and conciliatory*' during Thursday's encounter, the conduct of the petitioners was '*more pressing than on the first*' meeting and they '*said that they would insist on having a favourable answer to their petition.*'[291]

Darling reasoned at some length with the petitioners and even sent his chief-clerk, a Mr Fauchier, into the government archives to fetch a copy of the Land Tax Ordinance, which Darling subsequently read out to the petitioners. Fauchier translated the text into Kwéyòl, along with Darling's comments and additional explanations. Darling repeated that he did not have the power to alter the law and emphasized that the tax was intended for the benefit of the people who paid it and would be devoted, amongst other things, to the education of their children. He reportedly told the petitioners:

> *Have not some of you gardens, perhaps cattle, sheep or goats? If a man plunders your garden or steals your cattle, do you not go before a Magistrate, employ a Police Constable to arrest? Has the plunderer not to be maintained in gaol both before and after his conviction? Must there not be Judges to try, a Crown Counsel to prosecute?'Who,' he asked them, 'was to pay for all this? from what funds was this expenditure to be derived, if not from all who thus enjoyed the privileges of society and the protection of the laws?'* [292]

By his own admission, Darling felt that '*Some of the people appeared to admit the truth of my observations, but others were evidently impatient and dissatisfied and as I broke up the Conference, one of them dropped some expressions about a "Mauvais desordre" to which I attached no importance at the moment but the Significance of which Subsequent events have left little reason to doubt.*' The man who predicted the '*Mauvais desordre*' ('a nasty disturbance') was later identified as Henry Boy (or Boye).

His prophecy came true five days later. On the morning of Monday 5 March, on his way to the government office in town, Darling noticed that the street in front of the office of the Stipendiary Magistrate for Castries, Dr James Drysdale, was crowded by

> *... 25 to 30 Men and Women from the Country, most of them Carrying Sticks, and amongst whom I recognized some of those who had presented the Petition on the previous Thursday. They followed me so closely that by the time I was seated in the Council Chamber, the Street, into which that apartment looks, was occupied by them, their number however having considerably increased. They at once became tumultuous and noisy, directing threatening and impatient looks and gestures to the Council Chamber Windows.*[293]

Darling sent out '*an intelligent coloured Man, who is the Government Messenger*' to ask the crowd to send in five of their number to speak with him, whilst requesting the others to disperse. When this message produced no effect, Darling sent the Commissary of Police and Dr Drysdale (both of whom happened to be in the building) to address the crowd with the same request. He explicitly cautioned them to avoid a confrontation with the mob. Darling later recalled:

> *It was with difficulty however, they obtained a hearing while the people became more violent and tumultuous, every moment, flourishing their Sticks and Showing every indication of a determination to engage in a riot. Three or four Policemen had by this time Joined the Crowd, and I have been informed by more than one Bystander that they did not interfere until one of them had been first Struck on the back of the head by a Woman. An immediate conflict ensued, the Magistrate and Police were Completely overpowered and driven into the Government Buildings, the Chief of Police, and the Men having all received Severe injuries from the blows of heavy sticks and paving Stones. The mob immediately commenced an attack upon the Council Chamber, with the Paving Stones, which from the bad State of the pavement lay but too ready to their hands. Two or three Minutes Sufficed to destroy the Windows and the Shower of Missiles rendered it utterly impossible to remain in any part of the Buildings that was within their reach.*

Witness accounts vary a little but the attack appears to have gone on for between ten and 30 minutes. During this time

> *... almost all the windows of Government-office were broken; stones were thrown in crowds; the Lieutenant-Governor was during that time placed in personal danger; witness saw a dent in the chair usually occupied by His Excellency, but did not see it struck ... The attack continued about a quarter of an hour; the insurgents were masters of the street during that time; the Executive were on their defence, and powerless; the Lieut.-Governor, the Colonial Secretary, and the Attorney-General were there, and were powerless.*[294]

William Hanley, the Colonial Secretary and Treasurer, later testified:

> *A large quantity of very large stones came through the windows into the Council Chamber, and went farther; some of the stones passed through two apartments and fell into the gallery. The Governor was in danger, for he would most certainly have been killed if those stones had struck him. ... The frames of the windows and the panes were shattered; the partitions and maps, and several chairs, were damaged by the stones; the shoulder of one of the chairs was nearly dismounted; the left arm of the Governor's chair, at the Council table, was damaged. Witness saw a person come quickly up the step and throw a brick, which passed near the Governor, and struck between a bolt and the wall, where it stuck; saw the person who threw that brick, and the Governor was near at the time. Other apartments of the Public Buildings, besides the Council-room, were assaulted. The insurgents were masters of the street for some time; and the civil power was for some time unable to restrain them or establish peace. ... Witness saw two or three men come into the office for refuge, covered with blood; the floor of the passage was covered with blood; the Government Messenger was wounded in the groin, and was, witness believes, considered to be in danger.*[295]

Darling and the frightened government employees were saved from further injury and threat '*by the Sudden appearance of a few men of the Guard placed over the Ordnance Stores in Town.*'[296] The crowd, mistaking them for the advance guards of a larger police force, scampered off. But the attack left the Lieutenant-Governor thoroughly shaken and the news, carried by Dr Drysdale, that people in the crowd '*had boldly Said that they would not be refused, and that they would try whether the Government or themselves were the Stronger*' only further harnessed Darling's revulsion of '*the Sudden and extreme Violence*' of the crowd '*and Convinced me that the Law must be at once upheld, and the Question they had been unhappily advised to raise brought to an immediate issue.*' And so Darling adopted a hard line. He ordered the stipendiary magistrates to swear in as many special constables as they could muster, he asked the crew and officers of the merchant ships in Castries harbour to volunteer in that capacity, and called in a further 50 soldiers from the local militia. '*Before these arrangements were completed however, the Chief of Police aided by a few of the Special Constables ... endeavoured to apprehend Some of the Rioters.*' Darling had wanted to wait until he had gathered a sufficiently large police force before seeking such a confrontation, but his hands were tied. '*The Rioters even at this period of the day fought with Savage fury; one Special Constable received a wound from which his life was for some time considered in danger, and others together with the Chief of Police himself were very severely injured.*'

As soon as the impromptu volunteer police force was sworn in, Darling put stipendiary magistrates Drysdale and de Brossard at the head of two contingents and directed them to arrest the ringleaders and make an example of a few tax defaulters residing close to town '*against whom Warrants were out, and who were also among the Rioters.*' By early afternoon, 25 rioters had been arrested and put in gaol - but not before militiamen had needed to fire their muskets in the air to disperse the angry crowd. According to Darling, this was done '*without however occasioning any loss of life or it is believed even wounding any of them.*'

Simultaneously, Darling tried a last-ditch attempt at diplomacy by engaging a Roman Catholic Priest by the name of Abbé Lecaillet (to whose flock many of the rioters belonged) asking him '*to endeavour to induce them to disperse, and point out the awful consequences which a persistence in the Course they were pursuing must infallibly involve.*' With 25 rioters in gaol and the Abbé out on his diplomatic mission, Darling '*anxiously hoped that the disturbance was quelled, and that the people would depart to their houses in the Country.*' It was not to be.

Abbé Lecaillet told Darling afterwards that the people had been '*deaf to his arguments and advice, and even threatened him with personal Violence.*' As the afternoon passed, more and more rioters from the Gros Islet district arrived in Castries, full of fight and vexation and '*not an hour had elapsed, before they were in Complete possession of the "Chaussée" a long Street which forms the inland Eastern Boundary of the Town having been recruited by large numbers from the Northern District of the Island, armed with Cutlasses, heavy Sticks, Stones, broken Bottles and a few it is said, Carrying Muskets.*'

By now, Darling was close to panic, as were the '*inhabitants*' of Castries (presumably those of the middle and upper-classes). '*Many removed their Wives, Children and effects to the Shipping and to places in the direction of the Government House, or on the Sea Board of the Town. The Rioters threatened to burn the Town and release the Prisoners who had been Captured in the Morning and in fact, matters had arrived at such a point that the discharge of my duty to Her Majesty's loyal and peaceful Subjects, left me no alternative.*'

Darling sent in all the civil and military troops he had at his disposal, warning the rioters they would be removed from the Chaussée at any cost, but the protestors were not fazed and put up a '*determined resistance*'. At five o'clock in the afternoon, fighting continued unabated and '*the firing was so frequent, while night was fast approaching, that I thought it better to be prepared for any result.*'

Preparing for a worst-case scenario, Darling requested another 50 military troops to be sent down from the Morne (where soldiers had been observing the day's fighting through telescopes) along with two pieces of field artillery. '*When the latter arrived, I proceeded with them to the Chaussée, intending that the responsibility of employing them if Circumstances appeared to render that course inevitable should rest with nobody but myself.*' At the Chaussée Road, Darling was met with police officers and soldiers '*bringing in Several Prisoners and the Bodies of those who had paid the penalty of their rashness and infatuation.*' Although Darling had reportedly asked the troops to cause as little bloodshed as possible, the '*painful*' conclusion was that the riot

> *... only terminated when Eight had been Shot dead upon the Spot. (One killed and one wounded were women who were observed during the day to be Conspicuous for their Violence and determination.) Two more were wounded and fell into the hands of the Magistrates, who caused them to be Conveyed to the Asylum where they now are. There is no doubt that others also were wounded, and among them one of the most active Ringleaders, so dangerously as to render it impossible that he can survive, especially as he has not been taken and must be without Surgical Assistance.*

By nightfall of that turbulent 5 March 1849, the town of Castries was licking its wounds. '*The necessary measures were taken that night for the protection of the Town, but no further Attempt upon it was made by the Rioters.*'

The same could not be said for the rural northern districts. In the night of 5 to 6 March 1849, the sugar works and some other buildings on the Bellevue estate (quarter of Gros Islet) belonging to Madame St Jore Catherine were burnt down by angry tax protestors. The same fate befell the *mogass* (bagasse) house and a cane field on the Bonneterre estate (property of Muter Miller) and a mogass house on the Marquis estate in the quarter of Dauphin, which at the time belonged to *Messieurs* Bennett and Guerin. The mogass house on the Choc estate (property of Pierre Auxliens Augier) nearly ended up in ashes as well but was saved by the intervention of labourers from the estate itself. According to witnesses, during the afternoon of 5 March, '*there was a great mob on the road of Choc*'. Frustrated at not being able to enter Castries, one of the protestors (a man by the name of Pelage Aquart) allegedly told his friends Vincent, Servé and Grand Xavier: '*as we cannot get into town, let us agree to set fire to the estate*'. The proposal was to first burn the negro-huts, followed by the mogass-house and other buildings. In the court case, it later emerged that:

> ... *Vincent said: 'let us go,' while Servé and Pelage each took up a firebrand from under the farine platine. They were opposed by the people of the estate, whom they resisted with sticks and cutlasses. Grand Xavier was not seen to do anything. Eloi, a witness for the defence, said, he met Vincent near the farine house at Choc at about 6 o'clock on the 5th March; heard him talk of setting fire, and saw him take a firebrand, and go with it towards the gate on the highroad; ran up to him, and begged him to stop, putting him in mind that he had a wife and children; Pelage and Servé were also present; Pelage said, 'if you hear a negro say so, he is against you, cut him down.' Vincent took his (Eloi's) advice, but the others did not heed it; when this witness took the fire from Vincent, Pelage made a cut at him with his cutlass, and the fire fell from his hand.*[297]

Although no fire was actually set at Choc Estate and no other damage done, Pelage Aquart, Servé and Vincent were all eventually convicted to one year's imprisonment with hard labour. Only Grand Xavier was discharged.

Following reports of arson on estates in the north, Darling took up an offer of assistance made by the captain of a French schooner of war, the *Légère*, to convey Stipendiary Magistrate de Brossard with a party of special constables and 25 military men to Gros Islet. Their immediate task was to arrest as many rioters as they could obtain information against. In particular, de Brossard was instructed to try and find '*one of the principal Ringleaders, who is Supposed to be lying, severely wounded, at a Small Settlement in the interior; from whence the most prominent Rioters Came*'. The settlement was probably Grande Rivière and the man in question Eugène Déslandes.

Interestingly, Déslandes was allegedly a Martiniquan fugitive - a former *Commis Greffier* of the court at Fort de France, who had been convicted of forgery in that island. On the same day the riots in Castries started, Darling had received a letter from the Governor of Martinique (delivered by the *Légère*) asking for help in apprehending and sending back Déslandes. The captain of the *Légère* told Darling that Déslandes had been implicated in unrests in Martinique and somehow, Darling and the captain arrived at the conclusion that Déslandes might have wanted to stir up mischief in St Lucia as well, perhaps so as to '*raise about him a Body of followers to enable him to resist any attempt at arrest.*' Déslandes was believed to be harboured by old-time Martiniquan refugees in what was described as a mountainous area on the windward side of the northern district.

Thus, for some time at least, Darling was convinced that Martiniquan refugees were behind the tax revolt. Slavery had been abolished in the French islands the year before (1848) and this had prompted several Martiniquan refugees to visit their relatives and friends back home. In doing so, Darling believed, they '*no doubt imbided many of the Extreme republican and Communist Doctrines, which have naturally followed upon the recent Revolutions in France, and the Circumstances, under which Emancipation took place in Martinique.*'

Darling reported accordingly to his superior officer:

> *Your Excellency will observe Dr Drysdale's Evidence to the assertion of an equal right to the Soil, in all the Children of God which was held by one of the Ringleaders who was a Refugee. Amongst the dead are two Refugees, and with one exception, the Bodies are all recognized as those of persons Coming from the Same Settlement as the Refugees. Many more of these people were distinctly Seen among the Ringleaders. At the last Conference with the Magistrate they declared they would not pay the Horse Tax, or the Gun Tax, thus refusing in fact, to pay every Tax to which they are Subject. I am assured by one of the Officers present with the detachment of the 54th that the Revolutionary Song of France 'Mourir pour la patrie' was distinctly heard and that many of them were so frantic and infatuated, as to face the Soldiers; and by Action, and gestures, invite them, to fire. The Statement made by many of the Negroes who flocked in from the Country is Simply that they Came because the Rioters told them that war (La Guerre) was declared in Castries, and by others that they were to fight to get rid of the 'Impôt locataire', which however I understand is in Martinique always levied upon the Landlord.*[298]

It is unclear from the available records whether Eugène Déslandes was ever apprehended, or if he died before the troops found him. His name certainly does not appear in the court cases. Instead, the Solicitor-General sighted another man in his cross-hairs: Henry Boy, one of the two '*respectable looking men*' who had had the audacity to stroll up to Government House on the morning of 26 February with a neatly drawn-up petition on behalf of '*The Labouring Class of St Lucia*'. In *The Queen vs. Henry Boy*, Boy was accused of nothing less than high treason - a charge that had never before been laid against anyone in St Lucia. Boy was accused on two counts: firstly of having levied a war, '*actually and directly*', against her Majesty's Government in St Lucia, '*for the purpose, by intimidation and violence, of forcing the repeal of the law imposing a tax on cultivated land*'. Secondly, he was accused '*for compassing (that is, conspiring) to levy war against Her Majesty, in order to compel her to change her measures and councils.*'

Solicitor-General John Grey Porter-Athill went to great lengths to try and convince the twelve jurors[299] that in a legal sense, the levying of war '*did not require military array, fire-arms or other military weapons.*' What Boy had done, he argued, was to take a series of steps aimed at loosening the ties of society and returning that society to a state of barbarism. These steps were: having a petition drawn up addressed to the Governor; the '*hurling*' of '*defiant expressions*' at the highest authority in the country; getting that petition delivered to the Governor; going to the Governor's office and demanding the withdrawal of the land tax; having uttered '*certain violent and traitorous words*' (a reference to his muttered warning that there would be a '*mauvais desordre*'); followed, finally, by '*the daring, the savage and rebellious attack on His Excellency the Governor and the Members of his Executive Council in the Council-room, and the other outrages committed at and in front of the Government-buildings on the 5th of March.*'

Henry Boy's defence lawyer was Henry Percin: the son of Francois Percin, signatory to the 1824 petition for equal rights for free people of colour. Despite his relatively humble background, Henry Percin had obtained a law degree in Paris. Like his father, he was a firm believer in political rights for the masses – but by 1848, the struggle had become radical. Henry Percin fought Boy's accusation of high treason from various angles: on technicalities of law, by cross-examining the Crown's witnesses and by sheer power of persuasion. He highlighted the fact that petitions were presented to the Governor all the time by other members of society; the fact that the rioters had been armed only with the commonest of weapons - stones, sticks and their normal working tool, the cutlass - and that relatively little physical damage had been done by them, especially in light of the fact that at least eight of their own had been shot and killed by police and many more wounded. Under cross-examination, Percin got some of the Crown's witnesses to admit that they had not at the time, and did not now, consider the riot a 'war'.

Whether it was thanks to Percin's defense tactics, the jurors' common sense or the fact that the Solicitor-General had lost one of his key witnesses (a white police officer who had drawn up the petition at Henry Boy's request but who, instead of testifying, had boarded a ship to Scotland shortly before the court case got underway), we cannot say. What we do know is that the jurors decided to acquit Boy of high treason. He was returned to gaol, convicted the following day of rioting and assault and sentenced to three years' imprisonment with hard labour.

Also charged and convicted during the '*tedious sitting of fifteen days*' (as the weary reporter for the *Palladium* newspaper described it) were the following persons: Marie-Louise, Azor and Jeannine (riot and assault: three to six months with hard labour); Jean Louis, Jean Charles Alexandre and Jean (riot and assault: one to two years with hard labour); Céleste, Zabeth *alias* Negresse and Charlery (riot and tumult: Céleste was found guilty and convicted of one year imprisonment with hard labour; the other two were discharged); Jean Marie *alias* Prosper, Noel, Ambroise, Basil and Celiane (riot and tumult: two were discharged while the others received four months and three years respectively with hard labour); Jean Charles, John Smith, Marie Noel and Louis Marie (riot and tumult: after long deliberation, one was found guilty; the others were later sentenced to one year each with hard labour); Dah, Prosper and Jeannot *alias* Jean Simson (riot and tumult: two were found guilty and one was acquitted); Salomez, St Louis, Michel and Coralie Rock (three were found guilty and received one and two years with hard labour, the third was acquitted); Crépin, Pierre Marianne, Francois and Louison (unlawful assembly: six months to one year with hard labour); Malgrétout, Félix and Ital *alias* Vidal (riot and tumult: six months, one year and two years with hard labour); Lyall Bastien, Magloire, Louis Luce and Victor Marie Claire (riot and tumult: all found guilty and sentenced to one, two and three years with hard labour). The final death toll of the riot is unknown but was at least eight and may have been as high as twenty.

Looking back on the tax riots of 1849, Lieutenant-Governor Darling was convinced that the level of force used by his troops had been in proportion to the threat exuded by the crowd. This, perhaps, is more telling of the perception of threat by planters, merchants and administrators than the actual danger they were in. Taken together, the events of early 1849 indicate that one decade after Emancipation, any form of determined political action by the working class was still immediately associated with the carnage, rampage and arson of the Brigand Wars half a century earlier, and it was this sort of fear which had primarily informed the authorities' response.

The nightmare of slavery was not shaken off that easily. Just as for some decades after Emancipation freed people kept alive rumours about the imminent reinstatement of slavery, so too did the plantocracy continue to live in fear of a sudden eruption of violence from their labourers, tenants and métayers. If the tax revolt of 1849 shows one thing, it is that the working class of St Lucia still had many hurdles to cross before its voice was accepted in local politics.

The treasury fraud

By the late 1840s, not only were the working class beginning to test the chains of their political power: so too were the planters. A catalytic event in political discontent for both workers and planters was the treasury fraud of 1849. It was the largest case of fraud ever uncovered in the island up until then and one which shook St Lucia to its core. According to radical lawyer Henry Percin, working class people's outrage over the treasury fraud and the lackadaisical manner in which the Lieutenant-Governor allowed the main culprit to get away, had positively aggravated the 1849 peasant tax revolt. This may well have been the case. The fraud sparked a decade-long correspondence of complaints between a group of St Lucian planters (headed by William

Muter) and the Colonial Office and Treasury in London, and it is certainly true that the planters considered the fraud a prime example of administrative lapses and incompetence.

Historian Henry Breen provides a full and, by all appearances, reliable account[300] of the treasury fraud, in the uncovering of which he himself was instrumental. The first clear sign that something was amiss came to light in 1840. In May of that year, St Lucia's treasurer and colonial secretary William Hanley obtained leave of absence for a trip to England. On 12 June 1840, Henry Breen was appointed his *locum tenens*. A few months after Hanley's departure, the Lords of the Treasury in London asked Breen for a statement of St. Lucia's accounts between 1829 and 1837. The Lords said they had repeatedly requested such a statement from the various treasurers but had never received one, nor had they been given an explanation beyond the lame excuse that some of the old cashbooks could not be found. Breen, curious by nature, took to the task like a fish to water. '*There was a large press in the office, full of old registers. I caused the contents to be placed on the floor, and after a careful examination I discovered the missing books, which had been stowed away under a heap of old registers.*'

In finding the books, Breen inadvertently stumbled upon considerable amounts of missing funds. Not just one but a series of treasurers had helped themselves to St Lucia's cash box, starting with a Mr Honoré de Bernard, who had died in 1829, leaving behind '*defalcations to a considerable amount*'. According to the custom of the time, public officials had to provide sureties upon accepting their positions. In the case of Honoré de Bernard, '*Fortunately for the colony his sureties were planters in an affluent position, and the defalcations were made good.*' But the island was less fortunate with some of de Bernard's successors. A certain Mr Clarke had received but failed to account for £1500: a huge sum of money at a time when field labourers earned just one shilling per day. Confronted with the charge, Clarke - by then occupied in a military position in Spain - promised to pay back the deficit but he died soon after. When his sureties in London were contacted, they were found to have gone out of business and the £1500 was lost forever. Clarke's immediate successor, Mr (afterwards Sir) Henry Edward Fox Young proved honest as a treasurer but after his promotion, another crooked official took over: a Mr Stephen Villiers Surtees. During the two years of his tenure, Surtees relieved the treasury box of no less than £700. By the time Breen's investigations brought this to light, Surtees had been knighted and was a judge at the Supreme Court in Mauritius. Anxious to keep his reputation and career intact, Surtees '*immediately remitted the amount of the surcharge*'.

But the machinations of Clarke and Surtees were nothing compared to those of Surtees' successor: William Hanley. Appointed to the post of treasurer and colonial secretary in 1837, Hanley worked for three years before applying for leave of absence. He left in May of 1840 and returned on 25 May 1842. By 26 May 1842, Hanley was back at the helm as treasurer.[301]

Breen implies later that it was during his trip to Europe, between 1840 and 1842, whilst dallying around Paris and the continent with '*some ladies and gentlemen of his acquaintance*' and living on '*nothing but his half salary (£300)*' that Hanley ran up a £5000 debt which he subsequently paid off out of the coffers of St Lucia. There is additional evidence, however, both from Breen and others, that Hanley had been under suspicion of fraud right from the start of his tenure. On 12 July 1837, a committee of the Legislative Council investigated charges of '*plunder and embezzlement of the Public Funds*' carried on '*by the Colonial Treasurer and his Clerks*' and sent a report to Lord Glenelg at the Colonial Office in London accusing Hanley of fraud. According to at least one planter (William Muter) the evidence against Hanley was strong even then. But, as Muter later complained: '*The Acting Governor ... protected the Colonial Treasurer, and reported the Charge was not made out, although the Evidence was in his own possession. The Home Authorities believed the Report of the Military Officer and the Embezzlement continued ...*'[302]

When nothing was done to stop the alleged fraud or to alleviate their tax burden, the planters, '*goaded on almost to madness by such treatment*' organized public meetings in Castries, formed a committee, wrote resolutions and petitioned the home authorities to step in. In William Muter's prolonged correspondence with the Colonial Office, one of the points he and his associates consistently raised (besides the need for tax relief) was the issue of security at the treasury. In 1838, they urged the Legislative Council to demand additional securities from the treasurer but the Council resolved that no such thing was required. The planters, unhappy, turned to Lord John Russell, who was then Secretary of State for the Colonies and in June 1840 repeated their urgent request. The response stated that '*the Lords of the Treasury had deferred any ... definite decision on the subject until Mr Hanley's arrival in this Country. Mr Hanley is now in communication with their Lordships and the Board of Audit.*'

This little note later proved pivotal. In 1849, William Hanley was arrested and charged with embezzling from the St Lucia treasury the staggering amount of £29,814-7-8 Sterling. When a grim William Muter subsequently requested that the British Government pay back to the planters of St Lucia every last penny of that amount, the Colonial Office did all it could to wriggle out of taking responsibility for Hanley's theft. But Muter had them squirming when he reminded them that whilst the planters had persistently requested more security, all the Colonial Office had done was to speak with the fraudster himself, who had glibly assured them that the Legislative Council in St Lucia had already decided there was no need for concern! A worried note, scribbled on the back of one of Muter's letters, went around the Colonial Office in 1853, stating '*There is nothing in this office to show why security was not taken, at the time, nor have the Treasury as yet been able to trace why it was not done.*'

For years, William Muter stubbornly nagged for compensation (to the intense irritation of some in the Colonial Office)[303] and he eventually managed to secure a hearing in front of the imperial Treasury Board.[304] His request for compensation was turned down, however, and the people of St Lucia - planters and workers alike – were left to shoulder the burden of Hanley's theft alone.

Even allowing for the fact that William Muter may have exaggerated the financial plight of the planters somewhat, £30 000 was a huge burden on the small colony. Moreover, the money was embezzled during a particularly dire period - between 1837 and 1849 - when three-quarters of all plantations in St Lucia were seized for debts and sold at judicial sales. Hanley's theft represented (using Muter's calculations) an average of £2,208 per year, or approximately one-seventh of the entire annual tax revenue of St Lucia. It is easy to see why, at times, planters' frustration with their lack of political sway in the administration of their own colony left them foaming at the mouth. Whilst their petitions were duly passed on to the colonial authorities in London (one advantage that they at least had over the labouring class) the result was little different: '*seeing that the representations of the Colonists were unheeded or at most were attended with no other result than a courteous expression of sympathy*' as Muter observed bitterly: '[t]*he Public Officers at length took full advantage of this state of things, and hence in a great measure, may be explained the systematic plunder of the Colonial Chest by the Public Officers themselves, in spite of all the efforts of the Colonists to bring that iniquity fully to light and to arrest it.*'[305]

Indeed, with hindsight, it is difficult to see how Hanley and his henchmen could have gotten away with their shenanigans for so long. It was only when a repentant and ill treasury clerk by the name of Henry Niochet, believing himself on the brink of death, asked to see a member of the Legislative Council (James Macfarlane) and cleared his conscience that the fraud was finally arrested. Niochet confessed that for several years, Hanley and two of his clerks (John William Todd and Jean Marie Papin) had pilfered large sums of money. Niochet explained: '*A man would call at the Treasury to pay, for instance, £10 duty on some articles imported, and a receipt would be handed to him for the amount. The receipts were always carefully made out for the sums paid; so that an out-sider could not suspect that there was anything wrong. The case was different as regards the entries in the cash-book; instead for £10, the amount carried as received would be 10 shillings.*'[306] James Macfarlane immediately put together a Commission of Enquiry and it was quickly discovered that '*the colony had been robbed at the rate of about £3,000 every year since Mr Hanley's return from England. On this discovery Hanley and Papin made their escape from the Island, but Todd was prosecuted for the frauds and sentenced to twelve months imprisonment.'*

Breen found himself in an awkward position because even during his own tenure as care-taking treasurer, between 1840 and 1842, the clerks Todd and Papin had stolen money from right from under his nose.[307] He later explained that Hanley had expressed '*great confidence*' in the '*fidelity and zeal*' of his clerks and indeed, said Breen, the treasury was run with '*apparent regularity*'. Breen had had plenty of other work to attend to and no reason to upset the apple cart. Only later did both Lieutenant-Governor Darling and Breen admit that there had been warning signs. Darling had found the treasury chest empty when he took up his post in January of 1848 and Breen, around the same time, was alerted one afternoon when he took shelter from the rain in Todd's cottage, St Leger Hill, and walked in on a sumptuous, well-attended dinner party which included a dish of ham boiled in champagne. '*I took Mr Todd aside and asked him how, with a salary of only £150 a year, he could afford to incur such extravagant expense. His answer was, that he had lately inherited a large sum of money from a deceased relative in Barbados.*'

How Hanley and Papin, despite being placed on bail, managed to escape and flee to Europe is not clear from the available documents. It was whispered that Lieutenant-Governor Darling connived in their escape: Hanley being, amongst other things, his personal secretary. Although there is no hard evidence to support this, the appearance of a cover-up by the colonial authorities certainly existed in the minds of labourers and planters and aggravated their distrust of the government. It also supports Henry Percin's notion that the 1848 tax revolt was partly fuelled by anger over the treasury fraud.

Just how precariously unjust St Lucian society still was in 1849 becomes clear from a simple comparison between the punishments handed down to these public servants who, for purely selfish motives, had robbed the colony of nearly £30 000 over the course of twelve years, and those who had spoken of, but did not actually perpetrate, arson following the shooting death by police of eight of their friends. While Hanley and Papin escaped scot-free and a blatantly unrepentant Todd (although initially sentenced to transportation)[308] appears to have spent just twelve months in prison,[309] Pelage Aquart, Servé and Vincent all received twelve month in prison with hard labour. Other rioters served up to three years with hard labour for throwing a few stones.

Although planters and labourers were far from united in their dislike of the manner in which colonial officers administered their country, they did share a deep resentment over the fact that in their poverty - some of it relative, much of it real - they always ended up shouldering the bill. The difference was, of course, that labourers were at the bottom of the food chain, whereas planters could still pass on some of their burden by reducing wages - as they did in 1847, when wages in several districts were cut by a quarter or half. Simultaneously, the Legislative Council refused to reduce the salaries of the island's public officials despite the crisis in the sugar industry, arguing that fluctuations in income were part and parcel of the business of agriculture - completely ignoring the fact that the bureaucratic burden in St Lucia was enormous in relation to the small size of its population.

The newly freed working class had no such luxuries. Their only escape from the pincer-like action of planters and administrators (reduction in wages on the one hand and increases in taxation on the other) lay in self-reliance through land ownership. Throughout the second half of the nineteenth century, taxes, laws, levies and low wages made it very difficult for newly freed people in St Lucia to earn a living, support their families and build autonomous futures. The fact that a peasantry arose nonetheless and that working class people did as well as they did is resounding proof of their resilience and hard work.[310] In Earl Lovelace's novel *The Wine of Astonishment* the main character, Eva, phrases it so well. '*We was going good - not the best but good enough for a people who bring their bare hands with us from Africa and go through trials and tribulations enough to make a weaker people surrender.*'[311]

8

The evolving face of St Lucia: roads, towns and villages in the mid-nineteenth century

Seventy tumultuous years have passed since our last virtual tour of St Lucia based on reports by d'Ennery (1767), de Nozière and de Tascher (1773) and Marquis de Bouillé (1778). Since then, the Brigand Wars, three more decades of slavery and, finally, Emancipation all dramatically changed the social make-up of St Lucia. By 1844, the physical landscape had changed as well. It was the year in which Henry Breen's book *St Lucia Historical, Statistical and Descriptive* was published. Henry Hegart Breen was mayor of Castries and went on to become administrator of St Lucia (1857-61). He was a white Englishman with an inquisitive mind, but self-righteous and exemplary of the prejudices of his colour, gender, rank and era. Breen's book is full of facts and opinions and quite often, the two intertwine. His view of the working class black and coloured population is at best paternalistic and at worst undeniably racist. Breen also does not shrink away from committing to paper some very irreverent views on Frenchmen, womenfolk, the Catholic clergy and other 'lesser beings'. Bearing these shortcomings in mind, though, his book possesses a wealth of historical information and paints a colourful tapestry of contemporary views and vistas. It is for this latter purpose that Breen serves us here as an eager guide, taking us on a virtual tour of St Lucia anno 1844.

The evolving face of Castries

Castries, wrote Breen in 1844, was bounded on the north by a bay and Sans Souci, on the east by the Chaussée Road and '*the lands of Leslie*', on the south by the river and Morne Fortuné, and on the west by the harbour. It contained 600 houses, and 4000 souls.

> *The streets are wide and well laid out, extending in parallel lines from east to west and from north to south. Most of them are paved, and some are ornamented with footpaths. The upper part, or Chaussée division, is chiefly occupied by the humbler orders, and the houses are all built of wood and covered with shingles. The lower, or Bord-de-mer division, is the resort*

> *of the wealthier classes. Here the houses are constructed of stone, brick, or wood, according to the taste of the owners, or the prevailing anxiety to guard against the consequences of fire, hurricane, or earthquake.*[312]

Castries had developed fast in the nineteenth century, irretrievably changing its natural landscape. The harbour of Castries was originally a volcanic crater, which flooded when its western wall collapsed. The Amerindians had made use of its small indented coves: fishing, hunting and gathering on the bay's six large coral reefs and in the thick mangroves. At the time, the Castries River was navigable all the way up to the present-day Marchand Bridge and ran with a strong flow of fresh water that kept the river mouth free of sand. Vigie Peninsula and La Toc were thickly wooded with bois d'orange, red cedar, calliandra, broom palms, agave and various cacti. Morne Fortuné and Morne Dudon were covered in mature hardwoods including balata, bwa-pen mawon and awalie, on which parrots thrived. Huge numbers of sea birds fed on the abundant marine life and hundreds of frigate birds feasted in mid-summer on the migrating schools of fish that sheltered in the bay. Caribbean manatees, seals and turtles were everywhere and large edible muskrats and mountain chickens flourished in the nearby creeks.

This first changed in the early eighteenth century, when Europeans established a small village at Vigie Peninsula, on the west side of Petit Carénage Bay (so named because of the ease with which ships could be careened here to remove the barnacles that attach themselves to wooden ships in warm seas). At the time, this narrow bay stretched almost entirely across the Vigie Peninsula. Today, half of it has disappeared under the Vigie Airport runway. In 1745, a village was laid out on the flat land at the base of Vigie Hill with a single street running from north to south, linking the sheltered Grand Carénage Bay across the Vigie isthmus with the more exposed Choc Bay. Fourteen houses stood along this street. French military headquarters were established on the Vigie Height, including three forts: Choc Fort facing Choc Bay, Fort St Victor protecting the entrance to Grand Carénage Bay (Castries Harbour) and Fort Montagu keeping watch over Petit Carénage Bay. The Governor's residence was located on the slope just below Fort Montagu and a small church was built a little further north. Near this church was a small public square and the road here made a 90-degree bend to the east, continuing along the coast towards the Choc settlement. The military defences were strengthened around 1756, when a barrier of entrenchments was established across the peninsula. A daring attempt was also made to open a boat channel across the peninsula to enable quick access between Carénage Bay and Choc Bay (effectively making Vigie an island) but waves from the north kept blocking the entrance with sand and the effort was eventually aborted.

In 1765, due to the high death rate, d'Ennery had the entire village relocated to the southern side of Grand Carénage Bay. By 1768, most houses had been rebuilt in an area near the river's mouth, behind a sandy beach from which the thick vegetation of seagrape, manchineel, almond, custard apple, fat pork and mangrove trees had been removed. The military headquarters and government administration buildings were relocated to Morne Dubuc, which from then on became known as Morne Fortuné. Under temporary English occupation (1780-2), Admiral Rodney established naval headquarters at Pigeon Island and constructed docking facilities and a shipyard in the now abandoned Petit Carénage Bay. In 1785, once again under French control, the relocated village of Carénage was renamed Castries town in honour of Maréchal de Castries, the French Minister for Navy and Colonies. The old town of Carénage became known as Vieille Ville ('old town'), the former Governor's residence as Vieille Ville House, the shoal at the entrance to Petit Carénage as Vieille Ville Shoal and Petit Carénage Bay itself as Vigie Cove and, later, Ganter's Bay.

Around the same time, Governor de Laborie (who was a military engineer by profession) set in motion a long-term plan for reclaiming the waterfront which formed the north-western boundary of the new town of Castries. Mangroves were cleared from low-lying areas on both sides of the town and de Laborie granted ownership rights to anyone who reclaimed waterfront lots from the sea. He also had a timber jetty built midway along the beach to accommodate small trading vessels. Some of Castries' streets were paved with cobblestones and several more waterfront lots were reclaimed from the sea, filled in and drained. What later became known as Jeremie Street began to extend westward as the town grew northward, expanding by several blocks into reclaimed areas of land. The expansion roughly followed a line from the ox-bow at the river's mouth that later became Prince Alfred's Basin to the edge of the Conway mangrove swamp that later came to accommodate the Castries market and the botanical garden.

In 1835, the western wharf was built, in time to make optimum use of the fact that steam vessels were revolutionizing seafaring transport. Ships' bunkers needed bituminous coal to fuel their engines and with the new wharf, Castries became one of the few ports in the region with deep water landing facilities, making it ready for the nascent coaling trade.

The town's ambition was reflected in the new design of St Lucia's crest (following the coronation of Queen Victoria in 1837) which used as its motto *Statio Haud Malefida Carinis* ('A Safe Harbour for Ships'). The first steamship to call at Port Castries and dock alongside the western wharf was RMS *Solway*, in late 1841. It was a relatively small trans-Atlantic vessel of 1700 tons, carrying just 100 passengers but it was the largest vessel and the first iron ship ever to visit Castries, and the many spectators were suitably awed.

In 1844, Henry Breen concluded that the reclamation of wet and swampy lands had been '*the means of wresting from the empire of the ocean a considerable portion of the space now occupied by the western extremity of the town.*' But he complained also that '*those who obtained concessions in the northern division have not exhibited the same zealous exertion, and to their negligence, in great measure, is to be attributed the existence of swamps in that part of the town.*' The swamps were not only inconvenient but also a threat to public health. Some 4000 people utilized the Castries River for drinking, washing and sewerage. '*The river ... from enjoying the privilege of traversing the 'capital', is converted into a noxious swamp. Not only is the upper portion of it used as a general washing place by all classes of the community, but the river itself, at the back of the streets, is established by law as a reservoir for every description of filth.*' Malaria and yellow fever, in particular, were serious concerns and in July 1839 and August 1842, epidemics of yellow fever killed thirteen and nineteen people respectively.[313] Smallpox, introduced in October 1848, increased mortality as well and Breen argued that only further draining of the swamps could improve the insalubrious climate of Castries. '*Nothing ... but the extension of the town to the base of the surrounding hills, from Sans Souci to the Four à Chaux, will effectually eradicate the evil.*'[314]

Government employed two town wardens but the '*filthy state of the streets*' bore testament to the difficulties involved. According to Breen, this was in part due to the absence of a clear chain of command at all levels of Government, with the result that the inspector of police, his three sergeants and twenty officers constantly tread on each other's toes. Many other things were not properly regulated either: the size or weight of bread; the cemeteries (one of which was located to windward of the town) and the locations where butchers slaughtered animals. Another thorn in Breen's side was the fact that the fire engines were left to '*rust and rot*'.

Complaints aside, though, Breen was proud of his hometown and its many recent modifications. In the centre of the town lay the *Place d'Armes* (later renamed Columbus Square and now Derek Walcott Square). It was on Governor Dudley Hill's orders that, in the 1830s, ornamental trees were planted at the *Place d'Armes*, the old court house was knocked down ('*an eye-sore that formerly stood in its centre*') and the market was moved to '*its present advantageous and more suitable position at the north-west corner of the wharf.*' Hill had also rationalized the public offices which used to be '*scattered through the town, each functionary being permitted to keep his office at his private residence.*' In 1835, all Government offices were brought together under one roof '*in Mr Muter's extensive premises in Mongiraud-street. ... The ground-floor is appropriated to the offices of Colonial Treasurer, Attorney-General, Solicitor-General, Registrar of the Courts, and Provost Marshal; and the upper story is occupied by the Court House, the Council Chamber, and the Secretary's Office.'*

The Government Office was damaged in the earthquake of 11 January 1839 but eventually rebuilt. On the eastern side of the *Place d'Armes* stood - and still stands - the Catholic church. In 1844, this was *'a substantial stone structure ... capable of containing eight hundred persons.'* After the foundations were laid out and the walls erected, *'the span of the building was found too great for any description of roof that could be devised. Sorely did this puzzle the ingenuity of the St Lucia architects, and many were the schemes proposed and rejected, until at length recourse was had to a carpenter from Barbados, under whose directions the present roof was planned and put up. It is a most complex affair - knit together in a curious fashion, and supported by eighteen pillars, which serve the double purpose of solidity and ornament.'*

Construction of the church was started around 1827 but petered out due to lack of funds. Abbé Florent Chevalier recommenced the works and, being from a wealthy family, personally guaranteed loans to be paid back from pew rents. On 27 January 1834, the corner stone was laid. The walls were completed a year later and after the problem with the roof was resolved, the Catholic church of Castries was blessed and dedicated on 12 May 1836. It was initially dedicated to *'Saint Florent, who was Bishop of Strasbourg in the seventh century'* in compliment to Fr Chevalier but was re-dedicated in 1855 to the Immaculate Conception.[315] Until the construction of this church, Castries had relied on temporary parish priests and visiting priests who had rented common buildings to say Mass. Not far from the Catholic church, across the river, stood the Royal Gaol: a large stone two-storey building that was finished in 1827. *'It is well ventilated, is surrounded with a strong wall, and provided with a residence for the Gaoler, apart from the inmates. There is a surgeon attached to the establishment, who visits the prisoners every day. This Gaol is one of the best in the West Indies.'*[316]

Another new addition was the Anglican church, which was built on church property known as Glebe Lands donated by the widow Marie Rosalie Feningre. The first stone was laid in 1830 by Colonel Farquharson and the church was finished two years later, by which time it could accommodate 200 people. In 1833, lightning damaged the steeple and ten years later, on 28 May 1843, the Bishop of Barbados christened the building in the name of the Holy Trinity. He also consecrated the adjacent cemetery. With additions made in 1894 (including a new sanctuary) Holy Trinity Church is now the oldest unaltered church in St Lucia.[317] In 1844, the building stood on high ground, offering a grand view of the town to one side, but overlooking swampy land to the other. Getting to the Anglican church from town required a strenuous walk over sloping ground (now the Chaussée Road and the extension of

Trinity Church Lane): an exercise which forced one to '*inhale more of the poison of miasma from the surrounding atmosphere, than of the spirit of God's holy word.*'

Tongue firmly in cheek, Breen commented that '*If Colonel Farquharson had been commissioned to devise the best means of checking the growth of Protestantism in St Lucia, he could not have succeeded more effectually, than by erecting the church in the heart of a swamp.*' Matters did not improve when, in 1834, Anglicans began to bury their dead separate from the Catholics in a cemetery just four yards away from their church.[318]

Infinitely better chosen, in Breen's eyes, was the location of the '*asylum for the destitute poor*'. When Government became responsible for care of the destitute poor and ill (after Emancipation), they acquired 90 acres of land and an assortment of buildings at Vieille Ville Estate. '*There are several minor buildings and offices attached, besides a lime-kiln, an alley of cocoa-nut trees, and an extensive tract of pasture ground. This delightful little spot, the favourite resort of maroon parties, commands an interesting view of the town, the harbour and the surrounding hills.*'

Across the harbour from Vieille Ville lay Government House, at the time commonly known as the Pavillion. Although Breen described it as '*a spacious wooden structure, tastefully laid out, and fitted up in a style of elegance worthy the representative of the Sovereign*', in truth, he was more enamoured with the view than the building. It was located on the western side of Morne Fortuné and today, there is a popular tourist stop just below Government House in honour of the site's glorious panoramic views. One early morning in 1844, '*an hour or two after sunrise*', Breen rode to the Pavillion and witnessed the following picturesque scene.

> *Below lies the bay of Castries ... - the wide-spread town with its shingled houses glittering in the sun - the quay skirted with vessels of every size - then Vieille Ville and the Vigie, clothed in undying verdure, as they jut into the sea - farther on the coast indented by a succession of lovely little bays - on the right several eminences topped with gardens and negro huts - in the distance Pigeon Island - and straight across the channel, as far as the eye can reach, the gray cliffs and woody mountains of Martinique. The prospect is bounded on the left by a bright expanse of ocean, and on the right by a curtain of 'mornes' fantastically drawn up before the rising sun.*

Elegant though it might look, Government House had a reputation for being ferociously unhealthy. '*During a period of little more than four years, from November 1829 to January 1834,*' wrote Breen

> *... no less than four Governors died at the Pavillion: Stewart, Mackie, Mallet and Farquharson. Farquharson himself, in an eccentric mood, once told the Bishop of the diocese, who lingered after dinner, waiting to be*

invited to stay over: 'My lord, perhaps this is the first time you have visited Government House: come with me and I'll show you the apartments. I suppose your Lordship has heard of the insalubrity of this place: every room in the house has already witnessed the death of some Governor; but none of them has had the honour of killing a Bishop: so, my Lord, you have only to make your selection; I leave you to the 'embarras du choix'.

The Bishop opted for a late ride back to town instead.

Not far from Government House, 800 feet tall and boasting commanding views of Castries to the north and Cul de Sac to the south, stood Morne Fortuné: '*clean, comfortable, English, with neat cottages, smiling flower gardens, ever-green fences, smooth grass plots and gravel walks*' even if recently '*sadly neglected.*' Over the course of some two centuries of intensive military action, this strategic mountain ridge had become '*studded with fastnesses and fortifications, as well as barracks and buildings of every description for the accommodation of the troops, the artillery and engineer departments, and the Ordnance Store-keeper. The barracks are a cluster of brick buildings of one story, situated within Fort Charlotte, and capable of receiving 240 men.*' The officers lived in the '*iron barracks*'. In 1844, there were just twenty officers and 231 rank and file left to defend St Lucia - all of them whites - with 800 working arms at their disposal. The St Lucia militia had been disbanded in February of 1839 and there were no more native troops.

Roads and infrastructure

In 1844, St Lucia had three principal roads and one minor one. The first extended from Castries to Soufrière along the west coast and from there on to Vieux Fort, covering a total distance of 60 miles and taking in '*Morne Fortune, Roseau, Soufrière and the Etangs.*' The second road ran 45 miles from Castries across '*the Trace, the Barabara and the Bamboos*' to Dennery on the east coast and south to Micoud and Vieux Fort, where it met up with the west coast road. In its totality, this round-the-island road was known as the *Chémin Royal.*

The third road was nine miles long and ran from Castries to the village of Gros Islet, along the north-west of the island. A fourth, minor road diverged from the Castries-Gros Islet road at Choc, turning east, crossing the northern tip of the island over the steep hill at Paix Bouche and on to the Marquis and Grande Anse Estates from there.

In 1839, construction of a fifth road was started which was to cut across the island's mountainous spine from Soufrière on the west coast to somewhere near Micoud on the east coast. The project was discontinued in 1841 after two-thirds of the budget of £150 had been spent and it was realised that another £600 would be required to finish it.[319] Although it was never completed, oral history confirms that as late as the 1960s, farming families habitually cut from east to west across the island on foot or with donkeys, carrying goods such as farine to the market in Soufrière where they fetched higher prices.

In Breen's days, travelling from Castries to Morne Fortuné was no problem: '*Even the most timid and delicate females daily ride up and down, without the slightest apprehension of danger.*'[320] Beyond Morne Fortuné, however, towards Grand Cul de Sac and Roseau, the road quickly deteriorated and bridges were made of '*loose hurdles covered over with clay*'. Breen recalled a trip in September 1841, when he and some companions had ridden on horseback from William Muter's estate in Roseau to Anse Galet Estate, several miles further south along the west coast. On their return that same night, following a minor shower of rain, Ravine Rouge had become impassable. With Muter's cottage in Roseau in sight, they had had no choice but to turn back to Anse Galet. On their second attempt, the following morning, the '*architects of the valley*' were just putting the last smears of clay on the new Ravine Rouge bridge.

South of Roseau, the west coast road was actually the best bridle road in the island, designed to be travelled on foot or horseback and built in 1786 by Baron de Laborie. '*A considerable portion of it is scraped from the solid rock ... The actual distance from Castries to Soufrière is no more than fifteen miles in a direct line; but the length of road ... may be computed at thirty-five miles, owing to its interminable windings and a continuous alternation of ravine and promontory, forming a sort of horizontal zig-zag along the coast.*

Nothing more is said about the road from Soufrière to Vieux Fort, except that it existed. Alternatively, one could travel from Castries to Dennery, Micoud and Vieux Fort along the east coast. Breen's fascinating description of this trip in 1844 stands in stark contrast to the modern-day 25-minute scenic but essentially easy drive from Castries to Dennery. In 1844, the road to Dennery was called the *Trace*. From Castries one rode up to Morne Fortuné and across the central mountain chain to Mr Guesneau's estate, which lay on top of a bare hill. There were miles of uninterrupted views '*of hills and valleys, mornes and ravines, covered with umbrageous forest trees and interspersed with cane fields, coffee bushes, and gardens in endless variety. The coup d'oeuil is at once picturesque and sublime.*'

Here the *Trace* started: running along the summit of the Barre de l'Isle mountain range, '*abruptly winding up and down through a labyrinth of brushwood and broken trees. The ridge in many places is so narrow as not to admit of two persons riding abreast; and the passage or track is extremely dangerous, being bounded on either side by tremendous and unfathomable precipices.*' During the rainy season, the Barre de l'Isle was shrouded in clouds, making for a '*wild and sombre*' scene of rock, tree roots and mist. But the real breath-taker, said Breen, was the descent from the summit of *Morne Barabara* to the valley of Mabouya. '*Here, while the traveller is panting for breath, he contemplates beneath him a declivity, 2000 feet in depth, and all the way down a perpendicular track, shaped into a corkscrew by the inequalities of the ground. As he proceeds his headlong course, hanging over the horse's neck, both man and horse appear suspended from the side of the precipice, as if supported by some invisible agency.'*

Serious accidents were rare despite the obvious dangers - or perhaps because of them. '*Some persons never dismount; others never do otherwise: this may depend upon the state or strength of a man's nerves. After a heavy fall of rain the earth becomes detached and slippery, and the danger is truly appalling. But in general it is much safer and less fatiguing to ride the whole way down than to lead your horse.*'

What to a stranger might seem '*totally impracticable, is daily accomplished with spirit and agility by numerous cavaliers and pedestrians.*' There simply was no alternative, and the local Creole horses, hardy and tenacious, were masters at negotiating the *Trace.*

The hazardous descent was richly rewarded by '*the beautiful prospect unfolded to his view in the rich, luxuriant valley of Mabouya.*' For miles, the Dennery River could be seen meandering to the Atlantic Ocean, its banks adorned with bamboo, fifty feet tall and each clump about seventy reeds thick. '*These clusters are thrown together in the most fantastic forms, having their tops so thickly interwoven as to exclude the rays of the sun, whilst admitting a sufficiency of light and air. The space between their base is formed into compartments of every size and shape, opening into each other through doors and gateways, arcades, arches and porticoes; and the ground, or rather floor, is free from vegetation, or lightly strewed with the small yellow leaf of the reed.*'

Breen considered it a natural curiosity surpassed only by the Soufrière volcano, '*while the stillness and solitude of the spot, unbroken save by the soothing murmur of the pebbled stream, point to it as the chief attraction for the lovers of pic-nic and maroon parties.*' The last 25 miles down the east coast were an unremarkable '*uphill, down dale*' stretch that ended in three miles of beautiful road between Aupicon and Vieux Fort (known as Malgrétoute Road), the only road in St Lucia suitable for carriages.

Considering the strain of travelling over land, it is not surprising that most transport in the nineteenth century was by sea. The east coast with its shoals, cliffs and onshore wind made coastal boating dangerous but the leeward side was well-suited to the five-oared boats that plied the waters between Castries and Soufrière. Weather permitting, a dozen *pirogues* belonging to the town of Soufrière were engaged in this business six days per week.

> *Sails are used during the voyage* [from Castries] *to Soufriere, which is generally performed in three hours and a half - the pirogue starting in the afternoon and reaching the entrance of the bay about sun-set. Passing along the coast you are presented with a succession of cliffs and coves, producing*

> *a corresponding alternation of calms and currents of air. Strong gusts of wind rush down through the valleys with such violence, as to require a constant look out on the part of the boatmen, who are often compelled to throw the whole of their weight on the starboard side to keep the pirogue steady.*

The vistas were lovely and the atmosphere dream-like: '*nor is there wanting either the silent serenity of the evening breeze, or the softening sadness of the creole boat-song, to breathe a halo over the solemn scene.*' The return trip could not be sailed and so was a lot harder on the boatmen. '*It takes five hours of hard rowing to accomplish the trip from Soufrière to Castries, and in order to avoid the risk of being carried adrift by the currents, the pirogue must be steered close to the shore.*' At Grand Caille, about a mile from Soufrière Bay, more than one boat had capsized and '*such is the feeling of awe by which the pirogue-men are impressed ... that they have caused an image of the Virgin Mary to be placed on the summit of the cliff, where it overhangs the dangerous shoal.*' Pirogues also travelled from Soufrière to Vieux Fort - but less regularly - and the trip was infamous for the perilous passage at *Balambouche*, where '*the sea, at a considerable distance from the land, rises up into mountains of foam, which succeed each other with great force and rapidity. The slightest contact with them is invariably attended with disastrous results; and the presence of mind, courage, adroitness, and physical force of the boatmen are put in requisition, to effect a passage between two breakers, without touching the one or being overtaken by the other.*'

Soufrière boatmen not only enabled travel along the west coast of St Lucia but also acquired regional reputations in the inter-island seafaring business.

The face of Soufrière

In Breen's day, St Lucia counted eleven parishes - Castries, Anse la Raye, Gros Islet, Dauphin, Soufrière, Choiseul, Vieux Fort, Laborie, Micoud, Praslin and Dennery - and each parish had a town or village by that name situated near the sea. But the majority of people lived scattered around the out districts: near plantations or on land they rented or owned. '*The villages are remarkable for nothing save their lonely little churches and deserted streets,*' wrote Breen. '*They are chiefly inhabited by females of retired habits, fishermen and other idlers of the male sex, and the infirm of both sexes and of all ages.*'

In 1844, the only towns with considerable permanent populations were Castries and Soufrière. Soufrière had been formally established in 1746 by the French as an agricultural settlement and military outpost. Land was fertile and the harbour calm and easily protected from the north and south. A town plan was laid out on flat land south of the Soufrière River, facing the bay. A grid of four by three blocks along the waterfront (with an open space in the centre to provide a town square for soldiers to parade in) created relatively narrow streets and small house lots. Many of the houses in town were two stories high, with overhanging balconies which cast shade onto the narrow streets while at the same time protecting pedestrians from the frequent showers of rain.[321] This original grid and the elaborate fretwork and diverse roof styles of the houses continue to lend Soufrière a uniquely picturesque character up to this day.

A century later, Soufrière contained 220 houses and had a population of 1500 souls. The people were generally healthy and '*there are several persons, chiefly females, both in town and on the estates, upwards of eighty years of age, pursuing their daily avocations*', wrote Breen.[322] '*The streets are badly paved, but there is more attention shown to cleanliness than in Castries.*' Over time, the town expanded eastwards. A Catholic Church was built on the east side of the square: '*a very pretty church, recently somewhat enlarged, but still too small for the wants of the population. Its steeple of cut stone, erected at the expense of the labourers of the district, was thrown down by the earthquake of 11th January 1839, and a neatly painted wooden spire now occupies its place.*' An Anglican Church and hospital were added in 1846, on a hill just south of the original grid. Soufrière town continued to grow, maintaining its tradition of wooden fretwork houses and narrow streets until 1959, when a fire destroyed half of it. The area north of the square was eventually rebuilt with masonry buildings and, in recent years, some large multi-storey concrete structures have also been added to the centre. Nevertheless, the south-side of Soufrière town continues to present a quaintly historical face.

Looking down on Soufrière town from a northern hill (perhaps Colombette or la Haut), Breen sketched a picture of '*gardens of flowers and fruit-trees ... overtopped by the cocoa-nut and the palm in full vigour and luxuriance.*' The landscape was like '*an extensive amphitheatre, encircled by steep, cloud-capped hills, and laid out into cane-fields of vivid green. And the whole is studded with the pretty little villas of the different proprietors, and their characteristic accompaniment of negro huts.*' At the time, Soufrière contained most of St Lucia's coffee plantations and they were of '*surpassing magnificence*'. In 1836, the presence of the sulphur springs attracted a small sulphur mining operation (run by business partners Bennett and Wood of Antigua) but the enterprise was quickly killed off when the Legislative Council imposed an export tax of sixteen shillings per ton.[323]

Breen did not write about any other villages in the south or east, unfortunately, but he did reflect on the general state of the island. Whilst cognizant of the problems facing the sugar industry, he believed that sugar would continue to dominate the landscape in the future. He compared the number of sugar estates per district in 1789 and 1843 and recorded an increase from 43 to 81, with twenty of those located around Soufrière, ten in the Quarter of Vieux Fort and nine each in the Castries and Gros Islet districts.[324] In 1843, sugar estates were larger than in 1789 and the mills had vastly improved as well. '*In 1789 the* matériel *of the sugar estates consisted of thirty-two water-mills, eighteen cattle-mills, and three windmills: now it comprises fifty-one water-mills, twenty-six cattle-mills, and six windmills, besides fourteen steam-engines, an improvement totally unknown at the period referred to.*'[325]

Free people: new hamlets and growing villages

District magistrates' reports of the 1840s complement Breen's sketch and show that around the island, freed labourers were establishing new communities. Not only was land ownership an important goal: so was having a private home. Just three years after Emancipation, by September 1841, some 60 newly freed labourers in the Soufrière/Choiseul area already owned their own houses and three new hamlets had arisen.

> *First, Mr Tisnés, owner of the Morne Belair estate, an abandoned coffee property, in the Fond St Jacques, has leased out this property in lots, varying from 3 acres to 10; and there are at present about 26 houses seated in the midst of their grounds, which are generally well cultivated in provisions and young coffee, where, before emancipation, scarcely a dwelling was to be seen. Secondly, the Hon. H. King has in the same way leased out a long-abandoned coffee estate, called St Jour; 22 men, 21 women, and 24 children are now living in houses built by themselves on this property, and seem to enjoy peace and plenty. The third hamlet which has newly sprung up is situated on the Hermitage estate ... About a dozen families are here established.*[326]

A few years later, a fourth new village was established not far from St Jour: '*This settlement, composed of about 40 houses, surrounded with luxuriant gardens, producing an abundance of every description of edibles, has been named 'Victoria'; a compliment which, according to their manner of perceiving things, has been conceived to be due by them to Her Most Gracious Majesty.*' Once their homes and provision gardens were established '*for the employment of their youths and women*', the working men of Victoria returned to '*the profitable employ of the sugar estates*', using their wages to enhance their new homes. The same trend continued elsewhere and in 1897 it was reported that wherever lands accessible by public road were put up for sale, '*they have been readily purchased - witness the 'Ravine Claire', the 'Diamond', the 'Pearl' and the 'Fond St Jacques' or 'Esperance' Estates ... all of which have been parcelled out since the failure of sugar, and sold at 20£ a carrée.*' In 1871, the village of Canaries came into existence, with a grand total population of 298 souls. Until then, squatters had occupied the area.[327]

Developments were slightly different in Vieux Fort and Laborie. The district magistrate here noticed in 1844 that '*several amongst the labourers have built small houses in the villages, but still continue to reside permanently on the Estate, where they work. These town houses are intended for the use of their families, when occasion calls them to the village either for business or devotion.*'[328] Thus, many houses in Laborie and Vieux Fort town were vacant during the week and used only on Saturdays (market days), Sundays and holidays. Others were occupied by '*an aged mother or a wife with a numerous family*' while the working son or husband visited on weekends, as likely as not riding into town on his own horse. It was also a way of allowing children to attend school in town or to have them apprenticed to artisans (cabinet makers, shoemakers, tailors, and so on) and prepare them for a future independent of agricultural wage labour. Several families living in town owned cattle but these were '*sent to graze on the Lands of their Country-friends, upon condition of the produce, both in calves and milk, being divided between the Owner & the Grazier.*' This may be seen as an adaptation of the métayage system.

Along the east coast, villages boomed in the years following Emancipation. '*The Towns of Micoud and Dennery, which ... were composed of nothing better than a rude ... mass of huts, serving chiefly as a temporary refuge and shelter to the fishermen of the Quarter, have now encreased in population to three times its former number, and though the houses, it is true, continue to be* [thatched] *yet order, cleanliness, and comfort characterize the whole*', wrote the stipendiary magistrate in August of 1843.

Around 1885, the Desruisseaux Estate went out of the sugar business and immediately became the site of a settlement '*of some 40 cottages and gardens. The squatters maintain a Roman Catholic school, at which there is an attendance of about 50 children.*' Despite the fact that the public byway to Desruisseaux had been abandoned by the Government and the highway passed '*through barren land*' along the coast, '*the Micoud Church gathers, on feast days, about 3000 members.*'[329] By the end of the nineteenth century, the Colonial Office recommended that the Government construct and maintain more byways and that abandoned estates be subdivided and sold off as a whole, to promote concentrated settlements rather than isolated squatter households.

In the Gros Islet and Dauphin districts, labourers similarly established themselves on freehold and leasehold land, growing provisions and some sugar cane. In 1845, there were '*not less than 40 small establishments of this kind*', at least ten of them miniature *sucréries* where peasants used small wooden hand mills or '*an ingenious contrivance, forming a sort of lever attached to some strong tree,* [to] *squeeze out the juice of their canes, which they boil down to a coarse syrup, and for which they find a ready sale in the town'*[330] - rather than take their canes to a large estate for processing. Home-made presses were also in use in the Vieux Fort and Laborie districts.

In conclusion, from the 1840s onwards, existing seaside villages expanded and new hamlets sprung up inland. Labourers aimed for independence in land and home ownership but were not averse to combining various income-earning strategies. Within rural households, women and children grew provision gardens and tended animals, while their husbands and fathers went out to work for wages. Some also grew sugar cane on rented, freehold or métayage land, contributing their crop to a large estate or processing it in home-made mills and selling the sugar in the local market. Other households commuted from the out districts to town on weekends or lived in town permanently while the main wage earner joined them on weekends.

Towns and shops

The seaside towns and villages soon developed into commercial centres with permanent stores to complement the Saturday market. While most estates had shops for their workers, prices were high and planters often tried to indebt workers to secure their future labour. Travelling saleswomen (*hucksters* or *marchands*) travelled from plantation to plantation, '*with trays on their heads, containing Madras headkerchiefs, prints, and so forth, which they retail at an enormous rate of profit.*' Most labourers preferred to carry their wages and some items of value (such as poultry and provisions) to town. '*He goes on the Saturday morning loaded with plantains, yam and other production of his garden, and returns in the evening with his purchase.*' Trade was brisk. Castries had just half a dozen '*true merchants in the English sense*'. '*They are a colony of shopkeepers*', wrote Breen. '*Every second house in Castries displays a shop of some description, or rather a nondescript character, crammed with every imaginable ware, from a pipe to a prayer-book. Even the most respectable ladies and the wives of the wealthiest merchants deem it not derogatory to have a shop and hawk goods about the streets.*'[331] Anse la Raye, Soufrière, Choiseul, Laborie, Vieux Fort, Micoud, Dennery and Gros Islet also had 'house-shops' in abundance. Elderly women bought left-over wares from the Saturday market cheaply and sold them from their balconies during the week. In 1841, Soufrière contained 228 houses, '*and nearly every third house is a shop, where something or other is sold. Six or seven are respectable enough to merit the name of "stores" where the usual assortment of a West India store can readily be obtained*', including '*cured provisions and dry goods*': salted beef, pork, mackerel, cod and smoked herring as well as lard, butter, oil, rice and tea. Cured goods were popular to the point where farmers sent their poultry and pigs to the market and used the money to buy salted wares instead.[332] Fresh meat was usually reserved for feast days.

Building styles: trash huts and wooden houses

The new hamlets and expanding villages of St Lucia basically knew three styles of dwelling house: bamboo or *trash huts*, wooden houses, and stone or brick buildings. Trash huts were used by '*the poorest class of natives who live in the bush*', wrote J.T. Rae, a Scotsman who published *Building in St Lucia* in 1898:

> *These are merely one-roomed hovels, about 16 feet by 8 feet ... The framework is made of wood cut from the nearest plantation, roughly squared and fastened together with wooden pins. The walls are constructed of horizontal strips of split bamboo, between which the blades of cocoanut leaves are vertically interlaced. The roof is of steep pitch, hipped at both ends, and thickly thatched with the 'trashed' or stripped ribbon-like tops of sugar-cane; the floor is of bare earth, and square apertures take the place of windows.*[333]

In villages and towns, most people lived in wooden houses rather than trash huts. In Castries, a bye-law ensured that wooden houses were at least 16 by 16 feet. They were usually semi-detached, with one or two rooms each. A narrow passage between houses led to a courtyard behind. Quite often, the rear of a house was sub-let, resulting in '*"overcrowding in unsanitary areas", that bugbear of medical officers of health.*' The houses' frames were built from pitch pine

> *... covered with weather boarding; the floors are of wood, while the roofs are also hipped at both ends and covered with shingles, and a bell-cast invariably given to the eaves aesthetically satisfies the eye. Split bamboos not infrequently form a substitute for eaves-gutters, and walls are often patched up with the sides of old tin cans - a ludicrous sight indeed. These 'packing-cases' as they are jeeringly termed, are of the most flimsy construction and it would not be difficult to knock a whole house down, especially as the structures rest on four or more big stones ... It is no uncommon spectacle to witness one of these negro huts being carried through the streets by less than a dozen men for the purpose of being deposited on* [a] *fresh site.*

Larger wooden houses of one and two stories were built by the middle and upper-classes. In 1898, the only stone buildings in St Lucia were public ones: the government offices, the Castries market, the Colonial Bank and the gaol, asylum, convent, hospital and churches.

An tan choléwa: the cholera epidemic of 1854

A short but sorrowful episode in St Lucia's history underscores the pitiful state of public health during the mid- and late nineteenth century. Cholera visited the Caribbean three times between 1833 and 1868, killing some 150 000 people.[334] Jamaica lost 40 000 inhabitants in 1851, and in 1854 cholera killed 20 000 people in Barbados, decimating the population. That same year, 3920 people died in St Kitts.[335] The Bahamas, Trinidad and the Eastern Caribbean islands were also affected and cholera claimed 12 per cent of Grenada's population.[336]

St Lucia proved not to be immune. On 12 June 1854, the first case of cholera was recorded, but the patient recovered. Hope flickered that an epidemic might be avoided but the end of July saw the first fatality and the floodgates on the scourge were opened. On 5 August 1854, the *Palladium* newspaper reported that cholera was '*back*' in Soufrière, where doctors were already exhausted, and that 42 deaths had occurred in Choiseul. Roseau had seen four deaths, Anse la Raye one and Canaries four. The newspaper estimated '*the mortality not to be less than 350, of which at least two-thirds have fallen in Soufriere.*' For a while, Laborie and Vieux Fort remained unaffected. People everywhere were trying to keep the disease at bay by frantically *lime-washing* (white-washing) their houses, which had proven an effective disinfectant against yellow fever. But what Beverley Steele wrote about the cholera epidemic in Grenada most likely held true for St Lucia as well: '*it was impossible to eradicate in such a short time the longstanding habits of neglecting sanitation measures* ... [and] *the abysmal ignorance of all concerned. For example, people carefully whitewashed their houses outside, leaving the more important insides untreated. Dwellings also needed to be well ventilated, free of dirt and other rubbish ... Stagnant pools of water near to where people lived needed to be drained.*'

Cholera is carried by bacteria which cause vomiting and profuse watery diarrhoea. Patients can lose a pint of liquid every hour and unless this is replaced by clean fluid and salts, death by dehydration will occur within hours or days. Patients drinking contaminated water reinforce the bacteria's toxic effect and stand no chance of recovery. Cholera manifests itself suddenly within one to five days after infection. The cholera strain of 1854 was called 'Asiatic cholera' as it was believed to have been brought to the Caribbean from South-East Asia (where it was endemic) by ships carrying indentured labourers. Once the drinking water was contaminated, little could be done to contain cholera and prevent it from spreading. '*European-trained physicians and surgeons were plentiful in the Caribbean, but their capacity to reduce mortality levels was limited. Public health was little understood. Epidemics were common, cholera being the most devastating,*' Engerman and Higman wrote.[337] Steele added to this: '*The lack of modern medicine, the reliance on folk remedies, and the reluctance to be treated, all contributed to the spread of the disease.*'[338]

True enough, the frenzied whitewashing of houses proved to be no panacea and just one week after cholera had returned to Soufrière, it started wreaking havoc in Vieux Fort as well. The *Palladium* of 12 August 1854 reported: '*The disease has commenced its ravages with great violence at Vieuxfort.*' Within one week, 30 deaths occurred (including a family with three children) and 300 were dead before the situation abated. Other villages were also hit. Micoud recorded three deaths and Gros Islet two. At Roseau, inhabitants fled the valley. The total death toll by then was estimated at 600 and that figure doubled in the next three weeks, after which the disease mercifully began its slow decline. On 2 September 1854, the *Palladium* recorded an overall death toll of 1280: Gros Islet 54; Union and Choc Estates 43; Castries (including gaol and asylum) 156; Soufrière 470; Roseau 34; Anse La Raye 41; Laborie 68; Vieux Fort 300; Micoud 72; houses near the public road 15; Military 27.

The last days of August saw no further deaths in Vieux Fort but the south was still reeling from the blows. Laborie, which had just 250 inhabitants, had suffered a devastating 68 deaths: more than one-quarter of its population. Victims from Laborie and Vieux Fort were buried in a make-shift cemetery on the cliffs at Black Bay: an area still today referred to as *senmityè choléwa* (cholera cemetery) and avoided at night time (when it is said that strange noises can be heard and fires are seen burning without leaving a trace). Balembouche Estate reportedly had its own cholera cemetery.[339] In Castries, a cholera cemetery was created at Vieille Ville. After three prisoners died in the town's gaol, the remainder (about 200) were transferred to Vieille Ville, where they were given the task of burying the town's dead. They were allocated double rations of food and '*a measure of spirits*' to help them cope with the dreadful task. Although some of them fell ill, no more prisoners died.[340]

For four interminable months, from late July until the end of November 1854, cholera swept through St Lucia, killing an average of 300 people per month. Although the precise death toll is not known, the disease claimed at least 1400 lives, possibly more, out of a total population of approximately 25 000 (roughly 5.5 per cent, or one in every eighteen souls).[341] Even after November 1854, people continued to die of cholera but death lists kept by parish priests gradually shortened and cholera finally disappeared in or about March 1855.

The epidemic's psychological impact was profound. Father Jesse found that '*an extraordinary number of marriages took place that year in St Lucia doubtless through the fear of the Lord. At Castries there were 173 weddings, against the usual 35 or so; at Soufrière there were 175, against the usual 20 or so. The months of September and October that year saw 50 marriages each at Castries.*'[342] In all, the marriage rate jumped from 138 in 1853, to 906 in 1854. But Governor Power was wrong in his prediction (made in June 1855) that '*Concubinage, the master evil of St Lucia*' had been '*crushed*' by cholera, '*I trust for ever*'. The following year, 1855, the marriage rate dropped right back again to a moderate 167.[343]

Nevertheless, the expression *An tan choléwa* ('in the time of cholera') remained a household term for several generations and is still occasionally used by elderly St Lucians today, more than 155 years later. In 1936, 82 years after the epidemic, an editorial in *The Voice* newspaper lamented the fate of an old beggar roaming the streets of Castries, '*who gives his name as Louis Placide. He says he was born about six years before Cholera.*' The editorial went on to say: '*This epidemic ... made such a deep impression on the minds of the poor illiterates of those days that such-and-such an event "took place so many years before or after cholera"; or I or he was "so many years old," or was "so big at cholera time".*'[344]

It is no exaggeration to say that as a historical landmark, the cholera epidemic of 1854 defined St Lucian communal memory in a way few other historical events (with the exception of slavery) have done.

9

Identity, church and education

Just as the infrastructural landscape diversified after Emancipation, so too did the social landscape. With the yoke of slavery lifted, working class people gained the scope to create their own social identities. Autonomy from the large plantations was a prime concern, and if and when freed people performed estate work, they now did so of their own volition. Land and home ownership - even a thatched hut on squatted land - were equally crucial. But beyond economic independence, freed people also keenly explored new ways to express their creativity and individuality.

Academics have used the terms 'respectability' and 'reputation' to understand these social ambitions. It is said that West Indian women, as well as older men, generally aim to display their respectability while younger men are primarily concerned with showing off their reputations (for vitality, popularity, sexual prowess and so on). While they do not fully capture the social landscape, respectability and reputation do provide a useful backdrop on which to pin the richly coloured pieces of evidence which, taken together, tell the fascinating story of increasing social diversification in St Lucia after Emancipation.

Name-giving practices

Names are obvious markers of social identity. Preciously little is known about name-giving practices during slavery beyond the fact that people themselves had little influence over the process. In 1808, an Order in Council directed that slaves seized from foreign ships were to be given a random but English-sounding name if their African name was '*not sufficiently clear*' and were to be called by that name until sufficiently instructed in the Christian faith to be baptised. After that, their baptismal name was to be prefixed to the given name, which from then on acted as surname.[345] It is possible that this was common practice even before 1808 and it might help to explain the still widespread phenomenon of first names serving as surnames. Almost immediately after Emancipation, freed people began to invent new names for themselves, as Breen recorded:

Some have the sobriquets of Moncoq, Montout, Fanfan, Laguerre. Others have their names mollified by means of certain dulcet, endearing terminations: thus, Anne becomes Annzie, Catherine Catiche, Besson Bessonnette: whilst the greater number, dropping altogether the names given them at the baptismal font, have adopted others of more modern vogue. Jean Baptiste is supplanted by Nelson; François by Francis, Cyprien by Camille... M. Jean Marie Beaurégard considers Jean Marie too vulgar, and adopts the name of Alfred; and his friends consider Beaurégard too long, and omit it altogether in their dealings with him. By this process M. Jean Marie Beaurégard is metamorphosed into plain M. Alfred; and his wife ... goes by the style and title of Madame Alfred.[346]

It is possible that such liberal name-giving practices hide a deeper process of reinvention of identity, particularly a distancing from names reminiscent of slavery.[347] What we do know for a fact is that freed people took enormous pride in being able to use the respectful terms of address of 'monsieur', 'madame', 'gentleman', 'lady' and 'mademoiselle' for each other, and applied them with a persistence which baffled Breen - who obviously missed its social significance and mistook it for a linguistic eccentricity:

A striking peculiarity in the language of the English negroes is their constant application to each other of the terms 'lady' and 'gentleman'. Your friend's groom brings you a letter and waits for the answer. You have forgotten all about it, and presently your cook comes to you and says - 'Sir, the gentleman is waiting for the answer.' You notice a decrepit negress at your gate, and you ask your butler what she wants. He goes to the old woman and comes back saying - 'Sir, the lady is very poor, and begs you'll give her a shilling'.[348]

Freed people reportedly also displayed a distinct absence of servility in their body language. '*Unlike the European peasant, who seldom presents himself before a clean coat without a feeling of crawling obsequiousness and degradation, the St Lucia Negro is polite to a point; he can touch his hat to any one, but he will not uncover himself in the open air, even for the Governor of the Colony.*'[349]

In similar vein, Breen marvelled at the leisurely fashion in which a man strolled down the street in pursuit of his blown-off hat, rather than destroy his cool by breaking into a concerned trot.

Dress sense and entertainment

Such self-possession and panache was further exemplified in newly freed people's dress sense. It was said in 1842 that

> *... it would be difficult to find a labourer, who does not possess a trunk or press, abundantly garnished with coats, and pantaloons of superfine broad cloth ... As for the women, nothing can surpass the sumptuousness of their Dress, which generally consists of 'jupes' or petticoats, made up of the finest chintz, with richly worked cambric chemises shown from the neck, to the waist, and madrass headkerchiefs, all of the most radiant colours and most costly description.*[350]

The district magistrate of Micoud and Dennery, in similar tones of begrudging admiration, commented on the money spent on '*dress and show*', as he called it.

> *... perhaps in 99 cases out of 100 a female will be seen with none other than gold earrings, costing from 2£ to 3£ sterling; and 15s. to 20s. are commonly paid for a chemise, to be worn on some particular occasion, and the stuff always of the finest texture. ... A labourer must be idle or worthless, indeed, if he has not his coat, value about 3£, or at least a jacket of half the worth, with a hat of good quality, and it is seldom that either male or female is seen on Sundays or holidays, without their shoes and stockings and silk parasols, cotton ones being little in fashion among them.*

There were relatively few public occasions that called for dressing up, but public dances and story-telling were two of them. In 1836, a prohibition on the beating of drums in Castries was repealed and Governor Dudley wrote: '*I know of no amusement to which the negro of both sexes looks forward with more delight than that of dancing to the beating of the drum.*' In 1841, the magistrate of Soufrière and Choiseul added that frequently, dance parties '*do not break up until three or four days have been wasted ... Sometimes, on moonlight nights, a party will assemble at the door of their house, and will remain the whole of the night attentively listening to some wild narrative of African origin, which some few amongst them have the talent to relate.*' Of course, dancing and story-telling are avenues *par excellence* by which people can establish their reputations.

Religious devotion

Whilst drum dances undoubtedly remained popular, as an avenue for showing off one's dress and respectability they were soon overshadowed by church-going events. White Creole women had always enjoyed dressing up, wrote Breen, but black and coloured women took such '*flutter and frivolity*' to new heights. By 1844, women of all complexions and backgrounds had developed a '*rage for devotional practices*'[351] and in a town of 4000 people, Sunday mornings brought out hundreds of fashionably attired females to parade the streets of Castries.

It was a remarkable about-turn, especially considering that between 1825 and 1830, not one slave habitually attended Mass in Castries or Soufrière[352] and even in 1837, the Governor found the apprenticed labourers '*in a perfect state of ignorance*' as far as '*religious or moral instruction*' was concerned. Yet just a few years later (in 1841) churches island-wide were full to overflowing with newly freed people. In Castries and Anse la Raye, it was said that: '*The chief ambition of the labouring population now is to dress themselves and their children, and conduct themselves in a manner that would even surpass our European peasantry; on Sundays and fête days the church is actually crowded with these persons, many of whom come a considerable distance from the country to attend the mass.*'

In Gros Islet and Dauphin, '*although the Church is spacious, and capable of affording accommodation for about a thousand persons, it seldom happens that there is sufficient room for all who attend.*' In Soufrière and Choiseul, too, worshippers were habitually forced to stand outside. In Laborie and Vieux Fort, 400 to 500 labourers attended Sunday Mass and they were '*particularly exact in their attendance on divine Service and the observance of all the religious obligations of their Church is on all occasions exemplary.*'

In Soufrière and Choiseul, once a year, the seats in Catholic churches were auctioned off publicly. The district magistrate expressed surprise when '*about 100 places were purchased by the newly freed, at prices varying from two to six dollars, mostly by women, who, I am sadly afraid, go to church principally to display their finery.*'

But it would be unjust to imply that freed people embraced Catholicism solely for the opportunity to showcase their clothes. They also duly subjected to religious instruction and rituals[353] and contributed very generously to the construction, extension and maintenance of church buildings and the priests' stipends. The Catholic church in Micoud, for instance, was largely built ('*both in money and labour*') by newly freed people and they even voluntarily maintained the curate there. In 1844, in Anse la Raye, the Roman Catholic church was '*rebuilt and fitted up for the purpose of Divine Worship, almost entirely at the expense of the labouring population, by voluntary contributions; and they have further subscribed funds to procure from France the usual pompous ornaments and sacred vases generally used in the Roman Catholic Churches.*'

Before 1838, the Catholic Church in St Lucia had served the white and free coloured populations to some extent but really played only a marginal role in the lives of slaves. Slaves were given Sundays off, presumably to attend Mass, but priests or chapels were rarely available. When St Lucia came permanently under English rule, in 1803, the unusual situation arose that while almost the entire population was Roman Catholic in name, those in authority were Anglicans. The divide was further accentuated by language: French and Kwéyòl being the languages of the Catholic Church and the working classes, whilst English acted as a mark of authority and Protestantism. The traditional planters class found itself somewhere in the middle, with French planters usually Catholic like their workers and most British planters Anglican.

The Catholic Church's presence in pre-Emancipation St Lucia was weak and inconsistent. Castries did not get a parish priest until 1812: a Franciscan by the name of Dom Sellent y Badia. He said Mass on the ground floor of a rented wooden building on Laborie Street while maintaining a presbytery upstairs: a situation that remained basically unaltered for the next 24 years. By 1820, St Lucia was administered as part of the Vicariate Apostolic of the West Indies but only three priests ministered in the island and Castries lingered on without a church building until 1834.[354] It was only with Emancipation that this situation of general indifference changed. It can be fairly stated that newly freed people's affiliation with the Catholic Church was immediate and absolute, and it was they who transformed St Lucia's lingering church into a network of vibrant parishes - for the specific purpose of their own social and spiritual enjoyment and benefit.

Flower societies: la Rose and la Marguerite

Hand in hand with the huge surge in interest in the Catholic Church after Emancipation, St Lucia also saw a revival of the *flower societies* of la Rose and la Marguerite. Like church-going, these provided a marvellous opportunity for dressing up, singing and entertainment under the mien of religious devotion. The once ailing flower societies were reportedly revived in 1839 '*with unusual éclat and solemnity*'[355] and their boisterous rivalry remained a dominant force in society until 1860, when both groups were excommunicated by the Catholic Church. While not putting a complete end to la Rose and la Marguerite, this did usher in a period of relative quiet.

Always the domain of the working people, flower societies are believed to have existed in the French Antilles since the earliest days of slavery (Breen spoke in particular of St Lucia, Dominica and Trinidad). Their first recorded mention in St Lucia was in a letter by a Mme Jeanne Le Vexier dated 15 September 1769, but their origins remain shrouded. Douglas Midgett posited that they were founded during slavery and Breen speculated that they had a political character: '*their occasional allusions to English and French, Republicans and Bonapartists would seem to confirm this impression.*' Austrian anthropologist Manfred Kremser believed the flower societies were originally charitable self-help organizations with roots in the Catholic Church, given that each society celebrates a patron saint's day.[356] Other researchers, however, believe the flower societies have African roots and that their association with the Catholic Church was merely a guise to render them more palatable to the

European masters. Karl Wernhart, for instance, has associated the la Rose and la Marguerite societies of St Lucia with sacred African kingdoms which, 900 years ago, existed across Africa from the Niger to the Nile and from Ethiopia to southern Congo and Rhodesia. In similar vein, Gerhard Kubik likens la Rose and la Marguerite to the *Congada* dance drama found in South Brazil which harks back to an old Congolese tradition. All of these groups share a hierarchically structured mock society with a king who has ambassadors, secretaries and other lower dignitaries at his service.[357]

Considering the similarities with such African traditions and the minimal influence exercised by the Catholic Church on slaves in St Lucia before Emancipation, it seems likely that the flower societies are indeed derivatives of an African concept that was carried across the Atlantic Ocean in slave ships, with Catholic elements added on later to legitimize the gatherings in the eyes of the colonizers. Patrick Anthony put it well when he described the flower festivals as '*rooted in the church, but ... outside the ambit of official church power.*'[358]

Either way, there can be no doubt that that la Rose and la Marguerite are, and always have been, 100 per cent folk organizations in the true sense of the word - 'belonging to the common people.' There was no island-wide organization and each group was autonomous at the local level.[359] Although the societies have gone through periods of repression and revival, surprisingly little of their essence has changed. Each flower society is still organized hierarchically, with a king and queen at the head, supported by lesser royalty and a range of pseudo-legal, military and professional personnel such as a governor-general, president, judge, magistrate, lawyer, sergeant, corporal, secretary, doctor, soldiers, ladies of parliament, policemen and women, nurses, flower girls and ordinary citizens.[360] In an 1819 source, the French terms were used: *Roi, Sénéchal, Procureur du Roi, Procureur Général,* and so on.

The two societies have rival patron saints: one celebrating the feast of St Rose de Lima (30 August) and the other that of Mary Marguerite of Alacoque (17 October).[361] Each society has an extensive body of traditional music which is performed once a year by the *shâtwèls*. The *shâtwèl* is a solo singer who sings the verses, while the other members sing the choruses. Instruments used may be '*any combination of banjo, acoustic guitar, cuatro, shak-shak (shaken rattles) or bâhâ, the last named, a long, hollow pipe played as a rhythm instrument. ... Drums are also used in some local societies, although apparently less often than in the past.*'[362]

During the eight weeks leading up to the feast day, members hold regular meetings (*séances*) '*at which old songs are revived, new compositions introduced, and money collected for the feast.*' Participants are fined small amounts of money by the police officers for perceived transgressions, as a means of raising funds. The meetings gradually increase in frequency until the final week, when seances are held nightly. '*On the day of the fête the society members, dressed in their best ... attend mass and, after a parade through the streets of the village, congregate at a meeting hall where they will spend the rest of the day. Drinks and food are consumed, speeches are given by prominent villagers, the king and queen address their loyal subjects, and once again the songs are aired.*'

Breen, describing the feast as he saw it celebrated in Castries in the 1840s, mentioned that the flower society members (all of them manual labourers or domestic servants in normal life) first visited their higher class friends, presenting them with gifts of flowers and cakes. On the day of the feast, the men dressed like European gentlemen and the women donned their jewellery, head dresses and *jupes*, looking '*bizarre yet brilliant, grotesque but gorgeous.*' Breen explicitly admired the clever musical and lyrical composition of the belairs (songs). The day ended, in Breen's book, with a *bamboula*: an outdoor ball.[363]

During slavery, the flower societies went through periods of growth and contraction. In January 1819, for instance, three free men of colour were fined and three slaves sentenced to nineteen lashes with the whip each for having organized a meeting in the name of '*Roses Marguerites*', as the *Procureur du Roi*'s verdict termed it. Governor Keane queried the verdict, saying he saw no harm in people dressing up in carnivalesque costumes and assuming pretend names and titles, but the *Procureur du Roi* defended his decision as being in the interest of public security. He stated that secret gatherings of slaves in past years had distracted them from work and could have dangerous consequences (undoubtedly, he had the recent Brigand Wars in mind). Sunday dances had been allowed until recently - but on express condition that they did not carry the title '*Roses Marguerites*' and that the colours of these societies (red and blue) would not be displayed. The slaves had promised to abide by this but, as the *Procureur* complained, instead of keeping their word, they had immediately gathered to select a king and other officers and invited participants to bring small sums of money for the benefit of the flower societies. The *Procureur du Roi* responded by having six men arrested and punished[364] and once again abolished all slave gatherings, including the Sunday dances. In short, the authorities' attitude towards the flower societies swayed between fear and indulgence, and periods of repression and tolerance varied accordingly.

After Emancipation, la Rose and la Marguerite bloomed. The labouring population was split into rival camps to the point where, in 1840, labourers from Anse Canot and Fond d'Or Estates resigned their employ and moved to the neighbouring Riche Fond Estate reportedly because the latter was a la Rose stronghold.[365] The societies were active year-round, not just on feast days, and between 1840 and 1860, it was the money raised by flower societies that built and extended Catholic churches island-wide. '*At Vieux Fort, the*

Roses helped to build the belfry, while the Marguerites had much to do with the addition of the side aisle to the church. In Micoud, the Marguerites also made significant contributions to the extension of the church between 1858 and 1860.'[366]

Despite their generous support, church authorities did not wholeheartedly embrace the flower societies. The reason for this was not a lack of devotional enthusiasm, but rather an overabundance thereof. In the 1840s and 1850s, la Rose and la Marguerite were so influential that everyone in society held allegiance to one group or the other, and rivalry was intense. More than once, the police had to intervene in order to resolve clashes between la Roses and la Marguerites. In August 1842, for instance, '*a dispute had arisen between the queen of the Roses and a coloured woman - a warm advocate for the Marguerites. During the altercation the parties came to blows, and the queen, being a strong, lusty woman, inflicted a pair of black eyes upon her antagonist.*'[367] The matter was brought before the Chief Justice who, in a court house '*crowded to suffocation by the friends and supporters of the accused*' wisely '*expressed his surprise that two such "respectable desmoiselles" should have so far forgotten what was due to themselves, as to have assaulted each other in the public streets.*'

The reference to 'respectability' restored peace and a feud was averted. However, a year earlier, a fight between rival members during which recourse was had '*to bludgeons, broken bottles, and other missiles*' had resulted in '*many broken heads and battered bones*'[368] and the town was nearly set on fire by flambeaus.[369] In 1840, la Marguerite members from Soufrière disturbed a la Rose meeting in Vieux Fort, and the violent riot which ensued was only '*checked by the Police, and order was with some difficulty restored.*'[370]

Such feuds were more than just a form of 'hooliganism' in support of one or another patron saint, they also reflected a difference in social outlook. The la Marguerites considered the la Roses common, garish and somewhat vulgar. Members of la Rose were said to enjoy '*movement and stimulation. They actually build their reputation by their spectacular performance in speech, playing, dancing, singing, or drinking.*' In the 1980s, Jocelyn Guilbault described the la Marguerites, by contrast, as '*socially reserved - practicing Catholics, and serious parents trying to give a solid and conventional education to their children. Many own small businesses or are spouses of regularly employed workers. They speak both Creole and English fluently. All can read and write. In general, the "La Marguerite" members can be said to belong to the middle class of St Lucian society.*'[371] At la Rose meetings (held on Saturdays), all sorts of spontaneous events could take place but in contrast, la Marguerite members sought to structure their meetings (held on Sundays) and preferred events to unfold more calmly.[372]

After twenty years of enthusiastic fêting in the name of la Rose and la Marguerite, mounting objection within the church spilled over. In 1860, the Apostolic Administrator of Port-of-Spain with jurisdiction over St Lucia, Monsignor Ethelridge, judged that the flower societies' '*extravagance, and ... the quarrelling and rioting engendered by them*'[373] had gone too far, and he excommunicated them both.[374]

Although la Rose and la Marguerite remained active, they could no longer closely associate their séances with the rituals of the church. This led to some curious spectacles. In June 1892, the parish priest of Soufrière was accused of damaging an English flag. He admitted to causing the damage but claimed that it had been a flag of the la Marguerites. '*I walked towards the banner of the Marguerite society ... and in order to make it the better understood by those around that they ought not to expose this flag during a fête so holy as that of Corpus Christi, I struck it one blow with the head of my umbrella. This single blow was sufficient to separate almost entirely two of the three bands which, sewn together, formed the banner.*'[375] Excommunication did not end the quarrelling. In 1865, it was said that larceny was increasing in Soufrière due to '*the resuscitation of the old negro societies of Roses and Marguerites under the novel appellations of Floridas and Dahlias.*'

The flower societies of la Rose and la Marguerite exist to this day, having gone through another folk revival in the 1970s. They no longer split the working class into rival camps, but their séances remain an exciting part of St Lucia's folk culture. Few St Lucians will not have heard of the late Dame Marie Selipha Descartes, better known as Sésenne, Queen of Culture, and one of the greatest la Rose chantwèls of the twentieth century. Dame Sessene passed away in August 2010 at the age of 96.

The flower societies provide a fine example of how the working people of St Lucia appropriated the Catholic faith (such as this had been introduced to them during slavery) and, drawing on their African roots, transformed it into something uniquely their own. As such, la Rose and la Marguerite have been hugely important channels for creativity, originality and assertion. Without doubt, their finest moments came in the decades immediately following Emancipation (1840-60) when newly freed people's urge for self-expression, identity-formation and social diversification was at its zenith.

Obeah

As interest in church and flower societies soared, witchcraft appears to have gone through an uncommonly active phase in St Lucia as well. While the Middle Passage did not wipe out African religious traditions, it cannot but have undermined their integrity and hierarchical working order. Even so, elements of non-Christian beliefs and practices persisted during slavery and, in fact, continue to exist to this day. For a brief period in the 1840s, malicious magical practices seem to have been more radical and more frequent than usual, but it is difficult to say exactly what role Emancipation played in this - if any. In any case, the magical universe formed an important part of people's worldview and any discussion of their social and spiritual world would be incomplete without an understanding of this aspect, which is commonly summed up with the term *obeah* or *kembois.*

It would be wrong to understand obeah as a comprehensive belief system with deities, a theology and doctrines of faith. The non-Christian beliefs that pervade(d) the consciousness and practices of St Lucian people do not offer an integrated explanation for the genesis of the world and all its natural and supernatural phenomena (*ontology*). Nor does it prescribe moral standards or offer recommendations for achieving a higher state of happiness in the after-life. Obeah is best loosely translated with the term 'magic': both black magic (witchcraft) and white or benevolent magic. Knowledge of bush medicine and poisonous plants plays an important role in obeah but essential is its concomitant magical quality, in the sense that it is believed that actions performed on one object bear an effect on another object that is not obviously connected to the first but is related to it by similarity (or analogy). The image of someone sticking needles into a doll in order to hurt the person represented by that figure is cartoonish but touches on the essence of magic and, by extension, obeah: causing an effect through analogous action, for better or for worse.[376]

Back in 1844, Breen said that peasants were 'addicted' to sorcery. '*This popular infatuation ... still prevails to an incredible extent amongst the uneducated classes.* 'Kembois' ... *does not always imply a direct intercourse with diabolical agents, nor indeed with any supernatural power; and its appliances are brought into play alike for beneficial and for evil purposes.*'[377]

Breen believed that Christianity would soon counteract it but he was wrong. Even after Christianity pervaded St Lucian society, obeah continued to play a central role in people's understanding and manipulation of their world. St Lucian priest and anthropologist Monsignor Patrick Anthony, who extensively studied the (ongoing) influence of African traditions on the mindsets of St Lucians of African descent[378] found that even as recently as 1998

> *... there are innumerable beliefs and practices shared by Catholics that reflect only marginal church influence, or no such influence at all. ...* [A]*lthough good is associated with God (Bondyé) and prayers (lapwiyè), there is a great fear of evil (mal) which is associated with wickedness, malevolent behavior, harmful spiritual forces and supernatural beings. These ... include jan gajé (witches), maji nwè (black magicians), lèspwi (spirits), bolom (small foetus-shaped being with amazing powers whose feet are turned backwards), ladjablès (a long-haired female with one human and one cow leg), and papa bwa (a forest spirit), to name a few. ...*

> *Besides the fear of supernatural beings ... there is the even greater dread of the wickedness of those who can use spiritual powers to harm others. ... In popular belief, there is none so powerful, and no tool as potent as obeah.*[379]

Obeahmen and -women, wrote Anthony, are believed to have the power to *'harm someone on your behalf, heal you of an illness, help you to be successful in business, foretell your future, and "see" things affecting your life which neither you nor others may be aware of.'*

The seer (*gadé*) or obeah practitioner is '*regarded as the principal source of wickedness and malevolence in the communities,* [and] *most tragedies or mishaps, especially personal ones, are attributed to the workings of obeah.'*

Obeah was criminalized in 1804 by Governor Brereton with an ordinance decreeing '*Slaves accused of poisoning, witchcraft, or sorcery, to be immediately arrested*' and tried by a *Civil Commissary*. A further ordinance in 1832 proclaimed that '*Practising Obeah or pretending to be Obeah People, or pretending to administer, or educe to be administered pounded Glass, or other deleterious substance or matter*' was punishable with 39 lashes of the whip or two months confinement (first and second offence) or criminal trial (third offence).[380]

Breen stated in 1844 that in earlier days, obeah had been used mostly for trivial matters but that lately, obeah-men had taken to the '*mutilation of male children and other revolting practices*'.[381] Indeed, the year 1841 had seen a disturbing case of alleged obeah which created much fear and controversy. A two-year-old boy left by his mother (a labourer) in the care of another woman who resided in a cottage in an uncultivated area of Grand Cul de Sac valley (between the Soucis and Pointe Estates) had wandered off and gone missing. Search parties could not recover the child but the following Sunday, a labourer found the boy's body in his plantain patch, half a mile from the cottage, in a state of advanced decomposition. The mother and a local magistrate were notified and, assuming the toddler had died of hunger and exposure, he was buried on the spot.

Three days later, however, a newly appointed coroner summoned a jury based on the fact that the child could not by himself have crossed the ravines between his nurse's house and the plantain patch. His body was disinterred and inspected by a doctor who reported that the boy's private parts had been cut off and his neck showed marks of strangulation. This finding was ridiculed by others, who believed the soft tissue had naturally decayed. They accused the jurors of being overly zealous in proclaiming wilful murder. Nevertheless, three men were arrested (including a neighbour of the nanny) on suspicion of murder for the alleged purpose of '*attempting to poison balls to fight a duel.*'[382] The charge was explained in the *Palladium* newspaper of 10 April 1841.

> *If a quarrel occurs, a duel must be fought - the principals immediately fly to the Obeahman, and ... procure a charmed ball, warranted never to miss its object, or get themselves immersed in a cauldron, and made invulnerable to pistol shot - and, in this 'hell-broth', the members of a murdered human being must be the chief ingredients. For this, about five years ago, Maitre Jacques committed a murder a few miles from this town - and for this again, an infant has recently been murdered in the Valley of Grand-Cul-de-Sac.*[383]

It was alleged that the nanny's neighbour, a man named Malalou, had worked together with one Servé Cornau to produce charmed bullets (balls) for a duel between two other men. Cornau was also accused of having disinterred bodies from a burial ground with the help of one Adelson. '*Their dwellings were searched, and in them were found phials of unaccountable decoctions, and oils, and rams' horns stuffed with we know not what.*'[384] Malalou and Cornau were arrested on the charge of '*having poisoned balls to fight a duel*' but were released a few days later when the authorities realized that actually, '*it was no crime to poison balls to be used in a duel.*' The newspaper report went on to say that: '*No less than four instances have occurred in different parts of the Island, during the last two or three months, of the mysterious disappearance of children. And it is, at least, generally believed, that they have been sacrificed to the occult purposes of the professors of obi.*' While suspicions were frequently voiced, obeah practices were by their nature '*secret and insidious*', making them difficult to prove, and hence few were ever convicted.

One man who did die on the gallows in an obeah conviction was actually believed to be innocent. But he held such faith in the protective powers of an obeah man that he declined to plead his innocence. Henry Breen recorded this unusual case,[385] which took place in 1841. A young woman by the name of Eucharisse had been murdered in her bed in Mabouya by a man named Aurelien Martelly. Martelly, with the help of an obeah man called Alphonse Guis, had convinced Eucharisse's landlord, Louis Elie, to let him enter Eucharisse's room so he could sexually assault her. In the struggle that ensued, Martelly ended up not only raping but also strangling and killing Eucharisse. The following day, blame fell on Elie the landlord but the obeah man assured him that no harm could come to him. On the strength of this promise, Elie forfeited to plead his innocence to the judge and jury. Although the jurors and everybody else in Mabouya knew that the real culprit was Martelly, '*such was the prevailing dread of sorcery ... that no one had the moral courage to come forward*' and so Elie was convicted. The '*big round tears*' glistening in his eyes on the day of his execution proved to Breen that '*all confidence in the protecting power of Kembois had now vanished, exhibiting to the gaze of the sympathising multitude nothing but the wretched victim of sorcery and superstition.'* But by it was too late and on 22 October 1842, Louis Elie was hanged.

By 1871, obeah was still so influential that Governor Des Voeux (1869-78) felt it necessary to draw up a new ordinance saying that the *'system of pretended sorcery and real intimidation called* [obeah] *is exceedingly prevalent in St Lucia. I doubt indeed whether there is any other English island, except perhaps Trinidad, where the fear of it is so general or where the belief in it exists among persons so high in the social scale.'*[386] Indeed, planters, too, occasionally accused each other of *'holding an interview with the devil.'* Des Voeux's ordinance contained detailed descriptions of 'obeah', 'obeah man' and 'instruments of obeah' as well as exact measures of punishment: six to twelve months prison with hard labour, whipping, solitary confinement and cutting of the hair. It was under this new piece of legislation that in early 1876 *'one of the most terrible obeah-men,'* Adolphe La Croix, was convicted and hanged. Governor Des Voeux later wrote:

> *One who had long been reputed to be a dangerous Obeahman was convicted before the Supreme Court on the clearest evidence of murdering a little child with the object of using the body for some of his abominable rites. The principal witnesses against him were his own children, examined separately; and the body of the victim was mutilated in a peculiar way, which was sworn to be the method employed for Obeah purposes. It came out subsequently, when after the man's death people were no longer afraid to speak out, that this wretch, Adolphe la Croix by name, had previously disposed of one of his own children in the same horrible manner. Further, it appeared that it was in the immediate neighbourhood of this man's house that a child had disappeared, for the discovery of whom I had some years before offered a large reward without success.*

Where a strictly logical approach to spirituality would ordain that Christianity and obeah (or any other non-Christian belief system for that matter) cannot be maintained side-by-side, practical experience shows that indeed, they very well can - and are. As long as the believers themselves do not perceive a contradiction, a contradiction simply does not exist. According to Patrick Anthony, the bottom-line is that St Lucians tend to be solution-oriented in their beliefs and will try 'remedies' from both systems until their quest is satisfied. In similar vein, bush medicine and modern medicine are used side-by-side as well.[387]

During the course of the twentieth century, a rise in literacy levels, better general education, Anglicization, influence of the mass media and the advent of strongly doctrinal Protestant denominations have conspired to somewhat reduce the influence of obeah in St Lucia, but it continues to be practised to some extent. There is usually a rise in (the mention of) obeah around election time but on any given day, even well-educated people may display irrational fear at apparently innocuous natural phenomena, such as toads. The old-time practice of sleeping with all doors and windows tightly shut is also said to have its roots in a fear of malignant spirit beings[388] and in every community, people can usually point out a (suspected) obeah man or woman. Magical characters such as *jan gajé, maji nwè, lèspwi, boloms, ladjablès* and *papa bwa* continue to populate the magical universe of St Lucia even in the twenty-first century.[389]

Social differentiation: founding education

Although educational advancement for the mass of the population remained marginal until well into the twentieth century, Emancipation brought the first schools to the island. In 1836, it could still be said that '*St Lucia has been more completely neglected, both by the government and people of England, than any other colony; and its black population is therefore more degraded and ignorant.*' Two Englishmen (Sturge and Harvey) who visited in December of that year were told by '*an enlightened and influential resident, that "not a ray of light has yet reached the island, from any of the religious or benevolent Societies of the mother country." Another gentleman assured us, that it has not received twenty pounds a year, for educational purposes from Government.*' Out of a labouring population of 14 000 people, no more than one hundred children attended school in 1836, yet many '*of the proprietors, we are assured, are ready to assist in furnishing suitable buildings for schools.*'[390]

True enough, in 1838, the Scotsman William Muter (a large planter, merchant and member of the Legislative Council and the Castries Anglican Vestry) sent an application to the trustees of the Lady Mico Trust in England, which held some £120 000 in funds to be used for the education of freed slaves' children in the British West Indies.[391] In 1836, Muter had started a school on his Roseau Estate: reportedly the only estate school in St Lucia at the time. '*The children are taught by a respectable colored man, who was formerly a carpenter on the plantation. There were about thirty present, from four to twelve years of age, who had been learning about eight months. Some of them read easy lessons of one and two syllables, and spell very correctly. Their pronunciation is extremely good, but we found they were ignorant of the meanings of many of the words.*'[392]

Muter promised to make further land available for schools and the Mico Trustees granted his request. The first Mico teacher arrived in St Lucia in May 1838 and in June, the first school opened its doors in Castries. Although all Mico schools were Protestant, they accepted children of different faiths. By September, a second Mico school was up and running at Roseau and a third one was started at Troumassée (not long-lived). In 1839, Mico schools opened in Gros Islet, Laborie and Vieux Fort. Meanwhile, Christine Lloyd-Alexander of the River Dorée Anglican Household Church approached the Mico trustees to establish a school '*to assist the poor Negro population on her estate*'[393], offering a schoolroom and free accommodation for the teacher.

Soufrière did not get a Mico school until August 1841 - possibly due to resistance from the Catholic population. By 1845, there were seven Mico schools in St Lucia. Although open to all faiths, bible study was compulsory and the Catholic clergy was concerned that the schools interfered with the religious upbringing of Catholic pupils. The Bishop of Trinidad asked the Colonial Secretary to have Catholic teachers appointed to the Mico schools, but the Mico trustees objected on the grounds that English-speaking Catholic teachers could not be found. They agreed, however, to instruct the Protestant teachers to be lenient in their approach to religious subjects. Nevertheless, several parish priests continued to oppose the Mico schools and in 1841, stipendiary magistrates island-wide reported that priests actively advised parents to withdraw their children from school.[394]

The Sisters of St Joseph of Cluny

In 1846, the parish priests of Castries invited the Sisters of St Joseph of Cluny to conduct schools in St Lucia. The sisters lacked numbers, but they started a small indigenous community known as the *Filles de Marie*. In June 1846, six postulants (including two St Lucians) sailed from Trinidad to St Lucia with the specific goal of establishing a Catholic education system. The Castries priests donated a house and on 12 July 1847, their convent *cum* school opened its doors. Boarding fees were initially their only source of income, but from 1852, day students were admitted as well. In 1854, the *Filles de Marie* amalgamated with the Sisters of St Joseph in Trinidad and, in January 1855, St Lucia welcomed its own community of Sisters of St Joseph of Cluny. The sisters extended their property on Micoud Street and eventually built a convent and various school buildings in and around Castries, where they have been teaching infants, primary and secondary level students ever since.

Catholic education came to Dennery in 1859, to Micoud in 1861, to Gros Islet in 1862 and to Soufrière in 1864. In Soufrière, the Sisters of St Joseph rented a house on Bridge Street to teach girls and infants. Two years later, they had 118 pupils and by 1880, there were 276. For some decades, housing problems hampered their expansion but in 1904, a convent, infant school and primary school were built in Soufrière. Laborie received a Catholic school in 1873. Choiseul, Anse la Raye and Canaries did so in 1879 and Vieux Fort in 1881. Sisters of St Joseph built a convent on Belvedere Hill in Vieux Fort in 1892 and started infant and primary boys' and girls' schools. Catholic schools were later also started in Aupicon and Derrière Morne. Gros Islet saw the opening of a Catholic girls' school in 1898, when the old presbytery was transformed into a convent and a nearby building turned into a school.

In 1890, all Mico schools were closed down in St Lucia following an Education Ordinance which increased government control over schools, and the appointment of an Inspector of Schools. The change was opposed by some, who believed the quality of education dropped under the new regime.[395] The Wesleyan Mission took over the Castries Mico school and a small number of trained teachers continued to arrive here from the Mico Institution in Antigua. By 1890, St Lucia boasted six Government schools, two Anglican schools, one Wesleyan school, four East Indian Mission schools and 24 Catholic schools.

St Mary's College

In 1883, the parish priest for Castries, Fr Tapon, proposed a secondary school for boys. Five years later, in May 1888, the cornerstone for St Mary's College for Boys was laid on the south side of Micoud Street. Much of the work was done by volunteers, often by moonlight, and even the priests themselves helped to carry stones to save on the cost of haulage. On 30 March 1890, St Mary's College opened its doors to 27 boys. The headmaster was Frederick Bundy who initially ran the school with just one assistant, a Mr O'Neil Traynor. The first hurdle was that '*A few of the boys were reasonably familiar with English, but most had hardly what we may call "a nodding acquaintance" with that language and a good many knew not one word of it.*' The ages of students varied widely: the youngest being just six and the oldest fifteen years of age. It took some effort on the part of the teachers to establish their regime as '*Fights were common and broken windows an everyday occurrence. It was a regular custom to "baptise" new boys under the tap.*'[396]

Finances were a concern at first and the college remained in debt for several years. Government started an annual grant in 1893 on condition that a certain number of scholarships (initially ten) were awarded each year to boys from elementary schools based on the results of an examination. In 1895, two St Mary's boys sat the Cambridge Preliminary Local Exams for the first time, travelling to Barbados to do so. In 1896, an examination centre was established at the school and seven out of eight pupils who sat the exam passed. The school continued to grow slowly but steadily, and by 1915, there were almost 80 students enrolled. The college remained in the same location until 1952, when it was transferred to the old Military Officers Mess building at Vigie. What more fitting tribute can be paid to St Mary's College other than the fact that two Nobel Prize laureates received '*a sound colonial education*'[397] within its walls? They are Sir Arthur Lewis (Economics, 1979) and Derek Walcott (Literature, 1992).

The limited impact of education

Between 1845 and 1850, between 452 and 906 children (2 to 4 per cent of the population) were enrolled in schools. In 1896, half a century after Emancipation, of a total population of 46 671 people (and an estimated 9500 to 10 000 children of school-going age, that is, children between the ages of five and fourteen) there with 36 schools, with 4182 students. On average, about half of those children (2256) attended classes with some regularity. This means that towards the end of the nineteenth century, approximately one in every four children (24 per cent) between ages five and fourteen received *some* form of basic education in St Lucia.[398] By way of comparison, in England at the same time, that figure was 70 per cent.

To make matters worse, in St Lucia, many schoolchildren barely understood the language in which they were taught and there was a pressing lack of staff. With 36 schools on the island, the total teaching corps consisted of 36 head teachers, four certified assistants and eight uncertified assistants - making for an average of about 60 pupils per (assistant)-teacher. Meanwhile, children of the upper-class were sent to schools in Europe, Barbados or Martinique - as had been the practice since the earliest days of the plantation economy.

Fred Bundy, the headmaster of St Mary's College, later became Inspector of Schools. In that capacity, he submitted a report to the Royal Commission of Enquiry which visited St Lucia in March 1897 as part of a wider investigation. Bundy revealed that outside Castries and Soufrière '*few children understand English before reaching Standard IV. ... This, in spite of the fact that they are taught in English. The method of teaching is almost purely mechanical ... Little trouble is taken to train the intelligence. Knowledge of English is confined generally to the few simple words of command. Out of school the children hear and speak nothing but Creole.*'[399]

His point was underscored in St Lucia's Annual Report of 1893 which stated that '*there is but little attempt at the cultivation of the reasoning faculties, an omission which becomes at once apparent when the pupil is asked a question involving in its answer the exercise of something more than the faculty of mere memory.*'[400] Bundy believed that the '*Bulk of people take little or no interest in education.*' Coupled with the fact that many parents were unable to provide clothing, school fees or books, this explained why '*The bulk of the children, especially in the country, do not go to school, or only irregularly.*'[401] The Anglican priest of Vieux Fort, R.J. Clarke, similarly found that parents '*regard church and school as privileges to be had for nothing or done without. They will* permit *their children to go rather than* send *them to school.*' Father Tapon, the parish priest of Castries, partly disagreed with these views, believing instead that '*Parents appreciate education*' and that '*Some keep up their education after they leave school.*' But Tapon did agree that they '*find it difficult to pay the fees*' and that as a result, non-attendance was a real problem, especially outside of Castries and the villages.

Truancy plagued the education system for decades. In 1936, an investigator found that '*In the West Indies attendance at school is often interfered with by such things as the need to give the school outfit its weekly washing; the children also help their peasant mothers to prepare on Friday for Saturday's market, and many go wage-earning in the cane fields.*'[402]

Both Bundy and Fr Tapon acknowledged that the Elementary Instruction Ordinance was not being enforced, but both also believed that having police officers force children to go to school would only make education more unpopular. Instead, they argued for abolition of the school fees, believing this '*would do away with the excuse of parents for withholding children from attendance.*'[403] Many schools did not enforce payment of fees anyway, which was one penny per child per week.

Bundy also suggested that a reformatory school for vagrant boys (*wharf rats*) be established in Castries, and that more practical subjects be taught in schools, such as agriculture. Bundy had great faith in the trickle-down effect of education: '*It would be the most direct way of bringing to the doors of labourers and small proprietors new industries and how to manage them. For the parents would hear of them through the children.*'

In addition, reasoned Bundy, agricultural schools '*would probably check the tendency among the boys who reach the higher classes to be dissatisfied with an agricultural life. At present these boys wish to become clerks, &c., and do not care to soil their hands.*' This observation was underscored by Castries Magistrate Thomas Dix, who lamented that many educated boys discovered that there were no white collar jobs available to them, with the result that '*many of the youths either "loaf about" commercial centres doing nothing, or emigrate to some speculative field of labour, and their services are thus totally lost to the colony. Were teachers to instil in their minds that there is no other pursuit more independent, healthy, and* honourable *than agriculture, this might easily be prevented.*' The St Lucia Agricultural Society offered to assist in the establishment of agricultural schools, as did the curator of the botanical gardens and two planters, Henry Devaux and Bennett. But such progressive ideas permeated only slowly and partially.

In summary, although the nineteenth century saw the first stirrings of education in St Lucia, pioneered by the Anglican and Catholic Churches and gradually taken over by Government, the level and quality of education remained '*defective*' for many decades. Attendance was scant and irregular and Kwéyòl-speaking children were taught in a language they could barely understand and with a method that favoured memory over comprehension.

Until well into the twentieth century, the only working class children who managed to reap real socio-economic benefits from education were those who lived in towns or villages, could be spared from farm labour and already had a good grasp of the English language (often due to having a (grand)parent from an English-speaking colony). If such children did well in primary school and captured a scholarship to St Mary's College or St Joseph's Convent, they could successfully climb the social ladder. But for the vast majority of children, school might teach them the alphabet, some basic arithmetic and a few skills such as needlework and singing, but did not fundamentally improve their position in society. Until the 1960s or so, education did not significantly alter the structure of opportunity for the mass of St Lucia's people and could not be considered a leading instrument in social differentiation or personal advancement.

History of the Anglican Church

By the Treaty of Versailles (1783) St Lucia established free exercise of religion. However, the number of Anglicans in the island to claim the prerogative was small, and British settlers and soldiers continued to depend on itinerant Anglican army chaplains for their spiritual welfare. An Anglican clergyman was appointed to Castries only after the Treaty of Paris (1814) which ceded St Lucia to Great Britain. He was supported by the Protestant population. From 1819 until 1831, services were held alternately in a rented building in Castries and the officers' mess at Morne Fortuné. In 1828, the Anglican Bishop in Barbados established a school for the poor in Castries ('Bishop's School') but this did not last long. In 1831, an Anglican church was built in Castries for the then approximately 200 Protestants.

In late 1842, an Anglican clergyman, Morle, settled in Soufriere where he ministered from a rented house. There were few Anglicans in Soufriere but Morle was stoutly supported by three Scottish sisters who lived twelve miles away at River Dorée Estate. During the 1830s, a visiting chaplain had baptized Robertina and Christine Alexander and with the help of a third sister, Janette, they started a vigorous Anglican household church which eventually earned them the sobriquet 'The Pious Ladies of River Dorée'. Morle performed regular ceremonies at River Dorée and Barbadian labourers reportedly 'flocked' to the district to work because they could attend an Anglican church. In 1844, Morle built an Anglican church south of Soufrière town and named it Christ Church. On 7 July 1845, the Alexander sisters laid the cornerstone for their own Anglican church at River Dorée, thanks to £300 from the Society for the Propagation of the Gospel and other sponsors. It was built of local stone, capable of seating 250 people and was finished in late 1846. A few modifications were added later but, today the River Dorée church still stands as one of the neatest churches in St Lucia. Reverend Boddy was appointed to River Dorée in 1847 and two years later, the Bishop of Barbados consecrated the building Grace Church. Clergymen lived in the estate house until 1885, when a rectory was added. Nowadays, the Anglican parish of River Dorée extends from Dennery to Soufriere.

Between 1886 and 1891, the Reverend R.J. Clarke built an Anglican church in Vieux Fort in honour of St Paul the Apostle at a cost of £355, some £200 of which was collected from outside the district. Still, Clarke was proud of the money his local congregation raised, considering that *'the Protestants are below 10 per cent of the population, and that they are Barbadian labourers accustomed to a free church, and unwilling to subscribe.'* The clergyman lived ten miles away at River Dorée. A fifth Anglican church was built in 1921-2 in Mabouya Valley, dedicated to Saint Mary the Virgin. Although the Anglican Church's following in St Lucia has always been small and its survival at times a struggle, the congregation proudly celebrated 150 years of worship in 1999.

10

Indentured labour: Europeans, Barbadians, liberated Africans and East Indians.

After Emancipation, planters resorted to various legal schemes to try and tie the newly freed workers to their sugar estates. In addition, their thoughts also turned to immigration. Although slavery had been abolished in all British colonies in 1838, foreign labour might still be contracted for a prescribed number of years in exchange for passage, accommodation, medical care, rations, provision grounds and a basic wage. Four such groups of contracted (or *indentured*) immigrants found their way to post-Emancipation St Lucia: Europeans, Barbadians, liberated Africans and East Indians.

European indentured labour

The earliest plantations in the West Indies had been operated with indentured labourers from the slums of Europe: men and women on the brink of starvation who had signed on to the contracts simply as a means of keeping body and soul together. They had died like flies under the hot tropical sun: from heat stroke, disease and exhaustion. Soon, their places were filled with African slaves. Two centuries later, anticipating the abolition of slavery, planter William Muter considered the European experiment worthy of retrial, particularly as he intended to introduce the plough to St Lucia and wanted experienced workers. In 1836, Muter imported five Irish families, settling them on the Roseau Estate. The swampy land proved a hostile environment and all the Irish contracted malaria and died. He tried again in 1837, with eighteen Scots, giving them the best food and medical attention available, but the same fate befell them. In 1840, another seventeen Scots succumbed to tropical diseases. Only six Frenchmen placed on Muter's Canelles Estate appear to have fared better: at least they do not show up as instant mortality statistics.

Climate and sobriety proved critical, as was demonstrated by Soufrière coffee planter Henry King, who recruited 29 destitute Germans he had met on the streets of London. Ten arrived on 1 April 1840 and another fourteen later that year. They were settled on the Belle Plaine coffee estate, where they appeared happy and healthy. One year later, the magistrate reported that the Germans had '*greatly bettered their condition in life*': two couples had married and other matrimonial arrangements were being contemplated.[404] A month later, another German family of five joined them. Two people died but the others continued '*in excellent health*' and their gardens '*abound in every description of European vegetable and tropical fruit, with which they supply the Soufrière market, and sometimes even that of Castries.*'[405] One year on, a third person had died, four had returned to England and eight more travelled elsewhere, but the remaining fourteen Germans at Belle Plaine Estate appear to have lived out their natural lives in St Lucia. It is unknown if they married into the black population, but it seems not unlikely.

In another private initiative, Dennery planter M.A.J. Beaucé, whilst visiting family in Lyons, induced 21 or 23 people there to come out to St Lucia. They were artisans, field labourers and domestic servants. They arrived in January 1842 and Beaucé installed them at Anse Canot Estate. By March, five had died. Three others died soon after, inspiring another seven to flee to Martinique to escape Anse Canot which they considered '*one of the most sickly*' locations in the island.[406] With this unhappy tale comes an end to St Lucian planters' post-Emancipation experiments with European indentured labour.

Barbadian immigration, 1840-1847

Other planters, meanwhile, turned their attention to the more densely populated British West Indian colonies, where newly freed people with no recourse to vacant land were competing for jobs. Barbados was the obvious choice and in 1840, the first 77 labourers arrived from Bridgetown, brought in by John Goodman. He settled them on Union Vale Estate near Soufrière, paying out £80 in wages every month and giving them houses, medical attention, provision grounds and rations until their gardens started bearing. The 49 men, eighteen women and ten children were reportedly happy, and the feeling was mutual. The district magistrate reported: '*The wages given by Mr Goodman are high, comparatively speaking; but the labour performed by the Barbadians is equivalent, for it is no less strange than true, that the Barbadian labourer will, with ease to himself, do in the week at least twice as much work as the Lucian.*'

Planters in Barbados were obviously not pleased to see pressure on their labour market alleviated and invented various '*obstructions & formalities*' to prevent outmigration. Nevertheless, another 72 Barbadian immigrants settled in St Lucia in August 1841, all of them

> *... most respectable agricultural labourers from the rural districts of Barbados; eight men and their families have located themselves on the Morne Courbaril estate, and the others have made engagements with the proprietors of the Union Vale and Black Bay estates. ... They appear delighted with their prospects in this country, and I need hardly say that the parties who have engaged their services seem well pleased at such an acquisition.*

The Barbadians were reportedly '*cheerful*' workers. Unfortunately, before long, several died, frightening the others into leaving the estates or abandoning St Lucia altogether. One magistrate said in December 1842: '*coming from a dry uniform climate to take up his abode in a place where the atmosphere is peculiarly variable and humide and the soil wet and marshy, the native of Barbados is eminently predisposed to the influence of Malaria.*' Health concerns notwithstanding, immigration continued. Between July 1845 and December 1847, another 159 Barbadians went to estates on the west coast. Planters were happy with their work ethic, and the only discordant note came from the stipendiary magistrate for Soufrière and Choiseul, in December 1847, who complained that: '*Mostly given to hard drinking and quarreling, they add to these the horrible habit of carrying with them knives and even razors, which, in fighting, they make use of and with which they inflict most fearful wounds.*'

No further organized immigration schemes from Barbados were undertaken after 1847. Although satisfactory workers, '*the outlay attending their removal and location has far exceeded the original estimate*'[407] and neither John Goodman nor the other planters involved (Todd of Union Estate and LaCorbinière of Corinth) were tempted to repeat the scheme.

But individual Barbadians continued to travel to St Lucia of their own volition. They went largely unrecorded (to the chagrin of the authorities)[408] but by 1897, an estimated 10 per cent of all labourers in Vieux Fort were Barbadians (750 to 800 people). River Dorée, too, had a sizeable Barbadian population, attracted in part by the presence of an Anglican church. People from other islands also freely travelled to St Lucia and by January 1897, the *St Lucia Gazette* estimated that St Lucia had 3211 West Indian immigrants: 8 per cent of the total population and 22 per cent of that in Castries. One-third of these were Barbadians. In 1899, the 58-member Royal St Lucia Police Force consisted entirely of non-St Lucian Anglophone West Indians, from Barbados (21), Antigua (14), St Vincent (9), Montserrat (4), Jamaica (3), Nevis (3), Tobago (2), Demerara (1) and Grenada (1).[409] St Lucians, in retaliation, referred to them as the '*Queen's Dogs*'.[410]

Liberated African immigration

Britain abolished the slave trade in 1807 and slavery altogether in 1838, but other nations continued trading slaves for many more decades. Between 1810 and 1870 alone, an estimated two million Africans made the Middle Passage, with the vast majority ending up in the sugar industries of Cuba and Brazil. Britain actively tried to intercept these shipments, liberating the slaves whenever possible. If this occurred on the Caribbean side of the Atlantic, rather than send them on a long return journey, the liberated Africans were brought to the British West Indies where they were settled as free men and women. If liberated in the eastern Atlantic, they were carried back to the British island of St Helena or to Sierra Leone in West Africa, where the *International Courts of Mixed Commission* were located. Here, the freed captives were housed in *Liberated African Yards* and encouraged to migrate as contract labourers to the British West Indies. Many liberated Africans complied (although the longer they lived in the yards, the less inclined they were to leave). In this manner, thousands of liberated Africans[411] eventually ended up in the British West Indies. Between 1841 and 1867, Trinidad received 8854 free African immigrants, Guyana 14 060 and Jamaica 11 391. Another 5027 liberated Africans migrated to St Lucia, St Vincent, Grenada, Dominica and St Kitts,[412] with St Lucia receiving a total of 1298.

The first ship with liberated Africans reached St Lucia on 6 February 1849. The *Una* had left Sierra Leone twenty days earlier with 367 people on board, two of whom died during the passage. The remaining 365 people were in good health and consisted of 179 men, 109 women, 37 boys under the age of fourteen and 40 girls.[413] The arrival of the *Una* embarrassed Governor Darling who *did* expect a ship with liberated Africans - but not until five or six weeks later, and not from Sierra Leone, but from St Helena. This being the first arrival of immigrants, '*no organization of any kind for the proper conduct of it, had been established* [and] *we were of course wholly unprepared for the reception of these people.*'[414]

Nevertheless, 362 of the 365 liberated Africans were soon settled. They were obliged to work for one year on an assigned estate (five or six days per week, nine hours per day with a one-hour break), in return for '*dry, wholesome and comfortable lodging*', half an acre of suitable garden, free medical attention and rations (including salt fish, beef or pork, bread and either farine or corn meal, rice, yams, sweet potatoes, eddoes or plantains). They also received two pence per day for the first six months and five pence for the second period of six months, when rations were reduced to half. A third article stipulated that the immigrants had to complete '*an industrial residence of five years*' after which they were entitled to '*a free passage back to the port or place whence he came*' or, alternatively, '*a piece or parcel of land.*'[415] The African immigrants from the *Una* were distributed as follows: Anse Galet (20), Anse Latoque (1), Beauchamp (14), Beausejour in Vieux Fort (14), Beausejour in Gros Islet (7), Belle Plaine (8), Bonneterre (15), Château Belair (15), Cocoa Nuts (5), Corinth (11), Entrepot (17), Fonds Estate (22), Grand Anse (18), La Redoute (10), Marquis (32), Morne Courbaril (12), Pointe Sable (6), Two Friends (13), Troumassée (39), Union (24) and Union Vale (40).

Interestingly, the authorities in St Lucia attempted to classify these immigrants according to tribal African affiliations, something which was never repeated with later groups. The stipendiary magistrates found 79 of the 332 people 'unidentifiable' but classified the others as follows: Ganomerly/Gammerly and Yeroba (44), Yarriba (20), Akoo (17), Ogirila/Oguila (7), Yoriba (18), Akoo/Adgo and D'Issa (22), Housa (54), Adamoura (2), Egba (13), Ifes (2), Onda (8), Oror (4), Sakatou/Jakatou (40) and Gabon (2). Austrian anthropologist Ernestine Kolar (who compiled a comprehensive study of St Lucia's colonial archives from this period) concluded that at least 70 Africans on board the *Una* spoke some form of Yoruba.[416]

The immigrants from the *Una* were reportedly content with their new lives, and the planters were likewise '*satisfied with the cheerful and willing performance of their allotted work*'. Before March was over, the '*principal Landed Proprietors and Merchants*' of St Lucia petitioned the Colonial Office to send '*us a further supply of freed Africans who are the most efficient labourers who can be sent to these Colonies.*'[417] In June 1849, they were praised in all districts as '*remarkably*' willing and cheerful workers, in excellent health, who came readily forward '*on more than one occasion when the native labourers have been dogged by obstinacy or refused to work.*' The Africans, for their part, soon discovered the métayage system and several started growing sugar cane in their spare time. In the south of the island, the native peasantry had initially manifested '*some bad feeling*' towards the newcomers, assaulting and wounding two of them, but '*a little legal coercion seasonably applied, soon restored them to their sense, they have since come to a better understanding, & live upon more friendly terms.*'

In fact, the liberated Africans fitted in so well that within one year after their arrival, the stipendiary magistrate for Gros Islet/Dauphin reported that they '*speak the Creole language remarkably well, in fact one would hardly know some of them to be Africans, were it not for the Tattoo marks on their faces.*'

At the expiration of their contracts, 303 out of 355 liberated Africans opted to remain on the estates they had been first sent to, although all declined to renew their contracts, preferring to become free labourers instead. Seven had died by then, and four children had been born to immigrant mothers.

On 4 January 1850, a second ship from Sierra Leone arrived in Castries after 27 days at sea. The *Tropic* had taken 186 immigrants on board: 105 men, 29 women, 34 boys and 18 girls. Three died during the crossing but the remainder were in good health: '*Two cases of sleight dysentery and of a wound in the thigh through accident*' being the only ailments. Much less fortunate were the passengers of the *Tuskar* which arrived four months later, on 11 May 1850. It reached Castries after a 72-day trip that had started in Sierra Leone where 92 immigrants were taken on board, followed by St Helena, where another 520 embarked. Forty-one people had died during the crossing, and three others succumbed shortly after arrival. The high death toll was attributed to cold weather and rainfall, overcrowding and the fact that the St Helena immigrants had only recently been rescued from badly overcrowded slave ships, without time to recuperate. Of the 568 arrivals, 156 were men, 146 women, 141 boys and 125 girls (under the ages of fourteen). It was an unusually high percentage of children.

The *Tuskar* immigrants were distributed to estates around the island, while 30 children (presumably orphans) were placed as domestic servants in Castries town. A few weeks later, the magistrate for the Vieux Fort/Laborie district described the immigrants as '*a miserable lucky set of beings, & fitter subjects for a Hospital than manual labour; the greater part of them were in such an emaciated state when they arrived that nine of the number died soon after coming into the district. Many still remain very ill, & will be unable ... to perform any ordinary quantity of work for some time yet to come, they have all had medical attention.*' But despite their ill health, they were found to be '*tractable & obedient, & those that are able, willingly attend to any kind of work pointed out to them, they are undoubtedly superior in every respect (except health) to those of the Tropic.*'

The last remark hinted at the fact that 52 of the liberated Africans from the *Tropic*, which had arrived six months earlier, had been causing the authorities trouble. The district magistrate for Vieux Fort/Laborie reported that they

> *... are of different tribes, & very dissimilar in character, they are generally indolent & appear to be fond of roving & unsettled life; several of them absconded from Estates where they were employed under Contract, & were settling themselves in the woods, in another district, when they were arrested; they had already commenced erecting thatched huts, for the purpose no doubt for enjoying life without the trouble of working, & at the expense of the community at large ... they were well supplied with provisions which they had obtained by pillaging; they have been punished for their delinquencies.*

Although the records are silent, it is quite possible that the 52 had absconded due to harsh living conditions on the plantations. The magistrate for Castries/Anse la Raye, for instance, found that some estate managers neglected their liberated Africans. He mentioned Soucis Estate as a case in point, where the immigrants looked '*wretched, and filthy, they wear tattered and dirty clothes.'* On Reduit Estate, too, African immigrants complained of neglect and want of food.

In general, however, the immigration of liberated Africans worked out fairly well, *'particularly upon the Anse Galet, Mont Pleasant, Roseau, La Pointe, Marigot and Entrepôt estates. The planters are unanimous as to their good behaviour, and their Value as labourers. They appear also quite happy, and satisfied with their Employers'*. By October 1850, twenty months after their arrival, thirteen liberated Africans in the Castries/Anse la Raye district were active as métayers and eight of those who had arrived on the *Una* had contracted Christian marriages. In Gros Islet/Dauphin, *Una* arrivals owned cattle, pigs and poultry and those at Grande Anse and Marquis Estates were said to be *'rich in stock'*. On the east coast (Dennery, Praslin, Micoud), African immigrants did equally well and planters *'desire an increase of their number.'*

The situation remained satisfactory throughout 1851, 1852 and 1853, with the annotation that increasingly, liberated Africans followed the example of native workers and set themselves up as independent peasants, away from the estates. By the middle of 1853, three to four years after their arrival, only 55 per cent (617) of the original 1119 immigrants still lived on large plantations.[418] Of this number, 59 per cent were regular church-goers and 7 per cent were children going to school. The remaining 502 *'have hired small portions of land which they till ... for their own consumption and the procuring of a little salt-fish and a few clothes, and they seldom trouble the Estates with their presence for the purpose of working - others again are employed by Creole laborers to assist them in the cultivation of their provision gardens, which employment the Immigrants appear to prefer to working in the Cane fields.'*[419]

In short, within four years of arrival, the majority of liberated African immigrants had blended in with the wider working population of St Lucia. Ironically, this was also the inherent weakness of the immigration scheme: while the liberated Africans satisfactorily fulfilled their contracted one year of labour, as soon as that obligation was fulfilled, like their Creole counterparts, they joined the emerging peasantry, thereby defeating the scheme's long-term purpose. This only got worse when the *Una* immigrants, approaching the end of their prescribed five years of industrious residence, started leaving St Lucia. In late 1853, several of them travelled to Barbados *'en route as they say for their native land.'* A perplexed stipendiary magistrate reported: '*several of those who have left, industrious & good labourers - stated that they were only stimulated to work as they did by the hope that they would be able to realize the means of returning to their own Country.'*

Another magistrate confirmed this trend, albeit with a twist of his own: *'A few african Immigrants have been induced of lately to Barbados, saying they were going to Sierra Leone, I rather suspect they have been kidnapped.'*

Other time-expired liberated Africans left for Trinidad, including a group of 36 who went there *'under the expectation of a higher rate of wages.'* Governor Power related how one of the Africans had shown him a letter *'which he said he had received from his sister in Trinidad, in which she advised him to lose no time in coming to that place, as he would be much better off there than in St Lucia.'* This reveals the fascinating fact that some liberated Africans apparently maintained family ties across the West Indies and communicated in writing. Travelling around the Caribbean as a black person was not without risk in those days, as Governor Power tried to impress on the would-be migrants: *'They invariably come to me, a day or two before the arrival of the Steamer, to obtain permission to leave, which I have always refused to grant them on the ground, that by leaving this Island, they would expose themselves to the danger of being carried into slavery. But they meet this argument by saying that they avoid all such risks, by going in the steamer.* ' It appears that despite the Governor's reluctance, and despite the fact that their full five years of residence were not quite up yet, these Africans were nevertheless allowed to travel to Barbados and Trinidad.

After 1853, no further mention is made of such travel requests. On the contrary, St Lucia became the recipient of liberated Africans fleeing ill-treatment in Martinique. On 3 April 1858, seven African immigrants arrived in a canoe from Martinique. They gave their names as '*Tom Nimble, Jim Crash, Jack Will, Africa, George, Tom Toly, Tom Peter*'[420] and claimed to have originally come from Grandees, near Sierra Leone. Administrator Breen classified them as '*Kroomen*'.[421] They said they had arrived in Martinique on board a French ship one year earlier as contract workers, on the promise of eventually being allowed to go home. Instead, their employer had treated them like slaves and so they fled. They promised to work in St Lucia for one year and intended to return to Africa after that. A subsequent group of refugees was less fortunate. On 10 July 1858, the *Palladium* reported that a French warship, *Lucifer*, had *'entered the Port of Castries in search of some Kroomen who had effected their escape from Martinique. It appears that during the preceding night twenty-three of these unfortunate beings, employed on the estate of Mr Sempé, in that island, had embarked in a canoe, and had directed their course towards the northern point of St Lucia.'* Breen later reported that the 23 Africans had never arrived in St Lucia and were presumed drowned. A month later, on 21 August 1858, another French warship came to Castries in search of eight African immigrant deserters. Nothing more is revealed about their fate.

Other refugees continued to arrive. On 1 September, five '*Kroomen*' asked for permission to stay in St Lucia. Three more '*Kroomen*' landed on 12 September, declaring they had worked in Martinique for one year and stating they were prepared to work in St Lucia as well. More than a year later, on 11 October 1859, six refugees from Martinique reached Anse Mahaut, claiming to have fled an abusive employer. The stipendiary magistrate reported: '*Their names are Richard, Freeman, Murcey, Tom, Mimlen, Joe. They appear to me to be boys of about 19 to 24 years of age. They declare being natives of Chissalmas near Sierra Leone, and came out two years and a half ago to Martinique.*'

In November, four others landed at Anse Mamin. '*Their names are Bergley, Guisseau, Antoine, and Quamie, and understand the Creole language. They informed me they are not Kroomen, but natives of Kiplaon in Africa; ... and in consequence of ill treatment, and not being paid their wages, they deserted.*' On the magistrate's recommendation, they were accepted as labourers at Anse Mamin Estate. Altogether, 25 African refugees from Martinique reached St Lucia alive during the course of 1858 and 1859. There is no further mention of them in later sources.

Meanwhile, planters in St Lucia were drawing their own conclusions. They applied for, and received, two more shipments of African immigrants but under new contractual terms. From now on, the liberated Africans were obliged to work for three years, not one.[422] Twelve years after the *Tuskar*, on 15 February 1862, the *Ulysses* cast its lines at Port Castries. The ship carried St Lucia's first batch of East Indian immigrants from Calcutta, but had also stopped at St Helena to take on board 63 adult African men. One day later, the *Damietta* arrived, carrying a further 116 African immigrants from St Helena (59 men and 57 women). They were in reasonably good health, although one man had died on the *Damietta* and one person from the *Ulysses* died shortly after landing.

The 62 immigrants from the *Ulysses* were distributed as follows: Grand Anse (4), Black Bay (10), Pointe Sable (10), Tourny (8), Beauchamp (6), Cap (5), Delcer (5), Diamond (4), Union Vale (6) and Terre Blanche (2). Two were kept in hospital. From the *Damietta*, they went to Cap (3), Reunion (9), Beausejour (11), Delcer (2), Diamond (3), Troumassée (6), Canelle (7), Volet (6), St Urban (8), Pensée (5), Belle Plaine (3), Pointe (7), Anse Galet (11), Bellevue (4), Jalousie (5), Pearl (3), Morne Courbaril (5), Fonds Doux (3), Beausejour (8) and Anse Mahaut (5). Two were taken to hospital.

Again, planters found the African immigrants '*docile, industrious and sober*' and '*excellent agricultural laborers*'. Moreover, a '*considerable number of them have been baptised by the Roman Catholic Clergy.*'[423] Within four to six years of arrival, the immigrants from the *Ulysses* and *Damietta* had followed the lead of earlier free African workers and merged almost seamlessly into the local population. By 1866-8, they had built their own homes, planted provision plots, were keeping animals and worked as wage labourers on the estates if and when it suited them. They lived island-wide: in the districts of Gros Islet, Castries, Anse la Raye, Soufrière, Choiseul, Laborie, Vieux Fort, Micoud and Dennery. Before long, '*many of them ... intermarried with the Creoles.*'

Simultaneously, at Aux Leon, Babonneau, Fond Assor, Resina, La Grace, Piaye, Dannezan, Guinee and Morne Cayenne, existing small settlements of '*old Africans*' from the *Una, Tropic* and *Tuskar* grew in size when some of the later immigrants joined them to '*employ their time in raising stock and growing provisions*' and working as wage labourers '*when it suits their purpose and then doing contract work.*'

Over time, those who retained an awareness of their recent African origins called themselves - and became known - by the St Lucian Kwéyòl terms of *Nègs Guinées* (or *Djinés*) and, less commonly, *Nègs Congos*, referring to their homelands along the coasts of Guinea and Congo. One source further claims that the Nèg Guinées were '*considered to be superior*' to the Nèg Congos '*and more versed in the mysteries of nature and magic.*'[424]

Nèg Djinés and the ceremonies of koutoumba and kélé

Colonial records of the day maintain that the African immigrants merged seamlessly into the black working class, converting to Christianity and intermarrying with and working alongside the former slaves, but at least one modern author holds a different view. In a 1993 article, Manfred Kremser stated that because '*the Djiné were deeply involved in the practice of religious rites directly imported from their African homeland*' which were considered '*"pagan customs" by the Christianized creole population, they were met with strong disapproval. Henceforth the Djiné were treated with great contempt by their fellow creole citizens, who used to scold them* 'Mal Djiné' *(meaning 'bad djiné') whenever they performed their religious ceremonies. This made their integration into the creole society extremely difficult.*'[425] With some qualifications, both views may have their merits.

First of all, there is no denying that the liberated Africans or Djinés were very much part of the same social and economic daily routines that characterized their Creole counterparts. They intermarried with non-Djiné partners, they worked alongside Creole labourers on the estates, they were employed by Creole farmers and they settled as métayers and peasants in Creole communities. They even went to the same church services. On the other hand, several generations after their arrival in St Lucia, the liberated Africans were still classified as a distinct ethnic group, with physical attributes allegedly peculiar to their Djiné origin (e.g., tall with large feet, big calves and '*very dark, blue-black skin*'[426]) and certain communities were considered Djiné strongholds. Finally, Nèg Djinés are associated with two distinctly African ceremonies, *koutoumba* and *kélé* (also known as *Plaisir Guinée*).[427] Before considering whether or not this made them outcasts from the wider Creole society, as Kremser claims, let us first take a closer look at these ceremonies.

36. Hustle and bustle around Minvielle & Chastanet's first department store, here seen in 1905. The building was originally constructed in 1864.
(Postcard courtesy Suzy Barnard collection)

37. Looking south down a cobble-stoned Bridge Street in 1890. Note the lack of telephone lines and electrical wires. (Photograph courtesy Robert Devaux collection)

38. Old Castries in 1898, before it was partly destroyed by the fire of May 1927. (Photograph courtesy Robert Devaux collection)

39. Coasting steamer RMS *Tees* loading passengers and cargo in Prince Alfred's Basin, 1900. (Postcard courtesy Robert Devaux collection)

40. A police officer in colonial uniform (white with yellow trim) guarding the bridge on Bridge Street, 1900. Note behind him the Police Headquarters, Royal Gaol and Dispensary.
(Postcard courtesy Nancy Dowd collection)

41. Barnard & Sons on the south-west corner of Jeremie and Bridge Streets (1900) with students from St Joseph's Convent and St Mary's College congregating outside. (Photograph courtesy Robert Devaux collection)

42. The same south-west corner of Jeremie and Bridge Streets 100 years later, now home to the modern head office of the Bank of Saint Lucia. (Photo: Robert Devaux)

43. Bridge Street looking south (circa 1908), showing telephone poles and gas lamps. The first telephone call in St Lucia was made on Christmas Day, 1895. (Photograph courtesy Robert Devaux collection)

44. Brazil Street looking west (circa 1910), looking down the Castries River and across to what is the oldest remaining Roman Catholic cemetery on the island. (Postcard courtesy Nancy Dowd collection)

45. Looking north along the Chaussée Road in 1916. Nobel Prize laureate Derek Walcott grew up in this area a few decades later.
(Postcard courtesy Suzy Barnard collection)

46. St Joseph's Convent and St Mary's College on Micoud Street, circa 1916. The college is the building to the fore. (Postcard courtesy Nancy Dowd collection)

47. Grace Anglican Church at River Dorée is the second-oldest Anglican church and housed the island's first school for emancipated black children. (Postcard courtesy Robert Devaux collection)

48. The Carnegie Library, originally built in June 1924.
(Postcard courtesy Robert Devaux collection)

49. Victoria Hospital, completed in 1887, was named to honour the occasion of Queen Victoria's Golden Jubilee.
(Postcard courtesy Nancy Dowd collection)

50. A lovely example of Caribbean architecture is this office of the curator at the botanical garden in Castries. (Postcard courtesy Nancy Dowd collection)

51. Church-goers milling about near Columbus Square after Sunday Mass. The picture shows the church still with its domed belfry. In 1895, the building was enlarged and the main entrance moved to Micoud Street. (Postcard courtesy Robert Devaux collection)

52. The new Government House was completed in January 1896 for Administrator V.S. Gouldsbury. Horseback was the main mode of transport at the time. (Postcard courtesy Robert Devaux collection)

53. St Louis Street looking east, around 1900, blissfully uncongested. (Postcard courtesy Robert Devaux collection)

54. Government buildings and Peter & Company, both built after the 1927 fire. The Peter & Company building survived the 1948 fire and is now one of Castries' historical highlights. (Postcard courtesy Nancy Dowd collection)

55. Anse la Raye Village was named after the impressive-looking manta ray fish which used to frequent the bay in large numbers.
(Postcard courtesy Robert Devaux collection)

56. The west-coast fishing village of Canaries got its name from the Amerindian clay cooking pots of that name.
(Postcard courtesy Nancy Dowd collection)

57. Soufrière Town in 1909. The original layout remains unchanged up to this day. (Photograph courtesy Robert Devaux collection)

58. A group of cadets from the Royal Navy (circa 1880) being shown around the Sulphur Springs by local tour guides.
(Picture from *The Graphic*, courtesy Suzy Barnard collection)

59. Soufrière *en fête* in 1910. People clearly enjoyed the chance to dress up.
(Postcard courtesy Nancy Dowd collection)

60. Drying cocoa beans on the Soufrière waterfront (circa 1910). The beans were spread out on tarpaulins which could be used to cover them in case of rain. (Postcard courtesy Robert Devaux collection)

61. Ecuelling limes to extract the precious oil from their skins (circa 1930). This was done at various estates around Soufriere, including Diamond Estate. (Postcard courtesy Nancy Dowd collection)

62. Choiseul (circa 1900), with its large Catholic church, long jetty and fishing canoes lined up on the beach. (Postcard courtesy Robert Devaux collection)

63. Laborie Village as seen from the jetty (circa 1910) has changed remarkably little. (Postcard courtesy Robert Devaux collection)

64. The fishing village of Vieux Fort only came to life on weekends, when people came in to visit the market and attend Mass.
(Postcard courtesy Robert Devaux collection)

65. The Vieux Fort mangroves, once rich fishing grounds, were partially drained in the 1940s due to concerns over malaria.
(Postcard courtesy Nancy Dowd collection)

66. Vieux Fort celebrating First Communion. Showing the lower end of Clarke Street looking down towards the Caribbean Sea.
(Postcard courtesy Robert Devaux collection)

67. *Ma Gilbert* (born circa 1880) in the doorway of her home in Church Road, Vieux Fort.
(Photograph courtesy of Mrs Idalia Theodore)

68. Micoud (circa 1910) was originally located further south at *Vieux Bourg*, where it was destroyed by the great hurricane of 1780.
(Postcard courtesy Robert Devaux collection)

69. Praslin Village was once an important sugar-producing area. Heading into the twenty-first century, Praslin seemed set to enter the age of tourism.
(Postcard courtesy Suzy Barnard collection)

70. Dennery Village was described in 1893 as 'a most beautiful place on the seashore. [I]f it were in Europe instead of the West Indies, it would be the most fashionable of watering places'. (Postcard courtesy Robert Devaux collection)

71. The waterfront of Gros Islet Village, named after the 'big island' in its bay, Pigeon Island. Note the fishing nets spread out to dry in the sun. (Postcard courtesy Robert Devaux collection)

72. Traditionally, whoever helps to pull in the seine fishing nets gets a share of the catch for their efforts. (Postcard courtesy Nancy Dowd collection)

73. A countryside *kay pay* ('straw house') with walls of woven sticks and a roof of thatched coconut branches or grass. Kerosene drums were used to store water and cook ground provisions. Circa 1920.
(Postcard courtesy Robert Devaux collection)

74. Fishermen mending nets and shooting the breeze near a make-shift shelter by the seaside, around 1920. Note the double-masted canoe and the bamboo fish pots. (Postcard courtesy Nancy Dowd collection)

75. A St Lucian belle dressed in an eighteenth century style *wob dwiyèt*. The head dress is called the *calendeuse*, the scarf a *foulard* and the full skirts the *madras*. (Postcard courtesy Suzy Barnard collection)

Koutoumba

Relatively little is known about koutoumba or *katumba* except that (in the words of St Lucian folklorist Harold Simmons) it '*appears to be another pure African survival*' performed by the '*Negre Guinee*' who '*claim to be descended from the Angola and the Awanda.*' Another source typified koutoumba as a '*unique song-dance*' found in the villages of La Grace, Laborie and Piaye. '*The koutoumba was only performed for the death of a djiné, a person descended from Africans who came to the island in the middle of the 19th century.*'[428] Simmons described '*katumba*' as follows:

> *On the death of a* [family] *member, this dance takes place at night in the yard of the house of the deceased, and the night afterwards, and also on the anniversary of the death. These songs are accompanied by one drum and a shak-shak or rattle. Dancers dance alone or in groups of three, held together by a cord or string of white cloth. The words are a mixture of African and Creole; the singers claim to know the meaning in a general way. The men sing in a groaning manner, the women in a piercing high tone, often raising their hands over their heads in supplication, miming grief.* [429]

Another description of koutoumba differs slightly. '*The koutoumba is unique among St Lucian folk dance in that it is performed by a sole dancer and using only two to four lines of text, which is evocative of the song's atmosphere rather than narrative.*' This source also claims that '*The last drummer who knew this tradition died in 1986.*'[430] Oral sources, however, hold that at the start of the twenty-first century, koutoumba was still occasionally performed in Piaye, Morne Cayenne and Belle Vue.

Kélé

The kélé ritual was more elaborate than koutoumba and is better documented. Kélé is reminiscent of the Shango ritual found in Trinidad, the Big Drum Dance in Grenada and Carriacou and other possession cults found in the Caribbean and South America. However, unlike those cults, kélé contained no Christian elements. Instead, kélé was a syncretization of two Yoruba cults: Shango and Ogun. In essence, kélé was '*a ceremony given to ask the African ancestors of present devotees for protection in all matters of importance - good crops, good health, and good fortune. In the course of the ceremony, ancestors are thanked for past favors.*'[431] Kélé participants communicated with their ancestors through the ceremonial use of 'thunder stones' or *pierres tonnerre* which are smooth stones that were '*believed to have fallen from the sky during a storm when there were loud claps of thunder and blinding flashes of "forked" lightning.*'[432] These stones were called Shango (or Chango) and symbolized African ancestors. Interestingly, several of the stones used during kélé ceremonies in Babonneau have been identified as Amerindian axes.[433]

During the kélé ritual, a high priest placed several Shango stones on the ground in a half circle or cross shape and then invited male participants to add their own Shango stones, as well as agricultural tools (cutlasses, hoes, axes, forks) and personal items symbolic of their requests for good fortune.[434] After some preliminary dancing, drumming and singing, the stones were washed and polished, and the high priest made a speech in which he asked the ancestors to intercede with a higher power on behalf of the person or family sponsoring the event and all other participants.[435] More drumming, singing and dancing followed. The men then retired to a secluded spot where they washed the legs of a ram and killed it with one swift stroke. The high priest drank some of the ram's blood, as did the other participants, and then sprinkled some onto the Shango stones, the agricultural tools and the ground. This served to make the stones more powerful and the tools more productive and safe for their users. Continued drumming, dancing and singing were used to induce a state of trance, particularly in the high priest. Meanwhile, the women sang and danced in a separate area, and were also occupied with the task of ritually cooking the ram and ground provisions, to be used along with water and white rum as offerings to the deities and sustenance for the devotees. In the final stage of kélé, the high priest carried a calabash gourd filled with a mixture known as *djinification* into the circle of devotees and smashed it to pieces on the ground. This was intended to dismiss the leading evil spirit known to kélé devotees as *Akeshew*.

Kélé ceremonies were usually held on the first Sunday in the New Year, the Sunday before Lent, the first Sunday in October and the last Sunday in November.[436] Anyone could call a kélé but only a high priest could officiate. Since kélé required the sacrifice of a mature ram and offerings of ground provisions and drinks for all participants, calling a kélé was a costly affair. The kélé ceremony and the function of high priest have been handed down from father to son for several generations. Kélé ceremonies were reportedly still performed in Aux Leon in 1955, in Soufrière in 1980[437] and in Resina (Babonneau) in 1957, 1973, 1983, 1984, 1985 and 1986.[438] Younger generations seem to have lost interest however, and nowhere does kélé appear to have survived beyond the end of the twentieth century.

Liberated Africans, kélé and wider society

Now, to return to the original question: how prevalent was kélé amongst the liberated Africans and did their adherence to it make *'their integration into the creole society extremely difficult'*, as Manfred Kremser alleges? If it is true, as Harold Simmons claimed, that kélé first appeared in St Lucia *'in about 1867, shortly after the arrival of families from Western Nigeria, of the Ekiti tribe, thirty years after the abolition of slavery'*[439] then the answer must be that kélé was brought to St Lucia by passengers of the 1862 ships *Ulysses* and *Damietta*. Although the records are silent on the origin of these 178 people (all of whom arrived via the Liberated Africans' Yards in St Helena) it is entirely possible that they were indeed Ekitri people from Western Nigeria. By then, the majority of liberated Africans who had arrived in 1849 and 1850 had already spent a dozen years in St Lucia without the benefit of kélé and were, by all reports, well-integrated into Creole society. It is unlikely that the subsequent introduction of kélé significantly altered that position, and it may even be wondered whether they participated in kélé to any large extent, or at all.

An exception may be made for those 1849-50 immigrants who had clustered together in Nèg Djiné strongholds of their own. It is quite possible that after 1865, when the immigrants from the 1862 ships *Ulysses* and *Damietta* reached the end of their 3-year contracts and went in search of land and independence, they joined these old-time Nèg Djiné communities and so caused a *renaissance* of African ceremonial and socio-political life, along with a (re)invention of kélé. Assuming Simmons is correct,[440] the timing certainly would fit perfectly: in or about 1867.

One man stands out in particular: a prominent liberated African by the name of Assau who, after working out his contract, bought large tracts of land in an area now known as Fond Assor and Morne Assor. Assau and his descendants (whose family names were Coutou, Joseph and Delaire) were high priests and custodians of kélé in Fond Assau and Resina (Babonneau) until the death, in 1984, of Noah Delaire and the subsequent demise of his successor, high-priest Etienne Wells Joseph.[441] For a century and more, high priests such as Assau, Coutou, Joseph and Delaire were not only *'the religious leaders of the Djiné, but also their political leaders, as well as the judges within their group of families. They organized themselves in small village communities with a pronounced group solidarity, and preferred to intermarry within their founder families.'* For these men, kélé functioned as a cohesive force, lending them not only spiritual credence within their extended families and local communities but also socio-political legitimacy and power.

However, it would be incorrect to claim on the basis of this evidence alone, that kélé was responsible for causing a rift in St Lucian society between liberated Africans and their Creole counterparts. Neither the timing of events nor the extent of kélé's influence can bear the weight of that allegation. Thus, the conclusion must be that while kélé, for more than a century, affirmed some of the Nèg Djinés' spiritual and moral orientation towards Africa as their homeland and the home of their ancestors - to an extent which, admittedly, had been lost among the former slave population - it was not a practice that alienated them from their fellow St Lucians. Not even in a strictly religious sense, since kélé devotees, including many high officiating members, were almost always devout and active Roman Catholics as well.[442]

Liberated Africans: summary

In all, 1298 liberated African immigrants arrived in St Lucia between 1849 and 1862 on board five ships. Fifty had died *en route* but added to their number are 25 refugees from Martinique. On balance, planters and local authorities viewed positively the contributions African contract labourers made to the export economy. The immigrants, in turn, made active use of local opportunities to become semi-independent peasant proprietors, after the example of their native Creole counterparts. Within one or two generations, the liberated Africans had merged into the black working and farming classes of St Lucia, with the annotation that some Djiné settlements maintained a strong African cultural and spiritual orientation, expressed in the rituals of koutoumba and kélé.

East Indians in St Lucia

The largest and most visible group of contract labourers brought to the Caribbean during post-Emancipation days were the Indians (who soon became known as 'East Indians'). Between 1845 and 1917, 25 000 people sailed from the south-Asian subcontinent to the Caribbean, forever changing the social and ethnic make-ups of Belize, Cayenne, Guyana, Suriname, Trinidad, Grenada, St Vincent, St Lucia, Martinique, Guadeloupe, St Kitts, Nevis, St Croix and Jamaica. In some colonies, Asians came to form half the population, successfully maintaining their distinct socio-ethnic identity and eventually forming influential political factions as well. In St Lucia, East Indians remained a modest numeric minority. Between 1859 and 1893, thirteen ships carried a total of 4427 Indian men, women and children from the ports of Calcutta and (at least once) Madras to the wharves of Castries. Just over half (2423) eventually re-migrated to India.[443] Others left St Lucia for Caribbean destinations, and a handful arrived in St Lucia from elsewhere.

The East Indians' relatively small number in St Lucia, their scattered residence and the transitory nature of their stay, all served to undermine their capacity to recreate the traditional Indian village community system of *panchayat*. Avoidance regulations could not be enforced, as Hindus of all castes were housed with Muslims and Christians in barracks where cooking, washing and cleaning took place in shared spaces. Finally, a skewed ratio between men and women considerably altered gender relations, further eroding the patriarchal Indian family system. Nevertheless, East Indian culture remains clearly visible in St Lucia, and 150 years after their first arrival, there are still communities with a strong Indian presence (e.g., Forestière and Jacmel in the north and Canelles, Cacao, Anse Ger, Blanchard, Augier and Balca in the south). The terms 'Indian' (or *coolie*) and 'half-Indian' (or *douglah*) are still in daily colloquial use, and Indian colour schemes, cuisine and music add a spicy flavour to St Lucia's Creole mixture.

Origins of East Indian immigrants in St Lucia

The Indians who came to St Lucia probably originated from the north-eastern states of Bihar and Uttar Pradesh. Researcher Richard Cheddie believes Bengal, in the south-east, was a catchment area, as well as Gorakhpur (Goruckpore), Varanasi (Benares), Sultanpur (Sultanpor), Azamgarh (Azimghur), Allahabad, Patna, Ara, Jaunpur (Jaunpore), Mirzapur (Mirzapore), Kanpur (Cawnpore), Lucknow, Firozabad (Fyazabad) and Ghazipur (Ghazeepore) in the north, and Vellore, Chittor, Vizianagaram (Vizagapatam) and Madras in the south. They were rural people - agricultural workers and small farmers, but not usually the poorest of the poor. Most were Hindus of fairly low caste, with a few members of the Brahmin and other higher castes mixed in (especially widowed women). Several others were Muslims, '*as can be seen in many of the names ending in Ali or Din or Khan*', while a few arrived in St Lucia as Christians, with English names.[444]

The indentured workers generally came from households that owned some farm land, cattle and property. The large majority came out to the West Indies with a specific purpose: to save money and return to India for a better future. Young men often saw it as a means of acquiring property, while others used it to overcome some form of hardship: drought, famine, an accident, and so on. For women, the situation was often different. To them, indentureship was a vehicle of emancipation, a means of achieving personal freedom. Two-thirds of women leaving India were single: Brahmin widows, 'deserted women', women on the run from an unhappy marriage, and unmarried mothers. Often, indentureship was their only alternative to prostitution.[445]

Terms of contract

Prospective emigrants were signed up in India by Government-authorized recruiters who carried forms in several local languages, as well as English, to be filled out in triplicate and signed by the prospective emigrant. In 1889, St Lucia's registering officer was a man named J. Haclann, who was based in the town of Ghazipur in Uttar Pradesh. One of the forms used by Haclann carried the following information: '*Date:* 15-12-[18]90. *Emigrant's name: Budhu. Father's name: Parahu. Sex: male. Age:* 20. *Caste: Turki Koiri. Occupation: labourer. Residence - district: Azamgarh; thana: Mohamdabad; village or town and mahala: Walidpur. Successor to estate in India - name: Gulap; father's name: Domon; relationship: uncle.*'

Next were spelled out the '*Conditions of service and terms of agreement*'. The emigrant committed himself to five years of agricultural or domestic service, six days per week (except holidays), in exchange for weekly wages of '*not less than one shilling, which is equal to ten annas*' for time-work, or nine pence for children aged 10 to 15. For task work, adults were paid '*at least one shilling*' per task but experienced workers could earn more.

Immigrants were to receive rations for three months after arrival, at a daily cost of five pence (adults) or half that for children (under age 15). '*Suitable dwellings will be assigned to emigrants under indenture free of rent and will be kept in good repair by the employers. When emigrants under indenture are ill they will be provided with hospital accommodation, medical attendance, medicines, medical comforts and food free of charge.*'

After five years of indentured service, immigrants were allowed to return to India at their own expense. Alternatively, after five years of indentureship plus another five years of '*industrious residence*', they were entitled to the choice between a free return passage (along with their children), a bounty of £10 or ten acres of land.[446] While about half eventually took the £10 bounty, no one ever opted for the ten acres of land,[447] obviously preferring to choose and buy their own instead.

Many emigrants signed their contracts without informing their family. Part of the registering officer's job was to establish the heir and next of kin of prospective emigrants, in case he or she should die overseas. But the authorities found that '*it often happens that no persuasion can make an intending emigrant give the correct name of any of his relations for fear that he may be discovered and identified before leaving India; but the same fear would not operate when he had once arrived in the colony and was beyond reach of capture.*' This can only mean that many people migrated against the express will of their relatives. To solve the problem, it was left to the Protector of Immigrants in St Lucia to confirm every worker's name, next of kin and heir back in India. Safely beyond the reach of their relatives, the indentured workers invariably willingly obliged.

Arrival of indentured East Indians

The East Indian immigration scheme was organized by the colonial Government and paid for out of public funds.[448] Who instigated it in St Lucia is unclear but '*about 1852 the supply of African labour fell off and efforts were made to obtain Chinese labourers. The scheme, however, was abandoned, and in 1854 steps were taken to procure labourers from the East Indies.*'[449]

The first ship to arrive with immigrants from Calcutta was the *Palmyra*, in 1859. It carried 240 men, 58 women, fifteen 'minors' and five infants, making for 318 souls. The *Francis Ridley* followed later that same year from Madras with 261 people (146 men, 63 women, 23 boys, twenty girls and nine young children). The next year, 1860, also saw two arrivals: the *Victor Emmanuel* with 393 Indians (294 men, 67 women, eighteen boys, seven girls, seven children) and the *Zemindar* with 316 (213 men, 66 women, fifteen boys, sixteen girls, six children). The *Ulysses* arrived in 1862, carrying 62 liberated Africans from St Helena and 320 Indians from Calcutta (239 men, 56 women, eleven boys, eight girls and six children). Sixteen men had died from diarrhoea (10), dysentery (3), fever (2) and '*debility*' (1).[450]

Sixteen years passed before the fifth ship arrived but in 1878, the *Leonidas* delivered 580 Indians to Castries (286 men, 158 women, 50 boys, 32 girls and 54 children), some of whom continued on to Trinidad and Demerara.[451] It was followed in 1879 by the *Chetah* with 221 people (116 men, 75 women, thirteen boys, ten girls, seven children); the *Foyle* in 1880 with 67 on board (40 men, seventeen women, three boys, four girls, three children) and the *Bann* in 1881, carrying 316 souls (202 men, 80 women, 22 boys, eight girls, four children).[452]

In 1881, Chinese immigration was briefly considered when Indian immigrants were scarce but by 1884, the bottleneck was resolved and the *Bracadaille* brought 619 more Indians to St Lucia (336 men, 127 women, fourteen boys, seven girls and 135 children).[453] Twenty people had died of cholera during the crossing and the ship was redirected to Gros Islet Bay and quarantined for twelve days, while huts were built on Pigeon Island. The crew and passengers spent another sixteen days on Pigeon Island but no more fatalities occurred, and they were subsequently distributed to the estates. Interestingly, 37 of the Indians aboard the *Bracadaille* were on their second tour of duty in St Lucia, having returned home on the *Jumna* a year earlier. Whether they were disappointed by what they found back in India or had planned to re-indenture themselves, is unknown.[454]

The *Bracadaille* was followed a year later, in 1885, by the *Poonah* with 306 passengers (163 men, 76 women, four boys, five girls, 58 children). Fourteen people suffered from yaws and were quarantined at the leper and yaws colony on Rat Island.[455]

It remained quiet on the quays of Castries for six years until the *Roumania* arrived in 1891, with 554 Indian labourers on board (309 men, 126 women, ten boys, eight girls and 101 children). '*In the case of ... the Roumania,*' it was said, '*the coolies were a particularly good lot, but the children suffered much from coming in a steam ship through the Mediterranean, and 18 died within four months. They arrived in a wretched condition. This is strong evidence in favour of the use of sailing ships and the Cape Route, thereby escaping the excessive vicissitudes of temperature.*'[456] Five passengers were re-indentureds from St Lucia who had returned to India in 1888. Another 45 on the *Roumania* were re-indentureds from other colonies: two had worked in Natal, twenty in Demerara, seven in Jamaica, five in Trinidad, one in Guadeloupe, five in Suriname and five in Mauritius.

The last ship to bring East Indian immigrants to St Lucia was the *Volga*, in 1893. She carried 633 immigrants: 156 for St Lucia and 487 for Jamaica. On the night of 10 December 1893, the *Volga* '*arrived off the port of Castries after a quick and so far safe voyage from Calcutta; but, unfortunately, owing to keeping too close inshore the vessel went aground at the Vigie Point and became a total wreck. Providentially, there was not much wind blowing and the sea was comparatively smooth, so that, with the aid of the ships' boats and those from shore, every soul on board was safely landed without the occurrence of a single accident.*'[457] Those destined for Jamaica boarded the *Jumna* on 22 December and continued on their way.

Distribution of Indians around the island

Once an immigrant vessel arrived in Castries, the Protector of Immigrants and the Colonial Surgeon boarded the ship, inspected everyone's papers and examined every Indian '*as to his general health and fitness for labour.*' They were then sent to the various estates. '*The minors are first divided, their parents and relations are sent to the same estates, and lastly, any friends who wish to remain together. The coolies on landing are not delayed in Castries, but are marched off straight to the estates.*'[458]

The immigrants from the first two ships (*Palmyra* and *Francis Ridley*, 1859) were sent to estates around the island, while those from the third ship (*Victor Emmanuel*, 1860) were sent to '*a low-lying valley*'. Subsequent arrivals were assigned to '*bottom-lands estates*' but no more precise records survive. By 1891, Indians were working island-wide: at St Lucia Crown Lands Estate in Cul de Sac, around the central factory in Roseau Valley (which included the estates of Roseau, Peru, Bellairs and Mont d'Or), at the Dennery Usine (including the Ressources, Richefonde and La Caye Estates in Mabouya Valley), on the south coast (on the Hope, Bellevue, Retraite and Point Sable Estates) and in the Soufrière district (at Perle and Pelut). Other estates or areas that at one time or another were mentioned in connection with free or indentured East Indians are Bois d'Orange, Soucis, Marquis, Espérance, Jacmel, Forestière, Mon Repos, Troumassée, Canelles, Anse Ger, Cacao, Ressources, Augier, Balca, River Dorée, Mont d'Or and Anse la Raye.

Centralization of the sugar industry in St Lucia

Not much is known about Indian workers' living conditions, especially between 1859 and 1878, but it is likely that on the relatively small, scattered sugar estates prevalent at the time, they lived in thatched huts with their provision gardens nearby - not unlike the native wage labourers of the time. From 1878 onwards, however, almost all newly arrived East Indians were sent to work at St Lucia's four new central sugar factories.

The first of these had been built in 1874 in Cul de Sac, followed by a central factory in Vieux Fort in 1882 and factories in Roseau and Dennery shortly thereafter. St Lucia's sugar industry had entered a new phase of crisis in the 1870s. With the British Government unwilling or unable to give protective sugar tariffs to the West Indies, St Lucia's small-scale, scattered and outdated sugar estates faced total ruin. It was swim or sink and so a group of the wealthier proprietors, including the DuBoulay, Devaux and Barnard families, with help from English sugar merchant houses and the local Government, started a major rationalization operation. They also turned to their relatives in Martinique and Guadeloupe, where central factories had been introduced in the 1830s, using techniques borrowed from beet sugar production.[459]By increasing the scale of operations, abandoning marginal lands and introducing modern technology and machinery, these four resulting central sugar factories managed to weather the onslaught of continuing low prices on the world market.[460] All four central factories used indentured Indian labour and before long, Indian communities sprang up around Roseau, Cul de Sac, Dennery and Vieux Fort.

Working conditions

Indentured men on day work earned one shilling for a nine-hour working day. Indentured women earned ten pence, although performing '*most of the different sorts of work that the men do, except cane-cutting and attending machinery in the usine buildings ... many women do men's full tasks.*' Women commonly worked up to their eighth month of pregnancy and '*Cooly women sometimes make over their infants to negro women during the day while work is going on in the field, paying a small sum for the trouble given.'* Children were paid according to their tasks, primarily '*carrying water, hauling trash, weeding, &c.*'

Indian workers in St Lucia had a harder time than their counterparts in Trinidad or Demerara, with lower wages and less liberal arrangements. Unlike indentureds elsewhere, for instance, newcomers in St Lucia had to pay for cutlasses, hoes, shovels and forks, which were given free of charge the first time in other colonies (as well as pots, pans, lamps and buckets). At the end of their indentureship (or '*cut bung*' as they called it),[461] Indians usually remained on or near their original estates, working as wage labourers whilst supplementing their incomes by keeping cattle, métayage (which was very popular with Indians), shop keeping, selling kerosene or working as butchers. A few also grew cocoa and vegetables for the local market.

Transgressions of East Indians' rights

In 1891, the British Government sent Surgeon-Major D.W.D. Comins to the West Indies to report on the welfare of the Indian immigrants there. Comins had lived in India, spoke Hindustani, and was not afraid to show up at plantations unannounced, demanding to see the wage records or lecturing managers on perceived transgressions. His report was published in 1893 along with several pages of a personal diary. His *Note on emigration from the East Indies to St Lucia* offers vivid and intimate snap-shots of East Indian life in St Lucia in 1891.[462]

Overall, Comins considered the free and indentured Indians to be fairly content with their lot, living amicably with employers and Creole co-workers alike. But he did report several breaches of contract. Indian workers were not always paid their full wages, were paid late, were given IOU's in lieu of wages and were sometimes forced to incur debts for rations they had not needed. '*Because a woman has been pregnant ... or because a man has been sick in hospital ... to confront him when he appears in the field with a bill for food supplied which he never asked for and possibly did not want, amounting to £5 or £6 ... is a direct incentive to make him an idler, a skulker, vagabond, or deserter, and is directly contrary to the laws for immigrants in the best managed colonies.*'[463] Comins also disliked the compulsory payment for rations, '*which is often in excess of their actual value, and is really a reduction of the coolies' wages by which the estate profits.*' Adding insult to injury, the rations received by workers were less than those of prisoners in India and urgently needed to be increased.

Time-expired Indian labourers were routinely paid less than black workers for doing the same work. At Retraite Estate in Vieux Fort, for instance, the foremen on the '*cooly gangs*' got one shilling, when the *negro* foreman got one shilling six pence. '*This appears to be contrary to the ordinance, which says that labour other than indentured shall be paid for at the same rates as obtained by the free population.'* In similar vein, indentured workers were often kept on day work instead of task work, a practice Comins deemed *'destructive of advancement and improvement.'* Worse still, when Indians *were* given task work, the tasks were commonly too large to be completed within one working day.

Following the economic crisis of 1884-5, planters struggled to keep their indentured labourers occupied. This, in turn, made it increasingly difficult for the Indians to earn a living wage, since they were only paid for the hours they worked. By 1891, Mondays and Saturdays had become half working days and the effective working week was reduced to five days for 'industrious men' and four for 'industrious women'.

The Protector of Immigrants in St Lucia, R.P. Cropper, although well-liked and trusted by the Indians and sympathetic to their cause, by his own admission was impotent in the face of the plantocracy's power. He complained bitterly to the 1897 West India Royal Commission.

> *I should say very positively that the supply of immigrant labour should not be continued or increased. The planters cannot afford to pay the immigrants sufficient wages. Sometime ago, when I complained to a planter that the tasks given were increased and were excessive, he honestly replied that if I insisted on smaller tasks, I must take away the indentured immigrants. In another case, when I complained that the immigrants did not get regular and full employment, I was flatly contradicted. But I was satisfied that the statements of the immigrants to me were absolutely correct.*[464]

By the mid 1890s, assigned tasks routinely and illegally exceeded seven working hours. '*If there is any dispute the magistrate calls in assessors to decide whether the task is a fair one. The assessors are always neighbouring planters or managers. They are all in one boat, and they declare the task a fair one.*' Cropper was reluctant to take planters to court because a favourable outcome merely increased his worries. '*Until the recent bad years he could always have found planters willing to take from him coolies moved away from any estate.*' But with the economy faltering, '*If any case resulted in his favour against an estate, he would have to take away the coolies, and could not find employment for them elsewhere.*'

Cropper once sued the Central Factory in Vieux Fort for '*illegal treatment of the coolies in the smallness of their earnings*' but the court case '*had no result*' and Cropper '*never, on any other occasion, reported or took any steps*' again, since he '*could not see what steps could be taken.*'

From the planters' point of view, the indentured workers had indeed become a millstone around their necks. Ordinary labourers could be sent home if work was slow, but indentureds had to be kept occupied, paid and maintained, no matter how unprofitable the price for sugar. In early 1895, the situation became so grave that '*the Government received notice from the authorities of the estates in Grand-Cul-de-Sac Valley that the indentured immigrants of those estates would, on the 31st of May, be given up to the Government.*'[465] No doubt to the Government's relief, '*before that date arrived a local syndicate was formed, which undertook to carry on the work of the estates and the usine for one year.*' A small rise in the price of sugar and further improvements to the Central Sugar Factory in Cul de Sac (including getting rid of an expensive diffusion plant which had proved useless and '*which is lying on the beach now, and which you can have for the price of old iron*') helped the new syndicate put the factory on a profitable footing once again.[466]

Another transgression of Indians' rights (albeit a debatable one) was that until 1891, their contracts failed to state in writing that after five years of indentureship, they were free to return to India at their own expense. They consistently claimed that the recruiting agents in India had verbally promised this, but their applications to leave were invariably denied by the Government. They were naturally upset about this and vented their anger to Comins. On 16 May 1891, at La Caye Estate, Comins met with 74 indentured workers (including children) and about 90 time-expired Indian workers. '*Some of the free coolies made the usual complaint about not being allowed to return to India at their own expense after expiry of indenture. I asked to see their contract paper, and they produced certificates of exemption from labour* [instead]. *Apparently they have no copy of the contract made in India. They say that all the coolies who arrived in the S.* Poona *more than five years ago wish to return to India, and that the common saying is that the Calcutta sahebs are liars.*'[467]

Comins found that '*certainly the St Lucia Agent in Calcutta was never authorized to include this condition in the terms offered by recruiters. But the ship* Roumania *brought for each immigrant an agreement paper in which this condition is expressly stipulated, with the knowledge and consent of the Protector of Emigrants at Calcutta. Arrangements have been made by which the permission will be granted in future.*' Although this resolved the matter, Comins did not expect that in practice, much would change. '*Many are deterred by the formidable expense of the passage, £14, and it remains to be seen how many will avail themselves of their right: not many, I fancy*', he noted in his diary.

Relations between Indians and St Lucians

Most Indians viewed their sojourn in St Lucia as temporary - certainly initially - and, feeling little affinity with the wider society, made little effort to integrate.[468] Whether as cause or consequence, a certain level of antipathy and ridicule proliferated between Indians and black people, with mutual accusations of body odour topping the list. Indians were considered more docile and dependable, but also physically weaker and so Indians and blacks usually worked in separate gangs. In 1897, the secretary of the Agricultural Society summed it up thus: '*Coolie labour is at best a poor makeshift. It is costly, of poor quality, and the East Indian does not fuse with the native population.*'[469] Indian children were occasionally bullied, and '*Coolie Calcutta*' was a common taunt well into the twentieth century. Sporadic miscegenation between Indians and blacks or whites started early on, but they rarely intermarried before the 1950s. After almost four decades of immigration, a St Lucian official recommended that '*a serious attempt should be made to induce the Coolie to intermarry with the negro. At the outset ... a strong prejudice arose between the parties ... and ... nothing was done to dissipate it. The races now understand each other better ... with encouragement, they would ... provide a useful and satisfactory progeny, who would be equal to the varied requirements of these tropical islands.*'[470]

Indian women were strongly encouraged by their families to marry within their community and even between Indian communities in the north and south of St Lucia, intermarriage was relatively rare with the result that even today, certain family names are tied to specific communities. Where sexual relationships did cross ethnic boundaries, they more commonly occurred between Indian women and black men than *vice versa*. This was partly because Indian men considered black women too assertive. Other reasons may have been black women's disdain for the Indian male physique and the fact that black men more often occupied positions of power, giving them the leverage to gain sexual favours from Indian women.

Gender relations amongst Indians

Throughout the period of indentured Indian labour, the ratio of women to men was highly uneven at 1:2, or approximately four women for every ten men.[471] Newly arrived single women usually settled down with Indian men who had been in St Lucia for some time. In 1881, so-called '*heathen marriages according to the Indian custom*' became legally recognized in St Lucia so long as they were registered at the immigration office and on the estate. Similarly, divorces were arranged by mutual consent and '*the parties usually divide the jewellery, etc., amongst themselves without reference to any authority.*'[472]

Their relative scarcity gave Indian women a level of negotiating power they had not known in India - but it also put them in the line of danger. Research from other colonies shows that domestic violence against Indian women was very prevalent and wife murder not uncommon. In St Lucia, three indentured workers were murdered between 1879 and 1891: two women and one man.[473] Indian men's insecurity about their (common-law) wives' fidelity was high, and women's relative independence - so contrary to cultural expectations in India -

only served to heighten men's anxiety and aggression.[474] Breen wrote that, whilst heinous crime was rare, '*more murders are committed by the coolie immigrants in proportion to their numbers, than by all the other classes of the population. ... The men are very jealous, and that feeling... becomes intensified in these islands, owing to the comparatively small number of women ... The men seldom seek intercourse with any but their own countrywomen, so that the few who have "wives" have to watch them very closely, and when a woman is found unfaithful, the chances are that the reputed husband will murder either the seducer or the seduced, and sometimes both.*'[475]

Drunkenness was a notorious contributing factor in violence, and Comins found that '*The coolies very readily fall into habits of intoxication*'. Drunkenness was often proffered as an excuse for violence, but generally '*these offences are committed between cooly and cooly, and no records are kept of such cases.*'[476] One is left to wonder how many of such unreported drunken attacks involved the battering of women and children. Occasionally, Indian men turned their violence on themselves and in St Lucia, as elsewhere, the rate of Indian male suicide was relatively high (nine cases between 1879 and 1891).[477] Troubled love affairs were reportedly the most common cause.

Caste and religion

By 1891, of the 2523 Indians in St Lucia, 1849 were Hindus, 475 Christians and 199 Muslims.[478] Muslims preferred to cluster together, but their requests were not always granted. Comins came across '*one Musulman and his wife*' at Retraite Estate near Vieux Fort. '*He says he asked to be allotted to the same estate as other Musulmans, but was not allowed.*'[479] The Christians were mostly recent converts to the Presbyterian Canadian Mission headquartered in Trinidad. Between 1890 and 1900, the Reverend John Morton established schools for East Indian children in Mabouya, Canelles, Mon Repos, Roseau and Forestière.[480]

From the outset, distinctions of caste and religion became blurred. Living arrangements did not allow for separate cooking or washing, and so ritual purity could not be upheld. Caste, said Comins, is '*not a subject which troubles either the Indians or the authorities in this island. Most of the coolies are of the lowest Hindu castes, and a few are Brahmin and of other high castes. The differences in caste are not recognized, and the immigrants soon lose most of their prejudices on this point.*'[481]

Local knowledge of Indian religion was minimal, to the point where even the Protector of Immigrants, Cropper, told Comins straight-faced that '*a marriage was recently solemnized between two immigrants. A Brahman priest brought a Koran! and read some passages. Of the two married, the man was a*

Muhammadan and the woman a Hindu of caste. The name of the Brahman priest was Nazir Ali! which is the name of a Muhammadan.' It was blatantly obvious to Comins that Cropper, despite good intentions, neither understood the caste system, nor conceived of Hinduism and Islam as distinct religions. None of the administrative staff in the immigration office or on the plantations spoke or understood Hindustani, and the interpreters in the hospital were old-time Indians who had learned some Kwéyòl.

On the estates, pork and beef were banned from the rations (substituted with salt fish) and no pigs were allowed to be kept. But in facilities designed for the general public, such religious sensitivity was absent. In the Castries hospital, for instance - an otherwise meticulously run facility - all soup was made with beef or pork. Some Indians believed it was part of a blatant conspiracy: '*A group of coolies ... mentioned that they tried to make Christians of them here, and on my asking them what could have put such an idea into their head, they said in hospital they made them eat beef and pork, a custom which to them constitutes one of the most important evidences of Christianity.'* By the same token, Colonial Surgeon Charles Dennehy, in 1897, observed a contrary trend: '*The coolies, to save money, run themselves down by underfeeding. When they come into hospital they pick up 10 or 12 lbs. in weight in as many days. Then they go out, work off their fat, and come in again to recruit.*'[482] Be that as it may, caste sensitivities stood no chance in the face of indentureship, and so they were either suspended or, in the case of those who remained in St Lucia, eventually discarded.

Evidence regarding the survival of other Indian religious traditions is scarce. One author claimed that until recently, a '*small percentage of East Indian immigrants ... with their Hindu pacificatory rites, practiced their religious traditions including harhi, vivah, mundon and dinder funeral ceremonies*'.[483] While it is true that Indian ceremonies including sacrifices of food to appease the soul of the deceased are still performed today,[484] it is difficult to assess to what extent this wider claim is based on observed facts. The same researcher asserted that on plantations in St Lucia, up to around 1953, the daily evening routine saw people listening '*to stories from India, which included Ramayana, Mahabarata and mythological historical and social stories. The men of the panchayats system formed small groups sitting among themselves and smoking marijuana, tobacco, and drinking strong white rum. As usual they sat in a community village shack. They used lamplight in the ramayana, during which a small group of villagers sang Indian folk songs accompanied by music.*'[485] Oral history collected in the mid 1990s confirms that second-generation Indians growing up in the 1930s, 40s ans 50s still learned Hindi songs and stories from their parents, but they in turn seem to have passed these on to their own children in Kwéyòl instead.

Comins' diary: a snapshot of East Indians' lives

The report and diary of D.W.D. Comins provides many touching insights into the lives of the first generation of Indian indentured labourers - keeping in mind that by 1891, the sugar industry was once again in crisis, and the earliest immigrants had already spent three decades in St Lucia.

Comins arrived on 12 May 1891. He spent a few days with the Protector of Immigrants, Cropper, in Castries, chatting with the '*many coolies who came to the office with various business to be settled. They all expressed themselves most happy and contented, and had an air of prosperity. I was struck by the complete confidence in, and affection evinced for, Mr Cropper, to whom they confide their little wants and hopes.*'[486] A man by the name of Durma, who had arrived on the *Bracadaille* six years earlier, told Comins that '*he is a chaukidar on the Roseau estate, and does 7 days' work in the week. He is quite satisfied, but would very much like to go home and see his father and mother; but he has no money - women and drink have taken it all.*' Rum sold on credit was many an immigrant's downfall and Comins felt that '*as far as the Indian coolies are concerned, it would be a good thing if no rum were sold.*'

On 15 May 1891, Comins rode on horseback to Crown Lands Estate in Cul de Sac, where he met '*numerous groups of coolies, who were delighted at hearing their own language spoken by a sahib. I interviewed several of them, who were all very contented and happy, and spoke well of the place.*' The '*cooly lines*' were '*comfortable and well-built*' of American pine, the floor raised two feet off the ground. Cooking was done inside the hut, '*the floor being protected from fire by a layer of clay, each hut having a separate* chula.' Rain water from the roof was stored in an iron tank for drinking. '*There are no latrines. The surroundings clean and free from rubbish and filth.*' Compared to the barracks, however, the cooly houses '*appeared to me unnecessarily low and damp, considering the space available on the hills round.*' Comins also inspected the wares in the local shop, from which the Indians' rations came, and visited the estate school, where 4 or 5 of the 15 students were '*cooly boys learning to read and write English.*'

The following day, Comins rode to Mabouya Valley: '*a richly cultivated valley ... with a large factory standing out against the sea in the distance. The second estate I came to was Ressources which, together with Richefonde and La Caye, belong to one company, which also owns the usine near the seashore.*' At Ressources, the '*cooly lines*' were again comfortable and clean, built of pine with raised floors and fronted by a long verandah which doubled as kitchen. '*There are three shops on the estate kept by old coolies. Purmanon, a 7th-year cooly, keeps a bania's shop. Debi, a 7th-year cooly, keeps a bania's shop. Kali Pershad also sells dál, rice. There are about 30 cows owned by coolies on the estate, and a few horses or ponies. There is a school where the 3 R's are taught.*'

From Ressources it was just a few minutes' ride to La Caye Estate, which was managed by a Mr Jore, '*a great favourite*' with the Indians. La Caye counted 74 new immigrants (including children) and about 90 time-expired Indians. Including Creole workers, there were some 250 labourers on the payroll. The day of Comins' visit was a Saturday and '*It being pay day, a sort of hát or fair is held under the trees, largely attended by Creoles selling fish, fruit and even beef, gay handkerchiefs, sweetmeats and cakes.*' The Indians' living quarters were similar to what he had seen before, with the added advantage of a separate cooking shed. '*The surroundings are very clean and free from rubbish and jungle. ... There are no latrines, but I noticed no nuisance caused thereby. The coolies as usual retire to the neighbouring cane piece. Washing, bathing, is done in the river, from which drinking water is also obtained.*'

Two miles on from La Caye, Comins came to Dennery,

> *... a most beautiful place on the seashore. From its natural advantages, if it were in Europe instead of the West Indies, it would be the most fashionable of watering places. The small town stretches along the shore of a land-locked bay. An island, a few hundred yards from the shore, adds much to the beauty of the place and the security of the harbour in which lie the sugar ships loading from the neighbouring usine in the Mabouya Valley. The town is surrounded by hills covered with scrub and trees. On one of these is situated the district hospital for immigrants. On the right is a sugar estate, the working of which is abandoned for want of money and owing to the low price of muscovado sugar. ... It seems a great pity that after so much money has been spent on the erection of dwelling-houses, cooly lines and a factory, the clearing and forming of ground into cane beds, it should be left to its fate.*

Comins met with the Resident Medical Officer, Dr Taboni and found the hospital (as in Castries and Vieux Fort) clean, airy, well-furnished, well-provisioned, well-managed and far superior to hospitals in India. Like the European and Barbadian immigrants, Indians were susceptible to malaria and '*spleen disease*' and Dr Taboni estimated that '*normally 25 to 30 per cent of the indentured coolie population* [is] *in hospital.*' Comins was disappointed to hear that doctors visited the estates only once a fortnight, whereas in other colonies this was done once or twice a week. Also, there were just the three hospitals available to Indian workers, along with an estate hospital at Cul de Sac, and '*if the medical officer of Dennery or Vieux Fort falls ill or is absent, the immigrants are left without medical attendance. The distance of these hospitals from estates is a serious bar to their efficiency.*' At Roseau and Cul de Sac, patients were taken by trolley to the sea and from there by boat to Castries. Leading up to Comins' visit, the Dennery hospital had been closed for renovations and the doctor gone overseas. Patients had had to be transported twelve miles on horseback or man-handled stretchers across the Barre de l'Isle to Castries. *'The Vieux Fort doctor has just fallen ill, and his place is taken by the two doctors at Castries, who on alternate weeks leave their own patients and work in Castries and spend a week in Vieux Fort.'* Comins concluded that *'The medical treatment of coolies on the estate is not arranged for with that completeness which is supposed to exist under the immigration laws.'*

After spending the night in Dennery, on 17 May 1891, Comins rode out towards Richefonde. On the way there,

> *I overtook an Indian dressed in European style, riding a pony. I addressed him in Hindustani, and he answered in French patois. I got into conversation with him and found out that his name was Umeer Sing, a Chettri by caste, who had been in the island about 10 or 11 years. He had forgotten much of his native tongue, and the patois seemed to come much more easily to him. He told me the history of his life in the island, which was one of contented work and increasing wealth. He now does no work, but owns 12 cows, 2 ponies and some goats, and is worth about Rs.1,000. He has a wife and two children, and has no wish to return to India, and a few months ago accepted £10 bounty to forego his right to a free return passage. I asked him about his relatives in India, and he said he was the only son, and his mother, he believed, was alive, but he had never written to her, and dreaded doing so as she was very fond of him, and would cry much if he did not return to her. I suggested that it was hard to let her live out her old age in uncertainty as to whether her only son was dead or alive, and told him how rejoiced she would be to hear of his welfare. So he promised to write her a letter, and I am to see that she gets it.*

Correspondence with home was limited to 153 letters sent from St Lucia to India between January 1884 and May 1890, and a total of 210 letters received during that same period. *'Here and there a cooly on an estate is able to write a letter'*. It is likely that they acted as scribes for others. If immigrants came from the same district in India, it is of course very possible that one letter carried news of several people at once.

At Richefonde Estate itself (his last stop on this first trip) Comins found some newly arrived immigrants. *'They were extremely delighted that I had come all the way from Calcutta to see them.'* Comins found them *'happy and contented, and look well and prosperous, they have nothing but good to say of the estate and their treatment.'* It being a Sunday, the estate was quiet and workers spent the day *'sitting still or visiting their friends on neighbouring estates.'*

Comins then returned to Castries, but the following week saw him back on a horse, this time visiting Roseau Estate. Along with the central sugar factory in Vieux Fort, Roseau was owned by the St Lucia Usines and Estates Company and managed by the brothers Theophine and Emmanuel DuBoulay.

'On topping the ridge beyond the Cul-de-Sac Valley the whole of the Roseau district was visible, the tall usine forming a prominent object in the centre near the sea.'

At Peru Estate, Comins met some indentured Indians, who said they had no complaints. Peru, Bellairs and Mont d'Or Estates all contributed canes to the Roseau central factory. Although it was late in the crop season, processing still continued at Roseau. *'All the workmen in the factory are negros, and there is not a single Indian cooly at work. This was accounted for by their not possessing the same physical strength as the negros, and because they have no knowledge of machinery.'* Next, Comins inspected *'the cooly lines. All the indentured coolies were out weeding, but I found a batch of old coolies in the lines. They seem a very lazy and dirty lot of loafers. Some of them are squatting under the cooly huts, and apparently intend doing nothing all day.'* Comins was not pleased with the estate shop either. The shop was run by *'a Creole negro, who pays the estate £95 a year as rent, and of course takes it out of the coolies by charging them more for the articles they have to buy. ... This negro also sells rum to the coolies, which Mr DuBoulay promised should not continue. As the license for selling rum costs £30, a good deal of cooly pay must be expended before it can pay to take out a rum license.'*

Some days later, Emmanuel DuBoulay showed Comins around the Vieux Fort Central Factory and surrounding estates. DuBoulay told Comins that he spent just four months per year in St Lucia and returned to Paris as soon as processing was finished. That year 1891, the Vieux Fort factory (the foundations of which can still be found on the west side of upper Clarke Street) had turned out 1500 tons of sugar, operating day and night by electric light. Operations had just ceased when Comins arrived.

Accompanied by the medical officer, Comins visited Retraite Estate, which was under French management at the time, and home to 33 indentured Indian workers plus their children. He ascertained several breaches of contract with respect to working hours, wages and debts being carried forward, but found the housing arrangements *'very good of their kind'* and was pleased to see that at the estate school, thirteen of the 23 children were Indian. In one house, Comins was surprised to see *'a shrine without a god.'*

Hope Estate came next and here, too, *'the ranges are very good and provided with standing bedsteads. Cooking is done in the verandah which is, of course, dangerous. The immigrants have not yet got accustomed to the strong trade-winds, and want boards put up to screen their* chulas.' The immigrants at Hope must have arrived on the *Roumania*, since at the time of writing, in May 1891, they were still new to their situation. *'They are a simple people, and to-day refused work because they were ordered to do task-work instead of by the day, although the task given, as is usual at first, was a light one. They are probably waiting to see what the neighbouring estate Retraite will do, where day work is still universal. ... The older coolies and Creoles are doing the tasks the newly arrived immigrants refused.'*

Comins subsequently sailed to St Vincent and Barbados and did not return to St Lucia until October to round off his recommendations.

Return migration

The first time-expired Indian workers were repatriated in 1867 on board the ship *Ganges*, seven years after having arrived in St Lucia. The *Ganges* returned 451 people to India: 263 men, 103 women, 36 boys, 33 girls and sixteen children. A year later, in 1868, the *Lincelles* took back another 298 (180 men, 56 women, 23 boys, twelve girls and 27 children) and in 1871, the *Harkaway* repatriated 162 people (87 men, 27 women, 25 boys, ten girls and thirteen children). Making no allowances for deaths and births, this would mean that during this initial period, 911 out of 1608 Indians went back to India: just over half.

No return journeys were made over the next twelve years but in 1883, the *Jumna* sailed for India with 95 re-migrants on board (35 men, 24 women, seven boys, three girls and 26 children). It was followed five years later, on 5 September 1888, by the *Moy* with 327 people (130 men, 70 women, eleven boys, thirteen girls and 103 children). Of these 327, one had arrived 29 years before on the *Victor Emmanuel* and another 28 years before, on the *Zamindar*. Some 182 others had come out on the *Leonidas* (ten years earlier), three on the *Chetah* (nine years earlier), five on the *Foyle* (eight years earlier), nine on the *Bann* (seven years earlier), 26 on the *Bracadaille* (four years earlier) and two on the *Poonah* (two years earlier). '*Those who went before the expiration of their ten years were permanently disabled coolies*', Comins noted.

In 1889, the *Rhone* carried home 132 people (51 men, 31 women, four boys, three girls and 43 children), followed in 1890 by a small contingent of 21 in the *Hereford* (twelve men, three women, two girls and four children). In 1893, the *Jumna* took on board 487 returning Indians but that included some labourers who had arrived just two weeks earlier on the ill-fated *Volga* and were destined for Jamaica. In 1894, the *British Peer* repatriated 450 Indians and in subsequent years two more ships sailed from St Lucia to India: the *Akin* and the *Atticar Jorhad*[487] but precise dates and passenger details for these are not available.

At the time of Comins' visit, in 1891, public funds for repatriation were running low and financial duress was causing the Government to become disinterested in the Indians' plight. Comins wrote: '*There are at present 163 applicants, who have every right to be returned without delay at the expense of the colony, but I cannot hear that there is the slightest chance of any ship being provided for this purpose. ... In like cases of detention coolies are paid £1 for every six months detained, but the time between the first day of arrival and September, the date of usual sailing, is not counted as detention. So that a cooly may serve six months over the time stated in his contract without compensation.'*[488]

Comins acknowledged the cause to the problem ('*St Lucia being so small a place, and the immigrants few, it can never be expected that there will be enough returning to fill a ship, while those who are anxious to go have to wait for years*') but was nevertheless outraged at the abuse of their rights, especially since in his eyes, there was a '*perfectly natural and easy solution*' to the problem: '*All these people should be allowed to go as 3rd class passengers to India. ... Coolies after ten years' colonial experience are very worldly wise, and as capable of taking care of themselves as any other class of people.*'

But Comins' recommendation was not heeded. In 1897, planters started lobbying for abolition of the special tax on sugar and cocoa that had paid for the cost of Indians' medical care and repatriation, saying they had never personally benefited from indentured labour (many estates had since changed hands) and cocoa plantations had hardly ever employed Indians to begin with.[489] Already struggling to keep the *Coolie Repatriation Fund* afloat, Government also knew that in 1901 and 1904, Indians from the *Roumania* and the *Volga* would become entitled to repatriation, at an estimated cost of more than £5000.[490] Just as 163 Indians languished in St Lucia for three years before the *British Peer* finally took them home in 1894, so must hundreds of others after them have waited several years before the *Akin* and the *Atticar Jorhad* sailed for India. It is likely that many more, against their wishes, never saw their home land again.

Remittances to India

Despite their hardships, Indian contract workers and return migrants accumulated considerable sums of money, much of which they sent or carried back to India with them. The *Ganges*, which returned to India in 1867 with 366 adults on board, also carried more than £10 000 in remittances, belonging to 341 depositors. Adding on the value of jewellery and remittances sent through the bank, the total amount came close to £12 000.[491] Such a spectacular sum was never repeated, as the number of depositors amongst adult return migrants dropped to about half on later ships, but even so, more than £17 000 in total was remitted to India between 1867 and 1890 by ship.[492]

Money was also remitted through banks[493] or sent back, along with property, to heirs in India whenever someone died intestate in St Lucia.[494] Towards the end of the nineteenth century, those who had accepted the bounty of £10 to remain in St Lucia were beginning to show signs of (relative) affluence. In October 1891, the Protector of Immigrants reported that there were 1640 immigrants on 22 estates, 228 of whom owned stock, including twenty horses, one donkey, 480 cattle, 109 sheep and 96 goats. '*The entire population of Indians being under 2500, this shows that a fair proportion of them are men of property*', Comins concluded. He commended the move by Government to open up Crown lands for purchase by Indians. Almost immediately, '*sixty acres were bought by three coolies in lots of 20 acres each. A good many purchases have been made from private owners, chiefly by the original coolies of 1859 and 1860. In the office for the Crown Lands Department there are now five applications for 64 acres.*' Comins saw this as a hopeful sign for the future, believing as he did that once East Indians could own large tracts of fertile land, like their counterparts in Trinidad and Demerara, they would develop into '*happy and contented permanent settlers and good citizens and tax-payers.*' He was not wrong.

11

Sugar stumbles: emigration, coaling, public works, Castries naval garrison, World War One 1884 - 1918

Half a century after Emancipation, St Lucian society remained essentially unaltered, with the majority of people still cogs in the wheels of an export-oriented plantation economy. 'King Sugar' reigned in 1884 in much the same way he had done during the 1760s or the 1820s: arrogantly, unapologetically and unchallenged. Anyone not bowing to his demands was considered a vagabond and a threat to society, and St Lucia's working population remained a means to an end, never an end in itself. The plantocracy had grudgingly accepted the rise of a peasantry, but society continued to be structured according to the demands of its main export crop. The question was always: 'How can the people best benefit the plantation economy?' It was never: 'Which economic activity best suits the needs of the population?' Even in the halls of London's Colonial Office, no one could see beyond plantation-grown sugar.

At the end of the day, métayage and immigrant labour were merely stopgap measures implemented to counteract the abolition of slavery, and to allow St Lucia's human and natural landscape to continue to be exploited for the mass production of sugar destined for the rich European and North-American markets. Profits flowed into the same few pockets as before Emancipation, while the working masses survived on wages of one shilling per day and whatever provisions they could grow on land which, more often than not, they had no legal title to. It was enough to subsist on, buy a few clothes and build or rent a small house, but precious little beyond that. The standard of living of labourers in post-Emancipation decades was not essentially different from that of slaves. Freedom had basically brought '*the substitution of a low wage for the previous outlay on the purchase and maintenance of slaves, besides absolving employers from responsibility.*'[495] Colonial Surgeon Dr Dennehy put it more bluntly in 1897 when he said: '*Sugar cannot pay if a fair wage is given to the labourers. For sugar to pay, a starvation wage must be given. Sugar can only be grown at the expense of the labourers.'*[496]

The crisis of 1884

Throughout the 1860s, 70s and early 80s, sugar prices were reasonable and St Lucia's political climate stable. Peasants and labourers managed to feed, clothe and house their families, send their children to school once in a while, and even donate a few pennies to the church, flower festivals and friendly societies. This changed abruptly in 1884 when, almost overnight, a sharp drop in the price for muscovado sugar sent planters reeling into debt. The crisis was '*as quick and unexpected in its advent as it was permanently disastrous in its effects*'.[497] Sugar estates island-wide went into bankruptcy. The export value of sugar, rum and molasses had been £190 360 in 1883. By 1886, this was slashed to one-third: £64 000. It recovered slightly in 1893 (£95 000) but a further drop followed in 1896 (£63 000).[498] Of 81 sugar estates operational in 1843, only thirteen remained active in 1897. The following table shows all large sugar estates operating in St Lucia in 1887-9 (shortly after the crisis set in) and their condition in 1896, nine years later.[499]

Table 2

List of all major sugar estates operational in 1887-9 showing acreage under sugar cane, average sugar crop and their status in 1896.
(Quantities in hogsheads)

Estate	Mill type	Average crop of muscovado sugar in 1887-89	Status in 1896
Anse Canot	steam	216	Abandoned
Anse Mahaut	steam	70	Partly abandoned
Anse Galet	water	40	Abandoned
Anse Mamin	steam	80	Abandoned
Anse la Raye	water	40	Abandoned
Anse Noire Black Bay	steam water	}250 }	}Contributors to }Vieux Fort factory
Bonne Fortune	cattle	40	Abandoned
Bois d'Orange	steam	80	Abandoned
Bonne Terre	steam	60	Abandoned

Estate	Mill type	Average crop of muscovado sugar in 1887-89	Status in 1896
Beausejour (Massade)	steam	60	Abandoned
Malgrétoute	water	130	Partly abandoned
Belle Plaine	cattle	50	Abandoned
Beausejour	steam	80	Abandoned
Beausejour & Au Repos	water	100	Contributor to Vieux Fort factory
Balembouche	water	180	Almost wholly abandoned
Belle Vue	wind	60	Contributor to Vieux Fort factory
Beauchamp	water	60	Almost wholly abandoned
Toc	steam	130	Abandoned
Corinthe	steam	80	Abandoned
Cap	steam	180	Abandoned
C. Belair	water	130	Almost wholly abandoned
Cannelles	water	200	Partly abandoned
Canaries	steam	300	Partly abandoned
Diamond	water	140	Abandoned
Dauphin	cattle	39	Abandoned
River Doree Desgatieres	water water	}286 }	Almost wholly abandoned
Entrepot	steam	60	Abandoned
Esperance	water	40	Abandoned
Esperance	water	50	Abandoned
Fond d'Or	steam	150	Contributor to Dennery factory.
Fond Doux	steam	80	Abandoned
Fond	steam	250	Abandoned
Grandanse	steam	40	Abandoned

Estate	Mill type	Average crop of muscovado sugar in 1887-89	Status in 1896
Hope	water	123	Part-contributor to Vieux Fort factory
Incommode	steam	80	Contributor to Cul de Sac factory
Jalousie	steam	78	Abandoned
La Pointe	steam	80	Part-contributor to Cul de Sac factory
La Resource	steam	60	Abandoned
Soucis	steam	100	Contributor to Cul de Sac factory
La Caye	steam	130	Contributor to Dennery factory
La Riche	cattle	40	Abandoned
Le Parc	water	100	Abandoned
Providence	wind	40	Abandoned
L'Orangerie	water	60	Abandoned
M. d'Or	water	40	Abandoned
Marigot	cattle	40	Abandoned
Marquis	steam	140	Almost wholly abandoned
M. Plaisant	steam	100	Abandoned
M. Courbaril	water	120	Abandoned
Malgrétoute	cattle	12	Abandoned
Malgrétoute	water	150	Partly abandoned
M. Lezard	water	30	Almost abandoned
Mondesir	water	50	Abandoned
Perou	steam	70	Contributor to Roseau factory
Pearl	water	250	Abandoned
Pt. Caraibe	water	100	Abandoned
Pointe Sable	steam	150	Contributor to Vieux Fort factory

Estate	Mill type	Average crop of muscovado sugar in 1887-89	Status in 1896
Palmiste	water	140	Partly abandoned
Roseau	steam	250	Contributor to Roseau factory
Richefond	water	100	Contributor to Dennery factory
Reduit	steam	50	Abandoned
Ravine Claire	water	30	Abandoned
Ruby	water	100	Abandoned
Rabat	water	50	Abandoned
Reunion	water	200	Abandoned
Retraite	water	120	Contributor to Vieux Fort factory
Ressource	steam	80	Contributor to Vieux Fort factory
Ressource	steam	60	Contributor to Vieux Fort factory
Rayne	steam	60	Abandoned
Soufriere	water	120	Partly abandoned
St Remy	steam	80	Abandoned
Saphir	steam	200	Almost wholly abandoned
St Urbain	steam	80	Part-contributor to Vieux Fort factory
Savannes	steam	40	Abandoned
Sans Soucis	steam	40	Abandoned
Soucis	steam	100	Contributor to Cul de Sac factory
Terre Blanche	water	25	Abandoned
Tourney	steam	100	Contributor to Vieux Fort factory
Troumassée	water	120	Partly abandoned
Union	water	200	Almost wholly abandoned

Estate	Mill type	Average crop of muscovado sugar in 1887-89	Status in 1896
Union Vale	water	140	Abandoned
Union Praslin	water	40	Abandoned
Vide Bouteille	water	25	Abandoned
Valet	steam	86	Abandoned

The conclusion is stark: within one decade of crisis, four-fifths of all large sugar plantations had been abandoned, their owners ruined or forced to find greener pastures.

Survivors after 1884: central sugar factories

The ruinous prices left just four survivors in St Lucia's sugar export industry: the central factories (*usines*) of Cul de Sac, Roseau, Dennery and Vieux Fort. By 1897, these four factories belonged to two companies: one a local syndicate which in 1896, with assistance from the Government, had bought over the failing Cul de Sac factory. The other was the *St Lucia Usines and Estates Company Ltd*, which owned the factories at Roseau and Vieux Fort as well as the Dennery Company. The St Lucia Usines and Estates Company Ltd was headquartered in London at the offices of Drake & Co., a large company of sugar brokers. Their London manager, Henry Hales, had never visited the West Indies and was, ironically, a dealer in beetroot sugar: the very product which had forced prices for cane sugar to hit rock bottom in 1884. '*We accidentally, so to speak, became West Indian proprietors by taking over an estate from a man who owed us money; that was it, practically*', Hales explained in 1897 to the members of the West India Royal Commission. By then, he had held the fate of thousands of St Lucian sugar workers in his hands for eight or ten years. According to Hales, all three factories had come into his company's possession around the same time. '*One of them we had to take, and the other we bought.*' He added sourly: '*... we had better left it alone.*'[500]

The genesis of St Lucia's four central factories is somewhat shrouded, but at some stage during the 1870s, a group of local planters and businessmen undertook to centralize and mechanize sugar production in order to improve efficiency. In 1874, the St Lucia Central Sugar Factory Company Ltd was started in Cul de Sac, with a £40 000 loan from the Government. '*Of this sum, £30 000 was borrowed in the period 1874 to 1877, and £10 000 in 1887. This money has been lost and the factory sold, but the persons who bought the factory, for a comparatively small sum, are believed to be working it at a profit,'*[501] Hales explained

In 1882, a second central factory was built in Vieux Fort. Roseau and Dennery followed soon after. The central sugar factories rationalized transportation and, where canes and hogsheads had previously been carried on cattle-drawn carts, railway tracks now linked estate fields to the factory and the nearest port. Railway carriages pulled by steam locomotives were stronger and faster, thereby increasing the overall carrying capacity. During crop time in Vieux Fort, the steam locomotives *Baby* and *John Bull* travelled non-stop, twelve hours per day, from cane fields at Black Bay, La Tourney, La Retraite, Aupicon, St Urbain and Mankoté to the factory in Vieux Fort town and down to the jetty from there.[502]

All four central factories failed around 1884 and changed hands at least once. As Henry Hales explained in 1897: '*Well, the factories were practically new ones a few years ago. The origin of the thing was that some French companies started to put up these factories, then fell short of money. The whole of the installation was perfectly new, the latest thing known.*'[503] Although perfectly capable of making high grade yellow grocery sugar, by 1897, the central factories instead produced a low class brown vacuum-pan centrifugal variety, which was the only type of sugar with which they could compete on the world market.

At Cul de Sac, the local syndicate (with Government assistance) owned or leased 2000 acres of land, of which just one-quarter (550 acres) was planted in cane. In Roseau and Vieux Fort, the St Lucia Usines and Estates Company Ltd owned or leased thirteen estates with a total area of 5925 acres, 2086 of which were under cane. At Vieux Fort and Roseau combined, the St Lucia Usines and Estates Company employed between 1700 and 2000 workers. The factory in Vieux Fort drew its labourers in equal measure from the Vieux Fort and Laborie districts and, in 1895, employed 7572 people. The Roseau factory drew 2516 people from the district of Anse la Raye and in Dennery, finally, the company owned or leased an area of 2000 acres (of which 560 acres were in canes) and employed 450 hands.

With more than 10 000 people on its payroll, the St Lucia Usines and Estates Company reckoned it provided nearly 22 per cent of St Lucia's population with '*their daily bread*', paying out in wages alone an average of £1100 per month out of crop time and £2000 per month during crop time, or approximately £17 000 per year.[504] The DuBoulay brothers, who managed the company, found it a grave responsibility. '*The closing of these factories, therefore, and consequent stoppage of work on the estates would cause widespread distress; many of the people would be starving, as they have nothing to fall back upon, no provision grounds, nor any sources open to them for earning a livelihood, save in connexion with the sugar industry.*'[505]

A country in poverty: 1884-97

The sudden failure of the sugar industry in 1884 sent shockwaves through all strata of society, which was about 46 000 souls strong at the time. Within fifteen years, most outlying estates were abandoned and even the central sugar factories of Dennery, Vieux Fort and Roseau had fallen into the hands of a London merchant house whose main interest was European beet sugar. Wages for agricultural workers fell by 40 per cent and reached a point where '*no further reduction is possible. Many of the owners of sugar plantations have stated that they would prefer to abandon the cultivation altogether rather than attempt to reduce wages still more.*'[506]

Henry Hales, the London-based manager of the St Lucia Usines and Estates Company Ltd, conceded that between 1896 and 1897, wages at the central factories in Roseau, Dennery and Vieux Fort had been reduced by one-third to one-quarter, while tasks were increased. Working days were now 10.5 hours instead of 8.5 hours, and where a labourer previously earned one shilling per day, he now barely made six pence. When asked if he thought '*a further reduction of wages probable*', Hales replied: '*No, I think we have them about as low as they can very well be got so as to enable a man to live decently.*'[507] Hales' local managers, Emmanuel and Theophine DuBoulay, felt the same way. '[W]*e consider a further reduction both impossible and impolitic; the result ... would be to drive the people to the gold fields at Cayenne, to which place there is already a considerable exodus. We have lately, by increasing the tasks, virtually decreased wages about 30 per cent, or 40 per cent; this reduction has been accepted by the labourers as a necessity of the time, but we believe the limit is now reached.*'[508]

What constituted a 'decent' living wage was debatable. The reverend R.J. Clarke, Anglican minister in Vieux Fort and River Dorée, asserted to the West India Royal Commissioners that '*the people were not getting more than could feed them.*' Those who grew provisions were slightly better off but even for them it was '*often a feast followed by a fast.*' Clarke explained: '*His clothing is an unfailing indication of the depth of a labourer's pocket. ... I have never seen the people so badly clad on Festivals as they were on Christmas Day, 1896, and New Year's Day, 1897. ... Clothing may often be made too much of by poor labourers, but the question here is not whether they should be excellently or meanly clad, but that their present shabby state is a sorry result of reduced rates, and lack of employment.*'[509]

The Roman-Catholic Vicar-General, Fr Tapon, concurred. He found that

> *... amongst the poor there is a certain number half-starved, if not totally. The great bulk of the poor ... do not suffer much from hunger, as those who enjoy health can work a garden, or go in for fishing, hunting, or picking up wild yams and fruits, or even stealing from their neighbours' gardens. But ... they ... have scarcely the necessaries for clothing ... When*

> *I ask people why do you not come to church? Why do you so seldom come to town? Very often I receive this answer: Oh, father, look at me, I have no other clothes, except what you see on me. Why do not you send your children to school? I have no clothes to give them. Now and then, on Sundays, I am called to the most remote places in the country to visit sick people; on my way I see some women washing clothes in a river. When I ask them why they do that work on a Sunday, the usual answer (a true one, too) is this: 'Father, my husband has nothing else to wear during the week, he left that suit last night, and I must give it back to him early to-morrow morning.'*[510]

Fr Tapon singled out two classes of people as particularly vulnerable: the sick and infirm in the lower-class and a group he termed the '*pauvres honteux*'. In the first group, some suffered actual starvation, going '*to bed as they got up in the morning (it is their saying), without any meal.*' The second group, although quite numerous, was almost invisible, '*because they try to keep an outside decorum, but when one happens to know the true state of things, there is something to break one's heart.*' The *pauvres honteux* (literally 'embarrassed poor') are '*those who while the sugar cane was a remunerative produce were well off, and since have been totally ruined with their family.*' Their dilemma stemmed from the fact that even if healthy '*they cannot do the work the lower class of people can do to relieve their distress ... men try to go away from the island to seek for something better elsewhere, and, in the meantime, the poor wife and children are starved at home. I know cases where people ... have to dispense, mostly every day, with one or two of their meals, and to take instead some tea, made with soursop or orange leaves to deceive their stomach.*'

Fr Tapon's observation regarding the *pauvres honteux* was underscored by Robert Plummer of Macfarlane, Moffat & Co. who told the commissioners that he '*now has in his possession the jewellery, including not a few heirlooms, of many respectable but impoverished families, owners of large quantities of land, and they are unable, though eager, to redeem these pledges for assistance given them, although they would sell their now useless land at any price in order to recover objects on which they set a high sentimental value.*'[511]

There was little disagreement, in short, that by the mid 1890s, St Lucia's population had reached an acute state of poverty due to a crisis that was sweeping broadside through society, bringing labourers and peasants to the brink of destitution, while even some planters, artisans, shopkeepers and professionals saw malnutrition and misery enter their homes.

Alternative sources of income

St Lucia was not alone in this crisis. Neighbouring colonies suffered as well, each enduring the crisis in its own particular way, whilst trying to lessen the effects as best it could. St Lucia, too, had some redeeming factors that helped to provide alternative sources of income or sustenance. Ample land and subsistence agriculture buffered the impact of heavily diminished wages somewhat, as did fishing, hunting and gathering. Labourers were allowed to settle on several abandoned estates and in 1890, the Government opened up Crown lands for sale also.

Alternative export crops were tried, in particular cocoa. Along with cotton and coffee, cocoa was an old-time export crop which had been elbowed out of the way to make space for sugar cane. After 1884, however, abandoned fields were restored to pasture for cattle or planted in cocoa, coffee or kola nut. On the west side of the island, where conditions of soil, shade, exposure and moisture were suitable, hundreds of acres were planted with cocoa trees. By 1897, even the St Lucia Usines and Estates Company had 100 acres in cocoa. On Crown Lands, small farmers jointly cultivated 2500 acres of land, 75 per cent of which was under cocoa.[512] Coffee was tried in various places also, with moderate success. Around Dennery ginger, nutmeg and kola trees flourished. These alternative crops were supported by the newly built botanical garden in Castries (1887), which raised tens of thousands of seedlings for distribution around the island. In the dry north, cattle husbandry was tried in a bid to provide meat for the British troops in Barbados, who imported large quantities of beef from Puerto Rico.

Cutting and exporting logwood (*Haematoxylum campechianum*, a natural source of dye) provided a welcome source of income, at one time coming second only to cocoa. In 1893, export of logwood reached a high of £37 752 but by 1896, it had dropped to just £4284, with reports that stocks were becoming depleted, especially since roots were being harvested along with the trees themselves. Henry Hales told the Royal Commissioners in 1897, that it '*must go on decreasing, because it is a thing that does not grow very rapidly; the negro cuts down in a week what has taken a year to grow.*' Logwood was cut on abandoned estates or Crown lands but also, occasionally, on land belonging to working plantations. This to the impotent annoyance of a man like Hales, who told the Commissioners: '*well, the logwood belongs to you, and the negro has no right to go and cut it, but then I say if you meet a gang of negroes with cutlasses as you are riding home, you do not like very much to interfere with them, and if you take them to a magistrate he will not convict.*' Asked if estate owners did not harvest logwood themselves, Hales replied: '*Yes, but I think the negroes steal five times as much as we cut ... they would come and cut during a day or a few days, and carry it on their backs down into the nearest village and it is collected by a local merchant - small merchants.*'[513]

But neither logwood harvesting nor cocoa, coffee, cotton, ginger or fresh fruit production, cattle breeding or subsistence farming could replace sugar production: neither in terms of labour-absorption nor revenue. Cocoa fetched a decent price on the world market, but over-production drove prices down. Lack of good shipping hampered the trade in fresh fruit with North America and the rest of the region, and deficient breeding meant that Puerto Rico maintained its prominence in the cattle market. The botanic garden, meanwhile, was staffed with just one curator, who had no horse or travel allowance, and no bulletin to promote good farming practices.

The Royal Commission concluded that sugar cane cultivation had ill-prepared St Lucia's workers for the requirements of peasant-farming. '*The failure therefore of a sugar estate not only leaves a destitute larger number of labourers than can be supported upon the land in other ways, but leaves them also without either the knowledge, skill, or habits requisite for making a good use of the land.*'[514] In this difficult situation, some solace came from non-agricultural pursuits: overseas emigration, the establishment of a coaling station at Port Castries and the advent of a military garrison to Castries.

Emigration to Colon: the Panama Canal

In 1876, the Geographical Society of Paris began to study the possibility of building a canal across the narrow Panama isthmus in Central America to save ships the arduous journey around the horn of South America. In January 1881, French engineers landed in Panama's capital, Colon, and the following year, blasting, digging and construction of the canal route was underway. While skilled labourers came from France and the United States, tens of thousands of unskilled workers were recruited from the West Indies. Island authorities were initially reluctant to let them leave, but as the economic crisis deepened, most yielded. Between 1882 and 1886, 30 to 40 per cent of all adult St Lucian men lived in Panama (about 10 per cent of the entire population). To say, as one planter did, that '*About every second labourer in St Lucia has been to Colon*' was no gross exaggeration.[515] Financially, the mass-emigration clearly benefited the island. D.G. Garraway, St Lucia's treasurer, calculated that between 1885 and 1890: '*£66 337, representing the American gold received here from Colon, was re-exported. Large sums were also received in drafts.*'[516] He added that opportunities in Panama had '*averted the misery that would have been entailed upon a large number of people suddenly thrown out of employment.*'

In 1888, the French company collapsed and 20 000 West Indian labourers were left stranded in Panama, unable to pay for their passage home. In 1889, the Government of St Lucia paid for the repatriation of some, but it was alleged that '*the greater number were left in Panama*'[517] to fend for themselves. Adding their number to those who died in Panama due to the very harsh conditions, about one-third of all migrants never saw St Lucia again.[518] Those who *did* return were said to have become '*a little restless*'[519] and unsuitable for plantation labour. The Panama Canal project was revived in 1894 by the United States, once more drawing a huge immigrant labour force until its completion in 1914, but by then, St Lucians were also seeking out opportunities elsewhere, particularly in Cayenne (French Guiana) where gold had been discovered.

Gold fever in Cayenne

From the late 1880s onwards, thousands of St Lucians travelled to the South American mainland - mostly men, but women as well. '*The men that go to Cayenne ... go as porters to carry loads through the forest from the canoe landing-place to the placer mines. They earn 10s. a day. ... It takes them two days to bring a load up and return. They are paid £1 a load, so that they can earn £3 a week. Some work in the mines on their own account. As hired labourers there they are paid 3s. a day with board.*'[520] But life in Cayenne was tough. John Quinlan, a land surveyor from Gros Islet who had been to Cayenne himself, told the Royal Commision in 1897 that '*At Cayenne he found St Lucians suffering much, though making more money than at home. Few people from the other islands can face the work; some run away. Barbadians will not face it. You go up the river 10 days. Living costs 5s. or 6s. a day for food. One bread costs 2s., coffee 1s., the smallest quantity of sugar 1s. Still at 10s. a day wages they make some profit.*'

Although death and disease were ever-present, many men managed to send regular remittances, and most eventually returned to St Lucia with money in their pockets. Treasurer Garraway reported: '*These savings are being utilised in the paying off of old debts, in many cases contracted for the purchase of land; in the purchase of lots, and in the erection of improved dwellings in the several towns and villages; in the fresh purchase of land, and in making deposits at the Colonial and savings banks ...*'

The *pauvres honteux* jostled with the lower classes for passage. '*Even those who have landed property and stock raise money to go to Cayenne and try their luck ... and it must be said they have been fairly successful on the whole, bringing or sending back a good deal of money. I have heard it estimated by a merchant ... that drafts of the Bank of French Guiana were sold in Castries ... at the value of £7000, in a single month.*'[521] That is a staggering amount of money in light of the prevailing poverty in rural St Lucia at the time. In River Dorée, where '*People sell a little provisions, and get a day's work occasionally*', wages were below six pence per day. Small wonder that '*More labourers go to Cayenne now than formerly.*'[522]

Most migrants had to borrow money for their journey. Interest rates became so high that Fr Tapon spoke of '*usury*'.[523] John Quinlan testified that '*Men borrow money to go to Cayenne at 100 per cent and even 200 per cent interest. Some borrow £3 to pay their passage, and pay £6 six months later when they return.*'[524]

Whilst bringing cash back into St Lucia, the migration of so many people in the prime of their lives also served to (temporarily or permanently) aggravate the crisis at home. Hundreds of men either died overseas or for other reasons did not return, leaving their dependents destitute and worse off than before.[525] Planters, unsurprisingly, resented the loss of their best workers. Emmanuel DuBoulay claimed that 300 to 400 of his labourers from the Dennery sugar factory had gone to Cayenne, forcing him to reduce the area under cane from 900 to 630 acres and bringing sugar production down from 1500 to 850 tons.[526] George Hudson, attorney at Errard and Bazile Line Estate in Dennery, similarly complained that '*In consequence of the exodus to the Cayenne Gold Fields, St Lucia cannot find sufficient men to do even the small quantity of agricultural work now offering.*'

The gold fields of Cayenne, Demerara and Venezuela continued to draw St Lucians until well into the twentieth century. The more they experienced new ways and standards of living overseas, the less willing they were to re-submit themselves to the abysmal wages and working conditions at home. Those who returned either became farmers in their own right or continued to search out opportunities overseas. Travel also widened people's social and political horizons, and it was not long into the twentieth century before St Lucia's plantocracy began to look on returned migrants as potentially dangerous '*agitators*'.[527] Not without reason, as we will see shortly.

The coaling industry in Castries

The crisis of 1884 also led to internal migration, as the nascent coaling industry drew young men and women from the countryside to Castries in search of hard cash. Castries had been a trading port since the earliest days of Governor de Laborie (1784-9) and shipping activities were levied since 1818, but it was not until July 1841 that the first steam ship docked at one of the timber-piled wharves. It belonged to the Royal Mail Steam Packet Company (RMSPC) and its arrival signalled the start of regular mail services to St Lucia. But the real impact came in the early 1860s, when merchants realized that Port Castries could do more than handle imports and exports: it could actually generate income from storing coal and selling this off to passing steam ships as fuel for their engines. To this end, the harbour was improved in 1861-2 (deepening the approach channel, creating a turning basin and piling the western wharf at its junction with Prince Alfred's Basin) and on 14 March 1863, a vessel of the Compagnie Générale Transatlantique was the first ship to be refuelled at Port Castries.

Soon, huge piles of coal brought in from Britain and the United States dominated the skyline. The transfer of coal to and from the ships was conducted by women porters, who carried on their heads baskets of coal weighing up to 110 pounds. Thus burdened, they negotiated the narrow, steep gang planks, boarded the ship and dumped their load into the hold. For each one of these feats, they received one coaling token worth between half a penny (day) and one penny (night shifts). The male scaffold riggers and loaders were paid for their time in tokens worth six pence or one shilling. Each coaling company (RMSPC, Peter Coaling Co., Barnard, Peter & Co. and Chastanet Coaling Co.) had its own tokens, which could be cashed at their offices. But coaling quickly became such an integrated feature of life that Castries shopkeepers routinely accepted tokens in lieu of money as well.

Castries: a garrison-protected naval station

Prompted by deteriorating relations between Great Britain and France, it was recommended in 1882 that the coaling depot at Castries be upgraded into a defended coaling station for the Royal Navy, and that a garrison of British and West Indian troops be relocated from Barbados to St Lucia to defend it. Two years later, the British Parliament allocated £500 000 to the new defence scheme, and in April of 1885, the Legislative Council in St Lucia authorized £50 000 for the improvement of Port Castries. It was music to the ears of St Lucian workers, who flocked to the capital in search of jobs. Over the next five years, the harbour was deepened to a minimum of 27 feet and the northern wharf widened 650 feet northwards until it met the beach at Conway. The dredged spoil (made up of coral and silt) was used to fill in low-lying areas near town, particularly the Conway Swamp. The land thus created became known as *Reclamation* - which was also the code name given to Port Castries in 1889. Following these improvements, the entire West Indies fleet of ten British war ships was able to enter the harbour (as it did in 1899) and several ships could now take on coal simultaneously.

The number of ships calling at Port Castries rose from 233 in 1887 to 435 in 1896 and the quantity of coal transferred increased during the same period from 17 758 to 44 816 tons.[528] Besides extension of the harbour, the advent of a garrisoned naval station to St Lucia also created the need for troop accommodation, new defensive batteries at La Toc, Morne Fortuné and Vigie and improvement of the infrastructure in and around Castries. Castries was becoming a town that could proudly live up to its motto *Statio Haud Malefida Carinis*: a safe harbour for ships.

Occupants of the old military buildings and squatters on land at Morne Fortuné were ordered to vacate the area, and hundreds of acres of land at Morne Fortuné, Ciceron, Courbaril, La Toc and Vigie were expropriated to accommodate the new defence plans. During the years 1890-3, extensive batteries were constructed at Morne Fortuné, La Toc and Vigie and in 1894, the remainder of the military personnel was transferred from Barbados to St Lucia.

It will come as no surprise that Castries' transformation into a coaling and naval station had some unplanned socio-economic effects as well. Authorities quickly noted, for instance, that prostitution and venereal disease were rampant in Castries. The unprecedented influx of people also led to an increase in crime - something which Administrator Gouldsbury, in 1893, explicitly blamed on '*the advance of Castries as a coaling port, the establishment of a garrison in its neighbourhood, and the influx from the neighbouring West Indian Colonies of persons of loose and bad character.*'[529]

The more serious complaint about immigrant workers was that military authorities preferred them to St Lucian labourers because they spoke English, and allegedly had more useful skills.[530] When confronted with this accusation, the Colonial Engineer denied it, but St Lucian artisans (or at least a vocal segment of them) insisted that they were '*systematically excluded*'. They claimed that foreigners were preferred, not only on the harbour works and in construction of the new general hospital (in 1887), but even in the public service, on public works and at the sugar factories. Some leading men in society, including John Quinlan and Robert G. McHugh (editor of *The Voice* and secretary of the Agricultural Society) drew up a resolution calling for an end to the '*rotten system*' of discrimination - to no avail, as they lamented to the Royal Commission in 1897. What is more, Quinlan (not unreasonably) accused the commissioners of practising discrimination themselves, given that they had interviewed not a single St Lucian labourer, but several English-speaking immigrants.

To what extent the alleged discrimination of workers was a matter of perception or fact is difficult to establish. W.G. Moore, the foreman of Public Works, whilst admitting that '*St Vincent men employed on the public works and on the military works are found more intelligent as artizans*', also stated that with the 600 men employed on public works, '*no choice was exercised between natives of different islands, as the pay sheets prove. Nearly all of those employed on the waterworks are St Lucians from the country districts.*'[531]

What *is* generally admitted though, even by those in positions of authority, is that in 1895 or '96, the managers of the central sugar factories in St Lucia deliberately and successfully used their influence to have wages on public, harbour and military works almost halved, so as not to compete too much with the wages they paid sugar workers. Skilled labourers who had earned between 3s.4d. and 5s. per day, suddenly received only 1s.8d., while unskilled labourers went down to 1s. per day.[532] John Quinlan was still livid about this when the Royal Commissioners interviewed him in 1897. '*Think of that. The War Department combines with the planter of St Lucia to deprive a poor working man of his fair and just remuneration - working men who, according to the evidence, could never be employed by the planter, in whose behalf the colonial surgeon proved in his evidence that ... the reduced wages are starvation wages*'.[533]

It did not, at the time, lead to overt labour unrest but resentment lingered and when strikes and political agitation did surface in subsequent years, the memory of this injustice undoubtedly fuelled workers' indignation.

Military tramway to Morne Fortuné

For a little while longer, construction projects alleviated the unemployment situation. Works on a naval dock and an additional coaling depot were announced in 1895 and extra military barracks were built on Morne Fortuné and Vigie in 1896, doubling the capacity of the garrison to 700 men. But by the middle of 1899, building works were drawing to a close, unskilled labourers were laid off and misery seemed set to return. To everyone's relief, in August 1900, new military works were announced, the biggest of which was the construction of a military tramway from Castries to Morne Fortuné.

Plans for a tramway up the steep Morne hill had been first floated in 1889, when a thousand tons of building materials had to be carried up on mules' backs, in horse-drawn carts and in trays on women's heads. But at the time, the authorities opted for an exceedingly steep military road through Pavée instead. Eleven years later, in February 1900, the plans for a tramway were resuscitated. The idea was to have two carts: one for transportation of goods and the other filled with water to act as a counter-weight. Each cart was to be attached at both ends to a cable running through a pulley fastened to a concrete anchor at the top of Morne Fortuné. The carts would run on rails atop massive concrete columns stretching between the Morne and the western wharf in Castries. The method of operation employed was gravity, controlled simply by changing the amount of water needed to counter-balance the load. It took a year and a half before work was started in earnest, but by October 1901, construction of the military tramway occupied 500 people. Work continued for almost three years and by June 1904, the water ballast railway system was operational.

Alas, just as it was completed, word reached St Lucia that the garrison was to abandon St Lucia the following year and all further military works were to be cancelled. After spending approximately £5 million over two decades, £500 000 of it in wages alone between 1895 and 1904, the global political and diplomatic landscape had shifted once again. Almost overnight, the military complexes at Morne Fortuné, Vigie and La Toc became obsolete and a thousand labourers were back on the streets without an income. As for the Morne Fortuné tramway: the iron girders, timber ties and rails were purchased by the Public Works Department, dismantled and re-used in the construction of bridges and roads island-wide.

The riot of 1907

To make matters worse, the abandonment of the Castries naval garrison led to a big reduction in the number of visiting warships, causing a slump in the coaling trade. Hundreds of unemployed workers - immigrants and St Lucians alike - tried their luck overseas. Those who stayed behind sought work on the sugar estates, in coaling or returned to the countryside. During the first decade of the new century, there was precious little to do in St Lucia, and in this climate of poverty and despondency, tensions rose.

The situation erupted on 19 April 1907, when coal carriers in Castries called a strike. When, three days later, a ship came in, they rushed the wharf to prevent those willing to work from loading it. Fighting ensued and several people were injured. The police, in an attempt to stop the crowd from marching on government offices, came under attack and fired three volleys. Four protestors were injured, but the crowd refused to disperse. That same night, several shops and the Castries market were looted and the following day, the strike spread to sugar workers at Cul de Sac, Roseau and Dennery.

> *On the 24th April, 1907, a detachment of 22 policemen went to the Cul-de-Sac Factory, followed shortly after by the Governor. The police were attacked, however, by a crowd from Roseau. They fired on the crowd, and four of the latter were killed, twenty-three wounded. A crowd from Dennery then went down to Castries, but were stopped at the bridge by armed police. The following day, reinforcements of police arrived from Barbados and St Vincent, but that day there was looting at Dennery. On the 29th April HMS 'Indefatigable' arrived at Castries, and the crowd on the wharf stampeded. By the 2nd May, work had resumed at Cul-de-Sac, and partially so at Roseau.*[534]

The 1907 strike left seven people shot dead by police and another 37 wounded, some seriously. In Castries, 58 people were arrested, fourteen in

Cul de Sac, 39 in Roseau and 71 in Dennery. Of these, 71 were convicted and sentenced to varying periods of imprisonment. The estimated direct cost of the riot was £1300 and indirect costs triple that amount. Similar labour unrest continued to flare throughout the 1910s, 20s and 30s.

Initially, the coaling industry recovered from its post-naval garrison slump. Coaling reached its peak in 1911, when the tonnage of shipping entered and cleared in St Lucia hit an all-time high of almost 3.5 million tons of coal. Castries ranked thirteenth on the list of principal shipping ports in the British Dominions and Colonies and in 1913, a record was set for manually loading coal when workers from the Peter Coaling Company placed 1116 tons into the bunkers of HMS *Cumberland* within five-and-a-half hours. But by 1914, the tide was turning again. The opening of the Panama Canal drew shipping away from St Lucia and coaling entered a permanent decline, exacerbated by the introduction of oil-burning ships. The First World War created a need for bunkers for allied warships, but it was only a temporary reprieve. In 1920, a coal carriers' strike was quietly settled, but other strikes followed and when Wall Street collapsed in 1929, Port Castries was left virtually destitute. Coal carriers went on strike for higher wages in November 1935 and again in May and June of 1941 - but by then, the industry was almost dead and the strikes merely served to hasten its demise. In 1942, almost exactly 100 years after its birth, the coal transshipment industry in St Lucia disappeared forever.

St Lucia during World War One

Although no fighting took place on St Lucian soil, St Lucia did play some part in the Great War of 1914-18. The conflict started when Britain declared war on Germany on 4 August, 1914. Soon after, German battleships started attacking British ships in the south Atlantic. On 1 November 1914, at the Battle of Coronel, the HMS *Good Hope* was sunk, taking 26 of the 34 St Lucian stokers on board tragically under with her. They were the island's first casualties.[535]

When the war broke out, Castries was virtually unprotected. The Local Defence Force under Captain Lionel Devaux did what it could, but the island's entire armoury consisted of just a few guns at La Toc and Vigie. The Acting-Governor of the Windward Islands requested help from the Canadian Government, and in April 1915, 68 Canadian troops landed in St Lucia. Another 48 arrived later that month and the St Lucia Detachment No. 6 Company, Royal Canadian Garrison Artillery (RCGA) was formed. In all, 450 Canadians served at La Toc and Vigie between 1915 and early 1919, with overall responsibility for the defence of the island.[536] Their presence created some welcome employment, both directly (military works) and indirectly (through entertainment of the troops). On the whole, relations appear to have been amicable, even resulting in a number of Canadian-St Lucian marriages. War action at home did not extend beyond occasionally guarding some prisoners-of-war from enemy ships at Morne Fortuné, or clearing a mine field in the Castries channel. St Lucia was under black-out regulations from December 1916 until November 1918 but apart from that, there was little to indicate that a World War was taking place. However, beneath this placid exterior, St Lucian men were sacrificing their lives on the battlefields of Europe, North Africa and the Middle East.

The British West Indies Regiment overseas

In June 1915, while the British House of Parliament still debated whether or not to accept black West Indians into its army, St Lucians were already joining military units in Canada, Britain and France.[537] When black volunteers were at last deemed acceptable, a recruiting committee was immediately established in St Lucia, aiming to sign up 100 volunteers. The local Government promised to pay for their passage (a cost estimated at £5000) and a ladies' committee started preparing warm clothes. A front-page advertisement in *The Voice* of 19 August 1915 attracted 80 young volunteers straight off the bat, and more young men followed closely behind.

During September 1915, 101 St Lucian recruits plus eighteen men from neighbouring islands received basic military training at Morne Fortuné. On 2 October, the first contingent of St Lucian troops left for England, after parading around Columbus Square to an enthusiastic send-off from the crowd. Nine more recruits left on 13 November to join the newly-established British West Indies Regiment (BWIR). In January 1916, Private Denis Fevrier died overseas of natural causes. On 23 March 1916, a second contingent of 100 St Lucians sailed for Europe. In August, Ferdinand Bundy was killed in action whilst serving with the 28th Royal Fusiliers. Other casualties hit the regiment later that year, as soldiers from the BWIR came under fire at the front. The survivors later received praise for their courage whilst under attack. On 12 December 1916, three soldiers from the first contingent returned home from Egypt, all of them in ill health: George Beausoleil, Nelson Shadrock and Joseph Ernest. Three days later, news was received of the death of Private Felix Roque and in February 1917, Lieutenant Kennier Ferguson died also. Shortly after, a supplementary vote of £2000 from local revenue was approved to raise the 3rd St Lucia Overseas Contingent, and by March 1917, volunteers were undergoing training at Vieille Ville barracks.

A conscription bill was introduced but never enforced, as there were plenty young St Lucians anxious to volunteer - if not out of patriotism, then from a desire to escape the malaise of poverty, boredom and unemployment.

In July 1917, the 3rd St Lucia Overseas Contingent under the command of Harold Lafitte and Henry Shingleton-Smith sailed for England. Several more St Lucians succumbed in Europe and the Middle East, including Privates Reginald Hepburn, Wilkinson Baptiste, Isaiah Williams, Joseph Patrick, Cornibert Gibbs, Joseph Auguste, Charles Severin, Ferguson Blanchard and Lieutenant-Corporal George Phillips. Although the regiment was not involved in frontline fighting, it performed valuable and sometimes dangerous services in supplying ammunition to the front. The last contingent left St Lucia on 4 December 1917 and as war continued to rage into 1918, eight battalions of the BWIR served overseas. Reports of casualties from war action or natural causes kept arriving in St Lucia, naming Privates William Cole, Myrville St Phor, John Price and Alfred Jones as victims, as well as Captain J.F. Henry (who died of typhoid at age 27) and Privates Ismael Florius, Ebenezar Williams, Charles George, Howard James and Eustace James, all of whom died in action. In early June 1918, three soldiers returned home in ill health, one of whom, Andrew Prospère, subsequently died. He was given a military funeral in Castries attended by the St Lucia Volunteers and the Canadian Artillery.

In the early morning of Monday, 11 November 1918, word of an armistice reached Castries. Great rejoicing ensued, but peace did not put an immediate stop to the deaths of St Lucian soldiers. Veteran Rudolph Wells died at Victoria hospital and Privates Eugene Cassius, Cherubin Monlouis, Joseph Ford and Rafael Mathurin died overseas from disease or injuries sustained earlier.

Meanwhile, back in St Lucia, charitable activities were organized to raise funds to help the returning soldiers settle back in. The Legislative Council decided to give each discharged soldier a sum of money sufficient to enable him to return to his former civilian occupation, as well as a grant of five acres of Crown lands. On 29 April 1919, eighteen sick and wounded soldiers arrived in Castries on board hospital ship *Grantilly Castle* and the following month, Private Raymond Flavien returned home on crutches, both feet amputated due to frostbite. On 28 May, 108 St Lucian veterans returned home to an enthusiastic welcome, a debriefing, civilian kit, £2 and the promise of a piece of land. One month later, 61 more vets returned home to a similar reception. Two last shipments followed in August and September 1919.

In total, more than 15 600 West Indians served overseas between 1915 and 1919, making up eleven battalions of the British West Indies Regiment. Over 1200 of them lost their lives. Some 625 St Lucians were enrolled in the BWIR, 359 of them in active duty overseas. In all, 37 St Lucian soldiers died overseas or shortly after demobilization. Two dozen men returned home disabled. A few years after the war, more than 100 veterans were honoured at Columbus Square and decorated with service and victory medals.[538]

It was not all plain sailing after peace returned to Europe and the rest of the world. A month after the armistice, in December 1918, disturbances broke out amongst soldiers of the BWIR overseas. This, combined with the fact that soldiers of the BWIR had formed a *Caribbean League*, caused the Secretary of State for the Colonies to fear that demobilized West Indian soldiers might seek to overthrow their local Governments. In a confidential dispatch, he warned island authorities to exercise great care with the disbanded troops. In St Lucia, the Government responded by delaying closure of the Canadian garrison in Castries by six months. The precaution was not made public and the official line was that the garrison's departure had been postponed until springtime out of concern for the effects the Canadian winter might have on the malaria-infected troops.

As it turned out, the veterans of World War One did not attempt a revolution in St Lucia. But the fact that colonial and local administrators believed them capable of it was a telling sign of changing times. In St Lucia, as elsewhere in the British West Indies, the population was becoming ripe for organized political action - and those holding the reigns of power could smell it.

12

'Mr Hard Times' and a wind of change: 1918-1940

Sometimes, history really does repeat itself. The late nineteenth century had seen a sudden economic crisis (1884) followed by decades of deep poverty, a West India Royal Commission of Enquiry (1897) and a World War (1914-18). This tragic pattern repeated itself when the Great Depression of the 1930s dragged St Lucia straight back into the black hole of poverty from which it had barely begun to scramble. Strikes and riots led to another West India Royal Commission (1938), followed by the Second World War (1939-45). The first time around, this sequence of events was a kind of dress rehearsal: not really altering the power structures in society. But when the cycle of crisis, unrest, imperial recommendations and war came around a second time, St Lucia emerged profoundly changed.

Sugar and bananas: 1918-1940.

The pain of the 1884 crisis was mitigated somewhat by stopgap solutions and incidental fortuities, but neither coaling, military projects or labour migration had changed the basic nature of St Lucia's economy. And so the plantation system entered the twentieth century: lurching from crisis to crisis, floundering and faltering but refusing to die. By the mid 1920s, sugar prices dropped once again and export earnings fell more than 40 per cent between 1924 and 1931. It was mirrored by a 40 per cent reduction in imports, which meant that more people had to make do with less. Planters and peasants tried alternative crops such as cocoa, limes, coconuts, bananas, fruits and vegetables to ease the crisis but disease, erosion, shipping problems and unreliable prices in the world market prevented any one of these crops from permanently replacing sugar.

Twice, it looked as though bananas might do it: the first time in 1924-6, when the local Swift Banana Company secured regular steamer services to Canada and New York. Banana exports jumped from 59 bunches in 1911 (valued at just £2) to 4190 bunches in 1924 (worth £256); 20 818 bunches in 1925 (worth £1374) and 46 209 bunches in 1926 (worth £4358). But in early 1927, whithertip disease set in, the shipping service was terminated and large and small banana planters alike faced serious losses. '*An effort was made to ship bananas to New York in ventilated holds but this was not successful, the fruit being largely decayed on arrival*', the 1927 Agricultural Report stated. And so '*The best of the banana lands* [were] *being turned into cane cultivation*' once more.[539]

A second attempt was made in April 1934, when the Canadian Banana Company offered a five-year contract to purchase all the suitable Gros Michel bananas St Lucia could grow, at 50 cents per bunch. The St Lucia Banana Association was incorporated and a vigorous campaign of banana extension commenced. The association provided peasants with healthy plants, offered inspection and treatment of disease areas and recommended improvements in grade and quality. Large tracts of forest land were opened up for banana farming. Interestingly, some of the new banana farmers were veterans of World War One who had not previously bothered to claim their reward of five acres of land, but now could see a future in agriculture.[540]

By 1935, 830 acres of land were under bananas (against 400 acres in 1934) and production increased 200 per cent. By 1936, bananas were competing with cocoa as the island's third-largest export crop, after sugar and limes. By 1937, 914 acres were under bananas and refrigerated vessels of the Canadian National Steamships made fortnightly calls at Port Castries. While the Canadian company bought all the bananas St Lucia produced, it did not ship all. The remainder was sold cheaply in the local market, helping the destitute poor to survive.

In 1935 and again in 1938, the local banana association took steps to improve the intra-island transport of bananas to port by forbidding drivers from carrying passengers or freight on top of the fruit. From the north-east coast, bananas were wrapped in banana leaves and carried in trucks to Castries. From the Micoud/Vieux Fort area, bananas were trucked to Vieux Fort and then forwarded by motor launch to the Canadian steamer in Castries. Transport by truck resulted in about 5 per cent spoilage. From the west coast, bananas were transported to Castries on board canoes, which caused less damage to the fruit. The Government also started an ambitious road project with the two-fold aim of alleviating unemployment and opening up '*the richest banana lands in the island*.'[541] It was the Murray Road (named after its Chief Engineer) and intended to connect Micoud and Soufrière with a paved, cross-island road. By 1938, the banana industry employed about 1100 people (compared to 3000 in the sugar industry out of crop time), producing 100 726 bunches and netting £13 568. The contract with the Canadian Banana Company was extended by another five years but, as it turned out, 1937 and 1938 had been the industry's best years. In 1939, production fell by 25 per cent and the export value halved. Things recovered somewhat in 1940, but the early enthusiasm for bananas waned fast. What had caused this?

Black Monday: the Ravine Poisson disaster

The clearing of mountainous rainforest to make space for banana fields had caused rapid and serious soil erosion. There existed a nascent understanding of sustainable ecological practice at the time and, in 1938, the Royal West India Commission had warned explicitly that *'The St Lucian is not a careful agriculturist and the ravages done to the land by burning and soil erosion is a problem which needs careful handling for the future welfare of the population.'* But a 1936 report by forestry expert Wimbush warning of deforestation (he cited a decline of 300 per cent in 50 years) and the dangerous environmental impact of the Murray Road were openly ridiculed in local newspapers, and banana peasants everywhere continued to slash and burn hillside lands.[542]

This time, the preachers of doom were right. On 21 and 22 November 1938, after three weeks of heavy rain which had brought down 50 to 65 inches of water, part of the waterlogged northern ridge of Ravine Poisson collapsed. The avalanche of soft, yellow clay swept away a school and several houses in the hamlets of L'Abbaye, Ravine Poisson, Ravine Chicole and Ravine Ecrivisse and buried a group of workmen who were repairing roads damaged by earlier, smaller landslides.[543] Rescuers dug out the dead and wounded and moved them to a more accessible site a quarter of a mile away in the Cul de Sac valley, but later that same morning, a second landslide occurred, burying alive the wounded, the survivors, the rescuers and a crowd of onlookers. *The Voice*'s headline wailed '*Black Monday*' and reported: '*Fifty dead and mutilated bodies, some of them beyond recognition, were recovered from a sea of clay at Ravine Poisson yesterday afternoon when a huge mountain collapsed and covered whole hamlets. The death list is mounting rapidly and conservative estimates place the figure around one hundred and fifty when excavation efforts completed. Twenty three injured persons were admitted to Victoria Hospital last night.*'[544]

Corporal Clebert d'Auvergne with a team of prisoners (who were given double rations of rum) along with some volunteers, performed the macabre task of extricating the mangled and decaying bodies. The final death toll was between 99 and 101. Another 700 people lost their homes. The road between Castries and Dennery remained blocked for days. There was no doubt in the minds of experts that deforestation had caused the Ravine Poisson disaster. Harold Box, a botanist with the British Museum who had been collecting specimens and was camped out on the northwest slopes of Morne Gimie on Black Monday, later wrote that the '*evil effects*' of deforestation were in evidence throughout the island and that '*not even the sources of the principal rivers, nor their watersheds, show evidence of protection.*' He described Ravine Poisson as consisting of two steep, almost completely deforested slopes on either side of a valley and pointed his finger squarely at the '*very serious encroachments*' made in 1934-5 '*in connexion with the development of the banana industry*'[545] as the cause for their collapse. The scope and horror of the Ravine Poisson disaster shocked St Lucians to the core and, as the 1940 Agricultural Report wrote, *'the disastrous effects of 1938 have left an indelible mark on the industry, clearly demonstrating the unwisdom of continuing to expand the cultivation of bananas in areas unsuitable for this purpose.'*

'At the mercy of Providence'

With bananas failing and sugar continuing to define the social and economic landscape of St Lucia - as it had done since the days of slavery - the vast majority of the population had never done more than survive at subsistence level, combining starvation wages with own-food production. Official documents reflected two basic views about working class living conditions in the 1920s and 30s: one which blamed the victim, and the other which blamed the economic state of the country. Administrator Alban Wright was a proponent of 'blaming the victim'. In 1938, he painted the following picture of St Lucians to the members of the West India Royal Commission.

> *The people ... form very poor material out of which a prosperous community can be established. ... To show zeal and energy when working for another is not fitting for a free man. The leisurely way in which workers of all categories move was one of the first features of West Indian life which struck me unfavourably. Their wages are low but their output is low. When a task is completed at an early hour, it is rare in St Lucia that a labourer will undertake a fresh task. It is not that he is exhausted or that he does not need the extra pay, although in a number of cases he has his own land on which he wishes to work. He is not willing to learn, he has no initiative, he lacks enterprise, he has very little skill with his hands.*

Despite basic education, *'their home life is dull, uncomfortable, uninspiring and discouraging'*, added Wright. Similar views were expressed by the manager of Roseau Estate, who was also a director of the Cul de Sac Sugar Company. In 1937, the *Crusader* quoted him as follows:

> *Other day work is performed by those who do not wish to overexert themselves, such as the old and infirm, or young women who are either too lazy or who may think it infra dig to weed canes, and they earn 1/- and 10d. per day respectively for men and women and they do not deserve more. Some are employed out of compassion. Children are employed to apply artificial manure and other light work and they receive rates varying from 5d. to 9d. per day and up to 10d. in the case of boys. Only about 8 or 9 receive the 5d. rate, and they are about 9 years of age.*[546]

By 1938, such condescending views (although still held by powerful men in society) were becoming increasingly scarce. Certainly, the Secretary of State for the Colonies, Malcolm MacDonald, who had initiated the 1938 West India Royal Commission, no longer shared them. He wrote: '*it is clear to me that the social and economic conditions of the coloured communities in some of the colonies are at least fifty years behind the times, and it is not too much to say that their condition constitutes a reproach to our Colonial administration.*'[547]

In St Lucia, doctors reporting on the prevalence of tuberculosis, malaria, helminthic infection, venereal disease and other widespread problems consistently lamented crowded living conditions, lack of sanitation and general ignorance about the prevention and treatment of contagious diseases as contributing factors in their misery. At the same time, however, they unequivocally stated that poverty was at the root of all evil. While there was no real shortage of food to 'fill the belly', they argued, poverty resulted in chronic malnutrition, rendering people vulnerable to infection and disease. Listen to the telling testimony of 23-year-old Joseph Assor who, in October 1937, had moved from his home in Vieux Fort to Errand estate near Dennery to look for work.

> *For the past 8 days I have been working at Errand cutlassing and collecting cocoa by the task. Sometimes I do not make more than 7d. per day. I pick, collect, cut open and carry the cocoa to the cocoa house and fill 4 boxes for 1s. Each box holds about 2 kerosene tins full. It is more than I can do in a day. Last Friday I made a big effort and I did make 1s. but dark overtook me with the last basket load. I estimate the work cutlassing to be about 200 yard square. I work 4 days in cocoa and 2 days cutlassing. I go to work at 6.30 a.m. and work until dark.*

When asked '*Are conditions better at Vieux fort?*' Joseph tartly replied: '*If conditions were better at Vieux fort I would not have been here. My complaint is the work is too much and the money is too small. I can get breadfruits free, that is, if I pick a dozen I get 4 free. ... I have been eating roast breadfruit for the last 8 days.*'[548]

Malnutrition and disease sapped people of the energy needed to perform the hard physical labour required on plantations, construction sites and the coaling industry. In 1937, Edith Floissac of the newly established St Lucia Child Welfare Association reported that the children her organization cared for were '*the victims of economic circumstances. They are improperly fed because the parents are unable to purchase milk, etc., and not because they do not know what is correct. ... The doctor had prescribed a mixture to be taken after meals twice a day. The mother said: "It is all very well to say twice a day after meals, but where are the meals to come from?"*'[549]

As Labour Secretary, elected member of the Legislative Council and chairman of the Castries Town Board, George Palmer, admitted in 1937, the bottom-line was that most St Lucians lived '*from hand to mouth*' and '*at the Mercy of Providence*'.[550]

Living conditions, 1918-1940

Meanwhile, the population grew steadily. In 1922, its total number stood at 51 949 (23 725 men and 28 224 women, reflecting the high rate of male out migration); by 1926, it was 55 698; in 1931, the population was 59 676; in 1936, it had grown to 66 230 and by 1939, there were 69 737 people in St Lucia.[551] By the end of the 1930s, there were 12 340 inhabited houses in St Lucia; more than 2000 of them thatched huts in the countryside and another 6000 wooden homes in the countryside. Castries and the villages had 3870 homes in all.[552]

People lived crowded together in dwellings that were often no larger than one room, twelve feet square. '*The houses are rarely painted inside or out. They present a drab and dilapidated appearance. ... There is little furniture, the occupants in very many cases sleep on the floor, and the bedding is an old sack. The kitchen is a "coal-pot" burning charcoal.*'[553]

In 1929 in Castries, it was '*a common sight on entering the premises of a very large number of houses in the Town to find every available yard-space occupied by rooms in which resides quite a number of persons of all ages; this is certainly a most unhealthy condition of affairs and is a serious menace from every point of view to sanitation.*'[554]

In Castries town, carriers of 'night soil' disposed of raw sewerage at sea while in some of the villages, public latrines were erected over the sea. Gastro-enteric disease and worm infections were rife. '*The towns of Castries, Dennery and Soufrière are supplied with good drinking water, but in the other towns and villages supplies are both inadequate and unsatisfactory. ... In the country districts the supplies for drinking purposes come from the rivers and ravines. River supplies are very unsatisfactory due to pollution.*'[555]

The prevalence of tuberculosis (TB or *consumption*) also caused much concern, since little could be done to prevent it. Those with tuberculosis usually lived in '*a room of no dimension badly ventilated and at night hermetically sealed and having or sharing improper and insufficient food and indiscriminately making use of all commodities in the room with an utter disregard of what must inevitably ensue*', the district medical officer for Castries reported in 1932. Tuberculosis was especially prevalent in Soufrière, Canaries and Vieux Fort, while the latter also had the dubious distinction of showing the highest rate of malaria, due to the proximity of extensive swamps. In 1934, helminthic disease (worm infections) affected almost one-fifth of the population. Dr Bristol said this was due to lack of personal hygiene '*and the economic impossibility of the inhabitants to wear boots and shoes continuously.'* He related how people walked barefoot from the countryside to town on Sundays, and only put their shoes on in town. '*I remember remonstrating with one man, who, whilst coming down the hill that leads to the town, broke his toe, though having a brand new pair of boots in his hands. Ah, he retorted, "God has been good to me for had I put my boots on, I may have broken that one instead."*'[556]

Oral hygiene was another area of neglect. '*"Clean your teeth" we say to them - "Pas Necessaire" they shout at us*', a medical officer reported in 1935. The prevalence of sugar cane perhaps did not help in that respect, as it was stated that during the sugar cane season and the mango season, St Lucians were noticeably fatter.

Two areas where the medical services did eventually make an impact were in the treatment of yaws (which became extinct around 1940 thanks to the new drug bisoxyl) and sexually transmitted diseases. In the 1920s and 30s, between a quarter and one-fifth of St Lucia's population suffered from gonorrhoea, syphilis or some other venereal disease. In 1928 and 1930, medical officers still bewailed the fact that '*many a young man ... has come to regard infection merely as an indication of manliness.*' Furthermore, '*Gonorrhoea would appear to have no more terrors to them than an ordinary cold, indeed they often state as the cause of this condition that they caught a cold by sitting on a hot stone ... their principal form of treatment being bush teas and quack remedies of various sorts.*'

But by 1932, patients were presenting themselves for early treatment and in 1936 Dr Weatherhead said the large increase in cases indicated '*how much the public appreciate this Clinic, and how anxious they are to seek treatment.*'[557] In 1930, in a two-pronged attempt to relieve unemployment and improve sanitary conditions, the Government initiated some housing and sanitation projects and in 1937, the Roseau and Cul de Sac companies built concrete houses with proper toilet facilities for their workers. Commendable as these initiatives were, in light of the persistent poverty, they were but drops in the ocean.

Meanwhile, disaster of another nature struck twice, in February 1935 and February 1937, when boating accidents in Laborie and Soufrière caused the deaths of 53 people.[558]

A wind of change

By the end of the 1930s, about one quarter of the population was wage-employed. The other three-quarters somehow eked out a living from subsistence agriculture, or depended on relatives or friends for their daily bread. Of those who *were* employed, about one quarter earned a wage in the sugar industry. Another quarter worked on plantations that grew limes, cocoa, coconuts, bananas, fruits or vegetables. Some 10 per cent worked as dress makers; another 10 per cent as domestic servants; 5 per cent worked on the public roads (paid for by Government) and the remaining 25 per cent were carpenters, cabinet makers, fishermen, boatmen, blacksmiths, mechanics, masons, nurses, coal carriers, laundresses, bakers, butchers, charcoal makers, shoemakers, shop assistants, messengers, porters and hucksters.[559] Unemployment was rife, with labour supply 30 to 40 per cent higher than demand. Even those who did have work found it almost impossible to make ends meet on the starvation wages they received. '*Mr Hard Times*' lived everywhere.

St Lucia was not alone in this. The Great Depression had halved export values and caused great poverty and unemployment everywhere in the Caribbean. Additionally, Cuba and Ste Domingue were closing their doors and sending thousands of migrant sugar workers back home. Like the war veterans before them, returning migrants drifted to the capitals in their homelands where they proved to be bitter and militant agitators. Mounting discontent over prolonged economic depression, frustration with policies designed to keep poor black people at the bottom of the pack and, more generally, a renewed state of despondency infected those who had never left. In 1935, 1937 and 1938, strikes, protests and disturbances reverberated around St Kitts, Trinidad, British Guiana, St Lucia, St Vincent and Jamaica, leaving 46 people killed, 429 injured and thousands more arrested and prosecuted.

In St Lucia, coal carriers and sugar workers in and around Castries formed a militant labour pool. In the absence of constitutional machinery to deal with workers' grievances, they too turned to strikes and riots as the only avenues of protest open to them. The British Secretary of State for the Colonies quickly realized that '*it is no use our trying to comfort ourselves by saying that all those disturbances were the work of agitators. If agitators were responsible - I say "if" - they must have had very fruitful soil on which to work.*'[560]

On 22 October 1935, disturbances in St Vincent turned violent. Three rioters were killed, shops were looted and officials' cars smashed. On that same day, in British Guiana, martial law was proclaimed to prevent a sugar workers' strike in Georgetown from turning violent. Two weeks later, on 4 November 1935, 300 coal workers in Castries went on strike, complaining that they were not being paid the regular two pence per basket and '*that they were forced, sometimes, by the men in charge to carry more than the 115 pounds they held was the right weight they should carry.*'[561] With recent regional events in mind, the Governor took no chances and proclaimed a state of emergency. He called out volunteers for military service, requested armed assistance from the police and from the HMS *Challenger* (which happened to be in port), and provided rifles and ammunition to police stations in the out-districts in case the strike spread. Representatives of the strikers met with the Governor, who tried to convince them that if wages were raised, the coaling industry would go bankrupt and this would only result in further unemployment and poverty. The strikers were not persuaded, and for several days they continued to withhold fuel from ships docked at Port Castries.

The coaling companies, meanwhile, attempted to break the strike by employing *'wharf boys, women of no occupation, girls and boys. Some of the boys should have been at school; there were at least half-a-dozen who were below the age of twelve years'* - paying them a full penny for baskets that were only half-filled. The strike ended on 12 November, after the Governor promised an official enquiry. The Coaling Industry Commission of Inquiry held public sittings in December, where workers vented their grievances, and some recommendations eventually resulted from this. The same scenario was repeated two years later, in August 1937, when a strike on a sugar estate spread through the island. Although relatively free of violence, Government authorities again immediately jumped to attention, appointed another Commission of Enquiry, and eventually introduced legislation for the improvement of working conditions of agricultural labourers.

By then, it was clear to authorities at home and in Britain that while they could not, and would not, tolerate riots in the islands, agitation was the direct result of an absence of constitutional mechanisms to redress workers' grievances. Lacking organized trade unions, labourers had no means of initiating collective bargaining or negotiating with employers. In truth and fact, the situation for workers in 1937 was no different from that which had pertained 40 years earlier, in 1897, when a stevedore in Castries complained: *'If a man wishes to make a bargain for wages beforehand he can get no employment. He has to go to work and take what is given him at the end. If he protests, the police are called in and he is dragged to the police station.'*[562]

Local and colonial authorities, afraid of the new militancy of the West Indian working class, realized that the old remedy for disorders (*'shoot a few hundreds'*)[563] was no longer valid and that they needed to start collaborating with emerging working class leaders. It was the start of a long process which ultimately led to a democratic constitution and full parliamentary self-governance in St Lucia. But it required a momentous shift in thinking: not only for the powers-that-be but for the rebelling working class itself as well.

Breaking away from the plantation economy

From colonial administrators to planters and even labourers themselves: the emphasis had always been on how the people of St Lucia could best serve their society's economy - never on how that economy might best serve its people. One of the first to shift away from this plantation paradigm was W.M. MacMillan. In 1936, on the eve of the riots, he published a book entitled *Warning from the West Indies.* In it, MacMillan predicted that the sugar industry would never again be lucrative enough to employ the entire population, and that peasants would never be able to rise above bare subsistence, working as they did with low levels of technical expertise and in badly organized markets. '*The black or coloured farmers are welcome in themselves as evidence that the children of ex-slaves can do even as well as they do; but there is no reason to think that they will do any better in the long run than the plantation owners before them.*' The '*great moral crusade*' of Emancipation, wrote MacMillan, had withered before it was fully completed and all subsequent effort had gone into keeping the plantation system alive *in spite* of abolition.

MacMillan clamoured for more democratic constitutions to give intelligent local talent direct responsibility. In the long run, he believed only universal franchise and full parliamentary self-governance could break the cycle of poverty and un(der)employment in the West Indies and build strong and prosperous civil societies. With this, MacMillan finally posed the crucial question: 'What constitutes the interest of the people of St Lucia and what best supports those needs?' - doing away with the old planter's cry of 'How can the people of St Lucia best be rallied to support the plantation economy?'

It took a while for this paradigm shift to register in St Lucia. When examining the (partly verbatim) reports of the 1938 Royal Commission, it is strikingly obvious that nobody, as yet, was able to think outside the box marked 'sugar'. No one demanded serious constitutional change. By 1938, an International Sugar Agreement was in force under which each West Indian island was allocated an annual sugar export quota which it was not allowed to exceed. Unable to expand its volume of sugar in a market where prices were steadily dropping, the future of St Lucia's sugar economy was bleaker than ever. But when interviewed by the Royal Commission, not only did planters, public servants and middle class men call for a resuscitation of the plantation economy: so did all the labourers and even the island's lone radical, the journalist John Pilgrim!

Pilgrim had started a newspaper in 1934 (the *West Indian Crusader*) dedicated to the cause of the working class. He was by far the most politically progressive man to be interviewed by the commissioners. Yet like everyone else, Pilgrim demanded a larger sugar quota for St Lucia and pressed for a 33 per cent increase in the minimum agricultural wage. He refused to be drawn into debating how that should be financed and, despite his initial boldness, when pressed, shied away from making radical political demands. '*The point here is this*', Pilgrim told the commissioners: '*We are telling you that the planters say that they cannot pay more for labour unless they get an increased price for sugar. ... The factory is not going to tell us their figures. They are only going to say they cannot pay more. We are telling you that the labourer cannot live on 1/3d a day.'*

Pilgrim rejected the excuse that Britain, too, was suffering an economic crisis at home. '*You have it all now, but you are too far away. If you were on the spot, you would not certainly have these conditions*', he told the commissioners. They smartly answered: '*And supposing that we say we are too far away to pay?*' Pilgrim retorted: '*We say that it is your "baby". You allowed us to get into this condition and it is up to you to get us out.*' The chairman of the Commission decided to find out just how far Pilgrim was prepared to go in his radicalism: '*Are you prepared to say that in return for complete freedom we should withdraw and say, very well, go ahead in your own way. Is that your point of view?*' Pilgrim quickly capitulated at the threat of abandonment implied in the prospect of independence. '*No one has suggested that.*'

It is a telling debate. Pilgrim's radical analysis of St Lucian society was similar to MacMillan's. For instance, he wrote: '*The abolition of Chattel Slavery in 1838 ushered in the present system of economic Slavery*'. Yet ultimately, Pilgrim's recommendation was the same as everyone else's: revitalization of the plantation economy. While it was abundantly clear to workers and their spokesmen, including Pilgrim, that radical change was necessary, paradoxically, it required a West India Royal Commission to channel that agitation into clear and progressive political objectives, in particular the formation of trade unions.[564]

Middle class constitutional change

It would be wrong to say there had never been indigenous calls for constitutional change before unionization started in 1939 - but it *is* fair to say that until then, such political agitation in St Lucia had been a muted and narrowly defined middle-class affair. To better understand this, and the subsequent radicalization of the political landscape in the late 1930s, we need to look a little more closely at the political and constitutional make-up of St Lucia.

St Lucia had been governed as a Crown Colony ever since the early nineteenth century, with a Resident Governor who was directly responsible to the Colonial Office in London, along with a Privy Council (consisting of five leading proprietors) which functioned as a Court of Appeal. In 1832, Legislative and Executive Councils replaced the Privy Council. The Executive Council consisted of the Governor, Colonial Secretary, Attorney-General, Colonial Treasurer and the Protector of Slaves. The Legislative Council consisted of all of the above, as well as the Chief Justice ('official members') plus five principal planters ('unofficial members').

In 1838, St Lucia was included in the Government of the Windward Islands under a Lieutenant-Governor who was headquartered first in Barbados and, after 1885, in Grenada. Meanwhile, an Administrator (subordinate to the Lieutenant-Governor of the Windward Islands) replaced the post of Resident Governor. Minor changes took place in the structure of the councils in 1844, but still, no one was elected and all members continued to be representatives of the colonial system and the planters' class.

Although St Lucia had seen several instances of black and coloured revolt before the twentieth century, the role of the educated coloured middle class had always been somewhat ambivalent. While some identified with the white ruling class and dissociated from their working class brethren, others had proven themselves fearless and uncompromising spokesmen for the black lower class. Between those two extremes, the majority of the black and coloured middle class tried to reconcile their personal ambitions for upward social mobility with a natural empathy for those in the lower class whose hopes and needs were obviously trampled on by the grossly unjust socio-political and economic system.

What helped to reinforce solidarity between the (coloured) middle class and the (black) working class was the fact that the white minority upper-class in St Lucia (although not nearly as racially prejudiced as, for instance, its counterpart in Barbados) continued to be socially exclusive. It emphasized family connections over colour, but the effect was similar in that it created a near-impenetrable class. In the words of Vernon Cooper (one of St Lucia's first coloured lawyers), in the 1920s and 30s, whites and middle class people of colour '*mingled but did not mix*.'[565] By the 1920s, the West Indian middle class was carefully forging its own political agenda. It started off with modest demands for middle class representation on the Legislative Council and more job openings in the civil service. In 1921, *Representative Government Associations* were formed in various islands and in 1924, the Colonial Office allowed the Windward Islands (as well as Trinidad and Dominica) a very limited franchise, making it possible to elect a minority of middle class members onto the islands' Legislative Councils.

In St Lucia, the first elections were held on 9 March 1925. Little campaigning took place, two of the candidates were unopposed, there were high income and property qualifications for membership of the Legislature, and universal suffrage was still three decades away - but it was a start. Thomas Hull was elected in district West, Thomas Westall in district North and George Palmer in district East. All three were re-elected in 1928 with no opposition and no campaigning, but the election of 1931 saw some more action when Belmar and DuBoulay conducted a heated campaign in district West.

It was only when the modest middle class political aspirations of the 1920s joined forces with the more radical working class agitation of the 1930s that new notions of race and colour were brought into play. British Secretary of State for the Colonies, Malcolm MacDonald, realized this very well when he wrote that *'modern ideas have been spreading amongst the coloured peoples ... with great rapidity. Discontent is now being fanned by an increase of racial animosity, which is being stirred by various causes, and which is likely to become really dangerous over the next few years unless something is done to remove the other causes of discontent'.*

Certainly in St Lucia, rarely a week passed in which *The Voice* did not carry an article on that illustrious Ethiopian icon, Haile Selassie, illustrated with photographs of Ras Tafari himself clothed in exotic African dress. Headlines such as *'Haile Selassie, a man of to-morrow'*[566] probably did little to ease the minds of white administrators and planters in St Lucia. Marcus Garvey, too, captivated the imagination of St Lucians. A branch of Garvey's Universal Negro Improvement Association (UNIA) was started in Castries in 1920, just three years after Garvey (himself Jamaican) had begun uniting black people in the United States and across the Caribbean region. Throughout the 1920s and 30s, meetings were held in St Lucia to discuss UNIA business and in October 1937, Marcus Garvey visited St Lucia and was given a rousing welcome at Clarke's Theatre.[567]

Administrator Alban Wright, for one, was *'strongly opposed'* to extension of the franchise, fearing it would bring council members *'without constructive ideas or ability, and who are more concerned with creating and expressing class and race feeling than with promoting the general interests of the Colony.'*[568] He believed St Lucian workers were *'greatly inferior in common sense, education, or general knowledge to the British working-man'* and with more than half the population speaking only *patois* and being illiterate to boot, he felt it was useless educating them through newspapers. In any case, said Wright, working class people were not interested in politics or voting, and with the existing franchise, a Workingmen's Association could adequately represent working class interests on the Legislative Council. In 1937, out of a population of 66 000 souls, only 1509 people (2.3 per cent) had the right to vote.[569]

Even so, between 1933 and 1938, various pieces of labour legislation were passed in St Lucia. Trade unions were legalized by Ordinance 26 of 1933 (but did not properly come into existence until 1940); 1934 saw a law regulating the employment of women, young persons and children, and in 1935, the first Labour (Minimum Wage) Ordinance was passed. Ordinance 14 of 1938 instituted the post of Labour Secretary, followed in 1940 by the Trade Disputes (Arbitration and Inquiry) Ordinance.[570] Some labour laws initially had no teeth or had a reverse effect - such as the minimum wage act for agricultural labourers, which resulted in adults being laid off in favour of teenagers who could perform nearly a full task at just half the wage, and were unprotected by labour laws.

All in all, the riots of the 1930s and the subsequent recommendations of the 1938 West India Royal Commission had a lasting effect, setting into motion a process of democratization and unionization which eventually led to universal franchise and the formation of an independent parliamentary democracy in St Lucia. In 1939, the St Lucia Workers Co-operative Union was launched and (thanks to a new law) allowed to be registered a year later, in 1940, with 4329 members. It was from this trade union movement that political parties emerged in the 1950s. While it still took time to mature, by 1938-9, a movement was emerging to the point where a young St Lucian economist by the name of Arthur Lewis could write, with hope in his heart: *'The major issues discussed today no longer revolve around the aspirations of the middle classes, but are set by working class demands. Federation and elective control ... are now desired in the interest of the masses, and side by side with them are new issues - industrial legislation, slum clearance, social services, land settlement, extension of franchise and others - which were seldom discussed before.'*[571]

Lewis, who won the Nobel Prize for Economics in 1979, was one of the very first to fully grasp the fact that constitutional change was about to break the stranglehold in which the plantocracy had kept St Lucia for three very long centuries.

13

'The Time of the Americans': World War Two

The Great Depression hit hardest in the south, where the Vieux Fort Sugar Company had been paying below-minimum wages since 1930. Vieux Fort had no peasantry, since all 4000 acres of land around the town were owned by the sugar company. Besides a few fishermen and tradespeople, Vieux Fortians formed a true proletariat. In 1936, faced with throwing good money after bad, the Vieux Fort Sugar Company opted to pull out altogether, leaving 1000 wage labourers and 6000 dependents staring starvation full in the eye.

The Barbados Settlement Scheme

On 13 June 1936, co-director of the Vieux Fort Sugar Company Joseph DuBoulay offered the Government 6400 acres of land at £15 000 for use as a settlement scheme. The company intended to retain the factory, rolling stock and 600 acres of coconut fields. Mindful of the imminent distress of 7000 people, the Government investigated the proposition. By November, it had drawn up plans for a factory-owned sugar plantation, surrounded by peasant cultivators. But lacking capital to finance the project and unable to raise private funds, the Government turned to its richer, overpopulated neighbour Barbados for succour. The St Lucian authorities proposed joint purchase of the property, followed by a land settlement scheme involving 50 per cent Barbadians and 50 per cent St Lucians.

The Barbados House of Assembly discussed the idea on 25 January 1937 and a week later, Joseph DuBoulay and Agricultural Superintendent Walters showed a Barbadian delegation around Vieux Fort. They also spoke at length with Barbadian immigrants who, as a people, had resided in the district for more than fifty years. The delegation's recommendation was favourable - but on condition that the factory building be included in the sale; two large swamps near Vieux Fort town be drained to reduce malaria; the water supply improved; a Barbadian be put in charge; the settlers allowed to become land owners (not just tenants); and two or more schools and churches be built. They estimated the total cost at £62 553 of which £18 000 was needed for the purchase of land and factory, and £2000 to improve the water supply. They also recommended that 200 houses be built for Barbadian families (£4000) on the Retraite and Black Bay Estates, away from the swamps. The plan was to settle 50 Barbadian families in Vieux Fort per year, for four years. Since the scheme provided for 400 St Lucian families to become settlers as well and would also benefit storekeepers and fishermen, it was agreed that the cost would be shared equally between Barbados and St Lucia.[572] A committee was appointed in Barbados to work out the logistics.

Meanwhile, things went quiet in St Lucia. After the sugar crop of 1937, expenses were cut to a minimum and labourers sent home. Only the coconut fields of Pointe Sable and La Tourney still offered some work. Uncertain of the future, Vieux Fortians were not only hungry but anxious as well. It took nine long months before the settlement scheme inched forward again. In November 1937, a Barbadian committee recommended that the land be divided into a 600-acre factory unit and a 1900-acre peasant unit to be farmed by 275 Barbadian and 200 St Lucian families, who would each receive a five-acre plot for homes and gardens as well. The factory unit was to come under direct control of a general manager, and would employ St Lucian wage labourers as well as Barbadian newcomers who would be temporarily employed until their gardens started yielding. Barbados was ready to move forward on the project immediately - but St Lucia could not pay for its share. The island Government appealed to the British treasury for a loan guarantee, but the request was denied and on 5 April 1938, the Secretary of State told the Government of Barbados that '*it would be best for the settlement to be confined entirely to Barbadian settlers.*'[573] In May 1938, the Barbados Legislature passed a resolution for £43 000 to purchase the Vieux Fort Sugar Company's land and factory. The sale was executed on 28 May 1938 and by June, the Barbados Settlement Company's new General Manager, L.A. Chase, was setting up shop in Vieux Fort.

And so the settlement scheme shifted from being a St Lucian initiative, to a 50/50 shared project with Barbados, to a fully Barbadian-owned project. By then, however, the relief that *something* at least was happening in Vieux Fort was so great that residents and commentators alike happily overlooked the fact that soon, 475 Barbadian families, comprising 2000 people, would come to own 1900 acres of prime, flat land around Vieux Fort - with not a single St Lucian among them. St Lucians' only benefit was the provision of wage labour on the 600-acre factory unit, plus some expected economic spin-off. But the consolation prize was gratefully embraced, and the Barbadians were given a warm welcome. Garnet Gordon, elected member of the St Lucia Legislative Council, told the Barbados Advocate that '*The scheme now has on its paylist between seven and eight hundred labourers ... and the demand which has been created for labour is already having a marked salutary effect on the district.*[574]

The Barbadians believed that with improved management and a modern factory, Vieux Fort could be turned into a profitable sugar-producing estate once again. Their first crop certainly attested to their capability.

The hitch, when it came, came from overseas. While plans for the Barbados Settlement Scheme were being hatched, a new International Sugar Agreement came into effect which placed limits on the amount of sugar each island could export. The export quota allotted to St Lucia for 1938-9 was just 9600 tons, with 2000 to 3000 tons for the Vieux Fort factory. For the Barbados Settlement Company to make a profit, it needed to develop to its full potential, which meant extending cultivation from 600 to 2500 acres, and production of 5000 tons of sugar, plus another 1000 tons from canes grown by independent contributors. Although the International Sugar Agreement was on the table at the time, the architects of the Barbados Settlement Scheme had gone ahead in the obvious hope that the Colonial Office would grant them a special concession. The company saved as many ratoon canes as it could for the 1939 crop and planted another 300 acres in new canes for the 1940 crop, aiming to reap 1500 tons. By August 1938, 700 St Lucians and old-time Barbadians were employed on the estate. The factory, rum still and store house were repaired, partial drainage of the La Tourney and Pointe Sable swamps got underway and wooden houses for the managers were erected at Black Bay. Optimism reigned. While the Barbados Government did not want to send any settlers until all of the swamps were drained, 200 Barbadians jumped the gun and made their own way to Vieux Fort to join the list of prospective settlers. Several were rejected. By December 1938, the Barbados Company employed 1200 labourers, almost all of them St Lucians, and put £1000 of wages into circulation monthly. General Manager Chase reported: '*The town itself has taken a new lease of life since the business of the Company got under way. After pay day, it reminds one of Swan Street on Saturday evening. Several new places of business have been opened, including branch stores of the large business houses in Castries.*'

The 1939 crop did as well as could be expected from the previously neglected fields, and by June 1939, construction of 25 houses for the first settlers got underway. Three months later, the Second World War broke out in Europe but for the time being, in Vieux Fort, preparations for the settlement scheme continued unabated. Eighteen miles of railway track linking the cane fields to the factory were overhauled, as were the locomotives and all the factory equipment. A new caterpillar tractor, a large plough and a Ford V8 lorry were imported and a laboratory was installed in the factory. The irrigation systems were cleaned and repaired, and some additional swamp land was purchased and drained. The company was keen to make sure that new settlers could hit the ground running.

On 20 December 1939, the first batch of Barbadian settlers arrived in Vieux Fort: six families, comprising nineteen people. '*From now on*', wrote the *Advocate*: '*the Barbados Settlement Company ... hopes to be able to dispatch groups of settlers at convenient intervals, until the 3850 acre estate has become a fully Barbadian colony.*' A mini-village of fifty newly-built wooden houses on quarter-acre lots along the road to La Retraite were awaiting them. Newcomers were given land with crops already growing and were free to work for wages on the company's plantation unit, in the factory during crop time, or as artisans. The company extended advances which would be deducted from the value of their crops when reaped. '*"Little England" is laying the foundation stone of prosperity for St Lucia*', the *Crusader* wrote in February 1940. By June 1940, the number of Barbadian settlers exceeded 300 people (almost 100 families) and things looked rosy.

But in October 1940, the music changed. Scouts from a United States mission arrived to survey the south of St Lucia for the possible construction of a military base - news of which was received with mixed feelings. While the war in Europe sent imported food prices soaring, the Barbados Company was instructed to curtail its sugar production for 1941 to just 2000 tons. This effectively sabotaged the scheme's potential for survival. At the same time, the food crops of several settlers failed and they began to complain about inadequate allowances. Perceiving no prospect of improvement, in November 1940, 43 settlers returned to Barbados. Of those who remained behind, some said they were happy with their overall situation, but most stated they were only waiting to see what would become of the United States base. Not long after, the United States was granted a lease on a large portion of the Barbados Company's acreage. This rendered continuation of the project impossible and on 30 June 1942, after just four years of operation, the Barbados Settlement Company wound down its business, showing a total loss of £25 794. It remains an open question whether or not the project would have succeeded had the Second World War not thrown a monkey wrench into the works.[575]

An tan Méwitjen: the time of the Americans

'The time of the Americans' is still collectively remembered as a period when Vieux Fort boomed and the living was high. The Americans put seemingly endless amounts of money into circulation, most of which was reportedly spent without a thought for tomorrow. An almost mythical tale is that of American soldiers drinking a shot of whisky, opening a bottle of beer, chasing down the liquor and - arm outstretched - running the rest into the gutter. St Lucians reportedly gladly imitated this kind of 'cool' behaviour. Another such exaggerated recollection is that of men wiping the sweat off their brows with dollar bills. Dance halls and rum shops flourished *an tan Méwitjen* and a retired Castries lady related how, as a little girl visiting Vieux Fort, she was awestruck by the sight of gorgeous-looking local women, dressed Hollywood-style in pleated slacks, wearing bright red lipstick and smoking cigarettes with dramatic hand gestures. '*All I could think was: Lord, I want to be like that when I grow up. Hah! Little did I realize that these were women of the night!*' How much of this 'gold rush memory' is sustained by actual fact and how does *The Time of the Americans* fit in with the rest of St Lucia's past?

War spreads to Martinique and the Americas

After a decade of mounting German aggression, on 1 September 1939, Germany invaded Poland. This act kicked off the Nazis' alarming march across Europe: invading Denmark, Norway, the Netherlands and Belgium in rapid succession. By May 1940, France was next in line and the British gravely foresaw that soon, they would be facing the Nazi scourge in Europe alone. During a secret meeting on 15 May 1940, British Prime-Minister Winston Churchill urged US President Franklin D. Roosevelt to help, asking for escort destroyers to protect the vital Atlantic supply line from German U-boat aggression around the British Isles and the Canadian Maritimes. Roosevelt, while sympathetic to Churchill's plight, was faced with an American public that regarded the war as a strictly European affair. Having publicly pledged neutrality, Roosevelt was searching for ways in which to help Britain without appearing to do so.

Matters deteriorated quickly when, on 29 May, Hitler's army forced 350 000 Allied troops at Dunkirk to retreat to Great Britain. The French Government, seeing that a German invasion was imminent, secretly loaded all the gold reserves of the *Banque de France* into the cruiser *Emile Bertin*: 800 tons of gold, packaged in 14 000 sacks, weighing 120 pounds each. Accompanied by her sister ship *Jeanne d'Arc*, and protected by the aircraft carrier *Berne*, the heavy destroyer *Le Terrible*, the armed auxiliary vessel *Barfleur* and several other ships with a total of 2000 French troops on board, the *Emile Bertin* headed across the Atlantic Ocean, first to Canada and subsequently to Martinique.

On 10 June 1940, Italy joined forces with Germany and four days later, France surrendered. The French Government was replaced with a puppet German-affiliated Government known as the Vichy regime. This single act of war catapulted St Lucia into a position of vital importance as Martinique's southerly neighbour. Now that it occupied France, Germany had potentially also gained access to the French Caribbean territories of Martinique, Guadeloupe and Cayenne. In particular, the Nazis were after the mainstay of the French fleet, which had escaped with all of France's gold reserves hidden in her bowels. That gold was now stored underground in the ancient Fort Desaix near Fort-de-France in Martinique, guarded by 2000 French troops. To prevent the gold, the warships and the troops from leaving and possibly joining the German navy, from 5 July 1940 onwards, British naval vessels blockaded Martinique, checking every vessel entering and leaving the island. Although this greatly annoyed Martinique's senior officials and inconvenienced its civilian population, the British deemed it absolutely necessary in order to curb Nazi aggression.[576]

On 21 July 1940, the Governments of Canada and the United States met in Ogdensburg, New York, to discuss the defence of North America. A second meeting on the protection of the Western Hemisphere was held on 17 August in Cuba, attended by 27 nations. Two concerns ranked top of the list: defence of the Panama Canal and containment of the French navy and gold deposits in Martinique, out of reach of the Nazis. On 2 September, the United States and Great Britain signed the *Destroyers-for-Bases Agreement*: the US would give Britain 50 obsolete destroyer ships along with twenty torpedo motor boats and a certain number of aircraft and rifles, in return for 99-year leases on seven selected base sites in the British Caribbean (Bermuda, the Bahamas, Jamaica, Antigua, St Lucia, Trinidad and British Guiana) and one in Newfoundland, Canada. By seemingly extracting its pound of flesh from Britain, the US hoped to appease Hitler while, at the same time, helping Britain defend the Atlantic. A week later, the Greenslade Board was appointed to select base sites in the Caribbean. Because of the urgent situation in Martinique, St Lucia was the first island identified for naval and army air bases.

St Lucians monitored the negotiations between the US and Britain closely. Enthusiasm for the war effort was high and by November 1940, excitement about the advent of an American base was mounting. '*The general feeling in Vieux Fort, and even at the village of Laborie three miles away, is one of jubilant expectancy. "Work will be increased and we will be well paid" a labourer at Vieux Fort told me, while one woman to whom I spoke ... said "I am sure I will get a good price for my yams and other provision, and my husband and my children will all get work".*'[577]

Parish priest Fr Charles Jesse and headmaster Henry Smith organized a scrap iron collection, which saw teachers and students of the Vieux Fort Boys' School going door to door, ringing hand bells and carrying placards. '*On reaching Laborie Street an old woman of 76 years of age brought up a piece of iron, saying, "This is the only piece of iron I have. Take it, for it is this piece that will be converted into a weapon to pluck out Hitler's eyes".*' Meanwhile, *The Voice* wrote: '*The man on the street ... looks forward to a new era of prosperity although remaining loyal to Britain. Americans are popular here, and American influence is strong.'*

On 17 October 1940, members of the Greenslade Board arrived in Port Castries on board USS *St Louis.* They inspected Gros Islet and Vieux Fort by sea, air and motor car and a week later, a team of engineers arrived from Puerto Rico to survey the proposed sites in detail. The upshot was that Vieux Fort would receive an airbase as part of an arc of bases to protect the Panama Canal, while Reduit Bay near Gros Islet would get a naval base to help monitor the urgent situation in Martinique. Priority was given to the Reduit Base.

Start of the Reduit base

On 1 November 1940, the USS *Goldsborough* anchored off Reduit Bay and began its duty as a base for American personnel in St Lucia. The US navy also took over the blockade of Martinique, releasing British vessels for deployment back in Europe. The blockade's aim was two-fold: to prevent the French warships and gold reserves from being smuggled out to the Germans, and to prevent German U-boats from refuelling in Martinique. By mid-November, the United States bought Reduit Estate from planter Charles Devaux for the purpose of constructing a seaplane base. St Lucians welcomed the news and one Gros Islet resident, '*her face wreathed in smiles*', told a reporter: '"*Monsieur, it is a god send. The sailors come ashore and we get a good price for our eggs*".'

On 8 December 1940, President Roosevelt anchored at Reduit Bay aboard the cruiser USS *Tuscaloosa* to discuss progress. He never set foot on land. On Boxing Day, US engineers established an office at no. 5 Mongiraud Street in Castries. Meanwhile, part of the northern wharf was fenced off for the Aluminium Company of America (ALCOA) Steamship Company, the official carrier for the US navy. In January 1941, a large landing-ship deposited heavy construction equipment directly onto the beach at Reduit.[578] In early February, some 200 coconut trees were uprooted and foundation work started. On 5 March, President Roosevelt finally signed the Lend-Lease Act, which detailed the Destroyers-for-Bases deal and formally granted the Americans acces to St Lucian soil. On 22 March, 60 marines arrived aboard the USS *Curtis* and set up camp at the Reduit Estate house. On 31 March 1941, a flag-raising ceremony was conducted at Reduit, accompanied by gun salutes from the USS *Goff* and speeches from the St Lucian administrator, the American consul and the most senior commanding officer. The naval base in Reduit was under way.

Start of the Vieux Fort Base

Meanwhile, the Vieux Fort airbase was coming along as well. On 27 March 1941, a lease was signed and that same day, US engineers began uprooting hundreds of coconut trees at Pointe Sable Estate. By April, work was in full swing with 40 Americans and 390 local employees. Their priority was construction of houses for the American engineers and drainage of the swamps. From the outset, the Americans were faced with a huge task, as First Lieutenant in the Corps of Engineers, Thomas Bentley, explained in a secret report. Vieux Fort was in a remote corner of St Lucia, lacking '*any semblance of modern civilization and facilities.*' It was connected to Castries '*only by a narrow, winding, hilly road. There were no railway systems, no water, sewage or power facilities ... All materials except stone and sand had to be imported and unloaded in a harbor devoid of any docking facilities save a few small lighters.*'

The Americans' first goal was to build a dock with a long jetty and good access - still known today as New Dock Road. '*Another great obstacle to normal production was the type of local labor available*', Bentley reported. '*Although not wanting in numbers, they were deficient in competence and endurance. It was often necessary to recruit labor completely unfamiliar with modern tools and methods of construction. These men had to be trained before beginning work and close supervision was necessary.*' As if that was not bad enough, '*During the construction period there was a great deal of stealing of all types of equipment and material. It became necessary to set up an auxiliary police system which at one time numbered close to 100 men.*'[579]

Nevertheless, by the middle of April 1941, ships were off-loading equipment and supplies in Vieux Fort for use by the contractor (Minder Construction Company) and on 16 June, a temporary runway permitted the first US bomber to land. The base's radio station (WVDQ) came into operation around this time as well. On 4 August, another fourteen American officers plus 296 enlisted men arrived in Vieux Fort, followed in October by a medical staff of three doctors and five nurses. The former Barbados Settlement headquarters at La Retraite/Beausejour were turned into an interim hospital, while a brand-new hospital was constructed at Cantonement. On 28 October 1941, the American flag was raised for the first time near base headquarters, which was located at Ralph Giraudy's former estate house at Pointe Sable. In November, 24 officers and 177 enlisted men arrived at the base to be trained as a bombardment squadron.

On 7 December 1941, America's role in the war changed forever, after a Japanese attack on Pearl Harbor in Hawaii killed 2000 US army personnel on home territory and dealt a devastating blow to the US Pacific fleet. America declared war on Japan the next day and US bases worldwide were placed on alert. Shortly thereafter, Vichy France became completely allied with the Rome/

Berlin axis and Germany and Italy declared war on the United States. After two years of ostrich-like policies about 'the distant European war', Americans suddenly found themselves right in the thick of things. In St Lucia, Lt. Colonel Ronald L. Ring assumed command of all military forces, including the Local Defence Force. At this time, the Vieux Fort base was protected by three 30 mm guns and two machine guns placed on both sides of the runway. Later, heavier arms were installed in strategic locations around the base, including small rapid-fire anti-aircraft guns and a mobile 155 mm gun on Moule à Chique. There was also a mobile cannon on a hill south of Laborie, at Anse Noir. At the north of the island, the US military was granted permission to build a coastal defence base at Cap Estate to keep watch over Martinique and protect the base at Reduit. The US defense secretary publicly announced America's determination to seize control of Martinique should the Germans attempt to occupy it.

The Reduit base in action

The base at Reduit was completed in December 1941. By then, it occupied 221 acres of estate land plus seventeen acres at Morne Pimant and the southern flank of Pigeon Island, which was used as a communication station (code-named 'Peter Item'). All the buildings had prefabricated steel frames, poured concrete foundations and stucco exteriors. There were barracks for 300 men, quarters for 25 officers, a ten-bed dispensary, a mess hall and kitchen, power plant, cold storage plant, two industrial buildings, three magazines, a concrete parking apron, two timber ramps, two timber piers, a huge concrete water catchment area with two tanks for rain storage, and ten steel tanks for gasoline. Three magazines were built on the hill to the south of the base. Reduit swamp was partially filled in (using half a million cubic yards of sand dredged from the bay) and over this reclaimed land, a public road to Gros Islet village was built, just outside the chain link fence that surrounded the base. Strict security measures were enforced and the public was obliged to use this new road instead of taking shortcuts through the base.

On 1 February 1942, Reduit base formally became a naval air station. It functioned as a sub-station of the Trinidad sector and could service a squadron of twelve VP airplanes. In practice, it never handled more than four or five amphibious planes at once. There was a navy complement of six officers and 46 enlisted men, plus a marine corps of three officers and 49 men. They undertook patrols, convoy and rescue missions in the Windward Islands and were responsible for the surveillance of Martinique, using Catalina ('flying boat') PBY-5s and Grumman ('goose') PBMs. In addition, 74 St Lucians were employed at the Reduit base, in jobs varying from powerhouse foreman (Lionel

Ellis) and truck driver (Walter Alleyne) to cook (Joseph Louis) and mess hall officer (Altenor Joseph).

War action at Port Castries

War came frighteningly close to St Lucia on 9 March 1942, when German submarine *U-161* entered Port Castries under cover of darkness and, at 10:50 pm, fired two torpedoes at ships berthed alongside the wharf. One was the CNS *Lady Nelson*, principal carrier of the Caribbean Fruit Trade, the other SS *Umtata* from Calcutta. Twenty people died in the attack: sixteen West Indians and four Indians. Nineteen others were hospitalized. The two ships had been under floodlights, handling passengers and cargo when the torpedoes were released. In the ensuing confusion, the German U-boat escaped unscathed, still on the surface line. Eyewitnesses from the Pavée area later reported dimly seeing a submarine leave the harbour. They also heard rifle fire, which was later discovered to have come from Sgt. Armstrong, a Barbadian policeman on duty in Vigie, who had fired on the departing submarine with a .303 rifle.

According to local legend,[580] the submarine fired a third torpedo at an ALCOA ship anchored in the northern part of the harbour but missed its target, leaving the torpedo buried in the soft ground of the cove. This story is often embellished by reports that the ALCOA *Evangeline* contained a full cargo of the explosive TNT for the Vieux Fort base, so had she been hit, all of Castries would have been blown to smithereens as well. Although the legend was persistent enough to eventually warrant an inspection of the cove, the fact is that a third torpedo was never actually fired. Captain Achilles of the *U-161* had been under orders to disrupt shipping at Port Castries. The best way to accomplish this was by blocking the northern wharf with two sunken ships. Indeed, it took the American salvage vessel USS *Killerig* six months to refloat the *Lady Nelson* and the *Umtata* and restore normalcy to the port. Achilles could have sunk the *Evangeline* as well, but doing so would have involved some complicated manoeuvering and added risk, without contributing to his primary goal. In any case, the *Evangeline* did not have TNT on board: she carried a small amount of (explosive) magnesium but for the most part was loaded with general supplies.

Marvelling at the fact that the *Evangeline* was left unharmed, some people have come up with yet another explanation - how true or false is hard to ascertain. Shortly before the commencement of Word War Two, in May of 1939, German naval training tall ship *Gorch Fock* visited St Lucia. The 200 sailors and officers were warmly welcomed and shown around the island by eager self-proclaimed tour guides. *The Voice*, in a striking display of naivety, reported at the time: '*During her stay of six days in St Lucia, some of the* [Germans] *visited the Sulphur Springs, and the landslides. They spoke very highly of St Lucia and its magnificent scenery, saying that it was not only the prettiest island they had visited on their cruise, but that it was the "key position" of the British West Indies.'*[581]

H.A. Clement Welch, in an exasperated letter to the editor, was much less in awe:

> *From all such friends, Good Lord deliver St Lucia. ... these men are Nazi naval Students in their last year's training and will be officers in 1940 in the various branches of the German Navy. In spite of all this, these men went all over the Island, the majority of them with cameras; I saw them myself at Vigie, the Morne, la Toc, and Rat Island taking photographs ... there were always a few Wharf Rats piloting them and readily answering their questions. I am sure I will never get 1st prize for politeness from the one who asked me to show him the road to Meadow's Battery. Are our authorities blind? ... A man in jail is no use to his country; otherwise I would have knocked down a few Huns last week.* [582]

Welch was spot-on: Captain Albrecht Achilles of *U-161* had indeed been one of the Nazi naval officers on board the *Gorch Fock* and exactly knew his way around Castries Harbour. Whether he spared Castries out of gratitude for his enjoyable stay some years previously - as popular lore has it - remains an open question. Incidentally, Achilles and his crew were sunk and killed in 1944 in an air attack during their third posting to the Western Atlantic and the Caribbean.[583]

St Lucians' response to the submarine attack of March 1942 was mixed. Some people began to resent the American presence, reasoning it made St Lucia an enemy target. Ships in Caribbean waters were regularly attacked and sunk by German submarines (including a tanker just 26 miles west of St Lucia) and from time to time, survivors washed up on St Lucian shores.[584] Many were afraid of what might follow. Others were more opportunistic and joined in the looting of cargo from the two damaged vessels. It was in the aftermath of this that St Lucia saw its first 'war victims on home soil': one man (Arnold Maynard) died from a ricocheting bullet after a US marine fired shots at the legs of a fleeing looter. Another person died from food poisoning after eating spoilt ice cream from one of the torpedoed ships. The damaged vessels soon became health hazards in themselves, as clouds of flies and other pests were attracted to their decaying cargo.[585]

After the attack in Castries, a steel anti-submarine net (made with the help of students from St Mary's College) was installed across the harbour mouth, and the US army offered increased coastal infantry protection to the Naval Air Station at Reduit. A public notice announced that any vessel approaching the shore inside an imaginary line between Labrelotte Point, Pigeon Island and

Gros Islet cemetery would be challenged by the US coast guards and, if it did not respond, be deemed enemy craft and fired upon.

German aggression in the region peaked in early and mid 1942. Initially unbeknown to the Allied Forces, from 20 April onwards, German U-tankers capable of refuelling and re-arming twelve submarines were deployed in the mid-Atlantic region. Meanwhile, the American destroyers USS *Blakeley* and USS *Ellis* continued to patrol Fort de France. Unbeknown to them, the German submarines *U-69* and *U-156* also watched Fort de France, to prevent French warships from slipping out and joining the US navy. They were under orders to sink any ship that tried.

On 26 May 1942, at two o'clock in the afternoon, four miles off the coast of Martinique, USS *Blakeley* was struck by one of two torpedoes fired from *U-156*. The missile ripped 30 feet of steel out of the bow but she did not sink. Captain Mitchell Matthews managed to manoeuvre his damaged ship into Fort-de-France harbour, where he berthed next to the carrier *Berne*. Meanwhile, dozens of US ships and aircraft converged on the area to provide cover for the stricken ship and search for the submarine. Captain Matthews was given 24 hours to repair his ship (at what was, formally, a neutral port) and depart for the closest friendly port. He entered Port Castries under heavy escort two days later. According to one source, the USS *Blakeley* came under attack for a second time while entering Castries Harbour '*but this time she returned fire, and a short battle ensued right in the Castries harbour where thousands of townsfolk gathered to witness the spectacle. The submarine got away but it is believed that she suffered some damage.*'[586]

This is not quite what happened. As the damaged *Blakeley* reached the entrance to Port Castries, it was thought that another U-boat, probably *U-69*, was lurking outside the harbour intending to sink her for good. Grumman Hell Divers were scrambled from the Vieux Fort base along with escort destroyers from Reduit and began attacking an area one mile outside of Castries Harbour. Watched by amazed onlookers in Castries, the little planes vertically dive-bombed the suspected target with depth charges, which exploded a few seconds after sinking with a terrific noise and huge plumes of water.[587] The U-boat, unable to fire its torpedoes whilst under attack, nevertheless escaped. The USS *Blakeley* was safely moored on the western wharf and obtained assistance from the USS *Killerig*, which was there to repair the *Lady Nelson* and *Umtata*. Eleven days later, with a heavily reinforced timber bulkhead installed across her shattered bow and all loose metal plates cut away, the USS *Blakeley* proceeded to Puerto Rico for further repairs.

St Lucia was shaken by more war activity on the evening of 20 July 1942, when another of the *Gorch Fock* Nazi naval students, Captain Freidrick Markworth, brought his submarine *U-66* right up to the steel net across

Castries Harbour and put down six TMB mines along the outer channel, slowly retreating seaward in the process. The next day, a huge explosion alerted St Lucia to the grim reality that the Caribbean Sea had been mined. A small US coast guard cutter, on anti-submarine patrol, had struck one of the mines. She was towed back to port but shortly after, a US army launch struck another mine. All on board were rescued and regular mine sweeping operations were implemented in all the ports of the Caribbean. At least four different mine sweepers operated off Port Castries during a twelve-month period between 1942-3.

As a result of the increased war activity, black-outs were implemented island-wide and the US stepped up its vigilance around Martinique. Six destroyers stood ready at Gros Islet to intervene at short notice, and US naval bombers from Puerto Rico checked the island daily. According to one source, this was initiated after the US learned that the German cargo-boat *Helgoland* was attempting to slip past US naval patrols in order to put German pilots into the cockpits of 110 dive bombers and pursuit planes that were stored in Martinique.[588] This may not be entirely true, however, since those planes had been tightly packed away under canvas with no runway at hand. They were regularly maintained but never flown and some remained there until the 1960s, when they were put to use for pesticide spraying.

The Free French refugees

By June 1943, the US planned to turn the tables on Germany by invading Martinique and thus ending the stand-off by force. While the US navy was rehearsing these invasion plans in Trinidad - widely publicizing its intentions - they also tightened their blockade of Martinique, and limited food supplies in an effort to force Admiral Georges Robert to the negotiating table. The extra pressure had the desired effect, and more and more high-ranking naval officers under Robert began to desert the Vichy regime to join the so-called *Free French* overseas. By the middle of July 1943, without need for an invasion, the allied forces saw Admiral Robert surrender his fleet and leave Martinique.

From September 1940, hundreds of Free French had fled Vichy-led Martinique, arriving in St Lucia by whatever means they could, including wooden rafts. Many hired local fishermen to drop them off at night. Some were robbed and dumped overboard mid-sea, and several never made it to St Lucia alive. The first successful escapee was a man by the name of Pujol, who landed at Cap Estate on 19 September 1940. More followed, at an average of ten or fifteen per month. Eighteen Czechs arrived in November and December 1940 along with two Poles, and were instrumental in saving Castries from fire on 14 January 1941.

On 22 September 1942, a group of men from the *Emile Bertin* escaped and made it to St Lucia. They were in bad shape, having spent several days without food or water. Some weeks later, the commander of the Martinique garrison made his escape and on 15 March 1943, the son of Governor Nigel and two other youngsters escaped to St Lucia as well. In St Lucia, they were formed into the Free French Fighting Force. Several moved on to Trinidad or the US and ended up fighting the Nazis in North Africa and Europe. After Admiral Georges Robert surrendered Martinique in July 1943, the remainder returned to Martinique.[589]

Decommissioning the Reduit Base

The surrender of Martinique in July 1943 rendered the Cap Estate encampment obsolete and it was de-activated, along with the the naval air station at Reduit (1 September). In 1945, public access through the base was reopened after the by-pass road began to subside. The Reduit base was formally closed on 1 June 1947 and turned over to the St Lucia Government on 1 July 1948. As a result of the Chaguaramas Agreement, all the leased territories in the British West Indies were handed back before their 99-year leases were up, and Reduit was returned to the British Government in a simple ceremony on 11 March 1959.[590]

Positive impacts of the Vieux Fort base

Whereas the Reduit base had existed for the specific purpose of containing enemy activity in Martinique, the Vieux Fort air force base was part of an arc of protection for the crucially important Panama Canal. The military presence in Vieux Fort was much larger and so, too, was its impact on the local community. At first, the effects of the base were mostly positive. Drainage of the remaining swamps and a larger market for produce, increased employment and higher wages led to better standards of living. A young reporter for *The Voice*, Clendon Mason, witnessed the changes first-hand. What had been a town '*of lifeless sandy streets lined on either side with a parade of closed and battered houses standing at drooping attention*' was changing before his eyes. '*The capital of yesterday, the busy town of today, and the metropolis of tomorrow is now seething with activity. On groggy legs, the town of the Old Fort struggles to shake off its senility and to raise its proud head once more atop rejuvenated limbs.*'[591]

At 8 a.m. on a Monday morning, Mason strolled from Vieux Fort town to the site of the new base.

> *Cars and trucks passed up and down in steady streams, some driven by Americans, some by local chauffeurs. ... Every other face almost was one from Castries, and nearly every other one was from Barbados or somewhere. And things were humming! There was the ... sight of a giant motor shovel cutting through earth like paper, and lifting several hundredweight to dump it onto the huge waiting truck. ... Americans in khaki pants and helmets, broad bare backs baked to a brown tan beneath the blazing sun.*

Mason walked as far as the newly named Beane Field area,[592] where the Pointe Sable estate house had been converted into modern offices for the contractors and army officials. '*Several ... desks, each with one or two or more persons seated at it, were scattered over the floor. Around the room were safes and lockers of every description. ... On the desks were streamlined typewriters, the latest models. Electric lights were burning all the while from the roof. ... In the inner office some lady stenographers were rattling the keys of their typewriters.*'

At the time, the base occupied 115 Americans and over 600 West Indian workers, who were paid £2500 weekly in local salaries. Between April 1941 and June 1942, the local work force expanded until it peaked at 4615 local employees, directed by 600 Americans.

Negatives impacts of the base: overcrowding

By 1942, the American military base was beginning to have some negative impacts as well. Within a year, Vieux Fort's population had quadrupled from 2000 to between 8000 and 9000 in mid 1942. The Government neglected mounting problems with water supply, garbage disposal, housing and policing and before long, Vieux Fort had turned into a breeding ground for pulmonary tuberculosis, venereal disease and gastro-enteric afflictions. '*Vieux Fort burns while government fiddles away*', *The Voice* exclaimed in December 1941.[593] House rents became '*excessive, exorbitant, cruel.*' In 1942, 296 residential buildings in Vieux Fort town served a population of 8000: making for an average of 27 persons per house! People slept under balconies and trees, on the pavement and in fishing boats. A small house cost five dollars a week, and so '*About ten and twenty and often more persons live in one of these houses. They have to squeeze together on the bare floor at night. In the smaller houses, sleeping is done by relays. The first relay would snatch as much rest as possible during the earlier part of the night. Later, another relay would come in, and the first relay goes out to accommodate them.* [Areas] *under houses, balconies, kitchens and outhouses are used as dormitories ...*'

And all these thousands of people depended for their drinking water on the muddy and increasingly polluted Vieux Fort River whose water was, reportedly, dark blue in colour.

Typhoid epidemic

The area adjacent to the place where drinking water was stored in old tanks was used as a bush latrine and so, unsurprisingly, the last three months of 1942 saw St Lucia's severest epidemic of typhoid yet, affecting 233 and killing 47 in Vieux Fort. '*This epidemic was the result of unsatisfactory housing and sanitary conditions due to overcrowding of the labourers on construction work at the United States Base and also to a grossly inadequate and polluted water supply.*'[594]

Government repaired and enclosed the storage tank area, administered inoculations and advised people to boil their drinking water, but more needed to be done to prevent a recurrence. During the course of 1943, a supply of filtered and chlorinated water was extended from the US base to the town of Vieux Fort, new communal latrines were constructed and 50 homes were supplied with fly-proof latrines. It prevented another outbreak of typhoid but protests over the lack of Government attention to general infrastructure and facilities in Vieux Fort continued. '*Every stranger who came to work in this part of the island had revolting remarks to make about the conditions that existed, and visitors turned their noses and never came back*', a delegation of Vieux Fortians[595] told the administrator in May 1943. They protested the still insufficient water supply, the disrepair of the jetty, the failing telephone system and the lack of personnel at the government office (where two clerks, one copyist and a bailiff were supposed to run the post office, the registry, the savings bank, the treasury, customs and the judiciary office).

Another backlash from the American base was more indirect. The huge demand for local produce resulted in a rapid increase in the stock of pigs and this, in turn, led to an epidemic of swine fever. Between July and September 1941, 90 per cent of the pigs in St Lucia were wiped out and it was explicitly suggested that the disease had emanated from the Reduit Base.[596]

Prostitution and STDs

High levels of prostitution and venereal disease are typically linked with the presence of military troops and immigrant workers, and the American bases in Reduit and Vieux Fort were no exception. In January 1943, the disease rate amongst military personnel was 283 per 1000 and a military report stated further that '*Venereal diseases were the rule rather then the exception among the natives.*'[597] It goes on to say:

> *Local government physicians could not obtain sulpha drugs, arsenicals or bismuth for the treatment of prostitutes even if they sought treatment. There was an almost total absence of white women in the area and the monotony of wartime disposition for combat in an essentially peacetime situation, led men to visit native shacks, drink a local rum called 'Smack' and have sexual intercourse with black native women practically all of whom were infected. The fact that native huts were dispersed throughout the Army area on private land increased control problems greatly. The Base Surgeon also considered the high rate due to the character of personnel of the worst offending unit which had an average I.Q. of 89.7 % (Grade 4, below average) and the long periods the troops had served in the tropics.*
>
> *In March of 1943, after consultation with the British Government physician at Vieux Fort, it was decided to open a clinic for prostitutes. On 3 April, 62 women of the 'on-limits' village of Beausejour had been examined and 42 cases of syphilis, 5 cases of gonorrhoea, 1 case of chanchroid and 3 cases of lymphogranuloma venereum were found. Every effort was made to get these women out of the infectious stages as rapidly as possible. No woman refused treatment. Extensive education programs were started among the troops and additional prophylaxis stations constructed. Athletic and recreation activities received increased attention, particularly between the hours of 5:30 PM and 11:00 PM. Overnight passes were issued only to those individuals whose past records of good conduct entitled them to reward. All intoxicated soldiers found in civilian areas were taken into custody and returned to the post. Venereal disease rates were lowered but remained unduly high and far above the goal of 20 per 1000 per annum. The Base Surgeon considered the rates 'theoretically' inexcusable, when in November 1943, after ten months of extensive control measures, the rate was 174 per 1000 per annum.*

To help lower STD's, military authorities recommended that men who had been in the Caribbean for two years or longer and '*who felt they were "forgotten men"*' be reassigned as soon as possible. '*Many men ceased to have an interest in themselves or their unit.*' At the same time, out of 400 '*supposedly healthy working men*' applying for jobs on the Vieux Fort base, one in five showed up positive on blood tests for syphilis, while '*Other types of venereal disease were seen in their usual large numbers.*' Oral history accounts dwell extensively on the aspects of STD's and soldiers engaging in sexual encounters with the local *belles.*[598] By 1945, the introduction of sulpha drugs and penicillin greatly helped the fight but until then, local men, women and American military personnel shared the afflictions alike.

Law and order

Law and order was another problem in Vieux Fort, with just eight local policemen to keep control over an increasingly rowdy population. The Americans had their own police force but at times, this only aggravated matters. In November 1941, for instance, a conflict between a military policeman and a St Lucian man turned nasty and the crowd started pelting stones at four local policemen who arrived to restore order. In the ensuing fracas, a young girl was shot in the leg by a stray bullet, allegedly fired by an American police officer.

Shooting incidents involving the American military police occurred more than once - to the point where in April 1942, military authorities saw it fit to make a public apology to the St Lucian people. Most cases did not incur the loss of life but at least one proved fatal. In August 1943, Joseph Wilson, a worker on the Vieux Fort base, was shot by an American guard after Wilson's dog had repeatedly attempted to follow him onto the base. Private Cook threatened to shoot the dog, after which Wilson told the American he needed shooting more than the dog. Private Cook tried to strike Wilson, who struck back. Cook then stepped back and shot Wilson in the abdomen, which resulted in his death two days later. Cook was court-martialled and found guilty.[599]

Theft and larceny also presented the American military commanders with a serious challenge. *The Voice* reported in July 1943: '*The shortage of tyres for motor vehicles ... resulted in wholesale larceny of tyres from the United States bases ... The larceny of gasolene from the bases gave rise to further complications and the disappearance of cigarettes in bulk showed that the incidence of robbery was on the increase. Up to last Saturday, a number of chits was stolen from the American Service Club in Castries.*[600] The Americans also battled with workers sabotaging or protracting their tasks with a view to prolonging their employment.

Without in any way wishing to legitimize the high incidence of theft from the base, it must be added that local workers had a reason to feel robbed as well. In oral history accounts, it is often attested that during the war, workers in Vieux Fort lit their cigarettes with dollar bills. Indeed, wages paid by the American army were four times higher than those paid in the sugar industry - but not as high as the Americans had initially intended them to be. As had happened in a previous era, under pressure from the remaining sugar companies, military authorities reduced the wages they paid to their workers. And, as before, the decision created much resentment, particularly in light of the fact that the cost of living had risen spectacularly at the same time.[601]

Completion and decline of the base

Despite some negative impacts and incidents, work on the Vieux Fort base progressed well. With the exception of one or two buildings, construction was completed on 15 November 1942 and in March 1943, the engineering department handed over the completed Beane Field Air Base to the Post Engineer. By then, the base occupied over 3000 acres of land and had cost over ten million US dollars. It was divided into two sections: 1289 acres at Beane Field (just north of Vieux Fort town) and another 671 acres at Cantonement (now St Jude's Highway). '*As originally built*', Thomas Bentley reported, '*the base consisted of 352 buildings, two 5000 ft concrete runways, with taxiways, hardstands, revetments, two nose hangars and other Air Corps maintenance buildings. There are housing facilities for 4673 Enlisted Men and 649 Officers on the base, making a total troop capacity of 5332 men. There is 96 951 sq ft of warehouse area, a 1000 man Laundry and a completely equipped 150 bed Hospital.*'

The Americans installed systems for generating electricity, distribution of drinking water and sewerage disposal and built a fire station, radio station, fuel depots, incinerator, garage, barber shop, general store, movie theatre, stockade, a 50-line telephone exchange, cold storage and ice plant, docks and warehousing and an officer's club with a day room and library. At nearby Mankoté mangrove, they created an intricate network of dirt roads to deceive spying German aircraft into believing that this was where the American airplanes were hidden. In reality however, low bunkers covered with soil and vegetation located on the flat terrain north of Vieux Fort town acted as hangars to keep the aircraft safe. St Lucians nicknamed these mounds in the landscape *kai plane* and, after the war, commonly used them as pig pens.

Military men were trained in Vieux Fort in navigation flying, instrument flying, transition flying, cross-country flying, formation flying (day and night), and all types of bombing. In addition, ground training involved armament, bombardment, communications, engineering, link training, medical training, intelligence, navigation, photography and radar. Also included were submarine warfare training, tactics, sheet metal work and instruction on engines and aircraft structure. Although Vieux Fort was essentially a training base, a certain number of casualties occurred nonetheless. On 23 April 1942, a B-18 bomber and a P-39 fighter plane of the 5th Bomber Squadron based in Vieux Fort failed to return from patrol over open water. The bodies of the seven victims were never found.[602] Shortly before that, on 24 February, two planes had collided on take-off from the runway, causing one pilot to sustain a fractured skull. A year later, two men were killed when their US Marine Corps OS2N aircraft fell into the sea *en route* from Castries to Beane Field. The plane was never recovered.[603]

Once the base was completed, from mid 1943 onwards, the employment boom waned. In 1944, a Government report stated: '*Labour conditions generally reverted further to normal. There was little or no demand for labour on the United States Bases and, as a result, there was a noticeable increase in peasant agriculture as compared with previous years; most estates were able to obtain their labour requirements without difficulty.*' Once again, un(der)employment was business as usual in St Lucia.[604]

Immediate post-war period in the south

The Second World War ended in August 1945. To celebrate the victory over Japan and the new peace in Europe, flares were shot off at the base, much to the awe of spectators in Vieux Fort town. They were also treated to some radical air manoeuvres by three Lockheed P-38 fighters. Soon, however, Vieux Fort ceased to be the centre of attention and with no alternative sources of income the landless workers were once again thrown back onto their own resources. Many migrated - to Castries and beyond. Those who stayed on in town tried to make a living from fishing, charcoal-making, trades or small shop-keeping. Inevitably, the town slumped back into a state of desolation.

On 29 August 1949, the US army offered its remaining facilities for sale to the Government of St Lucia. For US$200 000, the administration bought 150 buildings, two 150 KW generators, a cold storage plant, a water filtration plant, gasolene storage and pipelines, sand washing tanks and various other items. At the same time, 700 acres of land were released back to the Government.[605] For a short while, the dismantling of the base triggered hopes for new development in Vieux Fort, including tourism. But none of the proposals materialized. The disposal of surplus material from the base created a climate of graft and corruption, and much was eventually sold at rock-bottom prices. In 1947, a new land settlement scheme was proposed for the landless workers of the south but the attempt was half-hearted and failed within eighteen months.

Vieux Fort entered the 1950s as a town dazed by its recent roller coaster-ride through economic and social upheaval. While some of the older inhabitants attempted to pick up the threads of their simple pre-war existence, a rising generation of young adults was desperate to leave this dull, poverty-stricken town and seek out brighter horizons.

14

The banana revolution: democracy and modernization 1945-1965.

After the Second World War, 'King Sugar' finally bowed out of St Lucia. As he did so, an army of peasants marched onto the stage, propelled there by the power of bananas as an export crop. The demise of the plantation system was accompanied by a process of democratization and modernization which changed the heart and soul, indeed the very structure of society. While initially, closure of the military bases resulted in yet another disenchanted return to the sugar fields and subsistence farming, change was in the air. The presence of the Americans had been a shot across the bow: giving St Lucians a glimpse of the kind of progress taking place in the wider world. Colonial support for unionization led to political awareness and a demand for working class representation and participation in Government. Before long, universal suffrage and the introduction of a two-party political system replaced the tradition of independent candidates from the propertied class. This took power away from the planters and handed it to the mass of the people. The return of war veterans further helped to open people's eyes, as did new opportunities for emigration. The Great Fire of Castries in 1948, although a great tragedy at the time, in the long run helped to erase class prejudices and opened the way for modern infrastructure. Most importantly of all, the demise of the sugar industry gave peasant-based banana production a chance, boosting modernization from the grass roots level up. For every door that closed, a new one opened and together, these post-war changes finalized the break with the old plantation system.

Post-war unemployment and early unionization

Due to the war, publication of the 1938 West India Royal (Moyne) Commission's report was delayed until 1945. One of its main recommendations was that trade unions needed to be developed in the British West Indies to provide people with legitimate avenues to voice their grievances over wages and working conditions. In St Lucia, an ambitious agricultural worker by the name of Charles Augustin picked up the ball and ran with it, raising enthusiasm for unionization among several influential members of society, including R.G.H. Clarke (a druggist and proprietor), John Pilgrim (editor of the *Crusader*), George Cooper (manager of T.R. Evans & Company), Randolph Roberts (clerk-treasurer of several friendly societies), Job James (a waterfront worker), J.B.D. Osbourne (a working class banker and ex-treasurer in government service), Lewis Clarke (a clerk with Peter & Company), Henry Pollard (active in friendly societies), Henry Belizaire (ex-school master) and R.L. Scott (secretary of several friendly societies).[606] On 9 March 1939, this illustrious company of men launched the St Lucia Workers Co-operative Society. Trade union legislation was introduced around the same time and in 1940, the St Lucia Workers Co-operative Union was formally recognized and able to start the monumental task of recruiting members, educating workers and becoming the collective bargaining partner for employers. Trade unionists themselves had a lot of new ground to cover as well and in the early years, they relied heavily on the British trade union movement, which supported its smaller St Lucian brother with funding, publications and invitations to conferences. Around the same time, the St Lucia Seamen and Waterfront Workers Union was formed.[607] In May of 1951, the St Lucia Civil Service Association was also registered.

The unions had their work cut out for them. The wartime boom had been followed by a post-wartime bust and by the time the Moyne Report was published, the situation in St Lucia was eerily reminiscent of the 1930s. Un(der)employment was rife and the *'psychology of discontent'* which the Moyne Commission had noted shortly before the war, loomed unabated. In the absence of a labour exchange, people daily turned up at the Labour Department's office urging the Commissioner to find them a job - an almost impossible task, as the desperate man reported. But whereas in the 1930s, the only option available to hungry and disgruntled workers had been wild-cat strikes and riots, this time the unions stepped up to the plate. On 29 October 1946, 800 members of the St Lucia Workers Co-operative Union paraded through the streets of Castries with banners, urging the Acting-Governor to commence public works to relieve unemployment, especially as the Christmas season was approaching. At the same time, the Seamen and Waterfront Workers Union conducted negotiations with an American shipping company and (with support from the Government) sent a representative to Curaçao and Aruba to try and secure employment there. One month later, 37 St Lucian seamen and 81 other workers emigrated to Curaçao.

In 1945, St Lucia received a grant from the new Colonial Development and Welfare Fund and several hundreds of thousands of pounds Sterling were allocated to projects such as housing development in Castries, extension of the Vigie airport (first opened in 1943), the Murray Road, education, and sewerage and water provision - all in an attempt to simultaneously create infrastructural development and jobs.[608] The sugar industry, meanwhile, employed 2000 to 3000 people during crop time and 1000 out of season. This still left thousands of people un(der)employed, particularly in Castries and Vieux Fort. Even those *with* jobs insisted that they could barely make ends meet. Although wages had increased somewhat, the cost of living had risen even faster, leaving workers out of pocket all the same. Four stoppages and strikes occurred in the sugar industry in 1946, one of which (at La Caye Estate) lasted eight days. Investigations by the Labour Commissioner revealed high levels of distrust between workers and employers, and a certain level of victimization of workers deemed 'unruly' by management.

It was fertile soil for the nascent labour movement. '*Very keen interest in Trade Unionism was manifested during the year*', wrote the Labour Commissioner in his report for 1946-7. '*Regular open air night meetings were held in Castries and in the outlying districts where branches have been formed.*'[609] Union leaders performed much basic work in those early years, from educating workers on the functions of trade unions and impressing upon them the value of worker organization, to teaching them how to write their own names and decipher pay slips. The St Lucia Workers Co-operative Union's membership soared from 778 in late 1945 to 5600 just twelve months later. Although employers (and administrators) were often uncomfortable with the role played by the unions, they realized that the alternative was riots and unrest, and so they supported unionization *malgré-eux*. Only the Labour Commissioner, continuously on the frontline of worker discontent, seemed more relieved than annoyed. '*There is no doubt that the enthusiasm shown in this movement is motivated by a genuine desire to raise local living standards. Under sober leadership it is possible to build a strong organisation which may be expected to play a vital influence in the economic and social life of the Colony.*'

If 1946 was a bad year for employment, 1947 was worse. The Labour Commissioner described it as '*a very lean year.*' The Workers Co-operative Union organized some strikes and demonstrations but also gained recognition from the sugar manufacturers for collective bargaining and negotiated its first-ever wage agreement.[610] The main glimmer of hope came from delegations from the Royal Dutch Oil Company (Shell) operating in Curaçao which conducted some recruitment drives for seamen and other skilled labourers. In 1947-8, 496 workers went to Aruba and Curaçao, enabling them to remit thousands of dollars home every year.

By 1948, the St Lucia Workers Co-operative Union had twenty branches island-wide and 6000 nominal members: about one-quarter of the island's entire labour force. Sugar workers especially had joined in droves. The Seamen and Waterfront Workers Union had 590 stevedores and seamen signed up. But the following year, membership of the Workers' Co-operative Union dropped dramatically: from 6000 in 1948 to just 2500 in 1949.[611] One of the explanations given for this was that people could no longer afford to pay their dues. A more likely cause may have been the easily doused high hopes of many members under the cold water of compromise. In addition, union leaders seem to have neglected their branches in the out districts, and spent too much time resolving individual complaints and too little on collective bargaining. Members became disillusioned and in 1950, despite a decade of unionization, a Commission of Inquiry was struck by the high level of helplessness displayed by St Lucian workers, '*evidenced in several instances by an air of resignation to their lot rather than by an expression of discontent.*' The attitude of the employers, wrote the commissioners, '*while not hostile, was disinterested and unsympathetic, and even the attitude of the Workers' Co-operative Union was not constructive.*'[612]

Nevertheless, a start had been made. For the first time in St Lucia's history, unionization provided a legitimate channel for workers' concerns and before long, out of the trade union movement evolved a political arm which became actively involved in governing the town of Castries and the country as a whole. As early trade unionist and later Chief Minister George F.L. Charles observed so rightly in his memoirs: '*... the flame that had been lit in the formation of a Union could not be extinguished.*'[613] Trade unionism eventually forced the worn-out plantocratic sugar economy to its knees and opened up the way for an alternative crop and a new, infinitely more democratic production process. But before bananas changed the physical and socio-economic landscape of St Lucia, employment relief came only after calamity had struck.

The Great Fire of Castries

On the evening of Saturday 19 June 1948, a live coal iron left unattended in a tailor's shop in the north-eastern part of Castries caused a wooden house to catch fire. The first cry of alarm went up at 8 p.m. but a strong south-easterly breeze rapidly fanned the flames, pushing the blaze deeper and deeper into town. The fire brigade was ill-prepared, lacking discipline and a clear structure of command. It failed to employ its full water power right from the start, and later failed to focus on extinguishing the flames when they reached Corporation Street. It did not help that the Town Board's mains water pipe lacked pressure. And so the fire was allowed to spread from house to house and jump from block to block, painting the sky deliriously red all night and greedily consuming everything in its path. Thankfully, no human life was lost but four-fifths of Castries was razed to the ground before a fire-fighting squad from the US Air Force Base in Vieux Fort finally managed to bring the flames under control, pumping water out of the Castries River.

The sight that presented itself in the thin light of early dawn, on 20 June, was abysmal: forty blocks of homes and businesses lay collapsed, their contents grotesquely exposed and wasted, the air filled with the acrid smell of still-smouldering wet wood, metal, fabric and stone. From Jeremie Street and the Public Works Complex on the north, to Micoud Street and the Castries River on the south; from Coral Street and Columbus Square on the east, to Rue Devaux and the western wharf on the west: everything had been consumed by flames. In one night, 809 families comprising 2293 men, women and children were rendered homeless and without possessions. Fire was not an unknown tragedy in St Lucia (in 1927, seventeen blocks in the north-west of Castries had burnt down, destroying much of the business sector) but the sheer scale of the 1948 fire easily made this *'the greatest calamity to befall a Colony of its size and resources in so short a space of time.'*[614]

The entire commercial district lay in ashes: numerous government buildings, including those housing the Administration, Customs, Treasury, Audit, Post Office, Executive Architect, Education, Printery, Supreme Court, Magistrate's Court, Registry (except for the contents of the fireproof vault!), Labour Department, Comptroller of Supplies and the Castries Town Board, as well as the Carnegie library with all its contents, Barclays Bank, Cable & Wireless and *The Voice* newspaper. The convent was saved just in time by quick thinking on the part of a Sergeant Monlouis and two young Devaux brothers (Vincent and Sylvester) who doused themselves with rain water scooped off the street before running towards the smouldering building with buckets of water, preventing fierce flames nearby from catching on. Eyewitness Father Jesse, in his meticulous *Outlines of St Lucia's History*, captured the enormity of the devastation.

> *All stores and their contents, apart from a few small shops on the outskirts of the town, were destroyed ... The value of property destroyed amounted to over nine million dollars. Irreparable damage was done to files, records and archives, to those of Government as well as to those of firms and individuals. ... Providentially, the electric power station and telephone exchanges escaped damage, as also did the buildings of the Police, Agricultural, Public works and Medical Departments. St Joseph's Convent, St Mary's College, the Presbytery and the Church of the Immaculate Conception, all in the path of the fire, were saved thanks to strenuous efforts. Very happily, no large school buildings were destroyed. Although the Post Office was destroyed, all letters and stamps and much material was saved.*

It was suspected (but never proven) that the fire was set deliberately by a shop owner looking to claim insurance benefits.

Swift action was needed to help the victims and check the looting. Emergency relief committees started re-distributing food, clothing, household goods and other comforts. Old military barracks and buildings on Morne Fortuné and Vigie were allocated to provide temporary housing. While the town still smouldered, emergency crews set to work: repairing power lines, restarting the water supply and installing a temporary telephone exchange on the north side of town. Three days after the fire, the Legislative Council passed the Emergency Powers (Castries) Fire Bill, giving the Governor-in-Council full power to maintain public order, take control or possession of property, regulate building operations and materials and suspend the obligations of banks.

Several offers of help arrived from other islands. The HMS *Sparrow* along with Red Cross and police detachments from Trinidad, Grenada and St Vincent arrived to help check the widespread looting which followed the catastrophe. '*During the days that followed the fire, steamers, motorvessels, sailing-craft and planes brought a steady and speedy flow of relief cargoes to Castries. The neighbouring colonies were particularly generous. His Majesty's Government contributed £168 000 as a free grant to relieve immediate distress. In London, the West Indian Committee started a public subscription in favour of the victims of the fire.*'

By December 1948, six months after the fire, the relief fund contained $446 040. The British Government offered '*substantial aid*' also, ultimately totalling £1 025 000.

Phoenix rising from the ashes: the reconstruction of Castries

While the Great Fire left 272 people unemployed, including shop assistants, domestic servants, clerks and tradesmen, reconstruction of the city and '*emergency measures to restore services and provide housing for fire victims created a building boom. Skilled workers in the building trade were chiefly affected.*'[615] The Government provided financial aid to those who had lost their homes and possessions. '*Tools were distributed to artisans to enable them ... to resume their occupations. Hucksters and pedlars were given cash advances so that they could recommence trading. Upon establishment in temporary quarters commercial firms re-engaged their assistants and clerks. By the close of the year the majority of those who were forced out of jobs by the fire had regained their employment,*' the Administrative Report for 1948 said.

There is nothing quite like a fire to initiate modernization projects. Castries was no exception. A few months before the fire, the Castries Town

Board had scrapped a proposal for a sewerage scheme, deeming it too expensive. After the fire, it became an integral part of the reconstruction of Castries. '*Those of us who suffered the inconvenience of the "nine o'clock parade" of yesteryear are in the best position to judge the great improvement in sanitation which has been brought about by the benefits of the sewerage scheme,*' Francis Carasco recalled in 1967.[616] The Government also started a housing project at Vide Bouteille which was initially meant to provide clean suburban housing for lower-income workers, while a housing scheme for '*better paid*' employees was planned for Castries proper - all in an attempt to decongest the centre of Castries and promote peripheral, suburban areas. As it turned out, the homes at Vide Bouteille were too expensive for lower-income workers and overcrowding continued.[617]

The Colonial Development Corporation (CDC), which was put in charge of redesigning and rebuilding Castries,[618] revealed its plans almost exactly one year after the fire. The density of residential accommodation was much reduced and central and lower Castries became zoned for commerce, warehousing and industry instead. '*This resulted in a great spate of building activity in the immediate environs of Castries,*' Carasco wrote in 1967, '*and today a substantial number of people who work in Castries live at Vigie, La Clery, the Morne and Marchand.*'[619] Conway and Sans Soucis became residential areas also and suburbanization continued from there. With more vehicles on the road and better public transport, commuters moved further and further away from Central Castries and residential areas eventually sprang up everywhere between Castries and Cap Estate.

The reconstruction and expansion of Castries provided jobs for 2000 people over the course of several years (final reconstruction was not finished until 1955). Around the same time, de-activation and dismantling of the American base in Vieux Fort provided employment for several hundreds more. Following the Castries Fire, prominent Vieux Fortians briefly floated the idea of moving the entire capital down to the south instead, where miles of flat land, a good seaport and decent infrastructure lay abandoned by the Americans. But the powers-that-be in Castries dismissed the idea out of hand, not even bothering to discuss it. Instead, several tons of building materials were dismantled in Vieux Fort, trucked to Castries and used in reconstruction works there. *The Voice* reported in 1949 that the CDC was getting lumber in Vieux Fort from 150 dismantled buildings for '*a ridiculously low price.*'[620]

The boom in employment attracted scores of people from the countryside to Castries, inadvertently putting more pressure on the already severely reduced housing stock. '*As a consequence rents for all types of accommodation were high and in some cases were double what they were before. The worker quite naturally complained persistently that his wages could not afford to pay for this item.*'[621] The cost of living index rose steadily from 100 in 1939, to 230 in September 1948, 241 in September 1949 and 252 in December 1949. Simply put, it meant that the necessities of life became two-and-a-half times more costly within the course of one decade. Trade unions had a hard time convincing employers to raise wages accordingly and in 1950, the Labour Commissioner admitted that '*there has been no marked improvement in the living standards of the people through wages.*'

Female labourers suffered disproportionately. Traditionally, women were the ones who carried stones and sand used in the construction of roads and buildings in wooden trays on their heads. But the Labour Commissioner noted in 1949 that '*Men with wheelbarrows and other labour saving devices have displaced the female labour force ...*' By 1950, typical women's jobs such as carrying coals and building materials had practically died out. The 1950 Administrative Report confirmed this, stating that while the reconstruction of Castries '*provided a greater continuity of employment throughout the Colony than has been experienced for a number of years*' by permanently employing 1145 people, '[g]*reat difficulty was encountered in securing employment for women*' who had been displaced in '*considerable numbers*'. This particularly worried the Government because '*in a large number of cases they are the breadwinners of the home.*'

The Great Fire, the great equalizer

The Great Fire of Castries had yet another unforeseen but profoundly modernizing effect on society: to a large extent, it erased the class and colour hierarchy of the time. The flames had destroyed the homes and businesses of rich and poor alike. All were left '*homeless and penniless, without food and almost without water*', as George Charles wrote in his memoirs. '*The class protagonists had been taught a goodly lesson which made a great deal of difference in the acceptance of the Labour Movement ... There was no discrimination in the long line of fire victims who yelled for food and who lived together as one family in the barracks.*' Charles even went so far as to say that the poor had felt a certain grim satisfaction in watching the rich merchant houses burn. '*The fire revealed a deep rooted feeling of social imbalance as the under-privileged looked on the burning of Castries with apparent delight that the wrath of God was leveling justice at last.*' [622]

Charles Cadet, interviewed in July 1992 for an oral history project of the Folk Research Centre, agreed that the 1948 Castries Fire had led to a welcome break-down in social class. Until 1948, he said, the elite had kept itself separate from the servant class, socializing at so-called house parties only with other high-class people or, at best, the *pov wespetab*, the respectable poor. Servants were there to ensure things ran smoothly but were not considered as people in their own right: '*they were there to grant service. That was what it was.*' If anything, observed Cadet, servants probably felt more loyalty towards their employers than *vice versa*. At the same time, Cadet took pains to explain that such social barriers were not racial barriers, even though '*whites were up there*', as he put it. '*They used the word béché - it was not used solely in respect of people who had a white complexion but also in respect of people who were rich ... people would tell you "tè béché-a," the white man's land and the land may not have been owned by a white man at all but by a black person who had money. So there was an association of race with money.*'[623]

The Great Fire became the great equalizer. In Cadet's own words:

> *The thing that had the leveling effect was the Castries Fire where people got up one morning and found their houses burnt down and they had to live next to the very people whom they wouldn't have associated with before. And for the first time people got to understand that there is a lot to be said for getting to know people a little bit more and not just having exaggerated views of people based on class. They found that the very same people who were their servants one day were living next to them and these were the people who had to help them because they were helpless people, they didn't know what to do. ... So that was the beginning of the breakdown of these social barriers.*

Few written records confirm this finding[624] but living memories of the many months spent at the Vigie barracks in close proximity to people from all walks of life invariably convey a sense of camaraderie mixed with bravura in the face of misfortune: something quite absent in social relations until then.

Just as trade unions were beginning to break the disdainful power of the plantocracy and the patronizing attitude of Government, so did the Great Fire of Castries smash the contrived bulwark of class and status. The train of modernization had been put in motion and, for better or worse, could not be stopped. The immediate post-war years ushered in a period in St Lucian history which was qualitatively different from anything that went before. The abolition of slavery had been a tremendous step forward, but the pervasive perpetuation of the plantocracy's power under the auspices of the governing authorities had prevented Emancipation from liberating the mass of the population from economic oppression, social injustice and physical deprivation. Unionization, politicization, democratization, collapse of the class structure and the advent of economic entrepreneurship for the masses in the form of reliable and lucrative banana contracts, finally opened the doors to the kind of real freedom that abolitionists had envisaged more than a century earlier.

The political awakening of St Lucia

If, in the mid-1930s, agitation for constitutional change had been a muted and narrowly defined middle-class affair, a decade later, it had turned into a deafening clamour supported by working and middle class people alike. While the first elections in St Lucia date back to 1925, until 1950, the right to vote and to be elected remained restricted to a tiny section of the population, based on property and income qualifications and literacy. On the eve of the introduction of universal suffrage, just 2553 people were eligible to vote out of a total population of some 79 500 souls.[625] Moreover, elected members formed only a minority (five out of twelve) of the total membership of the Legislative Council. The first step towards change came in 1947, when trade unions endorsed candidates for the Legislative Council and won two out of three of their favourites' seats. In 1950, union leaders were themselves elected as representatives to the Castries Town Board. Political change at the level of the Castries Town Board reflected the political wind of change on a national level. Unionists demanded universal adult suffrage, a fully elected Legislative Assembly and a majority of elected members on the Executive Council. In 1950, the British Government granted universal adult suffrage without income qualifications or literacy tests to St Lucia (and several other islands) and the time had come for the political arm of the trade union movement to branch off, allowing the unions to focus on industrial matters only.[626]

Thus, in October 1950, the St Lucia Labour Party was born. Its founding members were Allen Lewis, Martin JnBaptiste, Herman Collymore, Karl LaCorbiniere, Clive Compton, J.M.D. Bousquet, James Charles, J. Burke King, Horatius Phillip, Roy Skerrit, Thomas James, Charles Augustin, George Charles and Vernon Cooper. Also invited to the founding meeting were Francis Carasco and Louis McVane. '*The St Lucia Labour Party held its first public meeting at Clarke's Theater then seated on the Reclamation grounds after the Castries Fire where it was enthusiastically received by a very large crowd of citizens, many of whom joined immediately.*'[627] The picture of a tea cup became the party's emblem.

Universal adult suffrage

In 1951, Britain granted new constitutions to all of the Windward Islands and with the introduction of universal adult suffrage, new electoral districts were added to the existing ones, bringing the number in St Lucia to eight. Three nominated members remained on the Legislative Council but the majority were now subject to the people's vote. The Executive Council was to have three elected members as well, to be chosen by the Legislative Council. In preparation for the first general elections under universal adult suffrage (due in October 1951), a second political party was formed. Representative of the middle and upper-middle class, the People's Progressive Party (PPP) emerged in 1950 as the brain child of William Mallet, St Clair Daniel, Clifford Edwards, John Pilgrim, Charlie King, Oliver 'Starry' Branch, Antoine Theodore, Garnet Gordon, Henry Belizaire, Louis McVane, Ives John and N.G.L. 'Guatemala' Charles. A few independent candidates joined the campaign as well.[628] The 1951 elections fundamentally changed the structure of power in St Lucia. Carasco explained: '*The rising tide of a greater political consciousness was overtaking the mass of the community and the barriers of distinction ... which had dominated the political scene for decades under the old Colonial system were fast falling apart and a new political outlook based largely on socialist ideology was taking its place. The rival parties were at great pains to woo the great numerical strength of those they themselves described as "the common man". This political revolution was ... in the spirit of the times and was in fact taking place in all the West Indian islands.*'[629]

When the dust settled, the SLP emerged with four winners and the PPP with two. Two independent candidates were also elected, one of whom (Gilbert Mason) immediately joined the SLP.[630] The other independent candidate was Bermuda-born Walton St George Brown, elected to represent Anse la Raye/Canaries. In his radical campaign, Brown had promised sugar workers a wage increase to $2 per day. When, soon after the elections, sugar manufacturers (represented by the Sugar Association) sat down with the St Lucia Workers Co-operative Union (its recognized negotiating partner since 1947) to determine wages for the 1952 crop season, W.G. Brown attempted to infiltrate the process with his hastily formed Roseau Peasants and Workers Union. He was rebutted from the negotiating table, however, with the argument that his union had not been properly registered. The Workers Co-operative Union agreed to a salary increase to $1.50 for men and $1.20 for women.

W.G. Brown and the 1952 strike

W.G. Brown did not admit defeat so easily. He had fed and mustered the anger of sugar workers in Roseau and Cul de Sac, whom he now represented in the Legislative Council, and they would not go down without a fight. The Labour Commissioner later reported that '*The atmosphere in the sugar valleys was vibrant with the extravagant promises made to sugar workers during the 1951 election campaign*' by W.G. Brown, whom he called '*an irresponsible politician-cum-Trade Union leader.*' Workers had reportedly received the outcome of the Workers' Co-operative Union's allegedly '*protracted and hard fought negotiations*' with the Sugar Association '*with contempt and disgust*' and on the very day that harvesting operations started at La Caye Dennery, on 17 March

1952, workers downed their tools. Roseau and Cul de Sac soon followed and for two or three weeks, '*all field and factory operations in the entire industry were at a complete standstill.*' The strike, which involved some 5,500 workers, failed to gain further wage increases and in the end, workers lost a considerable amount of wages and the factories sustained '*substantial losses*'.[631]

With hindsight, George F.L. Charles admitted that the St Lucia Workers Co-operative Union had handled the strike badly and should have taken it over rather than shrink away from it. '[S]*ugar workers had become very hostile to St Lucia Workers Union Leaders and especially George Charles who had been recently elected to represent them in the Legislative Council. "Ti tas-la Kwasé" (The Tea Cup is broken) was the outcry. The presumption that an elected representative could dictate the wages and conditions of employment of sugar workers with or without a Trade Union had been established.*'[632] Commentators agree that the St Lucia Workers Co-operative Union's failure to effectively organize the sugar workers had allowed W.G. Brown to slip into the '*vacuum*'.[633] Due to bungling the 1952 strike, the St Lucia Workers Co-operative Union suffered '*a substantial loss of membership in the sugar valleys.*'

A Commission of Enquiry was established to investigate the circumstances of the strike. The Malone Report, published in November 1952, discovered a '*deep rooted dissatisfaction of the workers with regard to the method of payment for cutting, heading and loading canes.*' Workers' distrust of the way their wages were calculated was reinforced by the '*unsympathetic attitude of employers to their workers.*' Other contributing factors were the immaturity of the unions, high and rising costs of living, W.G. Brown's inflammatory campaign propaganda, and workers' belief that sugar companies were making huge profits.[634] The Malone Commission made some recommendations to improve the lines of communication between employers and workers and a Wages Council was instituted which would henceforth fix minimum wages in the sugar industry – replacing the St Lucia Workers Co-operative Union as the industry's negotiating partner.

Meanwhile, the strike's main culprit, W.G. Brown, was dealt with by the courts. In May 1952, Brown was accused of having falsely declared himself a fit candidate for the Legislative Council despite being an undischarged bankrupt. His seat was declared vacant and was taken over in an uncontested by-election by PPP-candidate, Henry Belmar. Not long after, Brown was '*charged and convicted for selling goods above the controlled price and an Order was made by the Courts for his deportation to Bermuda, his native land.*'[635] The St Lucia Workers Co-operative Union slowly regained some credibility after the 1952 strike, but mostly amongst domestic servants and skilled and unskilled workers. It took several more years for sugar workers in Cul de Sac and Roseau to reinvest their faith in the SLP and the union.

In March 1953, the company that owned and operated the Cul de Sac and Roseau Estates and Factories went into voluntary liquidation. The Government, fearful of yet more unemployment, threw its financial support behind a newly formed local company, Sugar Manufacturers Ltd, which in October 1953 bought up the assets in Roseau and Cul de Sac and continued operations.[636]

New blood in politics: John Compton's debut

Shortly after, two young St Lucian lawyers, freshly returned from university in Britain, joined the St Lucia Labour Party, determined to play their role in the working class struggle and the development of democratic rule in St Lucia. They were John Compton and Maurice Mason. '*The Labour Movement heralded this youthful and professional injection with enthusiasm*', George Charles recalled, '*and Messrs Compton and Mason were very quickly embraced in the leadership.*'[637]

General elections were due in September 1954 and the SLP nominated candidates for seven of the eight electoral districts. Despite his insistence on contesting the Dennery-Micoud seat, John Compton was not nominated. Frustrated, he ran as an Independent Labour candidate instead, and convincingly beat the SLP's James Charles. The SLP lost two seats (Dennery-Micoud and Choiseul) but won five overall, including two it had lost in 1951 (J.M.D. Bousquet in Soufrière and Clive Compton in Vieux Fort-Laborie). In South Castries, where George Charles '*had lost a considerable amount of support in the Sugar Valleys of Cul de Sac following the Brown strike in 1952*' the People's Progressive Party's candidate Charlie King did very well, but George Charles managed to hold on by his fingernails, with a margin of just 29 votes.[638]

In December 1954, the Secretary of State for the Colonies proposed further constitutional advances for St Lucia, including the introduction of a committee system (in 1955) to advise on the administration of three departmental areas of government. These committees were to be headed by three elected members of the Legislative Council, with an elected member of the Executive Council as chairman. Henry Belmar was put in charge of the Committee on Agriculture and Industry; Karl LaCorbinière headed Communications and Works and John Compton was given the Social Services Committee.[639] It was just an interim step in the process of democratization and on 1 March 1956, the ministerial system of government was introduced in St Lucia. Similar changes were introduced in other islands at around the same time.

Three ministers and a fourth elected member without portfolio were to be elected from amongst the members of the Legislative Council, which consisted at the time of five SLP candidates (Karl LaCorbiniere, Herman Collymore, George Charles, J.M.D. Bousquet and Clive Compton), two PPP candidates (Henry Belmar and Ives John), one independent (John Compton) and three nominated members (Maurice Salles-Miquelle, Grace Augustin and Joseph Devaux). The official members of the Legislative Council were not allowed to vote. Ballots were cast and recast, and the result was the first Labour Government of St Lucia. Karl LaCorbinière emerged as minister for Trade and Industry, Herman Collymore as Minister for Communications and Works, George Charles as Minister for Social Services, Clive Compton as Minister without portfolio and Maurice Salles Miquelle as Minister without portfolio nominated by the Governor. Despite the introduction of ministerial government, the Governor of the Windward Islands continued to have decisive overview powers. Heads of government departments, if they disagreed with a minister's direction, for instance, could write a memorandum to the Executive Council and ask for the Governor's ruling. In this way, elements of Crown Colony rule continued to influence politics in St Lucia. The Governor also maintained full responsibility for financial matters.[640]

New general elections followed on 18 September 1957. This time, the St Lucia Labour Party won seven of the eight seats in the Legislative Council, including the seat for Dennery-Micoud. A few months before the election, Compton had been welcomed back into the bosom of the St Lucia Labour Party and he once again convincingly won his seat. The reunion of John Compton with the SLP took place in the wake of six weeks of tumultuous strike action in the sugar valleys at the start of 1957, from which Compton emerged as an intrepid leader with considerable strategic insight. The popular image is that of a young John Compton, red bandana tied around his head, who had the audacity to face off with Dennis Barnard, a man who embodied all that St Lucia's plantocracy was infamous for, right inside Barnard's own sugar factory at La Caye, Dennery. Here is what happened.

The sugar strike of 1957

It took the St Lucia Workers Co-operative Union some years to regain the confidence of sugar workers after the 1952 Brown strike fiasco but by 1957, backed by the SLP, the union felt confident enough to once again make a bid for the role of rightful bargaining representative. When harvesting started in early 1957, the opposition People's Progressive Party which '*could by then see no rest and no gain*' according to George Charles, '*desperately ... attempted to organize a sham strike.*' Initially, it was a '*political wild-cat sham*' strike but the St Lucia Workers Co-operative Union had learned its lesson and this time did not hesitate. It '*virtually jumped in and activated that strike into a real industrial strike beginning at Roseau and spreading to Cul de Sac, Crown lands and Dennery*

Estates and Factories in a demand for increased wages for all workers employed by the day, task and in the factories.'[641]

The union demanded to once again be recognized as the sugar workers' representative body and asked for wage negotiations to be re-opened. But Francis Carasco, managing-director of the Sugar Manufacturers Company Ltd, stood by the rates that had been agreed with the Wages Council and refused to entertain the union's demand.[642] On 25 March 1957, union leaders George Charles, Martin JnBaptiste and J. Burke King went to Roseau and called workers off their jobs. They were joined shortly after by Karl LaCorbinière (Minister of Industry) and John Compton (in his capacity as independent district representative for Dennery-Micoud). This illustrious quintet then proceeded to Crown Lands Estate in Cul de Sac, where they caused a similar stoppage. Dennery was next. Having explained to the workers what was going on, they called for a vote on the decision to strike.

George Charles later narrated how the owner and manager of Dennery Estates and Factories, Dennis Barnard '*who had been jeering in the assumption that the workers would not obey the strike call,*' himself '*put up his hand first when the strike vote was being taken.*' It earned Barnard a snide riposte from union leader Martin JnBaptiste who told him: '*We will wipe the smile from your face.*' To Barnard's evident displeasure, the workers at Dennery Estate did vote to join the strike, and 25 March 1957 saw the beginning of six long weeks of industrial turmoil. What happened next was described by George Charles in his memoirs.

> *After all the workers of the Dennery Estates and Factories had walked out, John Compton walked into the factory to speak to someone, when Dennis Barnard smarting from the humiliation of the workers' walk-out arrived on the scene and told Compton to get* [out] *of his factory. It was reported that revolvers simultaneously appeared as if from nowhere, like Cowboys, menacing each other. That incident marked the beginning of Compton's physical involvement in the Strike.*[643]

Whether entirely factual or not: the image of a young John Compton, recently returned from law school in England, standing up to a man who was the very epitome of plantocratic power, has become emblematic of the final showdown between the plantocracy and the working class in St Lucia. The 1957 strike certainly served to build Compton's reputation as a natural and at times fearlessly uncompromising political leader. It was George Charles himself who wrote that by the end of the six-week strike, '*The personality of John Compton had ... become a symbol.*'

Around 28 March, three days into the strike (which thus far had seen little hostility, violence or damage to property) a British warship entered Castries

Harbour. Two more ships were seen patrolling just outside the port. When George Charles enquired of the Administrator to what purpose the ships were there, he was told that although he was Minister of Social Services, due to his involvement as a leader of the strike, he could no longer expect to be party to administrative decisions. As it was, the warships were part of Government's decision to declare a state of emergency in Castries. That things were heating up became clear later that same day. Whilst in a meeting with the Labour Commissioner, employers, the Wages Council and other union leaders, George Charles was called to the telephone and received a message from the Administrator informing him that a number of sugar workers from Cul de Sac were on their way to Castries to see him, Charles. The Administrator asked Charles to meet with the workers and persuade them to return to the valley. Charles immediately complied and, accompanied by John Compton, jumped into his car. They only got ...

> *half way up Bridge Street when fully armed police in battle gear obstructed the passage of the car and ordered us to take to our feet. Crowds leaving work during the luncheon hour ... gathered on the side walks. It was then we learnt that Magistrate Graham had just read the 'RIOT ACT' limited to the town of Castries. ... On walking towards the Morne, I was almost the victim of a police bayonet, had not John Compton pushed and fallen with me onto the sidewalk of the DuBoulay's Ice Selling Depot in Bridge Street. The bayonet thrust found its way into the arm of a worker among three who were walking behind us and he was ... arrested. This incident halted the mission to meet the workers who were then being dragged to Police Headquarters after arriving by police trucks while the police shouted inarticulate WAR cries of battle action.*

Charles returned home to find police in battle uniform guarding his residence, and the Administrator notifying him that whilst he was not under arrest, he was advised to '*stay home.*' This of course had the reverse effect and George Charles, this time accompanied by Martin JnBaptiste, immediately drove to the sugar valleys, shaking off police tag teams in the process. The Administrator called in Canadian warships and policemen from Grenada and Barbados to help maintain order[644] and for some weeks, the situation remained very tense. Unionists accused the police of '*acts of intimidation and brutality*'[645] and of indiscriminately arresting and charging workers. George Charles was himself fired upon by a police guard near the Roseau factory, although an official enquiry later claimed that the rifle had been discharged accidentally. Meanwhile, the union '*was at great expense having to assist workers on strike by way of token amounts to buy food, especially for their children. But there was no doubt of their determination and that of the union to hold on until the bitter end.*'

In the fifth week of the strike, banana carriers were briefly drawn into the conflict, but mediation by Allen Lewis prevented the strike from spreading. Lewis' personal association with the labour movement had earned him the trust and respect of both the union and the strikers and it was he who, in the course of the following week, brought union leaders and sugar manufacturers back to the negotiating table. On 29 April 1957, a settlement was reached which included '*an increase in wages for all hourly and daily paid workers in the fields and factories, increased rates for task workers, improved methods of transporting canes by the wagon to avoid spillage, constant inspection of scales, recognition for future bargaining with the St Lucia Workers Union and that there would be no victimization.*' After almost six weeks of bitter struggle, the strike was over. In the aftermath, some of the strike leaders '*continued to be arrested, heavily fined or imprisoned,*' including John Compton. It resulted in a rally of support from union leaders and workers, which underscored Compton's reputation. By the time general elections came around on 18 September 1957, the budding leader who had challenged party authority three years earlier, had been welcomed back into the St Lucia Labour Party - which went on to win seven of the eight seats in the Legislative Council.

Although the 1957 strike had raised wages for sugar workers, it was not a long-term victory. In 1958, the Dennery factory abandoned sugar production and converted to a new crop that was taking the island by storm: bananas. Cul de Sac and Roseau soon followed suit. Nevertheless, this is the real achievement of the 1957 strike in the history of St Lucia, the importance of which cannot be underestimated: the workers had forced 'King Sugar' to his knees. In John Compton's words, the strike '*effectively broke the power of the sugar barons*' and, in doing so, '*opened the way for a banana industry which enabled ... the emergence of an agricultural middle class. Almost overnight, St Lucia became a nation of entrepreneurs.*'

From sugar to bananas

Sugar production had been failing since the 1884 crisis, strangling the economy and causing widespread wage dependency, poverty and poor work ethics among agricultural workers. Accompanying this were an ill-developed peasantry characterized by poor security of land tenure, poor agricultural practices, high levels of praedial larceny (theft of crops) and disastrous environmental practices. Despite being the island's main source of income, in many ways the sugar industry had hampered St Lucia's social and economic advancement.

By the end of the Second World War, a new key objective in official colonial policy for St Lucia and the other Windward Islands was land reform linked to the development of bananas as a viable new export crop. It coincided with a growing demand in the British market for bananas and with the advent on the scene, in 1952, of Dutch-born, British-based businessman John van Geest. It was van Geest who, in 1954, brought together banana producers from four of the Windward Islands (St Lucia, St Vincent, Dominica and Grenada) to market their bananas through a single agent. He signed ten-year contracts with them, undertaking to ship and sell all the bananas of marketable quality that the four islands could produce. Within one year, the Government predicted that bananas would replace sugar as the island's main export crop. The St Lucia Banana Growers Association was resurrected and several abandoned sugar estates were planted in bananas.[646] Small subsistence peasants were initially reluctant to invest in a crop which had yet to demonstrate its worth and for a while, banana shoots imported by the Department of Agriculture from Central America and Dominica and freely distributed to rural communities, were left to rot by the roadside. Farmers were afraid to invest time and energy '*with no results. In addition, farming was associated with low status and poverty, characteristics which were reinforced by an educational system which taught that successful students become teachers and white collar workers while the poor and ignorant remain on the land.*' [647] Interestingly, the people who first started planting bananas in the small rural communities of St Lucia were those who had worked on the American military bases, returned migrants and those with other income-earning occupations (such as teachers and shopkeepers). Their success quickly proved contagious and within a few short years, between 1954 and '58, banana production island-wide expanded three-fold.[648] Meanwhile, sugar production stagnated and in 1957, bananas outpaced sugar as the biggest export crop. The *Geest Tide, Geest Crest* and other banana boats docked weekly in Castries and Vieux Fort to pick up the bananas, which were loaded by women carrying the bunches on their heads. From a crop of just 1904 tons in 1954, St Lucia's banana production soared to 21 329 tons in 1960 (making up 31 per cent of the entire Windward Islands production).

Sugar production declined just as fast, with the Dennery Estates and Factories going out of business in 1958, followed in 1959 by the Roseau and Cul de Sac Estates and Factories (owned by Sugar Manufacturers Ltd) which sold the majority of its shares to Geest Industries Ltd. Sugar Manufacturers Ltd had faced a difficult time following the 1957 strike and twice, in 1958 and '59, barely managed to avoid further industrial action. When Geest Industries Ltd took over the helm of Sugar Manufacturers Ltd, it immediately converted the Cul de Sac valley from sugar to bananas. Geest had promised the Government that it would continue sugar production at both Roseau and Cul de Sac (presumably in the interest of employment provision) but it soon reneged on this promise and put the estate lands of Roseau into banana cultivation as well.

'It gave as its reasons the continuing labour problems, the consequent unprofitability of the enterprises and the better economic prospects offered by bananas.'[649]

In summary, then, bananas conquered first the sugar estates that had been abandoned in the aftermath of the 1884 sugar crisis, then the small, badly impoverished subsistence peasants in the countryside, and finally the remaining three sugar-producing valleys of Dennery, Cul de Sac and Roseau. In 1963, St Lucia ceased to produce sugar altogether: exactly two centuries after the crop was first introduced.

Effects of the banana boom

As the banana industry expanded, a clearly defined structure for the Windward Islands banana industry emerged. The St Lucia Banana Growers Association was reinstated and in 1958, a Windward Islands Banana Association (WINBAN) - later renamed Windward Islands Banana Development and Exporting Company (WIBDECO) - was founded. Initially, its main responsibility was issuing hurricane insurance to farmers but in 1965, WINBAN's portfolio was expanded to include provision of technical and advisory services and scientific research for the industry. A WINBAN Research and Development Centre was established in Roseau, Dominica and WINBAN made great strides. Soon, it was negotiating with Geest on behalf of several banana growers' associations and representing the Windward Islands' industry in the international arena.

Meanwhile, the export value of bananas as a proportion of the total value of exports from St Lucia increased from 37.5 per cent in 1956 to almost 80 per cent in 1962.[650] Small farms (under ten acres) expanded most rapidly, due to the rationalization of family land being surveyed and subdivided among heirs, and vacant land being brought under cultivation. The total acreage of land under cultivation expanded from 66 727 in 1946, to 87 000 by 1961.[651]

For the first time, the villages sucked people away from Castries, where employment was low. '*The phenomenon is in keeping with the patterns of income distribution which accompanied the rise of the banana industry*' explained John Serieux in a 1986 study of patterns of settlement in St Lucia. '*The banana industry had its greatest effect on the small farmers planting on less than ten acres.*' The disposable income they earned with bananas did not immediately propel them into the middle class, but it did create a large increase in demand for basic goods and services, causing '*minor economic booms*' in the nearby villages '*with corresponding proportional and absolute increases in populations.*'

Bananas can be grown on very small plots of land, harvested every fortnight all year round, and new shoots mature and bear fruit within nine months. Soon, bananas were dubbed 'the green gold' and previously deeply impoverished farming households around St Lucia put their banana money to

76. A pedlar carrying coal pots to the market, circa 1910. They are still a popular means of cooking, allowing dishes to simmer for hours and adding a unique flavour.
(Photograph courtesy Robert Devaux collection)

77. The first motorcar in St Lucia was owned by George Barnard (second from the right). It got stuck in the mud of the Choiseul River during one of its first outings, in 1913.
(Photograph courtesy Robert Devaux collection)

78. During the First World War, the presence of Canadian soldiers created welcome income through various forms of entertainment for the troops (Vigie, 1916).
(Photograph courtesy Robert Devaux collection)

79. Canadian soldiers adopted the village of Canaries in an effort to help improve living conditions there. Here shown at their favourite rum shop, 1916.
(Photograph courtesy Robert Devaux collection)

80. People wandering through the desolate, smoking ruins of Castries after a large part of the town was burnt down in May 1927. The Carnegie Library stood unscathed. (Photograph courtesy Robert Devaux collection)

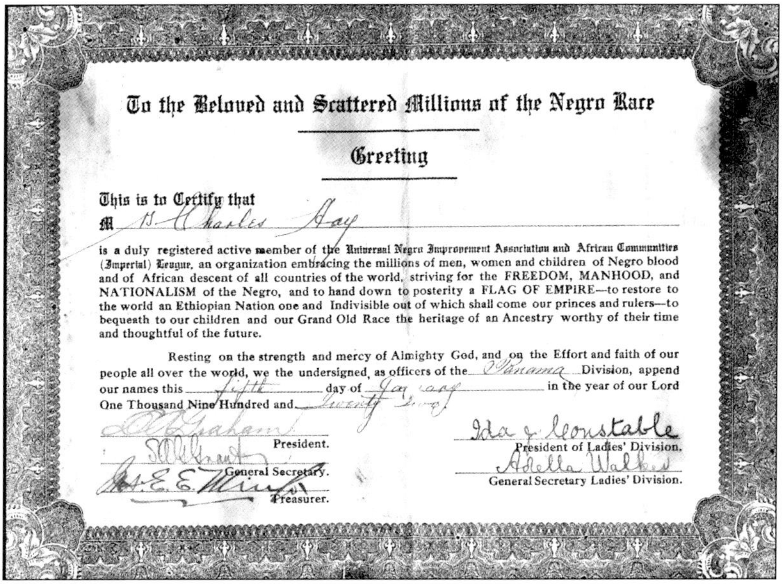

To the Beloved and Scattered Millions of the Negro Race

Greeting

This is to Certify that

M B. C. Charles Hay

is a duly registered active member of the Universal Negro Improvement Association and African Communities (Imperial) League, an organization embracing the millions of men, women and children of Negro blood and of African descent of all countries of the world, striving for the FREEDOM, MANHOOD, and NATIONALISM of the Negro, and to hand down to posterity a FLAG OF EMPIRE—to restore to the world an Ethiopian Nation one and Indivisible out of which shall come our princes and rulers—to bequeath to our children and our Grand Old Race the heritage of an Ancestry worthy of their time and thoughtful of the future.

Resting on the strength and mercy of Almighty God, and on the Effort and faith of our people all over the world, we the undersigned, as officers of the Panama Division, append our names this fifth day of January in the year of our Lord One Thousand Nine Hundred and Twenty two.

President.

General Secretary.

Treasurer.

Ida J. Constable
President of Ladies' Division.

Adella Walker
General Secretary Ladies' Division.

81. This 1922 certificate of the *United Negro Improvement Movement* demonstrates that Black Power existed in the West Indies, including St Lucia, well before the 1970s. (Courtesy Robert Devaux collection)

82. Watching the horse racing at Choc Pavilion, in 1916.
(Photograph courtesy Robert Devaux collection)

83. For centuries, women washing clothes in the river was a familiar sight all around St Lucia. (Postcard courtesy Robert Devaux collection)

84. A barber at work in the cooling sea breeze of a late afternoon.
(Postcard courtesy Suzy Barnard collection)

85. The first airmail delivered to St Lucia was carried on board a plane flown by Charles Lindbergh himself (22 September 1929). In 1930, there was a parking ramp for amphibian planes at La Toc.
(Photograph courtesy Robert Devaux collection)

86. On 22 November 1938, erosion and heavy rain caused a mountainside at Ravine Poisson to collapse, killing 100 people and leaving 700 homeless. (Photograph courtesy Robert Devaux collection)

87. The three soldiers' barracks at Vigie, built in the 1890s. One was demolished to accommodate the Vigie Airport; the others now house foreign embassies. (Postcard courtesy Robert Devaux collection)

88. A private of the West India Regiment is awarded a military medal during a ceremony on Columbus Square (early twentieth century).
(Postcard courtesy Robert Devaux collection)

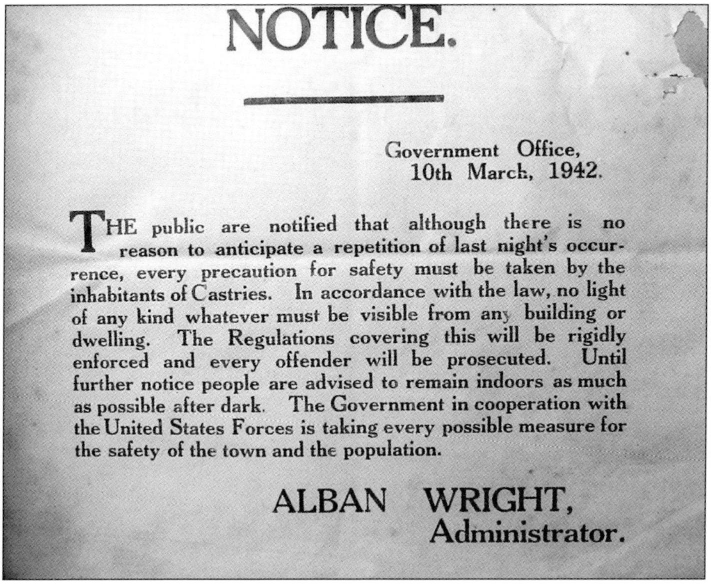

NOTICE.

Government Office,
10th March, 1942.

THE public are notified that although there is no reason to anticipate a repetition of last night's occurrence, every precaution for safety must be taken by the inhabitants of Castries. In accordance with the law, no light of any kind whatever must be visible from any building or dwelling. The Regulations covering this will be rigidly enforced and every offender will be prosecuted. Until further notice people are advised to remain indoors as much as possible after dark. The Government in cooperation with the United States Forces is taking every possible measure for the safety of the town and the population.

ALBAN WRIGHT,
Administrator.

89. St Lucia observed full black-outs after a German submarine torpedoed two ships in the harbour of Castries on 9 March 1942, leaving twenty dead and nineteen injured. (Courtesy Robert Devaux collection)

90. In October 1941, American troops raised the 'Stars and Stripes' in Vieux Fort. The wooden barracks were used as offices for administrative and engineering staff. (Photograph courtesy of *National Geographic*)

91. Pay-day for the local staff at the American Base in Vieux Fort, 1942. Workers came from far and wide to find employment in Vieux Fort. (Photograph courtesy of *National Geographic*)

92. The Great Fire of 20 June 1948 laid four-fifths of Castries into ashes, forever changing its face and character.
(Photograph courtesy of the St Lucia National Archives)

93. The destruction of Castries levelled not only buildings but social hierarchies as well. (Photograph courtesy of the St Lucia National Archives)

94. George F.L. Charles, founding member of the St Lucia Labour Party and Chief Minister from 1960 to 1964.
(Photograph courtesy of the St Lucia National Archives)

95. Sir Frederick J. Clarke became St Lucia's first native-born Governor-General when the island attained Associated Statehood in 1967.
(Photograph courtesy of the Folk Research Centre)

96. The banana industry often involved all members of a household, particularly on harvesting day. Here, women are seen washing bananas by hand. (Photograph courtesy of Guy Ellis)

97. Packing bananas in plastic bags (Roseau or Cul de Sac, 1967). The wagons were pulled along railroad tracks (a remnant of the sugar days) by a horse or small locomotive.
(Postcard courtesy Suzy Barnard collection)

98. Bananas were initially (1967) loaded onto the refrigerated Geest boats by women carrying large bunches of the fruit on their heads.
(Postcard courtesy Suzy Barnard collection)

99. Prime Minister John Compton joined in the work during a 1960s self-help programme to bring pipe-borne water to a community in his Micoud-south constituency.
(Photograph by M.C. Neil Jn Marie, courtesy Guy Ellis collection)

100. The charismatic, controversial George Odlum enthralled and outraged St Lucians with his work as political leader, journalist and commentator - but rarely bored them.
(Photograph courtesy Guy Ellis collection)

101. Aerial view of Reduit Beach, Rodney Bay and the marina in 1975. Before 1970, this area consisted mostly of mangrove swamps. Now, it sports much sought-after real estate.
(Photograph courtesy Suzy Barnard collection)

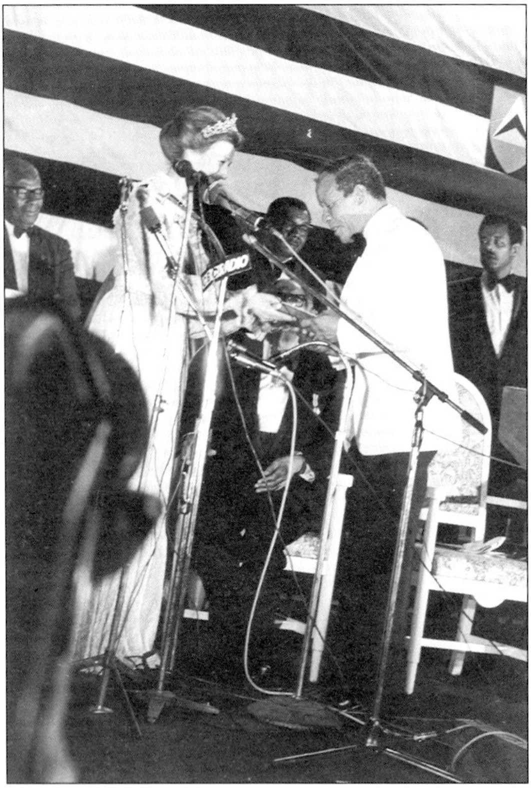

102. Independence Day, 22 February 1979, which Princess Alexandra attended on behalf of Queen Elizabeth II. John Compton was later called *'the father of Independence'*.
(Photograph courtesy of Guy Ellis)

103. Sir William Arthur Lewis, St Lucia's first-ever Nobel Prize laureate (Economics, 1979).The Community College on the Morne bears his distinguished name.
(Photograph courtesy of St Lucia National Archives)

104. Derek Walcott brought home the Nobel Prize for Literature in 1992, making St Lucia the country with the highest density of Nobel Prize winners per capita in the world.
(Photograph courtesy of Jenny Palmer)

105. Dame Pearlette Louisy was appointed Governor-General in 1997, the first woman to hold this office in St Lucia.
(Photograph courtesy of *St Lucia Mirror* archives)

106. Kenny Anthony came to power in a landslide election in 1997 and was re-elected with a handsome majority in 2002.
(Photo: David Vitalis)

107. United Workers Party supporters congratulating Sir John Compton on his party's victory on election night, 11 December 2006.
(Photo: David Vitalis)

good use. There was a boom in the construction of concrete houses to replace wooden ones, and the number of pickup trucks on the island multiplied virtually overnight, all of them bearing the tell-tale 'FAR'-number plates which indicated that they had been purchased under specially reduced duty concessions for farmers. It was said jokingly that 'FAR' was the acronym for 'Farmers Are Rich'. The Government began the huge task of extending modern amenities (pipe-borne water, electricity, telephone service and banana feeder roads) to rural communities, and countryside households increasingly acquired modern appliances: telephones, (transistor) radios, record players and televisions. Emigration and international travel further enhanced this trend of modernization.

Banana money brought not only prosperity but (at least as importantly) a level of security which, for the first time in the island's history, stimulated and allowed working class people to plan for the future. Rural households now dared to have ambitions for their offspring and freed up children from farm work to send them to school. Insistent calls went up for secondary education outside of St Mary's College and St Joseph's Convent in Castries, lest '*the boys and girls of the Districts must always be hewers of wood and drawers of water.*'[652] A petition to this effect bearing almost 1000 signatures was forwarded to the Government in 1957 and in September 1963, a secondary school opened its doors in Vieux Fort. It welcomed more than 400 students, 100 of whom stayed over at the school hostel during the week.[653] In that same year, a Teacher's College opened up at Vigie. Educating their children empowered the often illiterate and almost exclusively Kwéyòl-speaking banana farmers in very direct ways, giving them a trusted family member who could act as intermediary and translator between themselves and the often intimidating offices of Government institutions, banks, insurance companies, lawyers, and the like.

In these ways, banana money brought real economic and political power to small farmers. Those who profited the most from banana farming were usually male heads of households who had clear title to land, which they could use as collateral when applying for loans at the local banks. Those with undivided family land lacked this option, and hence were cut off from money to invest in equipment, vehicles and tools to improve and expand banana production. So while it is true that rural households on the whole benefitted tremendously from banana production, it must also be borne in mind that certain new socio-economic and gender distinctions surfaced in its wake.[654]

Another point worth making (as the OAS has done)[655] is that St Lucia's land mass is so small that in order to generate sufficient bananas to sustain a successful agricultural export economy, almost every square inch of the island needs to be cultivated. This, of course, impacts the water tables and unhinges the ecological balance.

Banana production peaked in 1964. By 1973, acreage under banana cultivation started a slow downward trend as St Lucia's economy began to diversify from solely agricultural exports to industrial development, tourism and some service industries.[656] Nevertheless, countryside communities prospered on the strength of bananas for another two decades (until the early 1990s) and so too did the nearby commercial centers which served them.

From patois to Kwéyòl

The domain of Kwéyòl and all that it signified in socio-cultural terms is an interesting one in light of the banana boom of the 1950s, 60s and 70s, because it shows the difficult paradox which accompanied the modernization of the countryside. Here, the stigma of slavery had never quite been shaken off, despite the fact that the great-grandchildren of slaves were fast becoming 'miniature capitalists' whose incomes often rivalled those of white-collar workers. No matter how modern the farming community quickly became, farming continued to be associated to some extent with slavery, backwardness, *blue-black* African-ness, superstition, illiteracy and all things old-fashioned.[657] The biggest mark of this alleged backwardness was rural people's inability to speak (or at least understand) English, the official language of St Lucia.

By the 1960s, *patois* (the colloquial name for what was long considered a 'Negro dialect' of French with some African elements) had become contaminated by the brush of modernization and was considered *'backward, rural, Negro, and unsophisticated'*[658] - despite the fact that virtually every St Lucian spoke it and, more importantly, enjoyed using it. English had been the language of Government and the courts for well over a century, but only in Castries was English heard to any large extent, and foreign visitors to St Lucia often marvelled at how it was possible to walk for hours in the streets '*wandering in and out of homes and shops*' without ever hearing a word of English. English had always been considered the language of the privileged, of those who '*by virtue of education, occupation, and manner of living*' did not rank in the same class as the common peasants, labourers, artisans and fishermen who formed the bulk of the population. Whites, or those who represented them or served their interests, spoke English: estate managers, bank tellers '*and sellers of expensive clothing and mechanical wares.*'[659]

Under the influence of the modernization process of the 1950s and 60s, *patois* became widely damned as an obstruction to progress. It was also considered to be the prime cause of persistently high rates of illiteracy in St Lucia (in 1948, almost 45 per cent of the population over ten years of age was illiterate).[660]

Douglas Midgett, in a 1970 study on bilingualism and linguistic change in St Lucia, found that among the local elite '*it required little effort to provoke comments concerning the inferior position of Patois and its role in obstructing progress in the island.*'[661] To give an example of just how zealously the eradication of patois was pursued at one time: on 30 November 1966, *The Voice* reported that: '*Shop-owners in Soufrière were asked ... to insist that their customers ask for their requirements in English. This was done as part of an "anti-Creole week", organised by the St Dominic Savio R.C. Boys School. Slogans, setting out that more English must be spoken and that Creole was not a recognised language, were stuck up around the town.*'

For some decades, St Lucians performed this regime of self-flagellation with respect to Kwéyòl, trying to rid themselves of the stigma of backwardness that clung to the practice of agriculture, no matter how profitable that industry had become and no matter how much they truly loved the expressiveness of their native tongue. Pearlette Louisy, in this context, has spoken of '*The ambivalence which creole speakers in St Lucia feel towards their language - an uneasy combination of pride and shame.*'[662] In the process, many more people learned to speak English - but Kwéyòl continues to be spoken widely today, particularly in the countryside, and there are few St Lucians who do not speak or at least understand Kwéyòl. There are no available statistics but for a sizeable section of the population (possibly even a majority) Kwéyòl remains their native tongue, with English being spoken as a second language at various levels of competency. Even today, it is not difficult to find people who speak very little English, or no English at all. They tend to be concentrated in the countryside and in the 45-plus age bracket, but not strictly so. Finally, it must be mentioned that the structure of Kwéyòl has changed under the influence of Anglicization, so that it increasingly uses English instead of French lexicon in a *patois* structural mold.[663]

The strongly negative associations with *patois* were reversed in the 1980s and 90s with the introduction of Kwéyòl TV and radio shows, Kwéyòl literature and dictionaries and the increasing use of Kwéyòl on political platforms and in Government.[664] If anything, the use of Kwéyòl is nowadays used as a sign of trust and a marker of unity. That, in itself, could never have come about had it not been for the socio-economic revolution of the banana industry which reversed the balance of power between workers and administrators to such an extent that it is now those in power who need to ingratiate themselves to the workers of the country, rather than the other way around.

Emigration

Migration was arguably the first force of modernization to hit St Lucia, back in the 1880s and 90s, when newly freed labourers eagerly grasped at job opportunities in South and Middle America and elsewhere. Migration remained a driving force behind modernization throughout the twentieth century. St Lucians emigrated to earn money, to escape the drudgery and oppression at home, to seek adventure and to broaden their minds.[665] Many returned to St Lucia - many more never did, or returned only for holidays. The numbers involved in emigration fluctuated in response to contraction and expansion in labour markets abroad but St Lucians' keen interest in migration remained constant.

In the 1920s, mortality rates began to drop in the British West Indies. With fertility still high and no avenues for migration available during the Great Depression of the 1930s, St Lucia's population increased sharply.[666] As soon as the Second World War was over, people once again sought out opportunities overseas. In the late 1940s, it was the Royal Dutch/Shell Oil Company in Curaçao which recruited seamen and other skilled labourers from nearby islands to work in its oil storage depot and refinery. The number of migrants from St Lucia was not very large and by 1952, Curaçao closed its doors again, but in 1953, there were still some 200 St Lucians living and working in Curaçao: as plant operators, laboratory assistants, electricians, car mechanics, deck hands, quartermasters, painters, and so on.

Although numerically small, the impact of migration to Curaçao was considerable in terms of the hope it offered during a particularly depressed period, the remittances it generated, and as an important first step up the social ladder for a new generation of young men and women keen to make their mark on the world. In 1953 Clendon Mason (previously a reporter for *The Voice*) was a social worker at the cultural centre in Curaçao, which was frequented by many migrants, including fellow-St Lucians. He explained that for middle and lower-middle class men in St Lucia, surviving on a clerk's salary was not easy. '*They are required to attend work clean and well-dressed, they must attend ... social engagements ... to be accepted as 'regular guys', they must meet certain domestic obligations - helping younger brothers and sisters through school, taking care of elderly parents or other relatives in need, or supporting their own wife and children.*' Naturally, for them, '*an opportunity to go abroad to secure employment at better wages is a God-send.*' Moreover, '*those who left the country to hover around the towns, ashamed to return to the good earth, unable to exist in the towns, are glad for the way out of the dilemma offered by migration.*'[667]

The St Lucians in Curaçao had their own cricket team and an active social club. Photographs show men and women in stylish evening dress, enjoying the fruits of their labour at social events. There is little or no echo of the tremendous physical hardships suffered by earlier migrants to the Panama Canal or the goldfields of French Cayenne. Several of the men and women who lived in Curaçao in the late 1940s and early 1950s subsequently moved on to other destinations rather than return to St Lucia. Those who did eventually return from abroad often ended up in powerful positions in society - John Compton being a case in point.

Other overseas opportunities presented themselves as well. On 24 June 1951, 149 St Lucians flew to Wisconsin to work as farm labourers for Green Giant Co. '*This was the first occasion on which labour was recruited from the Windward Islands for that country.*' The attempt was not as lucrative as expected, reported the Labour Commissioner, '*but nevertheless the workers themselves not only gained financially in most cases but amassed a great deal of experience.*'[668] Another 200 farm workers travelled to the USA in 1952 and '53 to work on tobacco farms in Connecticut and on citrus, cane and vegetable farms in Florida.[669] Between March and June 1953, 310 St Lucians helped haul in and process the sugar crop in Guadeloupe. Also in 1952-3, '*A steady exodus of both male and female continued to the territory of French Guiana. The total number of workers leaving St Lucia for that destination was 1,075.*'[670] While administrators said it was difficult to assess the sums of money sent home, they were confident that '*considerable economic relief is provided thereby.*' At the River Canning Company in River Fall, Wisconsin, St Lucians earned US$0.85 an hour, and paid US$1.85 per day for food and board.[671] Most contract workers returned to St Lucia once their contracts in the USA or the French territories ended.

While regional Caribbean destinations continued to rank high on the list of destinations for migration, after 1954, Great Britain started to come into focus as well - and not for St Lucians alone. Estimates hold that between 1948 and 1973, some 550 000 British West Indians migrated to Britain, with the vast majority of this number entering the country before 1962, when the Immigration Act effectively cut off new entries.[672] From St Lucia, an estimated 10 000 people moved to Great Britain in the course of the 1950s and 60s. In 1954, less than five per cent of all money remitted to St Lucia came from Britain[673] but in 1955-6, 910 St Lucians crossed the Atlantic and in September 1955, the *Crusader* wrote: '*St Lucians ... have seriously turned their attention to migration to the United Kingdom.*' Around the same time, 78 people went to British Guiana, 380 to Cayenne, 87 to the USA (as part of an organized labour scheme), 36 to Guadeloupe to cut cane and 31 to Martinique, also to cut cane. By 1956, Britain was the largest and most important migrant destination for St Lucians. Remittances from the UK exploded in value from $52 705 in 1955 to $208 790 in 1956, and $1 200 000 in 1962.[674] The annual report for 1956 stated that: '*Due to the increasing population and the limited avenues of employment available in the territory, emigration has been a safety valve by relieving the unemployment situation. As a consequence persons are always on the alert to discover new fields of employment abroad ...* [and] *considerable economic relief was provided to local persons from their relatives in the United Kingdom and elsewhere.'*

Meanwhile, the Government continued to search out organized labour contracts elsewhere. In 1957-8, a total of 584 men and women were placed overseas: 241 men as part of the US Farm Labour Programme; 68 workers to work in the Ascension Islands (where the BBC was installing broadcasting equipment); 53 cane cutters in Guadeloupe; 192 cane cutters in Antigua and 30 young women as domestic servants in Canada under the Canadian Special Scheme.[675] Organized migration schemes to the USA, Canada and Caribbean destinations continued to operate for several more decades, engaging hundreds of people annually, often on short-term contracts. Some people returned to overseas farms season after season, while others used it as a short term strategy to earn some cash to invest in farms or other projects back in St Lucia.[676] The Canadian Domestics Scheme, started in 1956, continued throughout the 1960s and had no difficulty filling its yearly quota of sixteen women. By 1966, a dozen or more St Lucians were still working on annual contracts in the Ascension Islands and until the early 1970s, hundreds of St Lucian men annually laboured on sugar cane estates and factories in Antigua, St Croix, St Thomas and Florida.[677]

St Lucians continue to migrate to this day, seeking out educational and employment opportunities in the wider Caribbean, the USA, Canada, Great Britain and elsewhere or joining relatives, friends and partners overseas. In many cases, it has become difficult to distinguish between temporary and permanent migration and a good number of St Lucians nowadays are part of so-called 'transnational households'[678] - moving between homes in St Lucia and abroad whilst maintaining financial and/or care-giving responsibilities in both places.

15

The rocky road to independence 1957-1979

The 1957 strike broke the back of the sugar barons and established John Compton's reputation as a political leader to be reckoned with. It also restored workers' faith in the St Lucia Labour Party. At the elections of September 1957, the SLP beat the middle-class People's Progressive Party and independents in a landslide victory, winning seven out of eight constituencies, and only narrowly losing in Soufriere. No candidate won more convincingly than John Compton, who carried 96.4 per cent of the votes in the Micoud-Dennery district.[679] New constitutional changes enlarged the Legislative Council from eight to ten members and made provision for a chief minister and three other ministers, appointed on his advice. Thus, on 7 January 1960, George Charles became Chief Minister in charge of the Treasury, Inland Revenue, Medical and Public relations; Herman Collymore became Minister of Labour and Social Affairs; John Compton Minister of Trade and Industry and Martin JnBaptiste the new Minister of Communications and Works.[680]

At the general elections of 1961, the SLP won nearly two-thirds of the vote and nine out of ten seats (including, this time, Soufriere), but lost the Central Castries seat to the PPP's George Mallet (who had won it earlier in a 1958 by-election)[681] and hung on to Vieux Fort and Soufrière with a margin of less than 1 per cent. Meanwhile, John Compton and his close friend Maurice Mason continued to poll well over 90 per cent in their districts (Micoud-Praslin and Dennery respectively). Compton and Mason were both London-trained lawyers and, along with physician/politician Vincent Monrose, were seen as the party's young intellectuals. They '*appeared to be the brightest stars*' of the SLP and it was their '*great popularity* [which] *would prove to define the lines along which the SLP disintegrated over the next three years,*' Douglas Midgett wrote.[682]

When, following the 1961 elections neither Mason nor Compton or Monrose was awarded a ministry, the three broke away from the SLP and, in December 1961, formed the National Labour Movement. This effectively reduced the SLP's 9-1 majority to a narrow 6-4 margin (three NLMs and one PPP). '*In the two years which followed, Compton effectively became leader of the opposition. On issues like the Eastern Caribbean federal plans, possible demise of sugar in the island, and management of the growing banana industry, he and his supporters took anti-government positions and intensified pressure on the SLP leadership.'*

The SLP's position was further weakened when its member for Choiseul, G.A. Mason, died in an accident, necessitating a by-election in July 1963. The SLP retained the seat with Joseph (J.M.D.) Bousquet, but it meant that the SLP now had two Bousquet brothers on its six-member team: a peril that became evident soon thereafter. By 1963-4, bananas had become St Lucia's number one export crop and sound management of the industry was of prime importance. To ensure this, the UK Government appointed a commission (known after its chairman, Biggs) to examine the organizational structure of the banana industry and recommend improvements. The commission suggested restructuring the Banana Association into a statutory organization, allowing for considerable Government control into what had been, up to that point, an independent organization. While the SLP accepted the recommendation, the Banana Association (voiced by its chairman Swithin Schouten) strongly opposed it.[683] As it turned out, '*The issue over regulation of the industry became the political hinge leading to the SLP's demise.*'[684] In March 1964, John Compton's National Labour Movement joined forces with the People's Progressive Party to form the United Workers Party (UWP) '*and the following day the Bousquet brothers, both representing areas where peasant cultivation of bananas was important, resigned from the government.*' With that, the SLP lost its majority in the Legislative Council and on 1 April 1964, the Labour Government fell.

The general election which followed on 25 June 1964 was to some degree '*a struggle between philosophies about the direction of St Lucia's economy. The SLP, with their strength still in a diminished labor union movement, had not yet grasped the new dynamic in the island's political and economic life, while their opponents galvanized support around the banana issue.*' The Bousquet brothers ran as independent candidates but were unopposed by the UWP, and when the final votes were tallied, the SLP was swept out of power. The UWP won six seats, the SLP two and the Bousquet brothers two. Joseph and Alan Bousquet '*promptly joined the victorious UWP government*' thus bringing the balance to 8-2. John Compton was appointed Chief Minister and Minister of Finance, Hunter François became Minister of Education, Health and Social Affairs, Joseph Bousquet was the new Minister of Communications & Works and Labour, George Mallet of Trade and Industry and Maurice Mason became Minister without portfolio.

Following its 1964 defeat, the SLP '*fell on hard times*' – a situation not helped by the fact that the demise of sugar resulted in a waning interest in unionization. For the next fifteen years, the UWP '*presided over the St Lucian political scene ... overseeing the economic growth of the banana industry and of tourism, and taking the island through constitutional stages into statehood and independence.*'

Associated statehood[685]

When the UWP Government under John Compton came into power in 1964, the movement towards independence in the English-speaking islands was already well underway. An attempt had been made in 1958 at a Federation of the West Indies, but the initiative collapsed within four years. A plan for a federation including the Windward Islands (minus Grenada), the Leeward Islands and Barbados (known as 'The Little Eight') foundered also and soon, each island was looking out for itself. Jamaica attained independence first, followed by Trinidad and Tobago in 1962. Barbados and Guyana were due to follow in 1966. In its election manifesto, the UWP promised to take St Lucia to a new constitutional status and in August 1965, the Legislative Council approved a resolution calling on the British Government to grant the island '*full internal self government by first January 1966, for and on behalf of the people of St Lucia.*' The resolution was passed with a nine-to-two vote. The two SLP representatives (former Chief Minister George F.L. Charles and Martin JnBaptiste) opposed the resolution, arguing that new general elections needed to be held in anticipation of the new constitutional status. An amendment to that effect was rejected, and Compton said his Government made no apology for seeking self-government, as St Lucians had achieved political maturity and financial stability.

Dominica, Grenada and St Vincent also expressed their desire for a new status and in December 1965, the Colonial Office dispatched proposals to all four islands for 'independence in association with Britain'. By March 1966, delegates from the four Windward Islands were attending a constitutional conference in London. It was not all plain sailing. Having taken a joint position that the talks should focus on financial aid, trade and migration, the delegates discovered to their surprise that the British Government was about to wash its hands of all such matters. Fred Lee, the Colonial Secretary and chief British negotiator, declared that the British Government desired '*to bring to an end, the colonial relationship in the Caribbean*' and that while Britain '*would continue to be responsible for your defence and external affairs*', St Lucia would have '*full control*' of domestic affairs and was free to unilaterally terminate associated statehood and proceed to independence.

John Compton was having none of it. He told Lee that the United Kingdom ought '*to prove the sincerity of her offer by providing opportunities for economic self-fulfilment.*' His fellow-leaders from St Vincent, Grenada and Dominica backed him up on this demand for economic support and development before full independence, but the Colonial Secretary was unrelenting. *'Aid, trade and immigration are out,'* he bluntly declared. The United Kingdom was not prepared, long-term, to build up the economies of the islands, nor would it give long-term guarantees of secure markets for the islands' exports or open up its closed-door immigration policy. The British delegation had come to the table, said Lee, on the basis that the new constitutional arrangement would leave the islands in exactly the same position with respect to developmental aid as they were. It was the only basis on which he had authority from his Government to take part in the deliberations.

Compton, in response, requested internal self-governance instead of independence in association. However, despite a few concessions, it soon became clear that associated statehood with Britain would not be accompanied by any special economic benefits for the Windward Islands. At the closing meeting, on Friday 6 May 1966, Compton launched a scathing attack on the British Government for what he saw as its failure to respond to the needs of the islands. In a no-nonsense speech that was widely covered in the media, Compton called the new constitution *'completely meaningless,'* saying that without economic support, it carried the seeds of its own futility. *'It would be less than honest to pretend that this proposed association could be termed voluntary.'* Compton added: *'The colour of our skins is against us and a government, even one that professes democracy, is pleased to legislate and to propound the doctrine of second class citizenship for people of another colour.'* Compton's parting shot - the diplomatic equivalent of a bombshell - took everyone by surprise, and delegation member Sir Garnet Gordon (who had served in Britain as Trade Commissioner for the Eastern Caribbean and was a nominated member of the St Lucia Legislative Council) explicitly dissociated himself from it.

But at home, many complimented Compton for his outspoken stance. Compton himself remarked: *'I have no apologies to make. All I had to say I said in Britain.'* The constitutional conference report sailed through the Legislative Council but in October, the SLP headed a demonstration in which hundreds demanded general elections. A petition to that effect was given to British Administrator Gerald Bryan for transmission to London, but the request was turned down. And so, at midnight on 28 February 1967, the brand-new yellow, blue, black and white St Lucia flag designed by the island's leading artist Dunstan St Omer took to the skies for the first time.

Associated Statehood gave the Government of St Lucia full control of all internal affairs, while Britain remained responsible for defence and foreign affairs (in consultation with St Lucia). The Executive and Legislative Councils were abolished and replaced by a Cabinet and House of Assembly. The post of Administrator was abolished and a local Governor came to represent the Queen.

St Lucia's first Governor under the new status was Dr (later Sir) Frederick J. Clarke. Chief Minister Compton became the first Premier of St Lucia. The Cabinet consisted of five full Ministers, an Attorney-General and the Cabinet Secretary. The House of Assembly comprised a Speaker, ten elected members, three nominated members and the Attorney-General. Compton considered associated statehood '*a bridge over which our people may pass to full independence*' but little could he suspect, in 1967, just how rocky the road to independence would be.

Courting Black Power

While British colonialism was drawing to an end, a new generation of indigenous political thinkers began to climb the ladder of leadership. Bringing back radical ideas from universities overseas, they re-shaped the political debate, aiming to change society from its roots up, and challenging systems and mind-sets that had become entrenched under colonial rule. Black Power, born in the USA in the late 1960s, quickly caught on in the Caribbean, advocating as it did black pride and the creation of political and cultural institutions to nurture and promote black collective interests, advance black values and secure black autonomy. In its extreme format, Black Power attained racist overtones, and a few adherents took the movement to its ultimate conclusion by advocating the use of violence.

In St Lucia, George Odlum was one of the first champions of Black Power. Born in 1934 as the son of a Castries barber, Odlum went from St Mary's College to Bristol University in the UK, where he made history by becoming the first black president of the Students' Union (then a 5000-strong gathering). With a degree in Literature from Bristol and one in Politics, Philosophy and Economics from Oxford University, Odlum returned to St Lucia and accepted a job at the Ministry of Trade. In 1962, backed by teachers keen to see a change in St Lucia's education system, he applied for the position of Education Officer. Not being a church-endorsed candidate, he was passed over. Odlum launched a furious campaign in the local press - to no avail. As Rick Wayne put it so inimitably in his 1986 book *Foolish Virgins*, the incident represented '*the painful deflowering of the virgin Odlum.*'[686]

Disgusted, Odlum returned to London, where he spent three years at the Commonwealth Secretariat. But by 1967, he was back home and working as Executive Secretary of the West Indies Associated States (WIAS). Odlum was young, ambitious and unhappy with what he saw as conditions of servitude left behind by slavery and colonialism. By August 1969, he wrote an article in *The Voice* explaining how he believed Black Power could help to overthrow the old '*master-overseer-slave relationship*' with its '*sharp colour correlation: white-*

mulate-black. This syndrome also had an economic relationship: rich-comfortable-poor.' Black Power, Odlum believed, could *'restore to the under privileged and dispossessed their dignity and self respect.'* He rejected violent action, but was critical of new economic developments such as tourism, which he dubbed *'a new form of economic slavery'*. He recommended that tourism development be *'phased and controlled'* and that foreign freehold ownership of land in St Lucia *'should not be encouraged.'*

Odlum's basic point was that the key factors of production - land, labour and capital - should never again be concentrated in *'the hands of the whites.'* St Lucian society was racially harmonious, he said, because the have-nots had always accepted inequality as a law of nature - but this was about to change. *'They want equal opportunities, they want to wipe away the unequal handicap of history; but most of all, they want to redefine the image of their race. They want to be an independent, bustling, self-conscious people who need not be haunted by the stigma of ghettoes, dish-water and cap-in-hand subservience.'* This was what Black Power had to offer St Lucia: *'a chance for a slighted and insecure people to pull themselves up by the bootstraps of their own self-consciousness.'*

The agenda of Black Power radically challenged the social and political status quo, and leaders everywhere spent time thrashing out their responses. The Caribbean Roman Catholic Bishops promised *'to seek out and vigorously promote the good to be found in the movement'* but many political leaders were uneasy with Black Power. Their fears were confirmed when, in 1970, a Trinidadian carnival band's portrayal of black revolutionary heroes resulted in marches, strikes, army mutinies involving hostages and the declaration of a state of emergency. Fifteen Black Power leaders were arrested and in many people's minds, the disturbances in Trinidad came to define what Black Power was 'really' all about.

Forum: encouraging St Lucians to think for themselves

By then, St Lucia was seeing the emergence of a group of critical voices, many of them civil servants, who adopted the name St Lucia Forum. Founding members included Peter Josie, Hilford Deterville, Primrose Bledman, Cyril Landers and Thomas Walcott. As soon as George Odlum joined, Forum became politicized – but without allying itself to any specific party. Odlum liked nothing better than a public discussion and referred to the Castries Market Steps as *'The People's University'*. On 24 October 1969, the St Lucia Forum was launched with a public meeting on Columbus Square. The movement hoped to induce a more nationalistic spirit and greater public participation in the development of the island. Its stated objectives were: to replace outdated colonial values with indigenous ones; eliminate foreign ownership and domination of the means of production; instill a sense of pride and dignity in black St Lucians and the cultural heritage of their race; create a more equitable distribution of wealth, and encourage people to think for themselves and solve their country's own problems. In his inaugural speech, Odlum (who was still Executive Secretary at WIAS), told St Lucians: '*We are not politicians and we do not want votes. So we will tell it like it is. We are going to be the 'Watch it' dogs of this society.*

While the president of the Civil Service Association felt that civil servants ought not to be allowed to participate in Forum, deputy Prime Minister Hunter Francois urged caution in muzzling people whose achievements could contribute to a better community, and Prime Minister Compton said he felt that the emergence of Forum would help provide civil servants and others with avenues to discuss problems facing the country. Elsewhere in the region, though, the response to similar movements was more hostile. In November 1969, the Associated States Council of Ministers in Grenada ruled that officials of the Secretariat could not take part in political activities and should not publicly criticize the Governments of the region. Odlum was therefore forced to resign from the WIAS. Forum, meanwhile, held meetings island-wide, engaged in community work and, if anything, was stepping up its criticisms of the Government - to the extent that there were now concerns *within* Forum that Odlum was using the organization as a smokescreen for his own political ambitions. It did not help that Forum never attracted much in the way of grass-roots support. Many people attended Forum meetings for their entertainment value, not because they identified with the - in their eyes - well-meaning but privileged young professionals who made up the organization.

SLAM: Odlum's entry into party politics

In 1972, both the UWP and the SLP went through rocky times and Odlum, sensing the weakness, took the opportunity to transform Forum from a pressure group into a political party. Some Forum members felt betrayed by the change but on 29 September 1972, in front of 3000 curious onlookers, the St Lucia Labour Action Movement (SLAM) was launched. SLAM's ideals were similar to those of Forum, but with the added conviction that electoral participation was necessary in order to effect the aspired changes in society. Within weeks, SLAM announced two candidates for the general elections (which it anticipated would be called early): Odlum for Castries East and Julian Hunte for Castries Central. But they had miscalculated. The elections remained set for 1974 and although Odlum had a loyal group of admirers and was a popular speaker, six months into its existence, SLAM was suffering from internal disagreements and had failed to attract other political *big-guns.* Allegations by the SLP and

UWP that SLAM was a communist-party-in-disguise fuelled suspicions that SLAM could not be trusted. That fear only grew when news leaked out that Odlum was hosting a secret meeting of Black Power supporters in St Lucia, many of whom had entered the island under false identities. Public reaction to the Rat Island meeting was highly unfavourable and SLAM subsequently disintegrated, leaving only Odlum, Peter Josie and Tom Walcott. In the 1974 elections, George Odlum ran as a member of the SLP, and Julian Hunte as an independent candidate. Odlum's dream of putting Black Power principles to work in St Lucian politics had failed, but he never stopped preaching its ideals. In nearby Grenada, Black Power ideals did eventually cause a (bloody) revolution when, in 1979, Maurice Bishop (one of the Rat Island meeting participants) led his New Jewel Movement into a coup and forcibly ousted Eric Gairy's elected Government.

Labour's opposition to independence without referendum

The independence clock was ticking in the Eastern Caribbean. Grenada was first, in 1974, followed four years later by Dominica. In 1974, the United Workers Party secured a third consecutive five-year term in office, after an election in which it had campaigned to proceed to independence '*alone if we must*'. And so, on 18 December 1975, the House of Assembly passed a resolution to proceed to independence. With hindsight, John Compton explained: '*We felt that having cleared all hurdles with seven years of successful self-government, with three consecutive electoral victories, with the mandate of the people, the party and the parliament, we would have been independent within a year.*' But the problems had just begun.

That same night, an SLP meeting on the Castries Market Steps ended with Member of Parliament, Evans Calderon, leading a group of protestors to the Premier's official residence at Vigie to express disagreement with independence. Before he knew it, Calderon found himself with a mob on his hands. Compton was not at home but his wife and three young children were. Three policemen guarding the residence were unable to prevent the protestors from hurling stones, one of which hit a senior police officer in the chest. Another stone smashed the windshield of the police commissioner's car. Police reinforcements were welcomed with more stones and bottles and in the end, the police used teargas to disperse the crowd.

It was not that the SLP did not want independence - it just strongly believed that general elections (or at least a referendum) should be held first.[687] Compton later said he believed that the SLP had quietly feared that St Lucia was not economically ready for independence. SLP opposition got so vehement that the British Government Representative reportedly warned in his dispatches to London that there could be bloodshed in St Lucia if the demands for postponement of independence were not heeded.

Nevertheless, in August 1976, the House adopted a resolution asking Britain to alter the constitution and grant St Lucia full independence. In April 1977, the British Government met in London with delegations from the St Lucia Government and the SLP for preliminary discussions on independence. This resulted in Britain asking the Government of St Lucia to publish a *Green Paper on Independence* in order to kick off a national consultation in the island. On 15 March 1978, another conference was held in London. The St Lucia Government was represented by John Compton and UWP chairman Henry Giraudy. The SLP team consisted of party leader and retired judge Allan Louisy, Member of Parliament Peter Josie and the SLP's new deputy political leader, George Odlum. Heading the British delegation was Ted Rowlands, Foreign Office Minister of State. The talks were predictable in that the St Lucia Government put forward its case for immediate independence, while the opposition delegation argued that nothing indicated that a majority of St Lucians urgently wanted independence.

Just as he had done at the Associated Statehood conference more than a decade before, Compton talked straight and was unapologetic. '*It is absolutely humiliating and intolerable, for a government that has been duly elected by the majority of the people of St Lucia since 1964 ... to be traveling at great expense of time and money to the United Kingdom, and then to trudge up and down the staircases of this office, like so many mendicants seeking favours from a master.*' He explained that under the terms of Associated Statehood, his Government had gained the right to unilaterally terminate relations with the UK, had indeed notified the British Government of this desire and had asked for St Lucia's freedom and independence to be restored. '*The government of St Lucia holds most fervently that it is the inalienable right of every country, however small, to be free and to preside over its own destiny*', Compton told Rowlands. He added that it was not St Lucia's '*duty to prove its right to have its freedom restored*' but rather Britain's duty '*to justify their unnatural action*' if it refused or delayed independence. As far as the continuing '*philosophical and ideological gulf*' between his Government and the SLP was concerned, Compton was short. '*We have over the past two years given every opportunity for debate about our constitutional future, but in any democratic society, when there is disagreement, the will of the majority must prevail.*'

Compton asked the British Government to take the constitutional steps needed to surrender its residual powers over the Government of St Lucia as soon as possible. He said he hoped independence could be declared on National Day: 13 December 1978. Compton, in turn, agreed to circulate a draft constitution for an independent St Lucia for public discussion and Rowlands promised that once he was satisfied that the process had been duly completed, a constitutional conference would be called within four months.

Although it was clear where the independence agenda was heading, the St Lucia Labour Party refused to throw in the towel. In London, Allan Louisy had asked Rowlands to devise some mechanism to test the opinion of the people of St Lucia on the issue, claiming that only 20 per cent of people favoured independence, while 45 per cent were against it and 30 per cent undecided. Before leaving London, Louisy issued a statement saying that Rowlands had requested the Government of St Lucia to consult the people further. '*It is now left for the people of St Lucia during the next four months consultation period to indicate firmly whether they want independence, and if they want independence, when*', Louisy's statement said.

While Compton was given a red carpet welcome by his party, in the Labour camp, a new mood of militancy emerged with anti-independence and anti-UWP campaigns led by Odlum. But Compton remained confident. In May 1978, the Government circulated the first 10 000 copies of a draft constitution for an independent St Lucia and in July 1978, news was received that Britain had promised Dominica full independence without elections or a referendum. Compton was elated and sent a congratulatory cable to his Dominican counterpart, Patrick John.

That same month, Compton and an opposition delegation flew back to London for the final constitutional conference. Compton told Rowlands that the draft constitution had been widely circulated with no objections raised against it, and promised that an independent St Lucia would remain within the Commonwealth and retain the British monarch as Head of State. The SLP's Allan Louisy repeated his party's opinion that the will of the people should be tested before independence. For four days, Government and opposition haggled over the draft constitution under Rowlands' mediation. The SLP provided substantial input, making it '*a much improved document*', according to Rowlands, including provisions for an ombudsman and a commission to supervise elections and determine constituency boundaries. The Government refused to yield to requests for an elected instead of a nominated senate and for a republican form of government but, at the end of the four days, Compton was optimistic that the remaining differences could be resolved at home. The British Foreign Office Minister was similarly hopeful and praised both sides of the St Lucia delegation for their constructive cooperation.

In some ways, cooperation is exactly what followed. In October, SLP members in the House of Assembly participated meaningfully when the draft constitution was adopted, with the Government agreeing to include an opposition-proposed amendment. But in other ways, the SLP continued its resistance to independence without elections. The newly amended draft constitution was greeted in late September with SLP-organized public marches and Odlum and Josie exhorted supporters at platform meetings to '*get ready for action*.' On 6 December 1978, Compton addressed the nation with the '*historic news*' that Britain would grant St Lucia independence on February 22, 1979. The following evening, two hundred people led by Odlum and Josie marched from an SLP meeting to the Malabar hotel, where the new British Government representative, James Stanley Arthur, was enjoying a holiday. Arthur was not in his room but in the heat of the moment, protestors smashed the glass sliding door to his room and the windscreen of a police vehicle. Damage was also done to several hotel cottages, which frightened guests. Compton sent a letter of apology to Arthur but his call to Louisy (who had not attended the public meeting) to condemn the attack went unheeded.

Compton pleaded with St Lucians to unite in nationhood. '*Now that victory has been won, let us not tarnish it by continued strife. Let us show to the world that whatever our political differences may be, we put on the mantle and accept the responsibility of independence and nationhood as a united people.*'

On 14 December 1978, the House of Commons in London approved the St Lucia Constitution Order, with only 15 of the 630 members present. Earlier, the House of Lords had taken just half an hour to approve it. On 13 February 1979, the St Lucia House of Assembly held its last meeting under Associated Statehood.

But just when Compton's Government thought the rocky road was behind them, new unrest reared its head - this time in the form of public servants clamouring for pay increases. As the date for independence drew closer, more and more public servants went on strike and the atmosphere in St Lucia became charged. With the wage dispute raging, foreign journalists pouring into St Lucia to cover the independence celebrations found unexpectedly exciting footage. On the day before independence, a meeting on the William Peter Boulevard, organized by striking teachers, was broken up by police using teargas. That same evening, in a television address to the nation, Compton called on St Lucians to be on their best behaviour while the eyes of the world were on them in their moment of glory. In town for the big occasion were Queen Elizabeth's cousin, Princess Alexandra and her husband Angus Ogilvy. Armed police were out in force on the night the St Lucian national flag was first raised on the Castries docks - and not without good reason. There had been rumours that teams consisting of some SLP members were planning disruptive incidents and general mayhem, including the use of explosives, but with the Special Services Unit of the police on full alert all remained quiet. In the end, the independence ceremony went off without a hitch and St Lucians, braving the threat of violence, turned out in large numbers to see the Union Jack lowered for the last time on St Lucian soil.

16

Independence turbulence and Compton's return 1979-1992

The first thirty months of independence brought much political drama to St Lucia. Trouble started within 24 hours of the euphoric flag-raising ceremony, when the century-old prison on Bridge Street in Castries was set on fire. A series of explosions rocked the city and before long, a raging fire swept through the prison. It was the culmination of months of unrest by inmates over conditions at the facility. Firemen and SSU-officers moved in swiftly to round up the inmates and tackle the blaze. In the months leading up to the riot, prison security had been extremely lax and prisoners were able to, more or less, walk in and out at will. With the Compton Government under pressure from public servants and the opposition SLP, and general elections around the corner, the prisoners clearly felt it was as good a time as any to take action.

The prison fire set the scene for a short 'reign of terror' for the UWP Government, which saw its campaign meetings routinely disrupted by agitators and hecklers. Following an historic 59-day strike by public servants, Prime Minister John Compton eventually restored peace, but the unrest had ushered in a mood of militancy which the country had not experienced since the 1957 sugar strike (led, ironically, by Compton himself).

The UWP Government was now at its most unpopular and few doubted that its days were numbered. Rumours of revenge, should the SLP lose the elections, were rife and with the Grenada Revolution just three months old, the police took no chances and raided the homes of several SLP members in search of weapons. None were found. The UWP accused the SLP of harbouring '*communist elements*' but the electorate was unimpressed and on 2 July 1979, accepted the SLP's invitation to chart a new direction for the country. Labour won twelve seats to the UWP's five and after three consecutive terms, Compton and his colleagues were booted out of office. For the first time, Labour made inroads into traditional UWP strongholds and three former UWP ministers lost their seats. A Labour victory had been widely anticipated but few were prepared for such a wide margin. Surprisingly, although political consciousness was believed to be at a zenith, there was a relatively low voter turn-out (63 per cent).

Plywood city

The new SLP Government never gave itself the chance to settle down. With election victory celebrations still ongoing, unknown to the party supporters, Prime Minister Allan Louisy verbally consented to hand over the reigns of power to George Odlum after six months. It was an agreement which came to shape the destiny of the SLP Government.

Fourteen days after the elections, the UWP announced its intention to hold a public meeting at William Peter Boulevard, its old stomping ground in the commercial heart of Castries, to thank voters for their support at the polls. The decision was fraught with danger, not least because in Castries, more than anywhere else, Compton's party was at its most unpopular. Still, 'thank you' meetings were a tradition, and no one seriously expected anything untoward to happen. This changed when, on the day of the planned meeting, George Odlum went on state radio and warned listeners that while Compton had obtained police permission for his meeting, '*it is only fair to warn him that he and his followers will be placing themselves at great risk.*' It became an unforgettable night in the annals of St Lucian history. Bags of human excrement were hurled onto the UWP platform shortly before speakers were due to address the audience. Attempts to clean up the mess or diffuse the stench proved futile. Once the meeting got underway, speakers were interrupted by heckling and booing, followed by stones and more bags of excrement. Within minutes, the Boulevard became chaotic and when the police moved in to quell the situation with teargas, all hell broke loose. Several UWP frontline members sustained injuries. Compton was attacked but managed to escape unhurt. The meeting was over – but a night of terror had just begun.

Over the next few hours, gangs wrecked the commercial sector of Castries, breaking shop windows and looting an estimated one million dollars worth of goods. Furniture, home appliances, cameras, shoes, handbags, firearms and ammunition were taken away amid the thickening clouds of teargas. When dawn broke, not a shop window on the Boulevard remained intact. Armed police were allegedly prevented from bringing the situation under control by the arrival of George Odlum, who ordered them off the scene. Eyewitnesses later swore they had heard Odlum call out from a bullhorn to groups of young men (allegedly mostly Rastafarians): '*Protect your revolution!*' Assistant Superintendent Martin Carasco, angered at being ordered off the scene, reportedly bluntly asked Prime Minister Louisy: '*Do we continue to take a low profile, as ordered by your Ministers, or do we do what the taxpayers pay* *us to do? Tell us what you want. We've had all the **** we're going to take.'* Louisy, afterwards, apportioned some blame to the police themselves, saying that if they had not resorted to teargas, the situation might not have escalated into looting. '*I will continue to stand by the police, but I will not endorse police brutality,*' Louisy said. The next day, carpenters and workmen boarded up the shattered shop windows with plywood and the incident has ever since been referred to as 'Plywood City'.

It was the start of a phase of unprecedented violence and crime. Several policemen were shot at by gunmen, culminating in the murder of Assistant Superintendent Etienne Alphonse, who was shot in the back one evening while having a drink in a restaurant in Castries. Prisoners took advantage of the lax security at the burnt-out prison and armed incidents occurred in several parts of Castries, including a daring daylight gunfight between rivalling gangs of youths. Months of political agitation had tarnished and undermined the authority of the police force, and by the end of that fateful July Prime Minister Louisy had to publicly call on escaped prisoners to return to their cells and implored people to turn in their illegal firearms. The violence abated somewhat - but it also shifted to new targets, in particular foreign visitors. Some were robbed and beaten, which understandably caused great anxiety amongst hoteliers. Minister George Odlum, who had Tourism in his portfolio, conceded that recent '*rampant violence*' had negatively impacted the tourism industry but promised that the culprits would be brought to justice.

Rastafarianism in St Lucia

By the late 1970s, Rastafarianism was becoming an established feature of life in St Lucia. Rastas had been strong supporters of the Labour Party during the 1979 election and were prominent participants in the Boulevard riot. Rastafarianism originated in Jamaica in the 1930s, out of anger over colonial oppression of blacks. It spread through the Caribbean and the first Rastas appeared in St Lucia in the late 1960s. Some were graduates from the University of the West Indies, returning from campus with dreadlocks in their hair, often to the despair of their parents. In 1975, an editorial in *The Voice* called for the eradication of Rastafarians, who were easily recognized by their *locked* hair and red, green and gold attire. Before long, Rastas were attracting extraordinary police interest and even George Odlum, who had initially suggested that they be used to guard Plywood City, openly blamed Rastas for the worsening crime. Their consumption of marijuana, which was (and is) illegal in St Lucia, but constitutes an important aspect of their religious practice, did not aid their case. The Iyanola Rastafarian Improvement Association was established in St Lucia in an attempt to better explain Rastafarian aims and beliefs. Meanwhile,

Jamaican Bob Marley popularized Rastafarianism and reggae music as a rallying cry for oppressed people worldwide.

In the early days, few employers hired Rastas and youngsters grew their dreadlocks at their own peril. But in the 1980s, Rastafarians began to emerge as a force to be reckoned with in society, particularly in the arts, sports and agriculture, both locally and international. Nowadays, Rastas are found in all areas of employment with little or no discrimination, but there continues to be some division (both real and perceived) between those who want to lift Rastafarianism to a level of higher consciousness and national respectability, and those merely using it as a cloak for nefarious activities.

The tug-of-war between Louisy and Odlum

In August 1979, the first political differences between Prime Minister Allan Louisy and his deputy George Odlum came to the fore after the UWP suggested Odlum had secretly sent young St Lucians for military training in Grenada, where self-proclaimed Marxist Maurice Bishop and his People's Revolutionary Government were now in power. Compton claimed to have a list with the names and passport numbers of the recruits, and shared that information with Louisy. Louisy denied that his Government was interested in forming a military branch, but Odlum expressed his preference for an army. With the six month-old Grenada revolution still echoing in everyone's ears, and continuing strife between Louisy and Odlum, speculation led to fears that a revolutionary faction within the Government might be planning to take control of the country.

For a little while, though, the Louisy Government seemed to be getting into its stride. In September 1979, St Lucia took its place as the 152nd member of the United Nations and George Odlum, as Minister of Foreign Affairs, made his first major foreign policy speech in which he articulated the special problems faced by small island states in light of their vulnerability within the wider world. There were some other, local achievements as well. But just when it seemed that Louisy was managing to get on with the business of governing the country, *The Voice* published an article claiming that George Odlum had written to Louisy asking him to '*confirm our previous arrangement*' and hand over power to Odlum by the end of 1979. The issue plunged the Government into renewed crisis. Louisy replied that he had decided to remain in his post and added that he was prepared to counter the possible use of '*undemocratic means*' to oust him. In January 1980, Odlum dismissed as '*nonsensical*' the suggestion that he planned a coup but he did, for the first time, admit that he had indeed sent young St Lucians to Grenada for military training. The reason, he said, was that some members of the SLP Government had been concerned about their personal safety and did not want to depend on the local police for protection. Louisy, in response, said Odlum had told him at the time that two men were trained in Grenada as bodyguards, but that he had later discovered that the number of trainees was much higher.

The leadership struggle deepened. Opposing factions within the Government began to trade words in the media and on political platforms, and it was not long before the UWP pressed for fresh elections. The first anniversary of independence came and went in a climate of national despair. On May Day 1980, Louisy and Odlum were enticed by party loyalists to shake hands during a trade union rally in a gesture that was intended to signify the end of the leadership controversy - but to no avail. The Chamber of Commerce joined the UWP in its call for new elections. This did not go down well with the SLP and Peter Josie, during a public meeting of the Odlum faction on the Castries Market Steps, predicted that there would be '*war*' if new elections were called. His declaration shocked Louisy, who said he would do everything in his power to prevent Josie from creating the kind of civil strife in which guns and teargas would be required to re-establish peace. By July 1980, on the first anniversary of the SLP's election to office, the feud had intensified further. Louisy reshuffled his Cabinet, stripping Odlum of his portfolio of Information and Broadcasting, and relieving him of his post as deputy-Prime Minister.

The man-made political disaster temporarily yielded the stage to a natural catastrophe which visited the island in the form of Hurricane Allen. Packing winds of up to 125 miles per hour, Allen ripped through the island on 4 August 1980, causing widespread devastation. Six people died, 9600 were rendered homeless and the bill of total damages was estimated at EC$235 million. The banana industry, life-line of the economy, was wiped out and no fruit was harvested for several months. The manufacturing sector and hotels also took a pounding, as did homes, schools and other public buildings. Foreign aid came flooding in, and the Hess Corporation voluntarily undertook to restore the island's schools - fourteen of which had been completely destroyed and 34 badly damaged.

Yet domestic strife still managed to get in the way. Charges of political interference in the allocation of relief supplies forced both Louisy and Compton to issue stern warnings. The UWP continued to call on the Government to resign, but attempts to undermine Louisy's support in the House of Assembly failed and 1980 ended with Louisy still in the saddle as Prime-Minister.

In March 1981, the SLP held a party convention which Odlum boycotted, leaving the door open for Louisy to be re-elected unopposed as party leader. Thus the Odlum faction was left without a single voice in the executive branch. Also in March 1981, Education Minister Kenny Anthony resigned, disenchanted with the power struggle. Odlum, increasingly embattled, announced that he intended to launch a new political party and he even spoke of an alliance with the UWP - an idea which was spurned by the UWP as '*a marriage of convenience and opportunism at its highest.*' On 14 April 1981, the controversy came to a head when Odlum and three allied ministers joined the UWP in opposing Louisy's budget. But Odlum was in for a surprise. Louisy agreed to resign as Prime Minister, but saved his Government: '*The vote against the budget was not constitutionally a vote of no confidence against the government but ... a vote against me personally*', he stated. For Louisy, it was the end of a brief political career that had started late in life with the promise that justice would be done in St Lucia '*though the heavens fall.*'[688]

Public disenchantment with the Government's course of action was high and erupted into industrial action by the Civil Service Association. The Chamber of Commerce followed suit and ordered a shutdown of the country while the UWP mounted the biggest public demonstration ever witnessed on the island - but the Government refused to back down. The names of various successors to the Prime Ministership were floated, including those of Peter Josie and George Odlum. However, Odlum stated he would accept the post only if he was given a free hand to select his own Cabinet - something that the other members of Parliament refused to accept.

The Cenac Government: 1981-2

The leadership wrangle was finally resolved during a meeting instigated by Governor General Boswell Williams in which Winston Cenac, who had earlier resigned as Attorney General, was accepted by his Cabinet colleagues as Prime Minister. Cenac was appointed in early May 1981 and his first act was to plead for '*a period of calm and stability*'. The call was in vain. Three days later, a UWP demonstration (which Odlum had urged his supporters to join) ended in chaos, with police officers using tear-gas against a small band of marchers who had broken through a cordon intended to keep them away from the city's main shopping centre. Gangs of youths smashed shop windows and armed police were brought in to restore order. On 16 May 1981, Odlum launched his Progressive Labour Party (PLP), finally breaking away completely from the SLP. His long-time ally Peter Josie opted to remain in the Government.

Cenac succeeded in getting a revised version of Louisy's budget through Parliament, and the SLP Government settled down for the first time since assuming office, almost two years earlier. The effect of the protracted power struggle on St Lucia's economy had been more traumatic than even Hurricane Allen, and restoration of the island's image overseas became a priority for the new administration. A trade mission was dispatched to North America to assure investors that St Lucia was once again safe and ready for an injection of foreign investment.

The tourism industry had declined precipitously, with hotels reporting occupancy rates of just 51.2 per cent compared to 83 per cent in the previous two years. The banana industry was getting back on its feet faster than expected after the hurricane, but declining prices in Britain left farmers disenchanted and banana workers were swelling the ranks of the unemployed. The coconut industry - the second-most important agricultural export crop - similarly faced a gloomy future. The only real milestone during this period was the inauguration, in January 1981, of the National Commercial Bank.

On 1 October 1981, the UWP filed a motion of no confidence in the Cenac Government, accusing it of sins ranging from corruption, mismanagement of public funds and contravention of financial regulations to gross inefficiency. The PLP's Michael Pilgrim seconded the motion and the Chamber of Commerce issued a statement at the same time, accusing the Government of running St Lucia '*aground on the reefs of economic collapse.*'

On Tuesday 27 October, Cenac's Government survived the vote of no confidence by nine votes to eight, but the meeting was very disorderly, with members of both sides using verbal invective of a kind unprecedented in the Parliament chamber, and Speaker of the House, Donald Alcee, barely able to exercise control. Small-scale violence and vandalism erupted around Castries and several vehicle windscreens were smashed, including Alcee's.

Compton's UWP did not yield, however, and proceeded to lay several specific charges of financial wrong-doing and corruption against SLP ministers and members of Parliament. This put the Government in a very uncomfortable position. Meanwhile, a World Bank memorandum found that in its second year of independence, St Lucia had recorded a negative economic growth of 6 per cent, an inflation rate of 21 per cent, a 6 per cent increase in unemployment and a $13 million deficit on the Government's current account.

Matters went downhill from there. On 17 December 1981, during another meeting of the House of Assembly, Michael Pilgrim spotted a pistol in Peter Josie's briefcase. Pilgrim informed Speaker Alcee of the fact and added a few choice words for Josie, letting him know what his fate would be if he opened the briefcase one more time. By the end of 1981, the Cenac administration was facing the prospect of industrial action by its own public servants, who had rejected the offer of a 45 per cent pay increase over a three year-period (holding out for 80 per cent instead). By then, the Government was hard-pressed to find money even to pay the regular monthly salaries. Banks had restricted their credit lines and the economy was in decline. The Cenac Government intended to present new legislation during a House of Assembly meeting on 11 January 1982 which would exonerate all those in Parliament whom Compton had accused of financial impropriety. On discovering this, Odlum's PLP hastily printed car stickers and handbills reading 'STOP THIS CRIME... THIS BILL MUST NOT PASS' and the UWP, too, had fliers made up. In the days leading up to the meeting, both the UWP and PLP held mass public meetings in Castries, exhorting their supporters to be prepared for action on the following Monday.

Long before the House assembled on Monday, 11 January 1982, the public gallery was jammed full to capacity. The meeting spun out of control almost immediately, with members on both sides of the House engaging in a tumultuous shouting match. Onlookers from the gallery joined in, hurling threats at Government MPs. Chaos reigned for several minutes, until Compton rose and suggested an adjournment in order to study the implications of the new bill, and give the Government time to withdraw it. The Speaker gratefully rapped his gavel and announced that the meeting was adjourned. However, as Compton pointed out, a motion for adjournment needed to be put to the MPs first. Recognizing his mistake, the Speaker turned to Prime Minister Cenac, who moved for the adjournment. Things happened quickly after that. Odlum, standing near an open window, produced a whistle from his pocket and blew it three times. A group of men, presumably Odlum supporters, rushed into the House and another round of parliamentary chaos got underway. One of the men grabbed the ceremonial mace (the symbol of authority in the House) and when the sergeant-at-arms attempted to remove it from his grasp, Odlum swiftly intercepted the sergeant, took hold of the mace and tossed it through the room. It sailed through the air and landed in the hands of Michael Pilgrim who, for a moment, seemed to contemplate throwing it into the mob outside. At that same moment the SSU arrived, and peace was restored to the House. The mace was briefly placed on the press table, before the sergeant-at-arms took possession of it once again. With that, another chaotic House of Assembly meeting ended - but not so the troubles of Cenac's SLP Government.

That same day, the Chamber of Commerce decided that enough was enough, and called on all businesses to close down. Prime Minister Cenac responded with an address to the nation, explaining that while the new legislation had intended to remove doubts about accountability for Government funds, he had since withdrawn the bill on the advice of the trade unions. But it was too late: public servants went on strike, the ports were shut down and calls for the resignation of the Government and fresh general elections went up everywhere. Four days into the national shutdown, Peter Josie announced on radio that he was ready to use force to compel the re-opening of businesses that had closed down in protest. '*As far as I am concerned it's time we smash it all up, even though we have to start building again from scratch,*' said Josie. The Civil Service Association, meanwhile, withdrew its members from all

Government departments except essential services '*until there has been a satisfactory resolution of salary negotiations and the political crisis to which the nation has been subjected.*' In a strange irony of history, the business sector and trade unions found themselves fighting on the same side.

Talks organized by Roman Catholic Church leaders between the three political parties eventually resulted in the decision that the SLP Government would resign, and an interim-Government headed by Michael Pilgrim (until then deputy-leader in George Odlum's PLP), would pave the way for new elections to be held in six months' time.

Pilgrim's interim-Government

The decision was announced by Prime Minister Cenac on the Castries Market Steps. '*In the interest of peace, harmony and tranquility, I have decided to resign tomorrow,*' declared Cenac, to thunderous applause from assembled PLP supporters. The UWP had more misgivings, deeming the conciliation a '*re-statement of the same problem in a different form.*' Nevertheless, on Sunday morning 17 January 1982, at the residence of Archbishop Kelvin Felix, Cenac handed in his letter of resignation. Pilgrim was sworn in as interim-Prime Minister on the same day, and with that, thirty months of SLP Government came to an end. When the dust cleared, Cenac was praised for having listened to the voices of popular revolt and commended for having possibly saved the country from bloodshed or even civil war during its infant years of independence.

Amazingly, precisely during the months when St Lucia was attracting so much negative attention at home and abroad, the island was struck by a ray of bright light when, in 1979, it provided the Caribbean Region with its first Nobel Prize winner. Sir William Arthur Lewis, brilliant academic, son of the soil and first President of the Caribbean Development Bank, was awarded the Nobel Prize for Economics, making him the first black person ever to win a Nobel Prize in a field other than Peace. It was a tremendous achievement and one which gave St Lucians a badly needed lift at a time when political bickering at home overshadowed almost everything else.

One island, two Nobel Prize laureates

Sir Arthur Lewis

St Lucia has the highest proportion of Nobel laureates per capita of any country in the world. Even more amazingly, the two laureates share the same birth date. Born on 23 January 1915, William Arthur Lewis won a scholarship to attend St Mary's College at the tender age of ten and completed secondary school with honours at fourteen. He won an Island Scholarship in 1933 but, not wishing to pursue the traditional fields of Law or Medicine and cognizant that jobs in Engineering (his first love) would be hard to come by for a young black man, he pursued Business Administration instead. After graduating in 1937 with first class honours, the London School of Economics offered Lewis a scholarship to do a Ph.D in Industrial Economics. By 1948, at age 33, Lewis was a full Professor at the University of Manchester and had served as Temporary Principal of the British Board of Trade and the Colonial Office. Over the next three decades, Lewis published extensively on problems of economic development and took up assignments in Asia, the Far East, Africa and the West Indies. A stint in Trinidad in 1957 to help the Eric Williams Government prepare a five-year development plan was followed by two decades as Professor of Economics at Princeton University in New Jersey, USA. When the Caribbean Development Bank was inaugurated in 1970, Lewis returned to serve as its first President. Sir Arthur Lewis died in 1991 at the age of 76.

Derek Walcott

Derek Alton Walcott was born on 23 January 1930 along with his twin brother Roderick. Both boys attended St Mary's College. By age sixteen, Derek was already composing serious poetry and by the time he reached 21, three volumes of his work were in publication.

In 1950, together with Roderick, Derek founded a theatre group at St Mary's College (the St Lucia Arts Guild) and wrote his first big play, *Henri Christophe*. Derek then made his way to UWI in Jamaica to study Liberal Arts, French, Latin and Spanish. After graduation, he returned home to teach at St Mary's. But 1955 saw Walcott back in Jamaica, where his reputation as a playwright soon spread. In 1957, Walcott was asked to write a play for the inauguration of the West Indies Federal Parliament (*Drums and Colours*) which subsequently won him an award to study theatre in the US. Two years later, Walcott set up the Trinidad Theatre Workshop, all the while producing plays and poetry. In 1961, he won the Guinness Award in the United Kingdom. The next year, his first major collection of poems was published (*In a Green Night*) followed three years later by *Selected Poems*. His third collection (*The Castaways*) won him a Royal Society of Literature Award in 1965, followed by the New Statesman Award for his epic *Another Life*. With an honorary doctorate from UWI, Walcott then moved to the United States to teach at Harvard and Yale (although frequently returning to the Caribbean). In 1979, *Star Apple Kingdom* came out and three years later *The Fortunate Traveler*. Along with his seminal book *Omeros* (1990), these works clinched Walcott's 1992 Nobel Prize for Literature.

Compton's second coming, 1982-1992

Apart from a scam involving blank St Lucian passports being sold overseas, it was relatively plain sailing for Michael Pilgrim's interim Government and on 3 May 1982, new general elections were held. Although St Lucians returned John Compton's United Workers Party to power with a clear 14-3 mandate, voter turn-out was low (56 per cent): a reflection of the deep political disillusionment in the country. The St Lucia Labour Party won two seats but nine SLP candidates lost their deposits, including Cenac and Josie, and so did Odlum. Even Michael Pilgrim, despite his well-received stint as interim-Prime Minister, was beaten by his UWP opponent. The Progressive Labour Party won one seat.

Back at the helm, John Compton painted a bleak picture of St Lucia, with an economy displaying negative growth, infrastructure in disrepair and the three major generators of foreign exchange - agriculture, manufacturing and tourism - all in decline. Compton proposed a tripartite consultative commission on wages, prices, productivity and employment, but the unions refused to cooperate and so Compton resorted to plain austerity measures instead. He called for a halt to the '*squandering*' of resources, cut back Cabinet members' salaries by 10 per cent and ordered all Ministries to cut expenditure by 20 per cent (referred to as the '*Compie Tax*'). It was the first calendar year of total political calm since independence but agriculture and manufacturing struggled. Tourism did a little better and, in 1982, Hess completed its $135 million oil transshipment terminal at Cul de Sac, which provided some encouragement,[689] and St Lucia was also helped somewhat by overseas assistance, in particular from the United States.

A history of infrastructural development in St Lucia

In his efforts to revive the economy, Compton reached back to a model of development he had held dear since he first ascended to power, in 1964. Compton firmly believed that the basis for a modern economy rested on solid infrastructure: expansion of utilities, good transportation networks, efficient ports and sound education and health facilities. He had been the main architect of the modernization programme of the 1960s and 70s, and it was here that Compton once again found his focus - and his critics their ammunition. Opposition politicians repeatedly called John Compton a 'dreamer' and even ordinary people sometimes thought his plans were pie-in-the-sky. Compton's response was invariably that big projects created opportunities for economic activity, employment and export. With historical hindsight, he was mostly correct, although on the down-side, his development model did lead to a high level of dependency on regional and international aid and loans determined by external factors over which St Lucia had little or no control.

Infrastructural modernization had started in St Lucia with the Great Fire of 1948. In the early 1960s, George Charles' SLP Government studied plans for an island-wide water supply system and expansion of the electricity grid. The telephone service was upgraded shortly after Charles' Government fell, with Cable & Wireless announcing a $15 million project to improve communications in the Eastern Caribbean. Before long, St Lucians were able to connect by telephone to other parts of the world. Compton's UWP Government took over in June of 1964 and upgrading and expansion of water, electricity and telecommunication services began immediately and in earnest. In addition, land was earmarked for housing development; air and seaports were improved to accommodate tourism expansion; factory shells were built to facilitate industrialization, and various corporations, each with a specific task, were established.

The electrification of St Lucia

In 1923, an editorial in *The Voice* complained that Castries was one of the worst-lit towns in the West Indies and that one could hardly read a book by the light of the petroleum wick lamps (known as *Kitson lamps*) which had illuminated Castries since 1904. The option of electrical light was floated and that same year, the St Lucia Electricity Company was formed. In 1931, the Government secured a loan from the Colonial Development Fund for the purpose of providing not only electrical street lights in Castries, but supply residents as well. In 1933, St Lucia got its first power station. It was located on Jeremie Street and on National Day in December of that same year, electrical lights were turned on in Columbus Square for the first time ever. The service was soon extended throughout Castries. It brought the Town Board several complaints from householders, including Leonty Cadet, who urged the removal of the lamp on the corner of Peynier Street, where he lived, because young men gathered on his doorstep every night.

In 1937, Soufrière resident Andre DuBoulay installed a water wheel and diesel engine on his estate to light up the streets of the village and supply a few residences. It gave Soufrière the scoop for hydro-electricity. Fourteen years later, Copra Manufacturers Ltd installed a 100 KW generator which powered the coconut oil factory and supplied about 50 residents. In December 1952, a hydro-electric plant was commissioned for Soufrière, using two 36 KW hydro-turbine generator units purchased from DuBoulay. The Government handed this system over to the specially formed South Western Electricity Board, managed by the Colonial Engineer, but took it back in 1957. In 1965, the Soufrière system was sold to the new national electricity company.

The American military had built a power station at the Beane Field Air Base in Vieux Fort during the war which was handed over to the Government in 1949. In 1952, a generating site was established at New Dock using two 150 KW units left behind by the Americans. Their performance was deemed unsatisfactory, however, and later that year, USAID donated two new units. These too were sold to the new electricity company in 1965.

Anse la Raye was the first village to be entirely electrified. This occurred in 1946 and relied on a 5 KW water wheel DC generator which was installed on a private estate belonging to the Adjodha family. The system operated for four hours only, from six p.m. till ten p.m. and whenever the water level in the river was low, lights were dim. Dennery got a generating set in 1960 but strictly for the benefit of the local hospital. In Choiseul, a generator was installed at the water reservoir near the Debreuil junction in 1962. A Lister engine was set up in Micoud in 1963 but it never worked well and was replaced two years later by a diesel generator. In Canaries, a small generator had been supplying electricity to the presbytery and a few surrounding homes since 1940 but community supply did not come until 1964 - the same year Laborie was connected to the Vieux Fort power grid. Although the US Naval Air Station at Reduit had had its own generating system, the village of Gros Islet (just a stone's throw away) did not get electricity until after 1965. In 1963, lights were installed on the runway of Vigie Airport.

In November 1964, Government, the CDC and the Castries Town Council came together and incorporated the St Lucia Electricity Services Limited company. LUCELEC took over responsibility for the entire island's electricity system on 1 July, 1965. By then, power station supplies in Castries were '*depleted*' and, according to the Electrical Engineer, '*in danger of collapse.*' The Castries Power Station on Jeremie Street, rebuilt in 1959, had lagged behind the growing demand, and in 1971 a new plant was commissioned at Union. When this, too, became obsolete, a state-of-the-art plant to the tune of $60 million was established at Cul de Sac in 1990.

Telecommunications

Telephones were first introduced in St Lucia in the last months of 1896.[690] The Director of Public Works, in 1897, revealed that it had 50 subscribers and added: '*The ultimate number will, probably, not exceed 100.*'[691] True enough, until the 1960s, very few people in St Lucia had telephones and the Government-operated service was an archaic system in which callers had to crank a handle to generate sufficient power to reach the telephone exchange, supply the operator with a telephone number, and wait to be connected. Outside of Castries, telephones were available only to a few upper-class households and the emergency services. Conversations had to be kept brief so as not to overload the system's capacity.

In 1964, British-owned Cable & Wireless moved into the Eastern Caribbean, including St Lucia, and set up an elaborate inter-island and international communications network with automatic telephone services. In the 1990s, the system was digitized. Cable & Wireless' 30-year monopoly ended in 2001, when St Lucia (and other territories) allowed other telecom companies to operate.

A spin-off of the expanded electricity and communications services was the introduction of television. In the early 1960s, television was received via Barbados, where the Caribbean Broadcasting Company was active. By 1967, St Lucia Television Service started limited local programming and by the middle of the 1980s, its successor, HTS (Helen Television Service) introduced satellite television, soon followed by DBS (Daher Broadcasting Service). By the start of the twenty-first century, almost every household in St Lucia was able to receive several dozen television channels from North America, Europe and the Caribbean region.

The story of pipe-borne water

By 1890, Castries had a fairly decent water supply, with the Castries Water Works sending 250 000 gallons of clean water daily to taps and standpipes around the town, whilst keeping another one million gallons in a backup reservoir. The system had cost £24 000, financed with a loan from England. Meanwhile, men, women and children in the rest of the island spent the early hours of every working day carrying containers of spring or river water on their heads for use at home. It was not until 1966 that the first Compton Government established a Central Water Authority with the aim of bringing potable water to the entire island. The organization went through various changes, as its name, role and character changed: in 1984, it became the Water and Sewerage Authority (WASA) and in 1998, the Water and Sewerage Company (WASCO).

Funded by the Canadian Government, the program expanded continuously and by the late 1980s, 90 per cent of St Lucia's population had access to pipe-borne water. Meanwhile, a permanent solution needed to be found for the increasing pressure on water supplies in the Castries-Cap Estate area, due to population expansion and the growth of tourism. The UWP Government found the solution in the Roseau Dam: with a capacity of 700 million gallons, 130 feet high, 600 feet long and 850 feet at its widest point, occupying nearly 200 acres of land and costing a massive $115 million, this was by far the largest infrastructural work ever undertaken in St Lucia. It was financed by the World Bank, the Canadian International Development Agency, the Caribbean Development Bank, the Organization of Petrol Exporting Countries and, of course, the Government itself. The dam was completed in 1996 and named, appropriately, after John Compton himself.

The expansion of pipe-born water around the island was not just a matter of convenience but also of public health. It led to the elimination of several water-borne diseases, including bilharzia, which afflicted and killed countless people up until the 1970s.

Air and seaports

The UWP Government also established a number of quasi-government entities: the National Development Corporation to spur (light) industrialization, the Housing and Urban Development Corporation to organize land development and housing projects, and the St Lucia Air and Sea Ports Authority to manage the island's air and sea ports. In the 1980s, Port Castries was upgraded with six cargo berths, a roll-on-roll-off pier, a container park and two cruise ship berths (later upgraded to six berths for mega-cruisers). Following the 1948 fire, the Conway area turned into a depressed slum, infamous for crime and poverty. Plans for redevelopment of the Castries waterfront started in 1966, when the Government transformed Sans Soucis into a modern residential area, and rationalized traffic in Castries by opening the Castries-Gros Islet Highway. In 1980, Conway was finally targetted, the residents re-housed and four high-rise office blocks erected, transforming the Castries waterfront into a modern business district.

In Vieux Fort, the air and sea ports were considerably expanded as well. Attempts for a 200-room luxury hotel in Vieux Fort failed in 1963 but on 1 May 1971, the 256-room Halcyon Days Hotel was opened (then St Lucia's largest hotel) and that same weekend, the upgraded Beane Field airport runway became *Hewanorra International Airport*: opening St Lucia's gateway to North America and Europe with its capacity to accommodate long-range jet planes.

Industrialization-by-invitation

Industrialization-by-invitation (a concept developed by our own Nobel laureate Sir Arthur Lewis) became popular in developing countries during the 1970s and the Government of St Lucia soon earmarked Vieux Fort for this purpose. Until then, manufacturing in St Lucia had consisted of relatively small-scale operations (paper products, soft drinks, cigarettes, copra products, bay rum, clay and furniture) but this changed in the early 1970s when WINERA opened a $5 million carton manufacturing plant (a joint venture between four Windward islands and a Venezuelan paper company) and the Windward and Leeward Brewery Ltd opened a large plant in Vieux Fort (1975). Other factories followed, producing household chemicals, adhesives, condiments, electronic sensors, clothing, toys, gloves, and so on.

When the Caribbean Development Bank was established in 1970, St Lucia took out loans to construct factory shells in order to attract new investors. Industrialization took off quite dramatically at first, quickly joining agriculture and tourism to form the tripod on which the island recorded successive years of economic growth. By 1989, a decade after independence, industrial exports totalled over $100 million, compared to just $30 million in 1979. There were more than 200 manufacturing enterprises on the island, the large majority of them locally owned. The Industrial Estate at Vieux Fort was the main hub of activity, providing employment and job training for several thousand people from all over the south. St Lucia was considered the most aggressive of the smaller Caribbean territories in pursuing trade with the US under the Caribbean Basin Initiative. But the decade of the 1990s was unkind to manufacturing in St Lucia. The sector suffered serious setbacks as several companies moved their operations to even lower wage cost centers in Asia and Middle and South America instead, and some 2000 jobs were lost. Attempts to shift the focus to the provision of information technology services instead were hampered by the relatively high cost of telecommunications in St Lucia.

Tourism, tourism, tourism

In 1979, St Lucia counted less than 2000 hotel rooms, received fewer than 100 000 visitors annually (both by air and by sea) and earned just $30 million per year in visitor expenditure. Two decades later, the number of rooms had doubled, arrivals soared to 630 000 and expenditure was estimated at $770 million. The upswing was primarily due to the arrival of all-inclusive resorts. The all-inclusive concept (in which guests pay for all aspects of their holiday in one lump sum before even setting foot on St Lucian soil) was initially accompanied by fears that it would undermine ordinary hotels and restaurants. Nevertheless, before long, all-inclusives accounted for half of all the hotel rooms and by 1994, out of St Lucia's twelve major hotels, eight were all-inclusive. It gave St Lucia the highest ratio of all-inclusive rooms in the entire Eastern Caribbean and the island was soon considered an all-inclusive holiday destination.[692] The advantages of all-inclusives were their high and continuous rates of occupancy, the demand for airlift they created and their marketing power - something which St Lucia's own meagre tourism budgets could never achieve. On the downside were concerns about a lack of linkages with the local economy (particularly agriculture), the absence of non-menial employment opportunities for St Lucians, and retention of profits overseas.

Cruise ship tourism also expanded phenomenally during this period. Thanks to the Government's foresight in upgrading Port Castries, St Lucia did not miss out on the sector's worldwide growth. Huge investments were made to create the Pointe Seraphine Complex, with berths built especially for cruise liners. It was a far cry from the days when cargo and passengers competed for space on the docks. Pointe Seraphine also took St Lucia into the era of shopping malls. Another success story was the St Lucia Jazz Festival, now widely acclaimed as one of the best in the world. First experimented with in 1992, the festival was intended to market the island abroad and cushion the effects of the traditionally quiet month of May. It quickly grew in stature and magnitude, raising St Lucia's profile as a holiday destination globally and introducing locals and visitors alike to some of the biggest entertainment artistes in the world.

Secondary education for all

Both the SLP and UWP placed education at the top of their agendas during their governance, and since the 1960s there has been a concerted effort to bring (junior) secondary schools to communities all around St Lucia. At the same time, the old military buildings on the Morne were transformed into a place of learning, becoming a Teacher's College in 1968 (until then located at Sans Souci), adding a Technical College in 1970 and an 'A'-level college in 1972. In 1985, The Morne Education Complex was renamed Sir Arthur Lewis Community College. By the start of the new millennium, the SLP Government attained the goal of guaranteeing a secondary school place for every St Lucian child who qualified for one.

The 1980s and early 90s: emerging social problems

By the mid 1980s, John Compton's Government was comfortably in control and the economy was back on track. Agriculture, manufacturing, tourism and construction all showed marked improvements, the economy was expanding once more and in November 1985, Compton announced that St Lucia had '*turned the corner and is now out of the woods.*' In 1986, banana production exceeded 100 000 tons and, with exchange rates for the British pound higher than they had been for some time, banana growers were enjoying some of their best returns in the industry's 30-year history. It was the year when bananas truly deserved their sobriquet 'Green Gold.'

But from a social and moral point of view, times were rapidly changing. In the wake of increased assertiveness, the lesser gods of aggression and recklessness began to rear their ugly heads. Although a certain level of violence in society was no novelty, the advent of drugs and gang brutality were. Vehicular accidents and their associated death toll started to rise and, increasingly, simple acts of indiscipline spiralled out of control. Despite more intensive patrolling, the police force was having a harder time keeping crime under control.

In 1985, St Lucia recorded its first deaths from Aids, marking the beginning of a new social and health problem which was to take a serious toll on the island's population. High unemployment, increasing drug abuse and the high rate of population growth were other burning concerns, threatening to nullify the progress that was being made in education and health care services. At 33 births per 1000 persons, St Lucia's birth rate was among the highest in the Western Hemisphere and a number of new strategies, including peer counselling for teenagers, expanding family planning services and a media education drive, were mounted in an effort to bring population growth under control.

Environmentally, St Lucia was beginning to lose ground as well. Islandwide, indiscriminate agricultural practices had bared hillsides, eroded soils and damaged watersheds. In November 1984, heavy rainfall resulted in a 10-acre landslide at Forestière caused by farmers having cleared land for bananas. Illegal sand mining for use in residential and commercial construction damaged dozens of small and large beaches, causing many of them to turn into rocky scars or disappear altogether.

Meanwhile, the militancy and angry partisanship of the 1979-82 period never lurked far beneath the surface. The St Lucia Labour Party had regained a level of unity under Julian Hunte and returned to the opposition benches. Odlum's Progressive Labour Party (PLP) was busy doing the same, organizing marches and other forms of protests. In 1983, police arrested fourteen young St Lucians attempting to travel to Libya under the auspices of the PLP. Odlum said they were legitimate recipients of scholarships from that North-African country, but Compton accused them of being terrorist recruits, claiming some of them had criminal records and others were illiterate. David England, a long-time British resident of St Lucia, was implicated in the affair and Government passed a special law to have him deported.

In 1985 and '86, George Odlum made repeated overtures to merge his PLP with the SLP to unite the opposition forces but he was rebuffed each time. Meanwhile, the SLP grew confident that it could once again assume the mantle of government at the next general elections. Those elections came on 6 April 1987 and again on 30 April: producing an historic double election within the span of just one month.

The SLP had promised it would bounce back and to some extent, it did. In the April 6 elections, the UWP barely scraped home with nine seats to the SLP's eight. It was a sharp rebuff for the UWP, which had entered the elections with a commanding 14-3 majority in the House of Assembly. A week later, Parliament convened but was promptly dissolved again by Compton. In an effort to obtain a better majority, Compton ordered new general elections for 30 April. Odlum's PLP had suffered badly in the April 6 election, and so the April 30 election became a direct fight between the SLP and UWP. For 24 hours, it looked like Compton had played his cards right. The UWP emerged with 10 seats to the SLP's seven. But in Anse la Raye/Canaries, the UWP candidate was ahead by just three votes and so a recount was ordered. In a charged atmosphere, the results were reversed, leaving the UWP once again with just a one-seat majority: 9-8. This time, Compton appeared resigned to the fact and on May 26, he presented his Government's new budget. But less than one week later, on June 1, as the House reconvened, the newly elected SLP

Member of Parliament for Laborie, Neville Cenac, strolled into the chamber and headed straight for a seat amongst the UWP parliamentarians - leaving his SLP colleagues (and even some in the UWP camp) dumbstruck. Cenac was appointed Minister of Foreign Affairs later that day. Cenac's crossing of the floor provided the governing UWP with the extra breathing space Compton so badly wanted - but it also caused much bad blood with the SLP.

The new UWP Government continued on its path of infrastructural development and economic growth but an escalating drug problem, high unemployment and a significant rise in (unresolved) crime commanded much of its main attention. The Royal St Lucia Police Force was repeatedly accused of inefficiency and in January 1988, Prime Minister Compton appointed a two-man Commission of Enquiry to investigate the force and make recommendations. Meanwhile, a spate of crime rocked the nation and the media soon spoke of '*Black September*'. In a raid on a suspected drug outlet, police discovered what they believed was a hit list with the names of several magistrates and senior police officers. In early October 1988, on the basis of the enquiry's findings, Compton announced the termination of three senior police officers, saying: '*A number of people are using the uniform as a cover-up for criminal activity and have been too intimately connected with persons involved in the drug trade for them not to bring suspicion on themselves.*' But by then, the illicit drug trade was flourishing in St Lucia. On the morning of 7 July 1988, 60 armed policemen swooped down on a house in Vieux Fort and seized cocaine, firearms and ammunition, $250 000 in suspected stolen jewellery and $93 000 in cash. Eight persons were arrested, charged with 32 offences and bailed to the sum of $260 000. It was one of the biggest drug raids ever on the island. In November, in a rare show of co-operation, Government and opposition members closed ranks in the House of Assembly to support a series of long-promised drug laws which significantly increased the penalties for offenders and allowed the state to confiscate property suspected of having been acquired with the spoils of the drug trade.

Despite the new legislation, St Lucia continued to struggle with a growing drug culture, which carried in its wake various social ills ranging from murder, robbery, shootings, addiction and HIV/Aids to sexual violence and domestic abuse. Until the 1980s, marijuana had been the major illegal narcotic substance in use on the island but by the start of the 1990s, cocaine and its cheap and ultra-addictive by-product, crack ,were gaining tremendously in popularity. St Lucia quickly became a busy transfer point, both by air and by sea, for hard drugs originating in South America *en route* for North America and Europe. At the same time, marijuana was routinely traded between islands on small fishing vessels. Police continued to intercept small and large shipments of drugs, both cocaine and marijuana, and even some trade union officials declared drugs to be the biggest threat to St Lucia's future.

At the same time, domestic abuse grew more violent as well. An absolute low point was the 1989 Rackliffe murder, in which Mary Rackliffe, a mother of four who had threatened to report her common-law husband (Sylvester 'Shaka' JnBaptiste) to the police for the alleged rape of one of her daughters, was hacked to death. JnBaptiste fled the country and was never tried. The murder generated much discussion and debate about the abuse of women and domestic violence in general, and prompted the St Lucia Crisis Center to raise its public profile.

General elections in 1992

In the run-up to the 1992 general elections, the UWP Government disclosed plans to change three electoral constituencies. SLP protesters led by Julian Hunte interrupted a meeting of the Electoral and Boundaries Commission and, in the commotion, a glass window was broken. A few days later, Compton referred to the incident in a speech, saying '*Some of us break ground, but others break glass.*' The remark annoyed Hunte, who approached Compton and, in front of eagerly-running television cameras, told him: '*We'll break the glass in your ass.*' Footage of the incident was greeted with widespread dismay and several commentators later insisted it was this incident, more than anything else, which cost Labour the election of 1992. After a campaign marked more by showbiz gimmicks and entertainment than substantial debate, on 27 April 1992, the UWP ran away with an 11-6 victory. A record number of four women were appointed to the Senate, where there had only ever been one at any given time in either the House of Assembly or the Senate. It was a sign that politics in St Lucia was coming of age.

Seeing his Prime Ministership extended into a third consecutive term, John Compton suggested early on that he might step down midway. Although the UWP was back in Government with a comfortable 11-6 margin, the party's political agility would be severely taxed as dark days lay ahead for St Lucia's main income-generating industry: bananas.

17

The rise and fall of 'green gold': globalization and New Labour

St Lucia's fate in the second half of the twentieth century revolved around the rise and fall of bananas. In the 1950s, bananas gave the island a radically new lease on life, breaking the power of the plantocracy and ushering in an unrivalled process of modernization and democratization. The 1990s found St Lucia grappling with a globalizing, post-colonial world which fast rendered its traditionally protected markets obsolete.

The banana industry was structured according to the original 1954 contract with Geest Industries Ltd, which gave that company the exclusive right to all Windward Islands bananas of exportable quality. While Geest took up exportable bananas at the docks, the returns to the St Lucia Banana Growers Association (SLBGA) and farmers were determined only after the sale of the consignment and the deduction of costs for shipping, grading, ripening, distribution and marketing. The contract was subject to periodic review but its original structure remained unaltered, giving Geest a relatively risk-free contractual position. The fact that, over the years, John van Geest had developed warm personal relationships with the powers-that-be in the Windward Islands, made re-negotiation awkward.

All the while, the Windward Islands were enjoying 'preferential treatment' in the British market by virtue of their status as former colonies. In 1986, Geest became a public company and Prime Minister Compton warned St Lucians that the new shareholders would not '*treat Geest as a social service concerned with the welfare of the Windward Islands farmers, but rather as a commercial entity which must return profits on their investment.*'

By the late 1980s, production costs were on the rise. At the same time, the market demanded higher quality. Anxiety about the future of the industry as Britain prepared to join the European Union sparked debate among politicians and industry officials. The worries compounded existing acrimony between the Government and the opposition SLP, who threw its support behind farmer agitation when low prices (due to falling exchange rates for the British pound) began to rock the industry. Banana revenue recovered somewhat in 1990 but farmers continued to agitate, demanding control over the SLBGA. In May

1993, a new pressure group emerged: the Banana Salvation Committee (BSC) led by activist farmers, Patrick Joseph and Abel Wilson.

As feared, on 1 January 1993, the European Single Market came into effect. On 1 July 1993, the banana exports of the Windward Islands became subjected to a regime of quotas and tariffs agreed under the Lomé Convention. In no time, the market became flooded with bananas and prices collapsed. The already worrisome situation was aggravated by a second scare when the Disputes Panel of the General Agreement on Tariff and Trade (GATT) ruled that what the European Community had agreed with respect to Britain's former colonies in Africa, the Caribbean and the Pacific constituted a preferential trading arrangement which violated the principles of free trade and therefore needed to be abolished. Implementation of this decision was postponed for a while but the ruling increased fears that soon, St Lucia's bananas would have to compete in a totally free market. The Government decided that streamlining the industry was now a matter of extreme urgency.

While the Government pursued its agenda of restructuring the banana industry, by the middle of September 1993, farmers in Mon Repos, backed by the BSC, decided to flex their muscles. They announced a strike, demanding a greater share in the money earned by Geest, a minimum price for their fruit, an end to mismanagement practices at the SLBGA, and a reduction in the costs of production. Two Government Ministers met with the BSC on 26 September, agreed on a five-point plan of action and left the meeting believing that the strike would be called off. They were wrong. The farmers insisted on personal guarantees from Prime Minster John Compton, who happened to be off-island at the time. Compton pleaded with them from the United States and urged them to avoid action that would jeopardise St Lucia's market position, but the farmers insisted on a face-to-face meeting with Compton, to be held two days before the strike notice expired. For reasons said to be connected with his flight arrangements, Compton did not arrive back in time for the October 5 deadline and the farmers went on strike.

The fatal banana strike of 1993

Within hours, barricades were burning along the east coast highway and mob rule was imposed in the Dennery valley. The nation saw television images of missile-pelting farmers doing battle with police officers trying to clear road blocks, and heard reports of intimidation and arson against farmers who had chosen to ignore the call to strike. Police restraint during the first two days of the protest was well in evidence and intensified further on the third day. Soon after his return to the island, Prime Minister Compton got a first-hand taste of the farmers' anger when a stone-throwing brigade near Richefond,

Dennery, attacked his car, barely allowing him to escape physical injury.[693] After commuters and visitors were left stranded as the road from the Vieux Fort airport to Castries was rendered impassable, Compton decided that enough was enough and ordered the police to do whatever was necessary to get the traffic flowing again. On Thursday 7 October, the third day of the strike, police officers moved in with tractors and automatic weapons. A confrontation ensued in the Mabouya Valley and, with fear and adrenaline running high on both sides, the police ended up shooting dead two young protestors: Julius and Randy Joseph. Several other people were injured, including two policemen. The country was shocked and outraged. Anderson Reynolds recorded: '*The funerals were national affairs. Motorcades of farmers originating as far as Micoud, with great pageantry and fanfare, joined their comrades in the valley, helping to mourn and bury their fallen brethren. The people, many waving placards calling for justice and the resignation of the Prime Minister ... came out in masses, causing traffic jams and chaos in the valley.*'[694]

In an address to the nation later that night, Compton said the action had been taken '*to preserve the industry and ensure that it is operated in the best interest of the farmers.*' Within hours, mediation by the Chamber of Commerce ended the strike and the farmers were given a price increase. The next day, in another nationwide address, Compton flayed and dissolved the SLBGA board, accusing it of bankrupting the association. Within the short space of three years, Compton revealead, the SLBGA had gone from a surplus of $16 million (in 1990) to a debt of $23 million (1993).

Not surprisingly, the St Lucia Labour Party condemned the Government's handling of the crisis. In January 1994, Compton established a committee to devise a structure to replace the SLBGA. Meanwhile, low prices were taking their toll. Farmers aligned with the Banana Salvation Committee (BSC) began to lobby the Government to open talks with American fruit company Chiquita, hoping for a better marketing deal than the one offered by Geest. In late 1993, a team of Chiquita officials visited the Windward Islands and held discussions with Government leaders. By February 1994, the BSC was organizing another 'no cut' strike, protesting Government's plans to put the debt-ridden SLBGA into receivership. A number of boxing plants were razed to the ground and defiant farmers at the Roseau Model Farms announced that they were prepared to defend themselves with force. Other non-BSC farmers requested police protection to be able to harvest their fruit.

In September 1994, tropical storm Debbie caused some of the worst flooding and landslides in recent memory, damaging roads and ravaging banana plantations. For the first time in seventeen years, production fell below 100 000 tons. But farmer agitation continued unabated and in, December, another strike was called. Once again, the action was marred by vandalism.

On east coast farms, 2800 bunches of fruit were maliciously destroyed and sixteen packing sheds burnt down. One farmer in Ti Rocher, Micoud, discovered that all his banana trees had been cut down overnight.

A glut on the market, continuing opposition from (US-owned) Latin American producers against preferential treatment of Windward Islands bananas in the European market, and plans by Geest to sell its banana interests did not help. But in April 1995, the Windward Islands Governments accepted plans for restructuring the banana industry which included less governmental control, a reclassification programme to eliminate marginal producers and the restoration of financial stability to the banana growers associations.

In March 1994, the Windward Islands Banana Development and Exporting Company (WIBDECO) was incorporated. A year later, WIBDECO negotiated a new contract with Geest, giving the islands more of a say and putting pressure on Geest to become more competitive. Not long after, Geest put its banana interests on the market. One of the interested parties was Chiquita Ltd: the same US-owned multinational company that had opposed preferential treatment of Windward Islands bananas in the EU market and was at the root of the current malaise. The Windward Islands fought back and, together with the British company Fyffes, successfully trumped Chiquita's bid. And so the Windward Islands started 1996 as the proud owners of the Geest banana business which included the shares of six Geest companies in England, Europe and Costa Rica as well as a number of subsidiary companies and the two ships *Geest St Lucia* and *Geest Dominica*.

Labour's vision for bananas

Elections were due in 1997 and naturally, the future of the banana industry took centre stage during the campaign. The Labour Party, in its manifesto, declared that '*the banana industry belongs to those whose land and labour produce bananas*' and promised it would '*restore trust and confidence in the industry*' by returning full control and ownership of the industry to the farmers. The SLP promised to transform the SLBGA into a commercial entity, enabling it to take decisions on the basis of cost-and-profit calculations and rendering it more agile to cope with competition. The SLP also promised to introduce profit-sharing by linking farmers' share ownership to their individual export earnings and the profitability of the new company.

The political mood in 1996 was one of excitement. There was a strong sense that the UWP was worn out by the banana troubles, industrial unrest and a damaging UN scandal, while a fresh team of 'New Labour' candidates stood champing at the bit and ready for another turn at governance. Around the same time that Kenny Anthony emerged as a promising SLP candidate for the prime ministerial seat, John Compton decided the time was ripe for him to bow out of active politics.

The UN scandal

To understand why Compton (along with his long-standing deputy George Mallet) threw in the towel, we need to go back to 1995. Coming hard on the heels of the prolonged problems in the banana industry, that year proved to be a watershed for Compton and the UWP. It was not only a year of scandal, industrial instability and political tension, but also a year in which the arrogance of power caused the Government to drift further and further away from the people.

By January 1995, the gulf between Government and trade unions had widened to such an extent that the unions joined together in an Industrial Solidarity Pact (ISP) and listed a *Charter of Demands*. But the biggest disturbance of 1995 was the United Nations scandal, which broke with a speculative newspaper article claiming that future UN aid to St Lucia was in jeopardy due to the embezzlement of earlier funds. Following widespread speculation and demands by the SLP and the press for an explanation, Compton eventually came out and stated that the Perez Guerrero Trust Fund (PGTF) had, in 1990 and 1991, provided US$110 800 for two projects in St Lucia, while the UN International Drug Programme had donated some other funds as well. Although these funds had been negotiated and received by St Lucia's then Ambassador to the UN, Charles Fleming, Compton said his Government had not consented to the transactions, nor had it been aware of them at the time.

In the flurry that followed, Fleming started spilling the beans. He said he had negotiated and accepted the funds on the orders of then-party chairman Henry Giraudy, with approval from Prime Minister Compton. Fleming claimed that Giraudy had suggested that a UN salary be arranged for political hopeful Rufus Bousquet, who indeed won the seat for Choiseul in 1992. Fleming also claimed that the UN funds had been used to finance the UWP's 1992 election campaign. Giraudy had since died, but Rufus Bousquet took to the media to clear his name. He admitted that Fleming had arranged a UN contract for him, but said he was not being paid by the PGTF nor had money from that agency been used to finance his election campaign. In a dramatic development, Compton subsequently stripped Bousquet of his ministerial responsibilities for having defied his gag orders.

In May 1995, a three-man Commission of Inquiry got underway. Thirteen witnesses, including Fleming and Compton, gave evidence. Fleming sought and was granted permission to go to New York to fetch crucial documents concerning the UN funds. He left the island and never returned to the inquiry, raising serious suspicions over the credibility of his claims. In its final report, the commission concluded that Fleming had indeed solicited and procured two PGTF grants and that the funds in question appeared to have been '*converted to Dr Fleming's personal use.*' But the really burning questions - who in the Government and the UWP had known about the grants and when; did any UWP politicians benefit from the funds; and did UN funds pay for the UWP's 1992 campaign or not - remained frustratingly unanswered.

Public sector strikes and sick-outs

Political storms like the UN scandal added spice and substance to the swelling tide of resentment against the Government but in the end, the straw that broke the camel's back, was the protracted wage negotiation for collective agreements with public servants (1992-5). Public sector unions asked for a 30 per cent general pay increase, to which Government responded with an offer of 3 per cent over three years. It did not help that, around the same time, top managers within the civil service were given salary increases of between 45 to 60 per cent plus benefits. In April 1995, the unions staged a two-day mass 'sick-out' to express their displeasure with salary negotiations, the disparity in salary increases and a number of other grievances. The country did not grind to a halt but it gave a taste of bigger things to come.

With the UN scandal raging, the Industrial Solidarity Pact unions became increasingly vocal in their condemnation of the Government. There was another two-day national strike in May, causing the (partial) closure of schools, Customs, post offices and sections of the port. Protest action continued to the point where the opposition SLP even boycotted the 1995-6 budget debate. For six more weeks, strikes affected schools, post offices and Customs but internal divisions within the Industrial Solidarity Pact eventually broke the spirit of the rank and file and the unions accepted an 8 per cent pay increase.

It did not, however, abate resentment against the Government. A controversial telephone tax was greeted with harsh criticism from consumers, the press and opposition political parties and resulted in protest marches. Besides industrial unrest, crime continued to be a major concern as well, with the St Lucia Hotel and Tourism Association condemning the Government for not grasping the full magnitude of the problem and the National Advisory Committee on Crime dismissing Government's promises to get tough with criminals as '*talk and more talk.*'

Changing the guard: anointing Vaughan Lewis

By late 1995, rumours were rife that the ageing and tiring leaders of the UWP were under pressure from within to give way to fresh blood. In January 1996, at an extraordinary party conference held in the UWP stronghold of Desruisseaux, political leader and Prime Minister of 32 years, John Compton, along with his deputy leader George Mallet, announced that they would not seek re-election. In a tearful farewell before a buzzing hall of delegates and supporters, Compton literally passed the torch (*flambeau* or *flanbo*, the symbol of the party) to his successor: technocrat and academic Dr Vaughan Lewis. What had been billed as the election of a new leader turned out to be the installation of an anointed one. Later that month, Queen Elizabeth II knighted John Compton in recognition of his service to the country. It was widely considered a worthy end to a long-standing political career and the start of a well-deserved retirement for *Sir* John. George Mallet gave up his seat for Castries Central (after 38 unbroken years),[695] Vaughan Lewis won the subsequent by-election and on 2 April 1996, Lewis was inaugurated as the island's sixth Prime Minister. But the manner of Lewis' rise to power did not sit well with many people, even within the UWP, and it was said that his fourteen years as Director-General of the Organization of Eastern Caribbean States had left him politically inexperienced. George Odlum (who, in a strange twist of fortune, had been appointed permanent representative to the UN by John Compton) took leave of his post to oppose Lewis in the by-election for Castries Central, telling St Lucians that with the pre-orchestrated transition they were being asked to buy '*a pig in a poke.*' The SLP supported this view but both the SLP and Odlum's latest political party, the *National Front*, were roundly beaten by Vaughan Lewis.

Hail Kenny Anthony: New Labour's landslide victory

With general elections fast approaching, the SLP's defeat in the by-election kicked the last leg out from underneath Julian Hunte's chair. After twelve unbroken years at the helm of the SLP, he resigned as political leader and leader of the opposition in the House of Assembly. Immediately, speculation about his successor soared. The name of Dr Kenny Anthony - then Counsel-General to the Caribbean Community in Guyana - quickly gained currency. On 21 April 1996, exactly three months after Vaughan Lewis was selected as the UWP's new political leader, the SLP elected an unopposed Kenny Anthony as its new leader. As 1996 rolled by, the SLP consolidated its reorganization, introducing what was heralded as '*a more participatory and democratic*' process of candidate selection and reintegrating into the party various factions of the opposition, most notably George Odlum, his younger brother Jon Odlum and Calixte George's Citizens Democratic Party (CDP).

By April 1997, there was still no indication as to when the next elections would be called but the SLP's well-oiled machine was under full steam. During the budget presentation that month, John Compton formally bowed out of local politics after 43 unbroken years as a Member of Parliament. The meeting was used to pay tribute to Compton and two other party stalwarts who departed the scene at the same time: George Mallet and Minister of Education Allan Bousquet. With these niceties out of the way, the date for the new general elections was announced.

On 23 May 1997, the most eagerly-awaited general election in St Lucia's post-independence history produced a sensational result: the landslide return to power of the St Lucia Labour Party and the complete routing of the UWP which had dominated the political scene for what seemed, to many, an eternity. So stunning was the result - SLP 16 seats, UWP 1 - that for months afterwards, the vanquished party remained in a seeming state of paralysis. One of the first results to come in was from Castries Central and the failure of UWP-leader Vaughan Lewis to recapture his own constituency sent early warning signals that something really dramatic was about to unfold. Lewis was upstaged by newcomer Sarah Flood, in a seat that had not voted Labour in 40 years. Over the next three hours of ballot counting, the bafflement continued with more and greater shocks as the Labour Party ended the evening winning all but one (Micoud North) of the seventeen seats. Even Kenny Anthony himself, Labour's new leader, expressed surprise at the margin of victory, describing it as '*an overwhelming mandate and an overwhelming responsibility*.' The new Prime Minister was magnanimous in victory and throwing out an olive branch to the opposition in recognition of the fact that traditional UWP supporters had contributed to his party's triumph.

The SLP won 60 per cent of the popular vote against just 35.8 per cent for the UWP: a clear indication that the tide had truly turned. There had been indications long before polling day that the UWP was in trouble, but it was the advent of Kenny Anthony to the leadership of the SLP which allowed that party to attract hordes of die-hard UWP's on polling day. With hindsight, many believed it was Vaughan Lewis' procrastination in calling the elections which allowed the SLP time to get its house in order and wipe the UWP off the board.

Labour had presented the electorate with a well-crafted manifesto, *Contract of Faith*, in which it promised a whole new direction for St Lucia on the eve of the new millennium. In obvious reference to the 1979-82 debacle, Labour promised that it had undergone '*fundamental change, both in direction and outlook*' and was offering St Lucians '*a new vision, a new Labour Party and a new St Lucia*.' It even referred to itself as 'New Labour' and, as such, promised transparency and accountability in all its handling of the country's affairs. What Kenny Anthony's new SLP emphasized, time and again, was that St Lucia needed not just a change of Government but a change in the way in which political leadership was exercised. It vowed to stamp out the abuse of public office for private gain and to appoint a Commission of Inquiry to *'review all cases of alleged corruption, determine which instances provide a basis for prosecution and ... to recommend measures to prevent recurrence of these abuses.'*

The Blom-Cooper investigation

True to his word, Prime Minister Anthony immediately appointed a commissioner to investigate alleged acts of impropriety and abuse of power under UWP rule. Retired Grenadian OECS Judge, Monica Joseph, made little headway, however, as former Prime Ministers Compton and Lewis challenged her appointment in court on the grounds of bias. The High Court denied the Compton/Lewis charge but the Court of Appeal upheld it. In the end, a new commissioner was appointed: British jurist Sir Louis Blom-Cooper. In the course of 1998, Blom-Cooper conducted his interviews and finished his investigation, but it took a long time before there was any hint that a final report was ready. In March 1999, Prime Minister Anthony finally acknowledged that he was in possession of the Blom-Cooper report and promised it would be made public. By July, the report was still under wraps. Eventually, Compton and Lewis appealed to Blom-Cooper directly for his intervention on the '*strength of his moral authority*' to get the Government to release the report, contending that their reputations were at stake. Incidentally, by then, John Compton had returned to lead and reorganize the UWP in the wake of his party's 1997 pummeling at the polls.

The report was finally published in early August 1999, two years after the commission's appointment. After all the hype, the conclusions were anti-climatic. Blom-Cooper reported he had found no evidence of corruption, '*only a high degree of maladministration in government, amounting to impropriety on the part of Ministers and, palpably, one public official.*' He did however add that bad governance was a breeding ground for corruption. '*I have discerned in St Lucia a culture of studied indifference, or at the very least, inattention to the practice, even the concept of public accountability.*' No criminal charges were laid on the basis of the report.

New Labour in action

Hardly a month into the job, the new SLP Government was served its first major challenge when prisoners in the antiquated and badly over-crowded prison on Bridge Street set fire to the facility, in an attempt to draw attention to their abysmal living conditions. The fire caused extensive damage but it would be some years before a new prison complex was opened at Bordelais, Dennery - along with a series of new police and fire stations around the island.

Meanwhile, the SLP started to put in place the administrative machinery needed to implement a range of new economic and social programmes. A party convention endorsing 'affirmative action' in the allocation of contracts and jobs sparked much debate, but only the new Foreign Affairs Minister, George Odlum, opposed the resolution and urged his colleagues to '*avoid spiteful firings and politically-motivated dismissals.*'

The SLP broke off diplomatic relations with Taiwan (after thirteen years) and established links with the People's Republic of China instead.

History was made in September 1997, when Dr Pearlette Louisy was sworn in as St Lucia's fifth Governal General since independence, making her the youngest Head of State (at age 52) and the first woman to hold the position. Prior to this, she had been principal of the Sir Arthur Lewis Community College. Having started as a pupil-teacher at the age of 12 in her home village of Laborie, Louisy had gone on to earn doctorate degrees in Linguistics and Education at Bristol University. Soon after her appointment, Dr Louisy was ennobled and thus became Dame Pearlette. She turned out to be a different type of Head of State to what the island had previously known: a staunch defender of traditional St Lucian culture who did not avoid burning social issues. She made no secret of her love for, and belief in, the positive value of St Lucian Kwéyòl and became the first Head of State to address the House of Assembly in that language, after the SLP Government enacted a measure allowing Parliament to be bilingual. This re-valuation of Kwéyòl was supported by the publication of a Kwéyòl New Testament[696] and a Kwéyòl dictionary. Radio and television talk shows increasingly featured Kwéyòl-speaking guests and callers as well.

Another undisputed highlight during the early tenure of Kenny Anthony's Government was the visit (in July 1998) of South African President, Nelson Mandela.[697]

But there were some low points as well. Concerns about crime continued unabated. The SLP Government declared a gun amnesty which yielded 33 firearms and some 2000 rounds of ammunition but before long, a reputed drug dealer was shot to death in his car in broad daylight, yielding St Lucia its first drive-by shooting. In February 1999, disturbances at the prison were followed by a search of the cells, revealing a host of illicit items including cutlasses, knives, screwdrivers, television sets and transformers. Just weeks later, in March 1999, the principal of the Vieux Fort Comprehensive Secondary School was attacked in her office and viciously wounded by a student whom she had suspended for possession of an illegal substance. The incident outraged the country and resulted in teachers, parents and students demonstrating for zero tolerance to violence. Another march, organised by the Seventh Day Adventist Church to protest against a range of social ills (including gun violence, gambling and drugs) brought 2000 people onto the streets. Nevertheless, the end of the year found St Lucia gripped by another wave of crime, including the brutal rape-murder of a school girl inside her family home.

The Helenair affair

It was not long before the new Labour Government's commitment to the principles of transparency and accountability was put to the test. In August 1999, three senators failed to support a Government guarantee for a $4 million loan to locally owned airline, Helenair. The measure had smoothly cleared the House of Assembly (thanks to Labour's 16-1 majority) but in the Senate, ruling party appointees Rick Wayne voted against the measure and Tessa Mangal and Patrick Joseph abstained. Wayne said he required a validation from the Government that would support the guarantee, Mangal called her abstention an act of conscience and Joseph said his decision was a reflection of his general disgust with the Senate. He did not elaborate. Prime Minister Anthony, displeased, fired all three senators, stating this was a '*political issue, where the government required political support and the credibility of the government and Prime Minister was an issue on that matter. When those occasions arise for any government it requires the support of those persons who are appointed in the Senate.*'

In a fiery retort, Mangal said it was '*a simple case of double standards*' for a Government which preached transparency and accountability to cast aside senators who refused to act as '*rubber stamps*'. The affair seriously scarred New Labour, not least because thwarted senator and talk show host *cum* newspaper editor Rick Wayne, used the incident at every opportunity to exemplify further alleged acts of governmental hypocrisy.

Disputed signs of economic growth

Another matter which cast an early shadow over the Labour Government was the repeated assurance from Dr Anthony that the country's economy had stabilised and that recovery was underway. The outgoing president of the Employers Federation, George Noon (along with several ordinary citizens) flatly contradicted this, saying that several businesses were in fact downsizing and that from all appearances, the economy had slowed down considerably.

Although the nation's economic figures in the late 1990s may have shown some cause for optimism, thousands of working St Lucians were tightening their belts and it undermined people's confidence that the Government appeared to be denying what they daily encountered in their lives.

The apparent disparity may be explained by the fact that money earned from tourism and manufacturing did not have the same income-multiplier effect as that earned from bananas. Banana revenue remained within the communities and circulated more extensively and more deeply due to the simple economic principle that the lower one's income, the more likely a person is to spend an additional dollar of income. In other words: a poor person will more easily spend an extra dollar, whereas a rich person (whose basic needs are already satisfied) is more likely to save it.[698] The transition from bananas to tourism may have looked good on paper but in practice, the disappearance of the 'green gold' touched many working class St Lucians where it hurt most, and no amount of happy talk could change that. A popular calypso highlighted the Prime Minister's alleged forked tongue by referring to him as '*Kenny and Tony*'. The nickname haunted Kenny Anthony for the rest of his term.

Patrick Joseph and the St Lucia Banana Corporation

Unrest in the banana industry had helped Labour to power in 1997, but the party's ascent did not magically solve the problems. True to its word, the Labour Government dissolved the SLBGA and in 1998, with much pomp and ceremony, the St Lucia Banana Corporation (SLBC) was born. The Government wiped out the SLBGA's $44 million debt burden and provided the SLBC with a clean slate, but many farmers were wary of the new organization and their trepidation only grew when the Government appointed Patrick Joseph as chairman of the SLBC. Many held Joseph and his Banana Salvation Committee responsible for the years of turmoil in the industry, and considered his appointment a payback measure by the Government for the strikes which had contributed to the downfall of Compton's UWP. While Dr Anthony called for an end to division in the industry, dissenting farmers took advantage of the newly liberalized environment to form their own banana trading company: Tropical Quality Fruit (TQF).

Around the same time, a ruling by the World Trade Organisation (WTO) put a conclusive end to preferential access for Windward Islands fruit in the European market, creating the kind of 'level playing field' which a truly globalized world market supposedly requires to function optimally. In effect, Windward Islands fruit grown by peasant-proprietors on small holdings were thrown into open competition with fruit produced on massive plantations in

Central or South America, owned by US multinational corporations such as Chiquita (which had backed the charge brought to the WTO) and employing cheap wage labour. St Lucian families felt the effects of globalization in their shrinking pockets. In 1998, out of 12 000 registered farmers, only half were still active. Production plummeted and by 1999, St Lucia exported only half the amount of bananas it had done in 1993. The industry was approaching the new millennium in very dire straits - and worse was yet to come.

Within months, farmers began to express concerns about the way executive chairman Patrick Joseph ruled the new St Lucia Banana Corporation. One of Joseph's first actions was to lock horns with WIBDECO, aiming to minimize or eliminate its middleman position in the banana industry. Next, Joseph sighted the Tropical Quality Fruit company in his cross hairs - but an attempt to restrain TQF from doing business with the SLBC was thrown out by the courts. By October 1999, a section of the leadership of the Banana Salvation Committee accused Joseph and his three staunchest allies of badly administering the SLBC; failing to pay farmers dividends earned from WIBDECO; indiscipline and arrogant behaviour towards farmers and BSC leadership, and abuse of power and authority. Things came to a head when BSC board member *cum* SLBC director Fred Flood (once a staunch ally of Joseph during the 'no cut' strikes), planned a vote of no confidence against Joseph and his allies. Joseph denied the allegations and when the 7000 SLBC-shareholders convened in October, Joseph prevailed and emerged in an even stronger position than before: none of the six directors nominated by the BSC were given the nod by the shareholders. Round two of Joseph's confrontation with disgruntled farmers came in May 2000, at the second part of the annual SLBC shareholders meeting. Again, Joseph had to fight off an attempt by unhappy farmers to topple him. Again, he survived. But the number of his critics within the SLBC was growing - as, for that matter, was farmer insecurity over the future.

To everyone's surprise, in October 2000, Patrick Joseph voluntarily resigned as executive chairman of the SLBC. Soon after, rumours were rife about questionable company transactions under Joseph's chairmanship, and the SLBC commissioned an independent audit into its financial affairs. By November 2000, a preliminary report by KPMG revealed a series of irregularities at the SLBC, including millions of dollars which had been signed away without the approval of the SLBC board. It was a terrible blow to morale. By February 2001, farmers had become so disillusioned with banana politics in general, and the SLBC in particular, that they no longer even bothered to attend shareholder meetings. At a meeting convened to select a new board, less than 100 of nearly 4000 registered shareholders showed up.

With the SLBC in shambles, production costs perennially on the rise and a price war in Europe further depressing revenues, St Lucia and the other Windward Islands were beginning to face up to the possibility of abandoning the banana industry altogether. As OECS Ambassador Edwin Laurent (a born St Lucian) explained it in August 2001, '*economic logic cannot be defied indefinitely*'. With their much higher costs of production, Windward Islands farmers simply could not compete with bananas from Latin America, and Laurent's advice to the Windward Islands was therefore to '*bite the bullet*': accept that painful change was inevitable and focus on exploring alternative crops and niche markets, such as the market for organically grown fruits.

His words were prophetic. By 2003, St Lucia's banana exports had dropped to a paltry 33 972 tonnes: the lowest in nearly 30 years and only a quarter of the 1990 crop. In June 2004, it was revealed that less than 8000 banana growers remained in the Windward Islands altogether. St Lucia alone had lost between 27 000 and 31 000 jobs in the banana industry between 1994 and 2000.

The mid and late 1990s were difficult times for St Lucia, especially its farming sector, whose origin and destiny had lain in the 'green gold'. That things did not get worse than they did, was in large part thanks to the emergence of tourism as a new pillar of St Lucia's economy.

18

The new millennium, the end of an era

The year 2000 started in St Lucia, as everywhere else in the world, with festivities and fireworks - but it ended with a uniquely heinous act. On Sunday 31 December, two young men invaded the Minor Basilica of the Immaculate Conception in Castries during early morning service. With Holy Communion in progress, they attacked worshippers, doused them with petrol and set them on fire. The attack caused pandemonium and sent people scampering for their lives. Most made it safely outside, but Irish nun Sister Mary Theresa Egan was bludgeoned to death and St Lucian priest Fr Charles Gaillard, pleading with his attackers to stop, was set on fire and died a few months later from the after-effects of injuries sustained on that fateful morning. Thirteen other worshippers suffered varying degrees of burns also. '*It was like a scene from hell,*' eyewitness Cletus Springer said. Walking back to his pew after receiving Holy Communion, Springer had heard wailing from the back of the church. '*I looked up and saw flames and I saw these men methodically going around setting people on fire.*' The attackers also set fire to the centre aisle carpet and torched the altar.

The Cathedral attack sent ripples of shock, anger, fear and revulsion through the island and, indeed, the world. The cold-blooded murder of Sister Egan, just four days after her 73rd birthday, outraged everyone. As a member of the Order of St Joseph of Cluny, she had lived in the Caribbean since 1949 and had worked in St Lucia for more than four decades as a teacher and administrator.[699] Everyone in St Lucia was desperate to know what could have prompted such violence on an essentially peaceful congregation? Two men were arrested and interrogated soon after the attack. Kim John (then 20) and Francis Phillip (then 32) both proclaimed that they had acted in the name of Haile Selassie, Ethiopia's late Emperor who is worshipped by Rastafarians in the Caribbean as the manifestation of God. They told police that they were 'prophets' sent to combat corruption in the Roman Catholic Church.[700] Although both claimed to be Rastafarians and wore dreadlocks, they were immediately denounced by other Rastas in St Lucia who stated that the men's actions flew in the face of the Rastafarian philosophy of peaceful coexistence.

In April 2003, Kim John and Francis Phillip were sentenced to hang for the murders of Sr Egan and Fr Gaillard. When the verdict was handed down, they showed little emotion beyond John's response: '*I rather the grave than be a slave in your evil society.*' Their defence lawyer argued that they were insane at the time of the attack and should be spared the death penalty. His appeal failed, as did their case at the Court of Appeal. But eight years after their sentencing, John and Phillip were yet to keep their date with the hangman.

The Cathedral attack heralded a wave of burglaries, robberies and violence. Soon, St Lucia was chalking up record murder rates. In response, the Kenny Anthony Government beefed up the police force, legislated stiffer penalties for gun crimes and started work on a new prison. The old facility in the heart of Castries had become the proverbial leaky sieve, and matters were not helped by the several fires lit by prisoners in protest over their living conditions. In January 2003, the Government honoured an election promise with the opening of the $48 million state-of-the-art Bordelais Correctional Facility in Dennery, designed for 500 inmates. The old prison in Castries, built in 1827 for 80 prisoners, had been housing as many as 400 by the time it was finally closed.

Global and local challenges

St Lucia's tourism industry was sent reeling in 2001-02 by the September 11 terrorist attacks in the United States. With one-third of the island's visitors coming from the US, St Lucian hotels were hard-hit. One of the casualties was the 256-room Club Med resort, which was the only large hotel in the south, leaving Vieux Fortians especially deprived.

Politically, these were troubling times as well. Since 1998, George Odlum had been quietly at loggerheads with his SLP colleagues (earning him the dubious sobriquet of '*Minister Moo-moo*'). But during the nationally televized April 2000 House of Assembly's budget debate, Odlum broke his silence. Putting his finger firmly on the sore spot, he pointed out that while the Government was patting itself on the back, the population felt strongly that the economy was in a state of malaise. He also accused the Government of alienating important sections of the community including the media, public servants and the opposition. Odlum's criticism of the SLP Government resonated strongly with sections of the press and the Chamber of Commerce. In 2001, Odlum broke ranks with the SLP altogether and announced his intention to bring together the opposition forces in a Government of National Unity.

Four years after its 1997 defeat, the UWP still had difficulty resurfacing as a major political force. When Odlum engaged the UWP in talks, it did not take long for a National Alliance to emerge. It had a three-cornered leadership structure: Odlum as political leader, Morella Joseph as vice-president and Sir John Compton as president. For a while, the Alliance attracted a strong following and there was a genuine feeling that it could beat the ruling SLP at the next polls. But confusion over leadership matters soon prompted observers to dub the Alliance *'a three-headed monster'* and leadership controversies coupled with an exceptionally unfortunate piece of political timing on the part of George Odlum[701] caused the National Alliance to self-destruct in October 2001.

Sensing the disarray, the Government decided to call snap elections. It proved a sensible decision and in December 2001, although polling 10 000 fewer votes than in 1997, the SLP won with a comfortable majority of fourteen seats against the UWP's three. A record number of five political parties took part in the elections but voter turn-out was low at 52 per cent. George Odlum lost disastrously in Castries South East, the constituency he had won so handsomely for the SLP in 1979 and 1997. Odlum never once won an election independent of the SLP and his dream of leading a government never materialized during his more than 30 years as a player on St Lucia's political stage. Nevertheless, he left an indelible and occasionally remarkable stamp on St Lucia's history. Odlum died of pancreatic cancer in 2003, aged 69.

The Hyatt and NCA scandals and Sarah Flood's stance

The shining armour of New Labour received a few more dents during its second term. The opposition UWP called for Kenny Anthony's resignation after it came to light that the Government had guaranteed '*$30 million*' in cost overruns to Rochamel, a French company, for the construction of a 284-room Hyatt hotel. It was initially believed that the $30 million was EC currency but Anthony eventually revealed that St Lucia had *'lost US$30 million'* on the project: a whopping EC$80 million. The project was to have produced a prestigious Hyatt resort, a brand name that could boost St Lucia's image as an upscale tourist destination, but it soon turned into a nightmare of construction delays and hopelessly low occupancy levels in the wake of 9/11. The matter came to a head in May 2003, when Anthony took a resolution to the House of Assembly asking to borrow money to refinance what he termed the Government's *'obligations'* to the Rochamel Group. As it turned out, few people had been aware that the Government had guaranteed the project at all and soon, the question was raised whether Government had acted properly and legally. Compton said it had not, and demanded Anthony's resignation. Attorney Martinus Francois took the case to court, alleging that Anthony had entered into the agreement without the authority of Parliament. He won in the High Court but the ruling was later reversed on appeal. Throughout the upheaval, Kenny Anthony defended his action, saying '*I believe that the investment was needed, it was justified, and that it would pay the value we have lost and pay it fairly quickly.*' The long-running Rochamel debate left many questions unanswered, and Anthony was dogged forever after with the suspicion that he had been reckless in using the country's money. The Hyatt hotel soon went into receivership and was taken over by the Jamaican group Sandals, which already owned two all-inclusive resorts in St Lucia.

Another matter which tainted the image of the Labour Government's second term was the National Conservation Authority controversy, which operated the Labour Government's flagship Short Term Employment Programme (STEP). An enquiry revealed that for four years, the NCA had failed to send financial statements to Parliament and further cited a range of financial irregularities, including missing cheques and people receiving pay for no work. The NCA proved the anti-thesis of transparency and accountability, the core ideals which had swept New Labour into power in 1997. Despite repeated calls, the responsible Minister, Menissa Rambally, refused to resign.

The Labour Government ran into more problems when, in 2003, it attempted to enact a controversial criminal code which included provisions to make abortion legal under special circumstances, such as rape. This time the challenge came from within, as Minister for Health and Gender Affairs Sarah Flood-Beaubrun objected to the provisions. A devout Roman Catholic, Flood-Beaubrun vociferously criticized her Cabinet colleagues, referring to them as '*baby killers*' and '*murderers*'. Not long before, a visibly pregnant Sarah Flood-Beaubrun had joined a church-organized anti-abortion march through Castries. Following her outburst in Parliament, Flood was fired from the Government and the Labour Party. She joined the opposition in the House of Assembly, where she continued to act as a thorn in the side of the Government, meticulously and sometimes audaciously questioning its every move.

The advent of Frederick and the return of Compton

Meanwhile, the opposition UWP kept trying to find its way back to the helm of power. A popular poll taken in late 2004 (said to have been commissioned by party leader Vaughan Lewis himself) concluded that 74 per cent of St Lucians felt the country was heading in the wrong direction under Labour, and that 63 per cent wanted to see John Compton return to lead the UWP. Compton re-entered the leadership contest during a conference of delegates in Soufrière on 13 March 2005, defeating Lewis by 265 votes to 135. Relations between Lewis and the UWP quickly went from bad to acrimonious. In early 2006, Sarah Flood-Beaubrun resigned her Castries Central seat in search of a new mandate. A by-election was slated for March. Vaughan Lewis opted out of running for the UWP and the party announced it would stay out of the by-election altogether. The SLP nominated Victor LaCorbinière (whose father Karl had twice held this seat for Labour in the 1950s) and, given the SLP's well-oiled election machine, it was widely expected that the SLP would leave Sarah Flood-Beaubrun's new Organization for National Empowerment to bite the dust in Castries-Central.

Then, less than two weeks before the election, Castries lawyer Richard Frederick entered the fray as an independent candidate. His entry created a buzz of excitement and mixed feelings. Prime Minister Kenny Anthony, referring to some incidents in which Frederick had allegedly brandished a firearm, called his candidacy '*frightening*'. But Frederick reminded Anthony that he had appeared on SLP political platforms in 1997 and they had seen nothing wrong with him then. Although running as an independent, Frederick joined the UWP, which led the SLP to accuse that party of descending to a '*new low*'. The launch of Frederick's campaign turned into a mass event. He launched a scathing attack on the Government in general and on Kenny Anthony in particular, threatening '*to run them out of town*'. If there were skeletons hiding in Richard Frederick's closet, as many insinuated, then no one was revealing them. The SLP platform did what it could to brand Frederick as an unacceptable candidate for Parliament but on 13 March 2006, the people of Castries Central sent Richard Frederick to the House of Assembly in a result that stunned the hitherto all-powerful Labour Party. With just ten days' of campaigning under his belt, Frederick captured 1516 votes to LaCorbiniere's 1267 and Flood-Beaubrun's 415. It was the first sign of a chink in Labour's armour.

With general elections due later that year, Frederick was quickly absorbed into the UWP. His entry into the *Flanbo* campaign, combined with Compton's return as leader, re-energized the party. But the SLP refused to play dead and staged an election show like no other, relaying live public meetings, staging popular overseas musicians and launching an advertising campaign unprecedented in scope and quality. The SLP also managed to lure Vaughan Lewis into its camp and another 'big gun' brought out for the upcoming poll was former leader Julian Hunte who, after being sidelined in 1997 in favour of Kenny Anthony, had pursued a distinguished diplomatic career which saw him elected President of the United Nations General Assembly. Hunte returned home to contest his old seat in Gros Islet for Labour. The SLP and UWP both fought determined campaigns, rousing massive rallies and motorcades. Still, no one was prepared for the results on that Monday 11 December 2006 when, at the advanced age of 82, Sir John Compton led the UWP to an emphatic election victory, winning eleven seats to the SLP's six.

Compton's troubled UWP Government

On the first working day of January 2007, the new Parliament created history when women were appointed to preside at both chambers: Sarah Flood-Beaubrun as Speaker of the House of Assembly and Rosemarie Husbands-Mathurin as President of the Senate. With Dame Pearlette Louisy into her ninth year as Governor General, three of the most important positions in the country were now held by women. In March and April, World Cup Cricket came to the Caribbean and St Lucia hosted matches at the brandnew Beausejour Cricket Grounds (a legacy of the Labour Government). The immediate economic returns of this event were not as expected, but the years of preparation did significantly increase the amount of local and foreign investment in the residential and tourism sectors. Crime, which had been a major topic during the campaign, began to nose-dive under Compton's UWP Government, thanks to the combined effects of security measures introduced for World Cup Cricket and additional resources made available to the police force by the former Labour Administration.

During April's budget presentation, Compton spent four hours outlining his detailed vision for the future of St Lucia. Two days later, he forewarned his Cabinet colleagues that whilst he would take them to the mountain top, he would not be there with them to enter the Promised Land. They were prophetic words.

Just as the Government was getting into its stride, the issue of diplomatic relations with either China or Taiwan came up, reigniting an old controversy. In 1984, Compton had established diplomatic ties with the Republic of China in Taiwan. In 1997, Anthony's SLP Government had severed those ties in favour of the People's Republic of China. With Compton back in power, the contest between the two Chinas started all over again - the underlying rationale being that China considered Taiwan a breakaway province and refused to acknowledge its legal status. By establishing diplomatic relations, Taiwan aimed to increase its legitimacy on the international scene and make a stronger case for recognition by the United Nations, which continued to deny Taiwan its status of independence.

The ink was barely dry on the December 2006 ballot forms when Taiwanese officials asked to meet with Compton. But Compton, on 22 December 2006, assured a two-man Chinese delegation that there would be no change in foreign policy. Foreign Minister Rufus Bousquet sat in on this meeting and later also met with the Chinese delegation on his own, thanking them for their continued support. However, Taiwan did not give up so easily. In March 2007, a Taiwanese delegation came to St Lucia to speak with the Compton Government (incidentally, China had done exactly the same thing in 1997, after the SLP's election victory.) Despite Compton's earlier assurances to China, he did meet with the Taiwanese this time, to the obvious displeasure of the Chinese. It sparked a diplomatic row between the two countries, just as it had done in 1997. Speculation was rife as to which way the Government would jump - but Compton revealed nothing. Then, out of the blue, Rufus Bousquet annouced during the budget debate that *'there is overwhelming consensus within the Cabinet for the renewal of full diplomatic relations with Taiwan at the earliest opportunity.'* Several Cabinet colleagues applauded and banged the table in support. The Chinese ambassador, furious, threatened to break off diplomatic relations if such an agreement with Taiwan were to be formalized. He did not have to wait long. On 30 April, Rufus Bousquet, with several Cabinet colleagues in tow, signed an agreement with the Taiwanese Foreign Minister. In response, China accused St Lucia of *'brutal interference'* in Chinese internal affairs and called it *'an open violation'* of the 1997 agreement between St Lucia and China.

One day after Bousquet signed with the Taiwanese, Prime Minister Compton left the island for New York, reportedly for a routine and pre-planned medical check-up. But a local radio station soon reported that actually, Compton had suffered a heart attack. Speculation soared that his sudden unannounced departure was directly connected to the China-Taiwan issue. Compton was said to have had second thoughts about breaking with China and had planned to give a television address to the nation that same evening to announce his Government's continued allegiance to China. He had come to feel that severing ties with a member of the UN Security Council (which China was, and Taiwan was not) would not be wise. Compton had scheduled a Cabinet meeting to inform his colleagues of this decision but before this meeting could take place, Bousquet and his consorts had rushed along and put their signatures on an agreement with the Taiwanese.[702] Accounts vary, but it is generally believed that an angry and distressed Compton suffered a stroke during the stormy Cabinet meeting following Bousquet's action.

After Compton's departure for New York, acting Prime Minister Stephenson King denied that there was a rift in Cabinet, and denied Compton's health problems. More than a week passed without further information and public apprehension mounted. In the end, Minister Lenard Montoute visited Compton in New York. He returned home with the news that Compton had suffered *'a series of small strokes beginning here (in St Lucia) and continuing in New York'* and said he did not think Compton would return to the office of Prime Minister. In late May, Compton returned home to recuperate. In early June, from his sickbed, he relieved Rufus Bousquet of his Foreign Affairs portfolio and, without further explanation, relegated him to the backbenches of the House of Assembly. In late July, under mounting pressure, acting

Prime Minister Stephenson King reassured the nation that despite the Prime Minister's ill health, the machinery of Government was running smoothly.

Meanwhile, in the third weekend of August 2007, Hurricane Dean passed between St Lucia and Martinique - the first big storm to come so close since 1980. One man died, agriculture and infrastructure took some blows and a few homes lost their roofs but on the whole, St Lucia had a lucky escape from this category two storm.

The passing of Sir John Compton

The Prime Minister never recovered. In early September, his vital organs failed and on Friday, 7 September 2007, Sir John George Melvin Compton passed away at Tapion hospital in Castries at the age of 82. For two weeks, the country mourned the death of '*The Father of the Nation.*' Compton's body was laid out in state in Castries and Micoud, his coffin transported on the back of his own pick-up van, according to his explicit wishes and in memory of his humble lifestyle. Daily television broadcasts showed attendance at the memorial services and reminisced about Compton's life and legacy. The funeral service was attended by dozens of regional leaders, past and present, and hundreds of other invited guests. The tiny island of Canouan in the Grenadines, where Compton was born in 1925, sent a 36-strong delegation. Children waving the national flag lined the route of the funeral procession which led to the two thousand-seat Basilica, packed to full capacity. Outside in Derek Walcott Square, hundreds watched the service on a video screen and thousands followed it live on television and the internet, at home and overseas. There were many emotional moments during the four-hour long funeral service in which one glowing tribute followed another, interspersed with performances of (school) choirs and dance groups. The sight of reigning Calypso Monarch Menelle Delice singing the song ('*Compi Holding On*') which had won her the title just two months earlier, tears streaming down her face, proved too much for many people in the audience and they in turn let their emotions run free. It was followed by calypsonian Morgie's emotional rendition of '*Island of Sir John.*' Unusually, Lady Janice Compton spoke at her husband's funeral service - to what many observed to be the obvious discomfort of some of the parliamentary representatives present.

Barbados' Prime Minister Owen Arthur, as Chairman of the Caribbean Community, saluted Compton as '*the major architect of the social transformation of this land*' saying that he '*laid the foundation for the creation of a modern economy in this nation and he ... has served to transform our region from a group of scattered and divided islands to a regional society with a common purpose, a common destiny.*' Sir Dwight Venner, head of the Eastern Caribbean Central

Bank who had worked closely with Compton's Government in the 1980s, hailed his infrastructural legacy: '*the Roseau Dam, the East Coast Road, the West Coast Road, The Gros Islet Highway, the Pigeon Island causeway, Rodney Bay, the tunnel to Cul de Sac, Hewanorra airport and the Castries and Vieux Fort harbours.*'

Compton was, said Venner, '*in the final analysis, what he was best at: a leader. He was a master mariner and sea captain par excellence and without fear who guided the nation with a sure and certain hand on the till, and so from a very early age he took on the mantle of leadership and from the bridge of the good ship* Helen ... *he steered this beautiful country into the modern age.*'

With the passing of Sir John Compton, St Lucia irrevocably ended an era - and entered another - in its long and colourful history.

Bibliography

Books, articles and pamphlets

Adrien, Peter. 1996. *Metayage, capitalism and peasant development in St Lucia 1840-1957*. New Generation Series No.4, Mona, Jamaica: Consortium Graduate School of Social Sciences, University of the West Indies.

Alleyne, Mervyn. 1973 [1961]. 'Language and society in St Lucia.' In: *Consequences of class and color. West Indian perspectives*. D. Lowenthal and L. Comitas (eds.):199-212. New York: Anchor Press. First published in *Caribbean Studies*. Vol.1(1):1-10.

Alleyne, Mervyn. 1985. 'A linguistic perspective on the Caribbean.' In: *Caribbean Contours*. S.W. Mintz and S. Price (eds.):155-179. Baltimore, London: Johns Hopkins University Press.

Anonymous. 1832a. *A reply to Mr Jeremie's pamphlet by an inhabitant of St Lucia*. London: Effingham Wilson.

Anonymous. 1832b. *Remarks on Mr Jeremie's conduct as President of the Royal Court by an inhabitant of that island*. London: Baylis and Leighton.

Anthony, Kenny. *Ca.*1988. 'Introduction. Society and the civil law tradition in Saint Lucia - a historical overview.' Unpublished paper.

Anthony, Patrick A.B. 1988. 'Encounter between Christianity and culture: the case of the 'Kélè' ceremony in St Lucia, West Indies.' In *Bulletin Secretarius Pro Non Christianis*. XXIII/3(69):287-300.

Anthony, Patrick A.B. 1990. 'Changing attitudes towards African traditional religion and the implications for Afro-Caribbean tradition in St Lucia.' In: *Ay Bo Bo. Afro-Caribbean Religions. 2nd International Conference of the Society for Caribbean Research*. M. Kremser (ed.):69-84. Vienna: Institut für Volkerkunde.

Anthony, Patrick A.B. 1998. 'Popular Catholicism and social change in St Lucia.' In: *Social Compass. International Review of Sociology of Religion*. Vol.45(4):555-74.

Anthony, Patrick A.B. 1999. 'St Lucia, West Indies. Garden of Eden?' In: *Popular Catholicism in a World Church*. T. Bamat and J.P. Wiest (eds.). Maryknoll, New York: Orbis Books.

Aspinall, Sir Algernon. 1939 [1907]. *The pocket guide to the West Indies. British Guiana, British Honduras, Bermuda, the Spanish Main, Suri-*

nam & the Panama Canal. London: Methuen & Co. In particular the section 'St Lucia':169-82.

Aubertin, Michael. 2000. *Nèg maron*. S.l.: Caribbean Diaspora Press.

Augier, F.R., S.C. Gordon, D.G. Hall and M. Reckord. 1988 [1960]. *The making of the West Indies*. Trinidad & Jamaica: Longman Caribbean.

Auguste, Joyce (comp.). 1986. *Oral and folk traditions of Saint Lucia*. Cultural Heritage Series no.1. Castries: Folk Research Centre.

Bailey, B., B. Brereton, V. Shepherd (eds.). 1995. *Engendering history. Caribbean women in historical perspective*. Kingston, Jamaica: Ian Randle.

Baptiste, André Fitzroy. 1988. *War, cooperation, and conflict. The European possessions in the Caribbean, 1939-1945*. New York: Greenwood Press.

Barrow, Christine. 1992. *Family land and development in St Lucia*. Monograph series no.1. Institute of Social and Economic Research, University of the West Indies. Cave Hill, Barbados.

Basch, L., N. Glick Schiller, C. Szanton Blanc. 1994. 'The making of West Indian transmigrant populations: examples from St Vincent and Grenada.' In: *Nations unbound. Transnational projects, postcolonial predicaments and deterritorialized nation-states*. L. Basch, N. Glick Schiller and C. Szanton Blanc:49-94. Amsterdam: Gordon and Breach Science Publishers.

Beard, J.S. 1949. *Natural vegetation of the Windward and Leeward islands*. Oxford Forestry Memoirs no.21. Oxford: Clarendon Press.

Beck, Jane. 1979. *To windward of the land. The occult world of Alexander Charles*. Bloomington & London: Indiana University Press.

Beckles, Hilary. 1991. 'Caribbean anti-slavery: the self-liberation ethos of enslaved blacks.' In: Beckles and Shepherd (eds.):363-72.

Beckles, Hilary and Verene Shepherd (eds.). 1991. *Caribbean slave society and economy. A student reader*. Kingston, Jamaica: Ian Randle.

Beckles, Hilary and Verene Shepherd (eds.). 1993. *Caribbean freedom. Economy and society from Emancipation to the present. A student reader*. Kingston, Jamaica: Ian Randle.

Bentley, Thomas E. 1945 (5 May). 'Acquisition of territory for US Air Base. Historical report.' Declassified secret report.

Box, Harold E. 1939. 'Observations on the landslides in St Lucia, BWI, in November 1938.' In: *The Empire Forestry Journal*. Vol.18:119-21.

Brathwaite, Edward (ed.). 1963. *Iouanaloa. Recent writings from St Lucia*. Castries: Department of Extra Mural Studies.

Breen, Henry. 1970 [1844]. *St Lucia: historical, statistical and descriptive*. London: Frank Cass. First published London: Longmans, Brown & Longmans.

Breen, Henry. 1879-1881. 'Fifty Years in the West Indies 1829-1879.' Seri-

alized in *The Chronicle* (Grenada) and *The Voice* (St Lucia).
Brereton, Bridget. 1985. *Social life in the Caribbean 1838-1938*. Oxford: Heinemann.
Bruce, John. 1983. *Family land tenure and agricultural development in St Lucia*. Research paper no.79. Land Tenure Center, University of Wisconsin-Madison.
Bruneau-Latouche, Eugène and Raymond. 1989. *Sainte-Lucie fille de la Martinique*. Paris: Imprimerie Pierron.
Buisseret, David. 1980. *Historic architecture of the Caribbean*. London: Heinemann.
Bullen, Ripley. 1966. 'The first English settlement on St Lucia.' In: *Caribbean Quarterly*. Vol.12(2):29-35.
Bundy, Frederick E. 1905. 'The system of education in Saint Lucia.' In: *Great Britain Educational Board. Special reports on educational subjects.* London. Vol.12(12):315-56.
Carasco, Francis. 1967. *Historical review of the Castries Municipality from 1785 to 1967*. Edited by John Pilgrim, published by authority of the Castries City Council.
Chamberlain, Mary.1997. *Narratives of exile and return*. Warwick University Caribbean Studies. London & Basingstoke: MacMillan.
Chaney, Elsa.1988. *Migration, smallholder agriculture, and food consumption in Jamaica and St Lucia*. Washington DC: Hemispheric Migration Project, Center for Immigration Studies.
Charles, George F.L. 1994. *The history of the labour movement in St Lucia 1945-1974. A personal memoir*. Castries: Folk Research Centre.
Chase, Vasantha. 1988. 'The economic and social context' and 'Empirical testimony. The case of the Mabouya Valley in Saint Lucia.'. In: *Caribbean women in agriculture*:27-37 and 97-103. Santiago, Chile: Food and Agriculture Organization.
Cheddie, Richard. Search online for his website on Indian immigration to the Caribbean, which carries extensive references to St Lucia.
Comins, Surgeon-Major D.W.D. 1893. *Note on emigration from the East Indies to St Lucia. Compiled at the request of the British Government.* Calcutta: Bengal Secretariat Press. Includes Comins' personal diary.
Crichlow, Michaeline. 1994. 'An alternative approach to family land tenure in the Anglophone Caribbean: the case of St Lucia.' In: *New West Indian Guide/Nieuwe West Indische Gids*. Vol.68(1&2):77-99.
Crowley, Daniel. 1955a. 'Supernatural beings in St Lucia.' In: *Caribbean Magazine*. Vol.8(11-12):231-4, 264-5.
Crowley, Daniel. 1956a. 'Naming customs in St Lucia.' In: *Social and Economic Studies*. Vol.5(1):87-92.

Crowley, Daniel. 1958b. 'La Rose and Marguerite societies in St Lucia.' In: *Journal of American Folklore.* Vol.71(282):541-52.

Dalphinis, Morgan. N.d. *Caribbean & African languages. Social history, language, literature and education. The case of St Lucia.* S.l.: Karia Press.

Des Voeux, G. William. 1903. *My colonial service.* Two volumes. London: John Murray.

Detaille and Jamet (comp.). 1849. 'Topographical map of St Lucia.' In: *Papers of the Royal Engineers.* Vol.10 (Oxford: Rhodes House Library, 1937). Map prepared in 1847 by Lt.Col. Reid.

Devaux, Robert. 1963b. 'The St Lucia Steam Conveyance Co. Ltd. Locals.' In: *Canadian Philatelist.* May/June:125-6,134.

Devaux, Robert. 1973. 'The wooden foot pirate of Fatigate.' In: *The Homemakers Guide.* Vol.1(1):22-3.

Devaux, Robert.1975a. *Saint Lucia Historic Sites: including monuments, buildings, parks, and open spaces.* Barbados: Letchworth Press.

Devaux, Robert.1975b. *A century of coaling in St Lucia, including a description of the coaling tokens.* Castries: St Lucia Archaeological and Historical Society. Reprinted from: *The Numismatic Circular.* London: Spink & Son (December 1974 to June 1975).

Devaux, Robert.1978. *Check list of the birds of St Lucia.* Castries: St Lucia Naturalist Society.

Devaux, Robert.1979. *Pigeon Island National Park. A brief history and guide.* St Lucia: Noah's Arkade.

Devaux, Robert. 1997. *They called us Brigands: the saga of St Lucia's freedom fighters.* Castries: Optimum Printers.

Devaux, Robert. 1994a. 'The May Rose disaster.' In: *Tropical Traveller.* July:22.

Devaux, Robert. 1994b. 'A pre-Columbian sundial.' In: *Tropical Traveller.* August:22.

Devaux, Robert. 1994-5. 'Mountains in the Arawak culture of St Lucia.' In: *Tropical Traveller.* November:22, December:22, January:22.

Dix, Jabetz. 1933. 'Adolphe - one of the most terrible of Obeah-men.' In: *Canada West Indies Magazine.* Vol.22(2):53-55.

Dix, Thomas. 1936. 'The three murderers of Monchy.' In: *West Indian Enterprise.* Vol.56(June):23-5.

Du Tertre, Père J.B. 1667-71. *Histoire Générale des Antilles.* Three volumes. Paris.

Dujon, Veronica. 1995. 'National actors against world market pressures: communal land, privatization and agricultural development in the Caribbean.' University of Wisconsin-Madison. Ph.D-thesis. Ann Arbor: University Microfilm International.

Durham, Harriet and Florence Lewisohn. 1971. *St Lucia. Tours and tales.* Wilmington, Delaware: published by authors.

Dyde, Brian. 1997. *The empty sleeve. The story of The West India Regiments of the British Army.* Antigua: Hansib.

Dyde, Brian. 2000. *A History of Antigua. The Unsuspected Isle.* London and Oxford: MacMillan.

Easter, B.H. 1965. *St Lucia and the French Revolution.* Tom Ferguson Memorial Lecture, 28 April. Castries: The Voice Publishing Co.

Easter, B.H. 1966. *A guide to Morne Fortune, St Lucia. On the occasion of the visit of Her Majesty the Queen and His Royal Highness the Prince Philip, Duke of Edinburgh on the 16th February, 1966.* Castries: St Lucia Archaeological and Historical Society.

Eastern Caribbean Natural Area Management Program 1983. *A report on a study of conservation and development requirements for the southeast coast of Saint Lucia.* ECNAMP Report no.1. Joint project with the Government of St Lucia.

Economic Commission for Latin America. 1981. *Social structural changes in St Lucia.* United Nations Economic and Social Council.

Economic Commission for Latin America. 1982. *Economic Survey of Latin America 1982. Saint Lucia.* United Nations Economic and Social Council.

Edwards, Bryan. 1793. *The History, civil and commercial of the British colonies in the West Indies.* Two volumes. London: Stockdale.

Ellis, Guy and Christian Zuber. 1981. *Saint Lucia.* S.l.: Éditions Delroisse.

Ellis, Guy and Lis Bhajan. N.d. *Sir Arthur Lewis.* Port-of-Spain: Imprint Caribbean.

Ellis, Guy. 1986. *Saint Lucia. Helen of the West Indies.* London and Basingstoke: MacMillan.

Engerman, Stanley and Barry Higman. 1997. 'The demographic structure of the Caribbean slave societies in the eighteenth and nineteenth centuries.' In: Knight (ed.):45-104.

Ferguson, Thomas. 1907. 'The quarter of Micoud.' In: *The Voice.* 3 October:6.

Ferguson, Thomas. 1909. 'St Lucia: 1778.' In: *The Voice.* 11 December:6

Ferguson, Thomas. 1927. 'Document history of Mamiku Estate.' Unpublished manuscript, compiled for Henry Shingleton-Smith.

Folk Research Centre. Ca.1995. 'Oral History Project, transcripts.' Unpublished research notes.

Folk Research Centre. 1992. *Religion and spirit power in St Lucia.* Cultural Education Kit. Castries: Folk Research Centre.

Fortescue, Sir John W. 1915. *History of the British Army.* Vol.4, part 1.

London: MacMillan & Co.

Foster Walker, Céline. 2005. *The Gaillard de Laubenque family of France and St Lucia*. Published by author. See also: www.Gaillard-deLaubenque.com

Francis, Claudia. 1979. 'A brief history of the United States Base in St Lucia during the Second World War.' Faculty of Arts and General Studies, University of the West Indies, Unpublished BA-thesis.

Frank, David (ed.). 2001. With Paul Crosbie, David Frank, Emanuel Leon and Peter Samuel. *Kwéyòl Dictionary*. Castries: Summer Institute of Linguistics International in co-operation with the Ministry of Education, Government of Saint Lucia.

Friesinger, Herwig and Robert Devaux. 1983. *Vorbericht über die Österreichischen Ausgrabungen auf St Lucia, Westindien. (Preliminary report on the Austrian excavations on St Lucia, West Indies)*. Vienna: Verlag der Österreichischen Akademie der Wissenschaften.

Gachet, Charles. 1975. *A history of the Roman Catholic Church in St Lucia*. Port-of-Spain, Trinidad: Key Caribbean Publications.

Gaspar, Barry and David Geggus. 1997. *A turbulent time. The French Revolution and the Greater Caribbean*. Bloomington and Indianapolis: Indiana University Press.

Gaspar, Barry. Ca. 1975. 'A fiction of freedom.' Unpublished manuscript.

Gaspar, Barry. 1983. '"The Best Years of My Life": James Johnston of St Lucia and Antigua 1819-1832.' Paper presented at the 15th Conference of Caribbean Historians: Mona, Jamaica, 15-20 April.

Gaspar, Barry. 1997. 'La Guerre des Bois. Revolution, war, and slavery in Saint Lucia, 1793-1838.' In: Gaspar and Geggus:102-30.

Geggus, David. 1991. 'The Haitian Revolution'. In Beckles and Shepherd (eds.):402-18.

Goveia, Elsa. 1991 [1970]. 'The West Indian slave laws of the eighteenth century.' In: Beckles and Shepherd (eds.): 346-62. First published London: Caribbean University Press.

Guilbault, Jocelyn. 1986 [1984]. 'Fitness and flexibility: funeral wakes in St Lucia, West Indies.' Revised version of a chapter from 'Musical events in the lives of the people of a Caribbean Island, St Lucia.' University of Guelph. Unpublished Ph.D-thesis.

Hall, Douglas. 1993 [1978]. 'The flight from the estates reconsidered: the British West Indies, 1838-1842.' In: Beckles and Shepherd (eds.):55-63. First published in *Journal of Caribbean History*. Vol.10-11:7-24.

Hamshere, Cyril. 1972. *The British in the Caribbean*. London: Weidenfeld and Nicolson.

Harmsen, Jolien. 1993. 'On analysing religion in social science: a masquerade of speculative ideas.' Unpublished paper, Erasmus University Rotterdam.

Harmsen, Jolien. 1994. *You gave us the Dreaming. Aboriginal law and Catholic law: changing religious identities of Arrernte people at Charles Creek, Arltunga and Santa Teresa in Central Australia, 1935-1991*. MA-thesis, Erasmus University Rotterdam. Nijmegen: Centre for Pacific Studies.

Harmsen, Jolien. 1997. 'From a child's point of view: intergenerational influences on the organization of household and labor.' In: *The History of the Family. An International Quarterly* 2(4):379-403.

Harmsen, Jolien. 1999a. *Sugar, slavery and settlement. A social history of Vieux Fort St Lucia from the Amerindians to the present*. Castries: St Lucia National Trust.

Harmsen, Jolien. 1999b. 'Down the line. Four generations in a Caribbean town, 1910-1998.' Erasmus University Rotterdam. Unpublished Ph.D-thesis.

Harmsen, Jolien. 2008. *Rum justice*. Oxford: MacMillan Caribbean. Published in 2003 as *Rum, roti, onrecht*. Amsterdam: Luitingh-Sijthoff.

Ho, Christine. 1993. 'The internationalization of kinship and the feminization of Caribbean migration: the case of Afro-Trinidadian immigrants in Los Angeles.' In: *Human Organization* 52(1):32-40.

Hofman, Corinne and Menno Hoogland. 1999. 'Expansion of the Taino Cacicazgos towards the Lesser Antilles.' In: *Journal de la Société des Américanistes*. Vol.85:93-113.

Hofman, Corinne, André Delpuech and Menno Hoogland. 2001. 'Les Amérindiens de Guadeloupe'. In: *Archéologia* no.376 (March):18-29.

Hofman, Corinne and Alistair Bright. 2003. 'From Suazoid to folk pottery. Pottery manufacturing traditions in a changing social and cultural environment on St Lucia (W.I.).' Draft of manuscript for *Newsletter of the Department of Pottery Technology*. Vol. 20-21. Leiden University.

Honychurch, Lennox. 1995 [1975]. *The Dominica story. A history of the island*. London and Basingstoke: MacMillan. Revised third edition.

Honychurch, Lennox. 2005. 'Ioüanalao people and the first resistance: peace and war among the Kalinago of St Lucia.' St Lucia Country Conference, University of the West Indies, 18-19 November 2004. Available online.

Hughes, Robert. 1987. *The fatal shore. A history of the transportation of convicts to Australia, 1787-1868*. London: Collins Harvell.

Hulme, Peter and Neil Whitehead. 1992. *Wild Majesty. Encounters with Caribs from Columbus to the present day: an anthology*. Oxford: Claren-

don Press.
Jacobs, Curtis. N.d. 'The Brigands' War in St Vincent: the view from the French records, 1794-1796.' Unpublished paper. Available online.
Jacobs, Curtis. 2005. 'Le Gibraltar des Antilles: the role of St Lucia during the Brigands' War, 1794-1796.' St Lucia Country Conference, University of the West Indies, 18-19 November 2004. Available online.
Jacquin, Pierre. 1961 [Ca.1796]. *La terreur sous les palmes.* Paris: Les Presses du Mail.
Jeremie, John. 1831. *Four essays on colonial slavery.* London: J. Hatchard & Son.
Jesse, Charles. 1968 [1960]. *The Amerindians in St Lucia (Iouanalao).* Castries: St Lucia Archaeological and Historical Society, The Voice Press. New and enlarged edition.
Jesse, Charles. 1994 [1956]. *Outlines of St Lucia's history.* Castries: St Lucia Archaeological and Historical Society.
Jesse, Charles and B.H. Easter. 1971. *A short history of the town and district of Vieux Fort (St Lucia).* Castries: St Lucia Archaeological and Historical Society.
Johnson, Howard and Karl Watson (eds.). 1998. *The white minority in the Caribbean.* Kingston, Jamaica: Ian Randle.
Keur, John and Dorothy. 1960. 'The Others believe: Obeah and "Jumbies".' In: *Windward children. A study in human ecology of the three Dutch Windward Islands in the Caribbean.* J. and D. Keur:176-83. Assen: Van Gorcum.
Koester, Stephen. 1986. 'From plantation agriculture to oil storage: economic development and social transformation.' University of Colorado, Boulder. Ph.D-thesis. Ann Arbor: University Microfilm International.
Kolar, Ernestine. 1985. 'St Lucia: Sklaverei, Emanzipation und Freiheit. Darstellung der Kultur sowie der sozialen, rechtlichen und ökonomischen Situation der schwarzen Bevölkerung St Lucias unter britischer Herrschaft im 19. Jhdt. - Ein Beitrag zur Ethnohistorie der Karibik.' ('*St Lucia: slavery, emancipation and freedom. Cultural, social, legal and economic situation of the black population of St Lucia under British dominion in the 19th century - A contribution to the ethnohistory of the Caribbean.*'). Universität Wien, Vienna. Unpublished Ph.D-thesis.
Kremser, Manfred. 1993a. 'Organizing charity since slavery. The example of the rivaling St Lucian flower societies "La Rose" and "La Marguerite".' In: *Slavery in the Americas.* W. Binder (ed.):305-15. Würzburg: Köningshausen & Nuemann.

Kremser, Manfred. 1993b. 'Visiting ancestors: St Lucian Djiné in communion with their African kin.' In: *Caribbean Quarterly*. Vol.39(3 & 4):82-99.

Larkin, Sherrie. 1989. 'West Indian workers and Ontario farmers: the reciprocal construction of a divided world' and 'Report on fieldwork in St Lucia, West Indies.' University of Western Ontario, London (Ontario). Unpublished MA-thesis.

Lefort de Latour, 1787. *Description général et particulière de l'Isle de Ste. Lucie.* Paris. Reproduced in Bruneau-Latouche 1989.

Levine, Barry B. (ed.). 1987. *The Caribbean exodus.* New York, London: Praeger.

Lewis, Arthur. 1993 [1938]. 'The 1930s social revolution.' In: Beckles and Shepherd (eds.): 376-392. First published as '*Labour in the West Indies: The birth of a workers' movement.*' London: Fabian Society.

Lobdell, Richard. 1988. 'British officials and the West Indian peasantry, 1842-1938.' In: *Labour in the Caribbean. From emancipation to independence.* M. Cross and G. Heuman (eds.): 195-207. Warwick University Caribbean Studies. London & Basingstoke: MacMillan.

Louis, Michael. 1981. 'An equal right to the soil: the rise of a peasantry in St Lucia, 1838-1900.' Johns Hopkins University, Baltimore. Ph.D-thesis. Ann Arbor: University Microfilm International.

Louis, Michael. 1999. 'The Revolt of 1849. Economic obstacles and peasant resistance in St Lucia.' Landmarks in St Lucian History. Unpublished manuscript.

Louis, Michael. 2003. *Was Empress Josephine born at Paix Bouche? Exploring a community's tradition.* Castries: St Lucia Heritage Tourism Programme.

Louis, Michael. 2005. 'Governing without consent: political resistance in St Lucia and the emergence of the Social Improvement Association 1838-1848.' St Lucia Country Conference, University of the West Indies, 18-19 November 2004. Available online.

Louisy, Pearlette. 1999. 'Creole: a language of our own.' Paper presented at the National Conference on Politics, Education and Culture. Encounters of Excellence Series. Castries, 18 February.

Lovelace, Earl. 1982. *The Wine of Astonishment.* Oxford: Heinemann International.

MacMillan, W.M. 1938 [1936]. *Warning from the West Indies. A tract for the Empire.* Harmondsworth: Penguin Books. Second revised edition.

Marshall, Dawn. 1982. 'Migration as an agent of change in Caribbean island ecosystems.' In: *International Social Science Journal* 34(3):451-67.

Marshall, Dawn. 1985. 'Migration and development in the Eastern Caribbean.' In: *Migration and development in the Caribbean: the unexplored connection.* R.A. Pastor (ed.): 91-116. Boulder, Colorado: Westview Press.

Marshall, Dawn. 1987. 'A history of West Indian migrations: overseas opportunities and 'safety-valve' policies.' In: *The Caribbean exodus.* B. Levine (ed.): 15-31. New York: Praeger.

Marshall, Woodville. 1993a [1965]. 'Metayage in the sugar industry of the British Windward islands, 1838-1865.' In: Beckles and Shepherd (eds.):64-79. First published in *Jamaican Historical Review.* Vol.5.

Marshall, Woodville. 1993b [1968]. 'Notes on peasant development in the West Indies since 1838.' In: Beckles and Shepherd (eds.):99-106. First published in *Social and Economic Studies.* Vol.17:1-14.

Mason, Clendon. 1953. *The greatest of these.* Castries: The Voice Publishing.

Mathurin, Lucille. 1954. 'St Lucia and the French Revolution.' In: *The Voice*, 28 November, 5 and 12 December.

Midgett, Douglas. 1970. 'Bilingualism and linguistic change in St Lucia.' In: *Anthropological linguistics.* Vol.12(4):158-70.

Midgett, Douglas. 1977. 'Performance roles and musical change in a Caribbean society.' In: *Ethnomusicology. Journal of the Society for Ethnomusicology.* (January):55-73.

Midgett, Douglas. 1983. *Eastern Caribbean elections, 1950-1982: Antigua, Dominica, Grenada, St Kitts-Nevis, St Lucia, and St Vincent.* Center for Development Studies, University of Iowa.

Mitchell's West Indian Bibliography - www.books.ai/index.html

Mohammed, Patricia. Ca.1996. 'A social history of post-migrant Indians in Trinidad from 1917 to 1947. A gender perspective.' Institute of Social Studies, The Hague. Ph.D-thesis.

Mondesir, Jones E. and Lawrence D. Carrington (eds). 1992. *Dictionary of St Lucian Creole.* Two volumes. Berlin: Mouton de Gruyter Co.

Moore, Sir John. 1904. *The diary of Sir John Moore.* Two volumes, edited by Sir J.F. Maurice. London: Edward Arnold.

Nicholl, John. 1992 [1607]. 'An Houre Glasse of Indian Newes' First published in London: Nathaniell Butter. Reprinted in *Caribbean Quarterly.* Vol.12(1) March 1966:46-67 and in Hulme and Whitehead (eds.) 1992: 64-79.

O'Loughlin, Carleen. 1968. *Economic and political change in the Leeward and Windward Islands.* New Haven and London: Yale University Press.

Organization of American States. 1987. *Saint Lucia Development Atlas.* Washington D.C.: General Secretariat, OAS.

Organization of American States. 1988. *Saint Lucia Human Settlements.* Washington, Department of Regional Development, OAS.

Organization of American States. 1991. *Integrated land development. The case of the Mabouya Valley in Saint Lucia.* Washington, Department of Regional Development and Environment, OAS.

Pattullo, Polly. 1996. *Last resorts. The cost of tourism in the Caribbean.* Kingston, Jamaica: Ian Randle.

Persaud, B., O. de Barry, P. Haynes, F.R. Hore, E. Mathurin and E.R. Ward. 1966. *Enquiry into the feasibility of re-introducing the sugar industry in St Lucia.* University of the West Indies, Institute of Social and Economic Research.

Purchas, Samuel. 1625. *Purchas his pilgrimes, contayning a history of the world in sea voyages and lande travells, by Englishmen and others.* Five volumes. London: printed by William Stansby for Henrie Featherstone. Reprinted in 1905-07. Glasgow: Maclehose.

Rampersad, Anthony. 1986a. 'Cultural resistance. Africans and East Indians in St Lucia.' University of the West Indies. Unpublished manuscript.

Rampersad, Anthony. 1986b. 'Traditional Indian heritage in St Lucia.' In: *The Voice* (14 June):9,13.

Rae, John Todd. 1898. *Building in St Lucia.* Inverness: Association of Surveyors.

Reddock, Rhoda. 1993 [1986]. 'Indian women and indentureship in Trinidad and Tobago 1845-1917: Freedom denied.' In: Beckles and Shepherd (eds.): 225-37. First published in: *Caribbean Quarterly* 32(3 & 4):27-49.

Reddock, Rhoda. 1994. *Women, labour & politics in Trinidad & Tobago.* Kingston, Jamaica: Ian Randle.

Renard, Rosamunde. 1983. 'The sugar industry in Vieux Fort, Saint Lucia. Participatory research and education.' Unpublished manuscript.

Renard, Rosamunde. 1993. 'Immigration and indentureship in the French West Indies, 1848-1870'. In: Beckles and Shepherd (eds.): 161-7.

Reynolds, Anderson, 2001. *Death by fire.* Vieux Fort: Jako Books.

Reynolds, Anderson, 2003. *The struggle for survival. An historical, political, and socio-economic perspective of St Lucia.* Vieux Fort: Jako Books.

Romalis, Coleman. 1970. 'Barbados and St Lucia: a comparative analysis of social and economic development in two British West Indian societies.' Washington University, Washington D.C. Ph.D-thesis. Ann Arbor: University Microfilm International.

Romalis, Rochelle. 1968. 'The rural community and the total society during economic change in St Lucia: a case study.' McGill University. MA-thesis. Ann Arbor: University Microfilm International.

Romalis, Rochelle. 1969. 'The rural entrepreneur and economic development: the case of St Lucia.' In: *McGill Studies in Caribbean Anthropology*, F. Henry (ed.): 93-109. Occassional Paper Series no.5. Centre for Developing-Area Studies, McGill University.

St Lucia Government. 1991. *St Lucia Country Environmental Profile*. Prepared under the aegis of the Caribbean Conservation Association (St Michael, Barbados) for the Government of St Lucia.

Serieux, John. 1986. 'Human settlements in a modified plantation economy: the case of St Lucia.' Unpublished MA-thesis.

Shingleton-Smith, Louise. 2001. *Mamiku: the tale of an 18th century sugar plantation in St Lucia*. Castries: Mamiku Gardens Ltd.

Simmons, Harold. 1963. 'Notes on folklore in St Lucia.' In Brathwaite (ed.):41-9. Department of Extra-Mural Studies. Castries.

Simpson, George E. 1970. 'The Kélé (Chango) cult in St Lucia.' In: *Caribbean Studies*. Vol.13(3):110-16.

Simpson, George E. 1980. *Religious cults of the Caribbean: Trinidad, Jamaica and Haiti*. Caribbean monograph series no.15. In particular: 'The Ras Tafari movement' (:208-28) and 'The Kélé (Chango) cult in St Lucia' (:313-9). Institute of Caribbean Studies, University of Puerto Rico.

Sio, Arnold. 1991 [1987]. 'Marginality and free coloured identity in Caribbean slave society.' In: Beckles and Shepherd (eds.): 150-9. First published in *Slavery and abolition*. Vol.8(2):166-82.

Sisters of St Joseph of Cluny. 1986. *150 Years of witness and worship. The Sisters of St Joseph of Cluny in the Caribbean 1836-1986*. Port-of-Spain, Trinidad: Sisters of St Joseph of Cluny.

Steele, Beverley. 2003. *Grenada. A history of its people*. Oxford: MacMillan.

Sturge, Joseph and Thomas Harvey. 1968 [1838]. *The West Indies in 1837; being the journal of a visit to Antigua, Montserrat, Dominica, St Lucia, Barbados and Jamaica; undertaken for the purpose of ascertaining the actual condition of the Negro population of those islands*. London: Hamilton, Adams & Co.; reprint London: Cass & Co.

Szeto, Linda and E.A. Cebotarev. 1990. 'Women's work patterns: a time allocation study of rural families in St Lucia.' In: *Canadian Journal of Development Studies*. Vol.XI(2):259-78.

Tapon, Rev. 1915. 'St Mary's College, St Lucia.' In: *The St Lucian*. Vol.1(1). Michaelmas Term. Trinidad: Muir, Marshall & Co.

Thornburg, John. 1990. 'Common property in the Eastern Caribbean: family land tenure in economy and society in St Lucia, W.I.' University of Wisconsin-Madison. Ph.D-thesis. Ann Arbor: University Microfilm International.

Uring, Nathaniel. 1725. *A relation of the late intended settlement of the islands of St Lucia and St Vincent in America, in right of the Duke of Montagu, and under His Grace's direction and orders, in the Year 1722.* London: J. Peele.

Vérin, Pierre M. 1961. 'Les Caraibes a Ste Lucie depuis les contacts coloniaux: monograph on the results of research in St Lucia.' In: *New West Indian Guide/Nieuwe West Indische Gids.* Vol.41(2):66-82.

Walcott, Derek. 1987. *The Arkansas Testament.* London, Boston: Faber and Faber.

Walcott, Derek. 1990. *Omeros.* New York: Farrar, Straus and Giroux.

Walcott, Derek. 1992. *Collected Poems 1948-1984.* London, Boston: Faber and Faber.

Walker, D.J.R. 1992. *Columbus and the Golden World of the Island Arawaks. The story of the First Americans and their Caribbean environment.* Kingston, Jamaica: Ian Randle.

Wayne Louis Foundation. 2000. *Indelible. The life and dreams of Stephen Wayne Louis: historian, youth leader, hero.* Castries: St Lucia National Youth Council.

Wayne, Rick. 2002 [1986]. *Foolish virgins.* St Lucia: Star Publishing Co. First published Los Angeles: Star Publications.

Wayne, Rick. 2003 [1979]. *It'll be alright in the morning. The fantastic true story of one Caribbean paradise on the brink of independence!* Castries: Star Publishing Co.

Wayne, Rick. N.d. [2010]. *Lapses and infelicities. An insider perspective of politics in the Caribbean.* Gros Islet: Star Publishing Co.

Weisbrod, B., R. Andreano, R. Baldwin, E. Epstein, A. Kelley, T. Helminiak.1973. *Disease and economic development. The impact of parasitic diseases in St Lucia.* Madison: University of Wisconsin Press.

Williams, Deirdre. 1993. 'Language, literacy, and libraries: St Lucia, West Indies.' University of Illinois, Urbana-Champaign. Unpublished manuscript.

Williams, Gregor (ed.). 2008. *Unsung war heroes of Saint Lucia. Honouring the servicemen and servicewomen of Saint Lucia & commemorating the 60th anniversary of the end of World War II, 2005.* Castries: The Saint Lucia ex-Service Legion.

Willyams, Cooper. 1990 [1796]. *An account of the campaign in the West Indies in the year 1794.* Basse-Terre: Société d'Histoire de la Guadeloupe. Facsimile reproduction. First published in London: T. Bensley.

Wolf, Eric. 1982. *Europe and the people without history.* Berkeley: Univer-

sity of California Press.
World Bank. 1985. St Lucia. *Economic performance and prospects. A World Bank country study.* Washington D.C.: World Bank.

Reports, letters and other documents.

Archives Nationales, Paris.

D/2C/74: St Lucia Census for the years 1730, 1732, 1744-7, 1756, 1758-60, 1769, 1773, 1787.

British Newspaper Library, Colindale, London.

C501 and MC501: *The Voice of St Lucia*, newspaper, 1885-1978; *The West Indian Crusader*, 1959-1979; *St Lucia Herald*, 1962-5.

Maxwell Air Force Base, Alabama.

Historical report Beane Air Force Base, 1941-1949. Dated 24 August 1949. Declassified secret report. Headquarters 5900th Composite Wing Ramey Air Force Base, Puerto Rico. Microfilm roll A0030. Copy provided by Air Force Historical Research Agency.

St Lucia National Archives.

The Voice newspaper.
The West Indian Crusader newspaper.
St Lucia Government Gazette. Ongoing since 1832, making this (one of) the longest-published official organs in the (former) British Empire.
Photographic records.

Koninklijk Instituut voor Taal-, Land- en Volkenkunde (Royal Netherlands Institute of Southeast Asian and Caribbean Studies), University of Leiden.

West India Royal Commission. 1897a. *Report of the West India Royal Commission, with subsidiary report by D. Morris and statistical tables and diagrams, and a map*. London: Eyre and Spottiswood.
West India Royal Commission. 1897b. *Report of the West India Royal Commission. Appendix C, volume 1, containing part 1, minutes of proceedings, reports of evidence, and copies of certain documents received in London.* London: Eyre and Spottiswood.

West India Royal Commission. 1897c. *Report of the West India Royal Commission. Appendix C, volume 3, parts VI-XIII. Proceedings, evidence, and documents relating to the Windward Islands, the Leeward Islands and Jamaica. Part VII, St Lucia.* London: Eyre and Spottiswood.
St Lucia, annual report for 1893 (no. 124) and 1930 (no. 1552).
Annual report on the social and economic progress of the people of St Lucia, 1931-38.

National Archives (formerly Public Record Office) Kew, London.

CO 253/1-150:
Original correspondence of the Secretary of State. Despatches, offices and individuals, 1709-1873 (150 volumes).
Specifically:
CO 253/1:
'Conveyance of the Indians of Sta. Lucia to the English.' Document outlining the conditions of the sale of St Lucia on 6 April 1663 by Thomas 'Indian' Warner, Annivatta D. Babba, Nicholas and Thomas to the English represented by: Thomas Pilgrim, John Hooker, John Harth, Thomas Lewis and Richard Lenon. Hand-copied from the original ca. 1780.
Letter from Henry Clinton to Maj. Gen. James Grant ordering him to attack and conquer St Lucia. Dated New York, 27 October 1778.
Letter from James Grant to Lord George Germain, reporting on Grant's conquest of St Lucia for the British. Written from Morne Fortune, 31 December 1778.
CO 253/2:
Letter from Commandant Brig. Gen. George Prevost to his Commander in Chief, 24 November 1789.
Extract from the 4th Article of Instructions to Brig. Gen. George Prevost by Commander in Chief Thomas Trigge, 14 March 1799.
State of the population of the Island of St Lucia for the year 1799.
'The humble Address of the inhabitants of the Colony of St Lucia' to the King of England. 10 April 1801. Attached are four pages of original signatures from planters in support of Brig. Gen. George Prevost.
CO 253/3:
Letter from Brig. Gen. R. Brereton to Lord Castlereagh, 27 October 1805, on the occasion of a large fire in Castries.
Letter from G.K. du Pemel to Brig. Gen. R. Brereton, on military plans to protect St Lucia. N.d., ca. 1806.
Letter from Brig. Gen. R. Brereton to the Right Honourable William Windham, discussing defensive strategies, 20 October 1806.

Unidentified letter on strategic plans for the defense of St Lucia, debating Morne Fortune versus Pigeon Island, 30 November 1806.
Translation of the Arrête of the Court of Appeals, by R. Drouilhet, Greffier en Chef, 7 April 1807.
CO 253/11:
Announcement by Governor Seymour on the occasion of the mutation of punishment laws for slaves, 27 February 1817.
Letter from Governor Seymour to the Earl of Bathurst in London on local controversy regarding slave punishments, 3 October 1817.
Letter from the Privy Council to His Royal Highness King George on the occasion of the destructive hurricane which killed Governor Seymour and others, dated 21 October 1817.
CO 253/26: Letter from Chief Justice John Jeremie to Governor-General Stewart, reporting on the effect of slave amelioration laws, 30 May 1829 (40 pages).
CO253/101: Lieutenant Governor Henry Darling to Governor-in-Chief Sir William Colebrook, Executive Despatch no.34, 9 March 1849.
CO 253/103: The Sentinel [*ca*. April] 1850, 'St Lucia Treasury Frauds.'
CO253/113: Memorandum on Taxation for the years 1844-51. Includes William Muter's 'Financial history of the British Colony of St Lucia. Its decay and the ruin of its Inhabitants by Fiscal Extractions. Enumeration of Public Acts and Efforts to obtain relief.'
CO 254/1-19: Entry books of correspondence, 1794-1872 (19 volumes).
CO 255/1-25: St Lucia Acts, 1818-1965 (25 volumes).
CO 256/1-30: Sessional Papers (Privy Council, Legislative Council, etc.): 1820-1965 (57 volumes and files).
CO 256/29: Annual Administration Reports 1922-25.
CO 256/32: Annual Administration Reports 1926-31.
CO 256/39: Annual Administration Reports 1932.
CO 256/40: Annual Administration Reports 1937-9.
CO 256/41: Annual Administration Reports 1940-5.
CO 256/42: Annual Administration Reports 1946-50.
CO 256/45: Annual Administration Reports 1951.
CO 256/47: Annual Administration Reports 1952-3.
CO 256/48: Annual Administration Reports 1954.
CO 256/49: Annual Administration Reports 1955.
CO 256/50: Annual Administration Reports 1956-8.
CO 256/51: Annual Administration Reports 1959-60.
CO 256/57: Annual Administration Reports 1963-5.
CO 257/1-25: Government Gazettes, 1857-1965 (102 volumes).
CO 258.: Miscellanea, 1722 - 1940 (136 volumes).

CO 258/3: Account of the Duke of Montague's settlement (1722).
CO 258/4: The memorials of the English and French Commissaries concerning St Lucia. London, 1755.
CO 258/5-15: Protector of Slaves. Includes half-yearly returns of punishment of slaves.
CO 258/1-2: *The St Lucia Palladium*, 1838-47 and 1848-56.
CO 258/16-17: Magistrates' Reports, 1845-53.
CO 258/121: Annual Blue Book of Statistics, 1925.
CO 321: Windward Islands Original Correspondence: correspondence after 1873.
CO 367: Register of Correspondence, 1850-81 (5 volumes).
CO 505: Register of Out-letters, 1872-82 (3 volumes).
CO 714/137: St Lucia: Governor's correspondence, 1816-1848.
CO 714/138: St Lucia: Correspondence, 1849-1866.
CO 714/139: St Lucia: Alphabetical index, 1816-1852.
CO 950/397-425: Interviews, records and reports by the West India Royal Commission of Enquiry under the chairmanship of Lord Moyne.
CAB 21/809: Extract from the House of Commons appointing a Royal Commission of Enquiry for the West Indies.
T 71/376-79: St Lucia: Plantation slaves (index and register) 1815.
T 71/380-390: St Lucia: Abstract of returns (plantation slaves) for the years 1819, 1822, 1825, 1828, 1831 and 1834.

Notes

Notes to chapter 1

1. St Lucia Country Environmental Profile, 1991.
2. Breen 1879-81 (*The Chronicle* 21 February 1880).

Notes to chapter 2

3. Honychurch 1995, p.20.
4. Hulme and Whitehead 1992, p.4.
5. *Ibid.*, p.68.
6. Jesse 1960, Devaux 1975.
7. In the mid twentieth century, Irving Rouse, Marshall McKusick, Wiliam Haag and Ripley Bullen performed archaeological research in St Lucia , while B.H. Easter, Harold Simmons, Father Jesse and 'the Trouble Chasers' rescued many Amerindian artefacts unearthed during construction work. Colonial Engineer Matthew Murphy (1905-19) collected 262 items which ended up in the Barbados Museum and Americans George Heye and Thomas Huckerby presented 414 specimens to the Gothenburg Museum in Sweden. Thomas Ferguson's collection of 482 items was partly lost in the 1948 Castries Fire but the remnants are with the St Lucia Archaeological and Historical Society, along with the Devaux/Canelles Rescue Collection of about 5000 pieces which remains in St Lucia also. In the mid 1980s, the University of Vienna undertook a major archaeological expedition at Pointe de Caille and since 2002, Corinne Hofmann and Menno Hoogland with teams from from the University of Leiden have performed several digs for Amerindian remains also.
8. Robert Devaux.
9. Wayne Louis Foundation 2000, p.108-12.
10. In the first three editions of Jesse's *Outlines*, this date is correct. In later editions, it was erroneously changed to 1502.
11. John Nicholl in Hulme and Whitehead 1992, p.68.
12. John Nicholl 1992 [1607], p.70, also CO253/1, vol. 4th Fol. 1255.
13. Walker 1992, p.26.
14. Honychurch 1995 [1975], p.37.
15. This and subsequent quotes: John Nicholl 1992 [1607], p.62, 68-77.
16. Augier *et. al.* 1988 [1960], p.27. The cave later collapsed in an earthquake.
17. CO 253/1, 'His Majesty's Title to Sta Lucia.'
18. Durham and Lewisohn 1971, p.45.
19. Jesse and Easter1971, p.4.
20. Jesse and Easter (1971) believe this fort was on the windward side but Lefort de Latour, in 1785, stated it was downwind of the Dutch fort, on top of a small hill. No ruins remained even then.
21. CO 253/1, 'His Majesty's Title to Sta Lucia.' An old copy of this deed of sale is kept at the National Archives in London.
22. They later accused the British of '*stealing all the church vestments.*' Durham and

Lewisohn 1971, p.46.

23. *Ibid.* The document states that this ceremony took place in 1664 but this is possibly wrong. Other records state the English sent took possession of St Lucia in 1663.
24. Bruneau-Latouche 1989, p.65.
25. CO 253/1, 'His Majesty's Title to Sta Lucia.'
26. Durham and Lewisohn 1971, p.47.
27. CO253/1, 'His Majesty's Title to Sta Lucia.'
28. CO 253/1. Letter from Mr Lillington: Representation to the Lords Commissioners of Trade. 31 October 1719.
29. A list with 263 named colonists remains: Bruneau-Latouche 1989, pp.299-302.
30. *Ibid.*, p.65.
31. CO 253/1.
32. CO253/1. Letter from Lord Commissioners for Trade to the Duke of Newcastle, 31 December 1729.
33. 'Recensement de 'Isle de Ste Lucia de l'année 1730'. D/2C/74, info provided by Jim Drouilhet.
34. *Ibid.*, 1732.
35. Bruneau-Latouche 1989, p.280.

Notes to chapter 3

36. This and subsequent quotes: Bruneau-Latouche 1989, p.30, 24, 33, 34.
37. Louis 2003, p.6. Josephine's birth place is still hotly debated. She was long presumed to have been born in Martinique but the case built by local historians such as Henry Breen, Vernon Cooper, Robert Devaux and Michael Louis is strong. See: Henry Breen, 'Birthplace of the Empress Josephine' in: *Palladium*, 16 April 1852; Vernon Cooper, 'St Lucians past and present' (undated manuscript); Robert Devaux, 'Josephine was born in St Lucia' in: *The Voice*, 23 June 1984.
38. Bruneau-Latouche 1989, p.104-5.
39. The dated key stone of this mill still survives. Personal communication, Robert Devaux.
40. For a detailed explanation and pictures of the various mills, see Buisseret, 1980, pp.29-38.
41. Breen 1844, p.167.
42. Personal communication, Jim Drouilhet.
43. Kolar 1985, pp.108-10.
44. Personal communication Jim Drouilhet, based on the 1745 census.
45. Bruneau-Latouche 1989, p.37. Letter written in Martinique, 27 May 1765 by D'Ennery and de Peynier to M. le Duc following their return from St Lucia. This and all following translations from the French kindly provided by Yves Renard.
46. This and subsequent quotes: Bruneau-Latouche 1989, p.37-38.
47. *Ibid.*, p.231-250.
48. *Ibid.*, p.251-98.
49. This and subsequent quote: Bruneau-Latouche 1989, pp.40-41.
50. Breen 1844.
51. Breen 1970 [1844], p.13.

52. This and subsequent quotes: Bruneau-Latouche 1989, p.41.
53. Dyde 2000, p.155; Augier *et. al.* 1988 [1960], p.125. In February 1794, an English vicar by the name of Cooper Willyams was part of the English army which conquered Martinique, St Lucia and some other islands. To his amazement, he found '*a fine breadfruit tree*' in the garden at Government House in St Pierre in Martinique, amongst a variety of fruit trees. '[H]*ow it came there, I could not learn, unless some French ships had paid a visit to the islands in the South Sea, for the same purpose that our ships of late have made that voyage; but then I think more of the trees would have been seen in this and the neighbouring French islands.*' (Willyams 1990 [1796], pp.44-5). Captain Bligh is also believed to have introduced the noni bush (*kossol djab* or *devil's soursop* in Kwéyòl) from Tahiti but its alleged medicinal value only recently became common knowledge in St Lucia following marketing drives for noni juice in the USA.
54. Henry Breen quoted in Devaux 1997, p.3.
55. Baron Claude Anne Guy de Micoud was Deputy-Governor from 1771-3, replacing his uncle, Governor Claude Anne de Micoud. In 1773, Deputy-Governor de Micoud was replaced by Monsieur de Karny, who remained in office until his death in 1775. Claude Anne Guy de Micoud (also known as Chevalier de Micoud) resumed provisional administration until arrival of Monsieur de Courcy in late 1775. In 1776, de Courcy was promoted and replaced by Governor de Joubert. De Joubert, however, preferred to live in Martinique and left Chevalier de Micoud to act once again as Deputy-Governor of St Lucia. Breen 1970 [1844], p.56.
56. They were remnants of the Infanterie de Marine and Regiments d'Armagnac and Auxerrois. De Micoud's forces at Morne Fortuné consisted of about 80 men of the Martinique Regiment, 16 gunners and two companies of local militia: a total of 158 men. (Shingleton-Smith 2001, p.16)
57. Bruneau-Latouche 1989, p.42. A letter by Marquis de Bouillé (dated 31 December 1778) mentions 3500 French troops clashing with approximately 2000 Englishmen.
58. Shingleton-Smith 2001, p.16.
59. The event haunted de Micoud for life. He was sent to England as a prisoner of war but soon released. In 1781, he was tried in France by an army war tribunal on charges of having surrendered Morne Fortuné too easily. Ironically, his former enemies General Grant and Admiral Barrington were the ones to defend de Micoud's bravery in resistance. He was cleared of wrongdoing but the trial ended his army career and annulled his army pension. He repeatedly imploring to be reinstated and even tried to redeem himself by acting as a French spy in Holland but he was betrayed and imprisoned. He eventually returned as a planter to St Lucia (Praslin and Soufriere).
60. Durham and Lewisohn 1971, p.14.
61. Mentioned in the 1789 Almanac. Personal communication, Jim Drouilhet.
62. The 1789 Almanac states that one reason the Maroons were successful in attacking white inhabitants was that upon capturing the island, the British had made the French colonists surrender their arms. Personal communication, Jim Drouilhet.
63. Bruneau-Latouche 1989, p.46.
64. Devaux 1997, p.4.
65. Augier *et. al.* 1988 [1960], p.109.
66. *Ibid.*, p.3. Also CO253/1.

67. Jean Zénon de Verron, Baron de Laborie, Brigadier des Armées, appointed Governor of Grenada in July 1782 and Governor of St Lucia from 1784 until his death in 1789.
68. Gachet 1975, letter from de Laborie, 8 June 1785.
69. Bruneau-Latouche 1989, p.50.
70. Hamshere 1972, p.156.
71. Dyde 2000, p.156.
72. The 1789 Almanac mentions in particular that up until 1775, '*Anglo-Americans*' did much trade at Entrepot. Personal communication, Jim Drouilhet.
73. Bruneau-Latouche 1989, p.46. State of the Colony on 1 January 1789. Subsequent quotes *ibid.*, p.43, 158, 163, 168, 173, 177.
74. Old maps show just one islet where today, there are two: Maria Major and Maria Minor. They were probably connected by a large blow hole that caved in at some time - perhaps during the 1780 hurricane?
75. Bruneau-Latouche 1989, p.220.
76. Breen 1970 [1844], p.131.
77. *Ibid.*, p.167.
78. Kolar 1985, pp.108-110.

Notes to chapter 4

79. Foster Walker 2005, p.6, quoting Bernard Boringe, *Le Journal de la France*, vol.V, Paris, 1978.
80. Easter 1965, p.8.
81. This chapter is based in large part on Robert Devaux's 1997 publication *They called us Brigands;* Barry Gaspar's 1997 article 'La Guerre des Bois. Revolution, war, and slavery in Saint Lucia, 1793-1838' and General John Moore's diary (published in 1904).
82. Easter 1965, p.6.
83. Augier *et. al.* 1988 [1960], p.112.
84. *Ibid.*, p.160.
85. Gaspar 1997, p.103. Lefort de Latour describes two estates in 1784: one belonging to the widow Viette and another to L'Ainé Viette. They are adjacent, just inland from Ance Mahaut and Ance Bonnet, a little south of Canaries.
86. *Ibid.* The incident was described in the *Gazette de Sainte Lucie, Nationale et Politique* on 6 January 1791.
87. Henry Breen (1970 [1844], p.78) wrote sarcastically: '*The slaves were freely roaming the towns and countryside under arms, discussing the rights of man.*'
88. '*Decret de la Convention Nationale. Du 16 jour de Pluviôse, an second de la République Française, une & indivisible. Qui abolit l'Esclavage des Nègres dans les Colonies. La Convention Nationale déclare que l'Esclavage des Nègres dans toutes les Colonies est aboli; en conséquence elle décrète que tous les hommes, sans distinction de couleur, domiciliés dans les colonies, sont citoyens Français, & jouiront de tous les droits assurés par la constitution.*'
89. '*The republican abolition of slavery was above all meant to turn the slave population against the British wherever they might land, thus adding to republican strength*'. Gaspar 1997, p.106.
90. Willyams 1990 [1796], p.78. John Jervis also commanded a brigade of light infantry under command of Major General Dundas; the 6th, 9th and 43rd

regiments commanded by Colonel Sir Charles Gordon; engineers under Colonel Dornford and a detachment of Royal Artillery with some light ordnance under Lieutenant Colonel Patterson.

91. Willyams 1990 [1796], pp.77-81 gave a detailed account of the English conquest: *'The gates of the fort were put into our possession the same evening by nine o'clock. On the 4th the enemy marched out of the fort, with the honours of war, to the glacis, where they piled their arms, and were embarked on board of transports, which conveyed them to France, under conditions that they should not serve against his Britannic Majesty during the war. The garrison that marched out with General Ricard, and laid down their arms as prisoners of war, were about three hundred men, troops of the line (among which one hundred and twenty-five were of the regiment d'Aunai), some artillery, and a few people of colour. General Ricard, at his own request, was sent to America, as had been General Rochambeau, who chose that place in preference to his own distracted country, where the system of blood that was then the order of the day under the tyranny of Robespierre, would have immolated even these men, who had with so much bravery defended the posts intrusted to them by their country.'*

92. Of these, 125 were of the regiment d'Aunai.

93. Gaspar 1997, p.106.

94. Willyams 1990 [1796] in a footnote on pp.129-130 described Gordon's trial in detail. *'At the taking of St Lucia, Colonel Sir Charles Gordon, who had repeatedly distinguished himself by his gallant conduct, was appointed governor of that island, and in the last promotion was advanced to the rank of brigadier general; soon after which some very unpleasant reports prevailed, of extortions and speculations by him, and taking bribes of the inhabitants, who were supposed to be disaffected, in order to suffer them to remain on the island, and then breaking his word with them. At length a regular complaint was laid before the Commander in Chief, who instantly ordered a court martial to be summoned, and sent an officer to St Lucia to arrest Sir Charles Gordon, and convey him to Martinique, in order for trial ... the event of which was, that the prisoner was found guilty of the crimes laid to his charge, and was sentenced to refund the money he had extorted, and to be rendered incapable of serving his majesty again; but, in consequence of some favourable circumstances that came out on the trial, he was allowed to sell his commission.'*

95. This and subsequent quotes cited in Gaspar 1997, p.105-07.

96. Easter 1965, p.8, quoting from Bryan Edwards' *History of the War in the West Indies.*

97. Curtis Jacobs, n.d. Curtis quotes military historian Sir John Fortescue on this fact.

98. Quoted in Easter 1965, p.8.

99. Quoted in J.F. Fortescue, *History of the British Army*. London: MacMillan, volume 4.

100. Easter 1965, p.10.

101. *'Whatever one's views may be on Republicanism as an abstract political creed, whatever one's views may be about the doctrine of the French Revolution, the fact is Republican rule in the 1790s meant a reign of anarchy, a reign of terror. There is no other island in the Lesser Antilles which fell victim to the event that St Lucia did,'* wrote Lucille Mathurin in 1954.

102. *The Voice*, 4 January 1906.

103. Robert Devaux, based on Anthony Gludon's article 'Quelques observations sur l'histoire de Sainte Lucie.' In: *St Lucia Palladium*, 3 September 1853.

104. Stewart's troops were made up of the 34th and the 61st as well as flank companies of the 9th and 68th and Malcolm's Rangers. Fortescue (1915, pp.433-6) dedicated four pages of his *History of the British Army* to the Battle of Rabot.
105. Fortescue 1915, p.434.
106. Tom Ferguson, 1906.
107. This and subsequent quotes: Fortescue 1915, p.434-6.
108. Quoted in Easter 1965, pp.10-11. Goyrand fulfilled his promise. John Moore (p.219) later described Goyrand as: '*a plain, honest man*' who '*has been always a military man ... He is a man of humanity, did good, and is much liked by the Colony.*'
109. Report by Goyrand, 1796.
110. This and subsequent quote: Breen 1970 [1844], p.85-6.
111. Curtis Jacobs, n.d.
112. Fortescue estimated 8000 men; Moore 11 000, and Breen 12 000. War Office records place the figure at well over 12 000.
113. This and subsequent quotes: Moore, pp.219-26.
114. '*The army is embarked and I remain with the 31st, 44th, 48th, 55th York Rangers, O'Meara's black corps, one hundred Royal Artillery, two engineers, asistants, &c., making in all for 4000 or 5000 men fit for duty, besides officers, sergeants, and drummers.*'
115. '*He is a man of property in the island, is reckoned clever, but is of a restless, ambitious temper. He was a principal agent of the Republic, but was permitted with many others to remain after the capture of the island. ... I sent for him ... I saw he depended much upon his eloquence, which consisted in declamation and protestations of innocence. ... I sent him to the Commodore at Castries to remain as a prisoner in his ship.*' In 1806, a Roche Rupes, former Praslin deputy to the *Assemblée Coloniale*, sold some land in Micoud; in 1818, a Sieur Roche de Rupes sold an estate at Praslin; and in 1827-8, Roche Rupes was listed as owner of Riche Fond estate. (CO258/5) Was this the same man? If so, he was either never deported or returned from exile. Praslin appears to have been a little white Republican hotbed, with sympathies in the Catholic Church. It was '*Madame Dubuc-Roche, residing at Trois-Islets, nowadays Praslin*' (Roche Rupes' mother?) who in 1749 '*had a Chapel built on her bay*' where Abbé Gerfroi, the Vieux Fort priest, '*used to come from time to time to celebrate Divine Worship.*' (Gachet 1975, p.16). It was the first church on the east of the island and points at a close relationship between the Roches and the local priests. The priest of Praslin later joined the Brigands.
116. This and subsequent quotes: *ibid.*, pp.227-30.
117. Moore 1904, p.230-1. In a list of half-yearly returns of punishment (CO258/5), Freeland and Rigby show up as owners of Canelle Estate. This fits in perfectly with Moore's description. The '*village on my flank in which more brigands might be placed*' would have been Micoud.
118. This and subsequent quotes: *ibid.*, p.231-450.
119. A 1771 record shows a Stanislaus, *Mulâtre Libre* with 20 carrés of land to the southwest of a runaway camp now known as *Ba Kan Nèg Mawon*. It is quite possible that this is the same man who later became an important Brigand leader.
120. Gaspar 1997, p.121.
121. Breen 1970 [1844], p.107.
122. Jeremie 1831, pp.47-8.
123. Gaspar 1997, p.121. The 1799 population stood at 13 391 slaves altogether:

3319 men, 5604 women and 4468 children. At the same time, there were 1364 free people of colour and 1195 whites. (CO253/2. '*State of the population of the Island of St Lucia for the year 1799, as by the Denombrements of the respective Districts.*').

124. Gaspar 1997, pp.121-2. Brigadier General Prevost's mortality figures for the period 28 May 1796 - October 1799 support this (CO253/2). The category '*Imported Negroes*' shows 949 deaths while '*Creole Negroes*' shows 1223 deaths, making for a total of 2172 slave deaths over those three years. At the same time, 730 children were born in slavery. Prevost hinted at the problem of starvation in an aside: '*N.B.: From the Year 1796 to the beginning of 1798 the Colony was in that distressed state from the calamities of the Civil War, that the Inhabitants could not reside on their Estates and consequently there was no sort of cultivation, even for supplying the Negroes with Food.*'

125. Gaspar 1997, p.121.

126. Devaux 1997.

127. Steele 2003, p.130.

Notes to chapter 5

128. Personal communication, Jim Drouilhet. National Archives London: volumes T 71/376-390.

129. Beckles 1991, p.363.

130. Beating drums and blowing horns (being means of communication with runaway slaves) was forbidden by law but this prohibition was not generally enforced. Goveia 1991, p.351.

131. Beckles 1991, p.364.

132. Philip Curtin (1972), cited in Kolar 1985, p.271.

133. Wolf 1982, pp.195-6.

134. CO 253/1.

135. Bruneau-Latouche, 1989, p.58, letter on 3 August 1719.

136. *Ibid.*, p.302. Letter by M. de Sennecterre dated 11 January 1723.

137. '*Affaires du Chatillon capitaine de malice qui veut chaser les negres marrons de Sainte Lucie.*' Dated 15 November 1726 and 1 July 1727. Documents at Archives Departmentales in Fort de France, Martinique: C8A/F0298 and C8A/37 F0320. Information provided by Jim Drouilhet.

138. Bruneau-Latouche, 1989, p.30.

139. Archives Departementales, Fort de France, Martinique: C8A/47 - F0305, 25 May 1736 and C8A/54 - F0321, 13 November 1742. Information provided by Jim Drouilhet.

140. Figures for free people of colour provided by Jim Drouilhet, using the 1745 census.

141. Archives Departementales, Fort de France, Martinique: C8A/57fo 136, 29 Dec 1746. Information provided by Jim Drouilhet.

142. Jeremie 1831, p.39.

143. CO 253/2.

144. Kolar 1985, pp.284-5. Also CO 253/14/1, 15 February 1819. This list formed the correction to another list drawn up in 1816, which unfortunately no longer exists.

145. *Ibid.*, pp.280-1. Also CO-253/23/2, period 1821-25.

146. *Ibid.*, p.282. Kolar spells the second name '*Valtou*' but it is clear that this reference is to the business partners Frederic Tharel and Valeton. Personal communication, Jim Drouilhet.
147. This may be a referral to the Madame Jacob whose tomb can still be seen in the front of one part of Riverside Cemetery in Castries today. Personal communication, Jim Drouilhet.
148. Probably Jacques de Ruaud. Personal communication, Jim Drouilhet.
149. Kolar 1985, pp.283-4.
150. *Ibid.*, pp.287-8. Also CO253/23/2. Indiana Sadler (f), Barbados; Waterloo Sadler (m), Barbados; John Sadler (m), Barbados; Antoine Sebrieto (m), Trinidad; Magdelaine Pegg (f), Trinidad; Francis Lacompe (m), Trinidad; John Grigg (m), Barbados; Casar (m), Barbados; Marie Victoire Soupiere (f), Bahamas; Jean Goodsir (m), Trinidad; Antoine Lancandier (m), England; Jean Fameux (m), unknown; Aimée Paresseuse (f), unknown; John Elliot (m), Grenada; Jeffery Hetherington (m), Grenada; Jean Artimise Jaque (f), Grenada; Ann Louis (f), Grenada; Marie Louise (f), St Vincent; Angelique Ange (f), Martinique; Joseph Ange (m), Martinique; Sabine Banane (f), Trinidad; Eugette Ann (f), Trinidad; Francis Wood (m), Jamaica; Alexander Danseur (m), St Vincent; Silvestre Figees (m), St Vincent; Richard Mango (m), St Vincent.
151. *Ibid.*, p.289.
152. Willyams 1990 [1796], p.13.
153. Shingleton-Smith 2001, p.24.
154. Augier *et. al.* 1988 [1960], p.163.
155. Kolar 1985, pp.60-1.
156. *Ibid.*, pp.168-70 for this and further quotes in this section.
157. *Ibid.*, p.150.
158. Goveia 1991, p.357.
159. Personal communication, Jim Drouilhet.
160. Bruneau-Latouche, 1989, p.251.
161. *Ibid.*, p.261.
162. *Ibid.*, p.263.
163. *Ibid.*, p.271. Similar marriage acts are found in pp.279-90.
164. *Ibid.*, p.265.
165. Personal communication, Jim Drouilhet.
166. Bruneau-Latouche, 1989, p.261.
167. *Ibid.*, p.259.
168. *Ibid.*, p.277.
169. *Ibid.*
170. *Ibid.*, p.277-8.
171. *Ibid.*, p.279.
172. *Ibid.*,, p.275.
173. *Ibid.*, p.276. It is unclear whether the marriage automatically freed Bruno Petit or whether Anne Marie had to buy her husband's manumission.
174. Kolar 1985, p.189, referring to British Parliamentary Papers: BPP/ST/71/2:16/3/1685, p.187 (National Archives, London).
175. The 1745 census mentions a Dubuq Letang in the company of Dezincher in Trois Ilets (Praslin) who was at the time the biggest slave owner in St Lucia with 50 *negres*, 23 *negresses* and 36 *negrillons* making a total of 109. Personal communication, Jim Drouilhet.

176. Kolar:1985, p.189. Also BPP/ST/71/2: 15/10/1786, p.207, National Archives, London.
177. This and subsequent quote: Kolar 1985, p.190-1.
178. CO253/11, letter dated 3 October 1817. Governor Seymour died eighteen days later in the 1817 hurricane.
179. Breen 1970 [1844], p.408-09.
180. It is sobering, in this context, to read Robert Hughes' book on the equally horrific treatment of white British prisoners in Australia around the same time.
181. Henry Breen (*The Chronicle*, 4 October, 1879) recounted how, on 30 November 1829, Scottish planters and merchants in Castries celebrated St Andrew's Day. '*A dinner party was organized, and in the evening the company (most of them in a state of intoxication), paraded the streets, headed by a man playing the bagpipes. ... In passing Mr Jeremie's house ... they assailed him and his wife with the most insulting language; and one of them took up a stone and threw it at his bedroom window. Mr Jeremie, who was in bed, rushed out in his shirt ... and boldly confronted them. No doubt there was in this a degree of intrepidity which* [is] *characteristic of the man; but there was also great temerity, for in the state in which the rioters were, they might have killed him. As it was, one of them took up a large carving knife and threw it at his head. It grazed his cheek and stuck in the partition behind him. Mr Jeremie now saw the danger and withdrew, followed by a volley of hisses and groans*'. Subsequent hostilities towards Jeremie were carried to a ludicrous extent. '*A lady, whose son was among the rioters, engaged a little black boy as a servant, and had him christened "Jeremie." She lived opposite the Court House, and whenever the First President came there on business, she would place the little boy in the street, under his windows, and assail him (the boy) with all manner of insulting language. It was "Jeremie! You scoundrel!" - "Jeremie! you blackguard!" - "Jeremie! you are nothing but a canaille!" And she went on in this strain, always addressing the boy, as long as Mr. Jeremie remained in his chambers.*'
182. Augier *et. al.*, 1988 [1960], pp.131-2.
183. Kolar 1985, p.65. Also CO 255/1/1: 1/6/1826, p.164.
184. *Ibid.*, p.67.
185. *Ibid.*, p.64. Also CO 253/19/2: 18/2/1825.
186. Anonymous. 1832a, pp.107-09.
187. *Ibid.*, pp.103 and 142. Subsequent quotes: *ibid.*, p.9, 24, 65
188. This and subsequent quotes: Jeremie 1831, pp.5-10.
189. *Ibid.*, p.16. Jeremie (p.9) mentions a case of multiple slave murder back in 1808, where the accused had been acquitted. The case was documented in detail by then greffier Raymond Drouilhet, who later became Procureur-General. The planter in question was Tyrone O'Neill. Following some relatively minor upset on his estate, O'Neill reportedly lined up six slaves, chose six other slaves and ordered the latter to bayonet the former. One of the six executors, a man named Vincent, objected on the grounds that the woman he was ordered to kill, Babet, was his godmother. O'Neill made Vincent join the six victims, found a seventh executor, and had all seven slaves murdered on his command. He then had their heads cut off and placed on pikes in the slaves' gardens. When neigbouring planters heard what happened, they were outraged and reported O'Neill to the *Procureur du Roi*. O'Neill was tried in the lower court and sentenced to death

but he appealed to the higher court, which was packed with his friends, and was acquitted. However, his neighbours and the members of the lower court did not back down and referred his case to the Privy Council in England for retrial. O'Neill skipped the island and eventually died before the matter was tried in the Privy Council. Personal communication, Jim Drouilhet.

190. Quoted in Goveia 1991, p.359.

191. Geggus 1991, p.406.

192. See Augier *et. al.* 1988 [1960], pp.148-58 for an excellent overview of the anti-slavery efforts in England.

193. CO 258/6, Protector of Slaves, Jan.-Sept. 1830.

194. CO 253/11.

195. Jeremie 1831, p.97. Two of these six estates were considered *'well-managed'* (Canelles and Noumacé).

196. *Ibid.*, pp.97-8. Ethnic background made no significant difference: there were Englishmen, Frenchmen, English Creoles and French Creoles in both groups. The one proprietor-run estate with very high returns of punishments was run by a man who had twice publicly petitioned to have the slave laws made more severe. Jeremie did not mention colour as a distinguishing factor in management style.

197. Jeremie was astounded to see how slaves' general treatment could be seen to impact on births and deaths. '*To say nothing of acts of wanton and atrocious barbarity, it is surprising how the want of nourishment, excessive labour, repeated corporal punishment, the want of sufficient clothing, damp and unhealthy cottages, and the leaving slaves to lie on the ground, - how all these causes affect population.*' Jeremie (1831, pp.98-9) provided another example of cruelty, which resulted in a trial against the culprit: '*The prisoner was said to have punished a boy, named Bastien, so severely as to have placed his life in danger, and then ordered that boy's mother to take care of him on her own day. She replied, that if so, she and her remaining children must starve. She, though quick with child, was flogged also. The result was, she was delivered of twins - both dead; - she died and Bastien died.*'

198. Anonymous 1832a, p.130.

199. Breen (1879-81) also remarked on this: '*Perhaps the worst days of slavery were those which immediately preceded emancipation. The planters were exasperated at the prospect of their property being taken from them; and they often vented their rage upon the poor slaves who were the innocent cause of their anticipated ruin.*' *The Voice* 10 April 1880, reprinted from Grenada's *The Chronicle*.

200. CO 258/15, complaint no. 79 (pp.599-614), Office of the Assistant Protector of Slaves, 3rd District, Vieux Fort, 28th April 1834. All subsequent quotes relating to this case are taken from this document.

Notes to chapter 6

201. CO 253/2/2. Also Kolar 1985, p.56. Prevost was succeeded in May 1802 by Brigadier-General George Henry Vansittart. The Peace of Amiens (signed 25 March 1802) restored St Lucia to the French, so Vansittart was replaced on 29 September 1802 by Captain-General of the French Antilles Admiral Villaret-Joyeuse, who sent Brigadier-General Jean Francois Xavier Noguès to act as administrator.

202. Kolar 1985, p.124.

203. CO 253/2, 24 November 1798.
204. Kolar 1985, p.125.
205. CO 253/2. First names deduced from other documents.
206. *Ibid.*, and Breen 1970 [1844], p.110-11.
207. Kolar 1985, p.55.
208. Sio 1991, p.150.
209. Breen 1970 [1844], p.127. Breen stated that the English drank like fish and died like flies, more so than the French: '*In July 1831 there were 142 European settlers in the island, 68 of whom, persons generally addicted to the use of ardent spirits, have been prematurely cut off - very few having attained the age of 35.*'
210. *Ibid.*, p.165.
211. Gaspar n.d. (*ca.*1975), p.3.
212. This and subsequent quotes: Jeremie 1831, p.30-1.
213. Sio 1991.
214. Gaspar n.d. (*ca.*1975), p.12.
215. This and subsequent quote: *ibid.*, quoting Governor Mainwaring (1826-27).
216. Augier *et. al.* 1988 [1960], pp.160-1. Of an 1819 list of fifteen Protestant free men of colour in Castries, eleven men owned a total of 83 slaves. John Patterson had seventeen, G. Hannim twelve, and Felicity Lee thirteen. '*Five years later ... both Patterson and Lee still owned more than 8 slaves each, and these were described as "personal slaves".*' Gaspar n.d. (*ca.*1975), p.7.
217. Gaspar n.d. (*ca.*1975), p.13, says '*the tone of the petitions was disarmingly modest*' and the language used '*conspicuously temperate*' Also: '*Absent was any note of militant opposition to the laws.*'
218. Gaspar 1983.
219. Jeremie 1831, p.49.
220. *Palladium*, 20 November 1858 (Henry Percin's obituary).
221. This and subsequent quotes: Gaspar 1983, p.2, 4 and 5.
222. This and subsequent quotes: Jeremie 1831, pp.50-1.
223. Breen 1970 [1844], p.166.
224. *Ibid.*, p.184.
225. Sturge and Harvey 1968 [1838], p.125.
226. This section based on Breen 1970 [1844], p.160-4.
227. Johnson and Watson (eds.) 1998. Also Brereton 1985, pp.15-17.
228. Renard 1983, p.10.
229. Augier et. al. 1988 [1960], p.127.
230. Jeremie, 30 May 1829. Also CO 253/26, p.23. '*... it has been usual to compute the value of an estate by the number of slaves attached to it, buildings and land being supposed to be, in themselves, of little value.*'
231. Breen 1970 [1844], p.278-9.
232. In 1927, Thomas Ferguson traced the history of Mamiku Estate. Also Shingleton-Smith (2001).
233. This and subsequent quotes: Breen 1970 [1844], p.279, 283, 285, 286. Pp.317-8 gives a list of all estates disposed by judicial sale between 1833 and 1844 and the prices obtained for them.
234. Renard 1983, p.18.
235. This and subsequent quote: Jeremie 1831, p.58, 60.
236. Romalis, Coleman 1970, pp.45-6.
237. Renard 1983, pp.18-19.

238. CO 253/3.
239. *Ibid.*, '*Translation of the Arrêté of the Court of Appeals at their Meeting of the 7th April 1807.*'
240. Breen 1970 [1844], pp.142-3.
241. *Ibid.*, p.138. Also Jesse 1994 [1956], p.38.
242. CO 253/11.
243. Breen 1970 [1844], p.139.
244. CO 253/26/6, 29 September 1829. Also in Kolar 1985, p.297.
245. This and subsequent quotes: Kolar 1985, pp.297-8.
246. Jeremie 1831, p.103.
247. *Ibid.*, p.51.
248. One refugee was returned: Sylvestre Pombarré, who stood accused of murder in Martinique. Breen 1970 [1844], p.180.
249. Anonymous 1832a, p.84.
250. Breen 1970 [1844], p.170.
251. Kolar 1985, p.330, citing a German magazine: '*Das Ausland*' 1836 vol.2, p.104.
252. Anonymous 1832a, p.87, footnote.
253. Breen 1970 [1844], pp.171-2.
254. Breen 1879-81 *The Chronicle* (Grenada) 10 August 1879.
255. Breen 1970 [1844], p.178.
256. Breen 1879-81, *The Chronicle* (Grenada) 10 August 1879.
257. Breen 1970 [1844], p.178.
258. Kolar 1985, p.327, using various sources.
259. CO253/62/6, 8 June 1838, stipendiary magistrate for Castries and Anse la Raye. Also quoted in Kolar 1985, p.332.
260. CO 253/62/9, 14 June 1838. Also in Kolar 1985, p.333.
261. CO 253/62/10, 2 June 1838. Also in Kolar 1985, p.334.
262. CO 253/62/7, 7 June 1838. Also in Kolar 1985, p.332.
263. CO 253/62/8, 18 June 1838. Also in Kolar 1985, p.333.
264. Jeremie 1831, pp.51-2.
265. Anonymous 1832a, p.86.
266. This and the subsequent quote: Sturge and Harvey 1968 [1838], pp.123-4.
267. Breen 1970 [1844], p.180.
268. This and subsequent quotes: Kolar 1985, p 329 (also CO 258/16/16, 1 July 1848); p.306 (also CO 253/40/7, 1 November 1832); p.304 (also CO 253/29/3, 28 June 1831); p.308 (also CO 256/2/3, 11 November 1833); p.307 (also CO 253/40/8, 3 November 1832; CO 253/40/9, 29 November 1832; CO 253/40/10, 30 November 1832 and CO 253/43/8, 31 January 1833).
269. Sturge and Harvey 1968 [1838], p.122.

Notes to chapter 7

270. Augier *et. al.* 1988 [1960], pp.183.
271. This and subsequent quote: Jeremie 1831, p.120-21.
272. West India Royal Commission 1897a (part III, 'Concluding observations and summary'), p.64.
273. Breen's memoirs (1879-81) at times, read like a nineteenth century soap opera. A good example is the *Polycarp letter* incident, regaled in *The Chronicle* (Grenada) of 11 October 1879.

274. In 1833, the unpopular Governor James Alexander Farquharson found his treasury much depleted as a result of planters' refusal to pay taxes. Whenever government could not pay a bill, Farquharson wrote '*Payable in plantation taxes*' on it. Planters subsequently hung an effigy of Farquharson from a tree, a sheet of paper pinned to its back with the words '*Payable in plantation taxes*'. Breen 1879-81, *The Chronicle* (Grenada) 10 August 1879.
275. Adrien 1996, p.16.
276. Marshall (Woodville) 1993a, p.64.
277. *Ibid.*, subsequent quotes: p.69, 64, 66, 65.
278. See for instance Lobdell 1988.
279. Adrien 1996, pp.30-1.
280. Augier et. al. 1988 [1960], p.211.
281. Administrator's Annual Report for St Lucia, 1851-2. Information provided by Robert Devaux.
282. Adrien 1996, p.33.
283. Marshall 1993a, p.72, also p.73, 75, 76.
284. CO253/113. Memorandum on Taxation for the years 1844-51, prepared for Mr Merivale, personal secretary to the Duke of Newcastle, Secretary of State for the Colonies, on the occasion of William Muter's allegation of over-taxation and his claim for reimbursement of funds embezzled by the treasurer, William Hanley.
285. Breen 1879-81, *The Voice* 6 December 1879.
286. CO253/113. Memorandum on Taxation, 1848-9.
287. St Lucian historian Michael Louis described in great detail the struggle of newly-freed people to gain access to the land, as well as the treasury fraud and the 1849 tax revolt in his 1981 Ph.D-thesis 'An equal right to the soil: the rise of a peasantry in St Lucia, 1838-1900.' (Baltimore: Johns Hopkins University). This thesis was distributed in microfilm format by University Microfilm International in Ann Arbor and printed copies can be found in specialist libraries worldwide, including the Folk Research Centre in Castries. A paper entitled 'The revolt of 1849: economic obstacles and peasant resistance in St Lucia' (based on a chapter from this thesis) was presented at the Landmarks in St Lucian History Conference in 1999. Another fascinating paper entitled 'Governing without consent: political resistance in St Lucia and the emergence of the Social Improvement Association 1838-1848' was presented at the 2005 St Lucia Country Conference and may be found online. Dr Louis has declined to grant permission to quote from any of these works for inclusion in this general history of St Lucia. A publication based on Louis' 1981 thesis is reportedly forthcoming. All of the sources quoted in this section are public records and were obtained directly by the authors from the National Archives in London.
288. This and subsequent quotes: CO253/101. Lieutenant Governor Henry Darling to Governor-in-Chief Sir William Colebrook, Executive Despatch no.34, 9 March 1849.
289. CO258/2, *St Lucia Palladium* and *Public Gazette*, 27 April 1848. Special session of the Criminal Court, 18 April 1848. Interrogation of Lieutenant Henry Whatley Tyler, private secretary to Lieutenant-Governor Darling.
290. This and subsequent quotes: CO253/101. Lieutenant Governor Henry Darling to Governor-in-Chief Sir William Colebrook, Executive Despatch

no.34, 9 March 1849.

291. CO258/2, *St Lucia Palladium* and *Public Gazette*, 27 April 1848. Special session of the Criminal Court, 18 April 1848. Interrogation of Lieutenant Henry Whatley Tyler, private secretary to Lieutenant-Governor Darling.

292. *St Lucia Palladium* 11 May 1849. Attorney-General J.G. Porter-Athill at a Special Session of the Criminal Court, 20 April 1849: The Queen *versus* Henry Boy.

293. This and subsequent quote: CO253/101. Lieutenant Governor Henry Darling to Governor-in-Chief Sir William Colebrook, Executive Despatch no.34, 9 March 1849.

294. CO258/2, *St Lucia Palladium* and *Public Gazette*, 27 April 1848. Special session of the Criminal Court, 18 April 1848. Interrogation of Lieutenant Henry Whatley Tyler, private secretary to Lieutenant-Governor Darling.

295. *Ibid.*, interrogation of William Hanley, Colonial Secretary.

296. This and subsequent quotes: CO253/101. Lieutenant Governor Henry Darling to Governor-in-Chief Sir William Colebrook, Executive Despatch no.34, 9 March 1849.

297. CO258/2, *St Lucia Palladium* and *Public Gazette*, 27 April 1848. Special session of the Criminal Court: The Queen *versus* Pelage Aquart, Servé, Grand Xavier and Vincent.

298. CO253/101. Lieutenant Governor Henry Darling to Governor-in-Chief Sir William Colebrook, Executive Despatch no.34, 9 March 1849.

299. The jurors in The Queen *versus* Henry Boy were: Henry Glace, Spencer Goodsir, Isaac Roche, Francis Peter, Charles Allarie, George Delomel, Alcide Bernier, Gustave de Rougemont, Joseph André, J.L. Romney, Ingenac Antoine and D. MacNachten.

300. Breen 1879-1881. *The Voice* 6 December 1879. Unless otherwise indicated, subsequent quotes are taken from this.

301. CO 253/103. *The Sentinel* [*ca.* April] 1850, 'St Lucia Treasury Frauds'.

302. This and subsequent quotes: CO253-113, William Muter, 'Financial history of the British Colony of St Lucia. Its decay and the ruin of its Inhabitants by Fiscal Extractions. Enumeration of Public Acts and Efforts to obtain relief.'

303. '*The Brothers Muter, one or other of them, have been for 20 years & more, steadily persisting in sending home elaborately false statements on St Lucia affairs which were for many years elaborately answered & whatever complaint they may have to make, they certainly cannot but know that they are unwarranted in complaining of not having been attended to. His method of proceeding has been to allow a certain lapse of time & then deliberately to reiterate his statements without taking any notice of the previous confutations & contradictions.*' Note scribbled on the back of a letter (CO253/13, headed Clapham Common, 19 Sept 1853) from William Muter to the Duke of Newcastle (Secretary of State for the Colonies), probably written by the Duke's secretary, Herman Merivale.

304. CO253/113, Minutes of the Treasury Board, 23 August 1853.

305. CO253/113. Letter by William Muter, dated 19 Sept 1853, to the Duke of Newcastle.

306. Breen 1879-81. *The Voice* 6 December 1879.

307. This and subsequent quotes: CO 253/103. Breen in *The Sentinel*, 1850 (*ca.* April).

308. CO253/103, enclosures 5, 6 and 7. John Todd, incarcerated at the Royal Gaol

in Castries, petitioning Governor Colebrooke. Lieutenant-Governor Darling returned the petition to Todd without forwarding it to his superior.

309. Breen 1879-81. *The Voice* 6 December 1879.

310. Breen 1879-81 (chapter XXV) wrote that forty year after Emancipation, ex-slaves had done well for themselves: '*They are intelligent, industrious, and, to some extent, educated, and they are, above all things, remarkably sober. The sons of those who were born in slavery have, in many instances, attained to a good position as tradesmen, shopkeepers, overseers on the estates, while many of the women are trusted housekeepers and domestic servants everywhere. The coloured people have risen in a still higher degree. They are now socially, and, to a great extent, intellectually the equals of the whites. The local schools, and the schools and colleges in Europe are extensively resorted to by them for the education of their children; and the consequence is seen in the number of coloured men who are now enrolled as members of the learned professions. In point of fact the prejudice against "colour" has almost entirely disppeared; and if a person is spoken of as a coloured man, or a coloured woman, it is no longer in the disparaging tone of former days, but merely for the purpose of stating a fact.*'

311. Lovelace 1982, p.33.

Notes to chapter 8

312. This and subsequent quotes: Breen 1970 [1844], pp.14-16.

313. *Ibid.*, p.118. Yellow fever is a mosquito-borne virus closely related to Dengue fever but more lethal.

314. This and subequent quotes: Breen 1970 [1844], p.16, 17, 18, 22, 23, 24.

315. The church was extended in the 1890s, bringing the seating capacity from 800 to 3000 and making it one of the largest churches in the region. Gachet (1975) described Fr Tapon's struggle to complete the work: '... *in December 1894 Fr. Tapon wrote this to his niece:* "I have not a penny left and I have become the greatest beggar in St Lucia. I beg everywhere, in church, at the market place, in the rum shops, in the streets and, though people are poor, they seldom refuse me a little penny." ... *Happily there was much generosity ... and many people helped freely with the carrying of stones and sand. The moonlight coups-de-mains were particularly popular.*' The newly extended church was blessed and consecrated on 11 May 1899 by Archbishop Flood. It became a Cathedral in 1957 and a Minor Basilica in 1999.

316. Breen 1970 [1844], pp.24-5.

317. Only the Roman Catholic Church in Vieux Fort is older (around 1805) but this was modified and enlarged around 1900.

318. This and subsequent quotes: Breen 1970 [1844], p.21, 22, 19-20, 119, 29, 28, 31.

319. The Legislative Council opted instead to allocate £450 to the construction of waterworks in Castries (*ibid.*, p.40).

320. This and subsequent quotes: Breen 1970 [1844], pp.33-39, 42-44, 13.

321. Hamilton *et. al.* N.d.

322. This and subsequent quotes: Breen 1970 [1844], p.117, 26, 292.

323. *Ibid.*, p.297. In 1841, wine-making became another brief experiment in Soufriere but the West India Wine Company failed to attract enough local capital and went under.

324. *Ibid.*, p.290. Number of sugar estates in 1789 and 1843 respectively, per

district. Castries 6 - 9; Anse La Raye 4 - 6; Soufriere 9 - 20; Choiseul 0 - 5; Laborie 5 - 8; Vieux Fort 8 - 10; Micoud 1 - 7; Praslin 3- 1; Dennery 1 - 4; Dauphin 2- 2; Gros-Ilet 4 - 9. Total: 43 in 1789 and 81 in 1843.

325. *Ibid.*, p.292.
326. This and subsequent quotes: Kolar 1985, pp.397-9.
327. Government Gazette, 22 March 1871.
328. This and subsequent quotes: Kolar 1985, p.400, 419, 401.
329. West India Royal Commission 1897c (app.C, part VII), p.76.
330. This and subsequent quotes: Kolar 1985, p.405, 411, 410.
331. Breen 1970 [1844], p.312.
332. Kolar 1985, p.411.
333. This and subsequent quote: Rae quoted in Kolar, pp.537-9.
334. Engerman and Higman 1997, p.92.
335. Augier *et. al.* 1988 [1960], p.216.
336. This and subsequent quote: Steele 2003, pp.213-14.
337. Engerman and Higman 1997, p.92.
338. Steele 2003, p.216.
339. Personal communication, Uta Lawaetz.
340. Colonial Annual Report for 1854.
341. Kolar 1985, p.339.
342. Jesse 1994 [1956], p.45.
343. Kolar 1985, p.551, 548.
344. *The Voice*, 15 October 1936.

Notes to chapter 9

345. Dyde1997, p.29.
346. Breen 1970 [1844], pp.186-7.
347. Kenny Anthony recorded one of the few cases known relating to name-giving (n.d., *ca.* 1988). In 1866, Mr DuBoulay, '*a member of a prominent and wealthy family of French origin*' sought to disposses a *mulatto* defendent, also called DuBoulay, of his name claiming '*he had a right in property to the name.*' The court rejected his claim outright. Anthony quotes from a 1905 *Report of the Judgments of the Windward Islands Court of Appeal*, 3 aff'd L.R. 2 P.C. 430.
348. Breen 1879-81, chapter XVI.
349. Breen 1970 [1844], p.204.
350. This and subsequent quotes: Kolar 1985, p.531, 414, 415.
351. Breen 1970 [1844], pp.182-3.
352. This and subsequent quotes: Kolar 1985, pp.562-4.
353. In 1843, the magistrate for Vieux Fort attended a catechism class and '*was surprised at the intelligence, piety, and devotion of the candidates. I have also attended at the Church on the occasion of a first communion at Vieux Fort, counted a great number of Labourers in attendance, and I was informed by the Curé that out of 26 communicants, 18 were plantation labourers, males and females.*' This and subsequent quotes: Kolar 1985, pp.564-6.
354. The first priests came across from Martinique in 1651. In 1665 a Père du Buisson left his signature on a document of restitution to the French. In 1719, Abbé François de Villeneuve was chaplain at Petit Carénage but it is doubtful there was even a chapel. By 1743, members of the Dominican

Order were in St Lucia, including a Fr O'Kelly at Petit Carénage and one or more other clergymen travelling around the island, which had about 2000 inhabitants at the time. Petit Carénage received a small church, Soufrière a chapel (1743, built by a Devaux near Coin de l'Ance) and in 1749, three parishes had resident priests. At Trois Islets (Praslin), Madame Dubuc-Roche built a chapel which was used by the priest from Vieux Fort, Abbé Gerfroy. But by 1752, none of these priests remained. In 1760, with more than 5000 inhabitants, there were still almost no priests. In 1762, Anse la Raye had a chapel but no priest and in 1763, only Abbé Gerfroy remained, now at River Dorée. Things improved once the economy expanded. By 1771, slave imports brought the population to over 15 000 and there were eleven parishes, most with resident priests, but Carénage still relied on a rented building. After the French Revolution, in 1795, no priests remained except for the one or two priests at Praslin who appear to have joined the Brigands. By 1802, there were once again three priests but for spells during 1810 and 1812, there were none. Ironically, Anglican British Governors Brereton (in 1807) and Wood (in 1809) were the ones to urge the population to build a Catholic church in Castries. Lack of funds delayed this for another three decades.

355. This and subsequent quote: Breen 1970 [1844], p.192, 191.
356. Kremser 1993a.
357. Cited in Kolar 1985, p.513.
358. Anthony (Patrick), 1999, p.112.
359. Midgett 1977, p.56.
360. Kremser 1993a, pp.310-11.
361. St Rose de Lima of Peru was born on April 20, 1586 and canonized as the first saint of the New World and patron of South America in 1671. St Mary Marguerite of Alacoque was born in 1647, died in 1690, was beatified in 1864 and canonized in 1920. Kremser 1993a, p.308.
362. This and subsequent quotes: Midgett 1977, pp.57-8.
363. Breen 1970 [1844], p.195.
364. Kolar 1985, pp.519-21.
365. The move was prompted by the estate owner who sponsored la Rose and had himself elected king in an attempt to tie labourers to his estate. But when the workers saw that their wages were as small, or even smaller than before, they deserted him all the same. Kolar 1985, pp.522-3 and Breen 1970 [1844], pp.198-9.
366. Kremser 1993a, p.309, citing Veronica Dujon.
367. This and subsequent quote: Breen 1970 [1844], p.202.
368. Kolar 1985, p.517.
369. Breen 1970 [1844], p.199.
370. Kolar 1985, pp.523-4.
371. Cited in Kremser 1993a, p.311.
372. *Ibid.*, p.312.
373. *Ibid.*, p.309, citing Crowley.
374. This excommunication was never officially reverted but the Church eventually condoned la Rose and la Marguerite again. Personal communication, Patrick Anthony.
375. This and subsequent quote: Kolar 1985, p.518, 517.
376. Harmsen 1993.

377. Breen 1970 [1844], p.249.
378. Anthony (Patrick) 1988. See also Anthony 1990, 1998 and 1999.
379. This and subsequent quote: Anthony (Patrick) 1988, pp.561-2.
380. Kolar 1985, pp.489-90.
381. Breen 1970 [1844], p.250.
382. Kolar 1985, p.494.
383. Cited in Kolar 1985, p.497.
384. This and subsequent quotes: Kolar 1985, pp.496-8.
385. Breen 1970 [1844], pp.251-3.
386. This and subsequent quote: Kolar 1985, pp.506-7. In 1933, an article written by one Jabetz Diz (or Dix) about 'Adolphe - one of the most terrible of Obeah-men' was published in the *Canada West Indies Magazine.*
387. Personal communication, Patrick Anthony.
388. Beck 1979.
389. E.g., 'White Magic' by Derek Walcott (1987). Also Keur and Keur 1960, pp.176-83.
390. Sturge and Harvey 1968 [1838], p.126.
391. In 1670, Lady Mico left £1000 to her nephew Samuel on condition that he marry one of his cousins, else the money would '*go to the ransom of any poor Christian seamen captured by the Barbary pirates of North Africa.*' Samuel refused and the money was invested instead. It was the abolitionist Thomas Fowell Buxton who convinced the trustees that using the money to educate the freed slave children instead was in the spirit of Lady Mico's original intentions. See Augier *et. al.* 1988 [1960], pp.179-80.
392. Sturge and Harvey 1968 [1838], p.123.
393. Gachet 1975.
394. Kolar 1985, p.569.
395. '*Many of the present teachers cannot answer the simplest questions at the teachers' examination, yet they are retained as masters. The people are kept in ignorance.*' John Quinlan, West India Royal Commission 1897c (app.C, part VII), p.74.
396. Tapon 1915, p.4.
397. '*I'm just a red nigger who love the sea, / I had a sound colonial education, / I have Dutch, nigger and English in me, / and either I'm nobody, or I'm a nation.*' 'The Schooner Flight', Walcott 1992, p.346.
398. The Anglican priest of Vieux Fort, Clarke, was more sombre: '*Sixty per cent of children receive no education whatever, 75 per cent are absent from school every day. Probably only 15 per cent are regular attendants.*' West India Royal Commission 1897c, app.C, vol VII, p.64.
399. *Ibid.*, p.70.
400. Annual Report for 1893, p.10.
401. This and subsequent quotes: West India Royal Commission 1897c, app.C, vol VII, p.71, 64 (emphasis in original), 73.
402. MacMillan 1938 [1936], p.133.
403. This and subsequent quotes: West India Royal Commission 1897c, app.C, vol VII, p.71, 66.

Notes to chapter 10

404. Kolar 1985, p.434.

405. Breen 1970 [1844], pp.305-06.
406. This and subsequent quotes: Kolar 1985, p.431, 434, 436-7, 441, 436, 438, 440. Out of twenty court cases, four concerned Barbadians, although no more than 150 or 200 Barbadians resided in his district.
407. Breen 1970 [1844], p.308.
408. Kolar 1985, p.439.
409. Renard 1983, pp.39-40.
410. West India Royal Commission 1897c (app.C, vol 3), p.68. J.W. Elliot, Magistrate for the 2nd & 3rd districts.
411. The term was first used in 1858 - until then, the records refer to them as *African immigrants.*
412. Kolar 1985, p.442.
413. This list was drawn up ten days later, when it became clear that the list of '*immigrants embarked*' did not correspond with the actual passengers. Kolar 1985, p.452.
414. Kolar 1985, p.446. Afraid he might not find licensed passengers in St Helena, the *Una*'s captain had opted instead to bring out this group from Sierra Leone, who had been in a yard for some time, at considerable expense and the risk of withdrawing their consent to emigrate. *Ibid.*, pp.444-5.
415. *Ibid.*, p.468. CO253/104/1:2/5/1850: 'An Ordinance promoting African Immigration into the Colony of Saint Lucia and the Industry of the Immigrants.'
416. Kolar (1985, pp.450-1) painstakingly traced these tribal affiliations to known ethnic or linguistic groups in Africa at the time.
417. This and subsequent quotes: *ibid.*, p.453-62.
418. There were 142 liberated Africans on estates in Castries/Anse la Raye; 122 in Gros Islet/Dauphin/Dennery; 246 in Soufrière/Choiseul and part of Laborie; and 107 in the remainder of Laborie and Vieux Fort/Micoud/Praslin. *Ibid.*, p.466.
419. This and subsequent quotes: *ibid.*, pp.467-9.
420. Henry Breen interviewed the men and found that they had adopted the names of British sailors on board of the ship they had crossed the Atlantic on. *Ibid.*, p.484.
421. This refers to speakers of the Kru language. Subsequent quotes: *ibid.*, pp.485-6.
422. Children initially worked until age eighteen but in 1862, it was further enacted that this period should be no less than three years. So a seventeen-year-old now had to work until age twenty.
423. This and subsequent quotes: Kolar 1985, pp.475-78.
424. Simmons 1963, p.45.
425. Kremser 1993b, p.85.
426. Frank (ed.) 2001, p.57.
427. This and subsequent quote: Simmons 1963, p.45, 47.
428. Online resource: Wikipedia. http://en.wikipedia.org/wiki/Music_of_Saint_Lucia
429. Simmons 1963, p.47.
430. Wikipedia.
431. Simpson 1980, p.313.
432. *Ibid.* In traditional African belief, Shango is the deity of thunder but in St Lucia, the stones themselves are referred to as Shango.
433. *Ibid.*, p.314 (footnote). A hypothesis is that it was the act of finding the

axes that prompted one or more liberated Africans around 1867 to create the ceremony of kélé out of the Yoruba Shango and Ogun traditions they remembered.

434. In modern times, this included car keys, school books, jewellery, dollar bills, etc.

435. Based on a ceremony he witnessed in the 1970s, Simpson (1980, p.315) wrote: '*Kele devotees believe that an African language is used during a ceremony. Actually, the participants, as do the shangoists in Trinidad, speak a patois that includes some African words.*'

436. Simmons 1963, p.45.

437. Simpson 1980, p.313.

438. In 1973, Patrick Anthony and the Folk Research Centre recorded a kélé ceremony performed by the Delaire family of Resina (Babonneau). Anthony attended again in 1983 and 1985. See: Anthony 1988.

439. Simmons 1963, p.45.

440. It is not clear what Simmons based this definite observation on. If he were wrong, then kélé could have arrived with the first liberated Africans or indeed the earliest slaves and been kept hidden from colonial eyes. Personal communication, Patrick Anthony.

441. This and subsequent quote: Kremser 1993b, p.88.

442. Simpson 1980, p.317, and Anthony 1988, p.292, footnote 23.

443. Rampersad 1986b mentions a total of 4354. Richard Cheddie uses the same figure and adds that of these, 2562 people remigrated and 1792 stayed on in St Lucia: a remigration rate of almost 59 per cent.

444. Cheddie claims to have seen several Emigration Passes, which carry immigrant's name, father's name, village, district, thanas, caste, next of kin, height, name of ship, registration number and body marks.

445. Reddock 1994, pp.28-31.

446. Comins 1893, appendix B, pp.*ii-iii*.

447. This and subsequent quote: *ibid.*, p.13, 6.

448. It was started in 1834 by the British colonial Government of India but was criticised by the reactivated Anti-Slavery Society as a guise for slavery. It went through phases of adaptation and prohibition in the 1840s, was resumed in 1851 and continued until 1917. Reddock 1993, pp.27-8. St Lucia had to institute labour laws acceptable to the Indian government first. Renard 1983, p.34.

449. Comins 1893, p.13.

450. Kolar 1985, p.470.

451. Cheddie mentioned by name: Dhoni (41) who was sent to Marquis Estate and imprisoned on 7 September 1878 for 14 days; Thaibdin Oree (35), 5'5' in height, sent to Perle Estate, returned to India on the *Moy* in 1888, and Bhookul Augnoo (43), sent to Esperance Estate.

452. Cheddie website. The *Bann* carried Sukram Mungh (38), 5'2.5 in height, and Dhowday Onsori (31), 5'4.5. Both were sent to Roseau.

453. Comins erroneously computed the total as 616. The Blue Book Report for 1884 mentions 626 people on board of the *Bracadaille*. Personal communication, Cheddie.

454. Comins 1893, p.13. Some of the passengers on the Bracadaille were: Hunoomansing (died 27 November 1884, aged 35) and his wife, both sent to the Dennery Usine, Badari Chadhary (22, Kurmi caste, sent to Bois d'Orange), Durman (sent to Roseau), Purmanon and Debi (sent to Ressource). Personal

communication, Cheddie.

455. Comins 1893, p.8. Comins visited Rat Island in May 1891. '*Altogether there were 33 confined and afflicted with one of these most loathsome diseases. Their quarters were comfortable and they had plenty to eat, but in the case of lepers no hope or interest in life. There were no cooly lepers, but 14 cases of yaws among the immigrants arriving in the Poonah.*' Yaws (*framboesia polypapilloma tropicum*) was curable by then.

456. Comins 1893, pp.14-15.

457. Annual Colonial Report for 1893, pp.8-9.

458. Comins 1893, p.6.

459. Renard 1983, p.22.

460. Comins, p.3. Subsequent quotes: p.7.

461. Cheddie.

462. Copy provided by Edward Phelps.

463. Based on Comins 1893, p.13, 6, 7-9.

464. This and subsequent quotes: West India Royal Commission 1897c, app.C, part *vii*, p.69.

465. *Ibid.*, Administrator Gouldsbury.

466. Diffusion (boiling canes rather than crushing them to extract the juice) was used in beetroot processing and hailed in the late 1880s as the latest innovation for sugar cane processing also. It failed. Henry Hales, West India Royal Commission 1897b, app.C, part 1, p.94.

467. This and subsequent quotes: Comins 1893, p.4, 14, 12.

468. Renard 1993, p.166.

469. R.G. McHugh, West India Royal Commission 1897, app.C, part *vii*, p.58.

470. Treasurer D.G. Garraway, *ibid.*, p.53.

471. Policies on '*the right kind of woman*' to serve as indentured immigrants varied over time.

472. Comins 1893, p.8. Possibly, some form of panchayat authority was in effect in these matters.

473. *Ibid.*, p.10.

474. Mohammed, n.d. (*ca.* 1996), pp.202-39.

475. Breen 1879-81, *The Chronicle*, 20 March 1880.

476. Comins 1893, p.10.

477. *Ibid.*

478. *Ibid.*, app. A

479. *Ibid.*, p.9.

480. Rampersad, 1986a. Copy provided by Richard Cheddie.

481. This and subsequent quotes: Comins 1893, p.8, 12, 2.

482. West India Royal Commission 1897c, app.C, part *vii*, p.65.

483. Rampersad 1986a.

484. Personal communication, Olivia Hackshaw.

485. Rampersad 1986a.

486. One man came to Cropper to withdraw some money from his savings bank book, which Cropper kept for him. He freely admitted not knowing the balance of his account (which was considerable) or the date of his last withdrawal. This and subsequent quotes: Comins 1893, p.1, 2, 5. Speaking of Richefond estate, Comins wrote: '*Some of the indentured, though not all, get drunk there and spend much of their pay, and when this is exhausted they are allowed credit.*' *Ibid.*, pp.3-6, 9, 12.

487. Personal communication, Richard Cheddie.
488. This and subsequent quote: Comins 1893, p.12.
489. West India Royal Commission, app.C, part *i*, p.80, Henry Hales.
490. *Ibid.*, p.43.
491. Comins 1893, p.10.
492. *Ibid.* The *Lincelles* (1868) remitted £2,397-18-8 with 236 adults, 119 of whom were depositors; the *Harkaway* (1871) carried £710-10-8 (236 adults, 119 depositors); the *Jumna* (1883) remitted £316-10-11 (59 adults, 29 depositors); the *Moy* (1888) remitted £1,832-4-11 (200 adults, 75 depositors); the *Rhone* (1889) remitted £1,603-16-2 (82 adults, 46 depositors); and the *Hereford* (1890) carried back £165-12-11 (15 adults, 8 depositors).
493. A total of £54-10-2 between 1885 and 1890. *Ibid.*, p.11.
494. A total of £164-14-0 between 1885 and 1890 was sent to India as '*remittances for the dead*' (*ibid.*) Another £40 or so was lodged in the treasury because no heirs could be traced by the agent in Calcutta. '*On the death of a cooly (indentured or otherwise) the proceeds are collected by the Protector and credited in the immigrant's name at the treasury, and a notice sent to the Agent in Calcutta to trace the heir. The Agent has funds at his disposal from the Crown Agents for the payment of the estate to the heir in India immediately on his identity being established. ... Deceased immigrants' estates usually consist of cattle, goats, occasionally horses, mules, money lent, jewellery, clothes, household furniture and utensils.*' *Ibid.*, p.15. Subsequent quotes: *ibid.*, p.9, 14, 3.

Notes to chapter 11

495. MacMillan 1938 [1936], pp.68-69, 78.
496. West India Royal Commission 1897c, p.65.
497. *Ibid.*, p.78.
498. *Ibid.*, 1897a, p.44.
499. *Ibid.*, 1897c, app. C, vol.*iii*, pp.356-7. G. Bennet, Memorandum: '*N.B. The above estates do not include sugar lands held by small peasant proprietors, and which probably contributed from 2000 to 3000 hogsheads yearly.*'
500. *Ibid.*, 1897a, app. C, part 1, p.93. Henry Hales, partner in the firm of Messr, J.V. Drake & Co., sugar brokers of 10, Mincing Lane, E.C., London. Hales mentioned that they also owned '*a smaller company, the Canelles Company.*' There was no central factory at Canelles but canes were grown there with East Indian labour. Oral history (collected by Harmsen in 1995) speaks of canes being transported from Canelles to Vieux Fort astride two fishing canoes.
501. *Ibid.*, 1897a, p.45.
502. Harmsen, interview with Mr. Senaie George, Vieux Fort, 1995.
503. West India Royal Commission 1897a, p.94.
504. *Ibid.*, p.57.
505. *Ibid.*, p.56.
506. *Ibid.*, p.15.
507. *Ibid.*, 1897c, p.99.
508. *Ibid.*, p.56.
509. *Ibid.*, pp.62-3.
510. This and subsequent quotes: *Ibid.*, p.72.
511. *Ibid.*, pp.78-79.

512. *Ibid.*, p.117.
513. *Ibid.*, p.97.
514. *Ibid.*, 1897a, p.66.
515. *Ibid.*, 1897c, p.62. George S. Hudson, attorney for Errard and Bazile Line Estate, Dennery.
516. *Ibid.*, p.52.
517. *Ibid.*, p.73. John E. Quinlan, sworn land surveyor, Castries.
518. *Ibid.*, p.66. Thomas Dix, Magistrate of Castries.
519. *Ibid.*, 1897b, p.99.
520. *Ibid.*, 1897c, p.62. George S. Hudson.
521. *Ibid.*, p.58. R.G. McHugh.
522. *Ibid.*, p.63. Rev. R.J. Clark.
523. *Ibid.*, p.72.
524. *Ibid.*, p.73.
525. *Ibid.*, p.72, Fr Tapon: '*Too often the women being deprived of the necessaries of life for themselves and their children fall into sin, and their last state is worse than the first.*'
526. *Ibid.*, p.57.
527. MacMillan 1938 [1936], p.99.
528. West India Royal Commission 1897a, p.45.
529. Annual Colonial Report 1893, p.18.
530. West India Royal Commission 1897a, p.45
531. *Ibid.*, 1897c, p.75.
532. *Ibid.*, J.E.F. Lashlie. On road works, wages had dropped even further: to three or three-and-a-half shilling for five-and-a-half days work. *Ibid.*, W.G. Moore, foreman of Public Works.
533. *Ibid.*, p.81.
534. Jesse 1994 [1956], p.40. Note that it took the HMS *Indefatigable* five days to reach Castries. After 1905, St Lucia was left without a defence force.
535. Their names were: Christopher Alexander, Edwin Arnot, George Blackman, Jordon Bolonge, Joseph Brathwaite, James Brown, Norman Chandler, Hamilton Charles, Matthew Francis, Henry Frederick, Maxim George, Regis Joseph, Percy Livingston, Joseph Mathurin, Joseph Mills, Henry Newman, Fatall Octave, Julien Philip, Eleuthere Solomon, Paul Solomon, Eudoxon Toussaint, Thomas Weatherhead, Frencis Wells, William Wilfred and Joseph Yard.
536. Five Canadian soldiers never returned home. Their bodies were buried at Choc cemetery.
537. They included Charles Dennehy, who was wounded at Ypres whilst serving with the 1st Canadian contingent overseas; two Lestrad brothers who were in London with the Scottish regiment; Harry McPhale with the Artillery Company; Elford Williams with the North Staffordshire Regiment; Sydney Ferguson with the Ordnance Department; Ernest Westall with the Canadian Forces 84th Regiment; Thomas Gittens with the French Infantry 26th Division; André Guignaud with the Zouaves; Charles de Laubenque with the French Army at Dardanelles and Robert Plissonneau who was transferred from the French to the British Army.
538. Robert Devaux has recorded the names of all St Lucians who served in four contingents of the BWIR; those who died (including the stokers on the HMS *Good Hope*) and those who have won distinctions or BWIR service medals.

Notes to chapter 12

539. CO 256/32. Annual Report (Agricultural Department), 1926-31.
540. *The Voice*, 14 May 1935, p.5. Also Devaux 2006.
541. *The Voice*, 7 July 1936, p.4.
542. '*What is needed ... is a general clearing of the forests and bush in which the island abounds, to be followed by a network of good roads and ... a bigger population. The forests in St Lucia serve no useful purpose.*' Henry Trotman in *The Voice*, 19 May 36, p.4.
543. Jesse 1994 [1956], p.45.
544. *The Voice*, 22 November 1938.
545. Box 1939, quoted in St Lucia Government 1991.
546. Joseph Cornibert DuBoulay, *Crusader* 21 August 1937. The editor responded angrily with: '*The strike is his only weapon.*'
547. CAB 21/809.
548. *Crusader*, 13 October 1937.
549. CO 256/40. Annual Report (Medical and Sanitary Departments), 1937.
550. CO 950/405, 19 December 1937.
551. CO 256/32, 39-40.
552. CO 950/405.
553. CO 950/411. Memorandum of Evidence, Administrator Alban Wright.
554. CO 256/32. Annual Report (Chief Medical Officer), 1929.
555. CO 950/405. Memorandum of Evidence, Labour Commissioner.
556. CO 256/39. Annual Report (Medical and Sanitary Departments), 1934, 1st en 3rd district.
557. *Ibid.*, 1936, by H.D. Weatherhead.
558. On 24 February 1935, the motor vessel *St George*, with 115 passengers, capsized one mile north of the reefs of Laborie Bay. One victim was from Laborie, two from Soufrière, '*but Choiseul, - poor Choiseul! - paid heaviest of all. ... No fewer than thirty-seven inhabitants of that village and the surrounding district perished. ... Now they say, "All girls of Choiseul have perished."*' *The Voice*, 28 February 1935, reprinted 17 November 2001, also *The Voice*, 25 June 1935. Two years later, on 13 February 1937, twelve people drowned when the *May Rose No. 349* tipped over at Pointe Grand Caille, two miles north of Soufrière.
559. CO 950/407, 'Reply to Labour Questionnaire (St Lucia)'.
560. CAB 21/809, Morgan Jones.
561. *The Voice*, 5 November 1935. Reputedly the highest weight at any coal-loading station in the world.
562. West India Royal Commission 1897c, p.76, David Clarke.
563. This and subsequent quotes: MacMillan 1938 [1936], p.178, 84, 53.
564. Sir Walter Citrine, General Secretary of the British Trade Union Congress was a member of the Royal Commission.
565. Interviewed by Harmsen, 9 October 1994. Cooper's father, George, was a middle-class coloured St Lucian in charge of a British-owned merchant house in Castries at the time of the 1935 coal carriers strike. His attempt to mediate between the strikers and the Governor led to the latter demanding from Cooper's employer that he be fired for '*anti-imperialist*' actions. Victimization was used '*mercilessly*' (Lewis 1993, p.386) to discourage early trade unionists. Cooper's employer ignored the Governor's request and in 1939, Cooper became

a founding member of the St Lucia Workers Co-operative Union. Charles 1994, pp.13-14.

566. *The Voice*, 30 July 1935, p.4.

567. Personal communication, Robert Devaux. See also: Martin 1993.

568. CO 950/411.

569. The eastern district (Micoud, Praslin, Dennery) counted 141 voters; the northern district (Castries, Gros Islet, Dauphin) 1118; the southern district (Choiseul, Laborie, Vieux Fort) 109 and the western district (Anse la Raye and Soufrière) 141. *Crusader*, 6 March 1937, p.4.

570. The 1939 Annual Report (Department of Agriculture) carried a list of all the labour laws in effect on 31 December 1939 (CO 256/40).

571. Lewis 1993, p.387, also p.391.

Notes to chapter 13

572. *Crusader*, 17 July 1937.

573. CO950/415.

574. This and following quotes: *Crusader*, 15 July 1938, 13 December 1938 (reprinted from *Barbados Advocate*), 28 December 1939, 17 October 1940.

575. Romalis 1970, pp.65-7.

576. *The Voice*, 9, 10, 11, 13 July and 10 August 1940.

577. This and subsequent quotes: *ibid.*, 13 November, 22 August, 5 September and 12 November 1940.

578. The Arundel Corporation was the contractor while Consolidated Engineering Company Inc. carried out the engineering works. All work was supervised from Puerto Rico.

579. Bentley 1945.

580. For variations on this event and hundreds of other war memories from St Lucians, see *Unsung war heroes of Saint Lucia*, edited by Gregor Williams (2008).

581. *The Voice*, 19 and 23 May 1939. The first report speaks of '*One hundred sailors* ...' the second of '... *a compliment* [sic] *of 200 sailors and officers.*'

582. *Ibid.*, 25 May 1939.

583. Personal communication, Robert Devaux.

584. Francis 1979, p.21. *The Voice* (24 March 1942) reported on the arrival in St Lucia of a rescue boat with survivors from a ship bound for Rio de Janeiro which had been torpedoed and sunk on the 28th of February. Throughout May, shipwrecked survivors landed in St Lucia and Martinique, some after as much as 46 days at sea.

585. CO 256/41 Annual Report (Health Department), 1942.

586. Francis 1979, p.21.

587. Personal communication Robert Devaux who, aged nine, witnessed this attack from the third floor balcony of his family home on No.11 High Street. A similar attack on a suspected U-boat occurred on 16 September 1942 and involved both US Navy and Airforce weaponry. Again, the enemy vessel escaped.

588. Francis 1979, pp.21-2.

589. Information on the Free French by Robert Devaux from Police Daily Occurrence Registers for Castries, 1940-1944 (copies at St Lucia National

Archives), *The Voice* (1940-1944) and Dubois, 1963.

590. Robert Devaux has collated a list with the names of all US personnel (Marines, Navy, Coast Guard and staff of the Arundel Corporation) based at Reduit.

591. *The Voice*, 23 May 1941.

592. *Ibid.*, 18 September 1941. Named after first lieutenant James S. Beane of New York City who was twice recommended for extraordinary heroism in battle during the First World War. Beane shot down five German aeroplanes before his own death in action on 30 October 1918. See also: 'Historical Report Beane Air Force Base, 1941-1949' (Maxwell Air Force Base, Alabama, microfilm roll A0030).

593. This and subsequent quotes: *The Voice*, 9 December and 12 November 1941. Also Auguste (comp.) 1986, p.10.

594. CO 256/41. Annual Report (Medical Department), 1943.

595. They were Eldridge Eudoxie, Antoine Theodore, Charles Moffat, Ralph Giraudy, Everton Williams and Oddie Leslin. *The Voice*, 22 June 1943.

596. CO 256/41. Annual Report (Department of Agriculture), 1941. Of note is also that the fishermen of Vieux Fort hardly benefitted from the increased demand for fish, partly because technological and ecological ceilings prevented them from significantly increasing their catches. St Lucian fishermen had been complaining about diminishing catches close to shore since the 1930s.

597. This and subsequent quotes: *Historical report Beane Air Force Base 1941-9*, p.21.

598. Harmsen 1999b, pp.35-48.

599. *The Voice*, 21 September 1943; Harmsen 1999b, pp.43-4.

600. Also *The Voice*, 26 September 1944. On the night of 2 October 1944, the officer's mess at Cantonment was robbed. An attempt on the officers' club was prevented.

601. E.g., Francis 1979, p.24; *The Voice*, 10 December 1940 and 9 December 1941; Jn.Baptiste 1986, p.54.

602. They were 1st Lt. William E. Johnson, Jr.; 2nd Lt. Ralph W. Mauch; 2nt Lt. Roy Mcnutt, Jr.; 2nd Lt. Frank P. Rott, Jr.; Cpl. Arthur J. Lupo; Cpl. Porter B. Armstrong and Cpl. Ashbury H. Dayton.

603. This happened on 28 September 1943. The plane's occupants were 2nd Lt. Edward S. Frantz, USMC rescue and Cpl. John H. Dearborn, AC.

604. CO256/41, Annual Report (Labour Department), 1944.

605. The base was partially reactived in 1955 as part of the US Space Program Long Range Proving Ground for Guided Missiles. Tracking facilities were constructed on Moule à Chique and on 2.51 acres of land at Morne le Blanc, north of Laborie. These remained in operation for about a decade. In early 1961, Beane Field (excluding the dock, two runways and the missile tracking stations) was handed back to the St Lucia Government. On 1 September 1964, St Lucia received the remaining lands and assets. The missile tracking stations followed shortly after.

Notes to chapter 14

606. Charles 1994, pp.13-14.

607. Charles mentions 1944. The Administrative Report (Labour Department) 1948 mentions that a union was established on 12 January 1939 which, if it referred to the Seamen and Waterfront Workers Union, would actually make this one

slightly older than the St Lucia Workers Co-operative Union. CO 256/42.

608. *Crusader*, 15 December 1945.
609. This and subsequent quote: CO 256/42, 1947-8.
610. Charles 1994, p.19.
611. According to the Annual Administration Report (CO 256/42), the drop in membership (from 6000 to 2500) occurred in 1949. George Charles (1994, pp.14-5) places it in 1945, as does Ezra Jn.Baptiste (1986) but as a primary source, the Adminstration Report must be accorded primary credence.
612. Economic Commission for Latin America 1981, p.112.
613. Charles 1994, p.15.
614. This and subsequent quotes: Jesse 1994 [1956], pp.73-76.
615. CO 256/42, Annual Administrative Report, 1947-8.
616. Carasco 1967, p.98.
617. CO 256/42, Annual Administrative Report, 1950. Construction staff was temporarily housed at George Fifth Park. After 1955, the buildings were converted to other uses, leading to neglect of the park's primary purpose as open space and its gradual ruin.
618. The CDC hired a British contractor: Holland, Hannen and Cubitts Ltd.
619. Carasco 1967, p.97.
620. *The Voice*, 16 August 1949.
621. This and subsequent quotes: CO 256/43, Annual Administrative Report, 1947-50.
622. Charles 1994, p.25 (emphasis in original).
623. Folk Research Centre n.d. (*ca.*1995). MB1, Charles Cadet.
624. George Oldum wrote that the fire '*scorched and ripped its way through decades of Victorian decadence. ... [L]ike a great leveller, the fire burned to ashes many notions of snobbery and favouritism.*' *The Voice*, 24 August 1974, p.7.
625. Midgett 1983, p.125.
626. Charles 1994, p.34.
627. *Ibid.* The year is erroneously printed as 1930 instead of 1950.
628. *Ibid.*, p.35.
629. Carasco 1967, p.114.
630. Charles 1994, p.36. Douglas Midgett (1983, p.126), noted that in St Lucia, labour candidates received less than 50 per cent of the total vote and that '*the results were nothing like the labor triumphs in most of the other islands.*'
631. CO 256/47, Annual Administrative Report, 1952-3.
632. Charles 1994, p.36.
633. Midgett 1983, p.126.
634. CO 256/47, Annual Administrative Report, 1952-3.
635. Charles 1994, p.37.
636. The Government lent the company $900 000 and bought one-sixth ($250 000) of all ordinary shares. (Midgett 1983, p.128). Charles (1994, p.46) placed the take-over in 1949. Midgett (1983, p.128) and Jesse (1994 [1956], p.79) both dated it 1953.
637. Charles 1994, p.39.
638. *bid.*, p.41.
639. *Ibid.*, p.42.
640. Under the ministerial constitution of 1956, the Executive Council was recognized as the instrument of policy and consisted of a chairman, three official members,

four elected members and one nominated member. The Legislative Council consisted of a president, two official members, three nominated members and eight selected members, three of whom were ministers.
641. Charles 1994, p.47.
642. See also Midgett 1983, p.130.
643. This and subsequent quotes: Charles 1994, p.48, 55, 52-3.
644. Jesse (1994 [1956], p.83; Charles 1994, p.53.
645. This and subsequent quotes: Charles 1994, pp.53-54 (emphasis in original).
646. For a good overview of the early history of bananas, see Reynolds 2003, pp.38-43.
647. Romalis 1969, pp.94-5.
648. Production rose from 306 000 stems in 1954 to 1 098 000 in 1958. CO 256/50, Annual Administrative Report, 1957-8.
649. Persaud *et. al.* 1966, p.5.
650. CO 257/25, Government Gazette, 1964.
651. This and subsequent quote: Serieux 1986, pp.129-31.
652. *Crusader* 14 December 1946, letter to the editor by Ralph Giraudy. Also *The Voice*, 14 September 1955.
653. *The Voice*, 18 May and 6 July 1963.
654. Quite a lot has been written about land tenure and gender issues in relation to St Lucia's banana industry. See e.g. Bruce 1983; Crichlow 1994; Dujon 1995; Organization of American States 1991; Szeto and Cebotarev 1990; Thornburg 1990.
655. Organization of American States 1987.
656. Serieux 1986, p.132.
657. Dalphinis n.d.
658. Midgett 1970, p.160. Also Dalphinis n.d., p.36. British administrators like Breen (1844) had always viewed *patois* negatively.
659. Weisbrod *et. al.* 1973, p.38.
660. Anthony n.d. (*ca.*1986), note 113, quoting from an unpublished paper by L. Carrington, 'Literacy & Rural development. A look at the St Lucian Initiative'. June 1981, p.5.
661. Midgett 1970, p.160.
662. Louisy 1999.
663. Dalphinis n.d., p.50.
664. A cultural renaissance started in 1970 but '*early attempts to integrate kweyol language and Creole structure into the established institutions were met with resistance*' and it took a decade before some headway was made. Charles 1999. See also Williams, 1993.
665. *Crusader*, 18 September 1955.
666. O'Loughlin 1968, p.59.
667. Mason, 1953.
668. CO 256/45, Annual Administrative Report, 1951.
669. *Crusader*, 21 May, 14 June and 29 November 1952.
670. This and subsequent quote: CO 256/47, Annual Administrative Report, 1952-3.
671. *Crusader*, 1 May 1955.
672. Chamberlain 1997, p.2.
673. CO 256/48, Annual Administrative Report, 1954. Money orders were received

from the UK, USA, Canada, Antigua, Barbados, Bermuda, British Guiana, Dominica, Grenada, Jamaica, Montserrat, St Kitts, St Vincent, Trinidad and Tortola to a total value of $142 030.

674. CO 256/49, Annual Administrative Report, 1955.

675. CO 256/50, Annual Administrative Report Administrative Report, 1957-8.

676. Larkin 1989.

677. *Crusader*, 12 October 1963, 19 February, 30 April and 26 October 1966; 6 March 1971.

678. Ho 1993; Marshall 1982, 1985 and 1987; Levine 1987.

Notes to chapter 15

679. Midgett 1983, pp.131-2.

680. Under the 1960 constitution, the Administrator became Her Majesty's representative in St Lucia; there were to be ten elected members instead of eight and two nominated members instead of three, with the Crown Attorney as the only official member of the Legislature. The Administrator ceased to be President of the House and a Speaker was elected from inside or outside the Legislature. The Executive Council continued to have general control over the Government and comprised of the President, Attorney-General, four ministers and one other person.

681. Mallet succeeded Karl LaCorbinière who had taken a seat in the Federal Parliament.

682. This and subsequent quote: Midgett 1983, pp.135-6.

683. Charles 1994, pp.78-9.

684. This and subsequent quotes: Midgett 1983, p.137, 139.

685. All unannotated information in the remainder of this book provided by Guy Ellis, who reported on all of these events first-hand for *The Voice* and *Mirror* newspapers.

686. Wayne 1986, p.30.

687. In fact, it was the SLP's George Charles who had first broached the idea of full internal self-government, in 1964.

Notes to chapter 16

688. Born in Laborie, Allan Louisy had been called to the bar in 1945 and went on to serve in various positions in the region, including Antigua, Dominica, Montserrat and Jamaica. A position on the bench of the West Indies Associated States Supreme Court capped his legal career. In 1973, Louisy retired from the judiciary and proclaimed to wish to devote the rest of his life to the task of creating a society based on the principles of justice and equality. At the time of his arrival on the political scene, the Labour Party was in the throes of an uproar over its leadership and Louisy, with his background in law and the judiciary, was seen as the perfect man to bring respectability back to the Labour Party image.

689. See Koester (1986) for a critical evaluation of the Hess facility.

690. West India Royal Commission 1897c, p.58, memorandum submitted by R. McHugh.

691. *Ibid.*, p.77, memorandum submitted by C. Messervy.

692. Pattullo 1996, p.74. gives an excellent overview of the history of (all-inclusive)

tourism in St Lucia and the Eastern Caribbean.

Notes to chapter 17

693. Reynolds (2003), pp.136-7 quotes John Compton reflecting on the peculiar historical irony of this event. '*About 36 years ago near the very spot, I looked down the barrel of the gun of the ... police during the sugar strike. On Wednesday I looked into the faces of hatred, heard the curses from the very same throats of the people to whom but a few weeks ago I was daddy Compton ... But I remember the lessons of ... the Bible that the same voices which shouted Hallelujah will shout "crucify him" without pausing for breath.*'

694. *Ibid.*, p.185.

695. In June, Mallet succeeded Sir Stanislaus James as Governor General: an appointment that was criticized as inappropriately partisan.

696. The result of a 15-year partnership between the St Lucian Kwéyòl Christians, American pastors and elders and the Bible Society of the Eastern Caribbean.

697. Mandela visit marked the 25th anniversary of the birth of the Caribbean Community, which was celebrated during a Caribbean Community Heads of Government Conference in St Lucia.

698. Reynolds (2003), pp.20-1.

Notes to chapter 18

699. Sr Egan was born on 27 December 1927 in Clonaslee, Ireland. She taught in Trinidad and Grenada before coming to St Lucia. '*Hers was a martyr's death,*' said Sister Paula Andrew, who lived with Sr Egan at St Joseph's Convent in Castries.

700. John's mother was baffled, saying her son had celebrated his First Holy Communion in the very same church. '*I asked him why he did that. He told me that they did it for the freedom of the nation, because we have to be free. He said if he had another chance to do it again, he will do it.*'

701. Odlum had suggested selling Windward Island bananas to Libya, with whose leader Muammar Ghadaffi he maintained ties of personal friendship. Even within the Alliance, many were uncomfortable with the proposal, which was a painful reminder of Compton's accusation in the mid 1980s that Odlum was sending young St Lucians to Tripoli for terrorist training. Just days later, the terrorist attacks of 9/11 occurred in the USA.

702. What did Taiwan offer to cause such a turn of events? Bousquet said Taiwanese aid would be invaluable in the agricultural sector, specifically mentionioning diversification, linkages with tourism, a livestock farm and an abattoir. In the preceding decade, China had given St Lucia a sports stadium, industrial free-zone (both completed), psychiatric hospital (nearing completion) and promised a new general hospital.

Notes to history of the Anglican Church

703. Gachet 1975, p.56.

704. Christine was the only sister who ever married, to a Scotsman by the name of Lloyd. A daughter died young but their son, Alexander Lloyd survived and in 1850, at the age of 21, took charge of the River Doree estate on behalf of his

mother and aunts. He ran River Dorée until his death in 1912.

705. 'Grace Church and its founders.' In: *The Voice*, 21 May 1999, pp.18-19.

706. As well as, reportedly, in memory of the late president of the United States of America, Franklin Roosevelt. *The Voice* 21 May 1999, p.20.

707. Rev. R.J. Clarke in West India Royal Commission 1897c, app.C, vol VII, p.62.

Index

NOTES

NOTES

NOTES

NOTES